Behind the Words

A Logical and Satirical Guide to The Impossible Defense of Jodi Arias

Volume I: Days 1-4 of Direct Examination

Kim Anne Whittemore

DEDICATION

To my daughter, **Rachel**, my best friend. She is a tireless encourager and the engine of this project. Without her ceaseless efforts, these words would remain forever locked in my computer.

To my husband, **Bob**, who listened to every recitation of every chapter, and who graciously agreed to give me the countless hours required to turn these individual pages into a book.

To my son, **Robert**, a man who is brilliant and reserved. You were the Carpathia when the Titanic was going down. My eternal love and gratitude belong to you.

To my father and friend, **Vincent**, a man who has an abundance of natural talent and an incredibly generous spirit. I hope I've made you proud, Dad.

And to my grandson, **Connor Logan.** Thank you for loaning me your Mommy for so many hours...days...weeks...months. If you should ever meet your own Jodi, speak to your Nana first. I love you, little man.

To the ladies of "The Fourth Incarnation", my first public audience, and now, my friends. Your laughter, lives, insight, and encouragement will never be forgotten. Thank you.

Maxine, Mary, Linda, Amber, Kaye, Tracy, and **Chris.**

And finally, to the late **Travis Alexander and his family.** May the malignancy of Jodi Arias ultimately be excised from their lives, and may they live secure in the knowledge that their late brother's legacy is neither tarnished or forgotten in the minds of the majority. **May God comfort and bless each of them, from the oldest to the youngest, and may they rest secure in the knowledge that they will see Travis, restored and radiant, in the life to come.**

CONTENTS

CHAPTER ONE

- Day 1 -

"If you tell the truth, you don't have to remember anything."
-Mark Twain

As we enter the courtroom, the trial is in the midst of its thirteenth day, and this is the day that Jodi Arias, the accused, will take the stand in her own defense. So, who is this defendant -- this Jodi Ann Arias? She is a 32 year-old former, part-time waitress from Yreka, California, a town situated in a county called Siskiyou. This county is so far north that it borders the neighboring state of Oregon. This Yrekan is on trial for the especially cruel, premeditated murder of her former boyfriend, Travis Alexander. He is a man who will be 30 years old forever. Alexander, a successful motivational speaker and insurance salesman, was slaughtered by Jodi Arias and left to decompose in the master bathroom of his spacious Mesa, Arizona home on June 4, 2008.

While Jodi Arias sat on the witness stand for an unprecedented 18 days, we will focus on her eight day direct examination, a procedure that was conducted by her court appointed attorney, Lawrence Kirk Nurmi (hereafter referred to as "Nurmi"), a public defender who is being paid the unconventional rate of $225 per hour (by the taxpayers) to represent Arias as his exclusive client.

He is going to attempt to do what ultimately proved to be impossible. He will try to bridge the gap between an essentially friendless, nomadic high school drop out with chronic money problems and a very popular, successful businessman who owned a well-appointed, exceptionally clean, noticeably organized, 3,800 square foot home in an upper middle-class Mesa suburb. Her attorney will try to minimize the differences between his client and her victim. He will attempt to paint her countless religious and philosophical dabblings as evidence of her intelligence and truth seeking, while at the same time painting her victim's adherence to his Mormon faith as evidence of his hypocritical double nature.

We will hear about her childhood. We will hear about her education. We will hear about her parents, and when we do, they will be called child abusers. We will hear about every romantic relationship Jodi Arias has ever had. We will hear about a waitressing job here and a waitressing job there. We will hear about teenage break-ups. We will hear about financial disaster, and we will hear about Arias' delusions of career grandeur. We will be bombarded with so much useless information that it may become difficult to care about this case. I urge you to hold on. There is much to be learned by listening to and dissecting both the carefully prepared and the off-script responses offered by Jodi Arias. We will learn so much about Arias that it will be easy to picture her doing exactly what she's been accused of doing.

The jury is not in the courtroom when Jodi Arias is first called to the stand. After the prior witness is excused, it is time for the star of the show to take her mark. The judge has just directed the jury to return to the jury room for three minutes. This gives the officer in charge of guarding Arias the time he needs to adjust her restraints. While sitting quietly at the defense table, any security devices restraining the defendant are not visible to the jury (or anyone else). However, she is about to walk. Adjustments need to be made, and this responsibility falls on one particular officer who is always right behind Jodi Arias as she sits with her legal team at a large table.

It isn't clear whether he's removing leg irons or attaching a stun device, but whatever he's about to do, it will be done outside of the jury's (and the camera's) presence. To preserve the presumption of innocence, something our legal system demands for a defendant, any visible indicator leading a jury to believe that Arias is dangerous is deemed too prejudicial. Too prejudicial – it's a defense team's big, pink eraser, and it's used frequently to limit the amount of information, both direct and indirect, given to a jury. Law enforcement, a grand jury, and a prosecutor have all determined that Jodi Arias is a murderer. The murder indictment creates a situation in which the accused either sits in jail awaiting her trial or she raises the money for her bail and is released from jail while she awaits trial. In the case of Jodi Arias, bail was set at an impossible $2M.

As she prepares to take the stand, Jodi Arias has been incarcerated in Arizona's Estrella Jail for almost five years. That jail, one of several in Maricopa County, is run by the infamous Sheriff Joe Arpaio. As an inmate, she is subjected to wearing a black and white horizontal striped uniform, pink underwear, and she is offered the notoriously bad food Sheriff Arpaio is famous for serving.

Donations from her supporters are plentiful, and Arias has found multiple ways to advise trial watchers that a good portion of her food (mostly snacks) is purchased at the jail store. On the days she is in court in front of a jury, she does not wear her stripes. She rotates a wardrobe of casual clothing her defense team brings to her. Once this jury convicts her and she stands before Judge Sherry K. Stephens for sentencing, Cinderella will find herself wearing her jail issued rags again.

Arias must be given some privacy so that she and the burly officer who shadows her can disappear behind a locked door to deal with the metal and technology that must be removed or affixed to her body. When she is outside of her jail cell, she must be restrained in some way. Actually, Arias now has two cells that she calls home. One is at the Estrella jail and the other is in the basement of this courthouse. Whenever the trial breaks for lunch, everyone assembled in the courtroom of Judge Stephens is free to patronize a local restaurant of their choosing – everyone except Jodi Arias. She has no such freedom. She is taken to her onsite holding cell and given a jail issued lunch consisting of peanut butter, cold milk, an apple, and a cookie (or so we hear).

Jennifer Willmott, the second chair defense attorney, approaches Arias after the judge announces, for the record, that the jury is not present. There is a brief interchange between Willmott and Arias. Willmott flashes a smile at Arias and then makes a request of the judge, Since she isn't speaking into a microphone, we can only guess as to the substance of her request . It must have something to do with Arias and her guard. The judge approves the request, and Willmott responds by turning toward the portly officer wearing a uniform consisting of a beige shirt and brown slacks. He's sitting about four feet behind Jodi Arias. Willmott cocks her head to the right – an obvious motion toward Arias and the door next to her. The officer immediately stands and walks a few inches toward the door. Without provocation, Arias stands and walks towards the same door, and once the two meet, the officer takes out a key ring and inserts a key into a lock that has been installed on the upper portion of the door frame.

Together they disappear into the room, the interior of which is familiar to Arias, but not to us, save for the ever diminishing slice of a room that a rapidly closing door affords. There is some movement in the courtroom gallery, but it is quiet movement. There is silence as we await the return of the defendant and her guard. After two minutes, we see that door open. The officer is pulling keys out of a lock that is on the inside of the door. I assume Arias has gotten used to every door being locked behind her. Arias emerges, and for now, she has been sufficiently processed in whatever way she needed to be processed. All visual prejudice has been erased. The stun device affixed to her thigh, hidden under her clothing, will stay in place as Arias testifies. Should she make any sudden or unapproved movements, the guard will hit a button and she will be stunned into submission.

We see the defense team at their table. They seem to be in good spirits. They are talking and smiling. By contrast, a shot of the prosecutor's table shows a serious, silent Juan Martinez, the man prosecuting Jodi Arias. He is patiently waiting for the jury to return. We see Arias walking toward her chair at the defense table, but she isn't afforded an opportunity to sit down before Judge Sherry Stephens says, "Miss Arias, you may come forward and take a seat, please". Arias complies, but she looks like the shy seventh grade student who, despite her best efforts to hide from the teacher's gaze, is still chosen to deliver her oral report to a class of students who have shunned her since the third grade.

Her dark brown hair falls below her shoulders, and she sports thin bangs, cut in a perfectly horizontal line across her forehead. The longer strands of hair are parted on the left, and the hair that is captured in a small pony tail falls down the right side of her head. This juvenile style, a questionable choice for a grown woman appearing in court, screams out for a big, ribboned bow to be tied around the elastic band. She wears over-sized, cockroach brown eyeglasses, and the outline of her face is uninterrupted as we look through their lenses. If they are prescription glasses – something she has never worn in her life – they are the weakest known to man. I believe they are a prop. Everything about her appearance is a prop.

So, this is the woman the media had branded "a bombshell"? Long gone are the banners of her past – the Marilyn Monroe bleached blond hair, the dark lip liner and lighter lip gloss, the eye make-up, and the cleavage. In their place, we see all of the physical attributes of someone who might be handing out fliers for her church's youth group retreat. She wears no jewelry or make-up, and if her eyeglasses had a piece of tape on the bridge of the nose, they could be marketed to those searching for geek Halloween costumes. All of this camouflaging is the result of a brainstorming session held in a defense attorney's conference room. The object, of course, is to force the jury to ask themselves, "How could this child, this shy, unpopular adolescent who could be waiting alone for the school bus, be a dangerous killer?".

Her baggy beige pants, topped with a plain, short sleeved black sweater, is part of her uniform of complete neutrality. It says nothing about her. As she approaches the bench, Arias drops her eyes and clasps her hands at her waist. Judge Stephens does not make eye contact with Arias. Instead, the judge closes her eyes and with her left index finger, she touches her eyelid. Once Arias has passed her, the judge looks to the right and watches the defendant. Arias drops her hands, and her arms swing back and forth as she approaches the steps to the witness stand. Mindlessly, Arias takes her right hand and swipes it against her upper lip. She shows no grace or femininity in her movements. Finally, she sits down.

In a soft and sweet voice, the judge says, "You can line the jury up. Line up the jury". Arias looks toward her left. That is where her legal team and supporters are to be found. She looks nervous and cagey. She wants to look in front of her – that's obvious – but she doesn't dare. If she did, she'd see Juan Martinez, the prosecutor. She'd see Esteban Flores, the detective who arrested and interrogated her. Behind them, she'd see the siblings and many friends of her victim, Travis Alexander. Instead, she drops her eyes. She's probably been instructed by her counsel to avoid looking at them. Their contempt for her, obvious in their faces, could weaken her resolve.

Superior Court Judge Sherry Stephens asks Nurmi if he is calling his client to the stand. Well, I hope he's calling his client to the stand, or Arias is about to get tased by her handler for moving around the courtroom without permission. Arias looks confused at this point, and her head snaps back and forth between the judge and Nurmi. Nurmi makes it official as he says, "The defense calls Jodi Arias". The judge then tells Arias to stand and be sworn in. Arias stands, pulls on the hem of her black sweater, raises her right hand, and swears, by God, to tell the truth, the whole truth and nothing but the truth. This is the first lie of many to come from her mouth during this trial. The truth is something she needs to conceal.

There is an obvious tension in the courtroom. After she is sworn in and takes her seat, we see Arias' eyes darting between the prosecutor, Juan Martinez, and her salvation, Kirk Nurmi. Martinez sits at the prosecutor's table, his hands in the steeple position. One index finger moves. The camera moves, and we see Nurmi, for the third time, reaching his hand behind his suit jacket He is tucking in his dress shirt.

Nurmi remains fixed at the podium. As he waits for his cue to begin, he rests on its surface and laces his fingers together. Occasionally, he glances up at Arias. A shot of Martinez shows him leaning towards the large, rugged faced, dark haired man sitting to his left. That man is Detective Esteban Flores, the lead investigator on this case. His contribution to this case cannot be underestimated. With a low key, polite, but tenacious approach, he built the foundation for the prosecutor. He will remain in this seat at the prosecutor's desk for the duration of this case. He has been on the witness stand, and he has been a target of the defense team. He did well on the stand, refusing to react to the arrows shot in his direction. The best words to describe him are strong and steady.

Martinez initiates a discussion with Flores. Nurmi's hands are now clasped behind his back as the silence is interrupted with the announcement, one issued from the woman I call Evidence Lady. In a serious tone of voice, she says, "Please stand for the jury".

The entire room is on their feet, with the exception of the lady in the black robe, Judge Sherry Stephens. For better or worse, she will oversee this trial. She is a pleasant looking, thin, middle-aged woman with dyed blond hair. She has a soft tone and a poker face that is usually unreadable. Her judicial record indicates that this is her first death penalty trial. Finally, the camera focuses on Jodi Arias. We see her interlocking her fingers;. It seems to be a trend this morning. It must be a sign of anxiety.

The camera lands on the defense table. We see Jennifer Willmott standing at attention. Nurmi is now standing next to Willmott. Evidently, he made his way back to the defense table before the jury was ushered into the courtroom. For the first time, I notice that the defense attorneys are color coordinated. Willmott is wearing an orange blouse and a brown blazer. Nurmi is wearing a beige suit, a long orange tie, and a white shirt.

Nurmi is told to proceed. He addresses his client and offers a flat, "Hi, Jodi". She answers, "Hi". Hi? This is the best introduction they could come up with? Okay, hi it is. It gets better. Nurmi asks, "How are you feeling right now?". How is she feeling right now? Is this a talk show or is this a trial? She does a few micro-swivels in her chair, gives a tense smile, and with all of the sincerity of a young girl about to undergo her first pelvic exam, she mumbles, "Ummm...nervous". Juan Martinez, the prosecutor, apparently shares my disinterest in how Arias is feeling right now. He interrupts and says, "Objection, relevance". The judge sustains the objection. Apparently she agrees with me. I don't care how Jodi Arias feels right now.

Nurmi fumbles around with his words, but finally he asks, "Well, let me ask you this – is this a position you ever thought you'd find yourself in?". No, Nurmi. She intended to get away with it. Does he not remember the "I wasn't there" story? How about the "two assassins killed him but let me go if I promised not to tell anyone what they did" story? Of course she never intended to find herself here. Even when those stories fell apart, she thought her threat to the state would seal the deal. Once the evidence came rolling in, she told the state, via legal motion, that she would accept a second degree murder plea deal, but she was careful to add that if the state didn't accept her offer, she would destroy the reputation of her victim on the stand. She promised that the LDS/Mormon church would be embarrassed. She claimed that marriages would be threatened by her disclosures. She said the surviving Alexander siblings would be devastated by her trial testimony. It was a red hot threat couched in Legalese, and the state ignored it. In the life of Jodi Arias, threats usually worked. This time, they didn't. She was on the stand, despite her best efforts to avoid being in this position. Again, Juan Martinez interrupts with, "Objection, relevance". Martinez taps his desk ever so slightly as the judge says, "Approach, please".

And so, it begins.

The camera now focuses on Sandy Allen Arias and Susan Allen Halterman (hereafter referred to as Sandy and Sue). They are identical twin sisters. Sandy is the mother of Jodi Arias. Sue is Jodi's maternal aunt. As the attorneys approach the bench, Sue, clad in a light blue sweater featuring two large white diamond patterns framed in navy blue and resting on each breast, reaches over to her sister, Sandy. Both women are middle-aged, overweight, rather homely, and are sporting two incarnations of a conventional, shoulder length, dark brown hair style. They both wear eyeglasses. Sue is wearing ear phones, and when she touches her sister, a woman clad in a black jacket worn over a black and white shirt, there is an acknowledgment by Sandy. The two women look at each other and smile. Actually, their interchange could be more accurately described as a mirror image of an anxious grin.

There is no pronouncement from Judge Sherry Stephens as to what was decided at the bench. Was the relevancy objection sustained or overruled? We don't know. We can surmise, and we'll do a lot of that, and we'll base our assumptions on how Nurmi proceeds after the sidebar is over. At this point, Nurmi returns to his podium and says that he wants to ask Arias a few important questions before he asks her about who she is and why she is here. There is no need to ask her why she is here, but we'd better get used to questions that are useless, if not insulting. They will be everywhere – but listen to the answers because that's how you're going to figure out who Jodi Arias really is. For 13 days, this jury has been totally informed as to why Jodi Arias is here. They've been a captive audience to expert after expert who have explained, in detail, and with accompanying evidence, why Jodi Arias is sitting at the defense table.

So, moving on to those "important questions". Nurmi asks Jodi, "Did you kill Travis Alexander on June 4, 2008?". Jodi pretends to steel herself for the answer. She tightens her mouth and closes her eyes before swiveling her chair towards the jury. Once faced in their direction, she opens her eyes and then drops them to avoid the gaze of the jurors, She doesn't speak while facing them. Instead, she immediately swivels her chair back toward Nurmi and answers this pivotal question while looking at the floor. She says softly, "Yes, I did". Nurmi responds, "Why?". Again, she repeats the same movements and answers, "Um, the simple answer is that he attacked me". Once she's back in position and looking at Nurmi, she suddenly remembers that she forgot to add the most important part of her answer. Without provocation, she swivels back toward the jury, looks down, repositions her chair toward her attorney, and, as an afterthought, says, "and I defended myself". Nurmi says, "Okay". No, Nurmi, it's not okay. It's not okay at all.

Nurmi continues, "It was also brought up during these proceedings, that you gave an interview with 'Inside Edition'. Do you remember seeing that tape?". Arias, somber as a widow at a wake, answers, "Yes, I do". Nurmi continues, "And in that tape, you said that no jury would ever convict you – something to that effect. Do you remember saying that?". It wasn't something "to that effect". It was far worse than that. She smiled and challenged the interviewer and the audience to "mark her words" that no jury would convict her. In fact, her demeanor was so casual that it was confusing. A viewer would believe that Jodi Arias was spending time in a hotel, not a jail.

However, today is a different day, and Arias dare not wear such a smug expression, and her voice cannot possibly carry that smiling tone as she addresses this question in front of the jury she previously challenged. Today, she looks like a guilty shoplifter caught on videotape, and she has no choice but to confess to her arrogance. With equal parts faux contrition and humiliation, she says, "Yeah. I did say that". Nurmi asks, "Why?".

You will now see why Arias was on the stand for a record 18 days. She does not give direct answers, and that is by design. She was just asked why she said "no jury will convict me". Instead of answering this very pointed question, she will cloud the issue by suggesting that her answer requires context to be understood. She will not say , "I said that because...". Instead, she will take us back to a period of time, and she will put a spotlight on that period of time while hoping that we all forget what the pointed question was. She is believing that the average listener will become far more interested in the context than the answer. Almost every important question will be deliberately framed with details that nobody asks her about, including her attorney.

Here's the first example: "Umm, I made that statement in September, 2008 (she pauses to display a look of indecision) – I think it was, and umm, at the time, I had plans to commit suicide, haaaah – (again with closed eyes, swiveling chair, and the added flourish of a huge exhale while looking at the ground). Um, so I was extremely confident that no jury would convict me because I didn't expect any of you to be here. I didn't expect to be here. So, I could have easily said no jury would acquit me either (except she didn't), but I didn't say that though, because there was an officer sitting five feet behind me, and had I told them the reason that no jury would convict me AT THAT TIME (she uses her hand to punctuate those words because they are so important), I would have been thrown into a padded cell and stripped down, and that would have been my life for a while – until I stabilized. Um, soooo, I was very confident that no jury would convict me because I planned to be dead – probably the most bitter words I'll ever eat".

Nurmi would like that last announcement repeated. So, as he will do from time to time, he pretends that he didn't hear what Arias just said. He asks, "I'm sorry, what was that?". Arias repeats, "I said, those are probably the most bitter words I'll ever eat". Really? That's hard to believe, isn't it? Don't you think there was some discussion she had with Travis before she slaughtered him? There were probably far more bitter words uttered on June 4, 2008, but since the general public will never know what those words were, she doesn't have to eat them.

Poor suicidal Jodi. She is so depressed, so hopeless, and so on target to die that she can smile and argue the absolute absurdity of the charges during a jailed, pretrial interview. Her higher brain functions were completely intact. She wants us to believe that she was so numb that she was prepared to take her own life, but inexplicably, she was still trying to figure out how she could guarantee herself a long and liberated future. The average potential suicide has their eye on the goal – to obtain peace through death. They give little thought to the days that might follow their demise, and if they do, their only concern is for those they may leave behind. But then there's Jodi. She not only notices the guard sitting five feet away from her, but she also knows what that guard will do to her if she doesn't hide her alleged suicidal ideations. She's planning to die by her own hand, anticipating her final exit, yet her strategic faculties are still completely intact.

There's that odd, uncomfortable feeling that often accompanies a lie that falls flat, but Nurmi knows when the silence becomes too awkward. He breaks the silence with, "Miss Arias, I want to clarify another thing as well. You were talking here – uh, um – your name has been pronounced, through most of this trial as Arias (Ah-ree-is). Is there another way to pronounce it, or have you always pronounced it Arias?". From suicide to name pronunciation in one question. Carry on, Nurmi. How does she pronounce her last name? I would assume that after years of being her attorney, Nurmi would have this information, but what's another diversion when your goal is to skirt around the real issue?

She reaches down to rub her leg and answers, "I've heard it pronounced about seven different ways. I say Arias, as does the rest of my family". That's it? I was expecting at least two alternate pronunciations – after all, according to Jodi, there are seven. What was the point of even asking this question? Was this interchange meant to impress upon a possible Hispanic juror that Jodi would have pronounced the family name differently had her parents not preferred to dilute its ethnic quality? Make no mistake, this seemingly insignificant interchange was more than a superfluous detail. It had a purpose.

Now that we know who we're talking to, Nurmi moves on. He asks, "So, let's back up a little bit and talk about your family. Who's in your immediate family?". Where are we going to back up to? She's been on the stand for less than four minutes. Okay, this is Nurmi's show. Let's play, "Meet the Murderer"!

Jodi says, "Um, my immediate family consists of...". The prosecutor, Juan Martinez, interrupts with an objection based on relevancy. It's overruled. She begins again, "Um, I'm the oldest of my parents, um, they also had another son about two years after I was born (so is she a son, too?) – my, um, brother. And then I have, um, another younger sister, and I have another younger brother. I also have an older sister from a previous marriage of my father's". It's family hour in court, and as Nurmi asks Jodi about her parents, he would like to know if they are still married (because this is supposed to give her a few extra points – as if she had anything to do with the longevity of her parents' marriage). Jodi tells us that her parents are Bill and Sandy Arias. Nurmi wants to know how long her parents have been married. She answers, "Yes, about 33 years". What's next? Are we going to hear how many tiers were on their wedding cake? Can we move along?

Nurmi goes through the Arias family members with a fine tooth comb. As we learn the first names of the forever branded Arias siblings (Carl, Angela, Joseph, and an older half-sister), I almost expect Nurmi to ask them to stand up, introduce themselves, and perhaps tell the audience a little something about themselves. It's getting that casual. Nurmi wants to know when the two younger siblings were born. Jodi informs anyone who cares that her sister. Angela, was born when Jodi was 11, and Joseph, the baby of the Arias tribe, was born when Jodi was 13. Armed with information that would only interest a genealogist, a census taker, or a family photographer, Nurmi proceeds. He asks Jodi what year she was born. She answers, "In 1980". He then asks, "Do you remember where you grew up?". Unless she was in a coma, I suspect she will say that she remembers.

Jodi answers, "Yeah. I grew up in a few different cities. I was born in Salinas, California, and I lived there until I was almost 12. Um (she looks at Nurmi for some direction as to whether or not she's supposed to go on with her answer or wait for another question)". Nurmi picks up the ball and asks her what life was like in Salinas. Remember what she says here. This is important, and it will come into play a little later in the trial.

She answers, "For the first years of my life, it was really good. Um...". Nurmi duly interrupts and asks for some clarification: What does Jodi mean by first years? She answers, "I would say until about age seven, it was a fairly ideal childhood". Ideal childhood? That sounds pretty good to me. However, Nurmi, the keen critical thinker, sees some ambiguity in his client's statement. He reminds the jury that everyone has a different concept of ideal. Right now, the only definition that matters is the definition hiding inside the head of Jodi Arias. He asks for that definition, and he is immediately rewarded with this answer, one he probably helped script: "Um, I have predominantly positive memories of my childhood at that time. Um, my brother and I lived in – when I was about four years old, we moved into a house in a cul-de-sac. We had the center lot, so it was a huge back yard, and we had a lot of places to play there. Um, there were trees to climb. There were other kids in the neighborhood and in the cul-de-sac that we played with, um – we were close in age, so we were, um – my family traveled a lot. We went camping. We went to all the theme parks in California (she waves her hand from left to right). Um...". Nurmi cuts her off and asks, "Did you go to school?". She answers, "Of course, yes, I went to school". Nurmi, she just used the word "predominantly". They don't teach five syllable filler words at camp sites and theme parks.

Jodi, looking dull and uninterested, stares at Nurmi as he asks if she went to grade school in Salinas. She answers, "Yes. I went to a private school for about three years, and a public school (she looks slightly nauseous as she nods her head once, looks at the jury, and then back toward Nurmi)". Nurmi asks her if she and her brother went to school together. While staring at the floor in front of her, she answers, "Uh, we were in school together. I was held back in kindergarten, so even though we were two years apart, he was only one grade behind me". Arias shows a distinct discomfort in disclosing this information. Perhaps she is still adjusting to life on the witness stand, or she may not like having to admit that she failed "A is for Apple and B is for Ball". She makes a weak gesture toward the jury with a few micro-swivels of her chair, but her eyes lift to meet them only once, and it is for a second or less.

I have always found it interesting that this is the first and last time we will hear about the little girl who failed kindergarten. The fact that the Arias family lived on the center lot of a cul-de-sac tells us nothing about little Jodi Arias, but a school's justification for choosing to remediate that same child after her first year of standardized education? Well, that could be enlightening. Statistically, boys are far more likely to be held back in kindergarten than girls. That's generally an issue of the two genders maturing at different rates. Is it unheard of for a young girl to be held back in kindergarten? Certainly not. However, that does become an issue one might want to look into if that remediated girl grows up to be a chronic underachiever with a sketchy work history and a brutal murder under her belt.

Kindergarten is the genesis of formal education. Why was Jodi Arias deemed too ill equipped to move forward to the first grade? Was she not coloring in the lines? Was she not able to tell the difference between red and blue? Was there an organic disability, perhaps dyslexia, that was diagnosed? Did she suffer a serious illness that year? Perhaps the issue was more social than intellectual. Perhaps she was oppositional, defiant, or unable to socialize. What happened? Surely, if the issue was not behavioral, the defense would have asked that question. Whatever the reason, it will remain a mystery. It will never be addressed again.

Jodi's first foray into the world of other children and a structured environment with new authority was met with failure and a need to try it all again. However, Nurmi is ready to leave the monkey bars and finger paints to ask about what really matters – the employment history of Sandy Arias, Jodi's mother. We learn that Sandy was a server (a/k/a waitress, but Jodi won't use that word) in Jodi's father's restaurants (plural) throughout most of Jodi's childhood. She adds that her father "always" owned restaurants. Apparently, Sandy had a career change in 1992, right about the time Jodi turned 12. Sandy became a dental assistant. Yawn.

Now, Nurmi wants to know what little Jodi's interests were during childhood. She answers, "Yes, I had pets – cats, dog, fish. I had a rat. I loved animals. We had a lot of pets. My brother had frogs...things like that. Um, we played a lot of hopscotch and two square when we were younger. We went roller-skating. They didn't really have rollerblades yet...or at least that we used. Um, we rode bikes a lot. We did a lot of camping. Um, I'm sorry. I kind of forgot the question". There's an almost perceptible chuckle in Nurmi's voice as he says, "You're speaking very quietly. Are you nervous today?". Isn't this sad? A random, geeky (33 year old) teen is being asked to tell us if questions about hopscotch and frogs are making her nervous. Well, it she's shaking while talking about Frank the Fish and Dan the Dog, how is she going to feel when we finally get to Travis the Human Being?

She answers, "Um, Yeah. Yes, I am, very nervous". Nurmi interrupts in the middle of her answer to say, "What's that?". Big deal. She's nervous. I'd be nervous facing a judge for a moving violation – and, in fact, I have been on several occasions. I'd assume I'd be paralyzed by nerves if the charge was Murder One. Nurmi tries to soothe Jodi's anxiety by telling her to pull the microphone closer to her. I don't know if that's going to help, but she complies. If you knew nothing about Jodi Arias (and this jury doesn't), this shy girl performance might actually be believable.

Let's get back to her answer, the one preceded by the forgotten question. Without even addressing the issue of a fish as a pet, can we talk about the dog? Jodi said, during her interrogation with Detective Esteban Flores back in 2008, that her family had a dog. Actually, the reason the dog was even mentioned was because Detective Flores asked Jodi if she had any issues with anger or rage. Initially, Jodi denied any such issues, but after a little more thought, she offered a sad and shameful story about Doggy Boy, the family pet. Detailing the events of an afternoon in which an adolescent Jodi was saddled with the care of her younger siblings, Jodi said that Doggy Boy, a dependent domestic animal her family failed to properly care for, got into some garbage bags and dragged discarded diapers all over the back yard of the family home. Jodi's' reaction was not to wave her finger and say, "Bad dog! Bad, bad dog!", and then proceed to pick up the diapers and rebag them. No. Jodi's reaction was to kick Doggy Boy in anger – possibly into eternity. She said he "only moved a couple of feet", but he ran, and they never saw him again. Does anyone else think she ruptured his spleen and buried him before her parents got home? I do. However, let's all remember that Jodi loves animals. During that confession, Jodi cried and said she needed to ask Doggy Boy for his forgiveness. Then, in that same room and In the presence of that same detective, she spent two days denying any involvement in the murder of Travis Alexander. She still hasn't asked for his forgiveness.

So, to sum up, we have a child who enjoyed a rather routine, status quo childhood in middle class suburbia. Seriously? A cul de sac? It doesn't get more clichéd than that. In her own monotone, barely audible words, we heard her say that her childhood was almost ideal -- a blend of California theme parks, camping trips, private school, and public school. This sounds like a good life for a child, until....the beatings began.

What beatings, you ask? Keep reading. The beatings are coming. The stage is being set. In fact, Bill and Sandy Arias will morph into child abusers right before your eyes (and it will be before your eyes because Sandy is in the gallery staring at her daughter. Jodi's father is hit and miss with trial attendance, and today, it's miss). The parents who indulged their young children with day trips, vacations, toys, and the expense of private school and music lessons, will become nothing more or less than sentient mitigating factors meant to spare Jodi Arias from the death penalty. In fact, they will be nothing more than descriptors attached to the stated mitigator, "Jodi suffered abuse and neglect as a child".

Back in the courtroom, Nurmi asks, "Jodi, one of the things that you said a couple of questions ago when we were speaking is that, um, your life was pretty ideal up until about age seven. Was there something different after age seven, or...". Jodi answers, "Um, it just seemed like our parents would spank us, or just hit us". Jodi says something changed when she reached the age of seven. What might that something be? Was there something, either pivotal or progressive, that made its presence known in 1987? A starting point might shed some light on her parents' transformation from guardians and caretakers to abusive dictators. How did that happen? Did 1987 mark the year that her parents began to drink just a little too much? Were their bills burying them in a grave of hopelessness and frustration? Did they face the death of an immediate family member? Did one of them introduce recreational drugs to the marriage? What happened? We are offered nothing to explain her parents' transformation from the providers of an ideal childhood to the instigators of emotional and mental distress in their oldest child. Nothing. I will concede that a seven year old might not be able to articulate the reasons for such a change, but I do not believe that this same child, having reached the age of 33, has not gained some clarity as to what marked the genesis of this change. The follow-up questions prove that Kirk Nurmi is not interested or prepared to explore those possibilities. Instead, he simply wants his witness to tell us about the result of the alleged change.

Nurmi's sentimental tone of voice is overplayed as he asks Jodi to explain the change. Referring to the spankings, she replies, "Well, I was spanked before, on occasion. It just seemed like the frequency and intensity of it increased around that age". Nurmi asks her what that means. I speak English, so I know what that means, but apparently, Jodi is having a little trouble comprehending the question. She looks unsure of herself as she answers, "Uhh, well just, (there's a lengthy pause here as she looks at Nurmi pleadingly. Her affect is questionable) I think that's the first year my dad started using the belt. Umm, (she pauses, looks down, licks her lips, rubs her leg, and finally, with her voice sounding like it's about to break, she continues), my mom began to carry a wooden spoon in her purse (now she's just about to cry)".

Juan Martinez interrupts with, "Objection, relevance", and the judge sustains the objection. While watching her, I can almost see Jodi thinking "Oh shit, and I was just about to push out a tear! Why did Martinez interrupt my performance?".

Nurmi doesn't like to be interrupted. He likes it even less when his client's Oscar worthy performance is ambushed, so he does something he will do many times during this direct examination. He looks at the judge and asks, "May we approach?". Judge Sherry Stephens, as she will do with only several exceptions in this trail, grants the request. "May we approach" is not the same as an objection. "May we approach" is exactly what it sound like. The attorneys from both sides – one side strutting and the other side shuffling (depending on which side wants to approach), stand in front of the judge's bench and argue their positions. The judge always turns on a white noise machine to prevent anyone outside of the inner circle from hearing the arguments going on at the bench. These bench conferences can be as quick as a minute, or they can last up to ten minutes or more. The majority of them – as in 90% – come from the defense, and they are often requested when the judge overrules a defense objection (or, as in this case, sustains a state objection). Many times, the argument the defense articulates at the bench causes the judge to give more latitude to the defense than her original decision allowed. Many judges don't allow side bars or bench conferences at all, some judges allow them in extreme situations, but this judge will allow them upon request. There will be more "may we approach" bench conferences than you can count in this trial.

While the secret arguments play out, the camera focuses on Sandy, Jodi's mother, and her twin sister, Sue. Sandy sits in the gallery with no expression on her face. Just before the camera leaves the sisters, we see Sue making a physical gesture of comfort. It appears as though she is either touching her sister's right leg or her right hand.

In this silent and awkward time out, the camera focuses on Jodi Arias. She is red-faced. She looks down, breathes noticeably, and then looks towards her left. This is where her attorneys and the prosecutor are arguing their positions before the judge as to the relevance of the portable wooden spoon Sandy carried in her purse, circa 1987.

The camera catches Jodi as she is watching her attorneys at the bench, and her lips have retracted into her mouth. She turns her head from her attorneys and looks down. This is an uncomfortably long side bar – a foreshadowing of things to come. The camera then focuses on Tanisha Alexander Sorenson and Samantha Alexander, sisters of the victim. Both bear the features of their brother, Travis Alexander, but Samantha is the female version of her brother. Tanisha stares at the lawyers congregated before Judge Stephen's bench. Samantha looks at Jodi Arias.

As the camera comes back to Jodi, it becomes obvious that she knows who is in her direct line of vision: Tanisha and Samantha. She keeps her head down. She does not want to meet their eyes in this still, formal silence. Still, she continues to turn her head to the left to steal a look at what is happening at the bench. After two minutes and thirty seconds, the judge finally breaks the uneasy silence with her ruling. Whatever was discussed at the bench, in the judge's estimation, it is not irrelevant to discuss the wooden spoon that Sandy Arias allegedly carried in her purse 26 years ago. Jodi's reaction to the ruling is crass -- she wipes her mouth with her hand. Then, she focuses on Kirk Nurmi, who has now returned to the podium.

Nurmi is now faced with the task of getting Jodi back into character. He begins, "Jodi, first of all, do us all a favor, and I know it's difficult, and I know you're nervous, you told us before, but if you could just speak up a little louder and make sure everybody can hear ya, okay?". Translation: We can move beyond the shy, frightened act. You've made your first impression. Let's take it to that Level 2 voice we talked about, okay?". Jodi agrees to speak up.

Nurmi continues, "You were just now telling us that your mother carried a spoon with her. What did she do with that spoon?". Jodi answers, "Um, it was a wooden kitchen spoon that she would keep in her purse". You would think, judging from her countenance and embarrassed tone, that she's talking about a canister of pepper spray or a stun gun that Sandy Arias used on her children.

Moving along, Jodi continues, "And, um, if we were misbehaving, my brother and I – this was before Angela and Joseph were born – um, although it continued through that point -- if we were misbehaving, she would use it on us (she flips her right hand quickly). Sometimes, she would pull the car over, and, you know, or if we were just being brats or something". She swivels back towards Nurmi just in time to meet his next question: "What do you mean by use it on you?". Well, what could she mean, Mr. Nurmi? Did Sandy stir them up as if they were ingredients in a mixing bowl? She beat them with it, of course. Let's get all of the ugly details, and let's pretend that she is actually answering questions that aren't in the script he authored and she rehearsed.

Jodi replies, "She would hit us with it". Nurmi, completely ignoring that a kitchen spoon is nowhere near as lethal as a knife or a gun, asks, "Did she hit you hard?". Arias, the nine year old on the stand, says, "It left welts". Nurmi, channeling a social worker, asks, "It left welts on your body?". No, Nurmi, it left welts on the car. Oh, how tragic this is. I think Travis Alexander, had he been given a choice, would have selected Sandy and her spoon as opposed to Jodi and her knife. Jodi looks traumatized as she answers, "Uh-huh, yes". Nurmi pretends to care as he asks, "When your dad hit you with the belt, did that leave welts on your body?". Juan Martinez interrupts and says, "Objection. Lack of foundation". Nurmi does his best "Huh, are you kidding me?" expression as he stares at the judge and moves his left hand up and down for emphasis. Nurmi is told to rephrase his question.

He rephrases, "You told us that you dad hit you with the belt". She answers, "Yes". Nurmi continues, "After age seven?". She answers, "Yes". Nurmi asks, "Did he leave welts?". Jodi answers, "Um, he didn't leave welts as often as my mom. She also used a belt. My dad was very intimidating, so I don't think he needed to hit us quite as hard to get the point across. My mom didn't carry that fear factor with her, so I think she used more force. So, her blows felt a lot worse, actually".

The camera pans to Sandy and Aunt Sue. Sandy is stone faced, staring straight ahead. Aunt Sue seems to be stifling a grin. Neither woman is remotely attractive, but Sandy is the more haggard of the two middle-aged women. She's more bloated than her sister, more affected, I suppose, by the fact that she gave birth to someone who grew into a human butcher. As if that isn't enough weight to carry in this world, that butcher, the woman who tortured and slaughtered a man, is now going to point a bony finger of accusation in her direction. I'm sorry, but as a mother, I would not be here.

So, what are we dealing with? Are we supposed to invest our emotions into this story? Are we supposed to picture Sandy Arias, circa 1987, pulling her car over, dramatically slamming on the brakes as the gravel flies on some dusty shoulder of the road? Are we supposed to see Sandy reaching into her purse to retrieve her weapon of choice? Are we supposed to cry when envisioning her reaching over her seat to start whacking at her children? If that's the case, Nurmi is out of luck. There's already a movie playing on the screen in my head, and it shows a man being stabbed, sliced, and shot.

Realizing that puddles of blood will always trump welts, Nurmi ask Jodi "to discern for us how many times a week your mother would beat her with this spoon". She replies, "Um, I don't recall how many times, particularly, but it seemed like it could go anywhere from four times a week to once every two weeks. It just depended". Instead of asking the obvious, "It depended on what?", Nurmi says, "Okay".

I find it interesting that Jodi can remember the schedule of spoon beatings from 26 years ago, but she draws a complete blank when she's asked what she and Travis Alexander argued about when she was circling his block in her U-Haul when pulling out of Mesa. She just couldn't seem to come up with anything on that subject. Oh wait, there was something she remembered about that event. She remembers mean old Travis standing in front of his house giving her a very rude gesture. With both middle fingers extended in the air, Travis gave Jodi her final goodbye as she carted her crap out of Mesa for the last time. I'm getting way ahead of the testimony, but try and remember the level of detail she can recall about 1987 when we finally get to 2008. Ask her about the decades old beatings that will become mitigating factors and she's a human video camera. Ask her why her victim cursed her as he finally cut the cord that bound them together and she can't remember anything.

Now we turn a corner. We're going to be regaled with details of second grade extracurricular activities. In a cottony soft tone of voice that will eventually have the same effect as razor blades assaulting your ears, Jodi recalls her lessons in piano, flute, and Karate. Her interests, she says, were art and reading books. This must be the ideal part of her childhood, unless her parents were beating her with her flute and she was defending herself with Karate moves.

Jodi says that her pets "were central" to her life, but Nurmi does not ask her to explain that. No matter. I suspect this little sociopath engaged in a few tree house surgeries ("Mom, I neutered the cat, but he won't wake up!") or some interesting science experiments ("Hey, Carl. I put your frog to bed in the freezer. He's all glittery with ice and sleeping very soundly"). Instead, Nurmi pounces on the art comment. He wants details. He wants to know what areas of the "art world" appealed to the second grader. Perhaps Nurmi is expecting a sophisticated answer – something like Impressionism or Surrealism, but I think he should temper his expectations. I think we're heading into the genre of the glitter, glue, paint, and poster board art. Still, he presses on.

She responds, and I'm not sure if I should laugh or roll my eyes. In total seriousness, she answers, "Yeah. I liked, well, when I was younger – I liked to color, just with Crayola's, and my older sister and I would color, and we – there were a lot of colors – just – she had the big box with all of the Crayola's, and so we would just draw pictures and watch cartoons, and that sort of thing. And, so, I would have coloring books, and I just began to take an interest in that because I wasn't able to draw what I saw, but I would see the art and it would fascinate me, so I slowly began to practice doing that". What did she just say? She liked to color? She just invoked the name, "Crayola" twice, and she seems to have little else to say about her early interest in the "art world". So, summing up, we're left to marvel at, "there were lots of colors".

This IS a murder trial, not a commercial for preschool activities, right? Art, indeed. Does Nurmi intend to magnify every mundane phase of this woman's life? She colored in coloring books as a child. Big deal. Every kid colors. Is that the point? Was little Jodi just like every other child as opposed to a budding sociopath who may have guillotined the crayons? Who cares? There is nothing of meaning here. And that big box of Crayola's with the built-in sharpener on the back of the box? Every kid wanted that. Coveting the 164 pack is not evidence of a budding artistic prodigy.

Wait a minute – what just happened? We were in the wonderful world of color, and now Nurmi is going to drag everyone back to – gasp – the beatings. He asks, "At this point in time, did the beatings from your mother and father, did they continue?". Jodi looks at Nurmi and says simply, "Yes". If we had to talk about the number of crayons she wanted, I'm assuming we're going to have to get some beating details.

Right on cue, Nurmi asks, "Did they increase in nature?". She answers, "They began to increase, I'd say, all the way through my teenage years (she waves her finger as she finishes her sentence)". That's a rather large span of time, isn't it? Is that why she waved her finger as she finished answering? Was she telling the jury that the beatings covered the entire six to seven years of her teenaged life? She will contradict this statement shortly, but for now, this is what Jodi and her lawyer would like the jury to believe. I find it interesting that Nurmi, a lawyer who seems intent on eliciting as much banality as possible from every answer, skips over details that are far more important than coloring books and crayons. Don't worry. We won't skip over anything.

He pushes further and asks, "Did the level of the brutality increase?". Jodi sighs before answering, "Yes, my brother and I would – we didn't like being hit – I know I didn't. So we would squirm around a little and the more we squirmed, the more, the harder they would try to whack us. So, just as that progressed, we – things would increase. At one point, I don't think she meant to, but my mom broke my brother's vein in his wrist. He was putting his hands behind his back to block one of her blows, and you know. Ever since I became a teenager, my dad would get rougher and rougher".

This story sounds familiar. Where have I heard this before? Oh, yes, that's right. I read this excerpt from a manuscript authored by Travis Alexander, her victim. Writing about his desperately sad and horrific childhood in his book "Raising You", Travis wrote: "I learned how to turn so that when she (his mother) hit me, she would strike my back and arms. The pain was less there".

Focusing on Jodi's testimony, try to remember what she just said – her father became "rougher and rougher" when she became a teenager. She will contradict that statement as well. For the moment, I'm wondering who is on trial here. Are Bill and Sandy Arias being pulled into Family Court twenty years too late to answer for crimes against their children, or is their daughter, Jodi Arias, in Superior Court fighting charges of premeditated, first degree murder? It is also interesting to note that Jodi shows no emotion or embarrassment as she recalls being "whacked" and "beaten" by her parents, despite the fact that her mother, now branded a child abuser, is sitting in the front row of the gallery, stone faced and staring at her daughter.

Before Nurmi gets to "rougher and rougher", which he said he intends to do, he asks, "How did you feel? How did it feel when your own mother was beating you?". It's a rhetorical question, of course. It was formulated to inject the jury with a healthy dose of contempt for Sandy Arias. It was also designed to paint Jodi Arias as a victim, not a perpetrator, as the state's evidence strongly suggests. Jodi answers, "When I was younger, I remember feeling – I didn't have a word for it then, but I can describe it as betrayed. And confused. As I got older, it would really make me mad because, I just didn't, I didn't get why, I don't know. I understood that I was being punished, but I would just be mad at her – a lot. Because it hurt". Oddly enough, there is an almost imperceptible grin on her face.

Now that the jury has heard about the physical and emotional pain that allegedly marred her childhood, Nurmi decides that this is the perfect climate in which to introduce the qualities of benevolence and forgiveness that are inherent in his client – the woman accused of a brutal murder. Referring to Sandy Arias, Nurmi asks, "But you still loved her". This is a declaration, not a question, and Jodi replies, "Yeah, I loved my mom". Nurmi interrupts and says, "Even though she was still beating you, you still loved her". Another declarative statement rather than a question. Again, there is nothing to answer, but Jodi says, "It put a strain on our relationship, but I still loved her, of course".

Jodi has an odd affect. Her tone is flat and any sign of emotion is missing. Aside from that one almost-grin, there is nothing to read in her vocal inflections, facial expressions, or body language. To recount crippling childhood brutality with such a consistent attitude of indifference, to maintain direct eye contact with the individual digging into the traumatic memories of an abused individual, to know that thousands and thousands of strangers are listening to something that has been locked away for years, and to recite those descriptions of abuse with such boredom makes Jodi seem disingenuous or heavily medicated. Frankly, her demeanor makes it difficult to believe that she was the victim of a raised voice, let alone chronic physical abuse.

Nurmi is trying desperately to paint an ugly picture of bruised and frightened children. If he is to be believed – rather, if his client is to be believed – there was a dark secret in the Arias home, and that secret was that the parents assaulted their children with frequency.

Nurmi asks Jodi to repeat the last thing she said, which was, "I still loved her". As I said, that is a tactic he uses when he wants Jodi to look better than the grand jury indictment and the evidence permits her to look. He'll also use this tactic when he wants Travis Alexander, the true victim in this trial, to look like a demon covered in happy flesh. Not surprisingly, Nurmi will not use this "would you repeat that" tactic during any testimony he elicits from his client that relates to the way in which she planned and carried out his brutal murder.

As if the point hasn't already been made, Nurmi wants to return to the slaps, whacks, and beatings of yesteryear. He asks, "Going back to what you said about your dad and the beatings getting rougher and rougher, could you describe for us what you mean by that?". Still looking like she's uninterested, Jodi answers, "Yeah, he, well, he never beat me with his fists or anything like that. He would just shove me into furniture, sometimes into the piano or things like that. Um, into tables, chairs, desks – whatever was around. He would just push me (she pushes the air with her hand), and I would go flying, really hard, and I would go flying into that. One time, I hit a door post – the side of my head hit a door post and it knocked me out, momentarily. I just remember waking up on the ground. My mom was there – we were all arguing. I was arguing with my mom, and he got involved. And so, I remember waking up and she was telling him to be careful". Oh, so Sandy, when not whacking the kids herself, played Igor to Bill's Dr. Frankenstein? Please. Nurmi asks her how old she was when she was knocked out after being pushed into a door post. She answers, "By then, I was age 17, maybe 16, but I think I was 17".

I think it's time to call her by her last name. The lies are just beginning, and I'm no longer comfortable calling a cold blooded killer by her childhood name. From now on, she's just Arias. She may go back to being Jodi later, but for time being, she's Arias.

She offered this story to Detective Esteban Flores during her interrogation in July, 2008. Of course, at that time, the story was a little different. She said her father pushed her, but she didn't believe that he meant to push her into a door post and knock her out. During that interrogation, she never mentioned being pushed into chairs, tables, desks, or "anything that was around", but that interrogation was five years ago. Maybe her father did push her and perhaps she hit her head, and if he did, he was absolutely wrong. By now, I'm already of the opinion that she hit her face as the result of a shove and then decided to fall down and pretend she had been knocked unconscious. Why? Maybe I'm just getting tired of hearing about physical abuse from a woman who not only butchered a man, but who terrorized him as he tried, like a mortally wounded animal, to crawl away from her and exhale for the last time without being assaulted by another blow or stab.

Nurmi says, "Let's back up a little bit (that's always a bad sign). You mentioned incidents like being pushed into a piano and furniture like there was just nothin' to it. Did this happen a lot?". She answers, "Not as often with my dad as with my mom, but, um, it just – I don't know, if I did something to upset them, it would, it would happen. Sometimes I got grounded. That became more the norm in high school so that the physical punishment was a little bit more farther apart, but more intense than it was prior".

Did she just say, "a little bit more farther apart"? Yes, she did. That was an awkwardly worded loophole, but one she thinks will help her if anyone on the jury is paying close enough attention to realize that she just contradicted her prior testimony. Earlier, in answer to a question about the frequency of the beatings, she said, "They began to increase, I'd say, all the way through my teenage years". Just now, she said the beatings didn't become more frequent in her teenage years. In fact, they were "a little bit more farther apart". The normal punishment in high school, if we are to believe her latest testimony, was grounding. And, as long as we're nitpicking, she blamed her father when she testified that she had been pushed into a piano, chairs, tables, desks, and a door post. That testimony was offered when she was qualifying "rougher and rougher", and "rougher and rougher" was a phrase used by Nurmi when he was asking about her father, not her mother. Now that Nurmi has made his statement that pushing Arias into furniture was a "nothin' to it" practice in Arias Land, she replies by saying that this didn't happen as often with her father as it did with her mother. So, I'm confused. Just who was pushing whom into furniture? Dad? Mom? Anyone?

Now that her father, a man who is not sitting next to his wife (or anywhere else in this courtroom), has been painted with the child abuser brush, it is time to revisit the sainthood of Jodi Arias. Nurmi asks, "At the time that you were getting these beating from your dad, did you love him, as well?". She answers, "Yes, of course". Of course.

Arias, the victim, has achieved a sense of inner peace when it comes to her abusive parents. She has taken their abuse in stride and matured into a completely normal killer. What a predictable foundation for a defense strategy. Abuse. We've heard this song a thousand times before, but this time, there are some differences. What Arias has described, if true, is parental discipline that crossed a line. Notice that she said, very clearly, that she understood she was being punished when "the beatings" were happening. She is never asked to explain the situation that lead to the discipline. She is never asked if SHE began the physical confrontation that resulted in someone pushing her away. We will learn, later on, that Arias admitted to having a rather violent streak that broke through when she was particularly angry. Several individuals who were close to Jodi Arias will publicly state that the Arias kids were spoiled. Her best friend will say that Arias had a great childhood. There were no signs or tales of beatings. This jury will never hear those statements.

A defense attorney will always probe into the childhood experiences of a client being charged with murder. Frequently, a murderer or serial killer will report horrendous childhood abuse, both physical and sexual. It is common to hear awful things that happened to murderers in their childhoods, and the type of abuse they describe, the type of abuse that breaks so many pieces of a child's heart and rewrites their future, is generally meted out at the hands of sadistic parents, substance abusing parents, or mentally ill parents. For those children, the abuse did not have a genesis in discipline. For those children, it was about being a receptacle for rage, sickness, or evil.

If the type of abuse Arias suffered was so significant as to factor into her murder trial, then I must ask, where is her brother? He's the sibling who suffered a "broken vein" at his mother's hand (and for what it's worth, I'm assuming the Arias parents did not take their son to a doctor for this diagnosis, so how would Jodi Arias, as a child, know that his vein was broken?). Did her brother kill anyone? No, he didn't. In fact, Arias said that she did not believe that her mother meant to break a vein in her brother's hand. For the truly sick and sadistic parent, they don't just mean to inflict serious injury, they enjoy it while it's happening. This is all immaterial, and I won't sicken anyone by listing out the hideous things that sadistic parents do to their children. However, I can tell you, it isn't a swat with a wooden spoon.

Referring again to the book, "Raising Me", written by Travis Alexander, we learn that he endured a childhood ruled by his drug addicted mother. He talks about the type of child abuse that a criminal might have experienced. I've fixed the punctuation for the reader's benefit, but these are his words: "My childhood, unfortunately, was very much like that of any child that had drug addicted parents. My father was never around, which left my siblings and I to the fate delivered by my mother. As she progressively got more involved with drugs, she progressively got less capable of raising children. Most commonly was a beating for waking her up. You see, when you are high on meth for a week, when you eventually come down, there is a lot of sleep to catch up on...there isn't any food cooked...what was rotten would be eaten too. To this day, I have one phobia, roaches. There was nothing more disgusting to me than to wake up to feel roaches crawling on my body. I have never heard, in any movie, on any street corner, or amongst the vilest of men, any string of words so offensive and hateful, said with such disgust, as the words my mother said to my sisters and I. I remember my mother emptying a revolver on the car my father was driving, and my father subsequently taking an axe to my mother's belongings and destroying them". That has the ring of truth. That, I believe.

He also wrote about his family being evicted from their squalid apartment and taking refuge in a broken down trailer. He talks about lice, not bathing, and having serious issues making friends in school because he smelled so bad. He talks about hunger assaulting him while his mother slept, and being taunted by a lone can a food and a can opener that none of the children knew how to use. He talks about eating molding bread. He talks about abuse, the type of abuse meted out by a sick individual. By comparison, Arias' story is weak, at best.

Perhaps we're done with this chapter in her life. Bill and Sandy Arias have endured the humiliation of having their sins – real or contrived – publicly proclaimed by their daughter, but she did say she loved them. Of course. If we believed her, she'd look great and they'd look terrible. But, that's exactly the plan, isn't it?

Nurmi is ready to change course. He asks, "In this time period now, you said you moved from Salinas at about age 11?". She answers, "Yes". Nurmi says, "This is where, in Santa Maria, your dad was pushing you into furniture, right?". She answers, "Yes, things really started in Santa Maria". Again, I have to point out a contradiction. When referring to being pushed into a door post and being knocked out – something she clearly framed as a solitary incident -- Arias said this happened when she was 16 or 17. Now, she's telling the jury that being pushed into furniture was something that happened when she was 11. This testimony doesn't even pass the "rougher and rougher/throughout her teenage years" clause that Nurmi just established.

Nurmi continues, "And is that where you went to – would that have been your junior high years, if I follow you correctly?". Pay attention, Nurmi. This woman was no intellectual prodigy, nor was she diagnosed as learning disabled (that we know of). So, taking into consideration her first failed attempt at kindergarten, she was 12 years old when she attended junior high school.

She answers, "Yes, sixth, seventh, and eighth grade". Nurmi asks, "And, did you go to school with Carl, then?". She answers, "I did". Nurmi asks, "What were your interests at that point in time?". Does anyone else realize that we are still 17 years from the date she murdered Travis Alexander? We aren't really going to go through all of her state mandated education, are we? Are we going to have to endure the scrapbooks of an uninspiring and failed life? Yes, I think we are.

She answers, "At that point, I was really focused on trying to make new friends. That was kind of difficult. In sixth grade, I went to an elementary school, and then I went to another new school. It was called junior high school, but it's now middle school, but it was, um, it seemed like I was constantly going to new schools. There was this new school, then another new school, and then, you know, we moved again, and so, you know, it was just hard to make friendships. I did make a few close friends, though". They moved again? If her testimony is true, this would have been the FIRST move of Jodi Arias' life.

As the defense portrait comes into focus, we see that Jodi Arias was not just a victim of physical abuse; Jodi Arias was also a victim of NSS (New School Syndrome). This could be the testimony of an army brat who was constantly uprooted, moving from home to home and school to school. I'm not sure she suffers from a serious case, but her attorney has muddied the waters enough to confuse the jury.

If you haven't already noticed, Nurmi is not putting on a linear defense, and that's because he can't. He must employ the element of confusion. He will jump around, and he has a very good reason for playing Scattergories. As she testifies, we hear about her experiences in second grade, but then, she's suddenly 17 (or maybe 16), then she's 11. Then, she's taking piano lessons – on a piano with which she will eventually collide as she's thrown around the room. She was knocked unconscious by her father at age 17, but Nurmi will then imply that the pushing began when she was a pre-adolescent. Why? Because picturing an 11 year being knocked out by her father is worse than picturing a 17 year old being knocked out by her father. Both are bad, but one is worse.

There are Crayola crayons immediately followed by a concealed wooden spoon hiding in her mother's purse. Then, we're suddenly back to where the Arias family lived. Oh, and don't forget all of the schools! That made it so hard for little Jodi Ann to establish friendships. Of course, her parents are the cause of that difficulty. Countless young families move when their children are in elementary school. Is it easy for a child? No, it isn't. But neither is it part of the recipe for making a killer.

Let's look at what we've already learned. Arias attended private school in Salinas for three years, and then, for whatever reason, one Nurmi never bothered to question, she was taken out (or expelled) of private school and placed in the public elementary school in the Salinas school district. Considering the fact that Arias was left back in kindergarten, we know that she would have left the private school in Salinas in first grade (at age seven). Arias then attended second, third, fourth, and fifth grade in a public elementary school in Salinas. That's a total of four years for Arias to make school friends. Then, her parents decided to move to Santa Maria.

As Arias refers to "another new school", it is worth remembering that every sixth grade student in Santa Maria was facing the prospect of a new school. Unless the family moved during the summer between fifth and sixth grade – another detail Nurmi is not interested in sharing with the jury – she had spent time in the Santa Maria school district in fifth grade. Each child in that class, including

Arias, was going to go to the local junior high school that particular September. There's at least a 50/50 chance that she did have time to make friends with other kids in that school district, and if she couldn't, it may have had more to do with her personality than her allegedly nomadic parents.

Now that Arias has broken our hearts with a family move, Nurmi wants to know if her passionate fifth grade art interest was still alive when she entered – gasp – yet another school. She answers, "Yes". By now, we all know the essay answer will follow. Nurmi gives her the essay question, and here it is: "Well, you mentioned that during your grade school years, you had an interest in art. Did that continue throughout junior high?". Can you guess what she said? She said, "Definitely. I don't remember so much in sixth grade focusing on my art, but in junior high, I took an art class, maybe two art classes, both years, um, and I had a really cool art teacher who mentored me".

Mentored? She said she was mentored. The rest of the students were being taught, but Arias was being mentored? This mentor, who is probably the teacher Arias mentioned on her blog, the instructor who "allowed her deviate from the linear curriculum", was not teaching a college art course. He wasn't even teaching a high school course for students who were selecting art electives. He was teaching the state mandated art curriculum required in every junior high school. He may be a good artist and a nice man, but too much is being made of this "mentoring". I would be far more impressed if she was a high school senior being mentored, but this is the best Nurmi can find. What is a mentor anyway (as opposed to a teacher)? According to the dictionary, the major difference seems to be that a teacher is instructing a group while a mentor is instructing an individual. Get it? Arias was so full of artistic potential that she was being mentored instead of being taught. Oddly enough, although her artist talent was listed as one of her mitigating factors (a reason to show her mercy), her artist mentor was never called to testify on her behalf.

So, according to Arias, she may have taken two art classes per year for two years. To which years does she refer? We'll never know, but we can suspect they were the junior high years. I didn't know that junior high school students were afforded so much flexibility when it came to scheduling their classes. My recollection is that junior high school classes are assigned, not chosen. I thought the type of freedom to which Arias refers is actually realized in high school – most frequently in the junior and senior years. Does anyone care?

Nurmi is no longer playing with the beatings or New School Syndrome. He plans to stay right here in the world of art. Don't get too comfortable – that could change without notice (we could be back in Sandy's car in fifteen seconds). He asks, "Let me ask you, as it relates to your parents, how was your interest in art received? Did they encourage that? How was it received by your parents?". Arias, a woman who corrected the prosecutor during her cross examination because he asked "a compound question", doesn't seem fazed by the fact that her attorney just asked her several questions at once. She doesn't even need to consider the questions before she answers, "Um, they didn't discourage me by any means, but they were lukewarm, I'd say. You know, they'd go, 'That's nice'. They weren't really moved by it. I was getting a lot of praise from my classmates, and my, um, art teacher, and other people, but I didn't really get that from them. They were just a little bit indifferent, but not disappointed". Well, the times have changed, haven't they? The Arias family is now making and selling prints of Arias' pieces. They're asking for large sums of money (as high as $9,000) for her original paintings. Maybe they took an art appreciation course because they aren't as indifferent as they used to be.

Let's get back to how her family used to respond to her art. They didn't discourage her art – not by any means. Those are HER words. However, her parents were not moved by her art. Whose fault is that? Does the blame lie with the artist or with the viewers? If an art critic, one who could discern innate and raw talent, had seen her junior high pieces and failed to respond enthusiastically, would he or she be subjected to the same level of scrutiny as the parents of Jodi Arias? I've seen the adult artwork of Jodi Arias -- the pieces her family sells while she sits in a closed custody cell at Estrella Jail. Can she copy an image? Well, even if I could allow myself to assume that she hadn't traced the copyrighted images that make up the bulk of her portfolio, I know that I could not call Jodi Arias an artist. Art, if it is art, evokes a visceral reaction in the beholder. That reaction could by a sense of awe, a sense of peace, a sense of sadness, a sense of anger, a sense of pride, a sense of nostalgia, or a sense of deep interest and introspection. It can be many things, but it is a feeling. I feel none of those things when I look at her "original" drawings of pinwheels, sailboats, or a cup of hot chocolate. Looking at an image and saying, "That looks good" is not the same as responding to the piece of a deeper level. That's what great artists do – regardless of the medium. A true artist does not copy, they create. A genuine connoisseur of art is not impressed by someone who can merely draw or paint well. A genuine connoisseur of art feels something stirring inside of them when they view an artist's original work. Jodi Arias has yet to create a single piece of work that would allow her to claim the title of artist. If that wasn't the case, the defense would have located a genuine art critic to testify during her mitigation phase (not that a genuine artist should be given a pass on murder). Even if such an individual would only point out unrealized potential in Arias, that would have been good enough. They didn't. They couldn't. What would have seen is what the Arias parents saw – nothing more than rendering skills.

Nurmi summarizes that Arias was, by the time she was an adolescent, used to her parents failing to foster her youthful artistic pursuits. My conclusion is that the Arias parents realized that their daughter was not going to be able to support herself as an artist. Their reaction to her art tells me that they saw it as her hobby, and I believe they were glad she had a hobby that made her happy. Is there anything so wrong with that? She may have been the best artist in the Arias family, but the real competition is not to be found in the family. Furthermore, they probably realized that their daughter lacked the discipline and tenacity to progress in the world of studios and gallery showings. Those are qualities (or deficits) that marked her adult life. We can safely assume they began in her childhood. Should her parents be condemned for not lying to their daughter? I don't think so. To this very day, Arias' supporters continue to refer to Arias as an artist, but they constitute the minority who are willing to say that the naked emperor is wearing clothes..

Nurmi asks, "Was that hard for you – not to get encouragement from your parents?". She answers, "It didn't really bother me at that time. Um, I would think it was kind of the norm. So, I was accustomed to it". The norm? There's that phrase again. It was used earlier when she was describing the discipline in her childhood home. Now it's being used in a broader sense – the "norm", in this instance, means no parental encouragement.

Nurmi jumps to a conclusion that seems slightly over reactive. He says, "By that point in your life, you were used to them now, not fostering your interests, right?". Slow down, Nurmi. These people spent money fostering her "interests". She was taking lessons to master two instruments – piano and flute. She was taking Karate classes. She never said they discouraged her artwork – not once. In fact, she specifically said they did not discourage her artistic interests. She didn't get the high praise from them to which she felt entitled, but that doesn't allow her attorney to make such a sweeping, generalized conclusion.

Arias attempts to answer. She begins, "Yeah...". Juan Martinez interrupts. He says, "Objection, leading". The objection is sustained. Nurmi drops his head and shifts his weight from foot to foot. His pen, something he doesn't use, remains a prop in left hand. For about ten seconds, he rocks back and forth in front of his podium silently. Finally, he says, "Let me ask you this. Did your parents ever show any interest, as you were growing up, in your artwork? Did they ever foster your interest in art?".

Arias answers, "Um, they did – minimally. At one point, yeah, I think this was after we moved to Santa Maria, uh, I was enrolled in one art class, which was after school (oh, is this the "second art class" to which she previously referred?), and it lasted a few weeks, and I created a few pieces, a few projects, and, um, I remember other family being more encouraging. I have a cousin who is a very accomplished artist, and he complimented my work, and, um, that was in the presence of my parents, so...". Nurmi, reading the signal that she has run out of words, interrupts with, "Okay". Suddenly, Arias decides to elaborate. She adds, "They never went out of their way to display it, or anything like that". She ends with a noise, not a word. It sounds like, "ehh".

How could her parents have gone "out of their way" to display her cousin-approved art? Oh, Mr. or Ms. Very Accomplished Artist Cousin – word to the wise: Don't tell anyone that Jodi Arias is your cousin, unless you're not so accomplished and could use the publicity.

Back to the original question – how could Bill and Sandy Arias have gone out of their way to display their daughter's junior high school art "pieces"? If they had just put one of her "pieces" on their front lawn with some spotlights focused on the work, would that have quelled Jodi Arias' murderous, sociopathic tendencies? If they had simply displayed her work in the foyer of their home – assuming they had a foyer – would Arias have believed her interests were being fostered? Maybe those pieces should have been displayed in the family restaurant. Would that have saved Travis Alexander's life?

Seriously, what were they supposed to do? I think the dynamic duo of Arias and Nurmi would be well advised to put this approach to bed. Jodi Arias, sixth grade artist, seventh grade artist – whatever – was not an art prodigy. Sandy Arias had four children to care for. Perhaps she was just too busy with maternal responsibilities and her full-time jobs as a server in her husband's restaurant(s) or her later position as a dental assistant to smother her daughter in false praise. Bill Arias was trying to run a business and pay the bills. Maybe Jodi Arias picked the wrong time to shove her latest "piece" in his face. Maybe he was changing the alternator on the family car when she decided to play Jodi Van Gogh. Is this what passes for abuse these days?

A hop, skip, and a jump, and now we're off of Arias' unappreciated art projects and onto her high school years. Nurmi asks, "And where did you go to high school?". She answers, "I went to high school, after eighth grade, we moved to northern California, to Yreka, and, umm, I went to Yreka Union High School". Will Nurmi ask why the family moved? Will he make even a single inquiry as to why the family left Santa Maria and headed for Yreka? Did they move because of a change in employment, an opportunity to live in a larger, more luxurious home, or did they move because their daughter, Jodi Arias, had made of mess of her life and needed a change of scenery? It's patently unfair for Nurmi to assume that the jury will blame her parents for the move. Perhaps they were moving because of their daughter. Perhaps they didn't, but unless he asks, we are free to ponder the possibilities, as is the jury.

Nurmi asks another school related question, and Arias replies, "At least, when I was there, it was called Yreka Union High School". My guess is that it is still called Yreka Union High School. With the unlimited tax payer money available to this particular defense team, it's safe to assume that they could have made a simple phone call to the school to see how the school identified the institution. Moving on...

Nurmi is shown on camera as he leans on the podium. He says, "And, I'll ask this because it's, uh, it's different in different places. What, what grades were you in when you entered Yreka High School?".

Is Nurmi about to introduce a few old Yreka High School yearbooks and ask that they be entered into evidence in this case? Does the fact that Jodi Arias went to high school impact this case in any way? Actually, the only thing I'm interested in is the fact that she began school with a failure and ended on the same note. She failed kindergarten and dropped out prior to graduation (in 11th grade). Other than that, unless she stabbed a student, started a fire in the bathroom, was caught slashing the tires on a teacher's car, or had a lengthy list of infractions, how is her high school experience relevant to a murder she committed a decade later and 1,000 miles from that campus?

Arias answers, "Um, that school is grades nine through 10. I'm sorry, nine through 12". Nurmi asks, "Okay. So what years, then, did you enter, then? Did you enter in your freshman year, or like...". Arias looks at the jury and says, "Freshman year". Nurmi continues, "Okay. And, so you were starting off at a new school again in high school, right?". She answers, "Yes". Again, much ado about nothing permeates the air. Nurmi wants the jury to believe that starting at a new school "again" is problematic. In reality, this is Arias' fifth school. Every other child has endured the agony of changing schools three times (elementary, junior high school, and high school), unless their sadistic parents moved at some point in their lives.

Nurmi continues, "Uh, just to give us a sense of things, uh, how far was Yreka from Santa Maria?". Arias answers, "I don't know the mileage, but let's see. From Salinas to Santa Maria, it's eight hours – I'm sorry, from Salinas to Yreka is eight hours, and then Santa Maria is another three hours south, so...yeah, over ten hours". Nurmi interrupts with, "Did you know anybody at Yreka High School?". Arias answers, "Um, I didn't know anybody when I moved there, but my mother, um, went to – I don't know if she went to school with or knew a woman about her age who had a daughter my age who was going to be a freshman – going into high school, as well. So, we hung out a little bit during the summer, so I knew her and her sister, and that was it". Sandy Arias played against type? The child abuser took the time to hook her daughter up with a friend? Why would she do that? Abusers don't do that kind of thing, do they?

Nurmi's drops his pen on the podium. It makes a loud noise, but we'll have to get used to that. This isn't the last time he will drop his pen next to a microphone. He replies, "Just a couple of people". It's not a question, yet Arias answers, "Yes".

Nurmi continues, "Now, you mentioned, uh, when you moved to – based on what you told us before – are we correct in understanding that the beatings and the pushing into furniture – that sort of thing with your dad -- continued throughout your high school years?". Nurmi, in case you weren't listening to what she told us before, "the beatings" took place during all of her teenaged years. As it stands, Bill Arias was beating his 19 year old daughter, despite the fact that she moved out of his home when she was 17 years old. If she was actually beaten during all of her teenaged years (as she testified to earlier), are we to assume she returned to her parents' home on the weekends for those beatings?

How many times is he going to revisit this issue? Arias seems comfortable answering these same questions again. She says, "Yes". She nods her head once to add a sense of conviction to her response. Nurmi asks, "Were those the incidents that you were talking about before about being pushed into the post and the furniture, or were there other incidents?". For those not keeping score, this is the third time in seven minutes that Nurmi has reminded the jury that Arias was allegedly knocked into a door post by her abusive father.

Arias answers, "That happened when I was in high school. Um, there were a few things that happened right before we moved. Um, a bunch of friends and I, one night, decided, like the last night that I was there, we tried to sneak out of the house and hang out and, um, my parents woke up and found out. So, when I came back, um, my dad asked where I had been, and um, I was, I had fallen asleep and he woke me up around six, and so when I s-s-sat. I sat up, you know, because I was disoriented because I had been sleeping, so I didn't give him a satisfactory answer, so he, um, he hit me across the face, and I fell back down, and so then he sat me up again and I didn't give him a satisfactory answer, again, and he hit me across the face, and I fell down, and um..." . How dare a father show his anger when he discovers that his fertile, eighth grade (14 year old) daughter is lying to his face as she refuses to admit that she left the house to party all night with her friends? What was the unsatisfactory answer she gave? Was it, "Screw you, and mind your own business"? Was it, "Huh? I wasn't out last night". Was it, "I'm sorry. My friends threw me a going away party and it got out of hand"? Once again, we're left to draw our own conclusions because Nurmi refuses to ask the right question.

Actually, I'm surprised she had any friends who were interested in spending the night with her. Until this point, I thought she was lonely Jodi Arias, chronically friendless. I am, however, delighted to know that she overcame her serious affliction of NSS (New School Syndrome). Much was made of that by Nurmi, and while it would have been nice to hear about her progress in more detail, I guess this will have to suffice.

Nurmi asks, "When you say he hit you across the face, did he punch you?". Much to Nurmi's dismay, Arias answers, "No, it was an open handed, hard slap". Oh, too bad, Mr. Nurmi. It was just an open handed slap, but it was a hard slap. Does that help?

Nurmi asks, "Do you recall, did you bleed?". She answers, "No, I didn't. Not that I recall". That means she didn't bleed. Nurmi continues, "Did you bruise?". More bad news. Arias answers, "Not that I recall". I guess we're going for the consolation prize. Nurmi asks, "Did it hurt?". Arias answers, "Yes". Yawn. Moving along.

Nurmi asks, "Just so we can clarify as well, your dad's a pretty big guy, right?". Well, Mr. Nurmi, for today's purposes, he'll be a pretty big guy. However, this jury will never hear what she told Detective Esteban Flores during her interrogation in 2008. Back then, she said that her father's health was declining, and it had been declining for ten years. It doesn't matter that 15 years later, he's still very much alive. What matters is that Mr. Solarflex smacked his daughter because she didn't give him a satisfactory response – nearly 20 years ago.

Arias answers, "He was very big at that time. His health is – he's frail now – but he was very big at the time". Okay. Let's assume he was very big at the time. Did he slaughter Travis Alexander on June 4, 2008? No, he didn't. The woman who failed to give a satisfactory answer to her bull of a father – twice – did that.

Nurmi has a lot riding on this. He continues "Can you give us an idea of how tall and how, uhh, much he weighed at that time?". She answers, "I don't know his weight, but he's about 5'11". He used to bench press 520 pounds. He, um, was a really big guy...for a while". Does Nurmi believe that the individuals on this jury are going to connect his dots? Is Bill Arias, the frail man who used to be a really big guy, going to be responsible for the murder of Travis Alexander?

Here's another example of Nurmi's selective hearing impairment: "You said he used to bench press 500 and something pounds". I wasn't at the table when these two were writing this script, and I remember the weight Bill Arias bench pressed. It was 520 pounds. However, Nurmi would like his client to repeat that number, and she's ready to do that. She responds, "Five twenty, yes".

Nurmi is like a dog with a bone. He asks, "Was that a hobby of his – weightlifting – or can you describe that for us?". Oh, I'm sure she can describe "that" for us. Arias answers, "Yes, he was very much into weight lifting. He had, um, I guess it was a Bowflex machine at home. I think it was called Solarflex (that's why she called it a Bowflex). It was one from like, the eighties, but he would use that a lot to work out. Um, he was into martial arts. We would watch a lot of movies like that. Um, you know, things like that. He went to the gym frequently".

What is the point of this testimony? Is Kirk Nurmi saying that a man who worked out and went to the gym frequently was engaging in that sort of physical development so that he could slap his daughter when she didn't give him satisfactory answers? Kirk Nurmi, along with a compliant Jodi Arias, is building Bill Godzilla Arias, and he's doing it right before our eyes. Does Mr. Nurmi have a single medical report to indicate that Daddy Sasquatch broke a single blood vessel in his daughter's body? Does Miss Arias, the defendant, have anything to offer beyond the brand name of Bill Arias' workout equipment? If not, can we move along? Will he at least drag either parent to the stand to say, "Yes, we were too hard on Jodi – physically speaking". No, he won't – not even when it really counts, which will be during her life or death mitigation phase.

Nurmi asks, "To your knowledge, was your mom aware – I know you mentioned the one incident where your mom was present – was your mom aware of your dad beating you?". Let me guess, mom was more than aware – she had a ring side seat. I can almost smell the Jiffy Pop wafting in from the Arias kitchen as dad danced around his 1980's Solarflex machine in satin shorts while punching the air to warm up for the beatings. Arias answers, "Um, well when she was present, yes, of course. Sometimes, we were on road trips together and, um, they would take turns (Arias uses both hands and does windshield wiper motion), if they, you know, if they had to pull the car over – not that it happened several times in one trip – but I remember it being both my mom and my dad punishing me, in the presence of each other".

Now, hold the phone. She just said, under oath, that her parents "took turns" beating her on road trips. She said it casually and easily. So, how did this work? Did an opportunity to inflict a vehicular beating arise and her mom would pull out the beating schedule from the glove compartment while saying, "You're right, Bill. You did beat them on the way to Mount Shasta. It is my turn. Let me get my purse".

Arias isn't done. She continues, "And, um, I don't know. When she was gone, I assumed they would talk about it". Well, of course they talked about it. They had to update the beating schedule for the next trip.

Arias swallows hard and looks at Nurmi. He asks, "We talked a little bit about your dad during high school, your mom with the wooden spoon – in your younger years, did your mom's beatings with the wooden spoon, did they continue in high school, as well?". This question has been asked and answered. Depending upon which answer you prefer to ascribe to this specific period of time, the beatings gave way to groundings in high school, or she was being shoved into pianos and furniture in high school...by her dad, or her mom, or her dad, or her mom...maybe.

Let's look at what's behind Door Number Three! Arias answers, "They continued for a short time, but I think as I turned 16, 17, she, I don't recall her carrying the wooden spoon around. She would just start grabbing for whatever was available, like a hairbrush or – she had acrylic nails, so sometimes she would grab me and dig her nails into my skin, things like that". Arias should copyright the phrase, "things like that". She uses that phrase as punctuation. It's her way of saying, "This sentence is finished". It typically follows one tale of abuse – a single tale she prefaced with a promise of multiple tales that are never delivered. Whether the alleged abuser is her mother, her father, or Travis Alexander, she trails off with "things like that". Well, in the case of acrylic nails, circa 1997, what are "things like that"?

Sandy Arias, the mother of the victim on the stand, stares at her daughter. Long gone are the days of acrylic nails and hairbrushes retrieved in an instant. Sandy wears the blank face of a corpse with its eyes opened. Nothing. We can read nothing. In her head, she's probably remembering hairbrushes thrown in her direction and losing an acrylic fingernail as the projectile bounced off her manicured hand. But for now, Sandy Arias has to accept the limited comfort her womb-mate, Sue Allen Halterman, can give her. I'm sure it's precious little comfort to a woman whose body nurtured the fetus that became Jodi Ann Arias.

Nurmi has turned another corner. He wants to know what Arias was interested in during high school. Arias, a woman who obviously likes to talk about herself, answers, "In high school, um, I was very interested in learning Spanish, so I took that in high school and middle school. Um, I was getting into art. Um, I was excited to get my driver's license. Um, I traveled abroad to Costa Rica (pause) – to learn Spanish better. Um (she's running out of interests, she clicks her tongue and sighs to fill the silence), I had a few friends – I didn't get – I didn't really make a lot of friends, close friends, like I had before. It just seemed like I was constantly making friends and then we were moving away".

I'm relieved that Juan Martinez interrupts and says, "Objection, beyond the scope. She was asked about what her interests were in high school". Judge Sherry Stephens sustains the objection.

I want to hear about Costa Rica. She went there "to learn Spanish better"? I thought you could learn Spanish in school, but maybe there are better ways – Costa Rican ways. Perhaps Costa Rica represents another case of educational mentoring in the life of Jodi Arias. I'll venture a guess that a young, tanned, male Costa Rican wanted to mentor Jodi in Spanish. We'll get back to Costa Rica later.

Now Nurmi is talking about Arias' friends in high school (or lack of them) – her amigos and her amigas. Where are they? I don't remember a single sentence that included the words, "lots of friends". True, she did mention sneaking out of her house the night before a family move to hang out with her friends, but that doesn't count because it was before high school. Besides, that incident wasn't raised to address the issue of friends in her life. That incident was raised to highlight her father's violent reaction to her all-nighter. Although Nurmi has portrayed his client as the lonely girl, if he needed to dig up some friends for her in order to sell the Story of the Smacks, then so be it.

Now that Nurmi is asking about high school, we are asked to put into place a foundation that does not exist. What friends is he talking about? Well, if her parents are to be blamed again, friends, or former friends, must be added to the equation to support Arias' claim of newly acquired social isolation (something she is claiming). It all goes back to her parents and their decision to move. Nurmi never asked if she was moving to a nicer home, a better school district, or an environment that would afford their children more opportunities. With no information, he suggested that the move socially damaged Arias.

We're about to get the inside scoop relating to the throngs of friends Arias had. When? Who knows? Here's what she said: "I had, um, I had a large circle of friends, but nobody I was very close with". Well, is that a premonition of the future? Does anyone recall PPL conventions? How about LDS wards and social gatherings? As I recall, those individuals were not her close friends. Those individuals allowed her to be a tag-along. Their motives were either to usher another associate into PPL or to usher another convert into the LDS fold. Jodi Arias is a person always on the fringes of whatever group to which she has attached herself.

Nurmi is finished with Jodi's friends (or lack thereof). He asks, "Would I be correct in assuming that your interest in art in high school moved beyond the Crayola crayon phase?". Really? He decided to remind the jury about crayons? Well, he's the guy earning $225 an hour, so let's see where he takes this. She answers, "Yeah, very much so". He replies, "Tell us about that". I'd much rather hear about the day she shot, stabbed, and sliced, but I guess we're going to get a lesson in art appreciation.

She answers, "Um, my grandmother – I was at my grandmother's house one day, and she had an old set of oil paint, and I knew what oil paint was – I'd never worked in that medium before, so umm, I didn't know what I was doing. I just took a piece of paper – printer paper – and started painting oil paint on this paper and it began to, oil began to spread around the paint. So, I figured that's not gonna work, so um, I went to Michael's, the arts and crafts store, and bought some supplies and began to experiment with that and, umm, started painting".

Maybe I'm expecting too much, but I was prepared to hear about her mentor, not her grandmother's kitchen table. The subject was her interest in art, right? We've already heard about the fact that she's being mentored, right? Now, I know we are supposed to be impressed by her use of the word, "medium", but I'm not. Printer paper? Isn't that a medium? Ancient oil paints? Crayola crayons? Is there anything to prove, beyond the word of Jodi Arias, that anyone believed she had artistic talent? Will a seventh grade art teacher show up in her mitigation phase? Spoiler alert – No.

Nurmi asks, "And did you work during high school?". Unless the answer is that she was painting portraits on the sidewalk during Yreka street festivals, why are we jumping from art into work? Actually, and I'm keeping score, we've jumped from scheduled beatings during road trips, acrylic fingernails as a weapon of choice, groups of friends, no friends, household moves, art appreciation, and now we're back to employment. Confusing, isn't it? Just as you begin to get a picture of Arias – true or contrived -- Nurmi changes the subject.

In answer to Nurmi's question about Arias working during high school, she replies, "I did. My dad owned a restaurant at the north end of town. It's now a Mexican restaurant, but he owned it then, and I would work as a server there. Um, from the time I was a freshman on through, I think 96 or 97 when he closed it". Nurmi asks, "So you started working when you were in ninth grade? How old were you then?". She answers, "In ninth grade, I was 15". Nurmi ask if there were a certain amount of days she worked while in high school. Arias answers, "Ahhh, he put me on a few afternoons and on the weekends". What an abuser. He gave his daughter a paying job. No job searches. No boring applications. No interviews.

There is a silence in the courtroom. With the exception of the noise made by Nurmi's pen being dropped on his podium, all is quiet. Nurmi must be getting ready to bring up something important. Finally he asks, "Did you graduate high school?". She answers, "No, I didn't". Okay, let's see how her inability to reach this typical American milestone was the fault of somebody else. I'm also wondering why she didn't opt to take the California High School Proficiency Exam. If she finished the tenth grade and was at least 16 years of age, she could have taken that test. California law says the CHSPE certificate is the equivalent of a high school diploma. She had years to take this test, or she could have taken a GED exam. Why didn't she? What kind of career could she hope for without a high school diploma? Well, perhaps the kind of career her father handed her.

Nurmi asks, "Why didn't you graduate high school?". The simple answer is that she dropped out. I don't think we're going to get the simple answer. She looks down and keeps her gaze fixed on the floor. There is a pause before she says, "At the time, I (long pause) – about three months (another pause) – well, it's kind of complicated. Should I?". It's kind of complicated? No, it isn't. The choices are very simple: expulsion, serious illness, too many failed classes, a personal choice, adherence to a religion that forbade formal education, or she was kidnapped and held hostage for two years. That's about as complicated as it gets.

She obviously needs some help with this one. She stares a Nurmi with her lips parted. Her large front teeth are on display. Nurmi is willing to help Arias explain the complicated scenario of dropping out of school. He suggests that they "talk about it", and talk about it, they do. He throws her the first question: "Did you drop out of high school?". She answers, "Yes, I did". Now, that wasn't so hard, was it? There's the answer to the question. Perhaps we can move on to something like, oh, I don't know, maybe the murder? She killed a man in 2008, and here we are stuck in the 1990s.

Nurmi asks, "Where were you living at the time you dropped out of high school?". Oh, here it comes -- the identity of the individual who caused Arias to drop out of school. A person who obviously never heard the old adage, "a mind is a terrible thing to waste", is about to be revealed. Arias answers, "Um, I was living with my boyfriend at the time, about six miles, it's a little town about six miles outside of Yreka". Wow. What a scandal! Who are we going to blame? Will it be the boyfriend who convinced Arias that it was more fun to stay at home and roll around in the sack than to finish her education, or will it be those awful parents who either allowed their high school age daughter to move in with her lover or made her living conditions so awful that she had no choice but to leave home?

Arias repeats an unsightly gesture I've just begun to notice. She sticks out her tongue and then retracts it. While her tongue is going back into her mouth, Nurmi says that this situation needs to be broken down. Of course it does. He asks, "Why did you leave – prior to that, were you living with your parents?". She turns her head toward the jury and says decisively, "Yes". Nurmi continues, "Why did you leave your parents' home to go live with your boyfriend". There you have it. It wasn't her boyfriend's fault that she left high school (despite the fact that she was under his roof when she pulled the plug on education); it was the fault of her parents. Apparently, their abusive and controlling tentacles can reach across town – six miles, in fact.

Her answer as to why she left her parents is on her lips. She says, "Um, I was kind of becoming tired of the discipline, and I was three months until I was 18, and um, one day they um, decided to ground me until I was 18 because I was, I had skipped one period in high school because there was a final for my um – I was taking a college history class, US History – and I wasn't – I didn't feel that I had adequately studied for the exam. So, I skipped that period to study for the exam and decided I would make it up the next day. So, I parked my car in the parking lot of Rite-Aid and just cracked open the book, and I was studying it for that hour, and my dad – somehow he found me – it's a small town. So, I guess the school notified him that I wasn't present for that class. So, he found me, and um, at that point, they didn't use physical discipline that day, but I was grounded 'til I was eighteen. So, I couldn't fathom being grounded three months. When you're grounded in my house, it meant no phone, no TV, no friends, no social functions of any kind. Um, you're in your room. Period. Um...". She was about to continue, but Nurmi cut her off.

Before we get to Nurmi, I'd like to summarize this so-called "complicated" explanation. It's actually not complicated at all. We learned a few things about Jodi Arias. She "was kind of getting tired of discipline". That means that nobody was going to tell Arias how to behave, particularly the people paying for the roof over her head and the food in her stomach. Groundings, of the conventional variety, were not something she was going to abide. Next, we learn that Arias, who later reveals that she finished this particular school year with nothing but Ds and Fs, wants applause and recognition because she was taking a college level US History course. Sorry, Arias, nobody is buying this. If she finished this "college course" with an A or a B, we would have heard about it. So far, all we know is that her final report card was full of Ds and Fs. So, she failed the course she's bragging about, in all probability. If she passed, it was by the skin of her teeth. Then, we learn that Arias "decided" that she was going to take the exam the next day, despite the fact that all of the other students had to take it on the day she cut class. So, we also know that Arias was a rule maker and a rule breaker. No discipline, exaggerated accomplishments, and the rules don't apply to her. This tells a lot about Jodi Arias – perhaps more than Nurmi intended.

Breaking this down a little more, we learn that Arias didn't like the new form of discipline her parents had adopted when she was in high school. We've heard about the beatings, but for some reason, groundings are what really pushed her buttons. She didn't leave home when she was pushed into a door post and was subsequently rendered unconscious at the age of 16 or 17 (she was sketchy on which year that assault occurred); she left home when she was grounded. The defense would also like the jury to hone in on the word "college". Why? Well she didn't go to college, so why even bother to use the word in her testimony? Simple. Nurmi must connect her aborted education to her parents. The implication is that they, with their brutal groundings, set in motion a set of circumstances that robbed Jodi Arias of her college education. Arias tries to add some verbal flourishes to detract from her own responsibility in this ill-conceived decision. She didn't cut the class the day of the exam, she just "wasn't present". She claims that she didn't feel she had "adequately studied" for the exam. In truth, she probably hadn't studied at all. Whose fault was that?

How did she remedy the situation? She made herself the exception to the rule. Every other student in that class was required to take that exam, and they were required to take it on one particular day. Without a legal absence, cutting the class – for whatever reason – would have earned Arias a righteous score of zero. Her casual attitude, as she told the jury that she had decided to study and take the exam the next day, was shocking. She actually appears to be totally unaware of the gravity of her admission.

Arias gets into her car – because the abusers let her have a car – and she drives to Rite Aid to "study". After hearing about the prior antics of violent Mr. Solarflex, I was expecting to hear that Bill Arias pulled his daughter out of her car while Sandy came running toward her waving a wooden spoon in the air. However, according to Arias, there was "no physical discipline that day". So, in short, we have a rule breaker. She has a problem with authority, whether it is parental authority or institutional authority. Oh, and the grounding? She lists out the restrictions as though they are unique to her situation, as though they are unique to incarcerated in prisons or internment camps. What she described was a typical American grounding. She shouldn't have had to concern herself with the "no friend" and "no social functions of any kind" restrictions since, according to Arias, her parentally driven, nomadic lifestyle left her with few friends (if any).

Now that we know that the Arias parents subjected their children to a Draconian form of grounding, Nurmi inquires as to when Arias experienced this punishment. Specifically, he wants to know if it happened in her junior year or her senior year of high school. I'm surprised he's asking this question. Left as it is, most jurors would remember that she was three months shy of her 18th birthday. That would lead to the assumption that she dropped out in April of her senior year. That's tragic. However, remember, she's a year older than everyone else in the 11th grade. She repeated kindergarten, so if this happened in her senior year, she would have said that she was three months shy of her 19th birthday, not her 18th birthday.

Arias does a mini song and dance, but finally admits that all of this drama occurred in her junior year of high school. Okay, so no senior portrait, prom, or cap and gown for Arias. What's next? Nurmi asks her if he understood her correctly – did she drop out in her junior year of high school? Arias answers, "I did finish my junior year, mostly with Ds and Fs".

For those of us who graduated high school, the grade of "F" means no credit was earned. If Arias earned mostly Ds and Fs, then we can assume that she failed at least several courses, and barely passed the rest of them. Those failed courses, if she was going to earn enough credits to graduate as a senior the following year, would have to be redone, retaken, and regraded. Technically, she finished her junior year, but she was going to have to stuff her senior schedule with those failed classes to actually graduate. This is all just a question of semantics, and the defense is hoping that we're not keeping score. I'm also confused, by design, as to how she dropped out of high school in April of her junior year (she said she dropped out in May quite audibly, but almost whispered when she corrected herself and said "April"), but still claims, under oath, that she finished her junior year. She did not. The jury is not stupid. I think they understand the bait and switch that's being presented to them.

The last word on this subject comes from Arias. She testifies that by the end of her junior year in high school, she "just let it all fall apart". Her mitigation specialist, Maria de la Rosa, is entitled to retrieve all of Arias' high school records. This would be the time to put "it all fell apart" on the overhead projector. Can we see some proof that college bound Arias let it all fall apart at the end of her junior year of high school? No. We'll have to take her word for it, and her word, even at this early stage of her testimony, isn't worth very much.

Nurmi runs away from Arias' decision to drop out. He just set the stage for some details, but now, as the author and director of this play, he is exercising his discretion to change course. He doesn't really want the jury to focus on the real situation surrounding Arias' impulsive and irresponsible decision to drop out of high school. He's decided that it's time to go back to discipline and groundings because he needs to link her decision to box herself into a life of minimum wages jobs with something that was beyond her control. It's an obvious and heavy handed tactic, and if I had been a juror, it would have never passed muster. It's time to take the spotlight off of the woman who signed the drop out papers and put it back on her parents. He says, “You talked about discipline and groundings.”

The camera lands on the Allen twins, sitting, as usual, in the front row of the gallery behind the defense table. I'm getting a clear picture of how this testimony is hitting Arias' mother, Sandy Allen Arias. She is not relaxed. She sits next to her twin sister, Sue Allen Halterman, in the front row. Aunt Sue sits with earphones in her ears, but her mouth is slightly upturned. Is that a grin? Well, it's certainly not a frown. By contrast, Sandy's mouth doesn't reflect a hint of a grin. She is frowning. Make of that what you will.

Now that Arias has described what a grounding is, Nurmi wants a little clarification. He says, “Well, let me ask you this. This was then towards the end of your senior year of high school, or was it in...”. He trails off as Arias interrupts and answers, “Yeah, it was in May...I think”. Arias tries to look confused, as though the question was which month she dropped out of high school, not which year. They really don't want the jury to know that she was a 17 year old, high school junior who called it quits. Unfortunately for Arias, Nurmi must be specific as he has no idea if Juan Martinez will clarify any ambiguity served to the jury as it relates to Arias and high school. He knows it would be better for Arias if he were to coax this information from his client rather than allowing Martinez to rip it out of her.
Nurmi's voice is heard as he says, “Okay, so your senior year or your junior year?”. Arias answers, “Maybe in April”. He is asking the year, and she obviously doesn't want to disclose the year. Finally she answers, “Um, my junior year...yes”. Nurmi responds, “So, you dropped out of high school before you finished your junior year, is that right?”. The woman is under oath. She just said she dropped out in May, probably April, of her junior year. To be specific, she just testified to the fact that she **finished her junior year.**

The school year ends in most states in June, some states in May, and no states in April (which she just said is probably when she dropped out). That means she didn't finish her junior year. She's about to backtrack. She answers, “No, I did finish the junior year, mostly with Ds and Fs, um, because toward the end of the year, I just let it all fall apart”. What actually happened is that her teachers submitted grades for her final report card (and they included every zero she earned). She was likely cutting school in the spring to be with her vampire boyfriend, Bobby Juarez. However, she still received a final, failing report card at the end of the year.

For all intents and purposed, Arias dropped out of school in April of her junior year. That is what she just told the jury – May, no actually April. Perhaps it wasn't official, or maybe it was. The bottom line, the truth, is that she made a final decision not to return to school after she got her final report card – the report card decorated with lots of sad Ds and Fs. If, as she says, she let it all fall apart at the end of the year, why would her final exam for the US History college course mean anything to her? She knew it was all falling apart, including the US History class. No, she didn't cut that class to study for a year that had, by her own admission, already been flushed down the toilet. She cut that class because high school was over, and it would take two years and a full schedule to graduate. Who wants to be the high school graduate who can combine their 20th birthday party with their graduation party? The answer? A person who realized, after failing her junior year that she had to change her ways and set some goals. Being two years behind her peers in college was preferable to being a minimum wage worker forever. Unfortunately, this was something she never realized.

Of course, Nurmi wants to move away from high school? Why? Simply put, most middle class American teenagers find a way to graduate on time. The warnings from the school are fast and furious when a student is in this kind of danger. There is no doubt that Arias was smart enough to graduate high school. Her issues have nothing to do with a lack of normal intelligence. Her issues have a lot to do with her unwillingness to conform to societal norms.

What are we dealing with at this point? We've got an unattractive, very obese attorney volleying softball questions to a woman on the stand, a 33 year old killer, who has been obviously and offensively disguised to look like an eighth grade student, and anyone with moderate intelligence can see through their game. She's a drop out – pure and simple. Their attempts to make it more complicated, more psychological, and more unique than that are falling flat. Nurmi must get off of his client's personal issues with authority and put the spotlight back on...anybody.

He asks, "You mentioned discipline. You talked about grounding. Was there a...any particular physical incident or incident of abuse that motivated you to leave your parents' home?". Just in case you weren't paying attention, abuse has been proven, according to L. Kirk Nurmi. I was listening carefully to her testimony. She just said that a three month grounding was something she couldn't "fathom". She made it crystal clear, with background elements of a college level exam and a quick school escape to the Rite Aid parking lot, that she decided to leave home because she was going to be caged in her room for the next three months (solitary confinement in the Estrella jail must be killing her). If that was not the motivating reason to leave her parents' home, the she perjured herself two minutes ago. I suspect she will perjure herself now. She's going to bring up a physical incident.

As predicted, she answers, "Um, one of the – yes – the incident I described where I was knocked against – I called it a door post, I guess it's a door frame – um, then at that point, I was, the guy I was dating, we started talking about me possibly moving in with him, so after that incident, I began to um, surreptitiously pack boxes of my things and start moving them out to his house...and um, then when it came, when they grounded me until I was 18, all of my stuff mostly was there, and I thought, I'm just gonna go ahead, I was gonna wait until I was 18 to move in with him, but, it was three months away, and it just made sense to me at the time – as a 17 year old, so, I just moved out". Oh, nicely played, Arias, nicely played. The hand gesture, the lifted brows that accompanied the "what's a teen to do?" facial expressions almost made that believable. On, and the use of the word "surreptitiously"? She knew it was too obvious to use that word instead of something more akin to an 11th grade drop-out. She could have said, "secretly". Yes. That would have made sense. Every individual in the jury box would have understood, "I began to secretly pack boxes of my things...", but surreptitiously? That's the clarion call of an intellectual, someone who, had she not been grounded – oh, no, change that – had she not been pushed into a door post – oh, no – change that – had she not been pushed into a door frame (because being exact on the details is so important), she could have been an intellectual giant. She's so smart, and damn her parents for robbing that degree from her!

Nurmi doesn't react to her five syllable word. We're just supposed to assume he knows that he's on equal footing with this could have been professional. He asks, "After you junior year, did you just not go back to high school? Is that...". Again, she cuts him off and answers, "Yeah, I turned 18 that summer. I got a job at another restaurant and began working there full time. I had bills to pay now – car insurance and credit cards and that kind of thing. Um, to me, it just made more sense to work so I could support myself and my boyfriend – he didn't have a job, so...".

Before we get into her boyfriend, can we talk about the bills she had to pay? Are we being asked to believe that the abusers were paying for her car insurance before she liberated herself from Hell House? Credit cards? Who gave Arias credit cards, and if they did, why should we feel sorry for her for using them? Biggest question? Do you know any woman who uses the word "surreptitiously" in conversational English who doesn't understand that moving in with an unemployed man is a bad idea? How does this reflect on Bill and Sandy Arias? (Truthfully, I believe they breathed a sigh of relief when she finally let them off the hook and moved in with her boyfriend).

Nurmi asks, "What was your boyfriend's name?". She answers, "His name was Bobby". Nurmi continues, "What was his last name?". She answers, "Juarez". Nurmi asks, "And Mr. Juarez...ehhhh...how old was he in relation to you?". She answers, "He was three years older than me". Nurmi continues, "So, he would have been out of school, I assume". Oh, save it Nurmi. You're not assuming anything – you're reading from a script.

Arias answers, "Yes, he was out of high school". Nurmi asks, "And, what did he do for a living?".

Arias answers, "Um, he had never been employed at that point, so...he...it was an isolated town we lived in, and it was difficult to obtain employment". Arias looks desperately at Nurmi as she cuts her answer short. The town was so isolated that it was difficult to obtain employment? How then, I wonder, did a high school dropout gain employment in that town while a 20 year old high school graduate just couldn't find a job? This is going to get interesting. Were there no convenience stores, no grocery stores, no gas stations, no construction companies, no bars willing to hire an able bodied, high school educated young man?

Nurmi continues, "Let me ask you this, as it relates to Mr. Juarez, where did you meet him?". The prosecutor, Juan Martinez, is hunched over his desk staring at Arias. When he hears this question, he visibly furrows his brow and wears an "are you serious?" expression on his face. That's because there was a more reasonable question Nurmi should have asked Arias at this point. " The Tale of the Truant Teen" is wearing thin, but at least Nurmi can keep up moving forward. The question on the minds of the jurors is probably, "Let me ask you this, as it relates to Mr. Juarez, how was he paying rent at your new address if he had never been employed?". Yes, I'd like an answer that that. How did he intend to add another mouth to feed at Casa Juarez if he had no income? Was he living off of government assistance?".

If Nurmi and his client are following the pattern they've already laid out, there is more to Mr. Juarez' employment problems than they care to discuss right now. First, they're going to have to make him human. They're going to have to make him attractive enough for a 17 year old girl to toss her most basic education out the window in exchange for living with him. That won't be easy when one considers that he has no job, no money, and lives in a hovel. However, they're going to try. Put on your BS masks, because the crap is out to fly.

Nurmi wants to know when Arias met Bobby Juarez. She answers, "I first met him the first summer that I moved to Yreka, when I was 15. Um, a carnival came to town, and so, I was there with the girl that I mentioned that my mom had introduced me to. Um, her, her sister, and I were there, and I saw him walking in the crowd with a few other friends, and he caught my eye. He was very intriguing looking. He was kind of dressed like 18th century goth, kind of". Arias smiles as she remember Count Dracula at the County Fair. The prosecutor, Juan Martinez, is hunched over his desk. He rolls his eyes without rolling his eyes. He knows what I know. We are being forced to watch Arias' mental home movies (we've gone back in time, yet again – further from the murder).

Nurmi, who chokes the life out of every sentence, wants more detail. In my opinion, he is insulting the jury with this plague of useless detail. He is also boring them to death. These stories are so drawn out, so dull, and so pedantic that they are eating up hours of time. This is a frightening foreshadow of things to come. These jurors didn't enlist in the army. They came here for a relatively brief period of time to complete their civic duty.

Nurmi asks, "For those who may not follow that reference, just kinda...". Nurmi is smiling and waving his left arm in the air as he speaks. Arias is smiling, too. She doesn't even wait for him to finish his question before she says, "He, Heee....". Nurmi cuts her off and finishes, "...kind of describe what he was wearing". I'm not sure if Nurmi was finished, but Arias really wants to talk about Bobby Juarez and his goth clothing. I don't know why. Were they found at the crime scene?

She cuts Nurmi off again and says, "Yeah, it was like July or August when I met him, and it's, maybe in the triple digits, the temperature, it's very hot. Yreka gets really hot – not quite like the desert, but in the triple digits in the summer. But this guy was dressed in a black suit and a high collar, white shirt, and he was on crutches. Um, he had long, dark, curly hair, and he just seemed intriguing to me as I remember seeing him walk by, and, I didn't approach him or anything, um, but, I noticed him. We spent the day there – my friends and I were walking around, and at one point, my friends and I, we were getting – they were getting in line for the Zipper. I didn't want to get on The Zipper. There was only two per cage anyway, so I was kind of the third, odd one out, so I just stood next to the line kind of waiting for them to get on The Zipper and come back. So, I was just looking around, and I caught his eye, and he was looking right at me, and he motioned for me to come over. He went like that (Arias raises her two hands and shows the jury a come hither gesture – using the index and middle fingers of both hands), and I didn't know if he was talking to me, so I looked around (she reenacts looking around, and if I'm not mistaken, she's blushing) and looked at him again, and he did it again. So, I walked up to him again and he said, in a very kind way, he said, "Do you want want to go...".

Juan Martinez throws metaphorical ice water on Arias as he interrupts with a hearsay objection. Arias responds with, "Oh, sorry". The objection is sustained. Nurmi would be well advised to move off of this subject. His client, someone who has already admitted to butchering a man, is almost swooning as she talks about her ninth grade encounter with a strange man, three years her senior, who prowled around county carnivals doing his best Barnabas Collins impression.

Apparently, Nurmi has no interest as to whether or not Arias ever rode The Zipper with Bobby Juarez. Good choice, Nurmi. Move on. He reminds her that he doesn't want to hear what Bobby Juarez might have said, but he does want the jury reminded that Juarez was 18 years old and Arias was 15 years old when the two met at a state fair. State fair, county carnival...who cares? Arias confirms what we already know.

Nurmi continues, "Tell us, then, do you begin a relationship at that point in time, or just kind of describe for us how that relationship was at that time". Any woman who walks over to a man who simply gestures for her is either lacking in self-esteem or is a child. In this case, we are dealing with a child. This crime has nothing to do with Jodi Arias, the child. This crime has to with Jodi Arias, the woman. I know Nurmi is trying to humanize Arias, but I hope he draws the line somewhere. Are we going to hear about the onset of her menstrual period and how her mother failed to prepare her for that milestone? Are we going to hear about her fiber intake, her visits to the dentists, and her birthday parties?

Oh, no. We're back to The Zipper. She answers, "No, he invited me to go on The Zipper with him, so we went on that ride with that and we talked a little bit as we were flipping around, and um, after that we parted and I didn't see him again...for a while". Nurmi replies, "Okay, when did you see him again?". Arias answers, "Um, I think it was in October – maybe November of that same year. Um, I was at at homecoming football game for my high school, and I saw him again. He was with some friends, and um, I was really shy, but I wanted to say hi to him, so I walked up to him and said, 'Do you remember me?', and he said he remembered me, but he couldn't remember my name. S so I told him I couldn't remember his name either, so we kind of reintroduced ourselves, and he said, 'Tell me your phone number and I promise I'll remember it", so I gave him the house phone, which was my parents' phone – we didn't have cell phones – um, and he remembered it and called me".

Remember, she approached him. He did not approach her. It is highly unlikely that he memorized her phone number. It is more probable that she wrote it on a piece of paper and gave it to him.

Nurmi insists on bringing this irrelevant testimony to the jury. Therefore, we are free to break it down. We are being asked to believe that a 15 year old Jodi Arias – the individual who just testified to the fact that her constant moving has left her with no friends – is attending the Yreka homecoming football game, and she just happens to spot the only "intriguing" individual she met in Yreka. He was not only inappropriately dressed for the season, but also for the century – hobbling on crutches – and she is expecting everyone to believe that she didn't remember his name? He was 18 years old.

I believe that this story rings hollow for every woman on that jury. A 15 year old girl who thinks an "intriguing" 18 year old has noticed her in a sea of summer clad, ripening girls at a county fair would be euphoric at the realization that the Johnny Depp of Yreka had chosen her to be "Babe for a Day". That he actually went a step further and gestured to her, inviting her to spend some thigh to thigh time with him on The Zipper, would have increased her excitement.

She not only knew his name when she saw him at that football game, but I'd say that she felt a few butterflies in her stomach as she met eyes with her fantasy lover sitting in the bleachers. In the weeks preceding this random encounter, she had probably written his name over and over in her summer diary. I'm sure her fall notebooks bore his name as well. She was not only looking forward to the day she saw him again, but she had spent several months fantasizing about it. She probably wished that all of the better looking girls in the ninth grade – the ones who wouldn't break ranks and allow her to join their social circle – were aware of the fact that she had an 18 year old, goth vampire admirer out there in Yreka...somewhere.

Make no mistake, when Jodi Arias saw Bobby Juarez at the homecoming football game in the fall of 1995, she knew his name. He may have forgotten her name, but she never forgot his name. Had she simply admitted that, she would have become more human to the women on the jury. Because she pretended differently, she appeared to be a narcissist. That doesn't help her.

Back to the bleachers...Nurmi asks, "Did you begin dating at that time?". Arias answers, "No, we were just friends. We just talked for a while. We weren't dating. He was actually seeing a girl, I think. I don't remember". Sure, he was seeing a girl – but maybe not – she couldn't remember. Then why bring it up? Friends? Ask yourself a question and answer it logically: What does an 18 year old man skipping through town while wearing 18th century goth attire have in common with a female, high school freshman? Oh, and while you're thinking logically, ask yourself why a man who was finished with high school was in the bleachers at a homecoming football game. If he was wearing the team colors, it might be an easy answer. But this particular alumnus was dressed like an 18th century vampire.

Nurmi asks, "So, you were just friends for a period of time?". Arias answers, "Yes, several months we were just friends". Nurmi continues, "So you were telling us he became your boyfriend at that point, so I'm assuming, at some point in time, um, you two began dating". Arias is quick to fill in the missing parts of this saga. She answers, "Yeah, the girl broke up with him and there was a period of time where he was single and I was single and we started just talking more and more, and then, I think it was on New Year's um – that followed that year, that year that I was a freshman – that we decided to become boyfriend and girlfriend".

So, this high school freshman considered herself "single"? I'm trying not to laugh. Even Nurmi is choking on this. He asks, "And you said that was your, that was the beginning of your sophomore year?". She doesn't respond the way Nurmi wants her to respond. Instead, without a hint of shame, Arias replies, "I would have still been a freshman, then". Obviously she sees nothing wrong with a ninth grader dating a man out of high school. Moving along...

Nurmi continues, "Was he in high school at that point in time?". Arias answers the same question for the fifth time, "No, he was out of high school". Nurmi continues, "And to your recollection, was he working at that time?". Well, here we are. Full circle. Nurmi took us down this rabbit trail after Arias had left home and moved in with Bobby Juarez. What took us from the straight and narrow was Bobby Juarez' lack of employment. According to Arias, at the time she moved in with him, he had never been employed. I don't know why Nurmi expected anything in the past to have changed, but maybe he'll learn his lesson as Arias says, "No, he wasn't working".

Nurmi says, "Well, describe for us what being boyfriend and girlfriend – at that stage of your life – meant for you and Mr. Juarez". Arias answers, "Um, for us, we, I didn't have a car, I didn't have a driver's license yet – I think I was getting my permit that year. So, he would come to town -- so during lunch, a lot of kids would leave campus – and there's a small gas station – USA gas station – near the high school, so I'd walk down there and he would be there. There's an arcade there – he really liked video games – so we would meet there and just hang out. Um, hold hands...that kind of thing".

If anyone believes that Count Juarez ventured out into the daylight, on foot, to travel to the local gas station to hold hands and play video games, then I thank God you weren't on that jury. Campus? What's next, varsity letters and pep rallies? Where were her parents? They already had enough on their hands with a daughter who was 15 and in the ninth grade. Did they not realize that she was also playing Fantasy Island behind the gas pumps with an 18 year old vampire?

Nurmi is looking for the inside info on a 15 year old freshman dating an 18 year old, never employed, guy in a costume. He stumbles through the awkward wording of his question, but essentially, he says, "Did you date Bobby exclusively from the age of 15 until the time you moved out of the home?". I'm having a hard time taking this seriously. She's 15. Nobody takes a 15 year old relationship seriously, except a 15 year old – and a 33 year old Jodi Arias.

She answers, "No. We stayed together for a while and I think – at age 15, I felt like the relationship was getting very intense. He was talking about being together forever, and, you know. I loved him, but I didn't feel like I was in love with him, and I knew that at age 15, there was no way I could decide who I was going to spend the rest of my life with, at that point. So, um, um, he wanted to move to San Francisco and – he had all kinds of wild ideas which were – they seemed fun, but they were just not where I was. So, at that point, I broke up with him".

Doesn't she sound mature for a 15 year old? She loved him, but was not "in love" with him. She knew, unlike most impulsive, hormonal 15 year olds, that she was far too young to take this relationship seriously. No, I'm not buying that. Jodi Arias didn't have the common sense to know, at this time in her life, that dropping out of high school was a terrible idea. Yet, here she sits, expecting everyone to believe that she understood the fraudulent nature of puppy love.

She talks about his wild ideas. I'm sure he had wild ideas. Anyone who goes to their closet in July and decides that his long black jacket and high collared white shirt are the perfect ensemble to wear to the county carnival in triple digit heat is an individual who thrives on wild ideas. Anything more ridiculous than that should not have come as a surprise to young Jodi Arias.

Nurmi is about to get specific. I know it, and you know it. He asks, "What do you mean, wild ideas?". She answers, "Um, well, he entertained the belief about vampires, and he thought, let's go to San Francisco and see if we can find some real vampires, and you know – I used to read Ann Rice novels all the time – and sometimes it seemed like – it didn't seem realistic to me, but it seemed like – it was just an idea that I would go along with, you know, with him". No, actually, we don't know. The man wanted to find "real vampires" as opposed to finding a "real job", For most of us, that would have been the moment we decided to placate him and plan our exit strategy. No, normal people don't believe the idea of finding real corpses who suck human blood intriguing, fun, interesting, or even possible. For us, it's aberrant. It's a red flag. But tell us, what happens next?

Nurmi asks, "And this was a time when you were about 15 years of age. He wanted to move to San Francisco and hunt vampires, right?". Arias barely lets Nurmi finish asking the question before she breaks in with, "Yeah! So yeah. So we could live together forever and be together forever". Then she stops smiling, snaps her head back toward Nurmi, and with a dead pan expression, waits for the next softball question.

Nurmi asks, "Was there a certain point in time, then, this was going on, when you said it was getting too intense for you, did you and Mr. Juarez break up?". She answers, "Yes, um, it was one afternoon. I broke up with him on the phone. I don't know where my parents were, but my Aunt Lisa was at the house. She was picking my brother and I up, and I was having this conversation with him – he was very upset. Um, and she, Lisa, wanted us to leave. She – I mean, she wanted to take us. We had to go somewhere with her. So, I didn't have time to stay on the phone with him a long time and talk through it with him. Um, so I had to abruptly end the phone call, shortly thereafter, and it was – I don't know. He didn't take that well".

Really? They were going to go to San Francisco to look for real vampires? They were going to be together forever (literally, because vampires are immortal). They were so connected, so in love, so spiritual that the break-up happened on the phone – while Aunt Lisa was trying to gather all the Arias siblings to go somewhere? Oh, what a gothic tragedy. She didn't even have time to talk Nosferatu Juarez through his grief. The phone call didn't end quickly – it ended "abruptly", and it ended "shortly thereafter". I wish she would be tased by the grammar police every time she added some superfluous word or phrase. It's beyond irritating and completely fraudulent. We just learned that she couldn't handle the eleventh grade (at 17).

This is the most irritating, ridiculous, and irrelevant direct examination I've ever seen. This sounds more like an interview taping (but at least the networks would know that all of this nonsense should be cut from the final tape). Who cares about ninth grade Jodi Arias? I don't. Unless she was kidnapped, raped, and set on fire in the ninth grade, why is the jury being tortured with this testimony? Who cares if the killer loved an unemployed, fake vampire in the ninth grade? How does this relate to the corpse she left behind in June. 2008? Why does anyone care how her boyfriend took the break-up? This is painfully boring.

Nurmi pretends he's hit upon the smoking gun. How did Bobby Juarez take the break-up? Arias, without skipping a beat, answers, "I found out a few years later that he...he". Thank God someone is still listening. Juan Martinez objects with, "Hearsay". Nurmi raises his left hand as if to say, "Huh? We were on a roll". The judge tells the attorneys to approach. I don't know why. It's obviously hearsay. Arias is about to tell the jury what she heard happened to Bobby Juarez after she broke his dead, vampire heart.

Juan Martinez is overruled. Judge Sherry Stephens has been convinced that a ninth grade break-up, thirteen years before the murder for which Arias is now standing trial, is somehow relevant to this case. The camera lands on Sandy Arias and Sue Halterman, Jodi's mother and aunt. They whisper to each other as the sidebar drags on. When the word "overruled" comes from Judge Stephens, the normally expressionless face of Sandy Arias breaks into a grin.

Nurmi irritates everyone besides Jodi Arias and the two twins on the defense side of the courtroom by asking, "I was asking – uh, describing that you understood that Mr. Juarez had not taken the break-up you had when you were 15 or so, so well. Describe for us what you mean by that". Arias answers, "Um, I learned a few years later that he had slit both of his wrists and tried to kill himself. And, he was committed to some, um, some kind of psychiatric ward in Citrus Heights, just north of Sacramento".

A very clear implication has just been presented to the jury. The way that interchange was just handled, it would seem as though Juarez tried to kill himself and was committed after his ninth grade girlfriend broke up with him. Remember, the attempted suicide story was offered in response to Nurmi's inquiry as to how Bobby Juarez handled the break-up. Arias said she learned, several years later, that he slit his wrists and was committed to a psychiatric facility. Does one incident necessarily follow the other, sequentially speaking? I don't think so. She could have just as easily have meant they broke up, and several years later he tried to kill himself. She could have found out about the suicide attempt several years later – when it happened. However, the defense is asking everyone to believe, without a shred of evidence, that Bobby Juarez tried to kill himself because Jodi Arias dumped him. Even if the attempted suicide followed the break-up as has been implied, has anyone considered the fact that he might have had other issues – more chronic in nature – that were really at the root of this (unsubstantiated) attempt?

According to Arias, he had no identification, no employment, no parents, was living in a hovel, and had been soothing his pain by living in a fantasy world of vampires. Could any of those reasons been behind a suicide attempt? Does anyone believe the name Jodi Arias came up often in his post-hospitalization psychiatric sessions? I tend to believe it had more to do with his life – not his ninth grade girlfriend. However, in the mind of Arias, it was simply the prospect of a life without her that caused him to choose death.

I find it hard to believe that Bobby Juarez' private medical history – psychiatric in nature – was just disclosed on national television. Juan Martinez did the right thing – he objected to this hearsay testimony before she able to spew it out of her mouth, but he was overruled. It's ironic that we know nothing of Arias' medical history (she's protected by HIPPA regulations), and yet somehow, someone who had nothing to do with this crime (or this decade) has now been identified as a committed psychiatric patient. I'd like to know if the sexually active Arias was on birth control. I'd like to know if the sexually active Arias was ever pregnant. I'd like to know if the "monogamous" Arias has ever contracted a sexually transmitted disease (you can bet we'd hear about any STD that Travis had contracted). I'd like to know what California surgeon performed a breast augmentation on Jodi Arias for $300 – and more importantly, why he/she charged one tenth of what the average surgeon would charge for such a procedure. The defense has made this trial about sex. Why are they being permitted to escape answering the medical questions that would normally accompany this kind of testimony?

Whatever personal information Arias is disclosing about an individual who had the misfortune of crossing paths with a murderer, we can rest assured that Juarez reached a level of success far superior to his ninth grade girlfriend. He went on to appear in a major television program (it was an extra role, several episodes – but it was one of the most popular television series of all time). I'm sure his agent is thrilled that his former adolescent girlfriend is attaching his name to a brutal murder and a suicide attempt. In this case, it doesn't matter who gets hurt. A motivational speaker is a pedophile and an actor is a failed suicide.

I'd like to hear about the woman on the stand. I would a few questions answered. How did a P/T waitress afford a home mortgage and an Nissan Infiniti?. That information is off limits. It was deemed too prejudicial by this court. We all know about the oldest profession in the world, and we've all seen the photos of her well used anatomy. You figure it out. In the meantime, she is permitted to slash the reputations and violate the privacy of any man who crossed her path.

Nurmi is tongue tied. He makes several aborted attempts to ask a follow-up question to "two slit wrists", but finally, he stops, starts over, and asks, "Well, let me ask you this way. It sounds like he was your boyfriend about the time you turned eighteen, right – a few months...". She interrupts him and says, "Yeah". He continues, "How did that come about?".

She answers, "We didn't talk, at that point, for a few years. It's kind of silly. There was this older man that used to come into my parents' restaurant. I'd say he was in his 60's, maybe 70's – and he always had his Bible – and it was a small pocket version of the New Testament (here comes the lies – they are always flanked by ridiculous details) – he had it all marked up – and he was always quoting Bible scripture and things (things? What things?). He had done the math in the Bible (what math in the Bible?), and determined that he knew when the second coming was going to occur, and he said it was going to occur on September 23, 1997 (will we hear about his personal medical history, as well?). So um, I was kind of naive and I believed him, so he would come in weekly – or several times a week – and continue to reiterate that (reiterate? Taze her!). So, at the time, I was a non-denominational Christian (former vampire). This seemed important, and I thought that Bobby should know because at the time, he wasn't religious (if she hadn't spoken to him in several years, how would she know whether or not he was religious?), and he was uncertain about his spirituality, at least when I had last known him (so this is the one person she thinks of warning? How about her parents? Did it matter if they burned in hell?). To me, it was important that he at least hear that information, so he could make a decision for himself. So I made contact with him again, and called him in, I think, September, mid-September, 2007 – I'm sorry, 1997". She's got quite the selective memory, doesn't she? She will later claim that she cannot remember what she and Travis Alexander were fighting about the day she left Mesa in 2008, but here she sits, 16 years after the fact, and she remembers that Jesus Christ was supposed to return to earth on September 23, 1997. Remarkable.

So, Arias is giving Bobby Juarez, a former mental patient who is now stabilized, a blast from his past. She just implied that he attempted to commit suicide when she broke up with him, but after several years, she decides that a phone call from the straw the broke the camel's back would be in Bobby Juarez' best interest. As if the identity of the caller isn't bad enough, let's examine the content of the call. She's passing on the good (or bad) news that she, a "non-denominational Christian", had garnered from an elderly man with religious delusions and too much time on his hands. Is this really the best she could come up with? I know she needed Bobby Juarez to secure her escape plan, but was this really the most brilliant plan she could think of in order to manipulate him into reconnecting with her? I watched her face as she told this story to the jury; she could barely keep from laughing. Even she knows how ridiculous this sounds.

Back to her story. She wasn't giving Bobby much time, was she? He has one week to make plans for his eternal destination. That's a nice way to treat a formerly unstable vampire who was probably trying to break free – with psychiatric assistance – from spiritual delusions. If she loved him, she would have left him alone. She needed him. She needed his house to replace her parents' house. She never cared about his spiritual destiny. She cared about herself.

Arias claims, in answer to Nurmi's question, that there were 19 months between the break-up phone call to Juarez and the "get your ticket to gospel express" phone call in 1997. In response, Nurmi repeats old testimony and finally asks what year of school Arias was in when she made this phone call to Bobby Juarez. She says she was just starting her junior year. Nurmi wants to know what happened when she made that phone call. She answers, "Well, when I first called, he – I asked – he answered the phone -- I could recognize his voice – and I said, 'Is Bobby there?', and he said, 'Who's this?", and I said, 'Jodi', and I immediately heard a click, and I thought, okay...".

Again, Arias shows us that she is practiced in the art of deception. She admitted that she recognized Bobby's voice when he answered the phone, but instead of saying, "Hi, Bobby", she asked if Bobby was there. She knew he was there. In fact, she knew she was talking to him. Then, when Bobby learned that Arias was calling him, he hung up on her. She prefers to use euphemisms like, "I immediately heard a click". In reality, she should have said, "He hung up on me". However, being the narcissist that she is, she won't actually say that. There's just too much rejection involved in admitting that someone chose to disconnect the call rather than engage her in a conversation.

It is obvious to me that Bobby Juarez had an impulsive reaction to the thought of speaking with Jodi Arias. Given what she's told us about his mental health history, she should have left him alone – especially if she was, as she claims, the reason for his failed suicide attempt. How dare she? Really, how dare she?

She continues, "So, I left it alone – because our last phone call, years back, didn't end well. And so, the next night, I tried one more time, and the same thing happened...". To begin with, their last phone call was not "some years back". She just admitted that the last phone call she had with him was about 19 months earlier. In order for the span of time between the two phone calls to qualify as "some years back", she needs, at the very least, another five months. This is what Arias does. She lies.

Beyond that, she didn't "leave it alone". She is saying she left it alone, but a second phone call is a clear indication that she wasn't leaving it (Bobby Juarez) alone. She was determined to have her way. This is Jodi Arias. She will not be ignored. Had Bobby Juarez not eventually taken her call, I have absolutely no doubt that she would have gotten into her car and driven to his home. She would have parked outside and waited for him until he finally agreed, out of frustration, to speak to her. The fact that he hung up on her a second time makes it clear that he did not want to speak to her. Did she allow him to exercise his freedom of choice? Let's see.

She continues, "...so I left it alone, and about, um...". Nurmi realizes, even if Arias doesn't, that she did not try "one last time" or "leave it alone". She is about to tell the jury about her third attempt to contact a man who has made it clear, in no uncertain terms, that he has absolutely no interest in speaking to her. Nurmi needs to shift gears; he needs to jury to forget that Arias is exposing herself as a determined and obsessive woman. He cuts her off and asks, "Well, let me ask you this – before we continue – um, you mentioned that Yreka was a pretty small town. Right?". Arias looks at him and answers, "Yes". Nurmi believes the jury is now invested in the size of Yreka instead of the stalker behavior of his client. He's wrong.

He continues, "Um, you never ran into Mr. Juarez in between these two phone calls?". What? The time frame that exists between the two phone calls is a single day. Yreka might be small, but it certainly isn't small enough that she was going to randomly run into a specific individual (who happened to live six miles away) in that 24 hour period of time. Arias answers, "No, he didn't live in Yreka. He lived in Montague, which is six miles from Yreka. It's even smaller. There's about 1,000 people in that town". She's already testified to the fact that Bobby Juarez lived six miles from Yreka. I doubt the jury cared the first time this subject matter was covered. I wonder if Nurmi thinks it's safe to go back to her third round of "leaving it alone".

Nurmi continues, "Okay. But never in this time did you run into him at all?". She answers, "No". Can we get back to the end of the world phone conversation? Nurmi asks, "Okay, so you talked about, you had called him a couple of times, you heard a click on the other end of the phone – how does the relationship progress from that point in time?". There is no relationship. Bobby Juarez has made it clear, in the rudest terms possible, that he has no interest in establishing a relationship with Jodi Arias.

Arias answers, "Um, I don't know how many days later – it was under a week – maybe four days, maybe five days (but she does remember the specific date of September 23, 1997), I was on the phone with a friend of mine – we were talking, and I heard the call waiting beep, so I clicked over and I heard someone say, 'Is Jodi there?', and I recognized his voice, so I clicked back over and I said, 'I have to call you back', and I clicked back over, and we started talking again". Sure. At this point, I believe she called him several times during this "under a week" period. In fact, knowing what I now know about Jodi Arias, I believe Bobby Juarez knew that if he didn't take her call, she would just keep calling and calling and calling.

Nurmi lifts his ample torso off of the podium and asks, "Okay. After that conversation, did you, did you become friends again, did you start dating again -- describe that for us". Why? Why does anyone in this courtroom care whether or not Jodi Arias and Bobby Juarez started dating again 11 years prior to the murder of Travis Alexander? Was he her murder accomplice? Did he fund her murder trip? Did he drive the get-away car? Did he beat her? Did he rape her? If not, why is this testimony even relevant?

Arias answers, "Yeah, um, I was, I felt kind of silly explaining to him why I was calling him – especially knowing that he, his religious beliefs at that time were not really defined, and um, I kind of expected him to laugh at me, but it was important to me, so um, I told him the reason I was calling, and...". Juan Martinez, the prosecutor, interrupts with, "Objection, hearsay". Good luck, Mr. Martinez. This entire portion of testimony has been nothing but hearsay. The objection is overruled. Arias is instructed by Judge Sherry Stephens to continue.

She does. She says, "Um, he expressed appreciation for that, which surprised me. Um, we just sort of picked up from there are began talking again". Nurmi smiles as he lifts his big left hand and asks, "Does talking mean dating?". Arias answers, "No, not yet".

There are a few questions worth asking. First of all, Arias began this portion of the testimony by saying that she wasn't sure of what Bobby Juarez' spiritual beliefs were in September, 1997. Actually, she said (under oath) that he wasn't religious. She offered that as a statement of fact. As she justified her harassment of Bobby Juarez , she changed her testimony and said that his religious beliefs were undefined in September, 1997. Which is it, and how would she even know what his personal religious beliefs were at that time? He won't even talk to her on the phone. He won't even say goodbye before he ends the call. In addition to that, we can all add. She claims she learned about the very important, second coming deadline in mid-September. In my world, mid-September is a few days, in either direction of September 15. With her two aborted phone calls eating up two days, we're at September 17. With the four to five days that elapsed between the last hang up and the actual conversation, we are at September 23 or 24 – give or take a day or two in either direction.

There is no doubt in my mind that if an actual phone conversation happened when she claims it did, she would remember whether or not the second coming was going to occur within the next few hours or whether it had come and gone without incident. Why do I believe that Nurmi will never even address this issue?

The judge calls for a lunch recess. Everyone heads to a restaurant – everyone but Arias. She will be taken to a holding cell in the basement of the court house to enjoy a peanut butter sandwich on stale bread, a soft apple, and an elementary school sized container of milk.

We're back from lunch. The camera focuses on Judge Sherry Stephens. I wonder if she has a mirror in her chambers. As she briefly grins at whomever from the bench, I notice that her white blouse collar is only visible on the right side. The left collar is buried beneath her black robe. No matter. She still has the best seat in the house.

Jodi is told by the judge to take the stand. Nurmi is front and center, and he's already talking to the judge about a discussion held in her chambers as Jodi parades right past him. The attorneys spend some time at a bench conference while everyone else is either whispering or staring blankly around the room. Finally, the attorneys finish and return to their respective seats.

Maria de la Rosa, the mitigation specialist assigned to the Jodi Arias case, is sitting in Jodi's usual seat at the defense table. Her job is to collect all of Jodi Arias' records – I assume that's everything from birth on. Records. It implies so much, doesn't it? De la Rosa is also responsible for finding people who will testify to something – anything – positive about Jodi. It would seem as though much of her work is done outside of the courtroom. In court, she doesn't do much. In fact, when Jodi isn't consuming days and days on the witness stand, De la Rosa sits alone at the second table, a bottle of water her only company. However, when Jodi is on the stand, De la Rosa seizes the opportunity to sit with the powerful people at the first table. She's right in the line of the camera, and she knows it. She's an attractive, middle-aged Latina. Actually, she's more than attractive – she's really quite pretty.

What follows is a rather long delay. Jodi, safely ensconced on the witness stand, looks like the kid in the cafeteria who is sitting alone. She looks down while desperately wanting to look up. She knows the free people are talking, but she has to sit silently and wait for the man who's paid $225 an hour to talk to her before she can speak. She adjusts her glasses, several times. The camera shows the defense table, and we see that something is amusing the professionals sitting there. De la Rosa, whispers in Willmott's ear while smiling. Willmott responds by popping something into her mouth and laughing. Nurmi looks at the two women and smiles. De la Rosa, in her shocking white jacket and saucer sized hoop earrings, takes the levity too far. She laughs, tosses her head, plays with her hair, and looks behind her. Is this a murder trial or a cocktail party?
On the other side of the room, at the prosecutor's table, there is stoic silence. Martinez looks straight ahead, and Esteban Flores, the lead detective in this case, looks down.

The delay is caused by a change in court reporters. The young woman with long blond hair, the individual who has been recording all of Jodi's testimony thus far, is now packing up her equipment to make way for Mike Babicky, the older gentleman who has become a fixture in this trial. Jodi stares at the young woman as she grabs her machinery and her plastic cup filled with a soft drink. She watches the woman, clad in a short, fashionable skirt and black stockings, as she walks out the door and into the free world. Jodi, by contrast, is dressed in baggy clothes that look like they've been donated to a lost cause.

Mike Babicky (the court reporter) is finally situated at his station in front of the witness stand. Just when it looks like court is ready to begin, we hear Jodi whisper, "Mr. Babicky". He doesn't hear her, but she realizes her microphone is on and she quickly shuts it off. She mouths his name again, and this time, he turns and looks at her. I've gotten rather adept at reading lips in this trial, and I'm reasonably sure she said. "If I'm talking too fast for you, just let me know and I'll slow down". Look at Jodi Arias making friends with the help. Isn't she considerate? She knows the protocol. If the court reporter is having trouble keeping up, or if two people are talking over each other, he motions to the judge, not the witness or the attorneys. There is no way the court reporter is ever going to look at Jodi while she's testifying and say, "Could you slow it down a little?". And she knows it.

So, what cliff were we left hanging from before everyone went off to forage for food? Oh, yes – Bobby Juarez. Nurmi looks prepared. I see no food stains on his white dress shirt, so I assume lunch proceeded without incident. The judge tells Nurmi to continue with his direct examination, and as he does, we can't help but notice the distraction being caused by Willmott, De la Rosa, and a court employee. The court employee, after approaching the defense table, leans over and begins talking to Willmott and De la Rosa. They have their heads together, and all three are laughing and gesturing. They seem oblivious to the fact that the jury has returned, and that Nurmi has already started asking Jodi questions.

Nurmi asks Jodi to take us back to the day she actually re-engaged Bobby Juarez on the phone some 19 months after their break-up. Specifically, he wants to know how the relationship progressed after she and Juarez had a full telephone conversation. Jodi, instead of answering the question, replies, "Well, at the time I had boyfriend. He lived in another country, so we corresponded". Well, congratulations. Now please, answer the question, not that it's relevant to Travis Alexander's murder.

She continues, "So, it wasn't a romantic reason, like I said, I reached out to him for a spiritual reason. Um, I don't know if he was seeing anybody at that time. I don't think he was. He used to call a party line a lot and meet people on that. I guess this was before, you know, the internet was in every single home". She was planning to go on, but Nurmi interrupted her. I'd like to interrupt her as well. There's a few things that need to be cleared up, but I'll wait until Nurmi is finished.

Nurmi wants to know what a party line is. She answers, "From my understanding – I didn't talk on it – but from my understanding, it was a 900 number that you could call, and it's like a chat room. It's on the telephone instead of the computer". Nurmi asks if that's how Jodi chatted with Juarez. She curtly replies, "I didn't. He chatted with other people that way". Of course SHE didn't use the lame party line. She would like that distinction duly noted.

Okay, my turn. In case you missed it, Jodi Arias is no two-timing woman, and we know that because she told us so. She had an international boyfriend back in September, 1997, but that boyfriend was not going to get in the way of a spiritual calling she had – a calling that didn't involve her current boyfriend. Her calling involved her former boyfriend – the far more local, Bobby Juarez. It is extremely important that we believe that Jodi was not interested in the body of Bobby Juarez. No. She was only interested in his eternal soul. She had spiritual reasons for contacting him. You see, she knew a guy who knew a guy who could get Bobby Juarez tickets for the one night only ride on The Gospel Express. Straight to paradise – all meals included. Hey, it's her story. Remember the old man who came into the diner and showed Jodi all of his Bible math? Remember, he knew the date of the second coming (I guess those who are waiting for the first coming are out of luck). She had absolutely no reason to believe that Juarez would care about her fire and brimstone warning, but that did not deter her.

I'd like to know if there is anyone willing to say that Jodi Arias was walking around Yreka, California, in September, 1997, with a sandwich board that read, "The End is Really Near. Repent". Did she warn her international boyfriend about the second coming? She never mentioned his soul or giving him the opportunity to "make his own decision". So, it seems as though Jodi had concern for only one soul – that of Bobby Juarez. It wasn't romantic, though. Not at all.

Remember those cheaply produced, late night commercials in the 1990s? They featured heavily made-up women and a few men sitting on couches, soaking in hot tubs, or reclining on beds. These "people" were all dressed up with no place to go. With their hair coiffed and lip-gloss shining, they'd all do the same thing – they'd pick up the phone. Why? Well, to join the festivities on the party line, of course. These commercials featured hypnotic voice overs that said, "Are you tired of the bar scene? Have you had it with being rejected? Well, meet real, live singles just like you, and do it from the comfort and privacy of your own home. Join the party line!". Then, the tiny print that flashed for 10 seconds on the screen explained the cost involved with dumping your loser life and exchanging it for a life of phone conversations. For a fee ranging from $1.99/minute to $9.99/minute, you could "join the party" and speak to other swinging singles looking for a social life.

That's what Jodi is referring to when she talked about chatting on a party line, and that's why she's making it clear that she never used those services. However, she claims that Juarez did. She claims that she was unaware as to whether or not he had a girlfriend at the time the world was supposed to end in September, 1997 (because, you know, Jodi isn't a stalker or anything), but she did know he chatted on the party lines. How would she know that?

Nurmi, satisfied that the jury now understands the complexities of the party line, wants to know about Jodi's international boyfriend. He starts with the basics. What was the new boyfriend's name? Just as she had done when she was asked about Bobby Juarez' name, Arias makes this a two part question. She answers, "Victor". Nurmi asks if Victor had a last name. She answers, "Arias, Ironically". She speaks rapidly, and it sounded like her international boyfriend's name is Victor Arias Ironically. Senor Ironically? Nurmi is confused. He replies, "I'm sorry?" Jodi says, "His last name was also Arias". Now it sounds like his name is Victor Also Arias. Can't she just say the man's name? I guess when you're asked to give your boyfriend's name, it's difficult to say your own last name and leave it hanging in the air without other words around it. So, Arias was dating an Arias.

Is this a kissing cousin situation? Of course, Martinez won't ask her about her boyfriend, Victor Arias. He is not going to waste time going through the mountains of lies she's already told on her first day on the stand. He's only going to cross examine her on testimony that is connected to the crime. That leaves Jodi free to pretend that Victor Arias was her boyfriend, not a distant family member.

How did Arias happen to meet Victor Arias?

My theory: Her father is probably related to his father, but I'm sure she's never going to admit that. She says, "Um, the summer that I turned 17, just before I turned 17, in July, I flew to Costa Rica on an exchange program, and I spent three weeks there with a family. Their name was also Arias, and they had, um, two sons and two daughters in that family, and the older son was just a little older than me. So, we kind of clicked and got to know each other and sort of had a little romance kind of blossom thing. I don't know. It was kind of like my first experience of the warm fuzzies – somebody that I felt, that I really cared for". As she recounts this tale, she struggles to maintain eye contact with the jury. She keeps snapping her head back to reconnect with Nurmi. Nurmi seems anxious to move on.

So, Jodi was a foreign exchange student? What comes to your mind when you think of a foreign exchange student? What comes to my mind is a student from a foreign country coming to an American high school and studying there for several months (if not longer). Typically, there is an American host family involved. The foreign exchange student's counterpart, the American student, will be studying in a school in the exchange student's country of origin. They will also be staying with a host family in the foreign country. The students who were accepted into these programs were often the best and the brightest. Nurmi and Jodi are leading us to believe that Jodi Arias met the criteria to not only compete for, but to win, this type of scholarship.

There are also school sponsored trips that allow students to visit foreign countries if they can pay their own way and have no problem with hostel or remote accommodations. It isn't necessary that school is in session during these trips, and counterpart students have nothing to do with the equation. It looks like this is the type of "program" for which Jodi qualified. To be honest, I'm not convinced it was even that unstructured. I truly believe Jodi Arias was a problem in her home, and I believe her behavior grew worse as she grew older. Remember, this was July, 1997, and she was dropping out of school just eight months later. I believe her parents needed a break, and they found a family member of her father's, secured her housing, and paid for her round trip flight to Costa Rica. There has never been an airline ticket produced. There has never been a photograph produced. There has never been any testimony produced that verifies Jodi's claim that she spent three weeks in Costa Rica in 1997. However, I think she did go to Costa Rice. If she didn't, and the entire story is a fabrication, she wouldn't have chosen the name "Arias" for her international boyfriend.

I'm going to refer to relevant testimony given by Jodi Arias that was not a part of this trial. During the retrial of her penalty phase (October, 2014 to March, 2015), Arias was given an opportunity by Judge Sherry Stephens to have the courtroom cleared, the media and public banned, and her testimony sealed. In other words, she was called to the stand to testify in her own behalf, but nobody was privy to that testimony except the jury, the attorneys, the victim's family members, and the judge. This unprecedented situation was quickly remedied when the press filed for emergency relief with the Arizona Court of Appeals. After two days of testimony, Judge Stephens was told that Jodi Arias and her bad case of nerves did not trump the US Constitution or the Arizona Constitution. The judge's ill-conceived ruling was overturned, and the doors of the courtroom were once again opened to the press and the public. Jodi Arias refused to continue to testify after she was told she was not entitled to the secrecy she demanded (and, for a short period of time, actually received).

Regarding this foreign exchange trip to Costa Rica, Jodi explained, during the period of time in which she believed her testimony would remain sealed until after sentencing, that the foreign exchange program was nothing more than an opportunity to go to Costa Rica in the summer of 1997. She said she saw a flier advertising the trip at school, came home, told her parents she was going, and she went. Who paid for it? She probably claimed she did, but it doesn't even matter anymore. That's it. No scholarship. No exchange. Just a trip. This is precisely what most thinking individuals had deduced two years earlier.

Back to 2013: They're moving fast here – flying by the details that would normally suck Nurmi into a morass of diversion. I can almost hear the clicking of castanets and the rattling of maracas as Jodi takes us to the home of Victor Arias and his family. After 21 whole days of simpatico, Jodi Arias labels Victor Arias "her boyfriend". Juan Martinez is shown enduring the testimony that sounds as if it's been lifted from the pages of a too often recycled teen romance novel, and with his clenched fist positioned firmly over his mouth, he's blinking slowly.

To sum up her relationship with Victor Arias, Jodi says, "It started to develop while I was in Costa Rica, and, um, I flew back – I had my 17th birthday there, in that country, and I flew back near the end of July, and we um, corresponded and talked occasionally on the phone in August, and then he flew to the United States um, that September and stayed in Redding – which is a city about 100 miles south of Yreka. Um, he had some um, people that he knew there. He stayed there about a week, I think, and then stayed at my house for two weeks – before flying back". He came to stay in Redding, California before he came to Yreka? He knew some people there? Yes, I'm sure he did. Quite a few of the Arias family members just happen to live in Redding, California. But, hey, those Arias family members aren't related to Victor Arias. It's all a huge coincidence. We just need to accept it. Victor Arias, a Costa Rican citizen, just happens to "know people" in Redding, California. This is so transparent.

Nurmi points out the obvious by asking Jodi when Victor Arias stayed with her for two weeks. She tells him that it was early September, 1997. Nurmi sums it up with, "So, this was about the time then, um, close to the time that you were in contact with Mr. Juarez, as well, right?". She answers, "Yes, it was, um, just right before that". So, Senor Arias was visiting Senorita Arias while Senorita Arias was trying to get in touch with Count Juarez for spiritual reasons. No wonder she was having a hard time in school. An international boyfriend on American soil, a vampire ex-boyfriend with an eternal decision to make, impending Biblical doom, and the beginning of her junior year at Yreka High School. What's a girl to do?

Nurmi asks, "And, you considered Mr. Arias to be a boyfriend?". She answers, "Yeah. Actually, he had actually given me a ring. It was kind of a promise ring, like we were going to get married, but we weren't officially engaged, but we were talking about marriage and children, and he wanted me to come live down there and start a family". Nurmi replies, "Okay. I guess this is your first experience of what we call young love". She answers, "Yeah, yeah, it was". Nurmi responds with, "Okay". Arias blurts out, "I wouldn't say totally in love, but it was my first taste of just feeling like, like being like, warm about somebody, if that makes sense". Just a thought – this guy made her feel warm, but she didn't bother telling him about the end of world that was coming that month?

No Jodi, it doesn't make sense. Why is any of this being discussed? Why is this jury being forced to consider the dull and uninteresting facets of the teenage life of Jodi Arias? Did Jodi Arias murder Bobby Juarez? No, she didn't. He's alive. How about Victor Arias? Is he dead or alive? He's alive. Travis Alexander? Alive or dead? Dead. Can we get to him? Unfortunately, we have at least two more living boyfriends to get through before we get to Travis Alexander.

Can I ask why the jury will be asked to consider the college level, US History course Arias was taking when she dropped out of high school? If she was sporting a promise ring and planning to escape to Costa Rica to have Arias babies while she was still in the eleventh grade, it's pretty clear she wasn't very serious about attending college.

Nurmi wraps Victor Arias up in a neat package. He reminds Jodi that he went back to Costa Rica. This resulted in their relationship being reduced to letters and phone calls. Jodi says, "Yeah, um, we wrote a lot. The postman actually got to know my name and face, and he would tease me every time I went to the post office to get it stamped for Costa Rice. And I would receive letters from him that were romantic – the Spanish language is very romantic – so he would write things like that. Very romantic". Nurmi, playing the pervert card again, asks, "Relative to your age, how old was Victor?". She's answered this question already.

She answers, "I don't remember his exact age. I wanna say he's about a year older than me. I think, actually, we were, I think, we were very close in age, but he was older than me". Big deal. Now Nurmi wants Jodi to explain how Bobby Juarez took the role of Jodi's boyfriend away from Victor Arias. A dual, perhaps? No?

She begins with, "Yes, Bobby and I would talk a few times a week, and then it became more frequent. Victor and I would – I couldn't see myself moving to Costa Rica and having that kind of life, and having children with him. Um, we argued over like, little, silly things. Victor was like, very jealous, and I couldn't talk to any of my high school friends who were like, guys. Like, I went through a drive-thru, and there was a classmate I had gone to school with two years – you know (she does the spinning hand motion again), over the years. He had a job there, and um, just, I was driving (she does the hands on the steering wheel hand motion), of course, because Victor was from out of the country, and we were just there to get ice cream, it was hot, and um, and he gets the ice cream, and we hadn't seen each other all summer – this person who served us – and um, the interaction I had with him um, Victor didn't like it. So, we argued over things like that. When we were in Costa Rica, he wanted me to always walk on the, on the sidewalk, on the inside away from the street. We were at a huge soccer game there um, it's a very big deal there – they call it football, but it's soccer um, and there was actually somebody who walked by (she waves her big hand in front of her face) who looked a lot like Bobby, and he kind of reminded me of him at the time. He had the long, dark, curly hair, and I glanced at him and Victor got upset. (She's smiling broadly, obviously traumatized by the memory of jealous Victor Arias). So um, things like that. I just didn't see myself being in a marriage with him, so I broke up with him around October – or maybe November. Uh, 1997. (Pause) On the phone". Adios Victor, hello Bobby. However, before we leave this Latin chapter of her dull life, let's pull this apart.

So, she and Bobby would talk a few times a week, and then it became more frequent. Well, isn't that interesting? Now we know why Nurmi tried to confuse the issues of Bobby Juarez and Victor Arias. The second coming of Christ was scheduled for September 23, 1997. Jodi claims that she contacted Juarez so that she could share that information. Then, in October, she's ready to break it off with Victor Arias because he was jealous of the guy serving them ice cream in the summer of 1997. She's sure it's a mistake to marry Victor because he made her walk to his right on the sidewalk. She also remembers seeing a man with long, dark curly hair, back on her foreign exchange trip, who reminded her of Bobby. Victor only knew that this stranger reminded her of Bobby because she told him that he reminded her of Bobby.

Put it all together and what do you get? You get a loser who's dating a man who doesn't speak English. The loser starts thinking about her old boyfriend, Bobby Juarez. It just so happens that just as she's had enough of the jealousy of her international boyfriend, she learns about the second coming of Christ, scheduled for the third week of September, 1997. Who comes to her mind? Is it the international boyfriend? No. It's her old boyfriend, former vampire and psychiatric patient, Bobby Juarez. She sticks to her story – she called him because the second coming was on the schedule. Hey, he had the right to know. Nurmi and Arias have hopped, skipped, and jumped around so frequently that the pieces of the puzzle are scattered. Long story short – Arias got tired of her second or third cousin once removed – a guy who was in another country – and she decided to call Bobby Juarez, her former boyfriend. It's not rocket science.

Bobby Juarez: The Sequel. Jodi claims that she started talking with Bobby again around the time that Victor went back to Costa Rica in September, 1997. Oh, they weren't involved or anything, and as Nurmi pointed out, he hadn't yet secured the soon-to-be available title of "Jodi's boyfriend", but it sounds like Count Dracula played his cards right. Jodi invites us to join her as she recounts New Year's Eve, 1998. She's celebrating with her ex-boyfriend, current friend, about to be bed mate, Bobby Juarez. She says, "It was again, around New Year's. I think we spent New Year's Eve, I had a car then, so we drove out to uh, this little white chapel, in little, it's called Little Shasta. It's a tiny, even smaller town – I don't even know if it's considered a town – and it's small, white chapel with a steeple (she makes the steeple hand gesture), and um, there was snow everywhere, and um (she phasing out now, not looking at the jury or Nurmi), we just kind of hung out there and rung in the new year – didn't really do any...(now she's awake and focused). I had developed, or began to develop, feelings for him right before Christmas, so I expressed that, and he expressed that he had feelings for me too, and so we decided to give things another try at that point".

Is this imagery lost on anyone? New Year's equals new beginnings. A chapel with a steeple equals a positive, spiritual destination. Snow everywhere equals a virginal, clean, and pure environment. In reality, she probably serviced him in the car and they timed his ejaculation to coincide with the ball falling in Times Square.

Nurmi wants to know if Bill and Sandy were aware of her blossoming relationship with Bobby Juarez. She says that they knew, but she doesn't know how they knew. She claims that she wasn't open about her relationships because of prior negative experiences with them on this subject. What prior experiences? We've dissected the love life of Jodi Arias up until this point in time, and exactly two boyfriends have been discussed – one of them a half a world away. The camera gives us a close-up of her mother and aunt, but there's nothing registering on their faces. Nothing.

Jodi cites the constraints of small town America as a way of explaining how her parents knew about her reconciliation with Bobby Juarez. Perhaps, she suggests, they saw her hanging out with him in the park, or perhaps someone else told her parents that they were together. When Nurmi asks if she knew whether her parents approved or disapproved of Bobby Juarez, she says that she didn't talk extensively with her father about Bobby. However, her mom "didn't like the fact that I was with him. She was basing her opinion of him on rumors she had heard about him". Could those rumors have been based on the fact that he was seen in eighteenth century clothing while wandering the streets of Yreka, California, in triple digit heat? We'll never know. Sandy Arias is not talking. She's not even emoting. Now we're going back to Jodi working at her father's restaurant. Why? I don't know.

Nurmi asks, "Um, when you, when you were, you described it in high school, how you were working for your father, in your father's restaurant, right? And you were in high school, your junior year, and this is going on at the point in time when you began dating Mr. Juarez, right?" Jodi adjusts her eyeglasses and places her extra-large hand on the side of her face before saying, "I think my dad's restaurant closed the year prior, when I was still (pause) a sophomore? (She seems confused, and looks up). No! (she raises her hand as if to say "stop') I think he closed in the spring, it would have been 98, it would have been 98. I can't remember. It was sometime in high school he closed his restaurant". Look, it's not an IRS investigation. The statute of limitations has passed on that. Who cares?

We're supposed to be wondering if she was a freshman, a sophomore, or a junior when her father closed his restaurant. We're supposed to be concerned as to whether it was 1996, 1997, or 1998. We're not, and neither is the jury. In fact, they are probably as irritated as I am. I believe that this is all quite deliberate. She just gave a long narrative, and she didn't just remember years, she remembered months. Now, she can't remember what year her father closed his restaurant?

Nurmi is trying to assist Jodi. He reminds her that she moved out of her parents' home in an effort to get her back on track. She swivels in her chair as she looks down and says, "Okay, yesss! I worked briefly as a hostess at a little restaurant called, 'Grandma's House'". Nurmi responds by asking, "And during this point in time, when you were a 17 year old high school student, Mr. Juarez is out of school, are you supplying him with money at this point, prior to when you left school?" Jodi answers, "Well, he lived (pause) with (pause) two people he called mom and dad. I think they were his grandparents. Um, Bobby said he was adopted so his um, actual, real parents, were kind of – I never really met them".

I don't know what she's hiding here, but this topic is making her unsure of herself and uncomfortable. She sums it up, "He lived with them. They would be his mom and dad, by definition. Um, so I think they were just supplying clothing and shelter and food and that kind of thing at that point". She means the basics of life. Even Nurmi is confused. He repeats, "So, going back to my question, were you supplying Mr. Juarez with money at this point?". "No", she says. Now we go back to where we were before lunch: "So, you leave high school and you move in with Mr. Juarez at this point, correct?"

Jodi swivels in her chair again, she's looking up as if she's trying to remember something she previously remembered with crystal clarity. She's halting in her speech. She's drawing out her words. She replies, "Mmmm, yes. In the spring". Nurmi continues, "And you mentioned he was living with persons you believed to be his parents, his adoptive parents?" She replies, "Yes. I don't know if they were like really related or if he just called them his parents, um, but if anything, they were more like his grandparents, but he called them mom and dad". She tells Nurmi that they were "very much older". Then she says that she saw the woman that most of the locals considered to be Juarez' biological mother, but Bobby Juarez wanted nothing to do with her.

Nurmi would like to rehabilitate the vampiric image of a previously 18 year old Bobby Juarez, and in so doing, hopefully rehabilitate the delusional 15 year old who found him so intriguing. That might go a long way in explaining her infatuation with the same loser two years later. Jodi tells us that he had matured "somewhat", but he still had his eccentricities. By way of explanation, she recounts Halloween. At age 20, Juarez would dress up as the Brandon Lee character from "The Crow" (a dead avenger). Can we just say it? This guy has a death fixation and a strong desire to be noticed. He liked wearing black leather, and he did the Brandon Lee character "really well", according to Jodi. She thought he was beautiful – inside and out. But, she's careful to add that at 20, he was a little bit more down to earth.

Now Nurmi is back to Jodi moving out of her parents' home. He wants to know what caused her to leave – what was the proverbial straw that broke the camel's back. I can answer this. If I were in the gallery, I'd have a hard time not raising my hand while saying, "They grounded her for three months for cutting a class, and then her father pushed her into a door post!". Is there anything I missed? Now she's rambling, and it's interesting to note that she is quite sure, at least at this point in her testimony, that her father definitely closed his restaurant before she left. There's no more stumbling over 1997 or 1998. She tells Nurmi that she was packing boxes because, she claims, she knew she'd be on her own soon (right, failing the eleventh grade, looking at two more years of high school, and she was fixated on preparing for an independent life?).

We can't have different precipitating events. Either she was preparing for an independent life and was "surreptitiously" packing boxes and sending them to Bobby's house, or she was grounded after cutting her American History exam and made a decision to flee. Which is it? She can't be sending boxes of independence over to Bobby's grandparents' home while simultaneously claiming that a grounding was the impetus for her escape. If she thought she'd be on her own soon and wanted to pack dishes her father gave her along with some old books, why the secrecy? She certainly didn't need to explain packing away extra dishes. The earlier version of leaving home – the story that had her escaping the hellish grounding – had Jodi staying up all night packing the rest of her belongings while her parents slept.

Jodi tells us that whenever she was grounded, her father would "unhook her car". She finally figured out what he unhooked, and she was able to fix it. The night she was planning to leave, she first checked her car. It started. Yay! She claims she walked back into the house to finish packing, but she heard one of her parents moving around at 4:30 AM. She dove on the couch and pretended to be asleep so she wouldn't have to face the music. She claims to have accidentally fallen asleep, and the next thing she knew, it was 7:30AM. Her abusive mother was in the kitchen making breakfast, and Jodi assumed she had missed her big opportunity to escape without saying goodbye. But then, she went into her room, grabbed her cat, and opened the front door. Her mother asked her what she was doing. Her reply? "Nothing". Then she closed the front door, threw the cat in the car, and drove to Bobby's house.

The camera pans to Sandy Arias. She's very still, and if it weren't for the people moving around her, you'd think you were looking at a photograph. This time, the corners of her mouth are down. She appears to be frowning. Sandy remembers the day her daughter left home. She remembers thinking that she, a high school graduate, was at least able to help her husband operate restaurants, and later on, get a job as a dental assistant. She realized that her daughter, Jodi, was nothing more than an insolent child attached to impossible dreams. She probably remembered all of the instances in which Jodi scolded her for not going on to college, for not thinking for herself, and for not reading more. She probably remembers not being able to endure the argument that would ensue if she reminded Jodi that she hadn't even made it out of the eleventh grade by the age of 17.

To drive the final nail into the coffin of the Arias parents, Nurmi wants to know what kind of environment Jodi was willing to live in to escape the alleged prison her parents had built. Jodi, the eleventh grade dropout, has enough architectural knowledge to tell us that the Juarez estate was in very good condition, structurally speaking. However, it was in very bad condition, aesthetically speaking. Bobby's grandparents were heavy smokers, so "tar was running down the walls", according to Jodi. She added that they were "hoarders", and the walls were packed with odds and ends – "just things" – from the floor the ceiling. Let's remember what Jodi's grandparents' crime scene photos looked like as we listen to her state her opinion of someone else's home, According to Jodi, the Juarez kitchen was very dirty. The bathroom was also very dirty. The linoleum was coming off the floor, and the shower was falling apart. "It was just a mess", she says.

She goes on, "All of the yard around the house was overgrown". Why didn't Nurmi ever ask why an unemployed 20 year old leech didn't bother to wash dishes or mow the grass for the senior citizens who were supporting him? I guess Bobby was too busy watching "Interview with a Vampire" or "The Crow" on their television to notice the squalor all around him. If you're not convinced of Jodi's sociopathy yet, this might do it. Two days later, after walking out of her parents' home without even so much as a goodbye, let alone an explanation, she waltzes back into their home to borrow their cleaning supplies. I guess she didn't want to spend her own $10 on a bottle of ammonia, a bottle of bleach, and fifteen roles of paper towels.

Nurmi, after citing the substandard living conditions in the Juarez hovel, decides to ask if Jodi was having sex with Bobby Juarez while sleeping in his bed. She doesn't remember. She doesn't remember? Oh, please. She thinks they might have waited a few months? Um, no, they didn't. This is one of the key problems in Jodi's life. She thinks she knows what people will believe. In her desperation to make others see this venture as a strategic move to insure her survival, she thinks older individuals have forgotten what it is to be young. I don't, and the jury doesn't, believe for a moment that a heterosexual male, 20 years of age, slept next to a heterosexual female, 17 years of age, and all that happened was cookies, milk, prayers, and sleep well. It's a biological improbability of huge proportion.

Now that the alarm clock has gone off and the pair are on their feet, we're learning that Bobby Juarez couldn't find his birth certificate. In addition to that, Bobby Juarez also couldn't find his social security card, although he had a social security number. These two hapless individuals (Bobby and Jodi) bounced from government agency to government agency trying to make him legal, but they always failed because they just couldn't get their paperwork in order. The camera goes to Juan Martinez, and he doesn't look like he's moved a muscle since we last saw him – fist over mouth, long blinks, and then finally, he lifts his yellow legal pad and turns the page.

The kept man and his woman then go to Chico, California. They stay there for a week while Jodi tries to secure a waitress position. She ends up at Denny's. I'm confused. Did she work at Denny's in Chico for a week or did they stay in Chico for a week to find her a job? Who cares? Nurmi asks her if this was the only full-time job she has had. She initially says yes, but then throws the Purple Plum into the mix. Remember the Purple Plum? It's important, or it will be once Juan Martinez gets a shot at Jodi. She says she did a short stint as a "busser" (someone hired to clear dirty plates, glasses, and flatware) at The Purple Plum. She explains that she worked there briefly before she thought she was going to move to Chico, but then came back and worked at Denny's. Make of that mess what you will.

Jodi ends up back in Bobby Juarez' grandparents' home. Now, it's been transformed into their honeymoon cottage. Suddenly, the parents/grandparents are in a rest home (when the hell did that happen?), and while Jodi used her money to buy food and clothes for Bobby Juarez, he remained unemployed. Nurmi asks a logical question – who was paying the utility expenses? Arias claims she wasn't paying them, but someone was, until the power was shut off.

The pair used candles for light until one of Bobby's friends came over and tinkered with their meter. Amazing. The power was restored, and not a dollar was spent. Of course, Jodi asked no questions. At this point, there's a long shot of Arias sitting on the stand. Under her cream colored slacks, the outline of some kind of rectangular device is evident above her right knee. For the first time in several hours, we are reminded that Jodi Arias is an accused killer, and there is attached to her a body an electronic device that will prevent her from moving from that chair. Thank you, camera person.

Next, there's a big convoluted story about how Jodi suspected that Bobby was interested in another woman. If electricity was a freebie in their home, you can safely assume the internet access and a home computer were luxuries they did without. Jodi tells the tale of the public library, the place the pair would go whenever they wanted to use computers and log onto the internet. On one fateful day, she stopped, with Bobby, at the library prior to going to work her shift at the Purple Plum. Together, they checked their email accounts and did whatever two poverty stricken individuals do when they have free access to the internet. While they were together, they would each use separate terminals – that's important if you're going to believe the next part of her story. On this particular day, after Jodi dropped 20 year old Bobby off for his play date, she didn't go to work at the Purple Plum. Instead, she went back to the library. She approached the computer Bobby had been using just a little earlier in the day, hit the backspace key, and she was able to access his email. Her worst fears were realized when she read the poetic letters he had been exchanging with another woman

Emotionally sick, Jodi called The Purple Plum and said she wouldn't be coming in for her shift that day. Then, she drove back to Bobby's friend's house and, not wanting to make a scene, pulled him aside and confronted him about his emotional cheating. Blah, blah, blah....you'll hear more of the same as the trial proceeds. Are you getting a picture of who Jodi Arias is yet? If not, there's plenty more to come. She claims that she broke up with Bobby on the spot, and then she went back to his house to pack and move her belongings to a friend's home. What friend? We haven't heard about any friends. In fact, we've only heard about Bobby's friends – the individual who restored their power without a dime exchanging hands and the other guy – the one who ran the all-day arcade for the unemployed.

We learn that Bobby visited Jodi in the unidentified friend's home in which she was now squatting. I'm falling asleep, but then I hear those words coming from Nurmi – "physical abuse". Of course there was physical abuse, Nurmi. Suddenly, Jodi is recounting an argument that led to her calling 911. She's smiling, chuckling at times, as she recalls the martial arts "strangle hold" Bobby used on her. Then she talks about how he almost broke her arm (but didn't), etc., etc., etc. Abuse, abuse, and more abuse. We haven't event touched on the subject of Travis Alexander. Jodi doesn't remember if she had sexual relations with Juarez after her nearly killed her and almost broke her arm, but Nurmi obviously believes that we believe she screwed him in the days following this horrible assault. Hey! What about the 911 call?

Nurmi asks Jodi why she would have sex with Bobby after the strangle hold and the 911 call. Her answer? "I still loved him".

Nurmi then begins to mention a name that will come up again: Matt. But before we go to boyfriend number three, we have to tie up the loose ends of Bobby Juarez. Jodi says she was preparing to leave the woman's home in which she was squatting so that she could squat with her grandparents back in Yreka. Nurmi wants a picture of her life at that point. Did she go home? Did she go back to school? Where did she go after leaving Bobby Juarez? I still want to know about the 911 call.

Jodi says that she earned vacation benefits after working at Denny's for a whole year. Where did Jodi take her vacation? Why, Costa Rica, of course.

Nurmi assumes, as we all do, that she went to see Victor Arias. Listen to her answer when he proposes that scenario: "No, he didn't live in the house anymore. I went to stay with my – the same family, but he had moved out and moved on". What was she going to say? My what? My aunt? My second cousin? It was, after all, the same house she stayed in when she was an alleged "foreign exchange student". I am more convinced than ever that Victor Arias was a family member. Oh, she does add that while she spent the week with Victor's family, and she did not see Victor (because he had "moved on"), Victor did show up three days before she left to take her to dinner. She calls this ten day period "a time of reflection and healing".

Jodi then testifies that she returned to Yreka, and returned to work. What does that mean, returned to Yreka? Was she living with her parents, her grandparents, in a motel, and in a shelter? As long as we are being forced to listen to this, can we at least know where she was living? Where is work? Is she working at her parents' restaurant or another restaurant? Is she at Denny's (which I though was in Chico), is she working at "Grandmas", or is she working at a convenience store?

She smiles as she says that she doesn't know if Bobby Juarez was watching the restaurant or not, but on her first day back from vacation – oh, we're at Denny's. I've really been listening, and if Denny's is in Chico's, and that's what she said, she would be driving over 2.5 hours to get to work from Yreka. That's why I hate this testimony. When you have the time to slow it down and look at what she's saying, it makes no sense. Who drives five hours a day for a waitressing job? Not even Jodi Arias could be that desperate, could she?

Okay, Denny's it is. Jodi says that upon returning to work, she saw Bobby sitting at the lunch counter. According to Jodi, "...He just had his face in his hands, and he has really beautiful eyes, and he was looking at me with these eyes, these puppy dog eyes, and um, I just stopped, and I was kind of shocked, and I felt stronger, um, not emotionally as weak, but um, I was coming up to my half hour break, and I said, 'Just wait a few minutes, and we'll go outside and talk', and so I went outside, and um, we ended up talking for a long time – I mean, we rounded the corner and then hugged, and it was emotional".

Nurmi asks, "Was that the last time you saw Bobby?" She's ready to answer, and she says, "No". Nurmi asks if they continued a relationship after that. Jodi answers, "We decided we were going to continue a relationship, but it didn't – we weren't getting along very well". Nurmi wants to know if the word relationship means friendship or romantic relationship. Jodi says it was a romantic relationship. Nurmi wants to know if romantic also means sexual. She answers, "Yeah, it would have meant that. I don't really remember, but it would have meant that". Nurmi asks the question every thinking person would ask – why was she open to a sexual and romantic relationship with a man who had choked her and abused her as she described? She responds, "Well, I guess I considered those incidents isolated and not a pattern of his. I still loved him, and he still loved me, and I didn't want to hurt him and I didn't want to – I don't know – we were, it just felt natural. I had been with him for some years. He was my first love, being with him, whether it was good or bad, it just felt natural, and it was what I was accustomed to".

Nurmi wants to know what ended the relationship. Jodi says that Costa Rica was the starting point of her healing, and if she hadn't seen Bobby Juarez again, she would have been alright. It becomes clear that Bobby is about to take his final bow, and we are about to be introduced to Matt McCartney. She says that Bobby moved to Medford, Oregon, and he had a roommate by the name of Matt. According to Jodi, after moving to Medford, Bobby Juarez reconnected with a woman who went to school with him, a Notary Public, and the powers that be accepted her word that Bobby was who he said he was . Is this true? Whether it is or isn't does really matter. Bobby Juarez is not on trial here. If he found a way to get around his identity problem, why should we care? This case is about the murder of Travis Alexander – a crime committed by Jodi Arias. We cannot put any stock in what Jodi Arias says, so this is all a moot point. Jodi claims that following Bobby's good fortune, she continued to purchase "South Park" T-shirts for Bobby Juarez. Why this matters, I don't know.

Jodi continued to visit Bobby several times in Medford, usually on the weekends. Hello, Matt. Apparently, Matt realized that Bobby was treating Jodi badly, so she felt comfortable venting with Matt. He saw her side of it, and that, she says, felt good. Arias recalls one weekend when she went to visit Bobby in Oregon, and Matt had a female friend visiting him. Her eyes were opened by his chivalrous behavior towards his lady friend (might that include the type of behavior she labeled as jealous and controlling about an hour and a half ago, when it was being displayed by Victor Arias?).

This chivalry was "jarring" to Arias. Jarring? Didn't she just testify that when her father would see a beautiful woman, he would react by saying that the beautiful woman could not compare to Jodi's mother? Jarring? Really? Why was it jarring? Because her parents argued, and apparently, in the fantasy world of Jodi Arias, people committed to a marriage must have the same opinion about everything under the sun? Can they not argue without negating all of the history and years between them? When they argued, Jodi said her father, being sarcastic, would say something uncouth, but he'd think it was funny. Her mother didn't think it was funny, so she'd slap him on the arm. Then, her father would respond by slapping her mother on the arm. Then, her mother would slap her father on the arm. The game ended when her father slapped her mother on the arm – but this time, with force, according to Jodi. This caused her mother to give up. This is now being described as physical abuse. Even Jodi is laughing.

There's a little dust-up at this point. Juan Martinez objects to Jodi telling us how her "gossipy" father degraded her mother. During the sidebar, we see Sandy and Aunt Sue whispering, giggling, and then composing themselves. Apparently, Nurmi won, because he gets to ask Jodi about a specific incident of husband-on-wife degradation. She's ready. She says, "One I recall specifically is um, my mom. My mother used to be very thin and she's like a size ten now, I guess, and he used to put up photos of her on the refrigerator when she was thinner, and um, he would make comments about her weight gain, and um, he would put little things like that around the house to remind her that he would prefer her with less weight. Things like that. I don't know how that affected her, but that was pretty constant. If somebody was crossing in the crosswalk that was overweight, he would yell at them. I don't remember what he said, but um, I don't know, things like that". Call 911 and have the man arrested. What an environment of abuse Jodi Arias was raised in.

There's a lot of prepared testimony that paints Sandy Arias as the long suffering wife of a verbally abusive idiot. If I wrote it all out, we'd never get to the relevant testimony. I will quote her testimony when her attorney actually addresses anything that matters, but for now, just accept my summarizations. There is some testimony that gives us the details of how Jodi Arias targeted and captured Matt McCartney as her new boyfriend. There is also some frivolous nonsense about Jodi, Matt, and Matt's nephew (the kid has some name I can neither pronounce or spell) playing on someone's front lawn with wooden swords.

Coincidentally, Bobby Juarez just happened to drive by, and after witnessing the frivolity from which he was excluded, he realized he was history. Be thankful, Bobby Juarez. It was the best think that could have happened to you. So, Bobby disappears, Matt's the new boyfriend. It is the end of Day One, and court is adjourned.

CHAPTER TWO

- Day 2 -

"People think that a liar gains a victory over his victim. What I've learned is that a lie is an act of self-abdication, because one surrenders one's reality to the person to whom one lies, making that person one's master, condemning oneself from then on to faking the sort of reality that person's view requires to be faked…The man who lies to the world, is the world's slave from then on…There are no white lies, there is only the blackest of destruction, and a white lie is the blackest of all."

- Ayn Rand, Atlas Shrugged

Well, good morning! We are starting bright and early at 10:30 AM, Jodi Arias is already on the stand when the viewing audience is invited to watch the testimony. She's lost the pony tail, so perhaps it's safe to assume we've exchanged the playground and school corridors for a chance to wander through Jodi's hungry years.

Jodi looks different today. More mature. More relaxed. More Casual. She could have been on the golf course prior to coming to court. Gone is the black, short sleeved sweater, and in its place is something that could have been pulled from a cardboard box labeled "Spring". It's a powder blue, short sleeved, cotton shirt, and only one button has been left unsecured. The shirt is tight enough to draw attention to her breast implants.

The judge's voice rings out as she reminds Jodi that she's still under oath, and Jodi smiles, looks at the judge, and replies, "Yes, thank you". Then she grabs a plastic cup, and while the judge is telling Nurmi that he may continue, Jodi, in a display of pure ambidexterity, pours herself a glass of water with her right hand.

Nurmi wants to get right into Matt McCartney. He asks, "Yesterday when we finished, we were talking, we were at a point in your life when you were about ready to move in with Matt McCartney. Do you recall that?". With a hint of a smile and a saccharine tinged tone, she says, "Yes". He continues, "And yesterday, I had asked you uh, if at this point in time, you were boyfriend and girlfriend. Um, and it seemed like you didn't have a definitive answer for that. Is that a label you two didn't use, or...?". As he trails off, Jodi picks it up just a little too quickly: "Um, I don't recall when we made things official, but he wasn't seeing anyone else and neither was I". So, that's it? No wonder Nurmi wanted to clean this up. All it takes for his client to share a man's residence and bed is a standard this low? Will there be any mention of love, commitment, common goals – anything at all? Basically, they were both unattached, so they decided to attach to each other. What are they, mating frogs?

So, what happened overnight? Did Nurmi decide that her ambiguity made her look just a little too easy for this jury? Obviously, this is something he believes needs to be fixed. Were Jodi Arias and Matt McCartney boyfriend and girlfriend when they moved in together? As infuriatingly irrelevant and absurd as this question is, we're going to have to listen to Jodi break it all down for us. The content is meaningless, but if you pay attention, you'll see an-the-spot technique Nurmi uses from time to time. It is meant to rehabilitate Arias, but she doesn't always comply.

Nurmi still doesn't like her answer. He heard what she said, but he lets her know that it's still not playing well. She'll need to refine it a little more. He uses the old stand-by line, "I'm sorry, what was that?". Jodi answers, "I don't recall when we made it official – our relationship (she is moving her hands randomly, and she looks right at the jury) – I mean, it definitely became that way, but I don't remember the exact date or time or circumstance, but we weren't seeing anybody else. Just each other". For most women, the time or circumstance would have been in the weeks leading up to the decision to move in together. That makes things pretty damn "official" in terms of being boyfriend and girlfriend. But Jodi Arias isn't most women. Nurmi really wanted her to make the relationship more than it was on moving day, but she didn't. Instead she focused on the fact that the relationship eventually became "official", and that should be good enough.

Nurmi sums it up the way he wants it summed up: "Okay, so when you moved in together, it was with the idea that this was gonna be a monogamous relationship". That wasn't even a question. It was a statement. He actually had to put the words in her mouth. This is called leading the witness. I wondered why Juan Martinez didn't object on those grounds, but he probably isn't interested in the status reports of a long dead relationship between this murderer and her ex-boyfriend. What he cares about is the long dead Travis Alexander.

Arias answers, "Yes". Too late. Nobody believes her. She just stated "it became that way", and that implies that it wasn't "that way" when they signed a lease together. Nurmi cannot rewrite history this time, especially when his client has stated, several times, that she and Matt were not boyfriend and girlfriend when they moved in together. There was no promise of a monogamous relationship. At best, it was a wait and see kind of deal, and it was based on their common need for pooled money and sex. I'm hoping Nurmi will move on.
Now we are going to explore the upwardly mobile careers of Jodi and Matt. She was working at Applebee's (I'm assuming it was P/T work or Nurmi would have wanted her to take credit for being a F/T employee). What about Matt? Jodi says, "Yes, he was a manager at Subway". A manager? Well, isn't that something? He wasn't slicing tomatoes and throwing slices of turkey on rolls, he was telling other people to slice tomatoes and throw slices of turkey on rolls. Fascinating work, if you can get it. Nurmi could ask how many hours a week these two individuals spent working, but he doesn't. He gives her a big, open ended question. He says, "Tell us what life was like. How did he treat you?".

Jodi responds, "Um, I see that period of time as probably one of the best times of my life. Um, he treated me very well. He was very kind. He was very respectful. He was very spiritual (Get it? He was all of the things that mean old Travis Alexander wasn't). Um, when I first met him, I was a little bit leery of some of the things that he was into. Um, I saw some books on witchcraft, and I thought 'uhhh' (all of her teeth are on display as she smiles at the jurors), but he explained to me that he was just seeking – that he had gone to church most of his life, and um, his family, he and his family are very much into the Native American culture, so he asked his pastor about the Native Americans, and he was told they went to hell – because they didn't have Jesus Christ (she's still smiling as she talks about Native Americans burning in hell). Um, so that turned him off to Christianity, and um, he decided to explore other religions, so about the time that I met him, he was not practicing Wicca, but he was studying it, and um, so he had kind of explained it a little bit to me so that I wasn't, I guess, frightened or suspicious – or superstitious, maybe – of the religion. Um, and so, I never practiced it myself, but I think he did prior to us getting together, and by the time I met him, he was sort of moving on to other – like studying eastern philosophy and Hinduism and Buddhism, and that kind of thing, too". Nurmi attempts to stop the flow of whatever the hell this is by saying "Okay". She's not ready to stop. She continues, "So, our relationship took a lot of spiritual turns and twists (she does a swimming hand motion for emphasis).

Does anyone remember the question? She was asked to describe what life was like while she was working at Applebee's and Matt was working at Subway. If she is to be believed, life was lived on a bookshelf filled with books about various religions. Witchcraft? Jodi claims she was frightened by witchcraft and Wicca. Really? Does she remember Bobby Juarez, the vampire she dated? Has she so quickly erased from her memory the long dark coat and high collared white shirt costume of the Undead? Does she remember talking about her love for Ann Rice novels? Suddenly, Jodi Arias, non-denominational Christian, is "frightened" by Wicca? It's interesting to note that Arias could not remember when she and Matt became official, but she knows that he had stopped practicing that bad Wicca stuff by the time "they got together". However, she also said that at the time they got together, he was studying Wicca and witchcraft.

So, let's get this straight, Matt studied witchcraft, practiced it, decided to stop practicing it, and then went back to merely studying it? Why would he go back to studying something he had already practiced and decided not to practice anymore? It doesn't matter. What matters is the jury believes that Arias was not dating a practitioner of witchcraft, just a student of witchcraft. Look at how dumb she's making Matt sound. It wasn't really Matt's fault that he was attracted to the occult. No, it was that ignorant pastor. After all, he's the one who told the life-long Christian that all Native Americans go to hell. Was Matt listening while he sat in church for all of those years? Was it suddenly news to him that the Christian church teaches that all those who fail to embrace Christ are damned? That isn't exactly something that hits you out of nowhere if you've spent your life in a Christian church. It's something they admit in their weekly church bulletins. It's right there under that heading, "We Believe...". I'd also like to know why Matt suddenly took up the cause of all damned Native Americans while ignoring the damned Hindus? I guess it was a case of selective disenchantment. Alright, enough of these lies.

Nurmi interrupts to say that this might be a good time to "back up a little bit" and talk about the subject of spirituality. He has to say that. Why? Because his client is running the show. She's not answering his questions. Instead, she's deciding what she's going to talk about. In order to save face, Nurmi has to pretend that spirituality is what he really wanted to address. So, put it in reverse. Nurmi asks, "At the time you met Matt, was there a particular religion that you were a member of? Can you describe that for us?". Sure, let's see if we get a different answer than the last time he asked this question. She has already said that she was a non-denominational Christian who called her ex-boyfriend, Bobby Juarez, to tell him that the second coming of Christ was going to happen in late September, 1997. Okay?

Jodi replies, "I was not a member of any denomination. I considered myself Christian". Fine. Question answered. Can we move on? No, she has more to say: "Um, I didn't attend church, and I didn't obey all the commandments that Christianity espouses". She knows nothing about Christianity. Christianity espouses repentance, salvation, and forgiveness. They do not espouse following the Ten Commandments.

So, how did she practice her Christianity? Just curious. Nurmi wants something more definitive. He wants to know if Jodi dumped her non-practicing Christianity and adopted Matt's beliefs. She could say yes. She could say no. However, she decides to give Mike Babicky, the court reporter, a run for his money with this rehearsed speech. She speaks in an unnaturally rapid fashion, and I believe this is why she gave Babicky a head's up this morning with her, "If I speak too fast, let me know, I'll slow it down" directive. She recites, "We sort of explored together and opened up to other beliefs. We began taking meditation seminars – kind of New Age seminars (free, of course, and with refreshments to follow), but they had their roots in Hinduism or Buddhism (she taps her left palm twice in rapid succession with her right hand as she rattles off two entirely different philosophies that share no common roots) – maybe some like, more modern version of transcendentalism – things like that (she's lying – her hands are moving furiously as they spin and threaten to hit her microphone) . We just took these little courses and classes, and we would drive to Portland or the Bay area". They would drive to Portland or the Bay area? Well, why didn't she just say so at the beginning? That sold me. All of the world's religions begin and end in Portland – or the Bay area.

Nurmi asks, "Was this a big part of your relationship with Matt?". She is proud of her recitation. Her shoulders are squared and her head is held high as she looks at the jury and says, "Yes, it was". Well, great. There must be a virtual party raging on the spiritual plane, but on the temporal plane, the bills are piling up. Can we get to that? Not yet...

Nurmi shifts gears without warning. Now he wants to examine the carnal areas of the couple's life. I'd rather go back to the spiritual plane. As vapid and pointless as it was, at least everyone was wearing clothes. Nurmi plows forward. He asks, "This may go without saying because you lived together – but, was this also a sexual relationship?". She's still sitting up strong – not looking at the jury – but still confident as she answers, "Yes". Nurmi asks, "Did you love Matt?". Jodi answers, "Very much. I was in love with him". Yawn.

Nurmi wants to know about money. She claims that all of the living expenses were split 50/50. Really? What was the rent? We don't even know if these two are working F/T or P/T. This woman's finances will remain a mystery throughout this trial. Arias says that they lived in "this small apartment" for five months (why do I believe they either fled under cover of night, or they were evicted). The spiritual lovebirds then settled into Crater Lake (I will refrain from pointing out the irony of the name of the town and certain parts of Jodi's anatomy). Nurmi wants to know why they chose Crater Lake. Her answer only solidifies my belief that they skipped out on their last landlord.

Does this sound like anything a normal person would say? For example, would you talk about the elevation of the town you were moving to if someone asked you why you moved? No, probably not. However, Jodi does. Remember, the question is, "Why did you move to Crater Lake". The answer? Jodi says, "Um, the seasonal work there is in the summer. It's a very high elevation, so the snow stays until about July and then comes back in October. So, it's quick season, it's a busy season, and um, they have staff housing there at the resort, and we got a dorm there for the season and worked there". Anything to avoid paying rent. It is the hallmark of her life. Going from an apartment to a dorm might be impressive if your spirituality demanded that you become detached from the material things in life, but it's not so impressive when you can't invite anyone to your home for dinner because there just isn't enough room on the dorm beds for everyone to balance their plates comfortably.

When Nurmi asks Jodi if her relationship with Matt was serious “at this point in time”, she responds, “Yes, we weren't like, heavily discussing marriage, but we were talking about children and what kind of lifestyle we would have if we decided to have a family”. Decided to have a family? Perhaps they should focus on deciding to have a couch or a coffee table first. As far as we can surmise, those items are still on the wish-list of life. Here's a good line -- they “weren't heavily discussing marriage”. Were they lightly discussing it? Was there a medium level of marriage discussion? She uses the word “heavily” because she will not say “seriously”. That is what a truthful person would say -- “We were not seriously discussing marriage”. See how much more normal that sounds?

I have a pretty clear picture of what transpired. She wanted to get married, and he said he didn't want to discuss it anymore. Children? Two people who are reduced to seeking resort work so they can have a dorm room to live in are hardly the individuals who would be talking about adding children to their lives. I cannot believe a word of this. In any event, Nurmi does his best to paint a picture of a happy, domesticated couple living in a dormitory, but with an eye on the future. They lived that lifestyle for almost two years – well, according to Jodi it was “approximately one year and eight months”.

Nurmi has been waiting for the opportunity to take this trial to an “R” rating. Out of nowhere, he asks her the following: “In the year and eight months, did he ever hit you? Arias does a mini-swivel of her chair, looks at the jury and says, “No”. Then she swivels back to face Nurmi. Nurmi asks, “Did he ever call you a whore?”. She repeats the same swivel action and faces the jury. She says, “No”. Then she's swiveling back to face Nurmi. He asks, “A slut?”. Again, it's a swivel to the right, “No”, and a swivel to the left. Pulling out the big guns, Nurmi asks, “A three hole wonder?”. She follows the swivel routine, answers, “No”, but this time, her face is super-duper sad by the time she's facing Nurmi again.

This language, of course, is a reference to the victim, Travis Alexander. These are the names he called Jodi Arias over the course of their “relationship”. Nurmi wants everyone to know that Jodi wasn't accustomed to those kinds of bad words – after all, Matt never used them. So, what's a girl to do when her former boyfriend calls her a slut or a whore? Well, if it's the first time she's been verbally assaulted with such pointed barbs, she gets to respond with a big butcher knife and a gun and call it self-defense. A few jurors probably woke up at this point, wondering what the hell they missed. There's a big, long, dramatic pause. Let those words sink in, jury...let them sink in.

Nurmi wants to know how and why the Jodi-Matt relationship ended. I don't care how or why it ended. The jury probably doesn't care how or why it ended. I doubt there is anyone who really cares about this relationship at all – beginning, middle, or end. Unfortunately, Nurmi shoves it down our throats anyway. As is her custom, Jodi Arias is going to talk about what she wants to talk about. So, when asked how her one year, eight month relationship with Matt ended, she starts talking about the irony of life. She says, "Well, after the first season at Crater Lake, we came back, and ironically, the same exact apartment opened up again (was this apartment in Matt's mother's basement or something? That a pretty big coincidence), so we rented the same place where we lived, prior to that. Um, we stayed there for some months (how did they pay the rent? Did either have a job? Nobody is asking). We began to argue over little things. It wasn't anything serious, but it wore on our relationship because it made things not so enjoyable (wow, this is commitment!). Um, so we began to take a breather from each other – not from each other (the truth slips out – it was a breather from each other), but from living together (oh, please), um, so he went back to Crater Lake for a season, and this time, I did not go. I move to Ashland, which is about 15 minutes south of Medford – it's in Oregon also...". Just so you remember, the question was, "How did the relationship end". If I needed topographical information and a geography lesson, this answer might work. So far, it all sounds like a huge distraction.

Nurmi cuts her off. He wants to know why they broke up. He wants her to describe what their little arguments were. She answers, "It was more like nagging. He would leave his clothes everywhere, and I'd be like, you know -- and what else? Sometimes I would leave a dish, sometimes in the living room if we were eating. So it was kind of about house – housekeeping, and that sort of thing. You know – living together. Those dynamics". This is ridiculous. They broke up – oh, pardon me, they didn't break up, they just took a breather – NOT from each other, mind you. The "breather" was caused by a plate in the living room and clothes all over.

Do I hear bagpipes? Is that the mournful cry of "Danny Boy"? Who died? Love died. Yes, the love between Jodi and Matt has left Medford, or Ashland, or Crater Lake, or wherever it is these two vagabonds are at this point in the story, and its gone onto the cosmic graveyard of dead relationships. How did something as benign as pile of clothes or a misplaced dish kill this relationship of spiritual seeking, little seminars, dorm rooms, and not heavily discussed marriage? Well, Jodi is about to fill us in on the details. She says, "Um, well, we um, decided to spend a little bit of time apart. We saw each other on our weekends. He would come in to town in Ashland and stay with me, and I remember I was with his dad's girlfriend, and she was trying to – I felt that we were sort of distancing, but I was hanging out with – I can't remember her name, but his dad's girlfriend, at the time. And uh, we were trying to download pictures on his dad's hard drive, and on the desktop there were some other pictures of this girl, and I didn't recognize her, but I recognized the setting, and it was inside the lodge at Crater Lake, so. The date was also current with this season, which would have been 2001. But, it was just labeled with I guess an initial – the letter B. So, I didn't know who she was, but I wasn't overly concerned about it (install laugh track here), ya know? I just kind of had a feeling, and so I let that go, and a few weeks later, I was working at Applebee's, and um, two – I was walking past the table and two people said, 'Hi, Jodi', and I stopped, and I didn't recognize them, and they explained that they worked with Matt at Crater Lake, and they were just in town for their days off, and um, they um, I just said hi to them and checked on them later as they were about to leave. They said they had taken a vote and we think we should know something, and they told me that he was seeing a girl named Bianca at Crater Lake. So that explained the initial B on the photo. And I kinda said did she have dark hair, and they said yes, and so I figured it was her".

There are so many holes in this story. Two people walked into an Applebee's restaurant. Jodi didn't know them, but they knew Jodi. They greeted her by name. The normal individual, the one telling the truth, would have asked, "Do I know you?". Not Jodi. She stopped and they started talking to her. They said, "We work with Matt at Crater Lake, and we are in town for our days off". Now, how they happened to walk in to an Applebee's that was almost two hours away from Crater Lake at exactly the same time as Jodi was working a shift is another mystery. Jodi's response to this information was not, "Who are you?". Jodi's response was to say, "Hi". Then she took off and decided to check on them later. Why? If she wasn't serving them, what more is there to say to them? Well, it's a good thing she checked back with them because during those minutes that elapsed between their first conversation and their second, the two mystery beings had taken a vote. A vote. With two people? In any event, these two people decided to put themselves right in the middle of a situation that most people would run from. They decided to tell Jodi that Matt was seeing Bianca. Now remember, Jodi has let all of that go – she just didn't let it go so far that she couldn't retrieve it at a moment's notice. Betrayed again, by the boyfriend who moved out on her months earlier.

Jodi is in the middle of smiling her way through a recitation of betrayal. Her lover, spiritual pilot, and roommate, Matt McCartney, has wandering eyes. Jodi believes the computer has, once again, helped to bust an unfaithful boyfriend. These are never HER computers – one belonged to the library and the other belonged to Matt's father's girlfriend – but grifters grift and usually, they get what they need.

So, two nameless individuals have filled in the missing pieces. In an instant, Sherlock Arias puts it all together on the spot. The initial "B" has come back to haunt her. Can you see her heart breaking? She has no heart, but if she did, it would be breaking. What she does have is an ego. I see her ego breaking, despite the fact that Jodi is pretty relaxed at this point. She's swiveling in her chair, and she's talking about this painful period of her life as if she's talking about what she's going to put on her next grocery list.

Nurmi asks what she did with this information. Jodi says "I was kind of reeling, because of all the boyfriends I'd ever had (and, according to her own testimony, that list is populated by exactly two other individuals), I'd expected him to not be the one that cheated on me. Um, he was very loyal. I trusted him completely (hand motions for emphasis) -- like implicitly. He could have said the sky was falling, and I would have believed him. I think I would have just looked out the window to see what it looked like. Um, but I asked my boss if I could go home a little early, and he said that was fine (sure, go home, server. We're not busy, after all, we're just Applebee's). So, I think I was let go. It was slow. I was let go around seven, and ….".

Now, wait just a minute. Nurmi interrupts here, but before he does, can I ask a question? Jodi was "reeling"? That's HER word. Does Miss Surreptitiously comprehend the meaning of that word? It means, "faint, weak, befuddled, dazed, and groggy". Basically, it means she was sucker punched in the psyche. If she was that dazed and weak, one would think the manager would say, "Jodi, are you alright? Why don't you punch out early". Poor Jodi. Nobody ever notices her when she's reeling.

Moving right along, Nurmi interrupts: "And just so we're clear, you were living with Matt at the time?". What is going on with Nurmi? Can he sleep while standing up, or is he thinking about lunch? He's the one dragging all of this useless information out of Jodi (the only one having a grand old time with the subject matter), and if we have to listen to it, so does he. She just spent the last four minutes telling us all about her independent life away from Matt. Matt is in Crater Lake. Jodi is in Ashland. She said they had housekeeping issues. Remember the clothes he left on the floor and the dinner plate she failed to wash? The last few minutes have been all about separation. Is this ringing a bell, counselor?

Secure in the knowledge that even her own attorney isn't following her testimony, Jodi answers, "No, he was living in Crater Lake and I was living in Ashland". Nurmi tries to recover without showing his embarrassment. "OK...". Nurmi stops talking, and Jodi continues, "Um, so I went home, and I changed my clothes, and I decided to – at this time, though, Matt was, on this night – Matt was in Borrego Springs, California, looking for my...".

Nurmi realizes he had better start paying attention, so he asks, "How far was that from where you were?". Jodi answers, "Very far, it's almost at the border, and Ashland is almost at the other California border, the northern border." Jodi and Matt were almost 14 hours apart that night. Nurmi neglected to point that out. Moving on.

Nurmi wants to know what happened after she left work early, went home, and changed her clothes. I can tell you. Now that we know all about Jodi's unsolicited spies (who are willing to report to her without any form of compensation whatsoever – not even money for gas or dessert on the house), we are going to take a trip back to Crater Lake, Oregon. Medford is in the rear view mirror as Jodi speeds down the highways and byways leading to her destination. She's charged up by the thought of an impending ambush. She's probably blasting music on the car stereo she finds personally empowering. She's hitting wrong notes everywhere as she sings, drowning out the studio recording of an actual vocalist, and she's probably thinking she should have recorded the song because she's just that good. Her desire to dominate is growing.

That's what I think happened. Unfortunately, we have to hear Jodi's version. Nurmi asks if she called Matt. Without missing a beat, she answers, "No, neither of us had cell phones at that time ". Fine, but Nurmi wants to know what Jodi did with that information after she went home and changed her clothes. She says, "Well, um, I decided that I wanted to find out if was true, so, it wasn't very late. It was about an hour and a half ride to Crater Lake, so after getting dressed, I drove up to Crater Lake to see if I could find out – I had friends that were still there – and the people that told didn't know. I wanted to find out from them, and, um, and I went – there were two dormitories there, so I went to the one that was closest to the lodge because that is where people would hang out, and I could find some people that I knew. Um, and I ran into a guy – I think his name was Steve – um, and I asked him...". Thank God, Juan Martinez objects by uttering "hearsay". The objection is sustained, and I'm delighted. I feel like I've been sitting in Jodi's therapy session. Of course, this opens the door for Nurmi to speak. Does he even know where we are?

There's some confusion about a juror's ability to hear the testimony. Judge Stephens brings us back to reality by asking if any of the jurors are having trouble hearing the testimony. False alarm. Apparently, all the jurors are wearing that "Who, me?" expression on their faces, so Nurmi is given the green light to continue. He says, "OK, Jodi, you were in the process of telling us uh, you're going to Crater Lake to find out whether or not Matt was being unfaithful to you." Jodi responds: "Right, I didn't want to continue in the relationship if that was the case. If it wasn't the case, then of course I would, because I loved him".
Nurmi wants to know the outcome of Detective Arias' investigation. She answers, "I knocked on Bianca's door, and Steve had run to warn her, and I could hear them talking (she wants to laugh, but she's controlling herself). I could hear them talking, and Steve was very frantic. Um, he's (smiling widely) – how do I say this? Um, well, he's gay, so he kind of – he's very animated, and he's kind of emotional (hands spinning wildly), and he's very animated, and he sounded very funny, and, um, and I could tell they were nervous (she's almost laughing), and she opens the door and I say 'Hi, are you Bianca?", and she says, 'Yeah'. And so, she invited me in because she knew who I was (of course – everyone knows who Jodi is). So, she invited me in, and we sat down, and um, there were two beds in this dorm, and she was staying with another relative, and they were both from Romania, and they were here for seasonal work, so she sat on her bed and I sat on the other bed, and we just talked for about an hour and a half. Maybe not quite that long, maybe an hour, and she just told me that she started...".

What's that refreshing breeze? What's the breath of spring in the midst of an Arctic freeze? Oh, that's the voice of Juan Martinez. He has an objection. Without even looking at the judge, he says, "Objection, hearsay". He's writing as he speaks. This particular objection shows us that Juan Martinez can multi-task with the best of them. He never looks up, not for a second. The objection is sustained. Nurmi looks at Jodi and asks, "Based on that conversation, could you confirm the idea that Matt McCartney and Bianca were having an affair?" Jodi looks directly at Nurmi, and without a laugh, without a smile, and in her most serious tone of voice, she said, "Yes".

Bianca, the Romanian Temptress, who, despite her modest living situation, has successfully lured that spiritual seeker, Matt McCartney, to her lair of sensual delights (a/k/a a dorm room with two twin beds), does not know what's about to hit her. Remember, Jodi was able to enlist the informational services of insider and (never mentioned before) effeminate guy-pal, Steve. Once she got back to Crater Lake staff housing, Jodi couldn't be seen running from door to door, banging wildly and yelling for Bianca to be woman enough to get outside and face her rival. No, no, no. Jodi had to enter the parking lot, find a parking spot, look sensually into the rear view mirror, toss her hair, adjust her breasts, and apply a fresh layer of lip gloss before she met her successor. She needed the room number. Thankfully, "Steve" served his purpose. Because of Steve, Jodi knew, with certainty, which door Bianca was hiding behind.

Nurmi asks the logical question: "During this hour and a half conversation, were you yelling at her?" Arias doesn't miss a beat. She clasps her hands and focuses her charcoal black eyes on Nurmi. No, there was no yelling. Jodi says it was "chit-chat". Chit chat? For a woman who probably smuggles a Thesaurus in her underpants for quick reference, I'm surprised that's the best word she could find to describe a late night interrogation she drove two hours to conduct. Chit chat? Idle gossip, casual talk, jaw flapping, small talk, tittle tattle – she would have found any of these phrases in her trusty Thesaurus under the entry "chit chat".

So, let's picture the scene, shall we? Once again, all of Jodi's crooked enamel is on display (because there's no photo-shopping in real life), and she's very relaxed as she remembers her ambush of Bianca. What probably saved Bianca's tires was the fact that Jodi, after questioning her suspect, did not believe that "this" was Bianca's fault. How did Jodi arrive at such a merciful judgment? Arias says, "...she (Bianca) had no idea (smile) – she was under the impression that he and I were no longer together...". Yes, I'm sure she was under that impression. I'm sure Matt was under that same impression. That is exactly the impression one leaves when they pack their meager belongings into a car, say goodbye to their significant other, and head off to another residence 97 miles away.

Jodi is smiling -- almost smirking at times. Nurmi is using his most serious tone of voice in an effort to make the jury feel her pain: "How did it feel when you had this information confirmed?". Jodi, sensing that she needs to mimic Nurmi's heartbroken tone of voice, responds, "Umm, I didn't really allow myself to have too much emotion about it until I left her presence. And um, and um, (deep sigh), at that point, I allowed myself to cry". What point? Mile marker 10, 20, or 30 on the highway? When was Jodi weeping? Nurmi really wants everyone to know where she was when she allowed herself to feel the weight of yet another betrayal. He asks, "Had you gone back home, or was this out in the parking lot?" Why would anyone care where Jodi Arias allegedly cried about the fact that her former boyfriend looked more appealing because he had moved on to another woman?

Jodi explains something, but it has nothing to do with Nurmi's question about crying. She tells Nurmi where she "crashed" that night: "I ended up crashing in my friend, Eddie's dorm. And um, he was um, just kind of a family friend, and he was from Yreka, and he was friends with Matt, and he was friends with me, and um, his father also owned a local restaurant, so we all knew each other (she makes an all-inclusive hand gesture)". Hey, fair question here – why doesn't Jodi know any women (unless they are interrogation victims)? Why are there always men around who are willing to come to her rescue? Nurmi never bothers to ask that question. According to Jodi, it wasn't a big deal to find a free local bed for the night (and in a moment's notice). She continues, "...so Eddie said, you can sleep here, and I'll sleep here, because there were two beds in that dorm, and um, I crashed there until about sunrise, and then I got up and drove back to Medford". Fascinating, and so relevant to the murder of Travis Alexander.

Nurmi would like to know if Jodi did the mature thing, the right thing, the logical thing (my words, not his) – did she talk to Matt about her ambush of Bianca? Jodi replies, "No." Of course she didn't. She's sitting stone faced now, staring at Nurmi, and she's wondering where to go next. Nurmi throws the bait and she bites, "What did you do when you got back to Medford?". Jodi replies, "I confronted Matt, and he confirmed it". Confirmed what? That Jodi broke up with him – or he broke up with Jodi? Does she need weekly reminders? What the hell did Matt confirm?

Nurmi wants details about this confrontation. If I'm not losing my memory, I thought we were given the details about the confrontation just now. We even met the supporting cast of characters, didn't we? Nurmi presses on. One would believe that Matt or Bianca were on trial. Nurmi wants to know if Matt was in Medford when she got back home the next day. Was he there to confront Jodi after her impromptu interrogation of Bianca? Jodi thinks, and then says that he may have been in Medford on "that day", "or the next day" – "or whenever".

Whenever? Could that be two weeks later, or whenever he happened to be in town – maybe for Thanksgiving or Christmas? Does it even matter? Her voice trailed off at "or whenever", and I doubt that even Mike Babicky, the long suffering court reporter sitting a foot away from Jodi, could have heard "or whenever". You'd have to be a lip reader to have picked that phrase up, and Babicky wasn't even looking in her direction. Anyone else in the courtroom would have had to strain to hear the words, "or whenever". In any event, Nurmi has now framed a picture that has Matt back in Medford within 24 hours (because, you know, if Jodi wants to get back together, it's worth a four hour round trip to talk about it).

Jodi says she went over to Matt's father's house on the day she "knew Matt was getting back" (the date she couldn't remember when she asked about it just ten seconds ago). Do you know what I'm picturing? I'm picturing this stalker sitting parked in her car waiting for the object of her wrath to pull into his father's driveway. There is no mention of her being invited to Matt's father's house, and there is no mention of a prearranged meeting with Matt. We just have to accept all of that.

Again, let's try and picture this. Mr. Matt's Father is relaxing at home. Suddenly, there's a knock at the front door, and when Mr. Matt's Father answers the door, who should be standing there but a bug eyed Jodi Arias. Mr. Matt's Father lets her in. Now, according to Jodi, Matt was on the phone when she walked in. Guess who he was talking to? No, really – guess? That's right. Bianca! This is such a cosmic coincidence that we almost forget to ask why the hell Jodi Arias is even at Mr. Matt's Father's house. Beyond that, why is Jodi standing near Matt as he talks to Bianca on the phone? Are we actually supposed to believe that Matt hung up, turned to Jodi, and said that he knew what she wanted to talk about? What are the chances of the timing be so perfect?

At this point, Jodi has acquired instant sophistication and decorum. She claims that she and Matt went to talk in her car so that his father wasn't "privy to this information". I always laugh when Arias speaks as though she holds some cabinet position in the White House. Privy to this information? What information? Childish breaking up/making up games? I'm sure Mr. Matt's Father was all ears as this compelling conversation started. In reality, this would be the kind of annoying discourse a person would try to drown out by turning up the television, and if that didn't work, a stern suggestion of, "Hey! Can you two take that someplace else?".

Just for the record, Jodi now wants to clarify that it wasn't the tone of the discussion that led the pair to head for her car. She claims it was "the information" to be discussed that was problematic. Jodi would have us believe that Matt was embarrassed for his father to learn that he and Jodi had separated, and after their break-up, Matt had a found a new girlfriend. That makes perfect sense, doesn't it? After all, his is the type of humiliating disclosure that will embarrass both Matt and his father for years. I'm sure Mr. Matt's Father was heavily invested in the dating life of his son.

Can we stop the BS? We know exactly how this went down. Matt had already talked to Bianca, and that discussion likely occurred right after Jodi ambushed her. Bianca was probably uneasy in the aftermath, and she probably warned Matt that Jodi was looking for someone to blame. Matt, in response, probably tried to calm Bianca by telling her that he could handle Jodi Arias. If he went back to Medford, it was only to confront Jodi and to tell her to stay away from Bianca. He would have the right – some would argue it was more of a responsibility – to confront Jodi after she showed up, unannounced, and knocked on Bianca's door at 10:00 PM to conduct her interrogation. There is no doubt that Bianca told Matt that Jodi wouldn't leave for over an hour. How do I know that? Because that's what normal people do.

I also believe that Matt did show up in Medford when Jodi returned home the next morning (after "crashing" in Eddie's room in Crater Lake). Initially she admitted as much, but, after thinking on her feet, she added "or the next day...or whenever". If she did stick with her original answer, "the next day", it would be clear that this man was angry.

Now, that we've gotten a good idea of what was actually happening, let's return to the fabrication being offered by Jodi Arias. She continues, "So, we kind of talked about it, and basically our relationship was over, and it was kind of sad". Her face reflects several emotions as she closes this chapter of her life, but sadness isn't one of them. It's safe to assume that Matt told her to back off. Their relationship had been over for a while, and I'm sure he didn't appreciate having to do face-to-face status conferences with Jodi to remind her that their relationship was still dead. Oh, and don't forget, according to Arias, she broke up with him. Yeah, right.

"When was this?", Nurmi asks. He looks down, prepared to write in his big lawyer notebook. Arias pauses, and then says, "Um, this would have been September – um, right before September 11. I just remembered that, so 2001". Okay. It's done. Can we move on? No. Nurmi wants to know if this was a heated conversation? Who cares? Unless Travis Alexander walked by the car and tapped on the windshield, why does any of this matter? Why? Why? Why? Jodi takes us back to that painful encounter. It wasn't heated, she says, but it was emotional. They were both crying, says Jodi. Boo-hoo. Oh, boo-hoo-hoo.

Jodi claims she needed to leave the area. There were too many reminders of Matt in Medford, Oregon. Like George Bailey in "It's a Wonderful Life", Arias saw the whole town differently without her beloved by her side. Medford was no longer quaint, happy Bedford Falls – it was just another ugly Pottersville, devoid of love, softness, rainbows, and banks that allow you to pay "whatever you can" on that mortgage you owe. Without her love and her "mostly good memories", living in southern Oregon was untenable. Where does Jodi go for advice as to where her next landing strip will be? Well, to a martial arts instructor, of course.

The Kung Fu master told Jodi to seek employment in Big Sur, California. Pack the car, guys! We're going on another road trip! Jodi's got a head's up about a resort called "Ventana Inn & Spa". Rumor has it that the resort was looking for high school drops-outs willing to serve their high end clientele (she didn't say that, but she's going to try sell it). Yay! Jodi knew what that meant. Ventana could be a gold digger's paradise – old men with stock portfolios and wrinkled wives with faces pulled back behind their diamond studded ears. Yeah, she could make a go of it there. Hell, even mistresses can live a great life of restaurants, jewelry, high fashion, and apartments in exchange for the required occasional Olympic event of arousing a man who hadn't had an erection since the Reagan administration. She could do this. Off she drove to Ventana Inn and Spa – her future, her Emerald City, her Shangri-La.

At this point, Jodi the witness, is shutting down. There are no more essay questions, and she spends some time replying quickly to Nurmi's inquiries, and then turning to Nurmi while waiting for him to relieve the awkward silence with another leading question. Here it is, "Is this where you met Darryl Brewer?. "Yes", says a solemn faced Jodi. Nurmi asks the rhetorical question, "You applied for a job, and you were interviewed by Darryl Brewer". Yes, she was, Nurmi. Move along.

Just when I thought we were going to revisit her interview, Nurmi throws in such an opened ended question that I'm dreading her answer. He wants to know about her life at this point, what she was doing, and how she was feeling. "Well, I drove down there, and interviewed with Darryl, and um, it was in the afternoon (what? Nothing about the weather? I feel cheated). I was kind of, I was, I was a little apprehensive about moving all the way out there – there was no place to live (aren't these the kinds of details people consider BEFORE taking a 500 mile, 7.5 hour trip to interview for a job?). There was staff housing at that resort as well, but nothing was open or available at that time (and nobody told her about this when she called to make an appointment for the interview?). Um, (she's being careful now, searching for her words), I was told when there was an overflow of employees, they are allowed to use the campgrounds, because this was in October now. I think my interview was actually on October 20, because I remember it was (voice cracking) Matt's birthday. So, um, during that time, that's the slow season in Big Sur, and things are slowing down, so the campground is almost all open, so um, though I was, I was thinking of trading in my car to get a trailer, but I wasn't really in a financial position to do that, so um, when Darryl hired me, I kind of scrambled around and went to an outdoor supply store and bought some equipment, and um, when Matt heard what I was doing – he was also looking for work – the position he thought he had at Borrego Springs didn't pan out, so he came down to Big Sur and also applied at Ventana".

When Matt heard what she was doing? How did Matt hear about that? What about Bianca? The last we heard of Matt, he was crying in a car over their old breakup – that had happened months earlier. Are they serious? Can I tell you probably happened?

My theory: Matt left Jodi. Who really cares which one did the dumping? Jodi tries to intimidate Bianca into recognizing that Jodi has permanently marked Matt with her scent, and he is to stay on the shelf waiting for Jodi (in case things don't work out with the next penis in line). Matt tells Bianca not to worry about Jodi – she's a whack job, but he will go set her straight – face to face. Jodi finds out that Matt is coming back to Medford, and she shows up at Mr. Matt's Father's house. Matt tells Jodi to hit the road. Jodi tries to be a big bad ass, and she tries to hit the road. Some martial arts guy tells Jodi that he knows of a place looking to hire servers – the only problem is that it's 500 miles away. Martial arts guy tells Jodi to speak to Darryl Brewer, and he tells her to use his name ("tell him that I told you to call"). Brewer tells her, on the phone, that staff housing isn't available. Jodi asks if it's true that there are campgrounds available. Brewer says yes, but asks her why that's relevant. Jodi brushes it off as inconsequential. She only adds the story about possibly trading her car in for a trailer so that the jury doesn't laugh about the whole convoluted tale during deliberations.

There's no way she's going to blow this interview before it even happens by letting Brewer know she's homeless. Jodi embraces her half-baked plan and gives Matt McCartney the middle finger, but she intends to drag him back into her life when necessary (and that's going to be very soon). Off she goes. Once she gets to Big Sur, seven hours later, she meets with Darryl Brewer. She pours on the charm as only Jodi can. She probably lies about her address. She probably says that she's moving in with an aunt, a cousin, or a girlfriend. However, Jodi then drives out to look at the campgrounds. She pretends that she can see herself living in a trailer. Hell, all she needs is running water, a mirror, and a bed. So, she claims that she drove her bank-owned car to a lot that sells used RVs. She wastes a salesman time, making him believe that she can afford one of the RVs on his crowded lot. When they get back to the office to start the paperwork, Jodi tells the salesman that she needs to trade her car in for a down payment on the RV – oh, and by the way, do they offer financing to poor people with no credit? The salesman plugs a few letters and numbers into his computer, and he realizes that some bank has a first lien on Jodi's car. It's not worth a penny. He sends her away, and he's a little pissed off. The salesman calls it a waste of time; Jodi calls it her financial position.

Not deterred, Jodi goes to Walmart and buys her house. She's thought of everything, except the fact that she doesn't like the idea of sleeping alone in an empty campground in October, November, and December. What does she do? I think she called Matt, told him that she got this great job with amazing staff housing, and, because the manager loves her so much, he told her that they are looking for a guy just like Matt. I think Jodi convinced Matt to drop the job in Borrego Springs and join her in Big Sur. Now, she won't be alone! As an added bonus, she can play Darryl against Matt. What fun! I can only imagine what went through poor Matt's mind as he drove up to Ventana Inn and was greeted by Jodi. I wonder what it felt like to be escorted to a canvas tent.

We're about to get through Matt McCartney. That will be followed by lots of Ventana Inn and Spa information (more than you'd ever want or need, unless you plan to apply for a job there), and we'll finish up with the advent of Darryl Brewer, her much older boyfriend). Nurmi wants Jodi to clarify a few things related to Matt. He says that it sounds as if the last conversation Matt and Jodi had was not the break-up conversation in her car – that personal conversation outside Matt's father's house.

A wide shot of the gallery shows Sandy Arias. She lifts her left hand and looks down at her watch as Nurmi speaks. I think I know why. She wants to see if three hours have passed since this day's testimony began (wrong, it's been 21 minutes). She's bored, and she realizes that Nurmi is moving in reverse now, and he's going to take us all back to irrelevant testimony that's been sufficiently covered. Is it not fairly obvious that Matt and Jodi talked after their break-up conversation? Didn't Jodi just say that Matt's job in Borrego Springs didn't "pan out"? How would she know that unless Matt told her? Didn't she just testify that "he heard" what she was doing in Big Sur? How else would Matt have gotten that information if not for Jodi? Carrier pigeon, perhaps? Maybe, smoke signals? Maybe he interrogated the martial arts guy. It really doesn't matter.

In any event, Nurmi wants to dissect how Matt "heard" about what Jodi was doing at Ventana. I just assumed Jodi told him, but maybe there's more pivotal information that will add to this (yawn) fascinating cliff-hanger. Jodi admits that after the break-up conversation in the car, she and Matt did not speak for a period of time (remember, this is according to Jodi). I thought she was going to define that period of time in terms of months. No. She defined it in days. It was a period of one week. Why am I not surprised? Seven days does not qualify as a period of estrangement. It simply means a week has gone by without communication. She certainly is dramatic.

Jodi explains, "We would say hi briefly; we would talk briefly on the phone, and then not again. It was – our feelings were tender, and it was just kind of (she makes a confused face that looks like she's either going to vomit or sneeze, and her hands are moving a lot) a sticky situation. It was – he was really ashamed of his behavior, ummm, I think his mother had shamed him a little, but eventually we began to talk again". Eventually? Seven days? Wow, talk about freezing someone out of your life. *His mother shamed him a little?*

I thought Jodi had visited Matt's father's girlfriend, and it was on the girlfriend's computer that Jodi found evidence of Matt's "shameful behavior" (the lodge pictures of the dark haired girl identified only as "B"). Now that I'm thinking about it, why would Matt's father's girlfriend have those pictures on his girlfriend's computer desktop unless Matt sent them to her? That doesn't sound clandestine to me. Did I miss something? And what shameful behavior did Matt engage in as it relates to Jodi Arias? A responsible mother may shame her son for posting nude pictures of an ex-girlfriend on the internet, or she may get a few words in if she discovered her son was cheating on his live-in girlfriend, but what father's girlfriend is going to inject herself into the private affairs of her boyfriend's lover's son AFTER his live-in girlfriend leaves and moves two hours away (and then seven hours away)? Is Bianca his "shameful behavior" (and are we to believe that anyone from Jodi's world actually uses phrases like "shameful behavior")? Are Jodi and "her team" really expecting anyone on this jury to believe that she and Matt were still a committed, exclusive couple after she left? Moving out and leaving someone behind is a distancing move, not a bonding move. She's lying. With a straight face and a calm voice, she's just reciting a story she crafted in her own head, after the fact.

Alright, let's frame the line of upcoming questions: Matt is coming to Big Sur to live in a tent and work with Jodi at Ventana Inn and Spa. Now, Nurmi wants to be clear again, and he is trying (and failing) to stifle a smile of embarrassment when he asks Jodi if Matt was going to be living with Jodi in "this tent". She actually straightens up, squares her shoulders, and just as if she's referring to a great apartment she leased, she says, "Yes, he was". Nurmi responds, "Just so we're clear, is this (and I swear, I thought he was going to ask if this was a two man tent) the rekindling of the romance, so to speak?" Nurmi looks creepy when he smiles, but Jodi doesn't seem to notice. She answers, "Not really. I mean, there were blurred boundaries because we were familiar with each other, comfortable with each other – ummm – we weren't actively trying to rekindle our relationship (it is not necessary to actively try to rekindle a relationship when two former lovers are sleeping two inches apart. Nature will just take its course, and everyone knows that), but there was still a lot of sentimentality (she means heat, not sentimentality)". Nurmi's favorite subject comes up: "Were you still sexual with him at this point in time?". Oh, please, let me guess.

Yes, but it was limited – based on the blurred boundaries, familiarity, and sentimentality. It's a guess, folks. Let's see what Jodi says. "One time (she lifts one finger in the air to make her point to the hard of hearing juror). We had sex one time after we broke up". I don't believe her. I think she considers "one time" to be one big sex session spread out over a month with a few day-long breaks in between. Either that, or Nurmi was able to convince her that normal people would never believe that there was no sex, given the dynamic, and she agreed to say it was one time. Nurmi follows up with, "After that, then, it was merely platonic?".

Here comes more equivocating: "Ummmm – I considered it platonic (she's looking confused). I still had some feelings for him, but we were not really together, and we were just – friends at that point (she wants to get off of this topic – not "really together", "some feelings for him", "blurred boundaries" – she had lots of sex in that tent). I got, actually, two weeks after living in the tent, I secured employee housing, and I think he stayed in the tent for some time, and then he got employee housing also". Right. That's just how it happened. I think Jodi used Matt to secure employee housing. I think she was flirting with Darryl, and Darryl, being at least seventeen years older than Jodi, enjoyed it. I think she made it very clear that she was being forced to live under a canvas canopy with her ex-boyfriend, and she probably added that Matt would make sexual advances to her as well – advances that Jodi had to fight off. Darryl, in his position as manager, could have helped get her employee housing quickly. One thing I'm sure of – there is no way Matt thought he was moving seven hours away to live in that canvas tent alone for weeks on end.

"Now, what was your job at this resort? What did Mr. Brewer initially hire you for?", asks Nurmi. Good, we're out of the tent (Matt's still stuck there, but that's what happens when you believe a pathological liar). Jodi responds, "Initially, I started as just a server in a restaurant (just a server? That's all she's ever been) – there's a restaurant at Ventana". I think the jurors rolled their eyes at Nurmi's next question because it is, without a doubt, the most pointless, irrelevant question he's asked – unless one of the jurors is thinking about visiting Ventana for dinner: "And, describe this restaurant for us...I mean is it a Denny's, or the equivalent of Denny's or was it this... ?" Jodi cuts him off, "No, it's considered, it's classified as fine dining. It was once rated four stars by Mobil Resorts. It was featured in Conde Nast Traveler, and (she's interested in her pant leg now. She's looking down at her right leg and touching it with her hand. It's the leg with the security device. Maybe it's irritating her skin) all kinds of different publications. It had a lot of accolades, and it's the kind of a resort where high profile celebrities and things would go to – to be in private and to get away from (she mumbles). And so, our guests were treated discreetly".

I get it. This makes Jodi a high class server. She's comfortable around the elite, and the elite are comfortable around her. Jodi goes on, and we learn about a classy restaurant that attracted celebrity patrons. A Denny's waitress would be far too inexperienced and unsophisticated to move seamlessly in this cultured environment. However, Nurmi is impressed. The jury is probably just hungry – too much restaurant talk.

The camera pans to the prosecutor's table. Juan Martinez, neat as a pin and sharp in his gray suit and yellow tie, is staring directly at Jodi. Even with his eyeglasses on, it is impossible to misinterpret what's behind that blazing stare. His face is a frozen mask of anticipation. He's holding a pen, but he's not writing, and he's not drifting, and he's certainly not looking at his watch. He's focused. Now, back to Nurmi, who by contrast, is slumping over the lectern...

He's talking about Jodi's "career" now, and he follows that word with other words – words like Denny's and The Purple Plum. He wants to know if Ventana represented one of the better positions Jodi held. I find myself wishing that Juan Martinez would leap to his feet and yell, "Objection... rhetorical question!" Didn't Jodi just make that clear? I guess Nurmi likes to talk about restaurants, especially one that attached his indigent client to a fine dining establishment peppered with "high profile celebrities and things", and he thinks this line of questioning indirectly ascribes to Jodi the first iota of sophistication she's had in her life.

Jodi answers, "As far as – well, most servers work for the tips, so as far as that goes, it was better paying. But, there was also a bigger tip out-go, so when you have a position like that, it's not just you, taking orders and delivering food. You have a lot of help from different people who make the restaurant run smoothly (she strokes her left arm), and so you have a lot of people...different people such as the bartender, the hostess, people that you tip out, so you – the tip pull is huge, and after the tip out, I was still walking away with more than at Applebee's (unless a juror is applying for a job at Ventana, why does anyone care how the tips were split? Can she stop now? The question has been more than answered). So, it was nicer".

Nurmi wants us to know how long Jodi was a server at Ventana. I'm actually shocked at her response. Three and a half years? Wow. What was going on in the background of her life to keep her attached to one place of employment for this long? Nurmi asks Jodi if being a server was her only position at the resort. Of course he knows it wasn't, or he wouldn't have asked. Let's see, what other skills did Jodi master in Big Sur? She answers, "No, um, in the summer of 2002, someone, the wedding coordinator, she had been having stomach pains that she had been ignoring, and she was ill for several months, and she finally went to the doctor, and found out she had pancreatic cancer, and she passed away in a month (Jodi looks sad. She's not, she just looks that way), so I filled her old position, temporarily, until they could find a more permanent replacement for wedding coordinating".

Can you imagine Jodi planning someone's wedding? She must have been living a slow torture as couple after couple were married. Jealousy must have consumed her as she saw each groom lovingly defer to his bride in the planning process.

Nurmi asks Jodi to describe her coordinating duties, and she gives the normal answer (negotiating contracts, showing the brides the spaces available for ceremonies and receptions, etc.). Nurmi doesn't ask how she ended up being replaced, but he does want the record to reflect that she was NOT dating Darryl Brewer when she was coordinating weddings. So, now we've segued into the relationship with Darryl Brewer.
Bobby Juarez? Check. Victor Arias? Check. Bobby Juarez, The Sequel? Check. Matt McCartney? Check. Who's next on the Arias boyfriend scorecard? Let's see, it's....it's....oh, that's right. It's the man old enough to be Jodi's father (or at least her two decade older, creepy uncle). Ladies and gentleman, may I present, Mr. Darryl Brewer! I can't wait! Let's hear all about this May-December

romance. According to what we know, this partnership evolved over time – "Professional" turned "Romantic" turned "I ruined my career so we don't have to have sex in the walk-in freezer at the restaurant anymore" turned " Really? Us? They're willing to give US a mortgage?" turned "They're predatory lenders who should have known better than to saddle us with this debt" turned "Don't you dare show my face on camera while I'm on the stand and you're at the defense table" turned "Hey! Why did you guys leave me standing in that hotel lobby when I spent all that money on a new tie so that I could mitigate in style?"

If none of that makes sense to you, it will by the time Nurmi and Arias have covered this long dead relationship. Darryl did testify for the defense during the guilt phase, but he required that his face remain off camera. Only his folded hands were ever seen by those watching the trial on television. Additionally, he was supposed to be called to testify for Arias during her sentencing phase, and he was ready to do so. The defense never called him, despite the fact that he was dressed and waiting to be called.

Nurmi wants to know how the relationship between these two discreet, Ventana Inn employees began and matured. Oh, yes, me too! In fact, I'm on the edge of my proverbial seat just waiting to hear how this "Once upon a time...." tale ran its course. Ahh, young love – or is it middle aged love? I'm not sure it was love at all. Well, it doesn't matter what we call it, after all, what really matters is that the mighty defense team has decided that this relationship is completely relevant to a human slaughter that occurred in 2008. The only connection I can see between this odd couple and Travis Alexander is that there were all breathing air back in 2001 and 2002. Oh, there was that sticky little detail about the gas cans Jodi borrowed from Darryl as she set off on her kill in 2008. Yes, I remember those gas cans. I think the Brewer gas cans helped the state prove premeditation. So, I guess we have to talk about Darryl Brewer.

Jodi's takes us back to her glory days at Ventana: "Um...during that summer...umm....(long pause) umm...well, in the May, in May, right prior to the summer, the restaurant, it was called Cielo's at the time, it closed for remodeling, and so, we moved the entire restaurant operation over to the inn, and I helped out with that, and Darryl was involved with that, and so we were working pretty closely together, and also, with the wedding, the wedding coordinating position, we worked more closely together, so I sorta began to develop a crush on him, but he was my boss, so I didn't ever let that on. Um, and then at one point, he pulled me aside and said, 'I'm going to resign from my position tonight at'--I think it was called (she's looking confused, as if the verdict depends on whether or not she can remember the official name of the meeting at which Darryl tendered his resignation) ...umm...the briefing – I think it was some kind of meeting we had before the shift started. So, he wanted to let me know that so it wasn't like, a shock. I think he let a few other manager know, at the time".

Well thanks for clearing that up, Jodi. What is she talking about? That's a lot of information to reduce to one run-on sentence. Let's break it down, shall we? Jodi is now an event coordinator.

She's giving tours, negotiating contracts, putting together reception packages, and she's handling emails, correspondence, and the phones. In fact, she's so busy coordinating weddings that she finds the time to hang up her smart, black blazer and exchange it for a T-shirt as she joins the troops in the trenches who are lugging restaurant equipment over to another building. She probably already realized that Darryl was her best male option at Dorm and Tent City. She probably volunteered her services, and Darryl gladly accepted them.

Jodi claims there was no relationship here. She'd like the jury to believe that she and Darryl Brewer were merely working together -- a lot. Why would Darryl Brewer tell a random employee about a resignation he was going to tender in several hours? Jodi admits that she had developed a secret crush on Darryl (something I've already defined as targeting the most eligible man on the premises), but she also guarantees that she never disclosed her feelings to Darryl. According to Jodi, Darryl did not make a general announcement to the staff. In fact, she said she thought he only told a few managers about his planned resignation. So, why let Jodi in on the secret? She claims that it was because Darryl didn't want to shock her. If we are to believe Jodi, she and Darryl were merely co-workers at this point, so why should Jodi's potential shock be any more important than another employee's potential shock? Did their potential shock not matter to Darryl? It has nothing to do with shock. I think that will become obvious.

Nurmi is not as slow as he appears to be. I'm confused as to the dates, and if the jurors are listening, so are they. Jodi said she broke up with Matt, and she remembers that it was September, 2001, because of the 9/11 attacks. She remembers the day she got to Ventana for an interview, because it was October 20, Matt's birthday. She was a server, a temporary wedding coordinator, and now she's talking about May, and her involvement in the restaurant relocation. I'm wondering how we got to May. If we are going to be forced to listen every banal detail of their relationship, we should at least hear about the more important dates. Nurmi brings us up to speed.

He asks Jodi how long she had been working at Ventana when Darryl Brewer told her that he was going to resign. Jodi tells us that it was a year (thankfully, we're out of 2001, and we're moving, albeit slowly, towards 2006, 2007, and 2008). This makes me wonder if we are being asked to believe that Jodi developed "a kind of crush" on Darryl Brewer, but she had the impulse control and maturity to keep that to herself? The She-Wolf? The Server-Succubus? The woman who confronted Bobby Juarez after she discovered evidence of his emotional affair with another woman (while hacking into his email account)? The woman who was ready to bear the children of Senor Victor Arias after 21 days of togetherness in Costa Rica? She was able to keep her predatory nature completely hidden from her intended target? Curious. Are we to assume that Darryl's quick decision to resign had nothing to do with anything that he and his subordinate were doing? With all of the questions posed about Ventana Inn and Spa, I'm left confused as to why Nurmi did not ask WHY Darryl was resigning. Let's see. Maybe Jodi will clarify. She's so good with the microscopic details.

Nurmi wants to allay our suspicions before they get out of hand, so he asks Jodi if she and Darryl had a romantic or platonic relationship at the time he resigned from his management position. Without missing a beat, Jodi answers, "I wouldn't even call it a friendship; we kept that separate. We never fraternized or anything like that. We just worked together". If they just worked together, didn't fraternize, or even have a friendship, then exactly WHAT did they keep separate? Nurmi continues, "So, he is advising you that he is changing positions. Do you begin dating at that period? Explain that for us". Did Jodi say that Darryl Brewer was changing positions, or did she say that he was resigning from his position? I recall her saying that he was "resigning".

Jodi responds, "No, after he had stepped down from his management position, umm...(she pauses, stares straight ahead, and she speaks in a robotic tone of voice, noticeably slower than usual), he stepped into a supervisory role, so I still didn't make any moves or he didn't express anything, and I didn't express anything, but...um, then he decided he was going to step out of that role too and, um, prior to actually doing that, we had a conversation, where we, um, discovered our mutual interest in each other, but we still couldn't do anything, because he was still technically my supervisor, and about a week later, he stepped out of that position, and we went on a date".

Nice and neat – and so terribly convenient. So, did Darryl Brewer win the lottery? Did Darryl Brewer inherit a fortune? Had Darryl Brewer already separated from his wife, and was he attempting to reduce his child support payments? Was Darryl Brewer divorced, and trying to reduce his spousal support payments? Or, was Darryl Brewer caught with his hand in the cookie jar and subsequently demoted? The world may never know. But, I have to ask, why would anybody willingly destroy their own career at the age of 42? The defense has certainly smoothed over quite a few of the rough edges here, and frankly, I'm far more interested in the back story of Darryl Brewer's rapidly devolving "positions" at Ventana Inn and Spa than I am in whether it was "an hour" or "an hour and a half" that Jodi spent interrogating Bianca.

Instead of moving right into the "it's now okay that we're dating" phase, can we talk about the several positions that Darryl willingly left after giving Jodi the inside information regarding his resignation? He left his "management position" and stepped into a "supervisory role"? To which supervisory role is Jodi referring? Is Darryl's new "role" on the same level as being the manager at Ventana, or is the new "supervisory role" subordinate to his previous management position? I believe it was a lower level job. If it was not, Jodi would have said that Darryl had officially resigned from his management position because he had been promoted to a higher position. People don't gloss over promotions – they gloss over demotions and terminations. Just who was Darryl supervising in his new role? The servers? Technically, he was still Jodi's boss (according to Jodi), so perhaps the position was supervisor of the servers. Perhaps Darryl wanted a demotion to be nearer to Jodi. Perhaps being nearer to Jodi caused some problems with reports of improper supervisor/employee fraternization between the two. Perhaps Darryl was given the option of quietly resigning from Ventana when their "relationship" was discovered, or humbly accepting a demotion. All we can do is guess. The ambiguity of the situation all seems rather ironic when we consider the fact that we've heard all about the stomach pains of the nameless, cancer afflicted, terminally ill wedding coordinator, as well as plenty of overload of completely superfluous details about Ventana.

Earlier on in the trial, there were those on social media who were wondering exactly what happened to Darryl's career at Ventana. There was one individual who was a chef at the spa during this time period, and he wrote that the two of them were caught together – as in "together". I won't give his name. You'll have to search if you're interested. In my mind, that makes complete sense.

Just as we're trying to figure out how and why Darryl Brewer offered to fall on his sword, Jodi's testimony clues us into the fact that we are now going to leave the murky waters of Darryl's Ventana employment and dive right into matters of the heart. We'll never know what happened at Ventana, but reasonably intelligent people can certainly connect the dots. I don't think he could handle the humiliation of his demotion, and ultimately, Darryl Brewer chose unemployment. Then he took what he paid for – Jodi Arias.

Nurmi would like us all to know that when the pair began dating, Jodi was 22, and Darryl was 42. Nurmi asks, "How did you feel about dating someone that much your senior?". Jodi responds, "Umm...I wasn't so much concerned about dating him as I was concerned about how other people might view it (she's doing the interlocked finger thing again – as in, "this is the church, this is the steeple, open the doors and here's all the people" – she's at the "here's all the people" stage). Umm....I found Darryl very attractive. He was tall, handsome, beautiful eyes, that kind of thing. We were very compatible, our personalities...um...I'm, I don't know, I kind of saw him as a George Clooney type – like he's older, but still attractive. And, umm...we had a lot of similar interests (how they knew they had similar interests is a mystery. They never fraternized, after all). So, I think he was more concerned about the age gap then I was (of course he was – he was a man in his forties dating a rather vapid 22 year old. What would you think?). He was a little concerned about how people would view him for dating somebody that young (valid concern, Mr. Clooney – oops, I mean, Mr. Brewer)".

Now we're going to get into Darryl Brewer's domestic situation at the time he was dating the Budding Butcher of Yreka. Nurmi asks, "At the time you began dating him, did you know Darryl had a son?". Jodi answers, "Yes. I had seen him a few times at the restaurant". Nurmi continues, "And, did you know he was divorced?". Jodi answers, "Yes". Nurmi wants to know if this was acceptable to her. Jodi responds, "It wasn't how I envisioned it, but I guess you can't always control like, where your heart's gonna go (like in a bathroom with a knife and a gun?). There were things I discovered about him, after the fact, that he kept very private, that I didn't care for, but I already loved him, so I accepted those things". Jodi turns away from the jury and faces Nurmi, and Nurmi responds with "Okay". I realize this is their signal that she's done answering the question, and he's free to move to the next inquiry.

Nurmi asks, "Before we start talking about those things (and you'd better believe we're going to talk about those things), let's talk about the evolution of the relationship from that first date. You're still living in staff housing, right?" Jodi answers, "Yes, I am". Nurmi continues, "Okay, just kind of take us through the process of other dates, how the relationship evolved – that sort of thing". Jodi's prepared, "Okay, umm...as soon as he stepped down from the supervisory position (this is a well-rehearsed phrase from which she never deviates), we went to San Francisco and went to a Forty-Niner game. We're both Forty-Niner fanatics, being from that area (Jodi is a football fanatic? Who knew?

Perhaps it was more about being a fanatic for a man who could afford tickets to an NFL game). Um, we just kind of toured the city a little – not like a whole bunch of touring, but we walked around Union Square ... umm....being in that business, you know other people that are in the business (what business? Darryl isn't IN any business, as far as we know. And Jodi? Well, she's a waitress. Is she referring to the football business, the touring business, or the restaurant business?), so we got a great deal on a hotel room, right near Union Square (oh, the hotel business – got it), and...umm....it was a good trip. We just continued to do that and began to come over and hang out, on our days off while his son was there (what days off? Is Darryl employed now?). His son got a little more used to me. He was very shy when he was younger (shy or freaked out? Children and dogs are good at assessing the character of the person invading their space). I think I started – I came into his life when he was about four – three and a half, four.

I am confused. I thought Darryl resigned before they started dating. Nurmi's next question, and Jodi's subsequent answer do nothing to clear up my confusion. Nurmi wants to know if Darryl was living in staff housing. Jodi says, "Yes". Doesn't the label "staff housing" connote that a person living in the housing is, in fact, staff? I hope they explain this. Nurmi knows something we don't. He asks, "Are you working together at this time, as well?". In an "Oh, did I forget to mention that?" moment, Jodi responds, "Yes. He actually became a server, so we're both kind of equal, as far as our positions go". I knew it. I knew it. From manager to supervisor to server. Can you say demotion(s)? How did she avoid disclosing this moments earlier?

Jodi's body language is showing signs of stress. Her deep breathing is evident in her just tight enough, powder blue, button down shirt. Nurmi allows her to exhale several times before asking her about the size of the serving staff at the time she and Darryl were on "the same level". She answers, "Umm....off the top of my head, I'd say, maybe twenty people...as far as just the servers." Nurmi would like to know how many women were employed there. Jodi thinks, and then answers, "There were (she goes through the child-like hand motion of lifting one finger after another, as if to show us that's she's mentally calculating and digitally recording – of course, she uses the hand with the crooked finger for her computation) maybe seven other women, I think". Going exactly where I suspected he was going, Nurmi asks Jodi if she, in light of their dating relationship, ever became jealous or angry when it came to the women on staff during the time that she and Darryl were dating and working as "equals". Jodi responds, "At him? No, I didn't". I wish he would have asked if she was angry at or jealous over any of the seven women as opposed to Darryl, but he didn't.

Nurmi is now moving us along; in fact, he's now asking about when the duo bought a home together. Can it be? Did we just get through three years? Are we actually landing in June, 2005? My interest is renewed when Nurmi asks, "When did you buy the home?". Jodi is visually fixated on something at the back of the court room, but she answers, "We bought the house in two thousand...five...I think we closed in June, 2005 (she's back from outer space, and swiveling comfortably in her chair)". Nurmi's backing up: "Prior to buying that home, what happened in...we were talking about 2002, you're dating, you're both living in staff housing, do you live together before you buy that house?" "No", Jodi says. She elaborates, "No, we had separate apartments. At that point, he had moved back to Monterey, and I had quit Ventana (huh?) and moved back to, moved to Monterey, as well, and we were working in separate jobs, separate apartments". Nurmi trudges forward, and he's using words like "monogamous" and "boyfriend/girlfriend". Jodi affirms that they were exclusive, but she can't remember the exact time that they moved to this level of commitment (right, sure...she knows the date, the hour, and the minute): "Yes...I don't remember the exact point in time. We were either at, in San Francisco at one of the games (season tickets?), or we were (she's tapping her fingers on her desk and swiveling in her chair)...I can't remember. We celebrated as soon as he was out of his supervisory role, we celebrated, decided to make things official around that time". Celebrated? I thought there was nothing to celebrate – they hadn't disclosed their unspoken love until after he was no longer a supervisor, right?

The defense is lucky that the jury is taking a nap. Darryl and Jodi, despite their cloudy, ambiguous, and vague beginnings, are now official. There has to be some drama between separate apartments and foreclosure, no?

So, Jodi Arias and Darryl Brewer were celebrating in San Francisco. They were celebrating love, or lust, or freedom; maybe all three, and, most likely, in varying degrees, depending upon which one of the two you ask. Jodi will fill us in on the details, fact or fiction, of that I'm sure. For now, we'll just have to picture them walking in the California sunshine while holding hands; Jodi snapping photos to memorialize this romantic get-away, the pair stopping for a latte at a trendy cafe, and finally, Jodi bouncing on a king sized bed while Darryl hangs the "Do Not Disturb" sign on the exterior handle of their shared hotel suite. She's probably squealing about room service, and he's probably footing the bill.

In light of what Ventana's Executive Chef has disclosed since Jodi's trial testimony, we can safely assume – if we already hadn't – that the evolution of their public relationship, as described by Jodi, has been nothing more than an strategically encapsulated version of the time period in question (although why it's in question is anyone's guess). While on the witness stand, Jodi will not yield to the truth by expanding upon this tale of repressed mutual affection. Jodi would like the jury to believe that she and Darryl were paragons of professionalism while working together at Ventana.

He was her boss, and she was his employee. Nothing more. It all rings hollow. Jodi Arias, despite being 32 years old at the time of this testimony is still an adolescent. She has been an adolescent since she was an adolescent – and that includes today, yesterday, yesteryear, and beyond. Her lack of ability to control her impulses is a topic that she and her attorney have inadvertently raised time and time again during this direct examination.

According to this eyewitness, the pair was not just impulsive, they were also reckless and brazen. Everyone at Ventana Inn and Spa knew that Darryl Brewer and Jodi Arias were involved in a sexual relationship, and beyond that, they resented the fact that as often as Jodi (the server) demanded Darryl's (the manager) protection, he gave it to her without reservation or investigation.

Jodi, despite just telling us about their mini-tour of Union Square following Darryl's resignation from some mysterious "supervisory role" at Ventana (we learned that he was promoted before he was demoted – several times), now wrestles with a loss of specificity when it comes to disclosing where they actually were when they "celebrated". Jodi indirectly informs us that the word "celebrated" is a euphemism for "making things official". Perhaps, she ponders, it was at one of the Forty-Niner games they attended (being the football fanatics they were, according to Jodi). She moves ahead, "He was a little nervous about it; he didn't want to get married, so he made that very clear right off the bat.... Yeah, he made his intentions very clear (she slaps her hand lightly on the desk, as if to reinforce the fact that his decision was not negotiable)... that he liked me, that he was attracted to me, and he was okay with being with me. But, he said, 'I don't see myself getting married again'". Nurmi asks Jodi, "How did that sit with you?". Jodi cocks her head the left, lifts her eyes to the right, and drops the left side of her mouth ever so slightly, before responding, "Umm...I was young at the time, and so it didn't bother me. I figured I still had many years left, and I enjoyed being with him. So, that's what I did. I enjoyed the time we had together".

I have no doubt that Darryl Brewer said those words to Jodi Arias. I believe he told her that he did not intend to marry her, or anyone else. This is, after all, the clarion call of the recently divorced. It's not the content I'm struggling with -- it's more the context. I just don't think this conversation happened during their celebration. I can see this conversation taking place in an entirely different environment – a far more private environment. Perhaps it reflects a few fragments of a conversation the two shared while they were hiding behind a Ventana building – both on the clock, she groping him with abandon, he with eyes darting back and forth on the look-out for passersby. He tells her, as delicately as he can, that he cares about her, but he doesn't intend to marry her. She pretends that his words never registered with her, and then she drops to her knees, and hopes that her oral skills impress him enough to render his declaration immediately inconsequential and eventually, negotiable. That's total speculation, of course, but it does fit the image of the Jodi Arias that is beginning to develop in my mind's eye.

Nurmi leads us from the celebration to the point at which Jodi claims to have fallen in love with Darryl. Nurmi asks if she did, in fact, fall in love with a man twenty years her senior. Jodi responds,

"Yes". This is not enough irrelevant information for a jury empanelled to determine whether or not the woman on the witness stand, Jodi Arias, butchered a man that Kirk Nurmi has failed to mention even once, thus far. If Darryl Brewer was Jodi's accomplice in the murder of Travis Alexander, this testimony might have some bearing on the case. Honestly, I'm baffled, and more than a little bored with the adolescent ramblings of a woman who is still as immature in 2013 as she was back in 2002.

Jodi swivels in her chair and faces the jury. She loves being interviewed. By watching the interchange between Arias and Nurmi, one could easily believe she was prepping for an Oprah interview. "I don't remember the case, I mean, the exact moment, it was....a gradual process. My crush just became more and more, and then I began to really love his son, and it just, we progressed in that regard". I'm sorry. I know everyone's story of finding true love is different, but this is so convoluted (despite being so practiced and scripted that it should be completely linear and status quo), that I'm having a problem following it. Paraphrased, she's saying, "He hired me. He's old. I'm young. He was my boss. I had a crush. I kept it to myself. We worked together. I was a wedding planner. We worked together more. We didn't talk about my crush. He resigned his position, and he told me about that before it happened. We waited. He took another position. We went on a tour of San Francisco. We were at a football game. We toured Union Square. We were free. His son was shy, but he liked me. Oh, he's in staff housing. Didn't I mention that he was a server now? There were no issues at work. He quit. I quit. We were at a football game, I think. He told me we weren't going to get married. My crush just got bigger. I loved his son".

Really, this mess is the best they could present? They had five years to get this story down; there was nobody who was going to edit anything Jodi had to say. Could they not, at the very least, have infused this tale with an aura of credibility – something that resonated as potentially truthful? Nothing, according to the dynamic duo, occurred in reasonable and believable increments.

Nurmi, doing what he does best (casting aspersions on people who are not present to defend themselves), finally gets to the point he's been aiming at for a while: "I asked because you said you were in love with him, but there were all these things, these flaws, you had to overlook". There's no "ummm" this time as Jodi answers Nurmi's question: "Yes....(insert inconsequential follow-up Nurmi babble meant to frame the insults that Jodi is about to hurl at Darryl Brewer)...I discovered, after I had already developed, ummm, some deep feelings for him, that he was a smoker...". Seriously? A black-lunger posing as a pink-lunger? Darryl waited to light up in front of Jodi until AFTER her crush got "bigger and bigger"? Oh my God! Say it's not so! Drag his ass into court now, and serve him with a citation and a nicotine patch! Where is that bastard? Judge Stephens – issue a subpoena! Bailiff – wake up and find Darryl Brewer! Where is that lowlife hiding? I'll just bet he's smoking a cigarette right now! I had no idea! Please, Jodi -- woman who confessed to stabbing a naked, wet man 27 times, chasing him down a hallway, essentially sawing his head off with a serrated knife, shooting him in the head, and propping him in the shower to decompose – tell us all about this fiend...this ...smoker!

"Ummm. He didn't like, he didn't advertise that", she replies, all the while grimacing as she pretends to remember the dirty smoker and the ashtray odor that lingered in his hair, on his clothes, and in his vehicle. Those damn smokers! Why don't they wear a sandwich board around their necks? This is so unfair! I just hate the ones who don't advertise it. Jodi was bamboozled. It's so obvious. "I never saw him smoking, so that was, ummm....(she extends her hand, palm up – even she feels like an idiot bringing this up) ...PAUSE ... (unusually long pause here, probably because the faces of the jurors are not registering the disgust she thought the smoking disclosure would elicit. In fact, she's probably irritated a few smokers on the jury, who'd like nothing more than to go outside and light up)... the only thing that bummed me out about it was, like, his health (the woman who killed a man who was a non-smoker, non-drinker, non-caffeine consumer, is now lamenting the fact that smoking cigarette is bad for her ex-boyfriend's health).... and I thought, okay, this is going to affect his health, so like, he didn't ever smell like smoke, I never knew it (liar...every smoker smells like an ashtray to a non-smoker – especially if you're close enough to them to smell their hair)...so he maintained, he had very good hygiene, but I was concerned about his health. And also, he admitted to me, one day, that he was an alcoholic".

Did we just listen to five minutes of testimony related to the dangers of smoking, but the entire line of questioning is footnoted by ALCOHOLISM? I'm really having some issues with this – issues related to the intelligence of the attorneys who mapped out this line of questioning and the testimony of their accused client. Okay....I'll roll with this. Let's talk about Darryl's alcoholism.

Nurmi asks if Darryl's issues were troubling to Jodi. "Yes. They were...I couldn't...I didn't ever want to... I didn't ever see myself being with a smoker, not that there's anything wrong with it (then why bring it up?. My grandparents were chain smokers (hey, how about bringing up Bobby Juarez' adopted parents/grandparents? Weren't they chain smokers, too? Such offenders that they actually had tar dripping down the walls of the hovel?) It wasn't a lifestyle I ever wanted. My grandparents, they were chain smokers, and I saw how it affected their health very negatively, until they finally quit. And just, I didn't want... I don't know (her voice is getting softer, she's looking concerned, she using her hands to make her point)... I just didn't want that kind of lifestyle... so..." (living in a tent is fine, though).

Nurmi wants to talk about Darryl's alcoholism: "Did that manifest itself throughout the relationship?". If Jodi was in a recliner, her feet would be higher than her head, at this point. She's so relaxed as she answers, "I didn't notice it until after he really talked about it. We would hang out, we would watch football, ummm, watch football during football season, and ummm. ...we would have dinner at his house, he was a very good cook, ummm....and I would notice after dinner, ummm, he would take some ummm, Stoli out of the fridge, some Smirnoff out of the freezer, and he would pour himself a drink, and okay, whatever, he's just relaxing, and umm, as the hours would go on, and I would go back in the kitchen to throw something away, and there would be an entire empty six pack of Sierra Nevada, and so, I didn't see him drink it (she's so relaxed that's she smiling now), and he wasn't changing his behavior, and he was the same...so, I didn't say anything really, but when he told me about it – one day, he was very troubled over it, and was trying to overcome it".

Nurmi is ready to get past the smoke and smell of booze. He wants to take us to where Jodi was working when she decided to buy a house with a smoking alcoholic who has little to no relevance in this trial.

Dirty little secrets. What type of socially unacceptable behavior does an outwardly respectable individual relegate to their closet of secrets? How about, "None of your damn business."? Well, that's not going to fly here. Even if you aren't on trial, the fact that a man – any man – crossed paths with a killer now makes that man a defendant in her murder trial. No, it makes no sense, but it's what's happening in a superior courtroom in Maricopa Country, Arizona. If any man actually engaged in sexual behavior with the murderer, the prospect is even worse. Their proverbial closets will be raided by a SWAT team (under the direction of General Nurmi and Captain Arias). So, let's consider the secrets in Darryl Brewer's closer. Why? Because we have no choice.

Thanks to the inside reporting of Jodi Arias, murderer, we learn that the secrets in Darryl Brewer's closet, circa 2002, included cigarettes and vodka. Too bad it wasn't cigars and Brandy. That pairing is far more acceptable than vodka and cigarettes, right? In the case of Travis Alexander, his secrets, circa 2007/2008, included prolific anal sex with Jodi Arias – a nomadic, unemployed waitress from Nowhere, California. So, in the world of closeted secrets, one man's booze and smokes was another man's murderer. Frankly I'd rather be the pack of 20 Class A Cigarettes (regular or menthol) than the crazy chick with the knife, but that's just me.

Shocking bottom line? Darryl Brewer, Jodi's lover, is a smoker and a drinker. Yawn. What kind of drinker is Darryl Brewer? I'm expecting tales of public vomiting, a few gutter face plants, and falling asleep on tables while his cigarette burns away and becomes ash. How about black outs? Were there any black outs? We won't know unless we get back to the court room.

But hey, we're not going there! Guess where we're going? Community College! We're going to fly by Darryl Brewer's alcoholism, and we'll hear what Jodi has to say about the behavior of the man she didn't murder in cold blood while she was taking college courses. Carry on, Jodi Arias... it's your show.

Master of Ceremonies, Kirk Nurmi, begins with a scripted question directed at the star of the show, Jodi Arias: "So, despite this, you said you know, you were in love with him. Before you, before you buy that house, you both lived in separate apartments in Monterey, right?" This is important. Separate apartments mean separate closets. How could poor, young, impressionable Jodi have known about Darryl's cigarettes and vodka?

Jodi, willing to wait to explain all of the gruesome details, affirms what Nurmi has suggested. Moving on, Nurmi inquires, "And, where are you working?". Wait, I thought we were focused on where she was living while Darryl was stocking his closet full of sin. Apparently not. We're back to Jodi. Where was the poor little lamb working while Darryl was smoking? Jodi responds, "I was working at – an Italian restaurant, called Piate, and also, California Pizza Kitchen had opened a restaurant there, out there, um, in their mall, and so I helped open that restaurant. And so, I was tending bar there." Jodi then swivels her chair back towards Nurmi. On cue, Nurmi asks, "And to your recollection, where was Darryl working?" Jodi places her left hand on her chin, all her long, bony fingers displayed, and as if she had never been asked this question before. She thinks out loud before replying in a half whisper: "Where was he working?". She massages her chin and pauses before saying, "I don't know why I can't remember – I think he was working in Pebble Beach, at a resort in Pebble Beach". Good enough. Nurmi responds, "Tell us about, um, the thinking behind the two of you deciding to, um, purchase a home together". I'm game. Let's hear all about it.

As expected, Arias begins her answer with the often used, "um". Picking it up from there: "Well, I was – I saw myself eventually becoming a real estate investor (what the hell is she talking about?). That's what I wanted to do, career wise (did she miss the day in class where the teacher explained that the word "investor" meant that disposable income was a requirement for investing in anything?), and obviously (a word injected to ascribe embarrassment to any juror who wasn't monitoring the real estate section of the newspaper back in 2005), the housing market was taking off in 2005, um, so, I wanted to buy a home and sit on it for a while, and um, I didn't have, I had good credit, but I didn't have quite the income required for that. So, I would, I began talking to Darryl about it (when he wasn't too drunk to converse or too hidden behind a cloud of cigarette smoke to locate), and he also really wanted to buy a home. The Monterey Peninsula was way out of our reach (it wouldn't have been if he had been able to report an income of a Beverage and Food Manager at a top rated resort) and, at that time, a dirt lot was going for $700,000, so there was no way we were able to purchase property in that area at the time (Jodi swivels her chair towards Nurmi before elaborating). Um, also, I should also probably mention that he had stopped drinking, otherwise I probably wouldn't have considered that (as long as Darryl was able to borrow money, his drinking habits were immaterial to Arias, and everyone knows that). So, (she taps her little desk multiple times for emphasis), um, so he's been sober since 2004. Um, so we decided to talk about buying a house together, and his wife, or ex-wife, was moving to LaQuita, California, which is in Riverside County, I think. And, um, it's right near Palm Desert, and so we began making plans to move to Sacramento since she was moving – we wanted to buy a home, but we wanted to stay nearer to Monterey, um and not come all the way down to the desert". Yeah, whatever.

Nurmi picks it up, "You said you wanted to become involved in the real estate market. Did you do anything besides just look at purchasing a home? Did you educate yourself – anything of that nature?". Let me guess – if the answer is no, there will be no leading question. Surprise, surprise: "Yes, I um, took real estate classes at Monterey Peninsula College (that Ivy League University) just to become more familiarized with the process of real estate, um, real estate economics and, um, I don't remember all the titles of the other classes I took, but it involved real estate, um, so I took those the same time I was taking more semesters of Spanish (Hey, can we see some of her transcripts from this period of time? No? How about a few grades? Is that possible? Can we delve into how an eleventh grade drop-out, who had not earned a GED, even qualified for enrollment in accredited college courses? Come on. She audited these courses, and because of her status, no professor cared whether or not Jodi Arias showed up to class. But then again, maybe California has no prerequisites). And um, I began studying it and just paying more attention to real estate market trends (are you laughing? I'm laughing) and listings, and...". Nurmi gives Jodi the okay to shut up.

He takes a deep breath, and he sounds as bored as I feel. He asks Jodi, "One of the things you spoke about earlier was, uh, you know, all throughout high school that you had an interest in art, photography (no, she never said photography), and these different mediums of art, um, was that a business that you were interested in, or were you more interested in the real estate business (the camera focuses on Sandy Arias – mother of the killer – and her odd twin, Sue. Sandy is stroking some hand sized object as she listen to her daughter create a college education)? Jodi responds, "Um, it was a business that I saw myself developing, but I wasn't actively, at that point in my life – I wasn't actively trying to start um, like a company. I was trying to start a real estate company". What? She wasn't actively trying to start a company, but she was trying to start a real estate company? Is anyone even listening?

Seriously? A woman who hadn't obtained a high school diploma (let alone as Associates Degree), a woman who had not even passed a state real estate licensing exam, was planning on opening "Arias Real Estate Investments, Inc."? Her lies are just offensive.

Jodi Arias, Real Estate Tycoon. Is there a single person in the universe, including Jodi Arias, willing to swallow this?

So, 25 year old Jodi Arias was secretly envisioning herself in the role of CEO in a real estate company, we have to adjust our vision -- just for a few minutes. We must now reconcile the image of the homely woman in the oversized glasses and discarded fashions on the stand, with a vision of a well-dressed woman, reclining in her executive chair and positioned behind a large, cherry wood desk. It won't be easy. She is a confessed murderess who hasn't done much to convince us that the mark she could have left on the world, had she not butchered Travis Alexander, would have been one worth noting; but let's indulge her (even if we know it's total BS). Can you see her (in a far better wardrobe) sitting behind the desk Travis owned? In her mind's eye, it's flanked by towering bookcases filled with titles that would tell us a lot about the intellect and interests of this successful business woman. I can see this narcissist telling her assistant to hold all her calls; that part is easy: Jodi Arias, steely, platinum haired business woman, someone who sees herself taking advantage of a boom real estate market in 2005, hiring and firing, while checking real estate listings, and lunching with her peers.

I wonder, how would this real estate tycoon manage to keep a business afloat during the crash that was right around the corner? That would take knowledge, planning, resources, commitment, and a very large umbrella for a very rainy day. People like Jodi Arias get to say these things, paint these pictures, elaborate on their dreams, but in reality, she, and others like her, are people with delusions of grandeur, opportunists, streamers, magical thinkers – these are the types who mentally gorge on the times of feast, but not a thought is given to the time of famine. These are the people who, in their imaginations, are being inundated with requests for their wisdom, but never see themselves hiding from the disturbing phone calls coming from their bankers or investors. If a business owner can negotiate and maintain their business through the lean times, then there's something to talk about. In this case, there is nothing to talk about, and it bothers me that we have to indulge a murderer this way. All the while, the camera rolls.

Kirk Nurmi, realizing that he's wrung this cloth dry, moves on. He doesn't want us to forget about the softer, more artistic side of Jodi Arias; after all, it's in his client's best interest to structure some frame work of marketability from her office behind bars. He knows, and we know, that it's far easier for a convicted murdereress to sell drawings from a prison cell than it is for a convicted murdereress to sell residential real estate from a prison cell, so I'm in agreement with him here.

We've heard two references to college as it relates to the forfeited life of Jodi Arias: the first time, it was a part of her failed eleventh grade curriculum; that college level, US History course she was taking right before she dropped out of high school. The second mention referenced a Monterey community college offering Spanish and Real Estate courses. Oh, and lest we forget, she also watched real estate listings, so she was super serious. It was a nice try Nurmi, but any way you slice it, dice it, and repackage it, nobody believes that Jodi Arias had, or has, a thirst for higher education. Even if she did, her own open-ended testimony has already shown us that Jodi lacks the discipline and character to follow conventional scholastic protocol. Whether Nurmi realizes it or not, his line of questioning, and his client's canned responses have put that issue soundly to bed. So, it's probably best that we get back to her "art".

"Were you still painting and drawing, and... ?", Nurmi's voice drops as he leaves the question unfinished. Arias knows what he's looking for, and without waiting for him to finish his question, she answers, "Occasionally. I didn't... it's very time consuming, so I didn't take a lot of time out of my schedule to do that, but every now and then, I did. Umm, for Valens – not Valentine's Day, for Father's Day, I gave Darryl a portrait of his son, and, umm, he really liked it". Oh, Jodi Arias is now a portrait artist. Who knew? Please, show us this portrait of the young Master Brewer. Then, can we subpoena a copy of any photographs that may resemble this so called, "portrait" that Arias created? I know, and so does everyone else who has looked at Jodi's portfolio, that she does not create – she copies. If Darryl Brewer's son actually sat for a portrait, you can bet Jodi's fog that we'd be hearing about it now.

Jodi licks her lips, and the words, "he really liked it" drop to the floor, much like the inconsequential art review they represent. Nurmi pauses. It's only a few seconds of silence, but it's long enough to jolt us, and remind us that this dialogue, this discourse, this conversation, is not at all normal or casual. It is false, foreign, and alien to anyone who is really listening. The soft feminine voice that is attempting to pull us into a world of relationships, restaurants, and road trips, is the same voice that was ringing in the ears of a young man as he lay dying on his bathroom floor. This voice, the one now telling us about market trends and her creation of a child's portrait, issues forth as a product of the same vocal chords that, in all probability, screamed the worst profanities imaginable, not to mention the animalistic grunts they produced, while she was making certain that her wet, naked victim choked and eventually drowned in his own blood. So, please, Jodi Arias, artist, tell us all about the time it takes to create your works of art, and we'll strive to remain focused, stay awake, stay alert, and not fall under the spell of a song, a lilt, a soft voice speaking of normal, human events. In reality, there is nothing normal or human about Jodi Arias. Nurmi's heavy breathing is finally punctuated by a question.

"Wa, wa... Did it... purchasing the home at this time, do you remember how much that home cost?". Jodi Arias purchased nothing more than a commitment to pay several interest payments. She never owned a home; she merely owned an image, a mirage, a sign that said "I have arrived". I find myself cheered by the hope that she is tortured by this memory, the memory of being free, of being able to select and purchase a house that belonged to her. I want her to remember, and despite the long and circuitous testimony that I know is right on the horizon, I'm willing to let her have free reign with it. I want her to remember. I want her to know what she had, and will never have again. I want her to crawl onto her jail cot at the conclusion of court on this particular day, and I want her to realize that real estate market trends will never matter to her again. I want her to know that she can ascribe value to her housing by looking at the figures put out by the professionals who calculate the per diem cost for housing an inmate – death row, or life in prison – it doesn't matter to me. She answers, "I believe it was 350....350,000". There's an air of pride as she speaks those words.

Nurmi continues, "And did you and Mr. Brewer (Jodi's tapping her fingers on the desk in anticipation of the question) have to put down a, a sizable down payment in order to buy that house?" Jodi pretends to think, but she remembers every detail as it relates to the acquisition of the home in question. She answers, "I think... I can't remember who put money down... but, I think it was one of those... ummm... I think it was, I think it was, (she's uncomfortable, and I know what's coming), umm... 100% financed, interest only, kind of thing." I hope the jurors realize, especially if there are any of them who have realized significant losses of home equity as a result of housing collapse, that Jodi Arias is not like them. The defense has been dancing around the issue and importance of Jodi's home ownership since Jennifer Willmott's opening statement. Jodi Arias owned nothing, and neither did her foolish, middle aged boyfriend, Darryl Brewer. Actually, I'm recalling something Darryl Brewer said in his post non-mitigation interview. Perhaps he was upset that he had been painted as a skirt chasing, career suiciding, alcoholic who was all dressed up with no place to go on mitigation day, but, he stated, on camera, that Jodi had saved $12,000 for a down payment on their shared home. Jennifer Willmott wants us all to believe that Jodi Arias and Darryl Brewer were victims of the housing collapse that began in 2008 and peaked in 2009. That has always rubbed me the wrong way. The truth is, it was the Jodi Arias/Darryl Brewer mortgages that CAUSED the housing collapse. I suspected this from the moment Willmott tried to push the collapse back by two years. As it turns out, the Arias/Brewer mortgage was one of those lethal, corrosive, sub-prime loans; a mortgage they never qualified for and should have never been given.

What a surprise that the house ended up in foreclosure within in year. What a devastation that so many of these mortgages were given out, and, predictably, the ripples affected decent, mortgage paying homeowners.

Nurmi says, “Okay”. That's it. We have been subjected to details that mean nothing. Well, I don't want to move on. I want to hear about this home purchase that Jodi Arias, educated in community college real estate courses, bought and then walked away from. That tells the jury a lot about Jodi Arias. It certainly trumps Crayola crayons, Costa Rica, Denny's, Bobby Juarez, and who bought Marlboro's every day. I suspect we'll be moving along.

The lies are about to continue. Nurmi would like to know what Jodi's financial position was when she purchased the house. She responds, “I was in a pretty solid financial position. I had a lot of money in the bank saved. Well, by a lot, I mean about ten or twelve thousand (it's probably less than $10,000, if it's even close to what she's saying)... ummm... (pause), which I think, at that point in my life, was the most I had saved ever, and ummm, I had very good credit. Darryl had good credit, he had, I think, umm, a Roth IRA that he was also, you know, saving for retirement, so he was investing as well”. Can we talk about the IRA? Did he cash it in? Did he lose it in the collapse? No ask, no tell. Where did the $10 – 12,000 go, if not on a down payment? Lawyer's fees, title searches, inspections? Will Nurmi ask?

No. He's not asking. He wants to know when they closed on the house and moved in. Jodi responds, “I believe it was June, 2005 that we actually... well... (she's directing her own examination now, and she wants to address issues Nurmi never raised)... we were actually going to move to Sacramento, and we were looking around the area there, ummm, so we made an offer on a house in Fair Oaks, which is a city right outside of Sacramento, and, ummm, the owners accepted our offer, and we checked out the house, we really liked it, and ummm, the day after our offer was accepted, ummm, the plan was, we were going to take his son, and keep him full-time (that would mean that Darryl wouldn't be paying child support; rather, he'd be receiving it), and you know, he would visit his mother, in LaQuita (you know, that town that Jodi thinks is in Riverside County), so, ummm, the day after our offer was accepted, she decided that she wanted him to be, to come live with her, and continue the same custody agreement. So, at that point, Sacramento wasn't feasible anymore for Darryl, and I wasn't able to buy a house without him, and, of course I wanted to be with him (of course, Jodi, of course) because we were still together, so ummmm.....”. Oh, thank God. Nurmi realizes that she has decided to add testimony they never agreed to bring up. She, for some reason, wants to answer a simple question that requires nothing more than a month, a day, and a year, with an irrelevant essay about some house they didn't buy. She wants us to know how badly she wanted it. She wants us to know that Darryl's ex-wife screwed her out of her dream home. She wants us to know that Darryl's ex-wife decided to pull the rug out from under them after their offer was accepted. Where is Darryl's ex-wife? I'd love to hear what she has to say, because I have a sneaking suspicion that her version of events would be drastically different than the one Jodi Arias just vomited all over the court room.

I just gave Nurmi too much credit. He cannot, or will not, control his client. I thought he was going to reign her in – remind her that his question required a day, a month, and a year – nothing more. Apparently, Nurmi's going with this testimony. He interrupts her long enough to ask if "she" is Darryl's ex-wife. Jodi licks her lips and smiles, "Yes, Jack's mother". Jodi, round two: "And so, I came over to his house, the day after, and we're just really high on the fact that we're going to get a house, and we're excited (she's hyped up as she's telling this story – hands waving, big smile on her evil face), and, ummm, he was just hanging up the phone, and he said, I don't remember what he said, but (she's almost laughing now), oh, I'm sorry" (Juan Martinez objected.... probably based on hearsay. He's irritated, and that's obvious). I don't know how the judge ruled, but Nurmi interjects, "Well, Jodi, why don't you just begin to, why don't we talk about the point in time where you make this offer on this house in Sacramento... tell us how you wind up in the house that you wind up in". Jodi knows the script better than Nurmi. I guess he decided to skip this portion, but she wanted to cover it. Now he's stuck, trying to cover it and move on, according to his notes.

Jodi's ready to shift subjects, and she answers, "Well, we decided that we needed to be, well, he needed to be, nearer to his son. So we checked out schools and real estate prices in Palm Desert, and umm, which was more affordable than LaQuita. LaQuita is more of a high end community with more expensive property. Ummm, in Palm Desert there was a very good school district (says the woman who put such a premium on her own education), ummm, and there were neighborhoods that had houses within our price range that was, that were in that school district. So, we made an offer on a house that I had seen online that I really liked". It's all about the children, isn't it? School districts... that's what mattered to Jodi Arias.

Jodi is now going to put away her defendant's hat and put on her business hat. Nurmi would like to know if she liked this house from a "business perspective" or a "personal perspective" (the only "business perspective" Jodi might have on this subject is whether or not the dining room was close enough to the kitchen for her to monitor the main course on the stove while she enjoyed appetizers with six dinner guests). If it isn't "do you want fries with that", she has no business perspective at all, and Nurmi is pushing his luck in this regard. Jodi is positively upbeat talking about this subject. You'd believe that she was the person in Mike Babicky's seat, and she was actually going home to this house, this sanctuary, tonight. "Well, I guess from a business perspective, because it was in our price range (that would actually fall squarely into the category of "personal perspective", but maybe that wasn't taught at community college), and a personal perspective because, well, just judging from the pictures of the house, it looked like a house that I could see myself living in. Of course, we needed to see it in person first, but...". N o, actually, Jodi Arias, Imaginary Real Estate Tycoon, that's not what you said. You said you made on offer on a house you saw online. Maybe she looked at it, but she had seen the pictures online, and she saw herself in her Egyptian cotton sheets in the master bedroom, and she pictured herself sipping white wine poolside. It was a done deal before they ever saw the place BECAUSE Jodi Arias could see herself in the house. If I'm wrong, blame Kirk Nurmi, because he has allowed his client to talk, talk, and talk. Jodi and her boyfriend, in my opinion, look like children playing grown-up.

Finally, after initially being asked what day they closed on the house, and after being suffocated with a never ending, non-answer about Mrs. Brewer, young Jack Brewer, a custody arrangement assumed but not confirmed, a lost home that she was not asked about, an on-line search of homes in another area, and the square footage of the house she purchased, we are given not a specific answer to the question, but a rather vague, "We finally moved there in the summer." Nurmi wants clarity: "Of...?". Jodi answers, "2005". Was there a day? She remembers that she got her Ventana Inn job on October 20, 2001. The closing date of her very first home? Uhhh.... she knows the year -- and the season. That's it.

Nurmi isn't ready to leave the house yet. I wonder if he's been listening, because he asks Jodi a question she just answered, regarding the square footage of the house. She repeats, "The house was... I can't remember the square footage of the house.... somewhere around 1400, maybe 1500. Umm, it had three bedrooms, two bathrooms, an open floor plan with living room, dining area, and kitchen. It had, umm, a pool in the back, fruit trees in the back, mature landscaping, palm trees, a front yard". A front yard is worth mentioning? Who knew. Was this a small snapshot into what Jodi Arias might actually sound like if she was selling real estate instead of tracings from a jail cell? Probably.

Nurmi has his thumb and middle finger pinched together as he punctuates his words by moving his left hand, "What was the living situation in terms of the bedrooms; did you and Darryl share one? Describe that". Yes, please, describe the living situation. Was a man named Travis Alexander living in one of those bedrooms – or perhaps in a finished basement in this 1400 square foot love shack? Was he a neighbor? Did he mow the lawn? Does he have any connection to the selection of the house, the financing of the house, the existence of the house? If not, why are we still at this house? Does anyone on the defense team remember a guy named Travis Victor Alexander? Wouldn't it be more relevant to talk about the home Travis purchased, paid for, and maintained, during this time period. Apparently not.

Nurmi wants to talk about sleeping arrangements in the Arias/Brewer homestead. Does Nurmi want to know if Darryl Brewer purchased a house with a woman who wasn't sharing his bed? Is he expecting Jodi to tell us who slept on the left side of the bed and who slept on the right? Will we soon be hearing about Darryl's green toothbrush and Jodi's pink toothbrush? Will we hear the inevitable "he left the toilet seat up" tale that led to her falling into the bowl in the middle of the night? Will we learn about which cabinet held the dishes, and if they argued over where the drinking glasses should be stored? How about appliances? Did their new home have a side by side refrigerator, a washer and dryer, or a dishwasher? How about flooring? Was it dingy wall to wall carpeting, or finished wood flooring? What about young Jack's accommodations? Did he need a night light? Was his bed linen covered in spaceships or dinosaurs? I'm beginning to feel like I'm in a real estate office, not a superior court.

Jodi answers, "We had... well, I had my bed, he has his bed, so we moved them both in, and I kind of kept the master bedroom as my own space, sort of (who's surprised that Jodi kept the big bedroom for herself? I'm sure this is where the second bathroom is located). He had another bedroom that he kind of like, when he came home from work, he would kind of (her hands are moving furiously; she's doing a windshield wiper movement with one hand), umm, call it his cave time ("cave time" would mean something completely different to me if I were Darryl Brewer, considering what I – and he – know about the demure Miss Arias' nether regions). When he came home from work, he needed about 45 minutes to decompress, and he kind of vegged out in front of CNN (not the instantly identifiable liberal MSNBC, or conservative Fox News – Darryl was solidly moderate. No jurors need be offended by CNN or the couple's political leanings)... something like that. And, umm, after that, we would sort of, hang out". Sorry Mr. Nurmi. You will not be hearing about what Darryl did to Jodi, or what Jodi did to Darryl, after decompressing and watching CNN.

Nurmi asks if Jack Brewer, Darryl's young son who visited on weekends, had his own room. Jodi answers, "Yes, Jack had the other bedroom". Nurmi continues, "And, how often did Jack, did Jack, live with the two of you?". Jodi responds, "He came on the weekends, two to three days a week".

Nurmi goes on, "And from your perspective, did you feel that you had a good relationship with Jack?". Oh, I see. This is all about Jodi Arias, Domestic Goddess. If Jack had issues with Jodi, we'd already know about it, so, I assume that Jodi is a friend to all children and small animals. She responds, "Yeah, ummm, we grew closer after moving to Palm Desert, ummm.... yeah, I did. I had a good relationship.. It wasn't like a motherly kind of role. I guess, having grown up with younger siblings, Jack felt more like a little brother to me".

Nurmi's walked away from the podium, and the camera catches him with his back to his client. We can barely hear the opening words of his next question, because he's in the midst of turning back to the microphone while beginning to speak: "In the relationship with Darryl, at this point in time in 2006, umm, 2005, excuse me, when you've moved into this home, what was the status of your romantic relationship with Darryl?"

I knew Nurmi wasn't going to be satisfied with the female, master bedroom thief, and the male who needed "cave time". Jodi answers, "Umm... we were boyfriend/girlfriend. We were in a committed, monogamous relationship (maybe so, but her voice belies the fact that things were a little tepid in the bedroom. Her voice is low, her face is non-expressive. She was far more excited recounting her ride on The Zipper with Bobby Juarez). Not necessarily headed for marriage, but I was in love with him (or his check book)". Nurmi wants some clarification on the "not necessarily headed for marriage".

He asks, "Darryl's perspective, as you saw it, did that change from that initial advisement, I guess, that he gave you a couple years prior?" Jodi answers, "I was not under any impression that he had changed his mind about his position on marriage (her face is like stone, and her voice is flat. She doesn't like this topic, or, she just doesn't care about it)".

Reading his client's flat affect, Nurmi asks the judge if this might be the time to take noon recess. Barely an hour of testimony on day two has gone by.

After Judge Sherry Stephen's tells the jurors to have a nice lunch, and then cautions them to remember "the admonition", we hear The Evidence Lady make her oft-repeated demand: "Please stand for the jury". The Evidence Lady has a good, commanding voice; it's strong, and it's clear. The voice of the soft-spoken Judge Stephens stands in stark contrast to that of The Evidence Lady. The judge's vocal inflections offer little insight into what she may be thinking; rather, it's her facial micro expressions, something she rarely displays, that indicate any level of frustration or irritation she may be hiding. She seems very laid back, and she's not excitable. In fact, Judge Stephens displays a level of patience and tolerance that might actually be her one noticeable, defining characteristic.

Jodi does as she's told. She stands. Jodi knows the camera is on her, and I assume she can't move without her restraints being adjusted or removed, but either way, she looks rather clueless as Mike Babicky, court reporter, moves out of frame. She looks toward her attorneys, and I assume she's sending a visual SOS. I guess she'll just have to wait for the deputy to assist her. The camera person, probably under court instruction to do so, moves off of Arias. The seal of the State of Arizona comes into focus: Ditat Deus. I saw those Latin words so many times during this trial, that I actually looked them up: God Enriches. Okay. That works for me.

I wonder if Jodi's styrofoam tray is already sitting on the bench in her courthouse cell in the basement of the building. Is there a lump or two of peanut butter sitting next to a few slightly stale pieces of dark bread wrapped in wax paper? Is there an apple? A cookie or two? Is she allowed to drink her child-sized carton of milk with a straw, or is a straw considered contraband? Oh, the indignities we never get to see her endure on camera. Will she pull the bread apart, as she did when she was given a sandwich during her interrogation? Will she demand that her attorneys spend some portion of their lunch hour talking with her in the basement? Will they flee and find a restaurant?

Court is in session.

The judge waves her finger from the defense table and points it towards the witness stand. "Miss Arias, please take the stand". Jodi looks rumpled and wrinkled in her too casual, short sleeved, slightly too tight, powder blue button up shirt and her baggy beige pants. She keeps her eyes down, and she's wearing a dead pan expression as she takes her seat. She immediately reaches for a plastic water cup (peanut butter has such a high salt content. I'm sure she's thirsty. Either that, or she just wants to look busy). She lifts the gold water carafe and with her right hand, and pours herself a half a glass of water. Then she carefully sets her water cup in front of her, straightens her already straightened horizontal microphone, puts her hands on the arm rests of her swivel chair, positions herself, and waits for Nurmi to begin Act II. She looks emotionless. Her mood is definitely deflated. The only thing that's moving on her face are her eyes. She looks toward the judge. She looks toward the defense table. She stares down at Mike Babicky.

"Please stand for the jury", says The Evidence Lady. Jodi is on her feet. She looks at the jury, and then she uses each hand to pull down either side of the hem of her cotton blouse. Mike Babicky's face is very red; I wonder if he has a blood pressure problem.

Jodi lifts her hands, and she places them right under her bust line. She's staring at the jury. She looks nervous. She's interlaces her fingers, and then pulls them apart. She's psyching herself out. She's getting ready. She's just waiting for her cue. She's forced to wait. Now, she's taken her left hand and has made what looks like a circle out of her fingers – the four long fingers are curved toward her body, and they are joined with her thumb. Then, she takes the other hand, and with four fingers outstretched, she inserts her right hand into what could best be described as a hole she made with her left hand. I wish I could interpret body language. This must mean something, and it looks odd.

Finally everyone is seated. Nurmi is instructed to continue with direct examination. His head in down as he begins, "Jodi, before we took our lunch break, I believe we were talking about a point in time when you and Darryl had purchased your home in Palm Desert (we hear a "yes", apparently coming from Jodi). Is that right? Okay. And, you'd also told us that Darryl's (Nurmi is searching for a word. His hand is moving up and down, and he seems amused by something) stance on not being married persisted all the way, to the point in time when you were buying this home". Jodi agrees, "Yes. I think there was a time when he may have wanted another child – he implied that (he implied it, or she inferred it?), but we never actively tried to get pregnant, or anything like that".

I am noticing a glaring omission in her testimony, and, if I'm not mistaken, it is an omission that is never addressed or modified as the testimony continues. How can we talk about conception, either attempting to facilitate it, or attempting to prevent it, while completely ignoring the subject of birth control? Why has the issue of birth control not been raised? It is a tame topic in the face of the testimony I know is just around the corner -- testimony that includes oral sex, vaginal sex, anal sex, fetish sex, semen, lubricants, Brazilian waxes and bondage. Let's not forget her dressing up in that closeted school girl costume that she wore when entering an adult book store to purchase male enhancement devices. So why is this very clinical, very inoffensive issue never raised when the woman being questioned was undoubtedly of childbearing age during her multiple relationships? I have my suspicions, and those suspicions relate to Jodi's need for birth control. I don't think Jodi Arias required birth control. I don't believe she is, was, or ever has been, fertile.

Nurmi continues, "So given that Mr. Brewer was not interested in getting married, and you had your separate lives, your separate bank accounts... let's see... you have the mortgage together... what was the... what was the plan... with this home? Were you going to live in it for years, what was, what was the idea?". Jodi tilts her neck, lifts her right hand, strokes back a portion of her hair that was not falling in her face, and then answers, "Ideally, if everything had worked out, and if the housing market had continued to increase, ummm, which, of course, it didn't... I think June was the year it peaked – or the month it peaked. Umm, then we would have stayed in it for two years, and umm, either rented it out, or flipped it, turned, near, ah... err... I mean, sold it, and reinvest in another place". Where are all the superfluous details? Her answers are clipped, short, and they answer his questions. And why is she choking on the term "flipped"? Perhaps this was not the love affair of the century. Perhaps for Jodi Arias, wannabe real estate tycoon, this was a means to a very personal, selfish end.

"So, you didn't have a plan to be permanently together, whether married or not", asks Nurmi. Jodi responds quickly, "Actually, I had hoped to maybe buy him out, on the house, if possible, so that I could own it. I had ideas of maybe (she's searching for her words, and her hands are moving rapidly) making it into a business investment... property". This is confusing. She's in love with Darryl, or so she claims. She was delighted when she was talking about buying this house. Either her peanut butter soufflé is not sitting well, or her mood has drastically shifted since this morning. She is no longer happy, and she obviously doesn't want to talk about this subject anymore. Maybe sitting in a basement cage, all alone, in the wake of a testimony that featured her autonomy and freedom, has depressed her.

In any event, I wonder why Jodi continues to talk out of her league. Flipping houses? Reinvesting her profit into another house? Buying Darryl out? Making the home a business investment? This is all so ridiculous that it doesn't warrant serious consideration. She was a server, and she was a server who was never going to be in a position of financial security to buy anyone out – especially in the short time span of two years. She'd need to come up with $175K, at the very least, to buy out Darryl Brewer. Is this the "magical thinking" that Darryl Brewer was talking about in his post non-mitigation interview?

Nurmi asks a reasonable question, and it is the one I would have asked after hearing the testimony she just gave – a testimony that made it very clear that she was using Darryl Brewer as a stepping stone to something that didn't include him, but included money and advancement for Jodi Arias.

Nurmi wants to know if Jodi was still "in love" with Darryl Brewer.

She isn't breaking into Nurmi's questions now – she's not answering before he's finished posing them. In fact, she needs clarification on what period of time Nurmi's referring to as it relates to her "love" for Darryl Brewer. She looks up before responding, "Wa, you mean while we owned the house together?" Nurmi answers, "Umm hmm". Jodi looks directly at the jury: "Yes". Nurmi continues, "Did you want to ma...to marry Darryl Brewer?" Jodi answers, "I probably would have.... oh, yeah... I would have married him. I don't know that... he was pretty clear that he didn't want to get married, so I didn't allow myself to entertain that idea, but I could see myself spending my life with him." I don't think she wanted to marry him. I think he had served his purpose. There was no way Jodi Arias was going to play step-mother to Darryl's son. She made it clear earlier in the testimony – she couldn't purchase a house alone. She needed Darryl.

Jodi looks at Nurmi, giving him the signal that she is finished with her answer. Nurmi continues, "So, as it relates to this, this plan that was hatched, that was actualized in 2005 (Nurmi's smiling again), to buy the house, and stay together in it for a couple of years, and make money, did that plan work?". Jodi sounds like a deflated balloon looks as she turns to the jury and says, "No. It didn't work at all". Nurmi wants to know how this foolproof, triple A plan failed. Jodi, despite her college education in real estate market trends, is about to offer her excuses for bad planning, complete lack of finances, and absolutely no knowledge as to how real estate investments actually work. She responds, "Ummm, the day before we signed on our house, our mortgage broker called and pushed up the terms, and she said it really fast, we were like, okay, whatever, we just really wanted the house. So, what we failed to remember or consider, was that in one year, the mortgage would index, umm, the current rate, so our mortgage payment jumped from $2,200 a month up to $2,800 a month, and, umm, it was a lot more than we were expecting". Her mouth is dry. She's licking her lips. Actually, she's doing more than licking her lips, she completely retracting her bottom lip into her mouth.

Their mortgage broker "said it really fast"? What "they failed to remember or consider" was the amount of the 13th mortgage payment? No. I don't believe this. I believe they were qualified for this predatory loan when they were prequalified – for this and nothing else. I think they accepted those terms in the beginning of the transaction. This is their fault. They didn't have to sign the deal, but they did. Why? Because, as Jodi said, she could see herself living in this house. Jodi crosses bridges when she comes to them (according to her). She had a full year to forget about impending doom.

In order to deflect the irresponsible behavior of Arias and Brewer, Nurmi attempts to rehabilitate his sucker of a client by asking if she was still working two jobs. She's on board, and she responds, "Yes, I was working (she appears to be thinking), ah, two jobs. Yes, in Palm Desert". Nurmi continues, "So, the, your half of the mortgage then, would have been $1400? Is that right". Of course that's right. Jodi affirms that Nurmi's simple division skills are intact, and then he progresses: "And that didn't include any of the other household expenses". Oh, please. Of course, it didn't include any of the other household expenses. All of those expenses would have been charted on an income/expense sheet they filled out when they were figuring out how much house they could afford. I have no sympathy for either of them. None.

Nurmi now asks if, between her two jobs, she could afford this new payment. Are we talking about a $300/month increase for her, or are we talking about Jodi Arias having to find an extra $800/month to pay her mortgage? She says, "I think I might have been able to. I would have been living very impoverished – it didn't quite cover the mortgage. I think I came up short every month". Impoverished: "being reduced to poverty, lacking material possessions and money". You are not impoverished if you own a house. You are impoverished if you don't have a roof over your head. You may be "house poor", but the responsible thing to do, the solution, is to get rid of your expensive car, your cell phone, the cable, you stop your road trips, and stop going to Starbucks. That's right off the top. Then, you cut everything from the budget besides the necessities. It's mortgage, utilities, Ramen noodles and canned vegetable (better than the diet of the third world), and insurance. You get a third job. You sell your car, and you buy one without a bank loan that doesn't require the added expense of collision coverage. You find a way. If you have a brain, you find a way. This increase, something they agreed to accept on the terms of their mortgage, was not massive. It was not a huge amount of money. I've known of people who accepted these ARM mortgages who had payments of $2,300 a month that jumped to $4,200 a month when the interest rate increased. That's a number that isn't workable. Each party having to find an extra $300 a month is something you deal with, and then you make a safe exit plan. You keep your mortgage payments up, and then you sell the house. If you take a loss, you take a loss, but you maintain a credit rating and you start again. You don't let the house fall into foreclosure without a fight. You don't, that is, unless you're Jodi Arias.

Now, what would be the worst idea you could think of in trying to solve this situation? How about the one Jodi Arias decided was workable? How about "I paid the mortgage with my credit card"? Yes, that was her answer. I wish Nurmi would delve into this low intellect plan, but he wants to talk about the value of the home versus the money owed on the home. Jodi Arias: Professional Victim. If equivocation was an art form, Arias would in galleries across the country:

Jodi Arias has just admitted to the fact that she tried to solve one huge problem by creating another problem – borrowing from one lender to pay another lender. I guess we should give her five points for not going to a loan shark. Despite her best efforts to sound older, but wiser, in the retelling of this chapter of her life, I am not buying her story. I'm quite confused -- nothing is fitting together neatly. The more she speaks, the more questions I have. My confusion isn't based on the fact that I wasn't listening to her testimony carefully; rather, my confusion is based on the fact that I was listening to every word of her testimony. Arias is the person who raised the issue of her credit card, and her usage of that credit card was described in her direct response to a very specific question: how did she manage the shortfall on her half of the mortgage payment after the monthly payment increased at the end of the first year of home ownership? If, as she implied, she actually began using the card to cover that extra $300/month increase as she claims, then this would have been a practice she began in June, 2006 (the first month their house payments increased, and the first time the mortgage was unmanageable for her).

Assuming that what she says is true (and that's a big assumption, but for the sake of argument, I'm willing to play along), that does not change the fact that in September, 2006, Jodi went to a PPL convention at the MGM Grand Hotel in Las Vegas. According to Darryl Brewer in his televised interview in May, 2013, Jodi's involvement with "PPL and the Mormon church" – simultaneous events – marked the beginning of her "irresponsible" behavior. Although she had signed up to be a PPL associate several months earlier in 2006, it was at this convention that her real involvement with the organization began. It was also at this convention that Travis Alexander's destiny was tragically sealed. The two met at The Rainforest Cafe at this particular convention, and Jodi, I have no doubt, found her shiny new upgrade of a man, and knowing what I now know, I don't think she was willing to leave Nevada without a prospective male upgrade.

Several questions now arise. If Jodi was actually paying her $1,100/month half of the mortgage faithfully until, as she claims, the payment increased in June, 2006, then how many months did she have to use her credit card to cover the increased payments? If she's being honest in her version of events, then she used it, at most, three times before the bank moved against them (June, July, August, 2006). If we're to believe her, it was that increase of $300/month that caused her to pull out the plastic in the first place. I don't believe her story. I think she began using that card to cover her payment shortfall far earlier than June, 2006. I don't believe she could even keep up with the original $1,100/month payment. Secondly, if she actually began using her credit card to cover the shortfall for several months, as she implied, then why did the house fall into foreclosure in August or September? If she used it several times because she seemed to fall short each month (after the increase), then it's reasonable to assume that the couple was current in August, 2006. She is either lying, or they had one hell of an aggressive lender. It is very doubtful that one missed payment would have caused their lender to initiate foreclosure proceedings. Legally, the lender has that right, but the bank doesn't want a 1400 square foot house in Palm Desert; they want their money.

It's also interesting to note that a woman who wasn't paying her September mortgage (a reasonable assumption, as Darryl was out of the house in December, 2006, and he testified to the fact that the house was lost in early 2007), found the disposable income (and the time off from those two jobs she was allegedly holding down) to jump into her car to embark on a 500 mile round trip from Palm Desert, California to Las Vegas, Nevada to attend a PPL convention. How did she fund that trip? Gas and food alone would be an expense, and does anyone believe that there was no PPL registration fee? How about lodging? While there may have been room blocks with discounts at the MGM Grand for attendees of this event, does anyone believe it was cheap to stay there for several days? Jodi claims that two, unidentified girlfriends accompanied her, but has anybody verified that? Where would she even meet these other PPL "friends/associates"? Jodi didn't know anyone in the organization. How about meals in places like Rainforest Cafe? There is a social element to this convention, and that element requires money.

My theory: She knew the house was going. She had known for months. She had tired of Darryl. She was starting a new life. She was reinventing herself again. I hope, at the very least, she said thank you to Darryl before she got into her car and started out on her 4.5 hour trip to Vegas. Maybe she left him a goodbye note that said, "Dear Darryl, Thanks for the job at Ventana. Thanks for throwing away your career at Ventana. Thanks for buying a home with an impossible mortgage because I needed to be a real estate investor. Oh, and thanks for allowing your credit to be destroyed after I decided that my signature on legally binding loan documents was only binding until I decided that I was bored with our life together. Oh, say good-bye to Jack for me. Think positive! Jodi".

So, now that we have a clearer financial picture than Jodi would like us to have, let's get back to court.

Nurmi would like to know if the woman who cared so little about the loan documents she signed ("we were like, whatever, we just really wanted the house"), gave some thought as to the value of the house at the time the lender was moving against them. He would like her to put a number on that – what was the house worth when they decided to stop honoring their agreement to pay for it? Jodi answers, "Ummm, the value obviously wasn't increasing anymore, ummm, I didn't, eh, I didn't really look into the value of the home I was living in, but I was paying attention to sale prices in my neighborhood, and they were going for almost $100,000 less, at this point, than what we closed on our home for. So, it was pretty apparent that the market was switching back to, umm, a buyer's market".

Wow. I'm impressed! There's that college education kicking in. It's a "buyer's market". I'm not college educated in real estate market trends or home listings, so I wonder what that could mean? Is that bad for the damsel in distress? She looks all sad and stuff. Yes, I think this was a bad thing. Naturally, Jodi couldn't be forced to face all of this negativity, and it just makes sense to do what she does when times get tough and the walls start to close in – take a long road trip!

Nurmi asks, "And how long were you and Darryl able to maintain the home with this increased mortgage payment?" Jodi swallows, and she still looks pretty down in the dumps, but she answers, "Ummm, I can't remember exactly when it mortgaged (when it mortgaged? Okay. Whatever), but it went south pretty quickly as far as us being able to maintain the payments. I think the last solid, well, the full half a payment that I made, was in November, 2006, and by December, I couldn't quite get $1,400, and by January, I couldn't pay. I think I paid even less. I think that was the last time I was able to even attempt it (translation: her credit card is at the limit), and, so by then, we decided that we would just let the property lapse into foreclosure". Interesting. According to Darryl Brewer, under direct examination several days earlier, he was already gone by December, 2006.

At this point, I went back to Darryl Brewer's direct testimony. These dates are bothering me. Under direct examination by Nurmi, Darryl testified that Jodi continued to maintain two jobs until the fall of 2006. Several minutes later, when asked another question (by Nurmi) that related to Jodi, he stated that she kept two jobs until the summer of 2006. He also stated that his ex-wife and the mother of his son, had moved back to Monterey. The home that Jack (Darryl's son) and his mother were moving to was a 9 -10 hour drive (Darryl's estimation) from the home that Darryl Brewer owned with Jodi Arias. Darryl Brewer made it clear that he intended to move to Monterey to be close to his son?). When Nurmi asked Darryl what was going to happen to the home that he and Jodi shared in Palm Desert, Darryl said that he intended to maintain his portion of the mortgage, and that eventually, he and Jodi would come to some resolution with that house.

Darryl made it clear that Jodi was not coming with him to Monterey. Darryl did testify that Jodi began having financial issues with the mortgage in the fall of 2006. He remembered her trip to a PPL convention in 2006, and he said it marked the beginning of her "irresponsible" behavior and her interest in PPL and the Mormon church. He said that he left the home in December, 2006, and as far as he knew, it went into foreclosure in early 2007 – maybe January or February (he's as vague as Jodi is). Darryl is obviously trying to portray Jodi Arias in the best light possible, so everything he says is suspect. I have no question as to why he's assumed a sympathetic position in regard to Jodi. I am sure that he has been asked to explain, more than once, how he didn't know that he was allowing his son to stay under the same roof as a woman who brutally slaughtered another human being. He has a vested interest in making Jodi appear to be a normal, not dangerous .

As far as the sketchy dates are concerned, we all know that there is a clear paper trail that will tell us exactly when the pair stopped paying the mortgage, when the foreclosure was initiated, and when the house was auctioned. I cannot understand why those dates are not being disclosed. I believe this is all an attempt to muddy the waters. I don't know what happened between Jodi and Darryl. Is he protecting her? Did he leave her? Did she leave him? We may never know. Do we really care?

As usual, Nurmi wants to move in reverse: "Moving back a few months to the fall of 2006, what was going on with your relationship with Brew...Mr. Brewer? Were you still happy, or – describe that for us". Jodi responds, "Well, I still loved him, but I think, umm, umm, that summer, I had a lot of things, like, reality kind of hit (like it's cheaper to live in a canvas tent than it is to live in a house?), ummm, we weren't really progressing in our relationship, umm, I was no longer 22, I was 26, so I began to question where I was going with my life (hint: Perryville), umm, was I going to have a family with this person (this person who had already told you that he was returning to Monterey – without you), so, it really didn't seem that way, and, at the time, my goal was marriage and children (not opening a real estate firm, as previously stated), and, umm, at least someday, and that's not just something you can just go out and get... you have to (go to a multi-level marketing conference and find the rising star) kind of invest time, and, so, at age 26, I was more than halfway through my twenties, and I wanted to begin focusing more on that. Umm, but we had the house together, so I wasn't sure how that was going to work, umm, so I became, I guess, a little more disenchanted with the relationship. He wasn't really focused on it (no, he wasn't. He was far more focused on a prior commitment named Jack). He had a lot of stress going on with his life and his bills, and his son, and his ex-wife, and that kind of thing. So, we just had, we were going in different directions, we had different visions for our futures".

Nurmi wants to talk about Jodi's personal life versus her business life. Well, at least there will be more content in her personal life because she has no business life. He reminds her that the Arias/Brewer estate was supposed to be the genesis of the business model Jodi was constructing. Nurmi points out the obvious, that nothing was going well. What, Nurmi asks, did Jodi want to do with her life, professionally speaking? We are in the realm of the ridiculous, once again. We've been here before, and I assume we'll be visiting frequently as she continues to answer completely irrelevant questions posed by her defense attorney.

Nurmi is still trying to float the waitress – artist – photographer - business person cartoon. Fine. Go ahead, Jodi. Answer his question. "Umm, well I was looking for other ways to get on my feet financially so that I could (snag Travis Alexander with a more appealing biography than an, 'I lost my home in foreclosure' tale of woe... not too impressive for a guy that was all about upward mobility, AND, 'Oh, by the way, I'm a business tycoon who happens to wait tables' footnote), invest in real estate, which was going to be my form of income, so that I could do more of the things that I enjoyed, which would also be forms of income; such as, umm, photography, and umm, I didn't, I didn't see myself yet making, umm, a career out of art. It was more of a hobby than a career role, but possibly that, and umm, I wanted to get my art into galleries. I wanted to, umm, I enjoyed the weddings that I had done at Ventana, but I enjoyed photography more than coordinating them... so I wanted to become a wedding photographer, also".

It's too much to break down.

So, what does Jodi Arias bring to the table – anyone's table – in the fall of 2006? The short answer is nothing but problems and far-fetched dreams. Her credit was destroyed. Beyond paying her bills with a credit card, she let her home "lapse into foreclosure", and she still had aspirations that included real estate investment, art gallery exhibitions, and a wedding photography business? At the very least, did she not realize that real estate just wasn't her thing? After suffering the devastation of a home foreclosure, wouldn't it turn her stomach – for quite a while – to merely pass an office building with a "Real Estate" shingle hanging out front? And, for what it's worth, can we ask what she actually does for a living? She's a waitress. Moving right along.

Nurmi gives us some hope of returning to the subjects that involve Jodi's "ventures", but for the moment, he wants to segue into her religious and spiritual life. That's a good idea. If the jury is given another five minutes to consider the three full-time occupations Jodi feels qualified to actively pursue, they'll be admonished by the judge for rolling their eyes or stifling laughter. It's far safer to address the parts of Jodi Arias that don't require an education or a resume. Let's talk about Jodi's spirituality.

What was going on with Jodi's soul back in the fall of 2006? I assume we're back to the essay questions. Jodi answers, "At that time, umm, I considered myself very open minded, uhh, spiritually, as far as religions go. Umm, I find good things in all kinds of religions, and truth in all religions, or things that resonate with me, and so I didn't have a particular (boyfriend with a religion she could duplicate) or a specific religion that I would identify with (although Mormonism was definitely on the front burner), or I considered to be my religion. It was kind of open and broad, but I still considered myself spiritual".

The camera now focuses on Juan Martinez, and I'm glad. I realize that I am lost in a maze of and legal manipulation. Juan Martinez is, for all intents and purposes, a bucket of cold water in the face of those whose eyes are glossing over. The man doesn't even have to move to make that kind of impact. In fact, if not for two eye movements, I would think I was looking at a still photograph. He's amazingly still for a man who doesn't stop moving when he's in the spotlight.

Nurmi asks, "Now, you mentioned looking for a financial mechanism, if you will, to allow you to make money while you worked on your art or your photography, and that sort of thing, right? Did you find one of those, or what you thought was one of those?". I'm surprised by her answer: "Umm, yes. The year before, umm, I went to work at California Pizza Kitchen (all great artists work at California Pizza Kitchen or some reasonable equivalent, just in case you hadn't googled that fact), and my manager asked me where I saw myself in five years (Hey! Now, wait just a minute. How many times do people ask you where you see yourself in five years? As far as Jodi Arias is concerned, that exact scenario has already played out in this testimony. Didn't some anonymous PPL missionary ask her the very same question a while ago? Now, the manager of a pizza restaurant, her boss, is asking the same question? What are the chances? Probably the same as being approached, several times, while on duty at work, by an individual or individuals who need to tell her that her boyfriend is cheating on her. Wow!), and, the first thought that jumped into my mind was real estate – something involving real estate. I think I mentioned that. Uh, he said he was going to be retired, and I thought that was a bold statement, considering he was about my age (wait... are we back to the original PPL guy, or does the Pizza Kitchen manager work for PPL on the side? I'm confused). And so, he gave me some information. The company was called Prepaid Legal (when did the clock turn back – we heard this already, right?). I think it was a magazine and a DVD, and, umm, he was really excited about it, and he, he, he asked me to look at it, review it, and I told him I would, and, umm, it wasn't anything that really got me excited. Initially, I took it – I mean, that day at work. I put it next to one of the computer terminals and I forgot about it, and it stayed at work for several weeks, almost a month, before I remembered to take it home..." (so this is the marketing literature she talked about earlier, much earlier, in her testimony. I'm just wondering, where is Jodi's home at this point in time? Staff housing at Ventana? Her separate apartment? The lost home? Why are we jumping all over the place?).

Nurmi doesn't seem confused. He asks, "Did you watch that DVD?". Jodi answers, "Not at that point. I took it home, I never looked at it, well, not never... I didn't look at it for a long time. Umm, it went into a closet, just a storage closet, and about six months later, maybe, five months later, I was cleaning it out, I was cleaning things out, and I came across the DVD, and I wanted to throw it away, but I didn't want to throw it away until I at least knew what was on it. So I stopped what I was doing, popped it into the DVD player, and I sat down, and I just gave it my attention for that time, so that I could at least throw it away knowing that I knew what was on it before I threw it away (her mood is lightening. She seems more animated, more invested, and more focused). Umm, and I just liked what I saw, and so, I called him back (Nurmi interjects, "Called who back?)...The person who gave it to me. I called him back. Umm, he said he wasn't in the business anymore, but he could refer me to someone up line. So, I got his number, and so I called that guy, and he told me he wasn't in the business anymore, but he told me that he would still get me some more material on it, and so I waited a few days, and still didn't hear from him, so I just went to Prepaid Legal's website and gave my information to get more information about it. I think I was able to sign up on the website... no... I don't think I was able to sign up then, but I submitted my information then, and a lady named Michelle finally called me back".

I actually had to reread her testimony to see if I had the facts straight, as previously stated. The first person who asked her where she saw herself five years from that point in time was not some patron at a restaurant she was working in (definitely the impression I had after she first addressed this under direct), but it was, in fact, her manager. He said he was going to be retired in five years, and he handed her the secret key to early retirement when he was no longer a part of the organization that held the key to early retirement. But, hey, he was still really excited about something he longer had any interest in. Right. Then, he gave Jodi the name of someone above him in the organization that he no longer belonged to, but she found out that that particular individual had also jumped ship. And this makes sense why? I want more details about this IQ test that she took. I am not seeing an intellect that is worth mentioning.

We've spent a lot of time doing what the jurors couldn't do (actually, we've been doing things that they strictly forbidden to do it); we've looked at public records regarding the home that Jodi and Darryl lost. We've filled in the blanks that Nurmi was hoping nobody was considering, despite the fact that the blanks were the highlights in each equation. I'm reasonably confident that the jurors didn't need all of these fine details to render a decision that Jodi Arias was not, nor was she ever going to be, a real estate investor.

Nurmi is now leading his powder blue client into the realm of her non-career with PrePaid Legal – an enterprise to which Travis Alexander devoted his adult life and energy, and something that Jodi Arias marked as the next host in a line of parasitic opportunities (side note: if you haven't watched a Travis Alexander motivational speech, you should. I watched a portion of on Youtube. It was in late April, 2008, and Travis was referring to a candidate named Barack Obama, and he said that he didn't know what kind of president he might be, but Travis did know that Barack Obama was an excellent marketer. This video impacted me because I specifically remember the months leading up to the 2008 election. I remember realizing, much like Travis, that Barack Obama was, in all likelihood, the next president of the United States. What really hit me was the fact that I know, definitely, how that election turned out... and the one after that). He was just too young. That's what always grabs me by the throat – his age.

Back on the stand, Jodi is rambling profusely, at Nurmi's urging, about her introduction into the world of PPL. She's speaking so quickly that Nurmi asks her to slow down. She's rambling about the woman who "signed her up", a woman named Michelle. Via Nurmi's promptings, we learn that Michelle checked her email, saw Jodi's message that contained her pertinent information, and then we learn that Michelle did what every telemarketer does: she called the prospect. I tell myself that I'm expecting some bombshell to highlight this line of questioning, but I know I'm lying to myself. Honestly, I'm not expecting anything of the sort. By now, I know that Nurmi's line of questioning, whatever the subject may be, will lead us to the same conclusion. Why does any of this testimony matter?

Regardless, I still find myself wondering how Michelle is connected to this case. Is there any connection between the murder of Travis Alexander and the protocol that a MLM solicitor uses to set the hook in the mouth of a bottom feeder who's looking to get in on the ground floor of a "sure thing"? Unless this portion of the trial will be edited into some PSA for young adults who need to learn the importance of just saying "no" to annoying solicitors on the telephone, why are we even listening to this?

At this point, Nurmi is acting as though too much critical data has been let out of the gate; he doesn't want this information to go over the jurors' heads, so he interrupts Jodi's streaming to say, "Let's, let's, before you get too far, what do you mean by 'signed up'?" Signed up? I think we all know what it means to sign up for something, don't we? How about Little League, the school play, a field trip, a gymnastics class, Weight Watchers, or jury duty? You put your name on a list – that's it. Has PPL been added as a co-defendant to the state's case? I have a feeling that PPL is about to suffer some public image damage, courtesy of Nurmi and his client.

After watching Jodi, I wonder if today's basement lunch consisted of a peanut butter entree followed by a dessert of amphetamines? What drug just kicked in? She's just vomiting out the words – almost tripping over them. She's back to peppering her answers with all the microscopic details we've come to despise. We will hear how the PPL system works, or according to Jodi, the way the system "used to work". Let's get started!

According to Jodi, someone is assigned to contact a prospective on-line "associate" according to their zip code or area code. We learn something critical here. No, the information offered has nothing to do with how many times Jodi Arias sawed Travis Alexander's neck with a knife before his voice box was eventually severed, but rather, where "Michelle", the PPL representative, lived when she contacted Jodi Arias: Hemet, California. Well, thank you for that, Jodi. We can all sleep tonight.

Nurmi is leading his client with his questions. She's a victim – a smart, verbally superior, artistic victim, but still, a victim. Jodi responds, "I didn't know what that meant at the time, but she just instructed me to go online, purchase the membership, and also pay the fee to become, umm, an independent associate with the company". I understand what that means. The jury understands what that means. Unfortunately, Jodi Arias, real estate tycoon, didn't understand what that meant. Nurmi, never willing to miss an opportunity to insult an individual or company not present to defend themselves, asks, "So, you, ahh, bought the product, and then you paid an additional fee to sell the product, right?"

I sense a tone of judgmental disdain in Nurmi's voice. I think he's implying that PPL rips people off (maybe they do, but Jodi Arias could have kept the credit card in her wallet instead of reading out those sixteen digits to Michelle). Nurmi's attitude is rich, ironic, and hypocritical; just as it would be if it were being projected by any individual who had used his client, his client's mother, and the court to execute an ambush maneuver that guaranteed him a pay rate far exceeding anything a peer could command for providing the same service. Before Nurmi finishes asking the question, Jodi answers, "Yes."

Nurmi asks Jodi why, at this point in time, she was interested in becoming an "associate" of this particular company. Put your feet up, folks – Jodi is now going to define her typical Modus Operandi (minimal work, maximum pay) with a new approach – one specific to PPL (every predator in Jodi's life gets their own back story, and PPL is no different). I think we're going to be here for a long time. Jodi answers: "Umm, I liked what I saw in the DVD. It was well represented by two executives in the company that have had a lot of success, and they were very eloquent, and they were able to explain it in very simple terms, umm, with simple math, and it just seemed like something that was, umm, that I might have success with".

There's an ugly head snap back to Nurmi (it's not the snap that is ugly, it's the head. Jodi is literally getting uglier as the hours go by). She looks at Nurmi like a dog who has just done a little trick, and as a reward, she's expecting a treat to be thrown in her general direction. If Jodi had a tail, it would be wagging in anticipation. Nurmi throws another dog biscuit; he wants to know if Jodi met with this individual, Michelle, and, if so, what was the outcome of their meeting. Jodi lifts her eyes, swivels her chair toward the jury, and responds, "Well, she sent me away with tons of supplies, DVDs to pass out to other people, magazines, umm, marketing materials, and, I really didn't do anything with it (Typical. I'm sure Michelle never really expected Jodi to pass them out to people, and that's why she wasted them on a woman who was going to toss them on the floor of a disordered, cluttered bedroom. Promotional items are always most effective when they're sitting under a pile of dirty Jodi laundry).

I just took it home, and it sat there and collected dust for a while (DING, DING, DING! Jodi tells the truth! The unabashed, God's honest, gospel truth! She did take that crap home and it did collect dust. No doubt). "At home? Were you still living with Mr. Brewer at that time?", Nurmi asks. Jodi tells us that she and Darryl were still living under one roof in March, 2006. This leads Nurmi to ask, again, about their level of intimacy. Although he uses the euphemism, "boyfriend/girlfriend" (the "boy" half of the equation is 46 years old), he really wants to know if Jodi and Darryl were still screwing around when Jodi embarked on her big business meeting with Michelle – in a diner – the meeting that netted her nothing more than a bunch of useless propaganda that nobody, especially Jodi, wanted or ascribed any value to.

"Yes", says Jodi, but there's no spark, no smile, no flush to the cheeks, nothing to indicate that Jodi was doing anything more than counting the slats in the bedroom window mini-blinds – if there were blinds as opposed to sheets stapled to the window frames – while Darryl was huffing and puffing his way to paradise. The dusty DVDs and magazines were probably in the same bedroom in which Brewer and Arias explored their desiccated feelings for each other (Nurmi's the one who wanted to connect sex and PPL propaganda, although I'm not sure why). He wants us to know that the pair was still motivated to make mediocre, apathetic, it's not really worth taking a shower for, kinda/sorta, faux love to each other. That's the impression I'm getting.

At this point, I despise the image Jodi Arias is portraying. Perhaps it's because I'm focused on her always moving hands, and I know what those hands are capable of doing. Perhaps it's because I've seen the crime scene photos; perhaps it's because I don't like looking at the bored faces and polyester tent shirts worn by her female family members in the gallery; perhaps it's because the Alexander family is being force fed a repulsive concoction made up of the mundane hours and epic failures of Jodi's life; perhaps it's because she's a liar; or, perhaps it's because she's just so damn boring. I don't care about the dandruff of her life, and neither, I assume, does the jury.

Nurmi would like to know if, between her forgettable sex sessions (my interpretation, not her admission) with Darryl, Jodi was actively trying to sell PPL memberships. Of course, she wasn't. Jodi responds, "Not at this point. She had called me, and told me that in the summer there was a team event (let me guess -- this event will have some kind of rah-rah name... Team Discover, Team Accomplish, Team Bravo, Team Victory, Team Champion... I wonder how much Team Foreclosure paid to attend this event), umm, at Daniel's Summit, Utah (this is a lovely, rustic lodge that has an array of winter activities and spa packages. The lodging, and, of course, you can book standard or different levels of luxury – begins at $150/night), and it was scheduled at the beginning of July that year, and I was scheduled to go to my cousin's wedding (most family members are invited to weddings, but not Jodi. She's "scheduled" to go to family weddings), and I wanted to build my wedding portfolio also (Oh, I see. Jodi is "scheduled" because she's a vendor, not a guest. I wonder how much this booking netted her. Let's see if Nurmi asks), so that was much more important to me, obviously (Obviously? Why would work obviously be more important to Jodi than lodge crawling? Perhaps Mike Babicky should give her a few pages of the transcript to read in the van on the ride back to Hotel Estrella. If her reading comprehension is as stellar as we are to believe, she'll understand that her own testimony, thus far, paints a much different picture)... umm, and to be with my family at that event, so, I didn't go to that, I didn't go to the company event that she invited me to ("invited" to a company event that has a registration fee attached, and "scheduled" for a family wedding? This is the woman with the expansive vocabulary?), but, I went to my cousin's wedding. The summer went by, and she called me in early August, and asked if I had bought my ticket for the convention which occurred in September, and I had told her that I had not, and she was very adamant that I go, and she told me that you can carpool with us, it's Las Vegas, it's not a far drive, umm, so kind of, at her behest, I bought the ticket (displaying a facial expression that, for a split second, looks like a child who has just tried spinach for the first time), umm, reluctantly".

This warrants some dissection. Let's begin with a few words that The Walking Thesaurus threw out in her breakdown of events. First of all, Jodi says Michelle "invited" her to the last company event. The next time around, Jodi wasn't issued such a cordial invitation; in fact, it sounds like Jodi was coerced by Michelle into attending this event. We've been through this testimony earlier, and Jodi never implied that she felt pressured to attend. She said that when she initially spoke to Michelle on the phone, after Jodi got the PPL information from the California Pizza Kitchen Manager, she was told by Michelle that it was too late to attend the March convention, but that there was plenty of time to register for the September convention (the convention she now says she was strong-armed into attending). She sounded so upbeat about it, that I assumed she booked it without having to reminded by a phone call from Michelle, at the end of the summer. I remember Jodi talking about getting into a car with "two girlfriends" and heading off the Las Vegas. It sounded like a girls' weekend the first time she told the story; now it sounds like she was forced into going).

Adamant? According to Jodi's favorite book (Thesaurus), this means that Michelle was rigid, stubborn, resolute, relentless, hard-nosed, and unshakable when it came to expressing her opinion that Jodi should attend the convention. Does Jodi not know how to deal with an individual who has their eye on your wallet and their ear on a telephone? Simple...you hang up. They hear the click, and there goes all of their huffy-puffy rigidity. Poof.

Behest? Again, referring to Jodi's favorite reference book, we can gain some clarity as to Michelle's demeanor on this phone call. Michelle didn't merely invite Jodi – no, no, no – Michelle demanded, dictated, directed, commanded, and ordered Jodi to attend. Oh, and let's not forget that Jodi gave in, "reluctantly". Reluctantly? So, Jodi packed her bags, and she drove to Las Vegas grudgingly, unwillingly, involuntarily, and unenthusiastically. That's how Jodi ended up at this convention?

There were several other inconsistencies I wish Nurmi would address, but I know he won't. Is

Michelle a girlfriend or a PPL solicitor? In version one, Michelle is simply referred to as one of two girlfriends who took the trip to Las Vegas with Jodi. In version two, Michelle is a telemarketer – someone who managed to toss her headset and crawl through the telephone and plant her ass in the same car Jodi was traveling in – just to make sure that Jodi realized how seriously adamant she was about Jodi's attendance. Secondly, does anyone else believe that a 4.5 hour drive qualifies as "not far"? Maybe I'm just a homebody at heart, but that constitutes a long drive to me. Isn't it amazing that Michelle already figured out that Wheels Arias would classify a 256 mile destination as "not far".

Now Nurmi is going to remind us, for the umpteenth time, that Jodi is working several jobs to cover her mortgage and expenses. He really needs to stop driving home the point that this woman does not earn enough money at one full-time job to support herself. He wants us to see motivation, discipline, and hard work every time he mentions her multiple jobs. Instead, we are beginning to see another picture develop. We see someone who is so lacking in marketable skills and a decent resume, that she needs several low paying jobs to equal what most people earn at one full-time job. Following right along, Jodi answers "Yes, I was going to go back to work at Cuistot (I don't remember hearing about her employment at Cuistot before this moment in the testimony, but it was a $30/entree, French bistro in Palm Desert, featuring either one or five star reviews back in 2006), but it closed in the summer for a few months, and the owners, umm, leave the desert. They umm, they go up to Monterey actually, and they open mid-September, or maybe it's...err...early September, whenever school starts (well, thanks for clearing that up, Jodi. This is, after all, February, 2013, in Mesa Arizona. Knowing which week of September, a small, French restaurant in Palm Desert, California, re-opened in 2006 is very helpful to the escargot deprived jurors. I'm sure they're taking notes), because he had children. So, umm, around that time, the restaurant reopened, and I still had my position (she's using her soft, smooth voice while speaking – and it's never more apparent than when she's drawing out the sound, "umm". She's putting far more thought into this restaurant's seasonal closing than she did when she was asked by the prosecutor to describe Travis Alexander's "linebacker" pose).

Now that we've randomly jumped all over the various months that made up every year from 2001 – 2006 (the Brewer years), Nurmi wants to return to the $10,000 - $12,000 cash that Jodi claims was in the bank, the most money she had ever saved in her life. Can we determine whether it was $10,000 or $12,000? That information has to be readily available, no? Sure it is, but we'll never know. Suffice it to say that if it had been $12,000, we'd be hearing $12,000 - $14,000.

Nurmi has muddied the waters enough to cause every juror to forget where that money went, although if they wrote it down, they probably made a notation that it was used for the purchase of the lost Palm Desert house (which we later found required no down payment). I think a little creative, forensic accounting will be involved in this line of questioning. Wrong. It's just a simple yes or no question, and she answers it that way. Nurmi asks if there was any of that money left by September, 2006. Let's guess, shall we? No? Jodi answers, "No. It was long gone". Nurmi responds, "Okay. So what is your financial situation in September, 2006?" (Juan Martinez has a perfect opportunity to object with "asked and answered", but I assume he's napping. I know the answer to this question. It's been asked three times already).

Jodi answers, "Umm, it's not... it's paycheck to paycheck. Struggling. I mean, we're not out on the street or anything, but I gave up all of the extra things that I liked (oh, now I understand why it was important to put a sad face on that MGM Grand convention trip she took. There was no money for extras, and a reasonable person would ask why she'd spend money on that kind of a trip – a trip we've already learned was at least a $1,400 expense. Now we know. It was all Michelle's fault), umm, Starbucks (why does everyone say Starbucks when talking about budgeting? Geez, just buy a $13 Proctor-Silex and a can of Maxwell House, and stop acting like it's a major sacrifice), just things like that, just little things that would chip away at your monthly income (how about some of the big things? Things that cost more than a strawberry frappucino?). I would... everything was very sparse... just whatever we could to makes ends meet (but they didn't meet, did they?)". Nurmi picks it up, "And, your relationship with Mr. Brewer, is it still going fine or are we at this dead end you were describing (are we going to get hourly updates on their relationship as it existed in 2006?)?

Jodi answers, "Umm, muh... it was sort of something I dreaded because I knew it wasn't going to last, but umm, we hadn't discussed it, I don't know where he was with things. I figured he was kind of in the same realm. Umm, I didn't realize his feelings were as deep for me as what he said on the stand. We had the conversation about a year later, or eight months afterward, and he told me that, umm, which surprised me. Umm, I just kind of figured he was in another place, and I was in another place (she lifts her right hand to signify her place and her left hand to signify his place – which certainly doesn't mean they were "in the same realm". Jodi should stop trying to speak above her pay grade. It gets confusing)".

We are now shown the faces of three tortured souls in the front row of the gallery; young, unlined faces focused on the object of their disdain. Samantha Alexander, rolling her eyes while looking straight ahead. Steven Alexander, wearing a persistent frown that's crowned by eyes that look almost closed. Tanisha Alexander-Sorenson, a, chisel featured, pretty face, wearing an expression that makes her look far more jaded than she would be if Jodi Arias has selected another victim. I suspect their counterparts on the other side of the aisle are either wearing their apathetic, bored faces, or they're all busy digging through bags to find candy or gum to pass around.

Nurmi continues, "Okay, this ticket for this convention, and this was in Las Vegas?" A barely audible "Yes" is heard, but we're still looking at the Alexander siblings . Tanisha brushes back a long lock of hair before Jodi smiles and answers, "Yes, it was held at the MGM Grand". There's a brief pause, perhaps so placed so that we can all marvel at the MGM Grand. Nurmi then asks a question that has been answered more times that I can remember: "So, did you go to this convention?" Does he not remember that this is the location of The Rainforest Cafe? Has he forgotten that this was the place that marked the meeting of Jodi Arias and Travis Alexander?

He asks, "How did you get there?". If I were a juror, I would be insulted. He is rehashing old testimony. I know how she got there, and I know that there were two other women in the car with her. Will we be forced to hear about bathroom stops? Here we go... for the third time (at least): "I drove to Hemet, and parked my car at Michelle's house (Michelle, the adamant PPL solicitor), and we took her – she had a brand new Honda Accord, so it was real spacious, and she, and Lenore (who's Lenore? I'm sure Nurmi will ask), and I, all drove, the three of us carpooled to Las Vegas". Nurmi does ask about Lenore. According to Jodi, she "became" a friend, but this was the first day Jodi met Lenore. Lenore was also a recruit of Michelle's. If Lenore was on the stand talking about Jodi, she'd probably say the same thing – that Jodi was a recruit of Michelle's. So, these are the types of relationships that qualify as "girlfriend" relationships in the mind of Jodi Arias? A telemarketer and a stranger? You couldn't pay me to take this road trip.

Nurmi calls the two "girlfriends" what they actually were: virtual strangers. Jodi says that Michelle was close to her mother's age – maybe a little younger – and that she had texted with Michelle. This made Jodi feel comfortable around her. Then she adds that despite the fact that she didn't know a single person attending this event, Jodi went because she felt she needed to give it, "an honest try".

Nurmi takes Jodi back to the moment she was checking into the MGM Grand. I'm serious. He finds legal merit in talking about the fact that she and her new girlfriends are checking into a hotel. Jodi remembers all of the specifics. She talks about all of the Americans and Canadians – some 12,000 of them – "descending upon the MGM Grand". Now, frugal Jodi, the woman who recently swore off Starbucks in favor of the mortgage, tells us that while everyone didn't necessarily stay at the MGM Grand, she did. She's careful to add a fourth person to the mix, perhaps to send a budgetary signal to the jury. This fourth individual has no name, and she's never mentioned again. Then, Jodi negates that helpful budgetary detail by telling us that while the convention didn't start until Friday evening (and spanned several days), the trio showed up on Wednesday. That must have been one hell of an expensive trip for a woman who couldn't make ends meet. I'm also considering the two jobs that gave her all of this time off. Nice bosses.

Nurmi wants to know what Jodi did after checking in. Will we learn that she went to the bathroom when she entered her room? Will we find out which bed she chose? How about art on the walls? Any input as to what designs were on the bedspreads? Jodi says that they went to their room, relaxed, got lunch, walked around, and got dinner. I'm so glad they got there early. It doesn't sound like they missed a thing. Nurmi wants more relevant information. Did they attend classes or meetings? Jodi answers, "I didn't understand (uncomfortably long pause here), I didn't know what to expect. I'd never been there before. She just told me 'it's going to be a great event, it's going to get you fired up'. Umm, I had never attended a convention, umm, not that kind of convention, so I didn't really know to expect". Nurmi continues, "Okay. (Jodi licks her lips while staring at Nurmi), and how long were you going to be there?". Jodi responds, "Umm, well, we were going to leave Sunday, so five days total".

Nurmi would like to know if that's when the convention ended. Jodi says, "No, my understanding was that it went all day Friday, all day Saturday, and there were smaller team events outside of those". Nurmi asks Jodi if there was a particular team she was supposed to be associated with. Jodi answers, "Umm, Michelle was on Team Freedom, so when she recruited me, that made me Team Freedom. No, I'm sorry (words the Alexander family will never hear from her mouth), I take that back. It was (pause while she's searching for the right word) – Team Renew. There was a lot of different teams in the company. Team Renew was the name".

Well, Jodi, you may have been part of Team Renew back in September, 2006, but today, it's February, 2013, and you're on Team Murder. Well, technically you're on Team Defendant, but we all know you're about to promoted, even with Nurmi "recruiting" you. How are the accommodations at this convention? Are you sharing your room with anyone? Having lunch (in the basement), walking around (in restraints), and having dinner (delivered through a slot in your door)? I have to remind myself that this testimony is all in the past, because she's just having too much fun remembering how important she felt while she was a guest at the MGM Grand (and why do I have a sneaking suspicion that she never made good on her part of the bill that was supposed to be split four ways?).

Nurmi wants us to relax with Jodi Arias, back in September, 2006. How did she relax after checking in? "We walked around a little. We went out to the swimming pool. There were a lot of people there. Uh, I didn't bring a bathing suit, I didn't even think we were...I was thinking business (oh, what? Did she leave her Jennifer Willmott Professional Collection back at the foreclosed house? What is professional wear for Jodi Arias? Black slacks and a white blouse?). So, umm, I felt, umm, I don't know, it was 100 degrees and everyone was out in bikinis, and hanging out in bathing suits, splashing around, so I just didn't – I felt awkward. I was just standing around there in my business clothes (what business clothes?). You know. I was getting introduced to a lot of people. I didn't really keep track of everyone. There were a lot of names".

What was preventing Jodi from buying a bathing suit? She's throwing that credit card around with abandon. Did they not sell Speedos in Las Vegas?

When asked how the quartet killed Thursday, Jodi tells us that they went to dinner at Applebee's. Nurmi isn't satisfied with that answer. Dinner might take a few hours, but what about the rest of the day? Jodi says that they walked around town. They killed time. Did they think of buying bathing suits? Apparently not. Jodi does remember meeting lots of other associates. All of this build up for the big day – Friday! Convention day. Oh, I can't wait. Do you think the girls set an alarm so that they could eat a continental breakfast and get front row seats? Do you think Jodi had to be pulled from her bed? Let's find out!

Jodi's not ready to get to Friday. She wants to interject a discovery she made. She found out that there was a pre-convention dinner on Thursday night. This was the Executive Director Banquet. I'm thinking that the room in which the banquet will be held is the room Jodi will be waiting around as the banquet takes place. She certainly won't be allowed inside – she hasn't earned a single PPL stripe, let alone the gold lapel pin that would grant her access to the big time. Still, I think she lingered on the periphery, whether or not she admits in on the stand.

Now, Nurmi asks a question, but I don't want you to think it actually means we're going to talk about the victim in this case. We've been here before, but Nurmi simply teases us with the mention of the victim's name. So, no promises. Nurmi asks, "While you were at this convention, did you ever meet an individual by the name of Travis Alexander?". She pauses for effect, and if this were a soap opera, there would be that music you'd expect to accompany a big disclosure. Jodi replies, "Yes". Will Nurmi actually pursue this line of questioning, or will he, as he has done each time we get to this point, say "Well, let's back up a little...."? Let's see.

Nurmi keeps his eyes to the floor as he says, "Describe where you were and what was going on when you met Travis Alexander". Jodi responds, "Umm, on Wednesday night, this would be early September, 2006, umm, Michelle and I, Michelle, Lenore and I (she is being very cautious as she speaks), were with her mother, and, I think, two other associates, and we were all sitting around this round table at the Rainforest Cafe, which is inside the casino and the hotel, umm, we were having dinner, and we were finishing up dinner, paid our check, and we left. We didn't leave the Rainforest Cafe, we sort of stayed in this kind of lobby area. I don't know how else to – we were right outside the entrance. Umm, still indoors. And, there's just tons of people everywhere. A lot of them are Prepaid Legal business associates, so I'm just standing close, I'm staying close to Michelle (once again, a gallery shot of the Alexander siblings. Their expressions have not changed, but they are all looking directly at Jodi. I can only imagine what they are thinking as the murderer invokes the name of their brother), because she's the only person I really know. And I'm meeting other people on my team, and she introduced me to people who are in my up line, and things like that. And, umm, there was just a crowd of people everywhere (she lifts her left hand, and with it outstretched, does a circular motion), and, out of the corner of my eye (she takes that flat hand, cups her fingers together, and outstretches her arm to the left, and pulls her hand, incrementally, back to chest) I see somebody walking, toward me, kind of fast paced, and, uh, umm, I noticed it was a guy, and I thought – I thought he was going somewhere because he looked like he had a purpose. So, I stepped out of the way because I thought he needed to walk past me, but he stopped right in front of me, and stuck his hand out (she reenacts the hand motion), and introduced himself". Yes, and?

Nurmi asks, and Jodi affirms, that this was Travis Alexander. Nurmi wants to know "What happened from that point in time". Jodi answers, "Umm, I shook his hand, and tried to just log the name, because there were a lot of people that I was meeting that weekend (oh, let's get this straight from Jump Street. He spotted her. He saw her and immediately knew that she was something he wanted. It was not the other way around. She was just logging his name along with the countless others she had been putting into her ample memory bank. When she found out what his level in PPL was, that's probably when she pulled out the Travis Alexander file for closer inspection), umm, so, we just kind of milled around the edge of The Rainforest Cafe a little longer, and then, our group began to wander throughout the casino – past restaurants, and sports bars, and slot machines, and all those kinds of things". Jodi looks at Nurmi, and he asks, "And you say, your group, does that mean the people you went to the restaurant with?". Jodi answers, "Yes".

Nurmi clarifies for the jury that Travis was not a part of the dinner group at Jodi's table. We already knew that. He does ask if Travis followed her around the casino. She responds, "He did make it a point to walk with us. He was also on, also on, Team Renew, but more like laterally. He was obviously higher, like as executive director (she's taken notice of his rank by now), as far as his position in the company, but, umm, so he knew all these people; he had met them all before. But, as we wandered throughout the casino, he made it a point to walk next to me and keep me engaged in conversation". She looks composed, as if this really didn't impact her. We all know that she was probably hogging the bathroom back in her shared hotel room, later that night. It would be the only place she could privately and gleefully memorialize the way he "walked next to her" in her beloved journal.

Nurmi would like us all to know how this fateful meeting ended. Jodi is ready to provide the answer: "Well, after wandering around, we kind of wandered back to the lobby, where that, there's a big, golden lion statue (she fans her hands out to mimic a lion's mane), and um, we took pictures there of people. And then, umm, after a while, umm, I kind of noticed that I had been ignoring everyone else in the group, and he and I were talking, talking, talking, and at one point, there was a lull in the conversation, and it kind of felt like everyone was staring at us, and so, it was a little awkward. And, so, I sort of began to talk to other people, and umm, we (Nurmi interrupts, Jodi apologizes, but Nurmi tells her to continue), umm, I don't remember how we parted (this was exactly what Nurmi asked), but we just said goodbye, and Lenore, and Michelle, and I just went back to our hotel room. And, I didn't really think anything of that meeting, but I think Lenore pointed out that she thought that (uncomfortable Jodi face and a pause), maybe he liked me, which made me feel differently, I guess, about reflecting on our conversation, because I didn't get that vibe from him".

Why can't she just tell the truth? This part of the testimony doesn't end in anyone having sex or being murdered. In fact, an eighth grade girl would know what it meant if, as Jodi testified, "I noticed he made it a point to walk next to me and keep me engaged in conversation". A ninth grade girl would be able to interpret that awkward silence as a group suddenly became aware that two people were "talking, talking, talking". The fact that Lenore pointed out that "maybe he (Travis) liked me (Jodi)" is such an adolescent reasoning that it makes Jodi look stupid. Please. Every adult woman knows when this is happening.

Nurmi wants to know the context of their next communication. Jodi elaborates, "Well, while Lenore, Michelle, and I were at Applebee's having dinner, Michelle's phone rang, and she answered it, and, I only heard her half of the conversation, and she hung up, and asked me, she told me that Travis wanted to know if I would go the executive director banquet with him". Nurmi and Jodi play a long verbal game that included questions relating to Jodi's understanding of the importance and honor associated with the banquet (no, she needed it all spelled out). Did she realize that Travis was a big league player with PPL (no, she needed it all spelled out), would she go (logistically impossible because it was less than an hour away, on the other side of Las Vegas, plus it was rush hour and the women dressed "to the nines". Remember, according to Jodi, she had only brought business outfits with her). Jodi tells us that she said, "thanks, but no thanks". Nurmi asks if she did attend the banquet, and Jodi says that she did. Let's hear all about Jodi's frantic search for a dress and how she got through the rush hour madness. This should be good.

Jodi says, "Well, after I said, I didn't, after I said no, Michelle was very, she encouraged me (was she adamant?), she said it would be a very good experience for me, umm, there are lots of executives that go that you should meet (i.e., screw). Umm, I think the idea was to get me inspired (i.e., laid), to become more active in the company, and to become more excited about the company, and both Lenore and Michelle were very encouraging, umm, saying that you really should go, this is a very good opportunity, not everyone gets this opportunity. Ahh, so kinda just said, 'okay, well, we gotta find something for me to wear'. So, we ran around town... I think Kohl's was near Applebee's. I didn't know if there were any suitable dresses at that store, but, we went in there, uhh, grabbed a few things off the rack, tried them on, nothing was really working out, so I was thinking I was probably going to call him back – well, actually I did call him right before that and said, 'Okay, I don't have a dress, but I'm going to look for one, and I'll let you know. And, umm, I was in the dressing room in Kohl's, and, umm, by that point he had my cell phone number, and called me and said...".

Thank you! I hear "objection"! I'm beginning to see a pattern with Juan Martinez' objections. You almost forget that the man is in the room. He could have objected on the hearsay rule multiple times, but he seems to wait until Jodi is in the middle of an exciting memory, something she's clearly enjoying, something she's reliving in excruciating detail, some piece of history in which she has all the power, and just as she's approaching the climax of the dialogue, he cuts her off.

Nurmi clearly understands the tactic. He looks noticeably unprepared and deflated as the judge sustains Juan Martinez' well placed objection. Nurmi is barely audible as he asks, "Did you end up buying a dress at Kohl's?". "No," says Jodi. Nurmi looks at the floor as he asks, "Did you end up obtaining a dress to wear to this banquet?" The cadence is broken. We're no longer in the Kohl's dressing room as Jodi's new girlfriends are tossing potential pieces over the dressing room door. We're back where we belong, back in the place the Alexander siblings are forced to be: a court room. It is anticlimactic as Jodi responds, "Yes, his friend packed an extra dress, and she was the same size as me, umm, I guess she heard about his predicament and said that I could wear that dress".

So, we have Jodi Arias, magically dressed up with someplace to go. But then, there's Darryl Brewer. He's waiting back in their home in Palm Desert. Did it ever occur to Jodi to say, "Oh, you do know I'm living with another man, right?" The voice of Jodi Arias, despite her obvious attempts to maintain soft, melodic tones and a volume that invites a frequent reminder to "speak up" or "pull the microphone closer", absolutely sets my teeth on edge. Scientists theorize that certain sounds disturb us. They point to infants screaming, nails on a black board, a knife on a glass, and styrofoam squeaking as the highest rated culprits. They have several theories as to why those sounds are so offensive to the human ear, but before they finish their research and render a final opinion, I want them to add one more sound: the courtroom voice of Jodi Arias. Her enunciation of consonants, the heaving clicking of "t" and "k" sounds, and the drawn out "s" sound that stops short of qualifying as a hiss, are all serious irritants. Her voice didn't bother me when she was undergoing seven hours of interrogation with Detective Flores, but now, all polished up and practiced, it infuriates me. How dare this raging murderer try to sound so controlled, so hypnotic, so life-coachy.

We're back to the big convention of September, 2006. Nurmi asks, "Did you find it strange that Mr. Alexander was asking you to this banquet, after only meeting him the day before?". Jodi looks down, and then turns to the jury, "I didn't really think of it as strange, umm, I think the whole week was strange (she flops her hands out in front of her, and they rest palm side up. That disfigured finger on her left hand makes so many appearances in this trial, I think it deserves its own exhibit number)...it wasn't really what I was accustomed to, so I was just going with the flow." I'm wondering if the jurors are catching all of this vital information. When they have an opportunity to drop their juror questions in the basket, will they ask about the trip to Kohl's to find a dress, or will they ask if she had oral sex with Travis Alexander the night before he invited her the prom? Hey, that's what I'd ask. Moving right along...

Jodi continues, "After we realized that there was a dress at the hotel, we dropped everything at Kohl's (I'm taking that "dropped" quite literally. Why would Jodi Arias care if some dressing room attendant making $8/hour had to go through the pile of pieces that Jodi and her new friends dumped on the dressing room counter as they flitted out of the store? What difference does it make to the homecoming princess that all of the pieces were, undoubtedly, inside out, and the hangers were left in the dressing room? None at all. Cinderella was going to the ball!). We hopped in the car, got on the freeway, and it was very slow traffic, but we just made it all the way back to the MGM Grand (she's using her left hand, disfigured finger featured prominently, to show us what traffic jams look like when they happen on your hands). We rushed to the hotel room where the dress was, and umm, I changed, and Travis and I, Travis met me there, met Michelle and me there, and we walked across the complex over to the ballroom where the banquet hall was being held. I'm sorry, where the banquet was being held, in the ballroom". Nurmi wants to know where Travis was able to secure a dinner dress for Jodi. Jodi answers, "Umm, his friend's wife, Sky Hughes". The next few interchanges are of no consequence. Did you know Sky Hughes? Did you know Chris Hughes? Was Travis in your hotel room when you were getting ready? No. No. Yes.

Nurmi would like a playback of the evening's events. Jodi pauses, and then responds, "It was uh, it was nah, it was nice. I was somewhat accustomed to that level of dining because of my server experience, but I was always a server, not a guest, and I was just very familiar with how the courses run, and table etiquette, and that sort of thing (wow, do you have to be a genuine server to know how the courses run? I must be a natural talent). So, that didn't move me a lot, but what was interesting was all of these people that were there and um, how successful they all were, and that kind of opened my eyes to the reality that you can really be successful in this company, and it's just not some fly-by-night or any kind of get rich quick scheme, or, things like that."

So, are we to believe that Jodi Arias failed to do her due diligence (that's a big PPL phrase) before she parted with more than $1,000 to cover registration, travel expenses, and accommodations?

Did it not occur to her that perhaps she had better do some research on this company before ditching her two jobs for a week? Was she already in so deep that another credit card charge for a dinner dress was of no consequence? Was all of this money lost worth being designated a member of "Team Renew"? There are easier and far less expensive ways to make these determinations, and none of them require parting with a dime. I wonder, does Nurmi think the jury will not see her flawed logic – her lies? While she was rambling about Kohl's, did a single one of them write the name Darryl Brewer and put a question mark after it? Reduced to the truth, her own testimony tells us that this whole expensive convention was a gamble, hardly a sure thing. I'm also wondering if she would have been so enlightened if she hadn't flirted her way into an executive banquet that she certainly had no business attending. I think not.

I am also amused at her response when asked to describe the banquet. The words, halting though they may be, are right. Her tone of voice? Wrong. Her facial expression? Wrong. "It was uh, it was nah, it was nice." Jodi Arias, Applebee's waitress and Ventana Inn server, knows her way around a restaurant of any caliber, and she clearly wasn't all that impressed. After all, she knows all about this "level" of dining (banquet hall food and fine dining are two different experiences, but since she will forever be relegated to experiencing slop delivered through a slot in a metal door with chipped paint, why educate her now?).

When Jodi claimed that she was familiar with table etiquette, I got a mental flash of her in her big, orange jumpsuit sitting in the interrogation room while writing a letter to Travis' grandmother, Norma Sarvey. The detective brought her a paper bag with a sandwich inside, and I was absolutely mortified by the way she ate that sandwich. She pulled it apart, put huge chunks of food in her mouth at one time, and even pulled chewed up food out of her mouth. I have an image of her tilting her head back, and dropping the pieces of food into her gaping mouth, but maybe that's just the way my mind summed it up. One thing is accurate, she looked like a chimpanzee. Table etiquette? She eats like a drunken man.

Nurmi suggests that Jodi was getting "intoxicated" by all of the success around her. I assume she'd find a better word than "intoxicated", because if anyone is going to pull out a big word, it will be Jodi. True to form, she answers, "I don't know if 'intoxicated' would quite be right (left hand on display again), but it definitely made a big impression on me". Nurmi wants details, and Jodi provides them: "Umm, it stuck out in my mind, Travis also challenged me, he said every person you take to the executive banquet....".

Juan's voice pierces the monotonous droning with, "Objection, hearsay". Before Judge Stephens can even rule on the objection, Nurmi drops his pen on the podium and asks, "May we approach, your honor?" Why, of course they can, and they do.

We see the Alexander siblings again. I always run past each face quickly, and then I stop to study their expressions. This time, it's different. The look on Samantha Alexander's face grabs me; it's a face that can only be described as controlled rage. She looks like a statue, her arms folded across her chest, her eyes focused directly on Jodi, and it is conceivable to believe that one movement, no matter how slight, would release that rage. Steven looks more sad than angry; he reminds me of a young man bearing up bravely at a funeral. Tanisha's icy stare is broken by her husband, who reaches out his arm toward his wife and whispers in her ear.

There is an extended pause here because of the sidebar. Jodi will not look at the Alexander siblings. She drops her head to the right, and she pretends that there is something interesting happening on the floor beneath her huge feet. The pause goes on, but Jodi will not give Samantha the satisfaction of looking at her. Jodi's stillness is finally broken by lifting her left hand, extending it, and playing with her fingers. Yes, Jodi, the jury saw your crooked finger.

Keeping up tradition, the defendant's side of the gallery has a new face of sophistication on which to focus. Directly behind Sandy Arias sits a rather obese, white haired man in a too tight blue shirt. He stares directly across the aisle at the Alexander family while scratching his bulbous gut. He apparently has forgotten about the television cameras. Then, he lets out a huge yawn – without covering his mouth, and proceeds to put his sneakers on his lap. All class, this group.

Finally Jodi's eyes are up, but she goes right past the gallery and focuses on her Hercules, Kirk Nurmi. "Miss Arias, did people at this banquet encourage you to become more involved in PrePaid Legal, umm, more involved in PrePaid Legal? Jodi looks up before answering, "Yes." She nods her head as she says it. I assume the sidebar was to determine whether or not Nurmi was allowed to single out Travis Alexander as the encourager, when actually, we all know that the entire convention has one objective: psyche people out with stories of wealth and success, only possible through deeper commitment to PrePaid Legal. Travis was doing his job, and Jodi was certainly aware of how this system worked, and if she wasn't, she's too stupid to get dressed by herself.

Now that Nurmi has established the foundation of his question, he is free to point to one individual: Travis Alexander. He asks if Travis was "one of those people" who encouraged her to become more involved. Jodi responds, "Yes, he encouraged me the most, of everybody." Jodi's demeanor suggests that she was being "encouraged" to join an international drug smuggling ring. Was there a single person at that event who was not being "encouraged" to become more involved? Why isn't pushy Michelle being mentioned? It was Michelle, after all, who told Jodi that the whole point of this event was to "fire her up". Bad Travis. Bad, bad Travis.

There is now talk of what it means to be an executive director at PPL, rings that are given out to people who make $100K a year, the fact that Travis didn't have a ring, but he did qualify for tickets to the banquet, blah, blah, blah. I'm wondering if I'm watching a murder trial or a PPL recruiting video. Just as I'm wondering about that, the camera focuses on Sandy Arias, and I am even more convinced that we're watching some propaganda video. She is in the front row, chatting, and laughing. The Alexanders are so tense they can hardly breathe, and the Arias family look like they're ready to kick their shoes off.

Jodi tells us all about the gold rings. One diamond, two diamonds, three diamonds, Yay! Beyond the talk of diamonds, she was also entertained by all the speeches given by those who used to be unsuccessful losers, but who were now enjoying lifestyles of the rich and famous. This is the stuff of those typical, late night infomercials that flooded the television landscape in the late 1990's. Are we seriously going to be subjected to tales of vacations, cruises, larger homes, second homes, sports cars, college educations for the kids, and banks vying for your business? Yes, I think we are.

Oh, before we learn why it is more fun to be rich than it is to be poor, Nurmi wants to know if all of the high roller talk was resonating with Jodi – you know, poor, broke, impoverished, losing her house, no more Starbucks, Jodi -- Jodi, circa September, 2006? "Yes", says Jodi.

Jodi begins, "Umm, their lifestyle, they no longer struggled with the, the impression I got, they no longer worried about paying the bills (so? neither did Jodi), they...(halting answer)...umm, no longer worried about where their money would come from (that kind of falls under the category of not worrying about how they're going to pay the bills, but, please, expound, Jodi Arias)...they were more concerned with things of a higher nature, I guess you could say (what?)...ahh, philanthropy, they could turn around and bless now that they've been blessed...(she is hemming and hawing)...and constructive ways they can now use their income to better society". Done. What was Jodi Arias doing at that banquet? Was she listening at all, because that was an easy question, and it shouldn't have caused her to stop and start and reach for answers. I bet she wasn't listening. She was probably scanning the room for diamond studded, gold rings while simultaneously playing under the table with her date's suit pants (all by accident, of course. Well, actually, it's going to happen soon...she later admits to Juan Martinez that the first time she had "oral intercourse" with Travis was one week after that convention).

Nurmi wants to know if philanthropy, the betterment of society – you know – things of a higher nature, also spoke to Jodi Arias. Oh yes, of course. And why shouldn't we believe that? Just forget the little man behind the curtain, that Darryl Brewer guy; he's nobody important, as he calls his ex-wife and admits that it all went to shit in a year. Really, he means nothing, and neither does Jodi's half of the mortgage. After all, she has all of society to better.

Nurmi wants to know what happened after the banquet. Well, it was photo-op time! Everybody walked around in their finery, grouping up, and taking photographs of each other. Jodi was important enough to be included in those pictures, all of them with executive directors, she's careful to add, because, I guess, once a PPL executive qualifies for banquet tickets, they also qualify to pose their "never earned a penny for the company or themselves" dinner date in photos of the event. Then, Jodi says, they went back to hotel room, and she changed out of her borrowed dress and into normal clothes. She says she picked up no "romantic vibes" from Travis, but she did notice that he was trying to impress her. How did she know that? Well, Jodi, the astute reader of all social cues, said that while Travis was talking about income levels while encouraging someone else, he was saying it "very loud" so she could hear it, too. Wow. Hot stuff for the journal entry tonight!

Nurmi would like to know if Travis told Jodi about his family, his life, or his work history. She replied, "He didn't talk about his family (of course he did, but it's more fun to let the people staring you down think they didn't really matter to Travis), but the night before, he said he was from Riverside (her voice is becoming softer, more childlike, more grating, and even Nurmi says he can't hear her), he told me he was a Forty-Niners fan (oh no! She just remembered Darryl, the guy who paid for her to go to the Forty-Niner games), which I kind of didn't believe because he was from southern California and most people like the Chargers in that area (did she really just say that?), umm, but it had to do with Steve Young, who was a member of the church, and he was a good quarterback (oh, so his affinity for the Forty-Niners had nothing to do with Jodi's feigned interest in the Forty-Niners – it was about a Mormon sports hero). He asked me about the UFC, it was an interest he had, and I was familiar with it, somewhat...it's an acronym for Ultimate Fighting Championship...it's cage fighting, no holds barred (so, the demure Miss Arias does know what a real body slam looks like)."

Now that we've segued into the church, Nurmi wants to know if Travis "conveyed his faith" to Jodi that evening. She replied, "Not that evening. We went to convention on Friday. He had invited me to sit down on the floor where the executive directors sit (I guess Jodi's "business attire" was acceptable for this event), it's just a bunch of chairs set up, but it's closer to the stage, instead of stadium seating (Yes, megalomaniac, we all what that means. It is completely unnecessary to remind us that you were not sitting with the plebes, where you belonged. I bet she was making enemies already)." Nurmi wants more details about this event. Jodi answers, "Yes. It was Friday morning. I had a ticket, but it was several seats up. It was with Michelle, and, umm, I got a text message from him saying there was an open seat down here if you want to sit closer to the stage". It would have been nice to offer that ticket to middle-aged Michelle. She did bring two new recruits in, and she had a history with the company; but, no, no, it's far more important that the Platinum Parasite be able to turn around in her orchestra seat and wave wildly to her chauffeur in the stadium seats.

I think everyone over the age of nine realizes that Jodi was given a special, undeserved privilege. That type of thing bothers people, so I would have left this topic quickly. They've made their point. Nurmi, however, wants to grind it in some more; maybe he will have Jodi describe the seat she was sitting in. I assume the point of all of this is to prove that Travis Alexander exerted a Svengali like hold over the sensitive, blond recruit from Palm Desert.
Nurmi asks, "And from your understanding, it sounds like this would be an area, an area in which you wouldn't be able to otherwise sit". Jodi answers, "Yes, you needed a special pass (or perhaps, a special ass) to get into that area". Point made again. Nurmi asks, "Do you know why?". Jodi answers, "Umm, it's reserved for executive director's only (how many times have they said this?), so, you have to be qualified for that position in order to get into that area".

I fear that we will be forced to relive an entire event I would have walked out of. Jodi begins, "I decided to make my way down...I don't remember how I got there...I think he made his way toward me, and, umm, he took me over to where the seat was, and I went and sat down there, and the event starts with the National Anthem (at least it wasn't "Oh, Holy Night"), and then the Canadian National Anthem, because they represent, the company is in both countries, ummm, and then different things just get started. There's, it's kind of mixed up, there's training, entertainment, so it's like, it's not entertainment, it's like speeches (how does one confuse speeches for entertainment?). They use the term, "entertrainment" (oh, I know who these people are...please, somebody take my seat!), it's entertaining trainment (hahaha – Jodi said "trainment"), umm, training. Enter...(and then, quite unbelievably, she laughs, she actually laughs, not a stifled giggle, but a laugh)...do you know what I'm saying?" She is alone in her laughter, and she's still smiling ear to ear as she says, "It's entertaining training, I guess you could say".

Jodi Arias -- look straight ahead of you – right in front of your eyes. Do you see those three haunted faces? Are those people laughing? Are they smiling? Are they even visibly breathing? I guess that special seat has put her in a great mood.

Jodi is on the witness stand, seeing the lighter side of things – laughing about the tongue twisting, non-word that combined the two areas of entertainment and training (hey, I've got one! How about finding a word that describes an aberrant defendant...a defaberrant! Hey, I've got the skills to start my own multi-level marking firm!).

She says, "We just did these, I mean, watched these speeches and, um, that kind of thing." Before we get to Nurmi's response to having heard his client laughing while testifying at her own murder trial, can we talk about Jodi's note taking at this convention? Did she just say that she was taking notes in her journal? Her journal? Isn't her journal the sacred book? Isn't this where she talks

about things like naughty fantasies, fruitful imaginations, and loving Travis Alexander as much as she loves the gospel? I know those specific entries came after the convention in question, but isn't it reasonable to assume that she had some other personal entries in that journal? Maybe there were entries about Darryl. Maybe there were personal musings. I'm not convinced that it is typical to bring a personal journal to a business meeting or a conference. That type of journal would not be a personal journal – it would be a day planner or professional journal. The only type of work notes Arias was used to taking fit neatly onto a preprinted food order pad. For a foray to a convention she reluctantly attended, does it make sense for her stop and purchase a new journal for business note taking? I think she took her own journal – her personal journal.
By her estimation, this convention was attended by 10,000 people. Hotels rooms were not private. So, in this situation, who would bring their personal journal with them? It is so easy to speculate when it comes to Jodi Arias, and at this point, it's easy to imagine her leaving her journal sitting on her convention chair while dashing away to get a few good photos of her new friends – leaving Travis just enough time to check the prior evening's entry to see if Jodi wrote anything about him. I don't think he was the type to read someone's journal, but we know she doesn't not respect the privacy of other people. She would seize that type of opportunity, so, it conceivable she believes others would do the same.

Back to court. Nurmi realizes how inappropriate his client's laughing response was, and he has to find some way to make her reaction palatable to the jury. He says, "What were these, and I'm not going to even try to repeat the word, because I'm sure I'd butcher it, but this entertainment/training, what was that, from your perspective, designed to do?". Composure has been regained as Jodi responds, "Um, it's designed tooooo (she does the inverted steeple gesture with her fingers) – well, you get more training. Sometimes there are new products that they roll out (how would she know what they "sometimes" do – this is her first event, ever), and they train on that, but at the same time, it is designed to not be boring, so it's something that you're usually riveted to (again, isn't it a little early for her to define "usually"). Um, there's a lot of note taking. Some people just come out and rally up the crowd. They're very good speakers, um, they have a lot of energy, um, the ring speeches, that were heard the night before, are also said on stage again, so that all the associates that were unable to attend the banquet also get to hear those speeches. They are generally very inspiring, because they are success stories".

Allow me to interrupt. Did she really just say that the "ring speeches were said on stage again" so that all the associates who "weren't able to attend the banquet" got to hear them? Forgive me, but who wants to hear those kinds of speeches? What, if anything at all, is interesting about plateau tokens when you haven't earned a single dollar with the company? You get a gold ring if you earn \$100K. Earn 150K, get a diamond in the ring. Earn \$300K, get a second diamond in the ring. Earn \$500K, get a third diamond in the ring. Let's be honest, for most of the people attending that convention, \$100K is no different than \$500K, because it's never going to happen, without a lottery win.

Here sits the most unqualified PPL "associate" in the MGM Grand, telling the jury that the other associates, those who were "unable to attend" the banquet, are happy to get a few nuggets from the king's table the next day. Those other associates weren't "unable" to attend the banquet, they weren't "allowed" to attend. My purpose is not to slam PPL, but to highlight the charade of this direct examination. This is obviously a typical multi-level marketing tactic, and Arias took to it like a duck to water.

If PPL is hitting me as a pyramid scheme, how is it hitting the jurors? If PPL is hitting me as an organization with some blurred lines between business and group-think, how is it hitting the jurors? They use phraseology that includes "because we've been blessed, we're free to bless others", and that's getting a little too far away from the black and white of balance sheets and into the gray tones of spirituality. I'm getting the impression that this is one of countless organizations that prey upon the desperate dreamer as well as those who are grabbing at any straw as they circle the drain. If I'm feeling that way about PPL, what is the jury thinking? Does it even matter to them?

The jurors were selected because they are "reasonable people" Therefore, they may be thinking what I'm thinking, or something very close to it. What does all of this say about the man who devoted his life to such a company? What does it say about a man who worked to bring people in to labor beneath him so that he could continue to attend banquets and earn gold rings? It says that he's getting toward the top tier of a pyramid organization. This extensive PPL testimony is designed to paint Travis Alexander as an exploiter. It may be a subconscious thought, but the seeds are being planted.

I am basing everything I know about PPL on a few Youtube videos I saw, some very negative reviews of their service, and Jodi Arias. My point is not to demean Travis Alexander. All of us work for someone, and worked for PPL – but he did work. My issue is that the defense is painting PPL as a predatory organization, with Travis moving up the food chain. I've come to the conclusion that even if this is the case, what difference does it make in terms of June 4, 2008? They were doing nothing illegal.

Nurmi continues, "And is this meeting in this large facility, is this something that lasts all day?". Jodi replies, "Yes, we start, I don't remember the time, we start somewhat mid to early morning (that would be early to mid-morning), go for lunch, break for lunch, and then come back in the afternoon, until late afternoon".

Another thing I just noticed is that Jodi continues to use the pronoun "we" instead of "they", and she has not deviated from that. Wow, powerful mind control going on over there at PPL. Here she sits, accused of murdering one of the rising stars in the PPL organization, and she still considers herself one of them. I doubt the feeling is mutual.

Nurmi asks the next logical question: Did Jodi have lunch with Travis that afternoon? She answers,

"No, that day I didn't. I went to get sushi with Michelle". Sushi? Expensive taste for a lady in foreclosure and holding down a server's job. Is there anything wrong with a chain restaurant? For a woman who gave up Starbucks, sushi seems to be a budget buster. Secondly, why do I feel that Michelle was a Plan B? I think Travis wanted to have lunch with someone else – perhaps a new recruit, someone he could "encourage". I can also guarantee that Jodi wanted to have lunch with Travis (Plan A), but had to settle for Michelle (Plan B). Whatever my opinion of PPL, I know the man was serious about doing his job. Jodi may have been fine for banquet time, but I think he tended to travel more in his own circle during lunch.

Nurmi wants us to know that not having lunch with Travis does not mean that Jodi had lost her good seat on the main floor. She says she returned to her seat after lunch on Friday, and continues, "I think he invited me one more time after that (she looks confused, and, once again, is spinning her hands), so, after that, I just stayed in that seat until the end of the convention". Nah...he didn't invite her a second time. Her entire face changed when she said that. She was jumpy. Her brow was furrowed. No, I'm not buying it. I think she just made sure that she got their early every day to take the seat before Travis could offer it to a worthy recruit. He'd be gentleman enough not to ask her to get up.

Nurmi restates the obvious: Jodi spent the "entire two days" sitting next to Travis in the front row seat. A close up of Juan Martinez shows a man who is fatigued; he's rubbing his eyes. Despite the fact that his glasses are slightly askew, he still looks sharp. Why can't we just fast forward to him? He's wearing a great suit, but I know we'll never see that suit in action – at least not today.

Now Nurmi wants to know if Travis took Jodi to dinner on Friday night. I'm going to guess that he didn't. Jodi answers, "No, not Friday night, we didn't. I don't really remember Friday night, actually." (Oh, right...she doesn't remember Friday night? I bet she was in some part of the hotel kicking holes in walls because two possible meal dates with Travis had come...and gone). Jodi takes a deep breath as Nurmi asks her to talk about Saturday night. She responds, "Okay. Saturday, I was again getting lunch with Michelle (Burn! Three meals have now gone by). We started texting each other, sort of back and forth. By this point, I, it was pretty clear, that he liked me, more than friends; he wasn't being overtly flirtatious, but he was being very friendly, and um, I decided that, well, Michelle had told him that I had a boyfriend...". I knew the objection was coming (the hearsay objection). Jodi was just starting to get that pink flush on her face, she was warming up to the memory, and she was going to want to drag this out. Good Juan, she doesn't deserve it.

Oh, and as long as there's an objection on deck, can I ask if anyone believes that it would be "pretty clear" that someone had a romantic interest in you if, after sitting next to you for a full day and a half, they had obviously passed up three opportunities to ask, "Hey, wanna grab something to eat?". I'm also interested in this "we started texting back and forth". When? It couldn't have been Friday night; Jodi can't remember Friday night. Maybe it was while they were sitting next to each other at the convention. No, I doubt it. I think it happened while Jodi was crying in her California Roll at the sushi bar and Michelle, in an exasperated tone, said, "just text him". I think Jodi is the one who made it clear that she liked Travis "as more than friends". I can't blame him for taking her up on her offer. I suspect that's where we're going, but she's going to change things around a little, and since there's no one alive, beyond Arias, who can tell us what really happened, we'll have to consider the source as we listen to the tale.

Thank you, Juan Martinez. He has such a way of dumping cold water onto Jodi's best memories, and he does it every time he sees the temperature rising – and I thought he was fading just a few seconds ago. Nurmi is forced to interject something that is as welcome in this dialogue as your mother would be on your honeymoon – Darryl Brewer. Nurmi has to ask, "Did you have a boyfriend at this time?". Jodi answers, "Yes, I was still with Darryl". Nurmi goes on, "Did you know, to your understanding, was Mr. Alexander aware of the fact that you had a boyfriend?" Boyfriend? How about live-in-lover/ co-borrower on an bundled mortgage? That's a little stronger than "boyfriend".

Jodi replies, "Yes, he was aware". How do we know that? Nurmi will now prove it to us by eliciting from his client the ways in which Travis gave her "the sense" that he was interested in her in ways that extended beyond the realm of the professional (can we start with the obvious – because she wasn't a professional? How's that?). Jodi answers, "Umm, he was texting me after the banquet (wait, the banquet's over? Was there a Saturday dinner? A Sunday lunch? Did they go anywhere alone together?), and he said really nice things. According to Jodi, Travis said, "You're a great girl". Beyond that, he was "friendlier and friendlier, but not inappropriate. But after I learned that he already knew I had a boyfriend and he continued to act that way, I thought it would be, I thought I needed to pull him aside and tell him that I had a boyfriend, so that he didn't get the wrong impression from me". The wrong impression? The problem, from the genesis of their relationship, is that he got the right impression of Jodi Arias.

Who do Nurmi and Arias think they're talking to? What day are we talking about. I've seen several opportunities for a budding romance to take root, and so far, Travis has taken none of them. Where is he getting friendlier and friendlier? Text messages? In the lobby of the hotel? And now, she starts talking about giving "the wrong impression"? She's already testified to the fact that she dropped everything at dinner on Thursday night, drove like a madwoman to a department store to find a dress to wear to a dinner that a man she met just hours earlier invited her to attend – at the last possible moment -- and NOW she's worried about a wrong impression? No. She was not worried about first impressions.

Nurmi wants some information about this heart to heart Jodi had with Travis. Jodi tells us it was at dinner on Saturday night. Do, they did have dinner in the same restaurant on of Saturday night – just don't forget to factor in the entire population of Team Renew. Their group was so large, they required an entire floor of The Rainforest Cafe. Heart to heart conversation at a private table for two – a nice little table in the back with a votive candle illuminating both of their faces?

Things are getting murky here. Jodi says that everyone had dinner together. Then, everyone hung out in the food court (good times), then, well, then Jodi needs to back up. She admits that she texted Travis earlier in the day to tell him that she needed to talk to him privately – when the time was appropriate. Apparently, the appropriate time was while everyone was hanging out in the food court after dinner. Jodi claims Travis said that if she needed to talk with him, they could go for a walk. I guess Travis must have been VERY concerned about this important personal conversation Jodi had previously arranged via text, because he waited until 1:00 AM to actually have the conversation (after being in her general vicinity all evening long). Now, that's a strong sign of romantic interest, I'll give her that. I'm actually wondering, has this woman ever been genuinely pursued – by anyone?

Let's hear it from the horse's mouth. She remembers that the casino was open, but the stores were closed. Arias claims that they wandered toward the closed stores and, "...I told him I liked him, but I'm in a relationship. I explained a little bit about the state of my relationship (what was the word Nurmi used to described it? Oh, that's right – dead end). I didn't go into a lot of detail, I just (she's warming up again, I can see it) – I didn't go into a lot of detail. I just said I wasn't sure where it was going, but he's my boyfriend. That's what I said".

Prepare yourself for a gem from the mouth of the Banquet Princess. She said she told Travis, "I'm monogamous. I'm with Darryl, so I'm with Darryl. I'm not with anybody else". Nurmi wants to know how Travis responded to this devastating news. Jodi is happy. Her chests moves up and down, her face is flushed, and she's smiling as she says, "He smiled. He was aware that that's what I – well, he assumed that's what I was going to talk to him about and, um, so at that point, it was clear. I thought, and I was able to relax a little more and be friends and we found a park bench (because right after you say you're monogamous to a guy you have your eye on, you find a park bench at 1:00 AM to talk about what great friends you're going to be). We sat down, and just ended up talking for a few more hours, just about everything".

Now, after sitting with a someone all through the night on a park bench, talking about everything, what would give the PPL predator (Travis) the impression that it was acceptable for him to give the monogamous PPL recruit an opinion as to how she should handle her boyfriend? Oh, we know that he did so because Nurmi just asked her if that came up during their all night talk. Juan objected to the question, but the judge allowed Jodi to answer the question. She answered, "Yes". Nurmi wants to know if Travis told Jodi that she shouldn't settle for a life with Darryl (although I doubt Jodi made it clear she had already come to that decision – all those pheromones must have been clouding her mind). Jodi answers, "Yes".

So, how did Travis know that she was settling for anything? After all, Jodi said she gave no details. This is so transparent. Just as I'm wondering if Jodi is going to say he moved in to kiss her, Nurmi changes the topic to religion. Did Travis share his faith with her? Yes, says Jodi, the topic did turn to religion. Now Michelle is made to look like an unkind person. You remember Michelle, right? She was the lady who really encouraged Jodi to go to this banquet with Travis? Well, as it turns out, Michelle "warned" Jodi that Travis was a Mormon. She repeated it twice. According to Jodi, "she said it as a warning". Jodi didn't really understand why she was being warned about Mormonism. As far as she knew, it was just another Christian denomination.

Jodi continues, "...I mean, I'd heard about Mormonism over the years. Mormonism is the butt of a lot of jokes on South Park, and some people just seem very antagonistic towards Mormons, um...". Enough already. What perfect timing. Guess what happens next? Objection. Beyond the scope of the question. The objection is sustained.

Nurmi wants to know if Jodi had any concerns about being around Travis because he was a Mormon. She answers, "No. Not at all. Someone's religion doesn't affect that at all". Isn't she politically correct? The only time someone's "undefined spiritual beliefs" really matter to Jodi Arias is if they are those of a former boyfriend/psychiatric patient who used to believe in vampires. If that happens, all bets are off. Just yesterday, Arias explained that she contacted Bobby Juarez because she got information (at the diner) the second coming of Christ was scheduled for September 23, 1997. At that point, religion didn't just matter – religion was everything. It wasn't just everything, it was the excuse she needed to call her ex-boyfriend, Bobby Juarez (while she was dating her international boyfriend, Victor Arias). She had to call Bobby Juarez, someone who had been free of Arias for 18 months, just so he could make a decision for himself. She never told the jury what the decision was, but she made it clear that it was one of eternal significance. Now, a day later, Arias is pretending that someone's spiritual beliefs don't matter to her. Okay. Moving right alone.

According to Arias, Travis didn't proselytize, but he "implied" it. He didn't kiss her "on the bench", leading us to wonder where he did kiss her. Upon further questioning, we learn he didn't actually kiss her at all, but she claims he wanted to. Lower the lights, turn up the saxophone, and picture it – he leaned in close, was licking his lips, and staring at her lips. But at the end of the day – or the beginning of the next day, as the case may be – no kiss and no conversion. But he wanted to. He really, really wanted to. We know that's true because the woman who killed him three times said it's true.

Will he or won't he? Does she or doesn't she? Let's find out.

We're are on the park bench at the MGM Grand. This park bench isn't in a park. Instead, it's inside a big mall, in a big hotel, in a big city. Following the time line Jodi has presented, Saturday night has turned into Sunday morning, and I'm assuming the big hand was on the twelve and the little hand was on the four (shameful), as their friendly conversation was drawing to a close. Soon, there would be no professional reason for Travis Alexander to ever converse with Jodi Arias again. It was time for Jodi to pull out all the stops – the low cut gown didn't do it, the platinum blond hair didn't do it, the flirtatious laugh didn't do it, the "I'm an empty vessel – fill me up" act didn't do it, and Michelle certainly hadn't helped by exposing Jodi's living situation (even if Jodi didn't tell us how damaging that was, we can all infer that this was not information she wanted disclosed to Travis). Nurmi parks us right in front of this odd couple who happen to meet on life's road as she is losing and he is winning. It's a shame that this wasn't the sum total of their relationship; two ships that passed in the night – a sleek, speed boat filled with people laughing and having fun and The SS Minnow, a typically docked vessel bound for a shipwreck on an unchartered desert isle. Unfortunately, it's just the beginning.

Nurmi asks, "Did he express a desire for you to learn more about his faith?". Jodi purses her lips, looks down, and pretends to actually think before answering, "No, um, he, not – he implied it (hands flopping in front of her, again), but he didn't openly start proselytizing or anything". So, the woman who knew nothing of the Mormon faith is familiar with the word proselytizing? In any event, we can assume the rabid Mormon was not willing to take on the complicated conversion of a bleached blond mess named Jodi Arias at an professional convention. Nurmi continues, "During this conversation, at the bench, in the MGM, did he ever attempt to kiss you?" Arias responds, "Not there on the bench, no". Nurmi continues, "But he did that night?". Arias is looking down while she says, "He leaned in very close, as if he wanted to kiss me, and he's licking his lips, and he was staring at my lips, and, like he wanted to kiss me, but – he didn't". Well, wasn't that a whole lot of build up to absolutely nothing? Notice that, according to Jodi, Travis was the only one showing outward signs of passion. Licking his lips? Staring at her lips? Well, if he was, it was probably because she was massaging them with her tongue. Unfortunately, his lips stopped moving almost seven years ago, so we'll never know. I suppose this is a lead-up to more sex talk on the defense agenda.

Nurmi asks, "And where did this occur?". Where did what occur? Her last words were "he didn't". So, there was no kiss. How could Jodi have an answer as to where something didn't happen? She says, "On the elevator". Wait a minute, are we talking about Travis staring at her lips or licking his lips? Where is he going with this?

Nurmi asks, "How close to you did he get?". Jodi responds, "Um, well, we got onto the elevator...". Wait! She forget to say that they pushed the elevator button! Doesn't Nurmi think it's important that the jury know which one of them actually pushed the elevator button? Every detail of the event that didn't happen is critical testimony.

Juan Martinez interrupts with, "Objection. Beyond the Scope. She was asked how close he was standing next to her on the elevator". I love the way he interrupts them, but by now, I know the drill. We're going to move into reverse to get back to where we are now.

The objection is sustained, and Nurmi, much to my surprise, just asks the same question again. Jodi is now being forced to answer the question, despite the fact that she really wanted to take that elevator ride one more time. She says, "Um, he got right in my face (there's a pause, and even Nurmi isn't filling it in). I'd say four inches, maybe five".

Nurmi moves on in his effort to make Jodi a victim. When referring to the close proximity of Travis Alexander and Jodi Arias in the elevator, Nurmi asks, "And this wasn't forced based on the size of the elevator, right?". She's quick to answer, "No. The elevator was empty." As Nurmi is saying his customary, "Okay", she interrupts and adds, "At one point, there was someone else who stepped on, but...". Nurmi continues, "A large elevator?", and Jodi answers, "Yes". Nurmi repeats, "And he got within four inches of your face?". Martinez objects, but it is barely audible. It is also overruled. I had to remind myself that he never actually kissed her. How are they making this look so deviant?

She has the demeanor of someone who's urging rape victims to come forward. I have to remind myself that just days from now, she will be revealed as a liar of monumental proportion. When Juan Martinez cross examines her, he will not be concerned with this elevator ride. Four inches or five? He won't care. He's going to ignore this nonsense and go for the jugular. For now, we are stuck in this box of lies, and it is getting cramped. I sense it's also about to get ugly.

Jodi is about to elaborate about her elevator ride. She puts her arms out, as if she's hugging an imaginary person in front of her, and she says, "Yes, he put his..". Juan Martinez objects. Beyond the scope. The objection is sustained. Nurmi rebounds and asks, "Once he got within four inches of your face – with his face, is that right?". A meek Jodi responds, "Yes". Nurmi continues, "Once he got within four inches of your face with his face, what did he do?" Jodi responds, "Um, he licked his lips, and said I wish you didn't have a boyfriend". Juan Martinez objects, but it is, again, inaudible. The objection is sustained.

Nurmi asks, "Did you kiss him?". Can we please throw this poor, deceased man a crumb? He's the one who has – allegedly – been so overcome with passion, just by virtue of being in an elevator with Jodi Arias, yet he did NOT kiss her. As we finish up the story, it was Jodi who gets the credit for not giving into a kiss that was never initiated. Now I understand why she didn't just say that he kissed her. There's plenty of that coming later. She's supposed to be monogamous at this point (and she is still living with Darryl), and Nurmi, somehow convinced her that this was the way to go with the story.

Nurmi asks, "Did he make contact with you, physical contact?". She answers, "Yes, um, he put his arm around me – when he walked me back to my hotel room (and then she makes that lifted eyebrow, kind of quizzical, one shoulder raised, "what else can I tell you?" face). Big deal. Jodi was doing photo ops all weekend. Plenty of arms were around her waist in those phony "best friends/never met 'em" pictures used for promotional literature (Hey! Come to convention! Look at how much fun and friendship abounds at convention!).
Nurmi throws in a curveball, and I hope Juan Martinez calls him on it. "When he walked you back

to your hotel room, did he attempt to kiss you again?" Again? He never tried to kiss her at all! Jodi responds, "No, he, it seemed very obvious...". Juan Martinez rightfully objects, and he barely looked up when he said this: "Seems like he attempted to kiss her the first time, when she said he did not". Nurmi then says, "No, that's not what she said". Oh, is that so? I've played this portion of testimony, backed it up, played it again, backed it up, etc., and I can promise you, that is exactly what she said. Unbelievably, the objection is overruled, and the defendant is instructed to answer the question. Juan Martinez is right. Judge Stephens is wrong. Kirk Nurmi is just lying.

"He made it very obvious that he wanted to kiss me, but he, like he was restraining himself...(pause)...it was very obvious restraint". Is she going to find another way to say that he was obviously restraining himself? Was he doubled over, barely able to walk, holding his groin, and asking her to quickly leave his visual field? We are talking about a kiss, not a sexual act. Actually, we're talking about a non-kiss, or, more accurately, two non-kisses. Suddenly, Arias is talking about the television show, South Park. She advises the jury that the writers of that show make Mormons the butt of many jokes (actually, they're equal opportunity offenders). Those two, former Mormon writers of South Park, would have a field day with testimony.

Now Nurmi wants to know if Travis tried to invite himself into her hotel room (because monogamous Jodi, acceptor of dates and all night talk sessions with strangers, would never do the inviting). Jodi responds, "No". Nurmi asks if there were still roommates in the hotel room. Jodi answers as we would expect: Yes, Michelle, Lenore, and Lenore's mother were in the room and asleep "at that hour". Jodi is obviously feeling rather victorious now (with that second kiss crap actually flying). Her arms are folded across her chest, and she looks rather superior – like she really has somewhere else to be.

"Is this the last time you see Mr. Alexander when you're in Las Vegas?", asks Nurmi. Jodi answers, "No...um, Sunday morning they had what's called a break-out (oh, now it's "they", not "we"?), and it was in a small theater near the MGM Grand, within walking distance, so that team, I guess, I think it was Team Renew (come on, Jodi! You remember Team Renew. You just had an intimate dinner with all of them last night), and a few other...people...not on that team were...present. Um, I saw him there (really, I thought she might have tripped over his unconscious body as she walked out of her hotel room on Sunday morning. I was under the impression that he was walking such a tightrope of restraint on Saturday night/Sunday morning, that he potentially exploded all over himself just as Jodi closed her hotel room door, and then he had fallen into a deep, satisfying sleep. Guess not). I didn't sit next to him (or, he didn't sit next to her?), um, and...". Juan Martinez is getting more active. Another objection: Beyond the Scope (he says that she wasn't asked where she saw him).
Sustained. Nurmi asks, "Where was he when you saw him?". She responds, "In a theater, and I was at the theater, and the, he invited me to...". Another objection: Beyond the scope. I see what Martinez is doing. If they want to give essay answers, he's going to at least stop the easy flow of information. The objection is sustained. Nurmi is irritated as he asks, "What did he invite you to

do?". Jodi responds, "He invited me to go to a buffet of some kind, back at the MGM, where he, and a few other people were having breakfast – or lunch". So, still, no private meal together? Wow, he is restrained (and I'm thinking this is a "pay your own way" buffet. Only the execs get to put their meals on the PPL expense account or credit card. Oh, and for what it's worth, when googling how to eat very cheaply on the LV strip, buffets come up right after "two for one" taco places. But please, go on, Jodi, tells us about your love omelet and toast).

Nurmi continues, "Did you accept his invitation to have breakfast?". "Yes", says Jodi. Nurmi continues, "And you said this was Mr. Alexander, and other individuals, right? (Yes, says Jodi) Were these people you knew previous to this point in time, or were these more individuals...(unintelligible)?" Nurmi, give them any identity you want. The fact that there is any individual there – beyond the two of them – mars the predatory picture you are trying to paint. Jodi answers, "I believe I had met them over the weekend. They were people who were on my team and in my up line". Nobody down line? Well, at her stage, it doesn't get much more down line than Jodi, so technically, everybody is up line of her. So, can we stop pretending she's playing Mrs. Trump to The Donald.

Nurmi asks, "Those people that you drove from California with – were they at this breakfast?". Jodi answers, "No". "Where were they, to your knowledge?", asks Nurmi. Can I take a guess? Looking for Jodi Arias. They had a 4.5 hour car ride in front of them, and they probably had to by checking out by 11:00 AM. Where is her part of the bill? There is no Jodi to be found. Apparently, she's up line somewhere.

Jodi answers, "Um, I don't know. I don't know where they went after the breakout". Maybe they went to a previously agreed upon meeting place? Maybe not. Nurmi continues with "the wining and dining at the breakfast buffet" chapter of the trip: "This breakfast with Mr. Alexander, is that the last time you saw him?" No, Nurmi. She saw him again on June 4, 2008. Did you forget? Jodi doesn't seem very excited when she's talking about this breakfast. Maybe she's tired. Let's see if she gives us a clue as to why she isn't happy.

Even Mike Babicky turns to looks at her (and that doesn't often happen) as she pronounces the word "no" so that it sounds like a weak and wounded animal: "Noooo, well...". Nurmi jumps in, "At the convention?". Jodi responds, "I stayed with him 'til he left, I think". Nurmi wants to know what the Buffet Buddies did after breakfast. Jodi says, "We walked over to the front desk, where he checked out, and, um, we walked out to the front where there were valets, and, um, he was loading his stuff into the taxi, and he was getting ready to go to the airport".

So, that's what she meant by "stayed with him until he left"? She means she followed him back to the hotel desk, watched him pay his bill, ask for a cab, and then stood there as his bags were packed into a taxi? Pretty hot. It's nice that Travis got to fly back to his 5 hour destination, while Jodi, who had probably alienated Michelle and company, was going to be shoved into the backseat of a Honda

Accord to drive back to her paradise, 4.5 hours away.

Nurmi asks, "Were there any arrangements made for you two to have contact with either other again? How did you leave things with Mr. Alexander?" There would have been no arrangements made had Jodi not pulled her butt out of bed and gone to the theater that morning (something she never said he mentioned or encouraged her to attend during their lovemaking in the elevator last night). Jodi answered, "Yeah. He indicated he would call me. I didn't really expect him to call me (probably true). But, that's kind of where we left it. We hugged." Nurmi asks, "Did he attempt to kiss you before he got in the taxi?". She quickly answers, "No".

Nurmi wants to sew this up. He wants to know when Jodi left the convention. She says, "Um, Michelle, Lenore, and I checked out a few hours – oh, we got lunch, at The Rainforest Cafe (how much food can this woman consume? Didn't she just eat?). Then we checked out after that". Hey, how much hotel property do you think was in her luggage? You know, towels, soaps, shampoos...stuff she'd never use, but took to display in her bathroom, just to prove that she'd been there?

The big convention of 2006 is now a memory. This was probably the highlight of her life. She was shown what an existence on the other side of the tracks looked like – a life that gave her the ability to lend evening dresses, not borrow them. She was going to grab it. If a picture has already been painted showing her as a manipulative, lazy, short-cut taking, covetous woman, then we need to be prepared for what's coming. That was all the training ground. She's about to gain entry into a world whose residents never really invited her, never truly welcomed her, and ultimately, asked her to leave. In fact, these conventioneers made more of an impression on Jodi Arias than Jodi Arias ever made on them.

After she murdered Travis Alexander and was in jail awaiting trial, she actually wrote to the leaders of PPL to state her case. The group was planning to host a memorial service for Travis Alexander. She wanted the leadership to remind everyone that she was innocent until proven guilty. Yes, she really did that. Here it is, dated September 1, 2008. This was three months after his murder, and it was immediately prior to PPL's first convention following his death (I assumed she guessed the first day of September would be the day to write it. In jail, she wouldn't have immediate access to the specific dates of PPL's bi-annual convention):

I am writing this letter in regards to Travis Alexander, whose life was taken last June. He was a good friend of mine. Am also, at present, in custody as I am being charged with his murder. I am not writing this solely to plead my own innocence. That goes without saying -- as Travis meant the world to me and I would never harm him. It is my understanding that his memory will be honored and recognized in Las Vegas this September. I would humbly remind those who say any different -- that I am innocent until proven guilty. It is with a spirit of humility that I would ask that if I am in any way referenced during Travis' memorial at the team breakout, that my implied innocence is taken into account.

With humble gratitude,
Jodi Ann Arias

Never before have I wished that the phrase., "What happens in Vegas, Stays in Vegas" was actually a statement of fact instead of an advertising slogan. The much-hyped convention was over. By Sunday afternoon, September 10, 2006, hotel and shift workers were already making noticeable progress in erasing any evidence that an organization named PrePaid Legal had ever descended on the MGM Grand Hotel. Guest rooms were cleaned and sanitized, and all that remained of Team Renew could be found in those plastic garbage bags sitting next to housekeeping carts in the hotel hallways.

Jodi Arias leaves Sin City exactly as Michelle had promised --"fired up". I have no doubt that Arias did leave fired up, but I think she was more excited about a potential romance than she was with the product she was being trained to sell. If Michelle had only known that her sales pitch to Jodi Arias would have altered the course of young man's abbreviated life, she would have opted to move onto the next hot (or cold) prospect. I suspect that most of the walk-on players in this tragedy would have handed in their resignations had they been shown a copy of the final script. Jodi Arias – how many people has she victimized?

Nurmi is taking us from Las Vegas, Nevada back to Palm Desert, California. Arias is heading home. I wonder what the car ride back to Palm Desert was like. Did Jodi freeze the other women out, preferring to stare out the car window while recalling the excitement leading up to the banquet? Did she sleep in the backseat while dreaming she was still at the MGM Grand, only to wake up as the car slowed down while pulling into a gas station? Did she talk incessantly about how PPL was going to change her life? We've heard about almost every hour of this trip, and I wonder if Nurmi will talk about the car ride home, or if will he just drop Jodi at Darryl's front door.

Nurmi begins, "Was it back to work, or, what did you do when you got back?" Jodi responds, "I did have to work...(pause)....umm...(left hand rises and falls)...just back in the same routine, except Travis began to call me". Nurmi asks if Jodi still considered Darryl Brewer to be her boyfriend when she came back to Palm Desert after the convention. She responds, "Yes". He follows that question by asking her whether or not she was still sexually active with Darryl Brewer. Jodi responds, "No". Nurmi asks, "Why not?".

Jodi responds, "I don't know – recall specifically why. Oh, because we broke up, I guess, that would be why. But, we didn't have sex after convention – prior to that was the last time, I would say". I don't know about anyone else, but that set off an alarm in my head: "I don't recall specifically why" suddenly morphed into "Oh, because we broke up...that would be why"? Did she forget the script for a moment? I am always amazed at the gnats of information that end up on the record, but the milestone events – like ending a five year relationship with her live-in boyfriend/co-borrower – seem like afterthoughts.

Nurmi wants to hear about the break-up. When did it happen? Jodi answers, "Well, I got back from convention on Sunday, and I broke up with Darryl on Thursday of that week". Nurmi asks, "Why did you break up with Darryl after the convention?". Jodi responds, "Umm...the relationship, as I mentioned, was already kind of fizzling...umm...I loved him very much, but there was no, it wasn't going anywhere, we had different visions for our future...umm...because it had been like that from day one...umm...it took me four and a half years to just let it go, because I really loved him. Also, on Wednesday night, I was invited to go out to some of Travis' friends' house, and I knew Travis would be there and, I didn't want to, I'm kind of like, one guy at a time kind of person, so I didn't want to have anything overlapping, and I knew there was an interest, ah, with Travis, and I was beginning to sort of develop just the seeds of interest with Travis, and I didn't want to be in a relationship when I went there because I didn't want there to be anything hindering...I didn't want to feel guilty for flirting or sitting next to him, or any of that. I wanted to be out of a relationship so I wouldn't be cheating on anybody...if that makes sense."

Jodi is using a bucket of morally superior verbiage to paint a structure of raw narcissism. It may look acceptable from a distance, but upon closer inspection, the cracks, the rot, and the decay are obvious. Jodi wants us to believe that she is a "one guy at a time kind of person". Okay. Let's see if that's true. There was Victor Arias, and although it has become obvious that he was a family member with whom she played kissing cousins, she puts him in the "boyfriend" category. She used Bobby Juarez to make Victor Arias jealous. She used Matt McCartney (Bobby's roommate) to make Bobby Juarez jealous. She used Darryl Brewer to make Matt McCartney jealous. She tried to use Travis Alexander to make Darryl Brewer jealous – although I think that plan failed. She used several men to make Travis Alexander jealous-- again, a plan that failed.

Jodi Arias never had the guts to move on as an independent woman. Because of the way she had ordered her life, men were a necessity. If she didn't have a replacement in the wings after a break-up, she may have had to humble herself, go back to her parents, admit that she had wasted more than a few years, and ask them if she could stay at their home while she enrolled in community college. She could have made up for a lot of lost time by age 30. If she had done that, she would have something to bring to table in terms of a relationship. In reality, this is all lip service – it's a "morality speech" she believes responsible people – people on the jury – will accept. In truth, she's has no moral tie to monogamy.

She knew "from day one" that her relationship with Darryl wasn't going anywhere, yet she affords herself the luxury of involving him in a real estate scheme that she couldn't pull off without him? Why? Her justification for that is that it took her four and half years "to just let it go". Did he know the terms of that agreement? Doubtful. The impact made on a person's credit after foreclosure is substantial, but, it is much easier for a 26 year old, single female (who will likely marry a man and simply use his credit for what she needs) to recover from that kind of hit than it is for a 50 year old, divorced male.

I'm wondering who invited Jodi to Travis' friends' house? Who are the friends? Did she get the invitation on Wednesday night, and put "break-up with Darryl" on her calendar for Thursday morning? How long did she travel to visit this stranger's home? She's already told us what her objective for the visit is: she plans to sit next to (and flirt with) Travis Alexander. I have such a sinking feeling – I know Travis is about to be trapped. I know there was a period where Travis actually dated Jodi Arias. I also know he didn't consider them a couple for at least another five months (their actual relationship is one of her shortest: February, 2007 to June, 2007), but still, this is the beginning of the end.

Nurmi would like to know if it is fair to say that Travis Alexander motivated Jodi to break up with Darryl Brewer. She doesn't miss a beat before responding, "The things he said made a big impression on me. It wasn't just about relationships, it was about my whole life, my career, the direction of my life, so, it made me take a step back and take a look at where I stood and where I was going, so that was part of the reason".

No, it wasn't part of the reason – the whole reason was just disclosed in her prior answer. She could not flirt with Travis while being Darryl's girlfriend – and that's what Travis said to her that motivated her. Besides, wasn't Travis, just moments ago, being portrayed as some kind of kissing bandit? Jodi knew exactly where she stood in life. She didn't need a fist-pumping event to sharpen her vision, and she didn't need after-care from a PPL executive to cement the truth. He caused her to look at her entire life? She looked at her career? She knew where she stood in her career. She hadn't earned the right to claim a career. She had a job. Sometimes. A low paying job that required her to accumulate other low paying jobs to earn the equivalent of a full time salary.

Nurmi continues, "You mentioned something that I think is interesting. You came back...you came back from the convention with a different vision of the future than when you left, right?" Jodi, predictably, answers, "Yes". Nurmi continues, "Describe for us, if you could, what was your vision of the future before you went to this convention in September, 2006". Jodi explains, "It was kind of...nebulous (she lifts her hands and makes a gesture as if she's resting her hands on a globe). It wasn't very clear (without a degree or specialized training/certification at the age of 26, what else could it be?). I just knew that I wanted basic things: I knew I wanted to have kids someday (a thank you to the power that made sure that never happened), I knew I wanted to be married someday (no from Victor, no from Bobby, no from Matt, no from Darryl, no from Travis – maybe she should accept that fact that the male gender has rendered her "not marriage material", but Travis was the first one with the guts to tell her the truth). I knew I didn't want to struggle paycheck to paycheck. I knew I didn't see myself living a life of excess, but definitely being able to pay the bills and being able to provide for a family, somewhat, or at least be a joint contributor to the household (she already had this opportunity with Darryl, but she found it not to her liking). I saw myself getting more into photography, and hopefully, I still had hopes of being successful in real estate, eventually (oh, please...don't even ask us to believe she hasn't learned that lesson)."

Now Nurmi want to knows what her vision of the future was after the convention. Jodi responds "I still had those desires, but leaving convention, I can't really describe it (bet she can). It was painful because I knew there was a lot of change on my horizon at that point. I couldn't continue with the same life that I had been living because, well, it's kind of like my eyes were opened to a lot of things that I had been ignoring, and the idea of change was uncomfortable. I really loved Darryl (she didn't "really love Darryl"...why does she kept repeating this mantra?), but I couldn't continue with him." Did they lift this paragraph from some life-coach book? Painful changes on her horizon? Please. She saw money. That's it. Same woman, different day.

Nurmi realizes that Jodi just spoke about all of the personal changes she was going to make. He realizes that we're probably wondering how a PrePaid Legal convention, a multi-level marketing carnival that was orchestrated to increase membership and revenue, caused so many monumental shifts in Jodi's heart. What about the impact the convention had on her, professionally speaking? Nurmi asks if she thought PPL was going to make her rich. Jodi answers, "Umm...the idea of selling the membership was uncomfortable to me (but without making that sacrifice, there was no other reason to keep communicating with Travis, so I'm guessing she swallowed her discomfort). I believe in the product, and, umm, but hitting up my friends and family seemed awkward (awkward, or impossible? She had alienated her family, and she doesn't seem to have friends), so I had that desire, but I couldn't quite see myself going out and doing it (where's the big internal shift?), at least, yet (stall tactics). Michelle invited me to an event about a week later, and it kind of re, re, (her hands start twirling around), reiterated some of the things I learned at convention, and I continued to go to these events from then on. I became more active, as far as plugging into those events (she means she showed up? Yes, we know), and how to sell the membership, and how to have success, and the general vision of it became crystalized in my mind".

Okay. So what does that mean? She drove from event to event, hoping that she'd have something to talk to Travis about? When did she actually make a sale? One sale? You can go to "how to" meetings forever, but eventually, you have to put all of that knowledge into practice. So, it's all crystalized in her mind now. Tell us about her first sale.

We're not going to hear about her first sale. Nurmi wants to know if there was a point in time in which she decided to go "all in". I'd settle for dipping her toe in. I'm not interested in hearing about where Jodi parked her car on a one-way street before going to someone's home with her written materials in hand, scoping out the room, finding a seat, drifting off while PPL members gave their testimonials, and then everyone headed for the coffee pot. I'm interested in Jodi pulling up to a house, gathering her courage, knocking on a door, and selling the damn product. Can we get there? She answers, "I had times in the company when I was very productive (WHEN?). The money I made was surprising (HOW MUCH?). I didn't realize the compensation plan was as generous as it was (oh please...the generous compensation plan is the hook! Between convention, literature, and meetings, if she wasn't familiar with the compensation plan, there's some intellectual issue Nurmi doesn't want to address). I liked that, but I found it difficult to maintain that level of production every month." Can we please get some specifics?

Here are all the specifics we need. Nurmi asks Jodi if she was still working "other jobs", despite the generous compensation from PPL. Answer: Yes. Nurmi then asks Jodi if she ever reached the point where PPL was her only source of income. Answer: No. Well, guess what? Travis was able to do that, so it was possible. I think we see where this is going.

Nurmi asks, "How much did you make with PrePaid Legal in your most productive year?". Jodi looks down, and then answers, "I really didn't make anything (she waves her hands in the air) for several months at a time, and one month I made (hands shifting back and forth) approximately (it's on her W2, certainly we don't have to be approximate), $1700, and then the next month, I made...(pause)...I wanna say a little over (hands shifting again)...umm, a little over a thousand...so those two months were really good." Wow. If this was in the period of a year, it might fall below the legally mandated standard for reporting that income to the IRS. She's estimating that the most productive year – the time frame she was limited to in her answer – was $2,700 (and we know she's estimating up). Let's just call it an even $2,300, because we know how Jodi's math works.

Nurmi wants to know how much time she invested in PPL to earn this small fortune. Jodi responds, "Not nearly as much as I should have been. Umm...they have goals in the company (why mention goals that, by her own admission, she never tried to reach), things they'd like you to commit to, such as, talking to a minimum number of people per day or per week, and, I don't remember them now, because it's been so long. But, just different Ten Core Commitments, at least that's what they were called then, and they tell you that if you just do these things systematically, then success follows". Right. However, Jodi just admitted that she didn't do these things the way she was supposed to.

Nurmi will now explain why Jodi didn't have the time to invest in PPL, or at least he's going to try. He wants to know how much time she was working her restaurant jobs. "At that time (what time?), I was still full time at Cuistot (wait, the last we heard, that position was available to her, but she said she wasn't working there. I'm confused), but eventually I quit that job (eventually? When?), and then I only had one job". Did Jodi use the word "nebulous" before? Did she learn that word when Nurmi told her that this was the strategy to cover her spotty work history? Why did a struggling woman quit a full time job? Why weren't those free hours eaten up with PPL efforts? What's the other job she's talking about? Where was it? How many hours did she work? We're done with this work history thing, aren't we? I know, as does everyone else, why she quit these restaurant jobs. They interfered with her weekend road trips.

Yes, we're done. We're going back to the break-up with Darryl, because, as Jodi points out, she "wasn't as specific as I thought I had been". She continues while addressing the jury, "You didn't get that impression, but we sat down, I had a conversation with him. We sat at our kitchen table, and I just told him, in essence, I told him, I know we're not getting married, but you know I'd like to have kids someday, and he said okay, and I said, well, umm, I think maybe we should, I might be pursuing that goal (Oh my! Juan Martinez was correct when he said she was looking for someone to "breed" with), and I know that you don't want to pursue that goal with me, and that's okay, umm, I know you're moving back, he was moving back to Monterey. I said I know you're moving back soon, so I kind of just left it at that. I wasn't very specific, but he was nodding his head like he understood what I was saying (yes...I'm certain he understood what she was saying), so, I was under the impression that we were no longer together, at that point. I mean, not in a committed relationship where we are boyfriend/girlfriend".

Wow. She even breaks up like a teenager. How about being woman enough to put it in black and white terms: "Darryl. I'm not in love with you. I see a new direction in my life, and that direction doesn't include you, and it doesn't include Jack. I've met a new man, and I intend to pursue that relationship. I'm going to see where it leads, but if it leads nowhere, that doesn't change the fact that I am pulling away and setting you free to pursue a life of your own. If you are interested in seeing other women, then I am not standing in your way". Then you end with all of the good stuff, thanks for the memories, etc. You walk away in tears. You walk away feeling like a piece of crap. You don't walk away saying, "I was under the impression he understood what I was saying".

Nurmi reminds us that Jodi fired Darryl before going to visit "Mr. Alexander" for the weekend. She responds, "Actually, I did it right after I was invited, but prior to going". Nurmi throws in an odd question about representatives of the Mormon Church visiting Jodi's home in Palm Desert, something, at this point, she denies has happened. Now, Nurmi is ready to talk about the weekend with Travis. Jodi says, "This would have been the weekend after convention". Nurmi asks, "How many hours away was it?" Jodi responds, "I don't remember the drive. Not far. Umm...It was in Murietta, California, either Murietta, or Temecula...I think Murietta. And I'd say an hour and fifteen minutes, maybe." Close enough, it's an hour and a half to the Hughes home.

Arias was invited to this private party, and she was hosted with comfortable, free, overnight accommodations for one reason – she was playing the part of a truth seeker. It was Step One in her plan to obtain a commodity named Travis Alexander. If he was a Mormon, she was going to be a Mormon. Likewise, if he had been a Jehovah's Witness, she would have feigned a deep interest in that faith. Remember, she played vampire games with Count Bobby Juarez, and she embraced Wicca, Buddhist teachings, and New Age philosophies because Matt McCartney embraced them. For Jodi Arias, the brand of non-denominational Christianity she allegedly embraced was as easily erased as chalk on a blackboard. Her quest to become a Mormon was merely a variation on a well-played out theme.

During these early days, Arias was doing her best to convince Travis and the Hughes that she wanted to learn all about their Mormon faith. She is so heavy handed when plying her deceit that I could easily picture her carrying a brand new notebook into the LDS Temple service on that Sunday morning ("Look, brothers and sisters! I have a notebook, and I'm going to take copious amounts of notes because I just know I'm going to want to replenish my spirit by going back and studying this sermon over and over again. I'm THAT serious about becoming a Latter Day Saint. Travis, wasn't it a great idea for me to bring this notebook?").

I have no doubt that the Hughes believed, with all sincerity and good faith, that they could lead Jodi Arias to the truth. I also know that this belief was based on the fact that Arias played her part convincingly. Remember, this is a woman who, when writing her post arrest letter to the Alexander family, made sure to add that Travis told her that he had never met anyone more ready to receive the gospel than her. Because she lies so frequently, it does become difficult to believe anything she says, but I do think Travis may have said something like this to her in the very early days. One thing is for sure – he stopped saying it. As far as the Hughes are concerned, they cannot be blamed for their lack of discernment in embracing Jodi Arias. They were dealing with a seasoned sociopath, and like most people, they would never realize it until the wreckage was finally unveiled.

Now we go back to the sexual encounter that occurred in the Hughes' guestroom. Nurmi listens as Jodi offers several different excuses – each based on what Travis allegedly wanted – for not stopping the escalating sexual encounter. He asks, "Why would rejecting him at that point in time be such a big deal for you?" Jodi answers, "At that point in time, I was not really accustomed to saying no. Umm...I wasn't... (pause, while she scratches her right cheek and searches for the right words)... I have a lot more backbone now than I used to. It was hard for me to tell somebody no. Umm...so, even though it was uncomfortable, I just kept going...with it". Jodi wasn't accustomed to saying no? Really?

Jodi was very accustomed to saying no. She said no to her parents. She said no to doing household chores. She said no to school administrators. She said no to homework. She said no to high school. She said no to college. She said no to Doggy Boy when she kicked him into eternity for the crime of being a typical dog. She said no to a cat when she decided to keep it locked in a closet without food or water for days. She said no to cigarettes (something she's very proud of). She said no to being grounded. She said no to Bobby Juarez. She said no to Victor Arias. She said no to Bobby Juarez a second time. She said no to Matt McCartney. She said no to Bianca. She said no to Darryl Brewer. She said no to employees with whom she worked when she destroyed a bathroom because another server wouldn't trade shifts with her. She said no to investing any real time into selling the PPL product. She said no to a PPL associate when she locked her in a bathroom and wouldn't let her leave until that woman understood that Travis belonged to Jodi. She said no to her mortgage lender. She said no to the company that financed the purchase of her car. She said no when her relationship with Travis ended and she responded by moving to his neighborhood. She said no to a few of the women Travis liked and dated. She said no to the tires on Travis' BMW – several times. She said no to Linda Ballard when Jodi took the diamond engagement ring Travis had purchased for Linda years earlier. She said no to privacy when she peered in the back window of Travis' home while he was romantically involved with another woman. She said no to her friends when they told her (and her mother) that she needed treatment for her mental issues. She said no to work when it was time to secure a full time job. She said no to her parents when they wanted to visit her in her Palm Desert home. She said no to the concept of locked accounts and personal correspondence. She said no to a Mormon wife and mother when that woman asked Jodi to leave her house because she was not welcome there. She said no to Travis by denying him life. She said no to Napoleon when she took Travis away. She said no to law enforcement when she was questioned about the murder. She said no to the Alexander family when they begged to know the truth. She said no, many times, to her own court appointed attorney. She said no when she was asked to show a shred of remorse for the murder she committed. She said no to the judge. Whether in word or deed, she said no to more things than any of us will ever know. She just never learned to say no to sex. She never said no to sex because it was on that stage that Jodi performed. The word no, in terms of trapping a man with sex, was foreign to Jodi Arias. We know it. She knows it. The defense knows it. The prosecutor knows it. She's hoping the jury missed it. So, own it, Jodi, and don't pretend you were uncomfortable with casual sex in a stranger's home.

Nurmi asks, "So, the discomfort you were feeling in going, in having your clothes removed, was less burdensome to you than the discomfort you would have felt saying no. Is that right?" Juan Martinez' temperature is not rising. In fact, he hasn't changed much from the last camera shot. He's still writing, but he utters an objection – again inaudible, again overruled. Nurmi continues, "Is that what we're hearing?". Jodi responds, "Umm...I can't really say, one way or the other, because I couldn't make the comparison, but at the time, it felt more uncomfortable to say – to push him off of me. I mean, he wasn't aggressive, but he was definitely doing the initiating at that point, and I kept going for it (she looks embarrassed, her voice is dropping, but she's smiling)".

Nurmi asks, "Did he, on this occasion, wind up removing your clothes?". Jodi answers, "Yes". Nurmi continues, "All your clothes?". Arias appears to stiffen, and she looks embarrassed as she replies, "Yes". Great. Naked Jodi. What's next?

"At this point in time, was Mr. Alexander dressed?", asks Nurmi. "Yes", responds Jodi. There's a pause as Arias does her best Hester Prynne-on-trial impersonation. Her eyes are down and she plays with her fingernails. She appears to be embarrassed, but not apologetic. She's trying to figure out how a woman – a Mormon woman – might act if she were exposed this way.

Nurmi continues, "Did that change?". Jodi answers, "Umm...not really, I think he kept his...his garments on. He was wearing garments". Nurmi wants to know what "garments" she's referring to. She responds, "Garments are, they're called Temple Garments, and they are, they are, it's like a (she puts her hand on her chest) T-Shirt, and umm, underwear, kind of likes briefs. They're a sort of an off white color. He had his Temple Garments under, I think, just like sweats. I think he had pajama bottoms over those".

Nice touch. Just in case the jury missed it (the Mormon clues have been so subtle, after all), the garments are mentioned to once again remind the jury of Mormonism and the hypocrisy of Travis Alexander. He's supposed to be a devout Mormon – so devout that he wears the sacred undergarments – but there he is, having premarital sex with some woman in his best friend's guestroom. Does anyone even believe this happened? Does anyone really believe that Travis would take this kind of chance with Chris Hughes – a man he claimed literally changed his life? There are several small children in this house. There are other adults in the house. I believe this a product of her imagination, but I also believe it is a story she particularly likes telling because it kills two birds with one stone. Not only does it make Travis look like a hypocrite, but it also insults Chris and Sky. She wants them to think that this was all going on right under their noses. She wants them to feel stupid. I have never believed this happened in their home, and I still don't.

Nurmi asks, "And, whatever else he was wearing over his garments, did he take those others off, or did you?". A shot of the gallery shows the three Alexander siblings (Steven, Samantha, and Tanisha). This must be very difficult testimony for them to hear. There is no reason any sibling should be forced to endure a play-by-play description of their brother engaging in intimate behavior. If you add to that the fodder that is being made of something that is sacred to many in their family, the garments, their discomfort becomes incalculable. This is what love looks like. It isn't being defined by Jodi Arias, a woman who easily attaches that word to every man with whom she's slept. It is being defined by these three people who love their brother enough to sit and listen to this, and all the while, hold themselves with dignity. In their stoic silence, they drown out her many words.

Arias answers as to whether or not she removed Travis' clothes, "I don't recall. I know I didn't. It might have been a joint effort, but...(unintelligible)...I don't really remember ". Then obviously, she does recall. "So, after you are undressed, and Mr. Alexander is in his undergarments, what happened?", asks Nurmi. Jodi answers, "Umm..this is embarrassing (she's stalling, and scratching the left side of her face with her left hand)...". Juan Martinez objects, again unintelligible, and it is sustained.

Nurmi asks, "Is it embarrassing for you to talk about this?". Before she can answer, Juan Martinez objects again with relevance. Overruled. Jodi answers, but so softly we can barely hear it: "Yes".

Jodi appears to have checked out. She won't look up. She's playing with her fingers. She examining debris on her fingertips. Nurmi interrupts, "I understand how it might be...but it's important to share this with us. So, if you could, please, tell us what happened". Nice act, Jodi. You can't wait to spill this, but isn't it fun to build the tension before you do? When she's sure she has everyone's undivided attention, she finally answers, "Umm...he began to perform oral sex...on me". Nurmi asks, "And was this...comfortable? You mentioned earlier that you had a certain level of discomfort with this act... being naked...were you uncomfortable while this oral sex was going on?". Nurmi can barely look up. He catches her eye one time, and he immediately looks back at the floor. Even he knows this is wrong.

Jodi answers, "I was...umm...it was uncomfortable. It was dark – I mean the lights were off – so I think that might have made it a little bit more tol...tolerable, but umm, it was, uhh – I don't know, he knew what he was doing, for sure, but it was just – it felt like too much, too soon, and I couldn't exactly rewind at that point, you know?". Did you hear it? She said he knew exactly what he was doing. Translation? She is now alleging that his skill level proved that this wasn't his first journey down the road of premarital sex.

I honestly don't care if it was or if it wasn't. That isn't the issue – at least not for me. Rather, I am thinking of what an awful prospect this is. Imagine, your life ends because you are murdered. As part of your killer's strategy to lessen their responsibility for your death, that individual sits on a witness stand and not only talks about your sex life, but talks about it in such detail that it includes what kind of underwear you wore. Imagine that most of what is being said is a pure fabrication, but still, the fabrications makes you look promiscuous, fetishistic, and even criminal (that's coming later). You will be gone. You won't hear it. However, people will. Your family, immediate and extended, will hear about it. Every member of the public who is sitting at the trial will hear about it. In this case, hundreds of thousands of people are hearing about it. It's even on the evening news. And you're dead. You can't do a thing about it. Your killer is at complete liberty to say whatever they want about a subject that most of us consider the most personal aspect of our lives. There are so many circles of hell in this trial, and this is just one of them.

Nurmi wants to know if Jodi voiced her "displeasure" with this event. Jodi answered, "No. I can't say it was displeasure, but it was uncomfortable." Nurmi wants to know if she voiced her "discomfort" with the event. Jodi answers, "No. I didn't want to give him that impression...". Objection from Juan Martinez. Beyond the scope. Sustained. Nurmi picks up, "Why not? Why not, Miss Arias?" Jodi answers, "Why not, what?". Nurmi answers, "Why didn't you voice your discomfort". I'll answer that – because she wasn't in any discomfort. Again, she repeats herself, "I didn't want him to have the impression – I wanted to – I wanted to, at least appear like I was enjoying it as much as he seemed to be". What a trooper.

Nurmi asks, "So, you were attempting to give him the impression that you were enjoying things?". She answers, "Yes". This line of questioning is taking longer than the sexual act probably took. Nurmi asks, "And why were you interested in doing that?". Jodi answers, "Umm...I guess, I guess it would have seemed, to me, to be unattractive for me to say anything different, or anything negative about the experience". Nurmi continues, "Okay. What happened after he performed oral sex upon you?". Oh, that's it? He's not going to take this to its biological conclusion? By the end of this trial, we will almost know what Travis' sperm count was, but when it comes to her, the question remains unasked. I guarantee that Nurmi will be all over orgasms when Travis is the subject, but now he just wants to know what happened next. Jodi says, "Umm... he asked for reciprocation".

"Well, at that point, I had taken it that far, and I was kind of glad he was done, so (putting his penis in her mouth seemed like the prudent thing to do)...and I was just willing to reciprocate at that point". Nurmi wants clarity. Does "reciprocate" mean "perform oral sex on him"? Now she is shy. Shy Jodi whispers, "Yes".

Nurmi asks if Travis removed his garments before she performed oral sex. No, Nurmi, she did it through the fabric. That's how skilled your client is. Of course, the garments were removed! How did that go, he asks. Jodi answers, "Umm...I don't really know if the garments, the bottom, came all the way off or just pushed down, but the shirt remained on, and umm, yeah". I knew this was coming (no pun intended). And here it is -- "Did he ejaculate?", Nurmi asks. Arias says that he did. Well, what else would she say? Hey, men on the jury, is this helping her?

Nurmi's not done with the details yet. There's one more critical piece of information he still needs. He has to know "where" Travis ejaculated. Jodi has an answer, and here it is, "In my mouth". I cannot believe I'm listening to this. Of what earthly relevance is this? Did she kill him because she allowed this to happen and regretted it later? Of course not. This woman knows the stages of arousal. That didn't have to happen and she knows it. Jodi Arias, the "shy" woman filled with nothing but discomfort during this alleged incident, still found the inner strength to put her special signature at the end of the encounter. We all know why she allowed this to happen. It was supposed to make his head spin and bring him back for more.

With the sex over, Nurmi picks up the pace. We learn that the two fell asleep in Jodi's bed. She doesn't remember falling asleep, and she doesn't know how they were both covered with blankets. She said she woke up, realized she was naked, put her pajamas back on, and got back into bed. Apparently, she didn't care very much if Chris or Sky Hughes caught them, because she didn't wake Travis up and send him back to his room. She says she remembers him waking up later, getting dressed, and leaving the room. She said this happened before anyone else in the house was awake. Nurmi reminds Jodi that it's now Sunday. Everyone is supposed to go to church. Nurmi wants Jodi to tell us about Sunday that morning.

She says, "Basically, the rest of the household began to wake up. I hadn't been to church since I was about eleven, so I didn't really have church clothes, so I went and bought two dresses before heading out there (did anyone ask about her church clothes? Is this to prove that "Miss I'm Broke" made a financial investment in going to church? Not one dress, but two? This is super serious). I asked Sky which one would be more appropriate (oh, really? So she asks Sky which dress is LDS appropriate, but didn't think to ask which sex acts are LDS appropriate?), and so then I put on an outfit, and the rest of the household was getting ready for church, and then we, umm, took separate cars. I took my car, Travis rode with me on that one, and I can't remember who else rode with me, maybe it was Jeff (is Travis ever willing to be alone with her in public?), umm, and the Hughes took their own vehicle".

Nurmi wants to know what the service was like. Was there a particular subject matter addressed that day? Suddenly, the human tape recorder draws a blank. She says, "I don't recall particularly what was said (actually, she can't even recall generally what was said), but I do remember that one of the speakers was Sky's brother, Zion, who had just gotten back from his mission. So he was giving a talk, something related to... maybe something related to... I don't remember the topic. It would have been related to his topic (a talk related to a topic? Wow, what a revolutionary concept!), because when you speak in church, you're given a topic to talk about (oh, please go on – this is fascinating), and I don't recall what the subject matter was. He was speaking from the podium". He was speaking from THE PODIUM? Well, why didn't she just say that when she was asked what the service was about? Wow. The podium. I had no idea that the main speaker would be speaking from the podium.

So, this was her big spiritual day. She can remember ONE speaker, and the implication is that there were several, and one podium. She can't remember the topic. What was going through her mind, I wonder? She was probably thinking about her exit-from-church plan. She was probably trying to figure out how to get Sky to ride home in her car instead of the car Sky arrived in. Why? Well, Jodi had planted something in the back seat of her car – something obvious and something Sky would probably pick up, look at, and show to Travis. I guess Jeff, the guy who rode with Travis and Jodi on the way to church, had no interest in that item. Jodi figured she'd have better luck with a woman. We'll hear all about it now.

Nurmi wants to know if Travis ever spoke to Jodi about the prior evening's encounter. She quietly says, "No". Asked about what happened after church, Jodi responds, "Well, we had the church service (that she cannot remember), and I drove back – well I rode back in my car. Travis rode shotgun, Jeff was behind me, and Sky was behind Travis (is she going to finally go home, or is she going to impose on the Hughes to give her lunch?). We were driving back and she found – in the back of my seat, she found a (strategically placed) portfolio of my photography, and she was flipping out looking through it, and there was a photograph of Darryl – a head shot that I had taken of him kind of growling at the camera. Umm...he looked gruff, and he was unshaven, and it was in black and white, and it looked really cool, and she showed it to, umm, to, to Travis, and that was the first time that Travis saw Darryl. So, that was – I kind of lost track of the question". I didn't lose track of the question. She was asked what happened after church. She answered by telling everyone that Travis saw a head shot of a handsome, gruff, growling Darryl – a guy Travis had nicknamed Grandpa.

That photograph placement was as accidental as the portfolio placement. The entire thing was deliberately staged by Jodi right before she left Palm Desert. She was hoping Travis would be reminded that she was taking her sex package back to another man, and she wanted him to know that Darryl was not just some middle-aged guy with an expanding gut and a receding hairline. She's so adolescent in her schemes.

Nurmi establishes that her portfolio testimony had no bearing on anything, and he moves on by asking if Jodi and Travis spent any time alone after church and before leaving the Hughes' home later that day. She says, "No, not that I recall". That's a firm no. This woman didn't get it – or maybe she did get it. However, she wasn't woman enough to look at the facts and accept them. We cannot argue that she fabricated her assertion that they dated each other. Other people have confirmed that they were, for a short time, a couple. We cannot argue that he had sex with her. The audio tape confirmed that. How much and how often is up for debate. I don't believe it was as frequent as she alleges. In fact, I don't believe it's any of our business. What is also up for debate is her allegation that he lied to her about his intentions. I believe he was forthcoming with her. He realized, pretty early on, that he was not going to marry her, and I think he told her that. If she didn't want to be what the defense team is calling "a dirty little secret", she certainly didn't have to be.

No woman HAS to be that secret.

Nurmi asks if she could have discussed the sexual encounter with Travis the next day. She makes it clear that "she could have pulled him aside, but it was not discussed". Nurmi asks if there were any plans to contact each other, and Jodi answers, "He walked me out to my car, kissed me, and I drove off". I wonder if she cried or raged until she got on the highway.

Jodi claims she heard from Travis either that night or Monday night. Nurmi wants to know who initiated contact. She answers, "Umm, we were calling each other back and forth at that point, so I don't remember who called who". Right. She remembers stopping for gas and Starbucks on the way home, but not who called whom after she had failed to make the serious connection with Travis she had been anticipating. I believe she waited all of Sunday night for his call. I believe she waited all of Monday for his call. By Monday night, she could wait no more. She called him on Monday night. When asked if the incident was discussed, she says, "There may have been reference to it, but he talked about church. He wanted to know how I liked it".

Nurmi wants to know when Mormon officials contacted her. She says, "Well, Travis gave me a book of Mormon Wednesday (how? Guess we'll be coming back to this), and I think at that time he contacted the officials of the church, and – I don't know how it works – but he gave them my information so that some of the missionaries in that area could come to my house". It's pretty clear how it works. He contacted church officials, gave them her name and address, and they dispatched missionaries to her house. She just explained how it works, so she can drop the neophyte act. It sounds like Travis turned her over to her local LDS Temple-- standard protocol, I'd assume.

Nurmi wants to know how Travis gave Jodi a book of Mormon on Wednesday. She says that she saw him again. She explains, "Umm... he was leaving Riverside and driving back to Mesa, and Palm Desert is on that stretch, it's on the I-10, and he called me on the way, and wanted to meet with me so that he could give me a copy of the Book of Mormon and meet him (let me guess? Round 2, and nobody else is there to witness their coupling). I didn't really know where we could meet though, because Darryl was home and I didn't want to bring some guy over ("some guy" she allegedly serviced like a pro two days earlier). We ended up meeting near a Starbucks which was near my house. He didn't give me the Book of Mormon right away. He had Napoleon with him, which was his dog – he's a black pug – on a leash, uh, I don't remember where Napoleon was, but we went into the store to get something to drink".

Juan Martinez looks up just long enough to object. Beyond the scope. The judge sustains the objection. Nurmi continues, "What is the subject matter of the conversation inside the Starbucks?" Jodi gets another opportunity to answer the same question. She says, "The Word of Wisdom, but we were sitting outside. It was a little hot, but it was somewhat – but we were sitting in the shade. It was cooler in the shade". Nurmi wants to know, for those of us who are not familiar with LDS doctrine, what the Word of Wisdom might be. Jodi answers, "The Word of Wisdom is LDS doctrine that states that it's – it prohibits the consumption of coffee, tea, alcohol, tobacco, and illegal drugs". Well, hey, I didn't see semen on that list, so if Jodi can give up Starbucks, she's home free.

"Did those same words apply to the Law of Chastity, or is that different?", asks Nurmi. Those same words? As in, are there two identical doctrines with two different names? I don't really see any connection between the word chastity and the words coffee, tea, alcohol, tobacco, and illegal drugs, but then again, I'm not a high powered defense attorney. Jodi answers, "The Law of Chastity is different". Really? Who saw that coming?

Travis is drinking Chai tea. Jodi says he had a legitimate excuse for consuming this form of tea, and it didn't count. He wasn't breaking any rules. She, being the in your face sinner she was, continued to slurp on her iced latte. There's more banter about caffeine, but she finally blurts out, "Umm...he was horny. That's what he said". Really? That's what he said? Well if he did, it's time to admit it. Jodi was a booty call. Had I been the recipient of that confession, I would have been so offended, I would have dumped my iced latte on his Mormon head, laughed at the fact that he had consumed caffeine, dropped his Book of Mormon at his feet, given Napoleon a pat on the head, and been off. If this happened – and again, that's a big if – she is to blame for the way she was treated, and no amount of pastel colored blouses, big ugly eyeglasses, hair scrunchies, and feigned embarrassment is going to change that.

Jodi admits that she was totally willing to help him think of a place they could go, after Starbucks, to help him deal with his "horny" status. They drove in their respective cars, "We both were, trying to figure out a place we could go. I don't know why, but I was also wanting to go with him to find some place, so we went, in our respective cars, we drove to a park near Starbucks – it was between my house and Starbucks – and it was the middle of the school day, and no one was there. There was a parking lot there, and we pulled into the parking lot, and he left Napoleon in the car with the air conditioner on and the windows rolled up, and he came into my car and sat in the passenger's seat".

We're going to hear another sexually explicit piece of testimony. I'm not giving it the treatment Jodi does. I'll hit the highlights, but I'm not making any of us endure her blow by blow (no pun intended, again) description on how he leaned over, unzipped his pants, etc. Unless there's something worth noting, I'll give you the basics. She says that she didn't really know what the point was when he was got into her car – at first. Juan Martinez is out of the gate with an objection: "Non-responsive. She knows the point". He's right, of course. She just said that he told her (in no uncertain terms) that he was in the mood, she was willing to help him think of a place they could go, she wanted to go with him to find that place, and she found a park that would suit their purposes because it was empty. To then add that wasn't sure why he was getting into her car was just too much.

There's cross talk between Martinez, Nurmi, and the judge, but Jodi is most clearly audible as she blurts out, "I did not know the point, then. I mean, I didn't know what he expected...". There's more background noise, and then the judge admonishes Jodi to wait until she is asked a question before she speaks. Jodi says, "I apologize". Now that the noise has subsided and Jodi has been put back in her place, Nurmi wants details. According to Jodi, Travis wanted oral sex, and he wanted to receive it, not give it.

She gave in, of course. Nurmi asks why. There's a lot of "I wanted to..." nonsense. She says she was attracted to him, blah, blah, blah. Yes, Jodi went down on Travis. Yes, Travis ejaculated. This time, she's not sure where he ejaculated (she probably changed the "in my mouth" answer after reading disgust on the jurors' faces). Everything is the same as the last story save a few minor details. This time, Jodi is not serviced. She claims Travis ended the session "by flipping the visor mirror back into place". Nurmi had a little heyday with that one, acting like he couldn't understand why the mirror had to be put back in place. Jodi filled in the blanks and said that Travis liked to watch her perform.

After it's over, Nurmi wants to know what happened. Travis refused to kiss her, but he pecked her on the cheek, and within minutes, he left the car and drove off. Jodi says she was deflated and disappointed with herself. The activity was not new to her, but the rapidity of the behavior was new to her. Jodi went home and got ready for work. While she was at work, Travis sent Jodi a text message. Through many objections, Jodi is finally able to say that Travis was expressing disappointment with himself for having had this encounter.

There's more end of day banter about lengthy emails – sexual and spiritual – and I have no doubt that Nurmi will delve into those in greater detail later. Jodi mentions that she saw Travis again a month later, in October. She met him in Ehrenberg, Arizona (a town on the border of Arizona and southern California). I know we'll be hearing about that trip again.

At this point in the story, Jodi is entertaining Mormon missionaries twice a week in her home. She claims that she was attending church and going through the baby steps of "Discussions", a form of religious instruction. Nurmi asks if The Vow of Chastity ever came up during the discussions. Jodi claims that she wasn't really familiar with that doctrine at the time, and, well, you know – those male missionaries who were coming to her house didn't really want to talk about sex with a young, single woman (one of the missionaries who were sent to Jodi's home was interviewed by a media outlet. He said that they told her about the Law of Chastity. They address it with every person they instruct. He rattled it off like it was second nature. There is nothing vague about The Law of Chastity. I heard it just that once, and I knew exactly what it meant. So did Jodi).

Nurmi is back to Ehrenberg. What were they going to do there? Jodi says they were going to hang out and, of course, Travis "strongly hinted at intimacy". Nurmi pretends to be confused. Didn't Travis have misgivings about the last intimate encounter? Jodi confirms that Travis did have misgivings about the last encounter, but intimacy was still one of the reasons they were getting together again. Nurmi asks if the two had not yet experienced what he refers to as "penile/vaginal" intercourse or anal intercourse. Why he asks is anyone's guess. He knows damn well she wouldn't have left that out of her already over-detailed sexual testimony. I guess it's supposed to be a teaser of things to come. Wow, so much to look forward to. Jodi is gonna get naked again!

Jodi admits that the moment Travis answered the door in Ehrenberg, he led her over to the bed, and the sex started. Passionate kissing, clothing removal, romantic weekend, etc. Thankfully, the judge wants to go home. This ends the second day of Jodi Arias' direct testimony. If you think Nurmi actually flew by that Ehrenberg testimony, don't worry. By the time he's done with it, you'll know what the bedspread in their motel room looked like.

CHAPTER THREE

- Day 3 -

"Things come apart so easily when they have been held together with lies."
Dorothy Allison

Jennifer Willmott is pretty in pink (think bubblegum, and you've got the shade), and she looks like she's ready to take a family Easter portrait at Sears. Nurmi is wearing an olive jacket, slate blue shirt, and a coordinating tie that matches the shade of the shirt so exactly that I'm left wondering if it is one of those shirt and tie combos packaged in cellophane and sold in Marshalls. Then I think about the size, and I realize that his ensemble didn't come from Marshalls.

Jodi takes the stand in a deep green top with a green patterned collar and matching cuffs on short sleeves. She wears a large black blazer over her junior department blouse. Maria De La Rose is in the shot as Nurmi takes the podium. She doesn't look bad, just overdone. I can see her light eye shadow, but her jewelry steals the spotlight. Rows and rows of gold colored balls are dripping from her neck and ears.

Nurmi begins by entering into evidence a disk that contains a recorded phone conversation between Jodi Arias and Travis Alexander. The judge asks if the state has any objection, and the camera goes to Juan Martinez. He looks rested, sharp in a pale gray suit, white shirt, and black tie with gray pin dots. He's up on his feet, and he says that the state, as indicated in the record, has never had an objection to this exhibit. With the stage clear, Nurmi is ready to continue.

He begins, "... We were just getting into the time you spent with Mr. Alexander in Ehrenberg... can you describe the town of Ehrenberg as it was back in October, 2006, when you were there?" Why does the jury need a description of some random town? Does it matter? If it does, can he at least explain why it matters? Jodi answers, "Umm... I don't recall its size, but it was very small. Umm... I think there was only one or two exits, maybe, and, umm... it's in the middle of the desert. I think it's actually in California, but it's right on the border". Nurmi would like to know if there was any reason, beyond it being a halfway point between Jodi and Travis, that they had chosen to meet in this town. Jodi responds, "I was driving out there specifically to hang out with Travis". Nurmi wants to know if there was anything -- a lake, park, or site that they were going to visit in Ehrenberg. Jodi responds, "Not that I was aware of, or had planned. It's not exactly a tourist destination". Oh, here we go again. Bad Travis picked a rendezvous point that was lacking in scenery.

Jodi makes it pretty clear that the only thing worth doing in Ehrenberg was Travis. Nurmi wants details about "their make-out session". Coincidentally, Jodi talks about this trip on the sex tape -- the one that was admitted into evidence this morning (which has yet to be played for the jury). On that tape, while speaking to Travis, she was rollicking with frivolity as she reminisced about this particular encounter. She reminded Travis, with great enthusiasm, that this encounter in Ehrenberg was the first time that they jumped on the bed, ripped each other's clothes off, and climaxed simultaneously. She also mentioned, on this tape, the amount of "jizz" that was everywhere. Sorry, but she did.

Let's see if she's still playing the Happy Hooker this time around, or will she pretend that was she was dazed, confused, and taken advantage of. Today's narration sounds a little different than what she said on the sex tape about the Ehrenberg trip, but this time, she's on trial for her life. She says, "He opened the door for me – because he had the room key – and he took my hand, and he led me over to the bed, sort of. He kind of pulled me, but walked me. I went willingly, of course (well, which is it – pulled, walked, or willingly?). We started kissing. It got a little bit more intense, a little bit more passionate, and then, soon we were both nude on the bed. And, umm...there were certain things that he said, well, like it's not, I don't know, we didn't have intercourse, so to speak. There was oral sex that weekend, but, that particular day, umm, we did at that time what was called – he called it grinding. So, it's kind of like being together (she pushes her hands together to show us what grinding looks like), but not actually having intercourse. It's something that I guess, I guess a lot of Mormons do, but they're not supposed to. Umm... there are different terms for it. Umm... like the Provo Push, and that's a Mormon implication, because it's in Utah. This is what I learned. So, umm..." Juan Martinez objects because, once again, Jodi has gone beyond the scope of the question. He says, "She was asked what she did". Jodi apologizes, and the judge sustains the objection.

The Provo Push? What else did they call it? The Salt Lake Slide? The Bountiful Bounce? The Holladay Hop? The Independence Initiative? The Ogden Offensive? The Orem Score 'Em? Like

Jodi, I have just listed "Mormon implications" – because these towns and cities are in Utah.

Nurmi encapsulates Slut-Fest, October, 2006. thusly: they grinded, they had oral sex, but there was no intercourse. Jodi keeps her eyes down and pretends to think before confirming, "Not...vaginal intercourse....or (unintelligible)". Oh great, I know what's coming... Jodi is about to get a prostate exam, isn't she? Nurmi wants the details. "Did you engage in anal intercourse?". Jodi answers, "No". Oh, fake out. It was just oral sex, after all.

Nurmi asks what day of the week this happened. Jodi says that while testifying yesterday, she had forgotten the day, but today, after all night to think about it, she now remembers it was on a Thursday. How can she be so certain? She explains, "Because we spent two nights there, and he had to leave on Saturday". Okay, and was Thursday not two days before Saturday when she was asked this question yesterday?

Nurmi wants to know what they did after "this encounter". I was expecting to hear, "take a shower", but I didn't. Instead, Jodi explains, "There wasn't really much to do. That night, we stayed in the room. He went to sleep. He flipped on the TV, and we watched umm – it might have been Friday night – but we watched some game shows, Deal or No Deal – he was just flipping through the channels...umm". Nurmi interrupts and asks, "Did you engage in any more sexual activity on Thursday night?". Jodi says that they did not.

Nurmi wants to know how they spent the day on Friday. Travis must have felt safe bringing the escort out into the sunlight, since it was far away from home. They drove to a city called Blythe, went to a movie theater, saw a movie, and went to Sizzler later that day. Sizzler? Is that the place with the cafeteria trays and a buffet? Wow, he really wanted to impress her.

Jodi is talking about movies and buffets, but Nurmi interrupts to ask if they engaged in sexual behavior before the movie. She answers, "I can't remember". He continues, "Did you engage in any sexual behavior after the movie?". Jodi answers, "Yes". Nurmi continues, "And what behavior did you engage in?". Jodi answers, "Umm, that was oral sex". Nurmi asks if the oral sex was mutual. Jodi confirms that it was.

Nurmi asks about the romance of the two day trip. I don't recall her saying that this was supposed to be a romantic weekend. I think what she actually said was that Travis "strongly hinted at intimacy". I was wondering why she suddenly used the word "intimacy". It seemed a little soft considering her usual vocabulary when it comes to sex. Now I know why. Intimacy can go either way. It can be romantic or it can be purely physical. I think she knew which definition Travis was using, but she's now going to pretend that she was led to believe that this was going to be a romantic get-away. Sure, whatever.

Nurmi asks if Travis treated her well when they were not having sex. Jodi answers, "He wasn't treating me bad. He just seemed, checked out. The whole time we were checked it, he was just sort of distant. Umm, we connected, I thought, we connected a lot over the phone. It was different when we were together. Umm, well, over the phone, we would talk for hours at a time, about things, not just about sex, but about other things – things of a spiritual nature – and um, just every subject you can imagine – pleasant things (pleasant things?) – and um, we were discovering things we had in common and things that were different and umm, when we, when we went to Ehrenberg, I was expecting the same kind of energy or connection, but it would just be in person. Ummm, there wasn't much of a mental or emotional connection like there was on the phone. It was primarily physical".

Whether or not Travis was breaking religious covenants is not important to me. The defense will use that framework to paint him as a hypocrite. I don't think he was a hypocrite -- not as far as Jodi was concerned. I think his behavior is sending a very clear message, and her behavior is saying "message received". It's apparent that he doesn't think she's a fascinating conversationalist. He does not find her opinions on "every subject you can imagine" particularly interesting or worth exploring when they are face to face. There is nothing I have heard from Jodi Arias that leads me to believe that she was not completely aware of the bargain they had struck. Whether deliberately or accidentally, Jodi has admitted that in their earliest days, they were more connected on the phone than they were when they were actually together. If she didn't like their face to face chemistry, she should have kissed him on the cheek and said goodbye. Dignity intact. Crisis averted.

Jodi wasn't going to do that. She was going to fix it. She was going to change her persona to make herself everything Travis was looking for. Changing your character is far more difficult that perfecting a sexual technique, and I like knowing that she tried (and failed) to be more than a sexual blow up doll to a man who needed far more than a sex toy. I want her to live with that knowledge. She could not stimulate anything in him beyond the most primitive and base of desires, and let's face it, almost any woman encountering a celibate man would be able to have that effect on him – at least temporarily.

Nurmi wants Jodi to tell us if she believed that she and Travis were in a relationship at this point. She says that they weren't. Really? Sizzler and a movie ticket? That's all it took for Jodi Arias to sexually service a man? Truth be told, it took far less. Wow, and she wonders why he didn't respect her?

Now Nurmi wants to get back to anal sex. Did Travis express a desire to have anal sex with Jodi Arias in Ehrenberg? Yes, she says. Did Travis express a desire to have vaginal sex with her that weekend? No, she says. Nurmi wants to know if Jodi declined Travis' invitation to have anal sex. Jodi answers, "Yeah, he – yeah, I did, I didn't. We did not have anal sex. It didn't just come up one time, he wasn't overly persistent about it, it was somewhat repeated...ly". Nurmi wants to know what other non-sexual activities they engaged in. She replies, "We did CDs, burned music CDs (illegal piracy of music?), some music that he liked that he was making for me. He shared more things from the Book of Mormon with me. Umm, what else did we do? Mostly, if we weren't in Blythe, he was watching television – other than those two activities".

Nurmi wants to know if either Travis or the Mormon missionaries visiting her home in Palm Desert had ever mentioned what Nurmi refers to as "The Vow of Chastity". Jodi says it was mentioned. Nurmi wants to know what Jodi's understanding of this vow was back in October, 2006. She responds, "The missionaries, sort of glossed over it. Well, they didn't gloss over it...". Another objection comes from Juan Martinez. He says, "She was asked what her understanding was." Jodi still isn't very good at this court thing, because she begins to answer Juan Martinez. She says, "My understanding was....". Judge Stephens interrupts her to tell her that she has to wait for a ruling and a question from her own attorney. Sustained.

Nurmi asks her what her understanding of the vow was, and if was sex prohibited. She looks confused and begins, "Hmm...no premarital sex". So she knew. She can't put this on Travis. She can't put it on the missionaries. She can put it on herself. She is not married. Therefore, no sex. Pretty simple, in terms of definition.

Given that admission, the superior intellect of Jodi Arias can now be called into question. I've never believed she was exceptionally intelligent, but that is the impression she hopes to give. I believe she is a chameleon. I believes she watches and duplicates what she sees. If her lawyers use words like "surreptitiously" and "contemporaneously", she'll add those words to her vocabulary. If her psychological reports use words like "incrementally", she'll adopt that word as well. Of course, you don't have to listen very long to see the real Jodi break through. She'll slip back into her slang speech quite a bit (i.e., using the word "grand" instead of "thousand", "shot gun" instead of passenger seat, or even more telling, the word "jizz" instead of "semen"). She ascribes a certain value to words, and that's why it's rather hard to believe that she couldn't comprehend the definition of two very basic words, typically joined together: "premarital sex".

Jodi Arias did not need to search the Bible, the Koran, the Book of Mormon, or any other sacred text to discover the ways in which the term "premarital sex" is defined.

Merriam-Webster's Dictionary, as good for the atheist as it is for the zealot, has a very comprehensive definition. It's Jodi's choice to either indulge in or abstain from premarital sex, but feigning ignorance as to what activities are listed under such a heading is not only unbelievable, it contradicts the high intellect she tries to wield with abandon.

Nurmi will now continue in his Sex 101 course, but before he does, he has a problem to solve. Jodi has just been forced, via Martinez' objection, to stop blaming the Mormon missionaries for "glossing over" the Law of Chastity (something Nurmi is suddenly referring to as The Vow of Chastity). Nurmi is going to have her back up and equivocate...again.

Before we listen to Jodi tell more lies, it is interesting to note that I put "Law of Chastity Mormon" into the search bar, and Mormon.org popped up as the first entry. I clicked on the site, and guess what was on the very first page? Yes, The Law of Chastity. It had a drop down feature and when you click it, you read: "The power and holiness of sexual intimacy requires careful protection so it can be a source of joy and closeness". It goes on to explain that it requires abstinence from sex before marriage, and it extends to the areas of dress, speech, and action. It makes sense to me that a religion which has a stated position on immodest dress would also have a pretty clear position on oral sex between two unmarried people. If Jodi had spent more time googling subjects she claimed were central to her life instead of hacking into peoples' email accounts, she may not be sitting here today.

Nurmi asks how premarital sex was defined, according to the Law of Chastity. Did it mean penile/vaginal intercourse or did it mean kissing? Jodi breathes deeply before explaining, "Well, it was explained to me...(very deliberate pause and stare)...by Travis...(another deliberate pause and stare), umm...". Juan Martinez is getting tired of Jodi's nonsense, and it's beginning to show. This time, he words his objection slowly (as if his enunciation will enhance her comprehension). He says, "What is her understanding – not who's telling her what". Sustained. Nurmi asks, "What was your understanding?". Jodi, satisfied that she was able to accuse Travis just before she was cut off, is now willing to play by the rules, "My understanding was that vaginal sex was off limits, but that everything else was more or less okay". More or less? Nurmi asks, "And who gave you that understanding?". Jodi answers, "Travis did".

The cold, fake weekend is about to come to a close. Nurmi wants to know about Saturday, the morning they left. Jodi answers, "We got breakfast at the neighboring truck stop (Sizzler and a truck stop? Good times). Um, again there wasn't much connection, there wasn't a lot of conversation, umm, I'm sorry, I forgot the question". So did I.

Nurmi brings her back to 2013, and she continues, "After breakfast...(pause)...he, we left at the same time. We checked out, and I took a picture of him. He was in a suit and tie. He had to go to a Super Saturday – it was here in Phoenix, one of the regional events in PrePaid Legal, and I – he hit the road for Arizona – I mean Phoenix, and I went back to Palm Desert". Jodi lets us know that she traveled three hours for this whirlwind of sex, crappy food, games shows, and a photograph. I wonder what she told Darryl when she got home. I wonder if she even cared that her flagrant carousing might be hurtful to him.

"Well, when we parted, there wasn't a lot of affection, so I kind of felt disappointed...um, not upset, just kind of bummed out a little bit. Umm, I don't know, I kind of felt stupid. Umm, I was replaying the weekend – it was my weekend – I was replaying that weekend, and I kind of wished things had gone a little bit differently – maybe just – I just wish there had a little bit more of a umm, a connection, a meeting of minds, rather. Well, I didn't...(pause)... I didn't dislike the physical part, but it seemed like it was missing an important element". The only thing missing was a desired reaction on Travis' part. She anticipated it, but it never came. It came with Bobby. It came with Matt. It came with Darryl. With Travis? He really had somewhere else he needed to be – an entirely different world in which he was needed. For Travis, when recess was over, he hit the ground running. Jodi was expecting Travis to drop everything for her, and she thought her sexual expertise had sealed that deal. It sounds like she's beginning to feel used – at least that's what she and Nurmi would like us to believe. As I listen, I am acutely aware of the fact that this is the sworn testimony of a woman who cannot stop lying, and her attorney – a man who has co-written this script intended to save her life – has been given a lot of latitude in allowing her to talk until she runs out of words or breath.

Jodi tells us that what was lacking in Ehrenberg (and in the park in Palm Desert and in the house in Murietta, California) was an emotional connection between the two of them – something she refers to as "being on the same page". Being on the same page? Jodi Arias is a picture book, not heavy reading. She doesn't have very many pages that would catch the eye an extroverted, motivated, organized man who is fully enjoying his life. For most couples, three disappointing dates means there is no real connection. If a couple finds themselves awkwardly eating and not conversing while on their third date, the relationship is probably doomed. A good connection would leave one of the parties looking down at their plates and saying, "Oh, wow... my food's getting cold!"

Nurmi is beating a dead horse. He is asking variations of the same question over and over. It is irritating, but he's doing it because it allows Jodi to continue to build her foundation. At this point, she takes her grievances with Travis to the next level. When asked if she felt they had grown closer during the weekend, Jodi answers, "I felt we had grown more distant". Nurmi follows up with a sexual question. He wants to know if Jodi was still feeling "too much, too soon" (sorry, Nurmi – that ship has sailed – three times). Jodi answers, "It didn't feel like too much, too soon anymore, because over that month, we had really gotten to know each other very well. Umm, I developed feelings for him, and... (pause).... it just seemed confusing though, even though it wasn't – it just seemed confusing – the umm, sex". This is sounding like a therapy session. Nurmi asks, "What do you mean?". Jodi answers, "Well...(long pause)... I mean, I guess just where the line should be drawn, I guess". The time for line drawing has come and gone. The time for line drawing was when Chris and Sky Hughes put Travis in one bedroom, and Jodi in the other. That was the line.

Nurmi wants to know what kind of line Jodi is talking about. She answers, "Well, to me...hmm...sex is sex. There's just different ways to have sex. And it seemed like, it seemed like, Travis was kind of... (long pause)...umm...I don't know how to put it, but he just sort of seemed like he had the Bill Clinton version, where, over here (she moves her hand), it seemed like oral and anal sex were also sex to me, but not for him". Bill Clinton? Did she really just invoke the name of a former president? Okay, moving right along.

Nurmi will now feed Jodi another question about lines. He's stepped up the phrasing. Now he's calling it "a line of demarcation". He thinks the line of demarcation "deals with the Law of

Chastity". Jodi agrees, but I don't really know what they are talking about. There was no Law of Chastity being respected here. I don't believe Travis would say he was being faithful to the Law of Chastity. Why does that phrase keep coming up between blow jobs? I'm not even close to being a Mormon, and it's completely offending me.

Nurmi needs to write down "Law of Chastity" on a piece of paper and put it in front of him on the podium. He consistently interchanges the word "law" for "vow", and vice versa. It doesn't reflect well on him (kind of like the way Detective Rachel Blaney kept telling Jodi that she needed to tell Travis' parents why their son was killed, and Arias was having a good time realizing that this detective didn't even realize that Travis' parents had both been dead for years). Nurmi brings us back to Jodi reflecting on the weekend. He wants to know if, during that time, she thought about her own behavior as it related to the Law of Chastity. She responds, "I considered it". Yes? And? Nurmi spoon feeds her, "How did you feel about that?". She's going to blame someone – maybe Bill Clinton, maybe Travis Alexander, maybe Joseph Smith – but someone's in trouble. She says, "Well, I trusted what I was told by him. I didn't feel like we were sinning. I just felt (messy, ugly, screwed up face) – I felt a little bit – I felt a little bit used, but umm, I knew I had gone there on my own, willingly...so...".

Nurmi wants to know why Jodi felt bad. Maybe because she felt "a little bit used". Wouldn't that explain why she felt bad? Can we skip this question? No, we can't. Jodi answers, "Well, you know, he gets a hotel room, I show up, we hang out, we have sex, he's not really there – I mean presently, he's not mentally present – umm, I'm getting a lot of attention, but only while we're engaging in sexual activity, and then, we check out and he takes off, and I kind of felt like a prostitute, sort of". Woe! I thought she said she felt a little used, but now she's morphed into a prostitute – sort of? Is that what her Mormon experience has done for her? Well, there's something worth sharing at Family Home Evening. Oh, listen to Nurmi. He likes the prostitute reference. He likes it so much that he wants her to elaborate. She says, "I was more upset with myself. I didn't feel like he mistreated me, but I didn't feel like he was treating me as well as he had been (unintelligible)."

Is this what Travis Alexander had to deal with? She feels a little used. No, she feels like a prostitute – sort of. Hold it, that doesn't mean that the guy who makes her feel like a prostitute – sort of – is mistreating her, because he's not. All it means is that he isn't treating her well enough. So, if Jodi Arias is not being treated exactly the way she wants to be treated, she feels like a prostitute? That's a head case. Poor Travis.

Nurmi asks if Jodi spoke to Travis after she got back to Palm Desert on Saturday. She says that she called him, but he didn't return her call. Wow. Can you imagine what poor Darryl Brewer had to deal with that evening? The slammed doors. The thrown phones. The drawings of men with their heads being chopped off. It must have been ugly. Maybe he even passed her his open bottle of vodka in an attempt to calm her down (or put her to sleep). Eek! It sounds like Sunday was no better than Saturday. Travis still hadn't returned her call, so she called again. No return call. I think

Darryl probably took little Jack to Chuck E. Cheese's for about seven hours. Suddenly we hear Jodi's soft voice. It sounds like it's about to break as she admits, "I left a voice mail, and...he didn't return my call".

Can you picture Travis? He's at church, and the phone is vibrating. He's at lunch after church with a large group of friends, and the phone is vibrating. He's driving home, and his phone is vibrating. Do you think Travis was regretting giving her that phone number yet?

Nurmi wants to know if not returning her calls was abnormal for Travis. She answers, "No, not one night. I did want to know if he made it home safely. I wasn't trying to be his mother, but I was concerned whether he made it back home safely". Isn't she amazing? I told you, this woman is a saint. There she is, feeling all used and prostitutey, and she's worried about whether or not the man who made her feel that way got home safely. Is there no end to her goodness? Actually, there is. This had nothing to do with her concern for Travis' safety. This was the beginning of her practice of keeping tabs on him.

Jodi continues, "He began to call me very late at night by this point, so I would leave a voice mail if I was going to sleep, and sometimes he wouldn't call me back if I told him I had to sleep to call anyway and wake me up, but by Monday, when he had an opportunity to return both of my calls...". If that sentence made no sense to you, rest assured it made no sense to me either. Something has happened. It's almost as though a drug has kicked in. The down, depressed, "I forgot the question" Jodi has been replaced by someone who is speaking very rapidly. I think she's trying to explain her weird little system for never missing a Travis call – regardless of the time of night. Sleep be damned – yes, I think that's what she's doing. I'm still unclear as to why she is leaving him voice mails to say that she needs to sleep if she plans on answering the phone anyway. Even Nurmi is confused. And that last comment about Travis having an opportunity to return both of her calls because it's Monday? Well, that sounds like she knows a little too much about his schedule, if you ask me.

Nurmi stops her. He says, "Let me back up. On Saturday, you're driving home, you're feeling used. You call him Saturday night, and you don't get a return call. How are you feeling on Sunday about the weekend? Are you feeling the same way? Have your feelings changed?" Jodi answers, "Umm, they hadn't really changed. I was trying not to think about it much, put too much thought into it, over analyze it (her hands are really moving)". That's a lie. She thought about nothing else. Nurmi asks a reasonable question. He wants to know why she wanted to speak to Travis at all if he made her feel used. She answers, "I had feelings for him. I wouldn't say in love, but I had warm feelings for him – still sort of in the crush realm, but a little stronger, I'd say". Uh-oh, Jodi's officially in Crush Realm Plus.

Nurmi continues, "So, those feelings for him were more prominent than your feelings for yourself (unintelligible). Is that what you're telling us?" No, Nurmi, that's not what she's telling us. She's only in Crush Realm Plus. She won't be pretending to care more about him than herself until she gets to "Crush Realm! Ultra Extreme! Super-Sized!" She's not there yet. She's still quite in love with herself. Juan Martinez objects with "leading". The objection is overruled. Jodi may answer, but before doing so, she looks up, shifts her left hand from side to side and says, "Can you repeat the question?". Yes, I knew she'd like that one. It may be the first time in her entire life that anyone has suggested she was thinking more of someone else than herself. Nurmi repeats his feeling question, but he adds a few more paragraphs. When he's done, she answers, "Yes, they were". Well, that's it, she's now officially in Crush Realm, Ultra Extreme, Super-Sized.

Nurmi inquires as to Jodi's "feelings of being used". He wants to know if Travis' failure to call her resulted in those feeling becoming stronger or weaker? She answers, "Umm...I think I began to think, well, I sent him a text message on Monday, so by that time, he still didn't return my call – any of those three attempts – I began to think that I had been very stupid, he had gotten what he wanted, and he wasn't interested anymore". Am I getting punchy, or did Nurmi ask her a simple question that required an answer of either "stronger feelings" or "weaker feelings"?

Nurmi wants to know if she was thinking of writing him off at this point. She says, "I wasn't thinking of writing him off. I think if he was moving on, I would have at least liked to have known, you know". There's another way of sending that "moving on" message. Actually, it's the way a lot of women get the message when they've given it up on the first, second, and third date. The communication stops. That's the "moving on" message.

Nurmi is really dragging this out. We all know that Travis and Jodi spoke on the phone again, so can we just get there? Finally, he asks when she got a response from Travis (you could have guessed it was Tuesday. If it was Thursday, he would have dragged everyone through questions about Tuesday and Wednesday). She answers, "Tuesday evening. I would have been at a business briefing, and he called in the middle of that, and I didn't hear my phone because it was turned off, the volume, the ringer was turned off, and so I checked afterward, and he had called and left me a very nice voice mail". Let me get this straight – Jodi Arias, the woman who sent text messages to Travis to tell him that he can call her anytime and wake her out of sound sleep, had the discipline to ignore a Travis call that she'd been waiting to receive for the three days? She just let it go to voicemail? Like hell she did.

First of all, why do I always want to roll my eyes every time Jodi Arias insinuates that she's a business woman at some important briefing. By her own admission, she has earned a PPL haul that hasn't broken $3,000, and she goes for months at a time earning nothing. Secondly, if she counts the days between their last sexual encounter and Tuesday night, can she not figure out why he's calling? It's been four days. What could he want? Sparkling conversation? Witty banter? Hmm... it's anyone's guess.

Nurmi wants to know if she ended up talking to Travis after the voice mail. She claims she called him after the meeting. She said, "He wasn't reassuring me, but the nature of the call was reassuring". Nurmi asks Jodi if she told Travis that she felt used after their weekend in Ehrenberg. Jodi says that she did not tell him that she felt used. When asked why not, Jodi responded, "I didn't want to make him feel bad. I also was telling myself that maybe this was all in my head and that's – I was misinterpreting it, or over-analyzing it, and it wasn't that big of a deal".

Nurmi establishes that everything returned to status quo. Jodi says the same routine began again – late night, spiritual phone conversations that morphed into sexual conversations. Nurmi wants to know when her next visit with Travis occurred. She says it was around Thanksgiving. Nurmi wants to know what the occasion was. Jodi answers, "He was driving to Riverside, where he was going to spend Thanksgiving, and Palm Desert is on the way, so he stopped at my house and we hung out for a little while...umm, and then he continued on to Riverside". Wow. Do you think Jodi was hoping for an invitation to an Alexander Family Thanksgiving? I do.

So, there's not much intel on how Jodi spent Thanksgiving, 2006. It looks like we're going to fly right past stuffing turkeys and talk about baptizing Jodi. Nurmi asks her when she was baptized. Without hesitation, she replies, "November 26, 2006". I know Nurmi will probably drag us through the eye of a needle to discover how Jodi Arias ended up positioned in front of a baptismal pool, but it really doesn't matter what she says. One way or the other, I believe Jodi manipulated the entire baptism to coincide with the Thanksgiving holiday. She probably announced her plan to be baptized, and then expected Travis to invite her to join him and his family for Thanksgiving dinner in Riverside. It's likely that she was imaging herself being introduced to his family as Jodi, the newest little lamb in the flock. I bet she thought they'd even make her a baptism cake (I don't know if Mormons make baptism cakes, but I can guarantee that Sister Jodi didn't know either). Let's find out how Jodi's sins were washed away (only to come back in the rinse cycle).

Nurmi asked, "Who baptized you?" Any guesses as to who might have baptized Jodi? She snaps her head toward the jury and says, "Travis baptized me". Then, she looks back at Nurmi. Nurmi asks, "This, this visit you're mentioning, was that when he baptized you, or was this a distinct visit?". I assume Nurmi is talking about the pre-Thanksgiving "hang-out" session at Jodi's house. She answers, "No, this was a distinct visit. It was right before Thanksgiving".

Nurmi continues, "Were you baptized before or after Thanksgiving?". Jodi answers, "After. Thanksgiving, I think was on the 22nd that year". Wrong – it fell on the 23rd that year. Maybe we should check Jodi's answers more often. Maybe she just sounds like she remembers every moment of every day of every month of every year. Jodi quickly realizes her mistake and says, "Well, the 26th would have been on a Sunday, so whatever the previous Thursday was". Seriously? She couldn't work that out on her fingers? She's always using them for something. This time it would have actually made sense.

We're not quite at the point of Jodi being ushered into salvation, because, as usual, Nurmi wants to know what happened when Travis visited Jodi in Palm Desert the day before Thanksgiving (November 22nd, the date she actually remembers). According to Jodi, Darryl was still living in the house, but she thinks he was at work. So, with dad out of the house, I guess the kids are going to engage in some hanky-panky.

Jodi says this was the first time that Travis had seen her house, so she walked him around the property. What is this, a farewell tour? By mid-January, just six short weeks away, the couple is going to be evicted. Jodi says, "... He wanted to see the pool...umm.... (long pause)...his dog jumped in the pool, and sank right to the bottom (I bet Jodi threw a ball into the pool to get the dog to jump in). That was scary, because Pugs don't swim. So, umm, he jumped in with his clothes and everything on to save his dog, and I took him and put him inside so he wouldn't do that again (wow, good thinking!). So Travis was soaking wet at that point, so he took a hot shower (oh, how convenient – she's got him naked again), because in November, the pool is freezing, and umm, I threw his clothes in the dryer so that they would dry off and warm up (yes, we know why clothes get thrown into a dryer), and we were intimate again, and then we said goodbye". Now, if Nurmi could leave it right there, we'd be fine. Unfortunately, Nurmi wants everything on the table – we know the drill.

Nurmi asks, "You said intimate; how were you intimate?". Jodi answers, "Umm, I don't recall exactly, it would have been oral sex or the grinding again. That's all we were doing at that point". Nurmi's bored with grinding and oral sex. He's ready to move on. He asks, "During this particular encounter, did he ask you to have anal sex again?". Jodi answers, "Yes". Nurmi continues, "But no anal sex took place on that day?". Jodi answers, "No, it was more like teasing, and I said no".

Nurmi continues, "After – did he ejaculate?" Jodi answers, "Yes". Nurmi asks, "And, after he ejaculated, he left?". Jodi answers, "Shortly thereafter". This is so completely unfair. If we are going to talk in this amount of excruciating detail about private sexual encounters between two consenting adults, then there should be ground rules. Why are we being sold a pornographic picture that leaves Jodi unfulfilled and sobbing into her pillow as Travis either rolls over and goes to sleep or walks out the door?

As a juror, this completely one-sided image would cause me to dismiss every bit of this salacious testimony. In fact, I'm starting to get irritated with this. I don't want to hear about it, and frankly, it's quite disgusting. Juan Martinez was exactly right when he said, during closing, that the defense has made this case about sex, but in reality, this case has nothing to do with sex. The sex means nothing. He's right. The sex means nothing, yet it eats up hour after hour of testimony.

Just when everyone listening to this testimony has really had enough, Nurmi elevates the sleaze by approaching Jodi with some photographs. After asking Judge Stephens for permission to approach, something she grants, Nurmi puts two 8.5" X 11" photographs (exhibits 393 and 394) in front of

Jodi. He asks her if she recognizes them. She does her best to treat them as if they were radioactive, picking them up, looking at them with disgust, and tossing them back down. Then she says, "Those are pictures of Travis' erection".

Nurmi continues, "And when did you, how did you, come into possession of these photos?". Jodi answers, "They were sent to me via his phone, a picture message, his phone to my phone". Nurmi moves to admit the penis pictures, but Juan Martinez objects due to a lack of foundation. He wants a date on the pictures. The objection is sustained, and Nurmi asks Jodi if she would like to see the photos again so that she can tell us when they were received. Jodi says, "I think I remember the day". Now we are getting to see some serious acting. Jodi Arias is handed the pictures again, and I'm surprised she didn't ask for latex gloves before she handled them. She is being that dramatic. In utter disgust, she says that they were sent to her on a Saturday. I am actually looking forward to the playing of the sex tape because I want these jurors to see that the Jodi Arias Travis knew would have squealed with delight if she had received those photographs. The real Jodi Arias is not the woman we're seeing play acting in court. Nobody deserves to have their sex tape played in front of the world more than this self-serving, lying, succubus.

Nurmi is so caught up in his penis exhibits (and Jodi is so busy feigning horror at Nurmi's penis exhibits) that everyone has forgotten about poor Juan Martinez and his objection. As Nurmi parades his heft right in front of the camera while bellowing something about Your Honor admitting these exhibits into evidence, Juan Martinez raises his left hand and pleads, "Again... what's the date? Can somebody just announce it?" Apparently, "Saturday" isn't cutting it.

Jodi is attempting to interrupt, and Nurmi interrupts her interruption to ask what date these photos were received. Jodi says that she received them on November 11, 2006. She's right, that would have been a Saturday. Wow. Hot date. Penis pics.

Jodi will now begin her Oscar worthy performance. As Nurmi asks, "Permission to publish, your honor", Jodi assumes the position (no, not on all fours). She looks down and refuses to look at the screen featuring Travis' penis. Yes, she's the one who decided that it was completely necessary to go the route of the X-Rated trial, but right now, you'd never know that she was the author of this entire thing. She didn't get her second degree plea deal, so we're getting exactly what she promised. Judging by the look on her face, you'd think it was Jodi's penis on the big screen. She does she look uncomfortable. Nurmi asks, "Is this something you solicited from him?". Say what you want, Jodi Arias, the sex tape is coming...

"Not directly. I didn't expect the photograph. We were flirting". Nurmi asks, "You were what?". Jodi responds, "Flirting (she looks like she's going to vomit, but she does sneak a quick peak of the penis on her monitor. Then she returns to her penitent nun posture)". There is a long pause at this point, and the camera remains focused on Jodi Arias. Suddenly, the camera shifts to the first row of the gallery. The Alexander siblings are in focus. The two women are looking down, and Steven is looking away. There's a big difference between Jodi and the Alexander siblings. Jodi's dying to look. The Alexanders are just dying.

Nurmi is asking questions as the camera remains fixed on the Alexander siblings. I hear his voice saying words like "flirting", but I'm not listening to him. I'm focused on these two ladies. They will not move. Tanisha has her right hand placed on her temple, and with her head tilted to the right, her eyes remain lowered. Samantha has her head tilted to the left, and her eyes remain lowered, in the exact same position as her sister's eyes. With their brother, Steven, sitting up in the middle, they almost look like two mirrored bookends. Back to the fraud on the witness stand...

Nurmi's voice becomes clearer as the camera leaves the Alexander siblings and focuses on Jodi. She is attempting to look like she's going to cry and/or vomit. Nurmi doesn't seem to care what she's about to do, he just wants to know what "flirting" means. Jodi answers, "I was at, I was in, Anaheim (she's pretending to cry), at the Anaheim Grove (oh, she's regained her composure – no crying), and I was at a Super Saturday for that area, and I was listening to the speakers, and we began to text, and I was... (Jodi wipes away nothing, but it's supposed to look like she's wiping away a tear)... (big, dramatic pause)... we were just text messaging back and forth, umm, it began, it turned flirty, and then it turned sexual, and it went on for hours, actually, just back and forth, just trying to be witty and top each other's last comments...".

I don't know the identity of the older lady sitting behind Samantha Alexander, but she is deeply affected by this testimony. She has her head down, and her hand is rubbing her forehead. She's in pain, or disbelief, or both.

Now we know that Jodi doesn't really pay attention during these so-called "business briefings" she claims to have frequented. Here she is at a Super Saturday event hosted for PrePaid Legal. She's there, she claims, to better her "career" with PPL, but like an obnoxious 16 year old sitting in an English Literature class that bored her, she's got her phone hidden from view while she's texting with her sex partner. I wonder, would Travis even turn his phone on while attending a Super Saturday event? Of course not. If he was texting her on a Saturday, then he was home. If he was at a Super Saturday event in his area, he wouldn't have been playing sexting games with Jodi Arias. That's why he was speaking at these events instead of attending them.

Nurmi asks Jodi if Travis tried to top her last comment by sending the penis picture. Remember, Jodi told us that they she and Travis were trying to outwit each other via text. Jodi answers, " It actually culminated at the restaurant after we left The Grove. Oh, he wasn't actually there, he was in Mesa. Umm, I was with other people (she's trying so hard to look like she's consumed with shame), so we were at the restaurant when my phone beeped. We didn't know – I hadn't received pictures on that phone before. So, when I opened, when I saw I had a message from him, and I couldn't find it, and then I realized it was a file that I had to – I don't know if I realized I had to go into another folder to see it, and then I shut my phone really quick. It was a flip phone".

Nurmi calls Jodi's attention to exhibit 393 and exhibit 394, (he puts one on the overhead projector, removes it, and replaces it with the second photo), and asks her if they are two different pictures. She states the obvious – that they are two different photos. Nurmi asks, "So, he sent you two photos that day?". With her head down and voice barely audible, Jodi mumbles, "Yes, consecutively".

Nurmi continues, "Miss Arias (what happened to "Jodi"? Now she's "Miss Arias"?"), when he did that, was he also requesting that you reciprocate with photos?". Jodi answers, "Yes". Yeah, right. Honestly, I am not convinced that these photographs depict the anatomy of Travis Alexander. There is a male hand in the pictures, and the shape of that man's nails are quite different than the nails we've seen in candid photos of Travis Alexander. Travis' nails had a curved base. The nails on the hand in the pictures are far more square than round. I first heard of this theory on social media – including suggestions as to whose hand might be seeing in the anatomy photos – and I decided to look for myself. From what I saw, I think this warrants a more closer investigation. I have no idea why the state did not follow that lead, but I am sure there is a reason.

In any event, I just don't believe her. Oh, I do believe Jodi Arias received penis pictures on her phone, but I'm not convinced that these particular exhibits are images of Travis. If there was ever a time that I wished ghosts and hauntings were real, this is that time. I would love for the ghost of Travis Alexander to expose this witch.

Nurmi asks, "Did you reciprocate?". Jodi answers, "No, not that day". If this were true, any of it, not only would she have reciprocated on the spot, she would have also captioned each of her photos with profanity laden descriptions. Nurmi asks, "Why not?". Jodi answers, "I was at a restaurant, and umm...(ridiculously long pause with an overdone confused expression)...I don't know how to really explain it, without (umm, lying?) saying...". Nurmi asks, "Well, did you want to reciprocate?". Oh, there's that Arias smirk we've grown accustomed to. She answers, "No, I didn't, but I knew he wanted me to, so I was a little bit conflicted, but I said no". Nurmi asks how Travis reacted to her answer. Let me guess! He yelled at her, insulted her, or threatened her? She answers, "He felt it should be fair, kind of like that. Like, he didn't say that (then why is she saying it?), but he had been requesting photos for a while, at this point, and...". Nurmi just wants to hear the word "vagina". He can't wait for her to finish, so he fast forward her answer by interrupting and asking her, "What was he requesting photos of?". Well, what does Nurmi think she implying? Her breasts? Her ass? Her vagina? All three? She answers, "Umm, naked pictures". Many people have seen the naked, close-up photos of Jodi Arias' genitalia. Frankly, it looks like a medical textbook. The fact that Travis did not realize that Jodi Arias does not look like a normal woman gives some credibility to the fact that he was not particularly familiar with the female anatomy – either in photograph form or in actual flesh. There are many theories as to why Jodi looks the way she does. Those theories would have never come up in court. HIPPA regulations.

Nurmi continues, “Of you?”. No, Nurmi. He wanted naked pictures of her mother. Please. No, not good enough. Naked pictures doesn't give us a clear enough mental image. Nurmi actually asks what specific body parts Travis wanted Jodi to photograph and forward to him. Jodi answers, “No, he didn't specify body parts, that I remember”. Nurmi continues, “Up to this point in time, where you received this picture, these pictures of his erection, you had not sent him any pictures, is that right?”. Jodi answers, “Yes”. Nurmi says that he doesn't want to get too far down the road, but he wants to know if Jodi felt guilty about not reciprocating. Juan Martinez objects because Nurmi is leading the witness. He is certainly leading the witness, and the place he's leading her is right inside her jail issued underpants. Oh, well. Objection overruled.

Jodi says she did feel guilty. I don't believe she's capable of feeling guilt, but I'll go along with it, for the sake of the trail. Jodi says she didn't want to disappoint Travis, but she ultimately realized that she had disappointed him. Suddenly, Nurmi doesn't want to talk about Jodi's lady-ish parts anymore. Now he wants to talk about her baptism. I assume he's jumping to that story because he knows how it will end, and that's exactly where he wants to be.

Nurmi switches gears and asks, “So, you say you were baptized on November 26, 2006, is that right?”. Gentle Jodi, meek and mild, affirms the date of her staged baptism. She keeps her head down, breathes very deeply, and she's noticeably swallowing. There's a large box of Kleenex right in front of her. I'm just waiting for her to start ripping the white tissues out of the box. She tends to rub them against her nose, but rarely do we see her wiping her eyes. It seems ironic that so much paper was wasted at the hands of this post-custody, rabid environmentalist. I guess she's a proponent of situational ethics.

Nurmi says, “We heard a little bit from Mr. Freeman about the process, but I wanna hear what you went through, umm, leading up to it, okay? I want to discuss that now, okay?” I didn't know an attorney needed permission to ask a question of his witness, but it makes no difference. Jodi approves of the topic. Nurmi continues, “So, you remember a particular point in time, maybe a month, a year, that you decided that you wanted to join the Mormon faith?”. Hell, Nurmi, I could answer that: September, October, or November, 2006. How's that for narrowing it down? She never wanted to join the Mormon Faith – she wanted to join Travis' faith. If he had been a practitioner of Hinduism, Jodi would have been looking for her place in the Caste System in the fall of 2006.

Jodi begins, “Umm...it was a series of experiences that brought me to make that decision ultimately”. This is so rehearsed that it's starting to look like a high school play. Jodi has been coached excessively, and her awkward pause and subsequent questioning look toward Nurmi lets us know that she has been told to break down these answers into tiny increments. There is absolutely no reason for Nurmi to have to ask her to “describe what she means” over and over again. They are making this script drag on and on, and it's painful.

Jodi obliges, "Well the first week, the missionaries came, they invited me to church that following Sunday. This time, I had actually slept (she gives the jurors a knowing smile), so I was actually able to pay attention to what was being said, and someone was giving a talk, and what that person said was very impactful, and it was something that I had not heard umm, other Christians embrace before, but it was something I personally embraced, and...". Nurmi cuts her off, but before we hear from him, let's take note of something she just said. She was able to pay attention this time because she actually slept? The implication is obvious; she couldn't remember the last church service because of Travis' alleged intrusion into the guest room at Chris Hughes' home.

If I remember correctly, Jodi did sleep that night. She even spoke about waking up, finding herself covered with blankets, getting up, getting dressed, and going back to sleep. Today, she'd like us to believe that Travis was the reason she never heard anything "impactful" in the first service. Actually, her recollection of the first service was limited to people giving talks after they got up to a podium.

Nurmi is about to quiz her, and how I wish there was a tape recording of that particular service so we could determine whether she actually listened, or whether she's just making this part up. Nurmi wants to know what she heard that moved her. Jodi answers, "Am I allowed to say what he said?". She's letting her lawyer know that she caught something he missed: a possible hearsay objection from her Napoleonic adversary, Juan Martinez. Nurmi instructs her, "Well, just tell us the general subject matter". Jodi continues, "It was, umm, it was (she looks up) an acceptance and tolerance of (Coffee? Tea? Grinding?) all faiths in the world, basically (doubt it, very much. She must have stumbled into a Unitarian Universalist church if that's what she heard. Faiths that honestly accept other faiths don't make conversion attempts the cornerstone of their faith). Nurmi continues, "And you found that aspect of the Mormon church to be in line with your own personal beliefs?". After listening to her ramble on at will for hours and hours now, I'm not convinced Jodi has any personal beliefs beyond those based in narcissism, short cuts, and self-preservation.

Jodi continues, "Yes". Nurmi would now like further clarification as to what other experiences led her to choose to be baptized into the Mormon faith. She answers, "The more – Travis and I talked about the Mormon church a lot, and I asked him any questions I had. I asked the missionaries also, but I was able to ask Travis a few more questions on a personal level, and, umm, not necessarily a sexual level, but just things I wasn't comfortable asking two 20 year old guys (all she needed to do was ask to speak with a woman in the church, but we've seen how much Jodi dislikes interchanges with females), so, umm, the more that I discovered about the church, the more I realized that it did not conflict with my beliefs. It was in alignment with a lot of the values that I had, and especially the family values, and the emphasis they place on families, and marriage, and the importance thereof (thereof? Did she just say "thereof"... scale it back, Jodi. It sounds fake), and, umm, I didn't like the no coffee rule (smiling broadly with a "Hey, call me a sinner, folks, but I love me some Starbucks!" expression on her face). I almost – I couldn't imagine giving up coffee at that point – I drink it every morning and sometimes in the evenings (not anymore). Umm, but that was the only thing that bothered me. There was no alcohol, but I wasn't really a drinker anyway, so that didn't really bother me. But, it just, everything seemed to line up for me as far as my beliefs, and the lifestyle that I was interested in leading".

Family values? Look directly in front of you, Jodi Arias. Look right over the heads of Juan Martinez and Esteban Flores. Focus. Do you see those people in the gallery? They're the ones with the tortured faces – alternating between imprisoned rage, disbelief, and abject sorrow. They are what we call a family. They have family values, very strong family values. Their family values are so strong that they are willing to suffer the humiliation of all humiliations by listening to, looking at, and cementing in their memories the most personal, sexual information being spewed about their brother, and it's coming from the mouth of his murderer. Family values? You depleted their family, Jodi Arias. You lessened it. You subtracted from it. You devastated the selfless matriarch of their family, likely hastening her death and blackening the countless hours contained in what should have been her last, peaceful years on this earth – her reward – and you did that after you savagely erased the life of another member of their family. Family values? You have never been able to function in your own family of origin. In fact, you disrespected your own family with such utterly contemptuous behavior that they were likely relieved when you fled like a coward, without even uttering so much as a goodbye, at the age of 17. Family values? You are the antithesis of family values.

What about this particular faith was so compelling to Jodi Arias? She has not convinced me, not in the slightest, even with the addition to her testimony of stuffy little adverbs like "thereof", that there was any epiphany or spiritual revelation that led her to sully the membership of the LDS church. Her tale of conversion sounds nothing like a tale of true conversion, regardless of the faith. Actually, Jodi's alleged life changing experiences are more akin to the thought processes of some random individual who preferred to order their spiritual convictions a la carte, but couldn't. When restricted to choosing from a set menu, she leaves on her plate what doesn't appeal to her ("I like that, I don't like that, but it comes with the entree I really like, so I guess I'll just push it to the side).

Again, back to Merriam-Webster's for a definition Jodi should have looked at before she claimed a genuine conversion experience. Conversion: "to change from one form or state to another, the act or process of changing from one religion, belief, etc. to another". Notice that she talks about things like alcohol; she wasn't a drinker, so no sacrifice was necessary. Check. She talks about coffee; that was her big challenge, and I don't believe she gave that up. Half a check – maybe. I'm surprised she didn't bring up the tobacco prohibition; that would have been a big check, and she does love to tell the world that she doesn't smoke. What about Jodi going on a two year mission? Did she ever do that?

What about the bigger issues – not coffee, not tea, not alcohol. What about issues of theology; this is, after all, a religion that's being discussed. What about her ideas concerning a supreme being, original sin, salvation, prophets, sacred texts, and eschatology? How did she feel about the meatier issues, the social positions of the church – the ones she won't address because the Mormon position might run counter to an individual juror's position. How about homosexuality? Does she know what the LDS doctrine says about homosexuals? How about abortion? Does she agree with their teachings on that subject? What about divorce? What about remarriage? Are those subjects too controversial for Nurmi to frame with faux interest? Any or all of these things are issues a true convert would speak about when talking about their conversion. She touches on none of them. Is he, at the very least, going to ask her to explain the spiritual relevance of baptism? Is she going to at least attempt to articulate the symbolism in terms of the LDS faith – the belief that she is, according to the LDS church, an entirely new creature when she is lifted from the water?

The specific faith is irrelevant, but if an individual, any individual, does not share the belief behind whatever rituals are being performed, they should have the human decency to sit in silence and not disrespect them by making them common and void, and above that, they should not be participating in them.

The biggest question, of course, and something Nurmi will most likely try to explain again via this rehearsed Q & A, is the issue of premarital sex. Despite all of her tortured feelings of emotional anguish, feeling used, feeling "bummed out", feeling stupid, and feeling like a prostitute, was the Law of Chastity ever on her check list? The huge issue for her was coffee? Are we seriously being asked to believe that?

Back to court. Nurmi asks, "Once you made this decision internally to be baptized, how do you move from, how do you, move from that point in time to November 26, when you were actually baptized? Is there a process you went through with the church? Can you just kind of describe, and explain that to us?". This should be good. Jodi answers, "Yes, umm, the missionaries finally asked me if I was ready to be baptized, and I told them yes, so they set up an interview with another... (searching for the word)... umm, young man. I think he was an elder, and he asked me a series of questions – it's like an interview you have right before you're baptized to see if you're ready to be baptized". She is uncomfortable with these questions. I understand why. She obviously lied to her interviewer, but it was a plan she couldn't cancel. Can you imagine the phone calls and texts to Travis in which she went on and on about how nervous she was about this interview?

Nurmi wants to know the date of the interview. Jodi claims she doesn't remember the date, but she does know it was close to her baptism date of November 26, 2006. Nurmi asks, "What sort of subjects were – what sort of questions were you asked? What was the subject matter, the questions you were asked during this pre-baptismal interview?". Jodi answers, "It was so long ago. I don't remember the exact questions, but they were... they asked umm, questions about your belief in Jesus

Christ and the veracity of the Book of Mormon and about your belief in Joseph Smith being a prophet of God and if you had been obeying The Word of Wisdom -- which is the coffee and tea, etc., and if you've been obeying the Law of Chastity – which, to my understanding at that time was, I guess, different. Umm...". Umm, indeed.

I did a little research, drawing from sites frequented by current and former Mormons, who are quite familiar with the questions Jodi Arias was asked during her baptismal interview. Then, I found a much more concise version of the baptismal interview from the site, LDS4U.com. This is from page 206 of the Mormon manual, "Preach My Gospel". If you do not give the textbook answers to these questions, you will be referred to the mission president to determine whether or not you qualify for baptism. Pay particular attention to 4a:

Do you believe that God is our Eternal Father? Do you believe that Jesus Christ is the Son of God, the Savior and Redeemer of the world?

1. Do you believe the Church and gospel of Jesus Christ have been restored through the Prophet Joseph Smith? Do you believe that [current Church President] is a prophet of God? What does this mean to you?

2. What does it mean to you to repent? Do you feel that you have repented of your past transgressions?

3. Have you ever committed a serious crime? If so, are you now on probation or parole? Have you ever participated in an abortion? a homosexual relationship?

4. You have been taught that membership in The Church of Jesus Christ of Latter-day Saints includes living gospel standards. What do you understand of the following standards? Are you willing to obey them?

a. The Law of Chastity, which prohibits any sexual relationship outside the bonds of a legal marriage between a man and a woman?

b. The Law of Tithing (correct answer: includes 10% of wages, lottery winnings, inheritances, settlements, monetary gifts, and every source of income).

c. The Word of Wisdom (correct answer: for the purposes of this interview, it refers to the coffee, tea, alcohol, tobacco, and illegal drug prohibitions).

d. The Sabbath day, including partaking of the sacrament weekly and rendering service to fellow members.

5. When you are baptized, you covenant with God that you are willing to take upon yourself the name of Christ and keep His commandments throughout your life. Are you ready to make this covenant and strive to be faithful to it?

Generally speaking, that's a tall order. Specially speaking, I have to ask, is it even remotely possible that Jodi Arias did not understand the totality of The Law of Chastity?

Nurmi continues, "...And your understanding of the Law of Chastity was abstaining from penile/vaginal intercourse. That's what your understanding was, is that correct?" Jodi answers, "Yes". Does Jodi speak English? Up until this moment, she's tried to convince us that she is a master of the English language – the one to rival. We are being asked to believe that the most verbally ostentatious individual I have ever seen on a television screen had this single, coincidentally self-serving, language failure. Forget all about Travis and his allegedly muddy teachings; the question, as posed by every LDS interviewer, is worded the same way. It says, "prohibits ANY sexual relationship outside the bonds of a legal marriage between a man and a woman". She was not simply asked, "Are you obeying the Law of Chastity?" They do not let their converts get away with what Jodi is implying. How she was able to sit there and recall the graphic images of oral sex while pretending that she was unaware that the word "any" actually meant "any", must drive every devout Mormon crazy. At the very least, and I'm talking about a convert with a lower than 70 IQ, someone being faced with this question after they had been told that the restriction was completely limited to one specific sexual act, would certainly take this issue up the food chain – if they were serious about their commitment.

Nurmi knows nobody is buying this – how could they? His only option is to try and break it down again. In fact, he plans to break it into such tiny pieces that nobody will see it anymore. He asks, "So, when you were asked this question, based on your understanding, you believed that you were in line with the Vow of Chastity (it's the Law of Chastity, Nurmi, not a Vow of Chastity), is that correct?" I don't think Jodi even believes what she's saying, "Yes, (she extends both of her hands, palm side up), in a technical sense, I believed I was". Funny, I didn't see the word "technical" in that interview. Again, for those of us still not swallowing this nonsense, Nurmi repeats part two of this mantra of lies, "And this belief was based on what Mr. Alexander was telling you?". Jodi answers, "Yes". I don't know if he'll revisit this subject again later, or if he hopes he's buried it for good, but now Nurmi is ready to move on.

He continues, "So, after this interview, were you approved to be baptized? What is the process from that point on?". Jodi responds, "I wasn't approved right away because I told the person that Darryl still lived in the house, and so he said he'd have to check, umm, since he's an ex-boyfriend and he's the opposite sex, and that's discouraged in the church – to live under the same roof as somebody of the opposite sex who's not family, or not your spouse. So, he checked, and I interviewed with another – I think it was a branch president – just to check, and he wanted to make sure that we were in separate bedrooms and that it wasn't going to be an ongoing living situation, and Darryl had plans to move in about another week or two, back to Monterey, so we were going to postpone the baptism, but the branch president said that he feels that the baptism should go forward as scheduled instead of postponing it until after Darryl moved". Nurmi responds, "Okay", but I beg to differ. This is not "okay".

Does this liar believe that her many words -- the silly detail about Darryl moving out in a week or two, telling us where's he's going (who cares if Darryl goes to Monterey or Timbuktu?), or her feigned uncertainty about the actual title of the second interviewer will make us all forget about the bottom line here? The fact is that she FAILED the interview, and she failed it because the interviewer found it problematic for an unmarried woman to merely be living under the same roof as a man to whom she was neither related or married. They were in separate bedrooms, and according to Jodi, the sex had stopped (which I believe). However, these people are so serious about the sexual restrictions inherent in their faith that merely living at the same address as a man to whom you are not legally connected is enough to stall a baptism and have it require special clearance from someone with more authority.

Nurmi would like to know how long her baptism application (for lack of a better word) was delayed. Suddenly, Jodi Arias, master of useless details, cannot tell us how long she had to wait to be ushered into the LDS faith. She responds, "I would say roughly a week... I don't remember...exactly...it wasn't...it was close to the date". This is good enough for Nurmi. He continues, "So, you were aware of your impending baptism when Mr. Alexander came to visit you at your home?". Jodi looks shifty eyed, like she doesn't trust where Nurmi is going with this, but she answers, "Yes. I believe I was". He continues, "Who baptized you into the Mormon faith?". Can a prosecutor object with "asked and answered", or is that solely a tool for a defense attorney who thinks his client is being badgered under cross-examination? We all know who baptized Jodi Arias, but let's all say it together with Jodi: "Travis baptized me (there's a new hand gesture, made to punctuate her statement. She quickly lifts both hands, places them close to each other, palm to palm, and after she puts them together, she rapidly points them down for emphasis)".

Nurmi asks, "How was that decision made, that he was to be the person who baptized you?". Jodi answers, "Umm, well, when I decided I was going to get baptized (she's looking a little confused), there was a period in early November, I think...(her speech slows down) or maybe it was mid-November, and Travis had been a little more distant again, so I was kind of questioning where we were going with things on that. I still wanted to get baptized, and umm, when I asked the missionaries – well, when they had told me – asked me if I was ready, and I told them yes, I asked them if – his name was Elder Jensen – I asked him if he would do it, because second to Travis, he had taught me so much about the church at that point, and he had said that it's better...".

Objection from Juan Martinez. Hearsay. Nurmi responds, "It's not being offered for the truth of the matter asserted". Judge Stephens instructs Nurmi to rephrase the question, which he does: "Did he accept your invitation to baptize you?". Arias, doing another messy face, responds, "No, he didn't accept it. He didn't...". Juan Martinez interrupts with another objection. Beyond the scope. The objection is sustained, and Nurmi moves on He asks, "To your understanding, why not?". Jodi responds, "I don't recall exactly what he said. He encouraged me to find somebody...". Another objection from the prosecutor. This time he says, "Hearsay. She doesn't recall exactly what he said".

The objection is overruled, and Jodi is instructed to answer. She continues, "I remember the essence of it, and that was that he encouraged me to find somebody – not him or his partner, not one of the missionaries". Nurmi continues, "Apart from those individuals and Mr. Alexander, did you have a close relationship with any other member of the church that would be – that would have the ability to baptize you?". Jodi answers, "Not a close relationship. I had acquaintances. Not really in that area, in that small branch. I didn't hang out with them too much at that point, so not really". Why wasn't she hanging out in her singles' ward? She made much ado about the importance of attending the singles' ward once she moved to Mesa into Travis' backyard. Why did it only matter in Arizona and not California?
"So, how did you come to the point in time that you, then, wanted Travis to baptize you?", asks Nurmi. Jodi answers, "He was the only other person I could think of and umm, he was the person I was initially thinking of also. So, I just decided to go ahead and, well, he asked me first if I was, if I decided whether or not I was going to be baptized, and he said, oh that's great...". Juan Martinez objects. This is hearsay, and she's referring to a conversation. The objection is sustained. Nurmi earns his pay by putting a few more words into the transcript. Waving his arm, he says, "Mr. Alexander was happy to learn that you were being baptized?". Jodi answers, "He was happy to learn that, yes". He was happy to learn she was being baptized, but disappointed to learn that she wasn't sending nude photos to him. What a whirlwind, crazy romance.

Nurmi asks, "Did you then invite him to baptize you?". Jodi answers, "Yes". Nurmi continues, "Do you recall when you made that invitation?". Jodi answers, "I don't. It would have been November. I don't remember the exact date (perhaps when she was at her business briefing in early November)". Nurmi asks, "Did this happen in person or over the phone?". Arias is clear, "It was over the phone". Nurmi continues, "Where did your baptism take place?". Jodi responds, "In Palm Desert". Nurmi asks, "What was involved – well just describe for us, your baptism. Was it just you and Mr. Alexander or were there other people involved?".

This was probably a highlight of Jodi's life. Despite some setbacks and recurring doubts, she's actually put a plan into place that has Travis Alexander coming back from Riverside to Palm Desert at the end of the Thanksgiving weekend to wash Jodi's sins away. I think she's going to be very clear on the details here. She says, "Many people were invited. I think it's open to anyone attending, especially church members. Non-members are encouraged to attend also. Umm, Travis...(long pause)...I don't remember if he invited them or I invited them, but the Hughes came out. Umm, a few other people in the business who were church members came to my baptism". Nurmi asks a reasonable question: "Did you invite your family?". Let's see how "Family Value Arias" answers this one. She says, "No, they lived 11, 12 hours away, so I didn't...I told them...". Another objection from Juan Martinez. This time, it's "Hearsay. Beyond the scope of the question. She was asked if she invited them". Sustained.

Nurmi continues, "You didn't invite them? Were you under the impression that they wouldn't have any interest in being there?". Oh, poor, poor Jodi. What's her answer? She's looking down, looking sad, looking rejected. Then, she pulls it together, looks up, and answers, "Well, if they could teleport there, they'd be there, but they certainly wouldn't make the effort to come out there for that event". Wow. Nurmi continues, "Prior to you being baptized, has your family expressed misgivings about you joining the church". A camera goes to the first row of the gallery on the defense side of the court room. Jodi's mother is looking down. She has no expression on her face, and her eyes remain downcast until Jodi utters the word, "Yes". Then, Sandy looks at her daughter. Her twin, Aunt Sue, has a head set on. She doesn't look quite as dead as Jodi's mother, but her expression doesn't tell us much. They'll do what they have to. It's quite embarrassing to be immediate family members of a contemporary Lizzie Borden. Sandy Arias adjusts the right collar of her red blazer, looks downs for an instant, and then she focuses on Jodi.

Nurmi continues, "We say your family...are we talking about your immediate family, your parents, your grandparents, your brothers and sisters?". Jodi answers, "Yes. Aunts. Parents. Siblings, and friends". Nurmi makes a sweeping statement – everyone in Jodi's immediate circle discouraged her from joining the church. Jodi agrees with Nurmi's summarization. We are about to go into the realm of the ridiculous – hold on.

Nurmi asks, "Did you invite Mr. Brewer to attend?". Jodi answers, "Yes". Nurmi continues, "Did he attend?". Jodi looks like she's very happy with the web of rejection that Nurmi has just woven. Of course Darryl Brewer wasn't going to attend Jodi's baptism. Was he invited to the Las Vegas conference? No. Was he invited to attend the party at the Hughes' home that was the impetus for their formal, kitchen table break-up? No. Was he invited to Starbucks a few days later to watch Jodi drink her strawberry frappuccino and perform oral sex on her new boyfriend? No. Was he around to take the farewell tour of the Brewer/Arias estate during which Travis dove into the pool to save his dog, took a hot shower in Darryl's bathroom, used Darryl's dryer to dry his wet clothes, or sit outside Jodi's bedroom door as she performed fellatio on Travis Alexander and allegedly declined his teasing invitations to engage in anal sex? No. Why the hell would Darryl Brewer agree to go to anything that had to do with Jodi's faux-conversion and new boy toy? Nurmi needs to tone it down. We've all been listening to his client's testimony. Darryl's refusal to attend Jodi's latest performance makes him look like the smartest person in a very mentally challenged room.

Aww...Poor Jodi. Nobody from her old life wants to see her cross the threshold to her new life. She tells Nurmi that she was nervous about the baptism, something Nurmi is now referring to as a "ceremony" (it's not a wedding Nurmi. I suspect his client will one day be married, but it will be one of those odd weddings that takes place between a lifer and some oddball who wants to be married to a woman who will never live with him...some man who's perfectly agreeable to a sex life defined by constant masturbation and two hands placed on opposite sides of an acrylic barrier . There will be no white wedding gown purchased at an LDS modesty approved bridal chain...no bouquets of Picasso calla lilies... no bridal party... no temple ceremony... and no back yard reception).

Jodi explains that chairs were set up, there was a podium set up – although not in the main chapel, and people took their seats. She continues, "There were some hymns, well, we opened with a prayer, there were some hymns that we sang, and a few talks that were given, umm, on a few different subjects, and I don't remember if another hymn was sang, but then I was led into the font, I went into the back, and Travis was already in the font...". Nurmi interrupts to ask what "the font" is. Good lord, even if you didn't know by definition , you could certainly figure it out by context. Jodi uses words like "giant bathtub", but we all know that it is the enclosure filled with water, and this particular church calls it a font. Fine, can we move along?

Nurmi asks, "And you said Mr. Alexander was already back there. What takes place as you move towards the font?". Jodi answers, "Well, before entering the font, I changed into, umm, an all white, kind of like a jump suit. Umm, and then there's some steps that lead into the font". Somehow, Jodi knows to look at Nurmi for the next question. He delivers: "And what happens when you go into the font?". Jodi answers, "It was a lot like Dan described. You walk up and, umm (pause), Travis held his hand up and said some kind of invocation, or prayer, or blessing, and I don't know what it's called, umm, he made a declaration, so to speak, and then I was dipped into the water and came back up". Nurmi wants to know if she felt elated or spiritual. He wants a description as to how Jodi felt after being baptized by her lover, Travis Alexander. She responds, "It was a very peaceful feeling". That's the best she can do.

Nurmi wants to know if there is a reception after the baptism. Jodi asks, "Are you talking about what happens after the baptism?". Nurmi says, "Umm hmm", and Jodi responds, "Okay. I went back into the designated area, for the ladies, I guess where they can change, ummm, was changing into my clothes, uhh, umm, Sky Hughes came into that area to see, to check on me. After that, we went back into the main area where everyone was still hanging out, and just talking about whatever, plans for week, whatever, things like that, umm, I think we might have closed with prayer, but I don't remember. I just remember everything sort of dispersing after that, after I was out of the water".

Nurmi asks, "And, how did you get back home that day?". Jodi responds, "That day....I, I drove". Travis comes into this equation, and I wish we could just get there. Ah, there he is: "Did you drive by yourself?", asks Nurmi. Jodi answers, "No, Travis came with me." Does anyone want to venture a guess as to what's next on the agenda?

"Tell us what happened when you got back to the house?", asks Nurmi. The spiritual is about to turn into the carnal.

She may look the same, but she's different. Old Jodi and her sins were either washed down the drain of the baptismal font, or they were bleached out of existence by chlorine. I don't know which sanitation approach the Palm Desert, California LDS temple uses in maintaining their baptismal fonts, but we're going to focus on what came out of that font on November 26, 2006: Jodi Arias, Genuine Mormon. For the record, I prefer the word "pool" to font, but when in Rome...

Arias has just given testimony detailing the religious protocol that led to her baptism into the Mormon faith. Her baptism, in all of its spiritual glory, was like any other baptism in the LDS church. She submitted a request for baptism and had an interview. What should have followed the interview was an approval, but a hold was placed on her baptism. Not one to give up, Arias pushed on, had a second interview, and finally received her approval. I assume there was quite a bit of anxiety on her part leading up to this baptism. The fact that she wasn't immediately approved could have thrown a monkey wrench into her long term plans (i.e. becoming Mrs. Alexander). It takes no stretch of the imagination to picture Arias pressuring the church to expedite the second interview. Travis would have been returning to Mesa, Arizona, from Riverside, California, on the night Arias wanted to be baptized. He would have spent Thanksgiving (November 23) in Riverside, and if he was planning on leaving on Sunday, it would have taken him about an hour to get to Palm Desert (the location of Arias' baptism). It's a pretty direct route, and for all intents and purposes, it was on the way. I wonder if he would have made the long trip to return to Palm Desert had her baptism been rescheduled. It was an imperative, in the mind of Jodi Arias, that Travis Alexander be the man who baptized her.

The LDS church operates with a lay priesthood (basically meaning that there is no formal seminary training or divinity degree required). In order to be qualified to baptize someone, the baptizer must be a priesthood holder (a person who has obtained LDS priesthood authority). It is not unusual for fathers to baptize their own children, or for close male friends to baptize new converts. As long as the baptizer is male, at least sixteen years of age, and has achieved the priesthood holder status, they are entitled to baptize converts. If we erase what we have been told about the sexual relationship between Travis and Arias, he would have been a candidate to baptize her.

However, none of this changes the fact that Arias lied in order to be baptized. In an interview with the Mormon missionary who spent about six weeks visiting and teaching Arias at her Palm Desert home, it was reported that she was very quiet and seemed quite normal When asked about whether or not he directly talked to Arias about the Law of Chastity, the missionary said he told her the same thing that he says when addressing the issue with any prospective Mormon. He used these words, "To live the Law of Chastity is to live a life completely abstinent of sexual relations outside a legal marriage". He didn't have to search his memory. It's a well-rehearsed statement.

I am reminded of something Arias said earlier. She claims that Travis had a "Bill Clinton" approach to sex, but that in her opinion, every sex act is sex. Using her own standard, she knew, despite anything she might now be attributing to Travis, that she was called to be completely abstinent if she wished to follow the Law of Chastity. I'm thinking it would be a good idea for the LDS church to add something to their pre-baptism interviews – call it the "Arias Clause". I'm only half kidding. Oh, and before we leave the baptism behind, I'd like to recall something Arias just said regarding the end of the baptismal service. She said she couldn't remember, but she thought they might have closed in prayer. They absolutely closed in prayer. It's a normal part of the process, and prayers are offered at the end of every baptism in the LDS church. In their doctrine, this practice is considered the laying on of hands to impart the gift of the Holy Spirit. It's a significant thing in terms of their theology, yet she doesn't even remember it happening. She does, however, have a very detailed recollection of the sexual encounter that allegedly followed her baptism.

We are now back in court, and Arias is going to tell us about the spiritual evening she spent with Travis after her baptism. She's already looking down in shame as Nurmi tells her that he wants to talk about what happened after she left church. He wants to know how she got home that day. She pretends to search her memory, and in an uncertain tone of voice, she begins, "That day...(questioning inflection and a pause)...I drove". Of course she drove. She had no friends at this particular church – none that we've heard about, and there is no bus back to her house, so I'm not sure why she feigned confusion as to how she got home that day. It's probably the same way she got home every time she left the church – if she ever attended, that is.

What happened next? Arias answers, "Umm...we got back to the house...his car was parked at my house. We took my car to church, so we got back to the house, went inside (what? No description of walking up the front path and putting the key in the lock?), and we (long pause, staring into the distance, flopping her hands – palm side up – in front of her) hugged...um...(she looks at Nurmi and waits for a question that doesn't come)...words were exchanged (small nervous chuckle)". Nurmi realizes she can't do this alone, so he asks the obvious: "What happened after you hugged and words were exchanged?". She's smiling nervously as she answers, "Aahhmmm...we began to kiss, and things got intimate again". She's letting her answers trail off. When she's said all happened?" There's a significant pause. She finally says, "His hands were wandering, um, and he lifted up my skirt, and...(long pause)...and he pulled down my underwear, and he was pressing against me...". Nurmi interrupts, "What do you mean, pressing against you?".

This is offensive. This woman is a seasoned sexual performer., and by now, we all know that. There is no way that she was traumatized by Travis lifting her skirt. If she didn't intend to have sexual relations with him, why not keep the conversation in the living room or the kitchen?. This is as nonsensical as what she said during her interrogation regarding their efforts to remain chaste. She said they would kneel down beside his bed, and they would argue about who was going to say the prayer that would ask "spirit" to stay. You know where "spirit" might have actually been hanging out? My guess is that it would have been in some public area of the house.

We will now learn what it means when someone is pressing against you, courtesy of Jodi Arias. She defines it thusly, "His whole body". Now we hear audible sighs. Her chest is rising and falling.

Her mouth is open. Her eyes are closed. Nurmi knows his client isn't going to have a panic attack or faint (that's not in the script), so he just pushes on, "Did he have an erection?" Arias answers, "I could feel an erection". Nurmi asks, "And what happened next?". I'm sorry, but I think Nurmi is enjoying this. There is absolutely no reason for this second by second playback. Actually, none of this testimony is necessary. It should have been summed up as an on-again, off-again, consensual sexual relationship.
Period.

Arias cannot sustain the trauma face. She suddenly seems a little more cogent as the next words fly out of her mouth. She says, "Um...he unzipped his pants, and (uh-oh, sad face again followed by a slower tempo), I guess he pulled them down. I didn't see, and he, um...he...he began to have anal sex with me and...". She's done. Without further prompts from Nurmi, there's nothing else she's going to offer except a lot of facial expressions. She pulls off an interesting angry look, and she turns her head to the left and to the right. She's trying to show that she's holding back the rage. She's watched the Alexander women doing this exact facial expression for several days. After practicing in her cell at night, she's gotten pretty close to mimicking the look.

Samantha Alexander just did the best eye-roll I have ever seen – I mean, award worthy. She's good at eye-rolls, but this time, she's topped herself. Her mouth actually opened, like she wanted to say something, but realized she couldn't. Her head actually moved this time – she shook it back and forth as if to say, "no". Tanisha Alexander Sorenson stared ahead, not showing much emotion. Then she picked up her water bottle and swallowed a few gulps. Steven Alexander has a different expression. He's got great posture, and he's still sitting up straight, but his frown has been replaced by a curled lip. He's angry.

Nurmi asks if this is something Arias was expecting to happen. She answers, "No, not that night". Well, what exactly was she expecting to happen as she led Travis into her bedroom? Were they going to reorganize her closet? Arias' face is flushed. I don't know if it's anger or humiliation, but it looks like the tears should be coming in short order. She adjusts her goggles as Nurmi asks, "Is this something that you wanted to happen?". She pauses before finally answering, "Well, I can't say I wanted to, but I didn't stop him".

Oh, seriously? Do we have to look at Sandy Arias as Nurmi utters the words, "When he entered you, you say you didn't stop him. Did you say anything? Did you tell him no?". Sandy Arias is frowning. It is a definite, corners of the mouth down, frown. This is the only facial expression I've seen her display, so far. She's usually poker faced. Aunt Sue is wearing a far less distressed expression. She's still, and she looks silly in her head set.

Arias' huge foot connects with the base of the witness stand. We hear the noise and see her body jerk very slightly. She answers, "No". Nurmi asks, "Was it pleasurable for you, physically?". She answers, "That time, it was painful, somewhat". Nurmi continues to talk about Arias' butt. He asks, “Given that it was painful, why didn't you tell him no?”. Good question, Nurmi. Why didn't she tell him no? I suspect we're going down the “I didn't want to disappoint him” road again. This excuse is wearing thin. She didn't say no. That's the bottom line. Therefore, she can stop playing rape victim. It's offensive.

Her voice is louder now, and she responds, “Eventually, I did. I probably would have just let him continue, but it became too painful (her voice cracks, but those tears are overdue)”. Nurmi asks, “Why did you say you probably would have just let him continue?”. Please, Nurmi, she said it because she meant it. Can he not take anything she says at face value?

Arias answers, “Because I knew that's what he had been wanting for a while, and I, I just, I trusted him (she trusted him? What has trust got to do with sticking things in rectums? I missed that day of school)...I had a lot of trust, and he...I just went with what he was...his agenda, I guess I could say”. Now it's an agenda? Juan Martinez must be seething.

Nurmi picks up on the same word everyone else did – agenda. He asks, “This agenda you describe him having, and this pain you were experiencing, did this go on for several minutes before you told him no?” A flash of the Alexanders shows them relatively unaffected by what they're hearing. Samantha almost looks like she's grinning as she shakes her head again. Steven looks more relaxed, and Tanisha could be anyone sitting in a crowd. There's no marked pain or anguish on any of their faces at this moment. Arias returns to the consensual sexual encounter. She says, “I don't think it went on too long...not several minutes, maybe a few minutes (is there really a big distinction between “several” and “a few”. I guess there is if you believe, as she most likely does, that several means seven).

Nurmi continues, “And from what you're telling us, it sounds like the only reason that you told him no, or told him to stop, was the pain, not your lack of interest in this activity”. Arias looks like a child being disciplined in the principal's office. She is definitely frowning, swiveling back and forth in her chair, and looking at her feet. She looks quite idiotic, actually. She comes out of her trance long enough to answer, “That's pretty accurate. I mean, I wasn't looking forward to it, but there was definitely pain – I had to – I had to have him stop...(her voice drops to a whisper)...otherwise, I probably would have had him continue”. Fascinating. Can we please put her clothes back on?

I truly believe that the only reason Jodi Arias is admitting to going along with this behavior is because she knows what will eventually be shown to the jury. There will be detailed images of Jodi Arias displayed on the courtroom Jumbotron. Every individual watching this trial will be able to look at the anatomy of Jodi Arias – including the areas of her body currently being discussed. It will soon be obvious that anal sex was something she engaged in frequently. She has no choice but to admit that she allowed it to happen. As repulsive and anti-erotic as those photographs are, I am glad they were found. Beyond that, there is the audio tape of Arias squealing with delight about this aspect of their sex life.

Nurmi asks if this marked the end of the intimacy on that day. Arias answered, "He finished...by ejaculating on my back, or somewhere, on me...um, and then we were finished. And then, I mean, shortly after, we parted. We kissed, embraced, and he left". Oh, Arias is sad. This is the same expression she wears every time she says, "he left",

Oh, just a thought? Did anyone care if Darryl Brewer came through the front door? He still lived in the house on "this spiritual day", and he was still paying the mortgage.

Nurmi's back to his greeting card sentiment: "After this encounter, on this spiritual day, how did you feel about yourself?". (Possible answer? "My butt hurt") She answers, "After he left, shortly after he left, I felt...I didn't feel very good...I kind of felt like a used piece of toilet paper (she chuckles, but it's confusing because she still looks depressed)." A shot of Samantha Alexander shows her holding back a smile and rolling her head. Her expression says, "Good for you, Travis. You made her feel like a used piece of toilet paper".

Arias continues, "I didn't continue feeling that way, just shortly thereafter, for a little while, I did". She continues to look down as Nurmi presses on. He asks, "Then, in late November, 2006, after your baptism, does Mr. Alexander stay in Palm Desert, to your knowledge, or does he go back?". Of course he went back. Unlike Arias, the man actually had a full time job and a home that wasn't in foreclosure.

In a voice that sounds like tears must accompany it, Arias answers, "He drove back to Mesa, to my knowledge". First tissue grab, and I knew it was coming. She wipes one side of her nose, and Nurmi asks with faux compassion, "Do you need a moment?" (Oh please, camera person, show us Samantha, show us Samantha!). Arias responds, "No...thank you". Nurmi continues, "After this incident on the 26th, when was the next time you spoke with Mr. Alexander?". She answers, "I can't remember if it was that night or the next night, but it was shortly after that". Nurmi asks, "Did the subject of the encounter, the anal sex you just described, did that come up in your conversation?". Arias answers, "Um...(tissue to nose, never to eyes, and this is happening frequently now that she has clutched a Kleenex)...he wrote me a letter about it, we didn't discuss it directly on the phone, we had discussed things of that nature in the past, and um...".

Nurmi interrupts, "Did you ever voice your displeasure with the incident, to him?". She responds, "Only when I said...". Oh, there's a voice of sanity. I can hardly hear it, but I know where it's coming from, and thankfully, it's coming from somebody who has all of their clothes on. Objection. Hearsay...it's what SHE said". Nurmi responds, "She's the declarant, judge". Overruled, but who cares? At this point, I like knowing that there is a straight shooter listening to every word of this trash.

Arias answers, "I kind of said through clenched teeth, stop, stop, stop, and he stopped, so I think he got the impression that it was not pleasurable at that point, but I never said anything about it after that, of a negative nature". Nurmi continues, "So, you never advised him that you felt like, as I think you said, a used piece of toilet paper? You never advised...". Arias interrupts and says, "No...I wouldn't have told him that...um...'cause I don't think that would have made him feel very good (as opposed to what? A lethal stab wound to the chest, followed by multiple stab wounds, a slit throat, and a gunshot to the face?)". Nurmi, the paternal counselor, asks, "How about how you felt?". Arias shrugs her shoulders before answering, "I was dealing with that".

Nurmi continues, "So after, after this incident, you say you talked to him. Did you talk to him again, on a near daily basis, or a near nightly basis?". She answers, "Yes". Nurmi asks, "And you mentioned these phone calls getting progressively later and later – what time are we talking about a majority of these phone calls taking place?". She's not falling apart anymore. She answers, "He...(long pause)...almost stopped calling me completely before eleven o'clock, eleven P.M. Usually, it was closer to midnight, and sometimes it was closer to 3:00 A.M...um...he would call, and we would talk". We all know that Nurmi wants to know what was discussed during these end of today, beginning of tomorrow phone conversations. He asks, "These talks, they were of a spiritual nature, a personal nature, and a sexual nature. Did that pattern persist in, throughout November – I should say November, December, subsequent to this incident?". Her lips are pursed, and she's staring down and to the right. She answers, "Yeah. New subject matters were incorporated...um...regarding our futures, things like that. But, for the most part, that same kind of thing continued".

Nurmi responds, "Well, let me ask you this. You say, regarding the future, did that future, was that related to the relationship prospects between yourself and Mr. Alexander?". Suddenly, Arias is no longer an emotional or physical rape victim. Her voice is clear and strong as she replies "Yes". Nurmi moves along and asks, "Prior to -- let's even make it specific to November 26 -- were you and Travis boyfriend and girlfriend?". She's very clear as she says, "No, we're not". Bad move, Nurmi. There isn't a woman on that jury (who isn't in the skin for sale business) who will sympathize with a woman who allows an uncommitted man to have anal sex with her. Bad move, Nurmi. Bad move.

"When did you, for the sake of discussion, become boyfriend/girlfriend?", asks Nurmi. For the sake of discussion? This is not a discussion, Nurmi. This is a sworn testimony in a death penalty case. Despite Nurmi's clumsily worded inquiry, Arias answers, "We became boyfriend/girlfriend – well, we didn't term it that (probably because he wasn't willing), but we became, not initially, we became exclusive, to my understanding, on February 2, 2007". Nurmi points out that "the incident" (a/k/a "this spiritual day") took place at least two months before they were dating each other exclusively. Arias agrees with his estimation.

Nurmi continues, "Now, as it relates to these times, and I want to back up a little bit, when you were in public with Mr. Alexander, prior to November 26th, did you act publicly as if you were boyfriend and girlfriend?". Arias gives the answer that paved the way for her baptism, "No, not in public". Nurmi continues, "What about the trip to Ehrenberg? Were you holding hands? Did you have your arms around each other? Was that different than most of the other times?". Arias answers this four questions in one inquiry by saying, "Inside the hotel room, definitely. Inside the truck stop -- the restaurant adjoins this mini-mart, and he...um...he grabbed my butt there – there were some men standing by, and he did that right in front of them -- and other than that, I think, he wasn't too affectionate at Sizzler. I don't really remember. But, he was very affectionate inside the hotel room while we were being physical".

Nurmi asks Arias is she was under the impression that her relationship with Travis was to remain a secret. Her answer is strange. She says, "I got that impression from different things, different clues and hints, and things his friends said...". How could this be a secret if his friends – plural – knew about it? Nurmi wants clarification. He's assuming that the secrecy was based on the fact that Travis wanted everyone to think he was adhering to The Law of Chastity. Arias answers, "I...don't...know. I believed that we were adhering to it. It was more – sorry". Nurmi's given her the "okay/shut-up" signal. He continues, "So, even at the point in time when you had this unwanted anal sex, you believed you were complying with the Vow of Chastity?". Dammit, Nurmi. It's the Law of Chastity, not the Vow of Chastity. For $225 an hour, you should get this right.

Arias answers, "By definition. It didn't really feel that way, but, by definition, I did believe that". Nurmi wants to know why she didn't tell anybody about all of her conflicted feelings in regard to her sex life and her spiritual life. Prepare yourself for the most ridiculous answer on record. She says, "I don't typically talk about my sex life with people – it was pretty much the simple reason". She looks arrogant now. There are no tears, no redness of the cheeks, and no visible deep breaths. In fact, she looks like the Chairman of the Board as she swivels back and forth in her executive chair. She's smirking and defiant. Even her saccharine voice sounds different.

Nurmi wants to know if Travis knew that Arias didn't discuss her sex life with other people. She responds, "He knew I was discreet (discreet? She's fooling around with him in another man's house. That's discreet? She serviced him in a playground parking lot in the middle of the afternoon. That's discreet?)...I didn't reveal anything about Darryl". Nurmi continues, "Did he ask?". This is one of Nurmi's most transparent and prurient questions thus far. Whether or not Travis asked about what Jodi and Darryl did in bed has absolutely no bearing on this case. I'm getting impatient with this line of questioning.

Arias answers, "In the beginning, he joked about it, but he didn't press for too many details. I didn't give him any.". So did he ask, or didn't he? She's the type of woman who made it an issue. She's the type of woman who dangled it in front of him. I know exactly who she is, and she should stop flattering herself. She's not that interesting, exotic, or mysterious, and if Travis didn't get that point across, perhaps she'll realize it once she reads the press coverage of her testimony.

Nurmi wants to know when Arias saw Travis the next time. She says that it was the Friday following her Sunday baptism (that would have been December 1, 2006). Arias got into her car and drove six hours to Mesa, Arizona to see him (big surprise). Nurmi wants to know what the purpose, the plan, the reason for the visit was. Arias answers, "There was another regional event happening, a Super Saturday in Phoenix, with a special guest speaker that was flying in, um, he was really big in the company. So, a ton of people were carpooling, caravanning out from California, and I was part of the caravan, and I think we were all – there were three or four vehicles...(wow, a ton of people)...they were coming from Paris, California, Murietta, other southern California towns, and Palm Desert is not on the way, so that was the last stop where I met them at Carls, Jr., and we all got on the road and drove together for most of the drive". Nurmi will make this testimony excruciatingly slow, and we are approaching the lunch break. I'll surmise the rest of the useless, pointless, irrelevant testimony.

Everyone showed up at Travis' house on Friday night. Jodi Arias was not a special guest. She simply glommed onto a mid-sized group of people who were heading toward Mesa. She had no special invite, and the last time we heard about Arias' attendance at a Super Saturday event, it concluded with her lamenting the fact that Travis sent her a penis pictures and requested her vagina picture in return. So, we know this is a super serious, business event for Jodi Arias.

Nurmi wants to know who ended up at Travis' house. She looks at him quizzically and asks if she is supposed to name names. Of course she isn't supposed to name names – there's too many of them. They finally agree to say that the group consisted of a lot of his friends and "people in the company". Why do I believe that Travis saw her get out of a car, put his hand to his forehead and said to himself, "Oh, shit. Who told her about this?". Like it or not, that's the impression they're giving everyone with this pathetic testimony.

Nurmi wants to know what purpose was served if everyone went to Travis' house. Remember, this answer is coming from the woman who slept under Travis' Christmas tree without his consent or knowledge. She answers, "Yes, a bunch of people from out of state were coming to his house, and we were all going to crash there". Like a parent with a promiscuous daughter, Nurmi asks, "And what were the sleeping arrangements to be?". She answers, "Well, the sleeping arrangements after we got, we got there, it was, we were determining those things...". Nurmi interrupts and asks if Travis knew she was coming to this event. She says that he knew. Nurmi then asks if Travis ever gave her the impression that he wanted to engage her sexually during that weekend. She answers, "No, it was just the opposite". Nurmi asks her if Travis told her that he didn't intend to engage her. Arias agrees with Nurmi's statement. Travis actually told Arias that there would be no sexual encounter during that weekend. I know this goes along with their "dirty little secret" storyline, but I actually think he was embarrassed. I don't think he wanted people to know he was sleeping with a woman who was as easy as Jodi Arias.

Nurmi wants to know if they had a sexual encounter that weekend. Arias says they didn't, but she has to elaborate. She says, "No, but he joked about oral sex, giving him, but he was concerned about his ex-girlfriend there, and he didn't want (her to know that he had sunken to the level of sleeping with a Jodi Arias type) us to be affectionate in front of her". Burn. He cares more about an ex-girlfriend's opinion than he does about Arias' feelings.

Arias hates this part. Nurmi asks if the girlfriend was Lisa Andrews.

No, says Jodi. It was the queen, Deanna Reid. Nurmi suggests that the issue would be one of Deanna being jealous of Arias. Even Arias knows that isn't the case, and she responds, "He didn't say jealous (because she wouldn't be jealous – she would just pity Travis)". Nurmi asks if Travis said anything about how Arias was to act around Deanna. Nurmi implies that Travis "warned" Jodi about Deanna Reid. Juan Martinez objects with a hearsay objection, and the judge dismisses everyone for lunch.

After excusing the jury for lunch, the judge wants to address the last objection made by Juan Martinez. Nurmi interrupts and asks if Miss Arias can step down. The judge gives Jodi permission to leave the witness stand. Jodi moves like a robot, and she descends the stand with a water cup in her right hand. The camera follows her as she passes in front of the judge's bench. She moves slowly and looks miserable. She's aware that there are people monitoring her every move, and right now, their only responsibility is to make sure that she maneuvers from point A to point B without hurting anyone.
Juan Martinez says, "She was going to talk about what Mr. Alexander told her. That's hearsay". Nurmi responds, "Ya know, hearsay has a much more complex definition that just the fact that something comes out of someone's mouth...it has to be an assertion, intended as an assertion by the declarant that was offered for the truth of the matter asserted. This goes to Ms. Arias' state of mind (don't get irritated, everyone. Miss Arias' "state of mind" will be the consistency of jello after her first year in solitary confinement) as it relates to how she was to act in front of this girlfriend, Deanna. It goes to the effect of the listener. I don't think it's hearsay because it's not being offered for the truth of the matter asserted as it pertains to the reasons why Mr. Alexander was concerned about his conduct in front of Miss Reid, and we're now going to the truth of the matter, the effect of how this affected Miss Arias' conduct and the behavior that weekend". Good lord, bring the jury back!

What is it with Kirk Nurmi? The jury leaves and he's suddenly on amphetamines? Juan says eleven words, and Nurmi responds by reciting a paragraph that he remembers reading in some law school textbook? Judge Stephens rules: "As we discussed at the bench yesterday, if you can redirect her by rephrasing the question, that is preferable, and will limit the number of bench conferences we need to have. So, just rephrase the question when the jury returns". Oh, and in case you haven't noticed, there is no limit on how many bench conferences they need to have.

Now, Nurmi, with lunch waiting, is willing to hang around for a few minutes to make "a record". He says he wants to address something to do with the sheriff's office and a request they have made. He intends to make an objection to whatever the sheriff's office has requested. Introducing Scott Dutcher , speaking on behalf of Sheriff Joe Arpaio (for your information, J. Scott Dutcher is listed online as the Deputy County Attorney, Maricopa County Office of General Litigation Services, Phoenix, AZ): "Good morning, your honor. Scott Dutcher speaking on behalf of Sheriff Joe Arpaio. Under the sheriff's objection, there have been some conferences in chambers and in unsecured areas of the court house with Miss Arias present, and that's not something the sheriff permits. I will – after we all discussed this this morning, before court began, I did explore some other options with the sheriff's office, and I know the defense has some concerns, and this may be an option, if everyone wants this, if there are short conferences, in lieu of everyone clearing the courtroom, right over here is a secure area (he gestures toward the door that Jodi disappears behind when leaving the court room). There aren't chairs; I don't know if you can get some chairs, but if it's a short conference, we can all enter this area of the court house, which is a secure area of the jail, and everyone can have – say what they need to say. I don't know if that's an option or what everyone wants, but that or the court room are the only options available, judge. It's a security issue to have inmates in unsecured areas of the jail, and this is not something the sheriff allows for, for any inmate, including Miss Arias". Judge Stephens replies, "Alright, and you wanted to make a record on that Mr. Nurmi?".

Nurmi definitely wants to make a record on that. The record Nurmi wants to make is that Jodi Arias, a sheriff's inmate, should not be treated like every other inmate who is subjected to a trial in this court room. Even inmates who have been charged with far lesser crimes are subjected to this security protocol, but Nurmi will now tell us why Jodi Arias, an inmate charged with first degree, premeditated murder, is somehow different from the regular assortment of car thieves, joint smokers, scofflaws, and drunk drivers who are the responsibility of Sheriff Joe Arpaio. He says, "Judge, I, I just wanna (his speech is much faster, and he uses slang contractions when the jury isn't around to hear him) recite...at least we know the sixth amendment guarantees my client's right to be present at all vital stages of these proceedings, and any denial of that would be a denial of due process and reason for mistrial (how many times is Nurmi going to throw the threat of mistrial into this mix?), umm, in this regard, obviously, based on whatever the reasons were when we were asking to do this, whatever party was, both parties have asked, and the court has understood that under those circumstances, without going into what they are, umm, that those were important, there were reasons for it...that is why some of those records have been sealed. So, judge, I believe, that at least for the record, and our assertion is that regardless – and I'm not trying to get in a dispute with the sheriff's office -- but Miss Arias is entitled to do that. I don't know about the viability from a logistics standpoint what the sheriff's office is suggesting, but I just want to make it clear, for the record, that we're asserting that she has an absolute right to be present, and if, if that means that is facilitated in some way, either through clearing the court room or through alternative means, and that is the basis of our assertion, and we will not waiver on that point. If it gets more contentious in that regard, I would be asking for a motion from the sheriff's office because, again, this is such an important right". Well, Nurmi, king of run on sentences and repetition, I guess all of those other public defenders just suck, or they are not aware of all the princess packages available to their clients. Nobody gets the special treatment Nurmi is demanding for his client, and I'm left with the impression that the sheriff's office has not had to send Scott Dutcher down to plead Joe Arpaio's case very often (he's quite nervous – maybe he's just not comfortable with the television cameras). Whatever the ruling, I hope that Sheriff Arpaio remembers this pain in the ass inmate when it comes time to serve her one of his delicious dinners tonight.

Judge Stephens rules, "The court will make the best determination it can in any given circumstance, including clearing a court room if necessary to accommodate the defense request for a confidential meeting."

I guess the ruling is almost neutral, although Nurmi did get his "clearing the courtroom" option rubber stamped by Judge Stephens. What's next? Jodi Arias is entitled to go to lunch with her legal team because they discuss the case over shrimp cocktail and a New York Strip? There is preferential treatment being shown here. Will it matter? Ultimately, no. Still, I don't like the fact that Jodi doesn't have to sit in the time out room when all the adults are busy talking about grown-up things. I wanted her to feel branded and isolated. I guess I'll take some comfort in knowing that the court will not allow her to be treated like the low security risk Nurmi wants everyone to believe she is. I'll take anything I can get that reminds her that she is not a reality star, but a dangerous inmate (who is soon to be a convict). Anyway, will somebody put her in the basement already?

Okay. Everyone is back from lunch, including Jodi Arias, the basement dweller who smells like peanut butter. When last seen, the murderess was attempting to convince everyone that she didn't inject herself into a group of people driving five hours away to attend a Super Saturday event in Mesa. No really, Jodi is super serious about PPL fist bump events. She was so serious about attending another event, that just happened to be hosted in Travis Alexanders' home, that she drove to Carl Jr's., and waited for someone in the caravan to pick her up. I wonder what was in her suitcase? A few thongs? Some personal lubricant?

Please, just forget her prior behavior at the last Super Saturday event she testified about; the one at the Anaheim Grove – the one at which she claims to have been sexting with Travis "for hours". By the time this California caravan was heading for Mesa (and, coincidentally, Travis Alexander's home), Jodi Arias was a new creation. She's been baptized. She will behave at Super Saturday events, because that's what good Mormons do. Oh, I figured this would be a good place to tell you that my question regarding whether or not Jodi actually completed the required two year LDS mission has been answered. Women are not required to do missions.

There is a lengthy sidebar. Then, the judge instructs Jodi to take the stand. Arias dutifully complies, her water cup in her hand. Everything is moving at a slow speed today. Finally, we hear, "Please stand for the jury".

The judge thanks the jury for their patience, and then she says she is sure they are accustomed to delays. What? Frankly, in my life, I'm not really accustomed to delays, but whatever. I guess she had to say something. Besides, if this group isn't accustomed to delays in their real lives, they will certainly become accustomed to them during their service in this trial. If the divine defendant says she has a headache – something she calls a migraine, all bets are off, regardless of whether or not getting to the court house was an inconvenience to a juror. By the way, the usual reason behind "we will adjourn for today" is based on Jodi's so called "migraines". Just because she's conned a jail doctor into giving her Imitrex, there is no evidence or medical history that suggests that Jodi Arias suffers from migraines, although I have to admit, I'd like it if she did. If you've ever had one, you know it's not a headache. It feels more like your brain is trying to break through your skull. It's horrendous pain, usually preceded by vomiting.

Jodi removes her jacket as the jury is being seated. Nurmi picks up where we left off: "Miss Arias, before lunch, we were talking about the time, weekend, that you and fellow members of PrePaid Legal were spending with Mr. Alexander, and that was at his home, is that right?". Jodi answers, "Yes". Nurmi continues, "You were talking about, you mentioned an individual by the name of Deanna. Did Deanna had a last name (oh please, for $250 an hour, Nurmi knows damn well what Deanna's last name is...in fact, he's already used it used it in his run-on speech after the jury left for lunch)?". Jodi responds, "Reid". Nurmi continues, "And this Miss Reid, what was your understanding of who she was?". Jodi responds, "My understanding, umm, was that she was an ex-girlfriend, umm...of Travis...yes, of Travis'...that she was somebody Travis had once been very serious with...umm...that he was once in love with, and they were both in love, and they separated. Umm, a lot of the history I know is through Travis. All of it, really, and his friends". Nurmi continues, "Umm, were you instructed to act a certain way with Travis when Miss Reid was present?". Nurmi also wants to know what Travis told Jodi about Deanna.

Gone is the rape victim. Gone is the PTSD afflicted flower. Gone is the red faced, downcast woman we saw before she was dosed with three ounces of peanut butter. Now this anally raped defendant is quite composed and clear as she says, "He warned me that she was emotionally unstable (she's happy saying this), she would freak out if she saw him with other girls, if he attempted to move on and at any time date somebody...". Travis was not "trying to date" Jodi Arias. The fact that this is clear to any adult woman just sets the foundation for the prosecution's expert mental health witnesses. Travis was embarrassed by Jodi Arias. Go for broke, Nurmi, but nothing you will say will convince anyone that Jodi Arias is anything less than a hateful, jealous bitch with huge projection issues.

Not that it's even worth arguing, but are we supposed to believe that Travis Alexander would leave his dog, an animal Jodi claimed he dove into a freezing pool to save without forethought or reservation, to an emotionally unstable woman in the event of his passing? No, of course not. There was a woman that Travis had labeled emotionally unstable, but her name wasn't Deanna; her name was Jodi. In fact, Travis made it very clear that any woman he married would have to accept the presence of Deanna Reid. She was going to be a part of his life until he no longer had a life.

Okay...we are now going to watch Jodi Arias paint Deanna Reid as Jodi Arias. According to Jodi, Travis instructed Jodi to act "a certain way when Miss Reid was present". Of course, nobody really believes Jodi, but she's oblivious to the fact. She actually thinks she winning this game. Jodi really should have given a little more thought to the fact that Deanna Reid is sitting in the gallery – not the witness box. The "unstable" Deanna is not the woman on trial for stabbing a man 27 times -- before she slit his throat and shot him in the face. I'm willing to give Dr. Jodi Arias the benefit of the doubt when she's handing out mental health diagnoses, aren't you? Let's not forget that one of her unbalanced fans has paid for her jail addressed subscription to "Psychology Today", so it's safe to assume that Jodi is a lay psychologist (and we already know she's a lawyer).

Jodi says that she believes that her December, 2006, ambush at Travis' house was the first time she saw Deanna Reid, but she is quick to add, "...He advised me to steer clear of her at his house, so I didn't...you know, seize the opportunity to go introduce myself, or anything like that". Oh, just stop it, Jodi Arias. You are trying to act like "one of us"...the normal people...the individuals whose lives are marked by spouses, jobs, bills, children, holidays, and those annoying jury duty summons letters that come in the mail. You are not us. You are them. You are the subject of grand jury indictments. You are the people we avoid talking to and interacting with. Just stop.

On the taxpayers' dime, Nurmi keeps this farce going: "These instructions, if you will, these instructions that were given to you regarding Miss Reid, was that some kind of constant dictate throughout the course of your relationship with Mr. Alexander?". Jodi, in her eighth grade attire, looks right at the jury as she says, "Yes. The entire time, even after we initially broke up". Nurmi continues, "Okay, because you weren't boyfriend and girlfriend in December, 2006?". Jodi answers, "No, we were not". Nurmi continues, "In that regard, you mentioned, umm, umm, and we'll talk about that...from the time you met Mr. Alexander to the time you were at his home in Mesa, for the first time, were you dating other people?".

Oh, Nurmi, were you not privy to her diary? She wrote about how amusing it was to have been invited on four separate dates on a Saturday night (first she wrote Friday, and then crossed it out and changed it to Saturday) – sometime in January, 2008. Word travels fast when the new school slut is in town. Jodi answers, "There were, umm, I was asked out on a few dates, some I turned down, and one I accepted during that time". Nurmi asks, "Did Mr. Alexander know about these dates?". I'm sure Jodi let Mr. Alexander know about "these dates" – whether they were real or imaginary.

My guess is that Mr. Alexander was desperately hoping that she'd accept every date offer that came her way.

Jodi answers, "YYYYYes...he knew about, he knew about when I was asked, and I think (she's now pretending to think out loud – eyes up, hands moving)...I think I did tell him...(she's left the annals of her memory and has rejoined the court room)...I don't remember...it was a church member. I don't remember if I told him". Does this alleged date have a name? If not, he doesn't exist.

Nurmi continues, "Okay. Before we move past December, 2006, based on what you're telling us, there was no sexual interaction between you and Travis during this weekend?". Jodi knows damn well that the answer is no, but she still has to mystify her audience with her false attempts at searching her memory bank for the answer to the question. She centers her chair, lifts her head in the air, closes her eyes, and finally responds, "No (and this should have been the end of her answer, but it isn't), but there were insinuations after everyone went to sleep, but he seemed almost paranoid that...". Juan Martinez objects. Nurmi doesn't like objections. He responds with, "May we approach, your honor". Judge Stephens never refuses a request for a white noise chat with attorneys.

Nurmi continues, "We were talking about the fact that no sexual interaction took place between you and Mr. Alexander, and you were explaining how he was paranoid about being caught, is that right?". Being caught? Inflammatory much, Nurmi? Jodi's on the same page as Nurmi, and she responds by saying, "Yes. He was hyper vigilant about us not having any physical contact, even just holding hands or hugging, or anything like that (Oh, seriously? How thick is this woman? She was nothing to him. Nothing. Why can't she see that?). Here's a novel approach: why doesn't her attorney ask her to define the big word she just used? Does she even know what hyper vigilant means, or is this a word, like so many others, that she has lifted from her multiple jail psych evaluations?

Holy cow...Nurmi asks what she means by hyper vigilant. He wants to know if they held hands, and things like that. Jodi is quite focused. Peanut butter must really agree with her. She says, "Well, even after Deanna left, when everyone found their sleeping arrangements, Travis and I slept in the front room; he had two leather couches, brown leather couches, and I slept on one, and he slept on the other, umm, and there were other people sleeping in an adjacent family room, and there were other people sleeping in the loft, and there were two ladies that were sleeping in his bed upstairs...umm, and even after all the lights were out, and it was dark, umm, we were laying on the couch talking, and he had his hand laying like that (nothing sexual or inviting – it's simply an arm hanging off of a couch), umm, just off the couch, and I just put my hand out and just touched his fingers – you know, nothing erotic or anything (BS – it was the invitation to engage in something erotic, and he knew it)...just being affectionate, and he kind of pulled away and sat up and looked around to see if anyone was awake, and then he just kind of turned over, toward me, and didn't reach out anymore".

So, are we expected to believe that Travis Alexander didn't usher Jodi Arias into the garage, or the front seat of his car, for his ration of fellatio? Isn't this the man who threw caution to the wind in his friend's home (Chris Hughes) after Jodi made it clear that she was offering her genitals to him on a silver platter? By the way, why did Mr. Paranoid allow Jodi Arias to sleep on the brown leather couch next to him? My thought is that he didn't. My thought is that somehow she manipulated the situation to end up right next to him. Women like this degrade all women. The more I hear about her desperate attempts to be serviced by Travis Alexander, the more disgusting she becomes.

Nurmi will now attempt to make this non-event an event: "So, based on your interaction with him over the weekend, you were left with the impression that he certainly didn't want anyone to know that you were involved in any way". Juan Martinez objects with "leading and speculation". Another non-ruling – Judge Stephens tells Nurmi to rephrase. He responds, "Based on this conduct when he pulls his hand away, out of fear of being seen, did that leave you with the impression that Mr. Alexander didn't want people to know that you were in any way intimately involved with him?". Not good enough, Nurmi. Juan Martinez objects again: "Speculation, maybe he didn't want to have sex with her". Judge Stephens says, "Overruled". What the hell? Maybe he didn't want to have sex with her. If he were here, he could certainly answer that for himself...but he isn't, is he?

Jodi triumphantly says, "Yes". I'm bothered by this judge's rulings. I know replacing her would be a disaster, but I have been carefully listening to what she sustains and overrules, and I can tell you, half of the time, either side has a right to be confused by her rulings. She confuses me more than any other judge I've seen. These rulings seem haphazard, random, and they appear to follow no theory. The longer this trial goes on, the more thankful I am that this jury convicted this murderer. The conviction belongs to the prosecutor and his witnesses.

Nurmi, basking in the glory of the nonsensical ruling, smiles broadly as he asks Jodi if she was there that weekend to have sex with Travis. Jodi responds, "No. It was a business trip. I was excited to see him because I liked him (she "liked" the man who, without warning or lubrication, put his erect penis into her rectum)...no, definitely not for that".

Nurmi continues, "Were you hoping he would bend you over the bed and have anal sex with you?". See, if you give someone like Nurmi an inch, he'll take five and three quarters inches. My intelligence is now officially offended. How is Nurmi getting away with this? What a wonderful actress Jodi Arias is – in a split second, in the wake of the anal sex inquiry, she's again wearing the face of the assaulted nun. It won't last long. Nurmi asks, "Now, you didn't have any physical or romantic contact with him this weekend because other people were there, and he wanted to keep it a secret. That was your understanding?". Jodi answers, "Yes, there was one romantic gesture (oh, let me guess – when Jodi went to bathroom to urinate, Travis followed her and hoped to watch? What the hell is she about to say?)...he walked me out to my car to load up my car, or my luggage, and, his friend, Chris, was sitting in their Lexus SUV on the street, and he was on the phone facing, I guess we were in the driveway, and we would have been facing west (the woman who told Det.

Flores that she gets lost all the time because of her poor sense of direction, can suddenly identify north, south, east, and west just by virtue of standing on a random street), because he was parked up near the house, and my car was parked in the driveway, and after the trunk shut, he looked around and saw that Chris was on the phone, and he said, kiss me quick while no one's looking. So, we just kissed, not, it was a brief kiss, umm, and that was it, and I...sorry".

Maybe Nurmi should focus more on the non-sexual aspects of this story. I was under the impression that Jodi drove out to a Carl's Jr.'s to be picked up by this caravan. I naturally thought she left her car parked in a parking lot and joined another car full of people headed for Mesa. If that wasn't the case, then why did she bother going through the details of telling everyone that Palm Desert was not on the way for the caravan, and she had to drive her car to a public restaurant to meet the caravan? Did she just follow everyone in her own car? Why do that? Did she not know how to get to his house on her own, the woman who spent half her life driving from point A to point B? Now, it seems like she drove herself, because she tells us that Travis is putting her luggage in her car. I guess none of that confusion will be addressed, because what really matters is that Travis kissed her on the cheek. In the sick, deranged, and perverted mind of Jodi Arias, that was a romantic gesture.

Travis Alexander is putting Jodi's luggage in her trunk (perhaps that was his way of saying, "No, you're not staying here tonight. Better get going, you have a long drive"). Jodi initially says he was loading bags into her trunk; then, she corrected herself and said it was luggage that was being loaded into the trunk. Umm, I'm going with bags. I'd put money on it. They were probably two, 30 gallon, black plastic trash bags. If she had just said "bags" and not felt the need to upgrade to "luggage", it wouldn't have even occurred to me that her clothing might not have been in suitcases.

As Jodi Arias finishes salivating over Chris Hughes' Lexus SUV (and if it were new, it would have had an MSRP between $40 - $65K – depending on the model), she looks to the west and makes a note to remember Travis Alexander's single romantic gesture that weekend: the quick peck on the cheek. If that constitutes a romantic gesture, I'm in serious trouble. I've apparently given many people the wrong impression. Nurmi doesn't question the validity of her statement, he accepts it and wants to explore the issue further. So, back we go to Jodi in Wonderland, drinking strange concoctions meant to shrink huge issues while magnifying tiny ones, meeting bizarre characters who talk in circles and leave us with more questions than answers, and, of course, sliding down rabbit holes.

I know we are going to learn more about Jodi's sex life – what she engaged in, and when she engaged in it. Travis couldn't win; have sex with her and be labeled a perverted hypocrite, don't have sex with her and be labeled a paranoid hypocrite. Nurmi begins, "Well, let me ask you this: at this point in time you had engaged in several, maybe half a dozen – well maybe not quite a half dozen (by my count, and I have been counting, we have five alleged encounters – Hughes' guest room, oral sex in the park, Ehrenberg and the fine dining experiences of Sizzler and the local truck stop, the farewell tour of the Arias/Brewer estate, and "this spiritual day" -- so I'm glad the detailed defense attorney took six off the table) instances of sexual contact with Mr. Alexander, correct?". Jodi responds, "Eee...yeah...well, how many did you say?". Nurmi's back to "around a half dozen, give or take". It would be take, but what difference does it really make? Jodi drops her head to the left and then to the right, furrows her brow, clasps her hands, and says, "Something close to that". With such attention being given to each encounter, including the penis pics, the spiritual/sexual late night conversations, and the blow by blow (no pun intended) descriptions of what each encounter included, did Nurmi and Jodi forget a few? It's five...in three months. That's it.

Nurmi continues, "Aaaaand, umm, he doesn't want anyone to know that you have any sort of relationship in December, 2006. My question is how did this make you feel?". Jodi's back to her frowny face. This is a serious question, and it is of monumental importance. We could ask Travis how she made him feel in December, 2006, but we wouldn't get an answer. Because she killed him. But, hey, let's all have a life coach moment and find out how Jodi felt when Travis didn't send out "We're Dating" announcements to his family, friends, colleagues, and church acquaintances. She stalls for effect, keeps her eyes lowered and to the right, and without looking at the jury, she raises her right hand and replies, "I didn't give it too much thought (now she's looking at the jury), it didn't make me feel good, but it didn't make me upset (this is her way of saying, 'I didn't kill him because he used me'). It's something I kept ignoring (like the mortgage, right?), and putting out of my mind (she's waving her right hand as if to show us a washing away motion), and just ignoring". Ignoring, putting out of her mind, AND ignoring? Wow, serious denial here.

"Okay, so you weren't mad at him?", asks Nurmi. Without the slightest hesitation, and with the reinforcement of a micro-head shake, Jodi responds, "No". Then she lowers her eyes. What a martyr. Nurmi asks, "Did you ever think, at this point in time, I'm done with this guy?". Done with him? Doesn't being done with someone presuppose that you've started something with them? Beyond an occasional unpaid escort encounter, I don't see much of anything to be "done with" (except long, expensive car rides that serve to put Jodi in the same place as the object of her obsession). Jodi hesitates before answering. She's doing the blank stare again, eyes lowered, and then suddenly, it looks as if a light bulb will appear over her head. She furrows her brow, and tilts her head, and she suddenly answers, "Maybe not in the context that I think you're putting it". That was the great answer? That's the epiphany I thought I saw on her face. Does she think this "context" framing of her attorney's question makes her look intellectual, thoughtful, or deep? Perhaps a combination of all three? Let's see.

Nurmi says, "Well, ah, what context, I mean, at this point in time, you didn't say gee whiz, we're doing all of this activity and he doesn't even want to hold my hand in public (Nurmi takes two horizontal fingers and begins to madly rub his nostrils, and then he holds up his hand to punctuate his question. Quite disgusting). It's time to end this?". Wow, why doesn't he just end it with, "I mean seriously, Miss Arias. You did know that you were looking more and more foolish with every secret encounter, did you not?". Maybe I've been watching too long, and like someone stranded in a desert, I'm seeing mirages. Maybe I'm not seeing what I think I'm seeing, but I am beginning to wonder if Jodi Arias looks so miserable because Nurmi is having some personal fun while making her seem like a desperate, easy, pliable, stalker, loser (for her own good, of course). These questions would be tough to answer, especially if the picture Nurmi is painting is accurate. Remember, he doesn't like her, and I suspect there may be a little bit of payback going on here.

Jodi looks up, stares at something, and answers, "A little bit. We talked about the status of our relationship the next day". Oh perfect timing – just as Nurmi is letting everyone know that Jodi may have actually assessed their relationship accurately when she described feeling like a prostitute, Jodi counters with a claim that she requested a relationship report card the day after Travis pecked her on the cheek (and basically told her to hit the road) after the Super Saturday event at his house.

Nurmi asks, "And based on that conversation...what was the status of that relationship, based on this conversation – to your understanding, what was the status?". Jodi answers, "After talking, I was encouraged to date other people".

Really? How can they make Travis look bad for telling her the truth, and what steps did Jodi take to reverse that decision? How did she go from "thanks, but no thanks" to an official dating relationship as of February 2, 2007 ? Let's find out. Nurmi asks, "And, we talked a moment ago about how you were asked out on one date, or a few dates in December. At this point in time, when you're going to Ehrenberg and all those things, were you of the mind that Mr. Alexander wasn't dating anyone else?". Really, all Jodi was entitled to know was the Mr. Alexander wasn't dating her. However, I'm sure she has some inside information she was able to extract.

Jodi answers, "I had that impression. I found out it was false". She had that impression because she began interviewing his friends. She is a piece of work. Nurmi continues, "We'll talk about that in a bit, but in January, 2007, after December, 2006, excuse me, you said that you were encouraged to date other individuals (Jodi answers, 'Yes'). Was there are certain type of individual you were encouraged to date (yes...perhaps a mental health professional was suggested...)?" Jodi answers, "Uh, eh, yeah...he wasn't specific that first time, but then he got more specific afterward".

Alright, I know that this duo is attempting to paint Travis Alexander as someone who tried to control Jodi's life, even going as far as listing the specific qualifications of the men she is supposed to be dating. Unfortunately for the defense, the impression they are giving the jury is something else completely. There is only one lingering question, and it isn't "what were those specifications". In the real world, one would want to know how many times Travis had to tell Jodi to date other people. Why did it have to be more than once? She was harassing him with this subject matter.

Nurmi asks, "Let me ask you this: did you go on dates (Jodi answers, 'Yes')...do you know, to your knowledge, did Mr. Alexander learn about these dates (Jodi answers, 'Yes')...and where were these, you were in, is this in December, or is this in January of the following year?". Jodi answers, "I think, umm, it, it would have been January".

Nurmi continues, "And, where, you were still living in Palm, I got the sense that maybe you were moved out of your Palm Desert home by then, is that correct?". Jodi answers, "No, I stayed (a/k/a squatted) in Palm Desert until early May, I think". Lucky woman. They stopped paying the mortgage at the end of 2006, the bank officially foreclosed on January 24, 2008, and Jodi Arias was allowed to live their mortgage free home until May, 2007? That's better than leasing an apartment for six months or a year.

Nurmi is satisfied. He says, "Okay, so, you were back in...did these dates take place in Palm Desert (Jodi answers, 'No')? Where did they take place (Jodi answers, 'Pasadena' – and just for some context, Pasadena is over 120 miles away from Palm Desert. Does she always have to travel so far to go on dates?)? Okay. And, was there one particular individual, or did you go on several dates?". She had better mention Abe Abdelhadi. He testified to the fact that he went out with her in January, 2007. They ended up in a bookstore, and found themselves in the spirituality/philosophy section, and he remembered Jodi telling him that she was "dabbling in Mormonism", despite the fact that she had been baptized into the LDS faith six weeks earlier. Who knows...maybe Abe had a bigger checkbook, a better job, and a different religion. She certainly didn't want to be dogmatic if doing so was going to close doors to her.

"I went on dates with two different individuals – umm, yeah (she looks confused), two official dates". I still can't believe we are listening to a butcher talk about who she was dating "officially" back in 2007. Nurmi continues, "Two actual dates. And you mention Pasadena. You weren't living there. Why were these dates taking place in Pasadena?" Jodi answers, "I had a doctor's appointment in Pasadena, so there was (she walking carefully here...measuring her words) a guy that I had met. He was sitting next to me at the Super Saturday event, the one that I was texting Travis at (the texting that went on for hours and culminated in penis pics? That event?), and he was very lively, and he asked me out, not right away -- he was talking to me, getting to know me during the event (her hands are spinning), and he said, I don't know how he worded it, maybe we should go out sometime, ummm". Oh, I'm sure that seemed like a great idea to the young man who sat next a woman who was sexting with some other guy for hours. A few glances at her screen would tell him exactly what was on the menu. I'm going to predict that this dating relationship might have lasted one or two dates. Just a guess.

Nurmi's got me on the edge of my chair with this line of questioning. The fireworks continue as he asks, "And this Super Saturday event that you met this particular individual, when did this take place?". Jodi responds, "It would have been the same date as the photographs, so November 11, 2006". Is she casually inserting a reference to the radioactive penis pics that she could barely touch, let alone look at, when Nurmi was tossing them around? Now, the words, "the photographs" just roll off her tongue as if she were speaking about normal pictures, the type that are suitable for framing? Why does she want the jury to recall that she was sexting one boyfriend while simultaneously flirting with another? How can this help her?

Nurmi asks, "And did this individual ask you out on November 11, 2006?'. Jodi answers, "Yes, but nothing confirmed or concrete – just threw it out there and I said okay, maybe, sure, you know?". Nurmi asks, "Did you feel like it would have been, at that point in time, considering your relationship with Mr. Alexander, that it would have been inappropriate to date this individual?" Jodi answers, "Not just to date, I wouldn't have considered it inappropriate, umm...I would not have, if it was just a date".

I am now beginning to wonder if Nurmi and Willmott have thought this storyline through. In the twisted mind of Jodi Arias, all of this might make perfect sense, but to the normal mind, it's quite illogical. For example, Jodi has already told the jury that she was having oral and anal sex with Travis, a man with whom she did not have a dating relationship. In fact, he refused to date her, or even take her to a nice restaurant and pay the bill. The closest they got to having an actual date was when he took her to the movies and two cheap restaurants during a weekend hotel tryst (I don't count the PPL banquet as a date). However, Jodi sees nothing inappropriate about going on an actual date with another man while everyone knows that she is desperate to attach herself to Travis. Does she not realize that people could reasonably assume that a woman who will engage in multiple sex acts with a man who will not date her is very likely to do that and more when she is going out with a man who is actually willing to take her on a date? I do not understand her morality or her logic.

Nurmi continues, "So, you run into this individual again down the road...you mentioned Pasadena, you have a date with this individual". Jodi responds, "We agreed to meet in Pasadena (she is retracting her lips again)". Nurmi wants to know who this individual is, and Jodi responds, "His name is Abe Abdelhadi". Answering Nurmi's next question, Jodi has to admit that she only had one date with Abe. Jodi's on a losing streak. She does much better with South American cousins, unemployed vampires, tent dwelling Wiccans with no place special to be, and middle-aged divorced men with a cigarette in one hand and a bottle of vodka in the other. She just doesn't seem to be what ambitious, working young men are looking for.

Nurmi continues, "And, you dated another individual?". Jodi answers, "I went on another...what I thought was going to be a date. It turned out to be more platonic, and that was someone else". Nurmi wants a name. Jodi answers, "His name is John...Dixon". Poor Jodi. Nobody wants to date Jodi. Nurmi continues, "So, you said the date with Mr. Dixon was, if I heard you correctly, platonic, right?". Jodi answers, "That, well we, he invited me to get lunch. We got sushi, we chit-chatted, I didn't get any vibes or major chemistry (but I'll bet she got a lovely plate of deluxe sushi with a pink orchid artistically decorating the plate), so that's the impression I was left with". Is there any chance, even a 50% chance, that Mr. Dixon didn't get any "vibes"? No, of course not. It was Jodi's choice to eat and run.

Nurmi won't give up on the two non-dates: "And the date with Mr. Abdelhadi, was that more, umm, or I should say, a less platonic situation". She's going to lie here. We all know about the magic in her underpants, and that information, as far as I know, came from Abe Abdelhadi. He comes across as very cut and dried, forthright, and an honest speaker. He approached the prosecution, hoping to help the state. The prosecutor's office told him what they told so many others – if we need you, we'll get in touch with you.

I've heard Abe interviewed on television and telephonically in court, so I'm using that knowledge to form some opinion of who he is. I know Jodi is about to lie here, so I'm going to carefully study her face as she avoids talking about the real images in her mind. She answers, "Well, it developed into that, sort of, but you know...umm...(uncomfortable pause, confused face, hands in a palm-up searching position)...we were just on a date. It was not (remember, the use of two words instead of a contraction is a sign of dishonesty)...he wasn't as...umm...(she's looking down, her face is getting red, and her hand gestures are all over the map)...I don't know how to put it...(now she's looking around) it was different than the lunch date I had". She's done. That was pretty bad, even for an accomplished liar like Jodi Arias. Perhaps her complete insecurity in answering this question is based on her knowledge that Abe Abdelhadi will be speaking on the phone with Nurmi in court.

Nurmi goes on, "Did Mr. Alexander know of these dates?". Jodi responds, "Yes. He didn't know prior, but he knew afterwards". He didn't care about them prior to them happening (and I definitely think she made sure he knew about them prior to them happening. She was probably trying anything she could think of to generate his interest). Nurmi continues, "Did you, how did he know, did you tell him?".

Perhaps he knew because his friends were digging for information about who Jodi was dating, and they reported their findings back to Travis. That is the way it works in the world of Jodi Arias, right? Is that what happened here? Jodi answers, "Well, I didn't answer my phone that night, sooooo, actually I went to hang out with John Dixon again. Again, it was platonic. He wanted to show me...". Juan Martinez objects. This is beyond the scope of the question. Jodi does what she always does when Juan Martinez cuts her off to object: she says, "sorry".

It is difficult to hear what the judge says, but judging from Nurmi's response and attitude, I suspect it was an order to rephrase the question. He does, "Why were you with John Dixon again?". Jodi answers, "He wanted to bring me over so he could show me clips from the movie he was directing...umm, and he just played some of those clips on his computer, umm, and we watched some clips from Pirates of the Caribbean, and that was it. I think we might have hugged when I left. I don't remember".

He is an actor/stunt man, and he did work on the Pirates of the Caribbean movie that was released in 2007. He is older than Jodi – probably by ten years. He works steadily in films. There's no way I believe she walked away from him. I think his career may be the reason she was hesitant about mentioning his name (she did pause before giving Nurmi his last name). It cannot be helpful for any professional to be linked to Jodi Arias – especially when it's supposedly a love interest. Additionally, his bio says that he has been living in Los Angeles for many years, which would make sense. The distance between Los Angeles and Palm Desert is two hours. So, once again, it sounds like Jodi did some traveling to see the stunt work – but I am speculating, I don't know where he lived in 2007.

Back to Jodi's unanswered phone: "And it was at this time that you said Mr. Alexander called and you were unable to take his call at that moment?". Jodi answers, "Yes". Nurmi continues by asking if Travis was angry that Jodi didn't answer her phone. Jodi responds, "He wasn't angry, just inquisitive". If John Dixon is who I believe him to be, I'm sure that Travis was more interested in the Pirate clips than anything Jodi might have been doing. Nurmi continues, "And that inqui...inqui...inquisition, if you will (inquisition? Like the Spanish Inquisition? Everybody hide!), led to you describing the fact that you were with Mr. Dixon". She confirms Nurmi's assertion. Nurmi continues, "And how did that sit with Travis (Nurmi's finally on a first name basis with the victim)?" Jodi is breathing deeply, noticeably, as she answers, "Umm, he, it wasn't warmly received, he didn't appear to get angry, but he, I could tell he was upset in his, just in the way he, his tone (hands spinning again), his tone changed".

So, he didn't get angry, but she knew he was angry. So, he handled it like an adult, but he's still going to be treated like he freaked out. This is unbelievably unfair. This man, even in death, cannot catch a break.

I guess Nurmi is satisfied with Travis' cool tone of voice, and the fact that Jodi's date with John Dixon was not "warmly received". Who talks like that, by the way? He's back on the date with Abe Abdelhadi. Nurmi wants to know how Travis learned of and received that news. Jodi answers, "Same conversation, because both of those dates were in Pasadena on the same day". Did she actually just admit that she dated two different men on the same day? What is wrong with her?

Nurmi asks, "Was his distaste for your date with Mr. Abdelhadi, was it different than, umm, than with John Dixon?". Juan Martinez read my mind. He objects because Nurmi has inserted the word "distaste" to the question. It was not established that Travis displayed any level of distaste over the news of Jodi's dates (although dating two different men on the same day certainly indicated a certain level of distaste). Another confusing ruling. Overruled. Jodi sticks it to Juan by asking for the question to be repeated. Nurmi asks, "I'm gonna try. Was Travis angry about your date with Mr. Abdelhadi?"

Jodi answers, "It appeared to, it seemed to me, well, it was over the phone so I didn't see him (so nothing appeared to her), but from the tone of his voice, he seemed upset". Nurmi pushes on, "Was that at a different level than it was with Mr. Dixon?". Jodi plays with her hands while answering, "I think it was all sort of cumulative (hands spinning)...ummm". Nurmi is generating a whole lot of nothing here, but he refuses to move on.

He continues, “Well, you mentioned the fact that as far as being encouraged to date, you said there were certain people, initially you thought it didn't matter what types of people you dated, but then you said later on you were encouraged to date a particular type of person. So, what I was asking if there is some difference between Mr. Abdelhadi and Mr. Dixon that caused, to your understanding, extra anxiety with Mr. Alexander?”. Now, wait a minute. Who is monitoring this dialogue. It is going off the rails. Initially, the news was not warmly received. By her own admission, Travis was not angry. Now we're using words like “distasteful” and “anxiety” to describe a non-event? Was Travis expected to really care who she was dating or what they were doing? Was he simply disinterested? I really am confused.

Jodi answers, “I think it was that they both weren't church members. I was sort of reprimanded for that”. Oh please, now we're going to add “reprimanded” to the line-up. No problem, Jodi. We all know how you love to be reprimanded with a well-deserved spanking.

Nurmi has his Perry Mason moment: “By Mr. Alexander?”. Jodi nods and says, “Yes”. Nurmi is now repeating everything the two of them just said, and he's doing this in case the jury lost interest. He says that, in Jodi's mind, the problem was that she was dating non-church members. Nurmi wants Jodi to reiterate that Mr. Alexander only wanted Jodi to date church members. She looks right at the jury, nods her head, and gives a strong, clear, “Yes”. I wonder, did she tell Travis that she told the non-church member, Abe Abdelhadi, that she was merely “dabbling” in Mormonism. I don't even know why I ask these rhetorical questions anymore. Of course she didn't.

It sounds like Nurmi is coming up with a big one. He says, “I gotta ask, at this point in time, you've been encouraged to date, why would you care, or why would you allow Mr. Alexander to have any input on who you dated?” Jodi answers, “I sort of felt that way when he said that. I'm thinking, he can't tell me who to date (see jury, I'm normal, I'm normal...I think just like everyone else!). But, he explained to me the importance of dating within the church, so I agreed with him”.

We're going to leave it here. We're going to leave it at Travis didn't want to have sex with her, told her the next day that he was encouraging her to date others, Jodi thought he was dating other people, but found out that wasn't true (more evidence of her invasive tendencies, not his), Travis didn't get mad when she dated other people, but may have had a slight change in his warm tone of voice after discovering that she was on a date, Travis didn't warmly receive her dating news (probably because she was doing a two for one run to Pasadena), she realized she didn't have to accept his input, but chose to anyway. Wow, what a controlling, intrusive, domineering, abusive bastard. Each day, I finish these pages, and I think I've heard the worst defense imaginable. Each day, I hear objections sustained and overruled, and half of the time, I don't understand how the defense is allowed to substitute Jodi's secret knowledge for what she said actually happened. Each day it gets worse. In order for Jodi and Nurmi to have sold this to a jury, the panel would have to be made up of sixth grade students.

We'll begin with Nurmi's summary: Jodi agreed with Travis when he told her not to date outside the church. Nurmi is obviously trying to imply that Travis had more of an issue with Jodi potentially dating Abe Abdelhadi as opposed to her dating John Dixon. The implication is pretty clear. Travis must be a bigot. He's already been called a pedophile, an abuser, and a hypocrite, so throwing in "bigot" would be easy. It's as easy as adding in another alleged conversation that nobody can validate, but for whatever reason, Jodi isn't willing to paint Travis as a bigot. Maybe she does later, but at this point, she's not going there. If she has a reason for not playing the bigot card, I'm sure it's self-serving -- maybe she's just not willing to say she sleeps with bigots.

Nurmi begins, "How did it go from you dating other people, him encouraging you to date other people, to this relationship – this boyfriend/girlfriend label?". I find myself fatigued, already tired of hearing Jodi speak, and as I write this, she hasn't even opened her mouth. I have never seen a defendant so completely misinterpret her situation, and this delusion is of her own making. She still has a metric ton of resentment and animosity towards Travis Alexander. I think she may actually be surprised that killing him didn't also kill her rage.

What's happened in the wake of the murder is a near public canonization of the man she ultimately hated enough to slaughter (much like an unskilled butcher). The more she attacks, the more Travis is revered. For these days, hours, and moments, she has the bully pulpit. She will, with minor interruption, have her say. These are the moments I believe she's been waiting for.

Jodi begins, "Umm...he was...a lot of things happened in that three week period". Oh, no. Why can't she just spit it out all at once? Is this her way of dragging out her time in the spotlight? Why do I have a feeling that Nurmi is going to go back to day 1 of this 21 day period to ask Jodi what she had for breakfast? I bet this is going to start with "Well, let's talk about that...".

Nurmi does interrupt, and he says exactly what I thought he would: "Well , well, let's talk about that...what happened from your perspective to get you from dating other individuals to being Travis' girlfriend?" Maybe I'm getting punchy, but was his first question any different than his second question? Same subject, same predicate, same sentence. Jodi answers, "Well, the first thing I did was...he hung up on me that night (she looks right at the jury, as if this abusive behavior will shock them, then she lowers her voice and her sense of bravado)...he was upset, and, and, so it kind of jarred me a little bit, so I decided to write him an email (because conversations are far more fun when the other person can't speak). I don't know, but I felt like I was cheating on him, even though he had told me to date other people (she's happy, smiling, waving her arms around). I felt guilty about it, and I had expressed that to him, umm, and, while I was writing the email, he sent me a text message...(she looks at Nurmi, and with her hands clasped in the inverted steeple position, she almost whispers)...I don't know if I can say what he said". Instead of a clean, scholarly yes or no, Nurmi takes the opportunity to simply drag this out.

Didn't she say, just a little while ago, that she found nothing inappropriate about "just dating"? Wasn't this something Nurmi asked her about as she was talking about her two dates in Pasadena? Before, she said she didn't feel like she was cheating on Travis by going on those dates; now, she says she does feel like she was cheating on him. Beyond the obvious flip-flop, I want to make a small observation – it may mean something, it may not. If these dates were platonic, if there was nothing more than a possible hug that ended them, why would she feel like she was cheating on Travis? I know Jodi Arias uses a very unique barometer when determining what physical acts accompany private encounters, but she has repeatedly said that "just dating" was not an issue for her. She's talked about "making out" with Travis – before they were an official couple – and she has given us her opinion that making out is no big deal. In her past, as one boyfriend faded from view and the next one came into view, she expressed no sense of conflict with the obvious overlap. She confessed to one final sexual encounter in the tent with Matt McCartney, while she was obviously already working on Darryl. Why is this situation any different – especially considering the fact that Travis gave her his blessing to date other people? What was she doing with Abe or John that made her feel like she was cheating on Travis? It's even more unbelievable that she felt like she was cheating on Travis when we consider the fact that she dated Abe and John on the same day. That is a strange move, and not one made by a woman who is conflicted about dating. This is not adding up. If she felt like she was cheating, then she was doing more than walking through a bookstore with one man and having sushi with the other.

Nurmi asks her, "Well, uh, you write him this email, and you're expressing your feelings. Did you ever send it?". Jodi says, "Yes". For your information, during the retrial of the penalty phase, Abe Abedelhadi was questioned about this particular e-mail. He testified that Jodi never sent him the email currently being discussed. There is an email, composed by Jodi, that looked like it was written to Abe, and a copy of that email was forwarded by Jodi to Travis Alexander. In truth, it was only the copy to Travis that was ever sent from Jodi's email. Abe never received any such email from Jodi. It was written to make Travis jealous. Abe was absolutely sure of that. Keep that in mind as you listen to her testimony.

Nurmi continues, "Without telling us what was said, did this, is this the kind of discontent that led to you two deciding, well, that's it, we're going to be a couple, is that what you're telling us?". Nurmi, listen. The question was not if Jodi could give us another round of what she was feeling--the question is far simpler: can she repeat what he wrote in a text message. Easy.

Jodi responds, "Not at that moment. It was a process over a few weeks". Jodi wants to talk about those three weeks. That should eat up the rest of the afternoon.

Nurmi apparently doesn't want Jodi to back up and give us the day by day version of this "boyfriend/girlfriend" development. He tries, for a third time, to summarize it by saying that this type of "disconnect" is what eventually led to Jodi and Travis becoming a couple. Jodi responds, "I think it sort of started us on the path...to become official, you know?". Jodi is not giving up. She's still talking about "a path". Nurmi is letting her know that it is time to get to the destination. He knows, I assume, that they are losing the jury. They are definitely losing me, and I've had huge breaks between this torturous testimony.

Nurmi's addressing what it meant to be a couple. He is completely ignoring the path. Good. He asks, "So when you said you and Travis officially became a couple, what did that mean? Was there some sort of agreement or, you know, you sat down and said, you're not gonna date other people? Tell us about the day you and Travis decided you were going to become a couple, if you will". Nurmi smiled through the end of that sentence. His client, by contrast, is quite miserable. He wants to talk about "the day", and she wants to talk about the days leading up to "the day".

Jodi responds, "Umm...I went out to his house that weekend, the first weekend of February, umm, we hung out, we were watching – I don't know if we were watching a movie or if we were on the internet – we were just reading books, we were just doing this in the (his) house, all day...just hanging out. And we were reading – we were each reading our own books, umm, and we were sitting in this oversized chair next to his bed (do they hang out in any other area of a house), we both squeezed into it...". Nurmi wants to interrupt. What's wrong, does he want the color of the chair they were sitting in?

I've noticed that Jodi is using a lot of hand gestures as she begins to tell the tale of the over-sized chair. She tends to do that, but it seems more extreme now. There are consistent, open hand, palm up gestures. Body language experts say that this gesture indicates either honesty, or an appeal to be believed. It is also one of the most easily faked hand gestures, as it is meant to convince the listener that the speaker is telling the truth. What is interesting, is that Jodi also moves from the open hand gesture right into the interlocked fingers gesture. That gesture has an entirely different meaning – this means that she is experiencing frustration, negativity, and anxiety. While I've been looking at definitions for hand gestures and micro expressions, I've learned that Nurmi's fascination with his nose, as well as Arias' fascination with her nose (it is constantly assaulted by tissues when she pretends to cry) is very telling. That is universally known as the Pinocchio Effect. Because of an involuntary rise in blood pressure when a person is embellishing or fabricating, blood tends to flow to the ear lobes and the tip of the nose. Someone who touches or scratches their nose while talking may actually be reacting to the increased blood flow to those areas. Body language experts take this as a warning sign. It is commonly believed that this gesture is a strong indicator of fabrication, especially when it is happening as a person is recounting an event.

Jodi has just painted a picture of the happy couple reading books in the over-sized chair next to Travis' bed. Nurmi asks, "Umm, where were you?". She made it abundantly clear where they were -- unless Travis has moved his bed into the kitchen -- but Nurmi wants the words "in his bedroom" to be said all by themselves. He wants those words to hang in the air, and hopefully, this will reinvigorate the sleeping jurors.

Nurmi asks, "What brought you to his home, and this is February. Do you remember the day?" Before answering, Jodi repeats an eye motion that seems to be her default position lately, especially when asked to recall details of an event. She looks down and to the right, and then she speaks. It would be much easier to read this gesture if she was looking up and to the left. There is a big difference between the two: up and to the left indicates that the person is accessing their memory. Body language experts feel far more secure in ascribing validity to the facts when they are stated by a person looking toward the left. Actually, most left direction eye gestures indicate that the subject is accessing the memory area of their brain, whereas most right direction eye gestures indicate that the subject is accessing the creating or imagining sphere of the brain. Looking down and to the right indicates that the subject is accessing their feelings while recounting the event. Furthermore, it can indicate that the person is actually questioning the feelings they're expressing concerning the event. I'm not applying science to Jodi Arias and her facial and eye movements. I just found this subject matter interesting.

Jodi continues, "Not exactly, but it would have been the first, or the second, maybe the third". By the time she mentions February 3 as a possible date in response to Nurmi's question, her gaze is broken. She furrows her brow and lifts her hands as if to say that it doesn't really matter which of the three days it was. Nurmi asks, "You go to his house in early February, why were you there? I mean, there must have been some discussion about you coming to visit him, I assume." Jodi answers, "No, there wasn't, actually". She looks up and to the right (this is clear sign of fabrication, visually imagining, and lying), before grinning and closing her eyes. I believe she is lying.

Nurmi just wants to know how she came to be at Travis' house in early February. This is getting interesting – these eye gestures. She immediately looks up and to the right and begins, "Earlier that month (she looks at the jury), he showed up on my doorstep at 1:40 in the morning, without warning, and that's when I met Dan Freeman. So, a few weeks later, I thought I would repay him in kind (interlocked fingers, showing anxiety), and surprise him as well". Sure. I believe that, don't you?

Nurmi continues, "Before we fast forward back to February (what?), we heard about Mr. Freeman coming to your door at 1:40 in the morning, as you just talked about, uhh, you and Travis went back to the bedroom, is that accurate to your recollection?".

Jodi answers firmly, and very audibly, "Yes". Nurmi asks, "Mr. Freeman wasn't in that bedroom. Can you describe for us what happened in the bedroom while Mr. Freeman was outside the door?". As casually as if she were saying that she answered a ringing telephone, Jodi replies "We just made out". I don't know why Nurmi or Jodi believe that discussing what was happening behind the bedroom door would make either of them look good, or if they believe it would Travis look bad, but there is not a person in the room who doesn't know what making out is, so there really is no need to go any further here. I believe this is angering the jury. Nurmi actually asks, "What do you mean, just made out?".

Before speaking, her eyes go up and to the right (lying), then she focuses on the jury and says, "We didn't go very far. We were just kissing...and playing around (hands extended, palms up), having fun". She's so casual about this. There isn't a hint of embarrassment. In fact, she sounds like the fast girl in junior high – the one who draws power from regaling all of the virgins in pastel sleeping bags with her tales of back seat groping. Nurmi continues, "No oral sex?". She looks directly at the jury and says, "No". Nurmi asks, "No anal sex?". She looks up and to the right and says, "No". Nurmi asks, "And, the clothing stayed on?". She looks at the jury and says, "Yes".

Nurmi is ready to move on from here. He wants to talk about things that happened a few weeks later. If that's the way he wants to play it, I think he should have ignored her bait and not addressed the Travis and Dan Freeman, middle of the night visit (and that was the point). Why was Travis bringing Dan Freeman to Jodi's house in the middle of the night? Dan Freeman seemed like a reasonably devout Mormon, or, at the very least, a well versed Mormon. Why would Travis even ask this kind of a favor from his friend, and why would Dan Freeman be willing to sit outside a bedroom door when what was going on behind that door was obviously in violation of the Law of Chastity? The mere appearance of impropriety is an issue for Mormons.

Jodi is hiding things here, and I now realize why Nurmi didn't want to go here. It's clear that Nurmi hadn't adequately prepared the foundation for this exchange (he made the statement about Dan Freeman being outside the bedroom door as though he was simply restating something that had already been addressed, but it hadn't been addressed at all). Now that Jodi has had her opportunity to convince everyone that Travis did a surprise, late night visit to her house before she made a surprise, late night visit to his house, we are ready to move on.

Nurmi asks Jodi if she remembers what time she arrived at Travis' home to "surprise" him. She has not stopped looking up and to the right in preparation for every answer, and this exchange is no exception, "I had to work that night, so I hit the road, I don't remember. I think it was about 2:30 or 3:00 in the morning". So, Arias does a five hour drive to Mesa, in the middle of the night, to surprise Travis.

Nurmi does establish Jodi's place of origin as Palm Desert as he continues to ask her about her trip to Mesa. I guess he believes it is better to leave the impression that Travis had done something as equally ridiculous as Jodi – in the name of lust. Nurmi asks, "So, tell us what happened when you arrived". Jodi answers – eyes very clearly up and to the right – with a smile on her face. She says, "I pulled up to his house, and I was kind of excited the whole trip, thinking – I mean, he thought it was hilarious when he came, so I thought it would be funny to do that (she continues to close her eyes as she speaks, and she is grinning so widely that her teeth are on full display. Her voice falls at the end of her sentence, and I get the impression that this is a very happy, private memory. Nurmi admonishes her to speak up, and she does). But, as I approached the door (hand out, palms up), I had doubts (hands touch her heart, very briefly, indicating truth), I thought..I kinda feel stupid, and

I thought, what is he going to think, I'm showing up at his house at three o'clock in the morning (she's very happy talking about this). Sooo...I started to go back and forth about it, and I'd waiver, and then I'd walk back to my car, and then I stopped (her eyes are closed for a lot of this testimony. I think she's blushing)...I was gonna get all the way in my car and just go back 'cause I felt silly, but I turned around and looked at the house one more time, and I noticed in the upper window, there were lights flashing – like that was the loft where the screen would have been for the, umm, television, or movies, or whatever – so somebody was awake. So, I decided, hey, what the heck? So, before I could change my mind, I went back to the front door and rang the doorbell".

I can only describe her affect during this testimony as giddiness under control. This would be the level of excitement you would expect to see from a sixteen year old who was being asked to the prom by someone incredibly popular and out of her league. This is so odd, the laughing, the smiling, the remembering. You would think she had married the man and was talking fondly about one of their early dating memories. But, that's not the case. She's fondly remembering an event featuring a man she killed. If this marks the day of the beginning of their official relationship, in her mind, they still haven't broken up...despite the fact that she slaughtered him, and despite the fact that he is quite dead.

Nurmi wants to know who answered the door. Jodi looks up and to the right again, in fact, I'm pointing it out so frequently, that it would probably be easier to tell you when she doesn't do this. I truly believe she is creating a story – probably based in a germ of truth – but she is embellishing wildly, making it far more amazing than it actually was. She answers, "Umm...Travis and Napoleon". I'm sorry, that is just stupid. Dogs don't answer doors. They follow after their masters who open the doors. Is she letting us know that Napoleon was an individual too? Jodi, lover of all animals...except the dog she kicked and the cat she squeezed (and there was another cat she almost dehydrated and starved). Nurmi establishes that Napoleon is a dog, and Jodi wants us to know that she heard Napoleon before she heard anything else (of course...dogs bark when the doorbell rings...whether it's morning, noon, or night).

Jodi is asked if Travis looked happy to see her (why am I wondering if he's implying a visible erection?). Jodi actually looks right at the jury, and says that Travis looked very happy, had a big grin on his face, and was surprised. What happened next, Nurmi asks. Jodi says, "He pulled me into the house (pulled? Really?). It was cold out, it was February, so I had on a jacket with a hood (she makes a hand gesture to show us what it looks like to pull a hood up over your head), and he just stood there – kind of a similar reaction as me, when he showed up, dumbfounded, but happy, like, hey, what the heck? Then, his roommate came downstairs, and he, umm, Travis yanked the hood off my head and said, well, this is Jodi (she's delighted, absolutely delighted)." She does a cute little shoulder shrug, almost imperceptible, looks at Nurmi with a toothy grin, and says in her best little girl voice, "So...".

The Alexander siblings are not as enchanted as Jodi, the storyteller. Tanisha looks absolutely disgusted, Steven is staring directly at Jodi with narrowed eyes, and Samantha doesn't appear to even be paying attention to this tale of relationship by ambush. She's got something in her lap that is far more interesting to her. This time, she's not even interested enough to exert the energy to do an eye roll.

We learn that the roommate's name was Thomas Brown. Nurmi asks, "So, after you met Mr. Brown, and he introduces you the way he does, what takes place?". Jodi answers, "The three of us go upstairs, we get comfortable on the love sacks -- they are like giant bean bag chairs. Umm, Travis and I took the center one (or more likely, Travis took the center one and Jodi glommed her ass onto it), and Thomas, I think he was on the other side – he would have been on my right (and this distinction as to Thomas being on her left or right would have only mattered if we were talking about June 4, 2008, at around 5:32 PM. Beyond that, who cares whether Thomas was on the right , the left, or stuck to the ceiling? Jodi wants him gone, not sitting in a love sack – which is precisely the message she's trying to send when she plops down with Travis instead of sitting in her own chair).

It's very late, Nurmi points out. Guess what's coming next? That's right. Nurmi wants details about sleeping arrangements. Jodi answers, "Well, based on the last time I was at his home, and how he reacted, I told him (let the games begin...she's going to make him beg for it, because she only drove five hours for friendly conversation)...it's okay if you want me to sleep on the couch – I'm okay with that (interlocked fingers indicating anxiety), and he (big, broad smile emerging) balked, and insisted that I stay in his bedroom with him".

I have to ask, because my life, when I was in my late 20's/early 30's, was marked by schedules. I would have been terrified by an impromptu knock on the door at 3:00 AM. I would have been furious if some person decided to camp out in my house, and I had to be up the next morning. I guess the point I'm making is, does anybody in this story have a normal, full-time job that requires them to go to sleep at night?

I don't know if we're going to get the details of another sexual exploit, but the camera goes to Sandy Arias. She puts something in her sister's lap, and appears to mouth the words, "Here, hold this for me", and she stands up and leaves. A bathroom break, or a humiliation break? I guess we'll find out. As for Aunt Sue, she still looks like an air traffic controller from 1975 with those earphones still secured to her head, and her butt is firmly planted on the bench. She's going nowhere.

Nurmi asks, "Did you spend the night in the bedroom?" Jodi utters a proud, "Yes". Isn't that enough? Please, please...let that be enough. It's not enough, is it? Nurmi begins to ask, "Did any sexual activity happen that night?".

Jodi answers, but not before she makes a very deliberate up and to the right eye motion, "Umm...(she almost sounds like she isn't quite sure)...yes, it did happen that night, and the next night". Details, Jodi, details. Remember, this transcript will eventually be a porn script for some skin production company.

Nurmi wants to know what happened. Jodi responds, "I don't recall specifics. I just know that we were intimate (they were not "intimate", so I wish they'd take that pretty label off of it. They were never lovers, not in the true sense of the word. Her use of that word is really starting to offend me). Umm...the same kinds of things we had done before, nothing different. No! Except we did the anal sex briefly, but there was none of that". I'm not sure what happened during this answer, and I backed it up several times to see if Nurmi interrupted while she was speaking to ask about penile/vaginal sex, because that's what "no" seems to be addressing. Nobody interrupted her. It almost seems like she heard another question in her head and is answering it. Bizarre.

Nurmi wants to know if there was penile/vaginal sex -- something Jodi just answered without being asked (maybe it's just a case of being overly rehearsed as opposed to hearing voices). Jodi, trying to sound virginal, says, "No", while shaking her head. Are we supposed to be impressed? We're not. Truthfully, I'm hearing too much about anal sex. I want to give the woman a diaper, because I think she'll eventually need one. Nurmi wants to know what the Palm Desert Parasite did the next day with Travis, and truthfully, that's a good question. If they aren't horizontal, they don't seem to have much in common – and that's according to Jodi.

Jodi answers, "Umm...we hung out all day. He was showing me a museum that had come through Phoenix recently (traveling museums? That's a new one on me. Most of the museums I've been to have been on cement foundations. Maybe she means an exhibit. I can't fault her on this one; she is unsophisticated, despite her attempts to paint herself as a Shakespeare fan). It was called "Body World", and he was showing me that museum online. It had just left town, otherwise he wanted to go take me to see it, but it was gone. Umm, so we just hung out at the house, I'm trying to remember if we left. I think we stayed at the house all day, and hung out". Was there nothing else to do in Mesa? How about Phoenix? He was willing to go there if the exhibit had still been in town, so why not look for something else to do? A quick search online shows that there a quite a few things to see in Phoenix: the Desert Botanical Gardens, the Challenger Space Center, not to mention the tons of restaurants. He wasn't interested in taking her out. This wasn't a date. When my husband was "courting" me (Jodi likes that word), sitting in his apartment for days on end, was not my idea of a great time. He spent money on me, and he did it without reservation. At the very least, did he take her dinner that night?

Nurmi asks if they went to see a movie, if he took her to dinner...anything? Jodi replies, "No. We may have gone out for a bite to eat, but I don't think so". Oh, this is sad. Not even a drive-thru McDonald's, really? Did he even run to the grocery store to get some food she may have liked? Was there even the suggestion of getting some interesting foods to prepare for dinner? No. He really doesn't want to be seen in public with her. Additionally, by not making plans to do anything, he may have been sending her a message that last night was fun, but he had other things to do. How did this woman not see that she wasn't valued for anything above her waist? This is so painfully obvious. I know they want us to hate Travis, but I can't. I don't blame him. I just wonder how he got to be 30 years old without figuring out the way the game works when sex is involved. If he were my son, and I knew this was going on, I would tell him to be very careful.

Nurmi has established that Thomas Brown and Aaron Dewey, the roommates, were home, at least part of the time. When asked if Travis showed Jodi any affection while they were in front of the roommates, Jodi responds, "No, we stayed in the bedroom a lot (big surprise), but when we hung out downstairs, if the roommates were there, we were just, reg...like friends". Nurmi asks if Travis was affectionate, not necessarily in a sexual way, when they were behind closed doors in the bedroom. Jodi answers, "Yes".

Nurmi wants to know what discussion got them to the point "where she was to be his girlfriend". Jodi answers, "Am I allowed to say what was said?". Well, why the hell not? That's what she's been doing for almost three full days, despite the hearsay objections. She had no problem telling us what happened and what he said when she was "pulled" into his house. Why are we playing this game now?

Nurmi is a little frustrated. This isn't the first time she has publicly challenged his legal ability (i.e., he asks a question, she implies the answer would be hearsay). He says, "Well, did the two of you have a conversation?". "Yes", says Jodi. Nurmi continues, "And what was the subject matter of that conversation?". Jodi answers, "My dating life (she purses her lips after she says that). She looks angry. There is no more smiling. It is hard to believe that merely a moment ago, she could barely contain her joy.

I'm beginning to believe that this alleged conversation was not a nice conversation. Not only does Jodi suddenly look miserable, but she did the hearsay question. She only does that when she wants to build a foundation, when she wants an opportunity to go beyond the scope of the question. Let's see where this goes. Nurmi asks, "And during that conversation, did Mr. Alexander express to you his desire that you not date other people?". Jodi drops her head, and in a lower vocal octave, she answers, "Yes".

So, was that it? Was that the boyfriend-girlfriend conversation Nurmi's been trying to locate?

Nurmi asks what was said in the conversation. Jodi answers, "Well, it was kind of a light hearted conversation. I didn't know if he was joking or not, because he was talking about my dating life, but not his (I thought she had already determined that although she thought he was dating other people, she found out he wasn't), so I looked at him like, what did you mean by that, and he clarified, and kind of laughed". Nurmi says, "You mentioned his dating life. Did you inquire if he was dating anyone else?". Jodi denies asking Travis if he was dating anyone else. That, I believe. Her usual method is by snooping around, never asking directly.

Nurmi continues, "Did he offer up any information that he might be dating anyone else?". Jodi answers, "Not during that conversation". Nurmi continues, "He did later? He offered them up himself?". Jodi answers, "Yes, I later found out that he was dating a girl named Chelsea around Christmas time, and it also would have been the time, I think, in December when I was there in December, but I'm not sure because it was close to Christmas". Nurmi continues, "And this was something he offered up to you when you were having this boyfriend-girlfriend talk, right (and there is a small smile on his face, which I read as "just agree with what I said")?". No, Nurmi – highly doubtful it played out that way. Listen to her words. She said she "found out". We all know how Jodi finds things out. She confronted him with her intel, he admitted it, and that's what happened – if any of this is true.

Jodi answers emphatically, "No". Nurmi is again frustrated. He begins, "Okay..". Jodi interrupts, "Oh, I'm sorry. I think it was near Thanksgiving, actually...I can't remember...the holidays...but they were separated by that time". Oh, so the two injections of the word "Christmas", and the two insertions of the word "December" in her previous answer – indications of her powerful memory – are to be discarded? Now it isn't December/Christmas, it's November/Thanksgiving. Okay, as Nurmi would say. Somehow she screwed up her phony story, and she just realized that without a correction, whatever she plans to say in the future won't make sense – if the jury is still listening, that is.

Oh, there we go. I just heard the tiny, little utterance that was barely audible at the end of her sentence. It trickled off, but she said, "It's in his emails". So, if she's lying, Juan Martinez will catch it. I knew it.

Nurmi begins, "So, this moment in time, when you became his girlfriend, were you happy about it?". Hold the phone! I've been listening to every mundane, repetitive, useless sentence here. When did the event actually occur? Did I miss it? I don't remember hearing the word, "exclusive", neither of us will date anyone else, we're officially a couple, or even the juvenile "we're going steady". Nothing. Did she read something huge into a non-event, again? Is Nurmi going to clarify here?

Jodi answers, "Yeah, I felt pretty good about it. It was...I don't know (big smile)...we had made a lot of progress over the last few weeks because of some things that had happened over the last three weeks (she is determined to get into that three week period), involving some other friends of his, and he had seemed to change, and really better himself (bettered himself? Who, besides Jodi Arias, believed Travis needed to better himself?), treating me very nicely, and when we became, what I believe (remember those words – it was HER belief), was exclusive, it was, it seemed like a natural, the natural next step". What the hell is going on here? I'm not sensing the evolution she's implying. Far from it, actually.

Nurmi asks, "What do you mean by some things that had happened with some friends of his? What do you mean by that...without telling us specifically what was said". Well, I guess he's going to let her have her way. Jodi answers, "Umm...Travis was a funny guy, and he would joke a lot, and he made some jokes toward me that were not very nice, but they were jokes, but still, they didn't sit well with me, so I expressed that to some of his friends (the unmitigated audacity of this woman! She's telling on him. Why not put on her big girl panties and do her own dirty work? How dare she inject herself into his personal relationships because things don't sit well with her. She is a manipulative, divisive coward). We were hanging out, and they advised me...". A hearsay objection. Guess what? When Jodi's doing it, it's not hearsay. When Dr. Janeen DeMarte, the stellar prototype for all mental health expert witnesses, is doing it, it is hearsay. Jodi is allowed to continue, "...and they advised me to stop dating him immediately".

Why am I picturing Travis calling this "advisory panel" to ask them if they gave her the "stop dating him immediately" line? I wonder if they had good news – that she bought it, hook, line, and sinker. What an absolute fool. At the very least, these people couldn't believe that they were being given this golden opportunity to tell her to get lost, leave their friend alone, and go back to wherever the hell she came from – and all the while, she's asking for it. This is rich.

Nurmi continues, "These jokes, you characterized them as jokes. What were they? What did he say to you?". Make it good, Jodi. He lost his life over the punch lines. Jodi answers, "Umm...he called me a skank (she is)...in front of his roommate, Josh Ward". If my daughter was called a skank by her boyfriend, and then he proceeded to laugh about it in front of his roommate, I believe she would have gotten into her car and left...for good. If she didn't, I've failed as a mother.

Nurmi asks, "And he thought that was funny? (I do, and as I've said, I hate words like skank and slut. However, when the shoe fits...)". Jodi responds, "He...I didn't react...and he said I'm just kidding, very quickly".

Just for reference, this is what Travis meant when he called Jodi a skank: "Derogatory term for a (usually younger) female, implying trashiness or tackiness, lower-class status, poor hygiene, flakiness, and a scrawny, pockmarked sort of ugliness. May also imply promiscuity, but not necessarily. Can apply to any race, but most commonly used to describe white trash". Courtesy of the Urban Dictionary.

Nurmi says, "He called you a skank in front of a roommate? Why not just hightail it out of there?". Jodi answers, "We were on the phone, actually (oh, one of the spiritual/sexual late night phone calls? Maybe it was all part of the game, and the roommate just happened to walk in?), and we were talking, and he began to have a conversation with somebody else, so I waited (oh, this is pathetic), and then he apologized and said, I'm sorry, Josh just got home, and I said, tell him I said hi, and he said, Jodi says hi, and I could hear a muffled response in the background. It sounded friendly, but Travis said, he said you're a skank. So I know it came from Travis, not Josh. Then he said, I'm just kidding. Sooo (smiling broadly at this traumatic recollection), I didn't know what to say. I just kind of, in a polite way, got off the phone with him. And then, the conversation h said. She said it was muffled. He probably called her a skank. So what? The woman shows up at Travis' house in the middle of the night, camps out in his bedroom, and doesn't even require dinner or a walk in the fresh air in return for her services? A roommate would know that. The fact that Travis really didn't care that his roommate called his "girlfriend" a skank should have told her all she needed to know. If anyone called me a skank when I was dating my husband, it would have ended with my husband being arrested.

Nurmi wants other name calling incidents recounted. Juan Martinez is going to object. It won't matter, I'm sure. We're going to hear the back of the school bus dialogue anyway. I like Juan's objection. He said, "Josh Ward called her a skank. She interpreted that to be Mr. Alexander". Yes, that's exactly what happened. Nurmi counters with "Judge, that's not accurate..(and here's the kicker)...these objections are inappropriate, judge". Nurmi should be thanking Juan Martinez for making objections. His voice is probably like an alarm call buzzer to the sleeping jurors. At least they wake up for a few minutes when there are objections. I find it amusing that Nurmi is frustrated by these objections; for every one of Juan Martinez' objections, he and Willmott will offer nine. At least Juan Martinez isn't stamping his feet and demanding that he be allowed to approach the bench every time he doesn't like the ruling. Overruled. Now I know why Juan Martinez flew out of the gate breathing fire. He's furious, and he should be.

Nurmi repeats, "Did Mr. Alexander call you other names besides 'skank' in a joking manner?". Attention, all junior high school boys: You are now on notice that calling someone a skank will be offered in court as a justifiable reason for killing you. Just thought you should know.

Jodi answers, "Yes. He called me Pollyanna (ouch!), and he called me Porn Star (no, actually, Jodi, you wanted to play porn star. Remember, you were going to put on extra make-up and hold you head up just so your breasts and profile were visible? You wanted an erect penis to serve as the centerpiece in this erotic image? The tape is coming, my dear)...ummm". Nurmi interrupts, "In front of people?". Jodi answers, "Pollyanna, yes. Porn star, no". So, isn't Pollyanna a compliment in the world of young Mormons? I would think so – Pollyanna, the image of innocence. Nurmi wants to know if Travis would stoop so low as to call Jodi Pollyanna in public. Get ready. This will be good.

"At the time, I had long, platinum blond hair (out of a bottle), and I think, because my demeanor at that point in time was kind of happy-go-lucky, positive, shrugged things off if they were negative, umm, I always looked at the bright side of things. That's kind of how I expressed myself, so with that demeanor, and plus, my blond hair -- he wanted me to wear braids sometimes -- so he gave me that nickname".

Happy-go-lucky? Positive? Shrugged off the negative? Looked at the bright side of things? That isn't what her journals, dating back to age of fifteen, have to say. By her own hand, she admits to feeling chronically empty inside and fixated on suicide. I can't wait until Dr. DeMarte can explain the happy-go-lucky world of suicidal ideation. That should be worth waiting for.

Oh, and I still don't see an insult here – not with Pollyanna, anyway. Beyond that, we have one episode featuring the word "skank" that was attributed to another person, and another of "porn star", which was not said in front of anyone. Travis seems like a pretty good guy right now. I would have had plenty of words for her. Bad move, Nurmi. You shouldn't have gone here. It blew up in your face.

Nurmi bellows on about the evils of the Pollyanna label, but I'm distracted by the antics of Maria de la Rosa and Jennifer Willmott. Why are they not being admonished to stop whispering and smiling? They are completely distracting. Maria de la Rosa should be out of the camera angle, sitting at the second table. Actually, she shouldn't be here at all. She isn't testifying. I don't believe she's even being paid.

Jodi is now rattling on about the skank comment opening a can of worms. There were three worms in the can: one named "Skank", one named "Porn Star", and one named "Pollyanna". It must have been a teeny, tiny can. Anyway, Jodi smiles as she remembers how this can of worms began a dialogue that ended in the resolution we've been hearing about for quite some time: He's my boyfriend!

Nurmi is asking Jodi how happy she is to have a boyfriend. She says she was happy "that day". I still can't find the boyfriend-girlfriend conversation, so in my mind, it didn't happen. Nurmi asks if Travis' public treatment of her improved after the boyfriend-girlfriend conversation. Jodi responds, "In front of Dan and Desiree Freeman, and in front of his roommate, Aaron Dewey, yes. But everyone else, no". Now, I'm actually laughing.

Nurmi wants to know why Jodi was only happy for one day. Jodi answers, "He got up, we had been looking at the Body World museum, and we're looking at all these different...I don't know if you're familiar with it (does she work for the Body World exhibition now?), but we were looking at all of these body parts, and it was fascinating (especially for a human butcher in training), the human body, the structure, and the organs (is this the best thing for a woman who tried to decapitate a man after stabbing him over 25 times to be talking about during her trial?), and all that. And after a while of clicking around on that website, he got up and, umm, started straightening up his room, and doing things, and I was looking at the website, and some of the things we looked at, we had gone over quickly, and I wanted to look at them again, and so I clicked the back button and I found what I was looking for, and I clicked back, back, back, and I went back too many times, and I was suddenly in his "MySpace" account (oh no! This happens to Jodi all the time! Let me guess, instead of leaving his account, she accidentally saw everything he was up to on MySpace)...Umm, first I was confused, I thought, I wonder why he didn't log out (and since it takes all of a mouse click to do that, she thought it was too much work to do that for him, and decided to snoop instead), and I didn't see anything immediately, he was in, uhh, inbox, and the temptation got the better of me, so I clicked on an email". The temptation got the better of her?

I am a person who does not want to know the things that other people wish to keep to themselves. Snooping absolutely sickens me. I never went through my children's' things when they were growing up. I don't see someone's journal and wish I knew what it said. People have a personal right to their own thoughts and documents. This may be one of the most despicable things about Jodi Arias – this love of intrusion, this invasion, this putting of her face where it doesn't belong.

My theory: Related to snoopers and eavesdroppers, if you hear or read something that hurts you, you deserve it.

I am not going to do a verbatim transcription of Jodi Arias making excuses for why she invaded someone's privacy (again). Suffice it to say that she opened up emails from women, and she was disturbed by the graphic art she saw. When asked to describe the offensive graphics, she said she saw pictures of lips and sparkly hearts. That pissed her off? Really? These graphics are something I'd expect to see from a twelve year old girl, not a sexually provocative woman sending an email to a man. This is silly. Apparently, happy-go-lucky, shrug it off, see the positive side of things, turn that frown upside down, Jodi Arias was miserable, obsessed, and negative.

Jodi gives the jurors a quick lesson in how MySpace messages work. I never used MySpace, so I have no idea if she's telling the truth. She says that she looked at one particular message, a message that was sent prior to the still undisclosed boyfriend-girlfriend conversation, and she looked at it because it was sent by a woman (probably Chelsea). She goes on and mentions something she calls a "wild experience", and she says that this experience was discussed in the message. Nurmi asks if the wild experience was sexual. Jodi says it was nonsexual.

Nurmi wants to give her another chance to call this wild experience "sexual". She takes it up a level, and while she still won't classify it as sexual, she will call it "hostile". I have no idea what they are talking about. Nurmi gives her a third opportunity to call the wild experience detailed in the email "sexual". Now, she gets it. Jodi replies, "In the beginning...". But, then she back pedals and calls it "flirty". She says, "It wasn't explicit, but there were innuendos". Seriously, if I did a verbatim here, it wouldn't help clarify what they're talking about. Nurmi wants to know if the message contained any discussion about "meeting". Jodi says, "Yes".

This goes absolutely nowhere. She said it was muffled. He probably called her a skank. So what? The woman shows up at Travis' house in the middle of the night, camps out in his bedroom, and doesn't even require dinner or a walk in the fresh air in return for her services? A roommate would know that. The fact that Travis really didn't care that his roommate called his "girlfriend" a skank should have told her all she needed to know. If anyone called me a skank when I was dating my husband, it would have ended with my husband being arrested.

This goes absolutely nowhere. Nowhere. Jodi admits that she snooped, but she tries to sound very cute and harmless when she says that her curiosity just got the better of her. She was afraid to tell Travis what she had done, so of course, she wouldn't ask him about anything she read. Jodi, not elated with the graphics of sparkles and lips, goes on to read another email. This one really outraged her. Why? Because this one, according to Jodi, was sexual in nature, and it came from "a married woman". When asked if she believed that this "married woman and Mr. Alexander were engaging in some sort of sexual affair", Jodi pauses before saying, "I don't know. She lived in southern California, but they were definitely making plans". I hate her. I really, really hate her. She's going to name this woman, isn't she? Jodi admits she didn't speak to Travis about the email. Instead, she went running to Sky Hughes with her latest intel. Par for the course.

Jodi Arias, in her never ending quest to drag down as many private citizens as she can while her life circles the drain, is on the verge of telling the world about a private email. It was not written by her, and it was not addressed to her. When the email was written and the response was sent, Jodi Arias was not in the minds or hearts of the sender or the recipient. Following a pattern that has marked her uninteresting and haphazard life, she is snooping – again.

She is stealing private thoughts and words. She is invading a conversation. She simply went into somebody's inbox, and, as if she were choosing from a menu, decided which private communication tickled her fancy. She is going to sit on the stand and cast aspersions on the behavior of other people, and she believes that the bombshell nature of her information will overshadow the way in which she accessed that information. She is morally corrupt. Here she sits, in a court of law, and the excuse for her offensive behavior is offered with a crooked toothed, silly grin, the admission that her curiosity got the better of her, and the assumption that absolution belongs to her by virtue of her find. Oh, and there's always the "he didn't log out" excuse. So, I assume, Travis – like the other men in her life – is being made to shoulder some of the blame for Jodi's snooping. I'm sorry, but I don't see how someone is able to steal something that doesn't belong to them – even if it is access to personal correspondence -- and then use that information to help themselves.

Jodi has already told us that this email was sexually explicit. She must have been thrilled as "sexually explicit" is a language in which she is fluent. Jodi has also told us that the woman who was involved in this email interchange was a married woman. As a footnote to this information, she throws in one more descriptor -- "an LDS woman". Jodi Arias appears to be the human LDS hypocrisy detector. Thanks to her, we now know that a married, LDS woman was exchanging R-rated emails with Travis. Did this married, LDS woman kill Travis, or did a homely, invasive, disordered, stalker (who also claimed to be a baptized Mormon) kill Travis? I seem to remember many of Jodi's emails and texts being redacted as they were placed on the overhead projector for the jury. I guess you have to actually kill someone to maintain some level of privacy in a court of law.

Nurmi begins his disgusting inquisition: "And, you said it was sexual in nature. Did you get the sense that this woman and Mr. Alexander were engaged in some sort of affair?". She's going to answer, but before she does, can I ask why anyone would care what a murderer senses – about anything? Why would anyone ascribe any veracity to this woman's intuition or understanding? She isn't normal. She sees things that are not there, and she is blind to the things that are there. Big things. Jodi pauses, and then she speaks: "I don't know. Um...she lived in Southern California, but they were definitely making plans". What? That's the shocking, sexual information? They were definitely making plans for what? Attending a conference? Attending a church event? Attending a party? Perhaps he wanted to take Mrs. Mormon to see the Body World exhibit.

Jodi is asked if she spoke to Travis about this hot email. She responds, "Eventually, I did. But, I spoke to Sky about it first. I wasn't sure what to do". She wasn't sure what to do? She's a baptized Mormon now, right? Here's what she's supposed to do: Repent. Quite frankly, I fail to see why Sky didn't tell Jodi, right off the bat, that she didn't want to hear the latest gossip. That's how you handle it when a gossip comes calling. They let you know they've got something juicy, and they're dying to talk about it. So much gossip gets passed around under the guise of "I need counseling" that I'm surprised more mature religious people haven't caught on to that yet. You cut them off at the pass, and you do that in the face of their contrived hand wringing. You tell them to take it to the source.

Nurmi asks, "You said you weren't sure what to do. Why not just break up with him?". Nurmi can try to anticipate every question the jurors might have, and he is consistently hitting the nail on the head in that respect, but her answers are weak, unconvincing, and not helping their case. This time, she'll either go with the Svengali hold Travis had on her, or some moral outrage she felt – after all, Jodi must have been concerned about the sanctity of Mrs. Mormon's marriage, right? She is leading a fine, upstanding Mormon lifestyle herself (with her hardcore sexual behavior, her violations of other people's privacy, and her love of caffeine).

There's something I'd like you to keep in mind when you're listening to Jodi Arias talking about these "sexually explicit" emails she allegedly found. Remember, at this point in time, we have heard Jodi and Nurmi describe the sex life that she and Travis shared. We've heard about oral sex, anal sex, vaginal sex, body fluids, and the sexual fantasies they had. There is no doubt that Jodi Arias was having actual, real, medically identifiable sexual intercourse with Travis Alexander. That is exactly what the defense wants you to be thinking about when Jodi talks about Travis "cheating" on her. They want you to picture Travis doing with other women what he did with a very willing Jodi Arias. However, as the layers are peeled back, you'll realize they are comparing apples and oranges.

When Ryan Burns (Jodi's failed murder alibi and alleged next love interest) was on the witness stand, he was asked to read parts of text message conversations that he and Jodi authored. In one of those excerpts, Jodi was telling Ryan why she broke up with Travis. Above the portion that he was directed to read, more of her texts were visible on the overhead projector. In those texts, she admitted that she went into Travis' phone and found messages to other women that were highly "flirtatious", and in several, he mentioned the possibly of getting together with a woman to "make-out". Make out? That's what a woman who's been consistently involved in an active and real sex life for the past decade deems "sexual content". Maybe if we were all in the seventh grade, that would fly.

Let's also compare "making out" to what Jodi Arias was willing to do with Ryan Burnes just four hours after meeting him for the first time. She was not only "making out" with him, but she was letting his hands roam below her waist. Ryan tried to be a gentleman on the stand. He wanted it to seem as though the decision to stop the encounter was one they reached mutually. He admitted no words were exchanged, but rather, they both "just stopped". Hours later, after spending several hours in a social environment, they went back to his house and took a nap. Ryan said they woke up an hour later and the "making out" started immediately. It was different this time. Jodi forcefully positioned him, mounted him, and then began grinding on him (remember, she just killed Travis about 30 hours earlier). Ryan, again trying to be a gentleman, said it could have gone further, but they decided to stop. As before, no words were exchanged. As the questioning intensified, it became very clear who stopped the encounter. Ryan, a lapsed Mormon, said he thought of what Jodi had told him about her Mormon beliefs. He liked her. He thought that if he allowed himself to have sexual intercourse with her on the first date, she would go home, feel guilty that she had allowed "temptation to take over", regret the trip, and he would lose his opportunity to develop a relationship with her. This is the woman who judges others for "making out" – or even just writing about it.

Back to court – Nurmi has just asked Jodi why she didn't break up with Travis after she found out about the "sexual" emails. Jodi answers, "Well, part of my, muh, my reasoning at the time was that this was also something that took place a few months back. It was before Christmas, and...(long pause)...I was a little disturbed by the fact – it made me question what his values were regarding marriage. Um...but...(long pause), I liked him (with her hands extended and her best "what's a girl to do" expression), and I wasn't going to break up with him". Oh, how nice. Another appearance by Family Values Arias. Truck stops. Out of town motel trysts. Jizz. Grinding. Anal sex on "This Spiritual Day (Nurmi's pet phrase for the day Jodi was baptized into the Mormon church)". Penis pics. These are all evidences of Family Values Arias' strong commitment to home and hearth.

Nurmi continues, "You said you liked him. You were his girlfriend at this point in time. Were you in love with him in February, 2007?". She answers, "I might have been. I don't recall being 'in love-in love' with him. I recall having feelings for him, but I don't know if I could say in love, yet". Well, let's look at the situation, shall we? She's living in a foreclosed home. Darryl is history. She has 12 – 14 weeks to find a new place in which to squat. She's not going home to her parents. She may be forced, if all else fails, to go live with her grandparents, but that would put some serious mileage between her vagina and Travis Alexander. No, I think she was intending to move into the lovely, large, nicely decorated home in Mesa, Arizona. You know, the one with the BMW in the garage? I bet she even dropped a few "roommate who will pay rent" hints to Travis, which, I'm sure were promptly shot down.

By the time that 12 -14 weeks passes and she's forced out of that home in Palm Desert, Jodi and Travis are just several weeks from breaking up. It all sounds so much more ridiculous when you're following the actual time line as opposed to hearing about these events in bits and pieces. The love affair that led to murder was little more than a seemingly benign coupling that quickly crashed and burned. Remember, it was only "official" from February to June. Four months. Sixteen weeks. For most of us, this type of miniature relationship would definitively be placed in the "fail" column.

So, Jodi, according to her own words, is not "in love-in love". She's in heavy like, with equal parts obsession, impending homelessness, and covetousness thrown into the mix. Nurmi asks, "After you left his home, as his girlfriend, did you go back to Palm Desert?". She answers, "Yes". Nurmi continues, "And at that point in time...uhh...well, describe the relationship. You're hundreds of miles away, anyway. Are we back to the phone calls, sort of thing?" Jodi answers, "Yes. He had to call me more often at that point, owing partially to, um, everything that had happened between his friends and I and him. So, he was a lot better in how he was treating me, so things began to develop a little more rapidly".

This is not a dating relationship. It sounds more like a punishment doled out by the LDS church. He HAD to call her more often because of what happened between "his friends and I and him"? Says who? Was she reporting all of his bad behavior back to Chris and Sky? Was some repentance plan mapped out that required Travis to call Jodi a certain amount of times per week to make up for the fact that he wasn't all that interested in treating her like a girlfriend? If that's not the case, Nurmi should at least make an effort to clarify what she just said. Secondly, how do "things develop", rapidly or otherwise, when you are five or six hours apart? I don't understand this relationship, and it is all hitting me as completely casual and unimportant.

Nurmi asks, "You say developed a little more rapidly. You're already boyfriend and girlfriend, um, what is it developing into?". Jodi looks puzzled, but answers, "Well, um, there was a lot more talk about marriage. We were not engaged. That, the subject of marriage, was almost discussed from very early on, not necessarily he and I, but he would throw out hypotheticals – if – and now, then it was more like, if he was making plans, it was always we, instead of he. So, it seemed like I was included more as...in his future, and his in mine". Almost discussed? That means it wasn't discussed. When the subject of marriage came up, she said, "...not necessarily he and I". Well, it that's the case, it takes a lot of nerve to tell a jury that this kind of meaningless conversation meant they were talking about marriage – to each other. Let's not forget that he was still charging Jodi half of all the expenses they incurred on their road trips. A man who really wanted to marry his travel partner would begin by absorbing her costs. He never did that. In fact, he charged her what she owed – down to the penny. If she wanted to be honest, which she doesn't, this would be the perfect time to remind the jury that he proposed to her once, on the phone, as a joke. Those are her words. He never intended to marry her, and I don't believe he ever implied as much. Again, that will become clear once the sex tape is played. Sorry, Jodi, you just can't be his dirty little secret and his prospective wife. It's clearly one or the other.

Nurmi continues, "And based on what you told us earlier, it would seem, at this point in time, being married and having a family was still one of your primary, primary goals in life, is that right?". Oh, now I see why Jodi didn't want her family to come to Ventana Inn or her baptism. The camera just settled on Sandy Arias. She's tired or bored, but I really didn't need the complete shot of her dental work. The family from Yreka would have embarrassed Jodi. I wonder, did no one tell Sandy Arias to cover her mouth when she's going to let out a serious, five second yawn? Yuck.

Where were we? Oh that's right, Jodi's primary goal is marriage and children. Sure. I thought she said her primary goal was her photography business. Oh, wait. Her primary goal was getting her drawings into art galleries – or was that her secondary goal? What about being a PPL executive? She spent quite a bit of time and money on those conventions and meetings. Curious. I know she wanted to be a real estate tycoon, but I think the foreclosure was the bucket of water that put that fire out. So, really, she does have time to breed while being an artist and photographer, right? Okay. Jodi really just wants to be Mrs. Mormon, and she envisions herself hosting Family Home Evening after baking cookies with her brood of children. Well, it seems that's not going to happen. Now, her secondary goal is to cheat the Alexander family out of the justice they need, which will be a byproduct of her primary goal: to avoid dying in Perryville Prison (one way or the other).

It's hardly worth mentioning, but when she's asked about marriage and family being her primary goal, she looks right at the jury and gives them a loud and strong "Yes".

Nurmi asks, "And in this time period in February, 2007, are you still involved in PrePaid Legal?". Jodi likes saying yes. She does it again – loud and strong. I'd like to hear about all the sales she made for PPL in February, 2007, but I doubt that's going to happen. When Nurmi says "involved in PPL", I think he's asking Jodi if she was still trailing Travis as opposed to digging up clients.

Nurmi wants a little detail on PPL. Was she actively involved, or just keeping up her membership? Does PPL make $2,000 earner rings? You know, like really tiny ones? Jodi's earned one of those, a whopping $2,700 smackers! Just think, if she had duplicated that figure in 2007, and earned an addition $97,300, she'd be right up there with Gus Searcy – just flashing that ring!

Jodi will now tell us all about her PPL exploits in February, 2007: "I would describe it as I was very actively involved, but I was not making any money (followed by that silly "what's a girl to do" expression)". So, is that "very actively involved" status the same status claimed by the Avon lady who constantly dumps those little catalogs in public places but never answers the phone if you actually want to order something? Is that what she means by very actively involved? Oh, wait, I get it – she's not actually working, she's just paying for a membership that allows her access to the events Travis goes to – those events with all the young, single ladies. Very. Actively. Involved.

Yes, I see.

Nurmi points out that Jodi's relationship with Travis is flourishing, but then he adds, "but largely over the phone". I'm serious. You cannot make this stuff up. They are actually having a discourse highlighting the blossoming, serious phone romance that Jodi is enjoying for a few fleeting months in 2007. Realizing that a romance isn't really a romance without some face time, Nurmi asks when Jodi next saw Travis. Jodi responds, "We began to see each other once or twice a month...I'm trying to remember the exact time (don't bother, Jodi. Don't exert the energy. We can all multiply. Given your four month "boyfriend-girlfriend" relationship, and allowing for one or two visits a month, you went on four to eight actual dates with Travis)...I came out to his house again in March...umm, just prior to convention". Hey, I have an idea! Why don't they just check her journals if they want to know how often the two long distance daters actually went on dates? We don't want to Jodi to guess. She journals about everything Travis-related. She even journaled about Travis when they were no longer "boyfriend-girlfriend". In fact, she journaled about little else. So, crack open those journals.

Nurmi continues, "You mentioned you'd try to see each other about every other week, right?". No, actually she made it clear that sometimes four weeks would elapse between their visits, but fine, slice it and dice it anyway you want, Nurmi. It was a benign, brief, crash and burn relationship in which the participants were separated by hundreds of miles. If those miles were not separating them, I think we'd be talking about an "official boyfriend-girlfriend relationship" that lasted all of six weeks. It was certainly not the love affair of the century.

Fueling the fantasy (untruth) put forth by Nurmi – that the pair tried to see each other every other week -- Jodi answers, "About. He would come out to California about once a month (and if the Hughes are to be believed -- and given the choice of the Hughes or Jodi Arias, I'm going with the Hughes – those visits were not to Jodi's house. They took place at the Hughes' house), and I started going to Arizona, on average, about once a month (but I bet she wanted to go there far more often than that)". Nurmi continues, "So, he would either come out to your house in Palm Desert, or you would go out to see him in Mesa?". Jodi answers, "Yes, until May, he would come to Palm Desert". Nurmi's not interested in talking about May. It's probably too close to the end of the official boyfriend-girlfriend relationship. He still has to milk all he can out of their four to eight dates.

Nurmi continues, "And at this point in time, if I understand you correctly, February 2006, you are boyfriend and girlfriend (wrong, 2007), but you have not had penile/vaginal intercourse, is that right?". Jodi answers, "That's right". Nurmi asks, "When did you first have penile/vaginal intercourse with Mr. Alexander?" Jodi answers, "It would have been April or May...I think May...I'm pretty sure May...but it could have been April. It was in the spring". She's acting like the difference of a few weeks matters. It doesn't.

Nurmi asks, "Apart from these trips back and forth between your two homes, did you, – we heard a little earlier about travels, did you, had you traveled together yet?". Oh, please don't make the Alexanders suffer anymore while listening to Jodi giddily recall their "travels together", and don't make them choke on "1000 Places to See Before You Die". I think they'd rather hear about their brother calling her the worst thing that ever happened to him. I know Jodi's life is in the past, and all she has left are these memories of events that are becoming more distanced from her as each day passes, but that's her fault. For the rest of us, 2007 has come and gone. I take some pleasure in knowing that if she wants to brighten her pointless, dull, isolated day, she has to reach back in time and think of the past. There is no future for Jodi Arias. It is gone.

Nurmi lets Jodi know he doesn't want to hear about field trips that involved other people (because they're easier to confirm, I assume). He wants to hear about the travels they took alone (you know, only the trips that Jodi would know about). She answers, "We...that month of March that I came out before convention was our first...umm...was the first time we traveled together...Umm...he wanted to show me, the ah, the places that were significant in Mormon church history, so we decided to go to...(she likes this part)...we flew to Kansas City, Missouri, to see places in Missouri, and we also drove to Nauvoo, Illinois". I do have to hand it to Nurmi. He is definitely picking up on what the jury would find suspicious. He's pretending that he's asking for the benefit of those who might not know about the history of the LDS church, but he wants to know what places of significance she saw.

Nurmi asks if they saw something in Missouri. She responds, "Not in Kansas City, but that was the nearest major airport". Then, he wants to know if the airport was the closest major airport to "Navahoo" (he actually mispronounced it), Illinois. Jodi answers, "No. The sites, in Missouri". Bad move, Nurmi. She doesn't remember what she saw on the Magical Mormon Mystery Tour, and you just announced that to the jury. In the future, when she flubs through an answer and just uses filler words, let it go. Her memory is quite selective. Ask her what sexual position she was in at 8:21 PM on March 13, 2007, and she will have an answer. Ask her about public, daylight sightseeing tours, and you're not going to get much. I'm not a Mormon, but even I know that Joseph Smith, who is the leader of that faith, is buried in Nauvoo, Illinois (after being killed in a Carthage jail). There is an unbelievable amount of church history in both states. Jodi wasn't paying attention.

Now that we've had our anti-lesson in historical church sites, we're ready to move on. Nurmi asks, "How long of a trip was this to be?". Jodi answers, "I don't remember how many days (he should have asked her how many nights), but we left a few days early to see those sites (what sites?), and then fly to, or maybe drive to Oklahoma City, where convention was in the spring". Nurmi asks, "And, you're boyfriend-girlfriend at this point (I feel like he's constantly refreshing a page on a computer. He raises the boyfriend-girlfriend question before or after third question). You go to Kansas City. Is there a difference in his behavior in terms of how publicly affectionate he is when you arrive in Kansas City as opposed to when you're back home in Arizona?" Jodi answers, "Umm, he's...(very long pause)...he's a little bit more distant...umm, we hold hands sometimes, but not often, and that's about the extent, some...I don't know...sometimes he wouldn't even hold my hand. He would just be like...he wouldn't introduce me to anybody...umm, anything like that". Nurmi continues, "In Kansas City?". Jodi answers, "Oh, no. I thought you meant at convention".

Nurmi says, "No. No. Not at convention, in Kansas City. We talked about, earlier, we talked about how you, he acted like just your friend, unless it was in front of Dan or Desiree Freeman, or Aaron Dewey, but he acted like just a friend in public. My question was whether or not, when you got to Kansas City, umm, and you were traveling together, where people didn't know you, did that change?".

She is embarrassed because she wasn't paying attention. She is embarrassed because she looks stupid. She answers Nurmi's question, "Yes. He was more affectionate in those cities when we were out of town". Nurmi now establishes that the Magical Mormon Mystery Tour was two or three days long. He mentions the fact that she must have seen multiple places of historical significance, and while she confirms that, we are still clueless as to what those places might be. Nurmi isn't really interested in the sites or the cities. He wants to talk about the hotels they stayed in. This is going to be painful. He asks, "Did you have two hotel rooms?". Jodi answers, "No, just one". Nurmi asks, "Two beds, or just one?". Jodi, the gal who can't remember looking at the highly polished, granite tomb of the so-called prophet Joseph Smith, answers, "One queen size bed (see, I told you she'd remember the sex details)". Nurmi asks their ages – she was 27, he was 31. They are supposedly a couple. He knows they shared a hotel room.

Nurmi asks, "Was there sexual behavior during this trip?". Jodi says, "Yes". Nurmi asks, "Oral sex?". Oh, look at this. Jodi is pretending she doesn't remember. She remembers, but says, after a lengthy pause, "I don't remember the nature of it, but it was not anything different than what we had been doing (oh, kind of like the Provo Push she mentioned, but this time it would be Nauvoo No-No?)". Nurmi continues to invade the privacy of the dead. He asks, "And was this something fairly consistent throughout the two or three days while you were on this trip?". Jodi answers, "I think it only occurred once during that portion of the trip". I'm sure. He was surrounded by the sites and teachings of his faith. That probably went a long way in cooling things down. Jodi must have been angry.

Now we're going to break down The Magical Mormon Mystery Tour for the fiftieth time – and we're doing it so that we can get a better backdrop for what this case has been reduced to: How many times and in what ways these two consenting adults had sex. Has anyone mentioned that he's dead yet? Jodi says, "We went to three of four place in Missouri (nameless, again), then we drove to Nauvoo, Illinois". Nurmi asks, "And then from Illinois you went to Oklahoma City?". Jodi answers, "Yes, we stayed the night in Nauvoo, Illinois, and...(Jodi's spacing out, big time)...then we spent the whole day, until it was dark again, and then drove most of the night (she strokes her beard...I mean chin), I think to Oklahoma. I remember driving a long time after leaving Nauvoo".

I don't think she enjoyed the Nauvoo portion of the trip. I think, given a choice, she would have preferred to stay in the hotel room instead of looking at a grave of a man who thought he was as important as Jesus Christ (even if it was really shiny and pretty, as far as tombs go). It sounds like he kept her outdoors for a long time. There is something on her face and in the tone of her voice that's giving me the impression that she couldn't wait for this tour to be over. It was especially evident earlier when she said that they spent "the entire day" touring Nauvoo. It was the way she said "entire", like she didn't sign up for this type of comprehensive tour. I'm speculating, but I think she tried, and failed, to keep him between the sheets.

Now we're going to convention. Nurmi repeats what anyone watching this trial could repeat: that this was one of the two big PPL conventions of the year. Then Jodi repeats what Nurmi just repeated: that this was one of the two big PPL conventions of the year. Always ready to out talk someone, Jodi adds that this convention was in the spring. Guess what, Jodi? In the United States, March is the spring. We all know it was the spring. Now, move along.

I've been avoiding mentioning how absolutely annoying Maria de la Rosa is when she knows she on camera (when she's just preening, not smuggling contraband). Every few minutes she whispering, smiling, shaking her head, or otherwise causing a visual disturbance. Jennifer Willmott isn't as bad, but she's an attorney, and as such, she should write a note to Maria and let her know that her conduct isn't appropriate. I hope they move her back to the second table tomorrow.

Okay, back to convention. Nurmi recalls the confusion that Jodi experienced earlier when she was asked about Travis' public displays of affection (PDAs) in Kansas City, but Jodi thought the subject was his PDAs during convention. I guess we're going to dissect that now. Oh, very nice close-up of Juan Martinez. He's a handsome man – one of those men who improves with age. His chiseled features barely move as he stares as Jodi.

Nurmi wants to know how Travis acted toward her at convention. Jodi answers, "Umm...just, I just sorta became, it seemed like, I was just another person there. Uh, maybe on a friend/acquaintance level. Umm...I wasn't expecting (BS), he had told me ahead of time that convention is crazy, and all that, but there were plenty of moments where we were all just hanging out, and he wasn't incredibly affectionate (why should he be "incredibly" affectionate in public?), umm, but there was one time when we were up very late, and we were in the hotel lobby, and, umm, I was really tired, but I stayed to hang out with everyone, and he put a pillow on his lap and let me lay there. So that was really nice of him".

We remember this, Jodi. You didn't look very appreciative in that video. In fact, you looked quite put upon; kind of like a hostess with a house full of friends who are not getting the hint that it's time for them to leave. Why not just take you butt back to your hotel room and go to sleep if you're so exhausted that you cannot remain in an upright position among a group of people who are all quite alert? He was obviously awake and ready to socialize. You, on the other hand, wanted to go and have sex. He preferred the company of other people – at least when given the choice of staying and talking or being alone with you. You were an anchor. Let's not even get into what he was talking about – his near death experience dream.

Also, I would like to know what Jodi Arias considers appropriate when it comes to PDAs. Should Travis have grabbed her by her hair, shoved his tongue down her throat, and his hand down her blouse? Does she not realize that many people find adolescent displays of affection off-putting and awkward?

Oh, I'm sorry. I cut Jodi off. She wasn't finished. She continues, "Other than that, he was actually very flirtatious with another woman (oh, could this be Clancy, the woman who was trapped in the bathroom with a territorial Jodi?)". Nurmi tells Jodi not to get into the details, but he wants to know if this flirtation happened in front of her? "Yes", says Jodi. Nurmi continues, "Did that hurt your feelings?". Jodi answers, "Yes, it hurt my feelings". Nurmi asks, "Did you ever say anything to him about it (I'd be more interested in what she said to the woman, frankly)?". Jodi answers, "Afterward, after the incident, we ended up talking about it". Nurmi reminds us all, including Jodi, that in the past, it had been very difficult for Jodi to bring "these things" up to Travis. He would like to know what gave her the strength to do it this time.

My theory: She had no choice. I suspect she confronted this woman, and word was going to get around. Jodi answered, "I didn't bring it up to him. He came to me. I think he knew he screwed up". No, absolutely not. He came to her, and he was probably very angry and embarrassed when he found out that she had cornered this woman in the bathroom. I have a very strong suspicion that she is talking about Clancy Talbot. Because this woman isn't testifying, Jodi is free to spin whatever tale she wants about this "incident".

Nurmi asks if all was forgiven after they talked about it. Jodi answers, "Eventually. We talked about it for a few minutes. Getting into it made me cry because it was very blatant, what he did (as blatant as 27 stab wounds, a slit throat, a bullet to the face, and a shower stall for a grave...that blatant, or was it more subtle than that?). And, he was very apologetic". There is an absolutely disgusting expression of smug victory on her face. Do you know what I just realized – as in, it just really hit me? I think any penalty Jodi Arias will pay will always be secondary to the fact that she truly believes she won. I just saw that look on her face. She wasn't reflecting or reacting to an incident in the past – that is her heart, and that is the way she feels today. She may pay a huge price for what she did, but the price he paid will always be bigger. Even if she dies by lethal injection, she will never know the absolute frenzy being experienced by a mortally wounded man trying, in vain, to crawl away from his attacker, only to feel her cold, blood drenched, bony fingers on his body again, pulling his head back, and ending his life. This is beginning to feel pornographic.

Jodi is now going to go into the realm of the ridiculous. Nurmi continues to hammer away at the PDA disparities based on location. Jodi says, as far as the convention was concerned, she didn't over analyze it. After all, she realized it was a business convention, and while there were other couples there who were sitting together and holding hands, she wasn't really upset that Travis wouldn't do that. What upset her is what he did with the other woman. She says, "...So it hurt my feelings a little bit, but it was very mild in comparison to the way he was actually acting with another woman".

Nurmi is back to sleeping arrangements. He wants to know if they shared a hotel room. She answers, "Definitely not. We were in separate hotel rooms (that makes me happy, and hopefully, he made her pay for her own room)". Nurmi pounces on "definitely not" (didn't see that coming), and he wants an explanation. Here we go. Travis the Mormon hypocrite, right? Jodi answers, "Well, he explained to me that it wasn't looked upon very well when...to stay in the same hotel room. Umm, plus, we weren't married, we weren't going to get the same hotel room. We would stay in the same...he would stay in a room full of guys, and I would stay in a room full of girls, and we would all split the cost".

Just a point that's dying to be made. Why did any of this need to be explained to New Creation Arias? Four months earlier, she was subjected to a stalled baptism because she lived under the same roof as a man who was not her husband and not a relative. If anyone should understand what the issue with a shared hotel room was, it would be Jodi Arias. By the way, let's not forget that she's allegedly as much of a Mormon as Travis Alexander. There was probably quite a bit of bitching about this. I can almost hear it: "We barely get to see each other as it is, and you care more about what a bunch of hypocrites think than what I think, blah, blah, blah". I think she would have loved to have gotten him out of that church. I think she would have loved to see him excommunicated from that church.

Nurmi says, "I'm a little confused then, because it seems like this man had concerns about appearances at the convention, but didn't have any concerns about sharing a hotel room with you a night or two before hand, right?". Nurmi should not be trying to make his point by feigning confusion. It's transparent, and it makes him sound stupid – or even worse, it makes the jurors believe that he thinks they're the stupid ones. Framing questions while pretending that you haven't been listening to all of the testimony you have elicited is a low level mistake. We all know why the sleeping situation was set up the way it was. If he has any further confusion on the subject, maybe he should stop trying to figure out the Mormon brain of the victim. Maybe he should look at his client, who also claims to have a Mormon brain, and ask her to explain the doctrinal issues of premarital sex. No. Instead he will act like he is talking to a woman who never pretended to be a Mormon, and he'll pretend the man she was dating suddenly foisted his odd Mormon beliefs on her at a convention.

Jodi says, "Yes". Nurmi asks, "Did you ever question him about that disparity?". Oh, I'll bet she did, whether or not she admits it now. There was no reason for her to question anything. She knew the rules. She was a baptized member of the faith. If she didn't like it, she could have told him that she wasn't willing to have this type of relationship. The truth is, she held onto this type of relationship with the same white knuckled fervor as a man hanging from a ledge.

Jodi answers, "No. I knew it was a church standard, and I knew we were going against the church standard when no one else knew about it, but, not that time. Eventually, it came up between us, but not at convention, I didn't".

Nurmi wants to know how they got back home from the convention. Jodi says she believes they flew directly back to Phoenix. Jodi makes it clear that they did not fly with a group of people. There may have been other people they knew on the plane, but they made their own reservations and flew together (you want to bet that she whispered, "It's a short flight, babe. Wanna join the mile high club?). Look at how things have changed for the waitress from Yreka. At the last convention in September, Jodi was left watching as Travis pulled away in a taxi to be driven to the airport. She was stuffed into the back seat of a Honda and subjected to a long car ride back to Palm Desert (and she wasn't even driving). Now, this non-earner, but very actively involved PPL associate, is flying in and out of conventions. It's so much fun to play house, isn't it?

Once they got back to Phoenix, Jodi did not get into her car and drive back home. Instead, she hung around Travis' house and wrangled herself an invitation to a weekly Sunday dinner Travis attended at someone's home. Nurmi wants to know if Jodi slept over. Of course, Jodi slept over. I think Travis might have even compensated Jodi for her travel expenses...just a guess. Does Jodi have a job she needed to be at on Monday morning at 8:00 AM (and Tuesday morning, a1nd Wednesday morning...all the way to Friday)? No, and even if she did, she'd just get up at 2:30 AM and start driving.

Back to the dinner. Jodi had not met these people. They are, at present, not being named. Nurmi wants to know if Travis introduced Jodi to this family as "his girlfriend". Jodi answers, "No, I was kind of just a friend". No, he didn't say, "Hey, this is Jodi. She's kind of just a friend. Do you mind feeding her?". Of course not. He said, "This is my friend, Jodi Arias. She's a PPL associate, and a recent convert". That's what he said.

Once again, we need to know if Jodi's feelings were hurt. She says "not particularly". Nurmi continues, "That evening, you went to this home and you were introduced as his buddy, again. When you go back to the home, is there more sexual activity?" Jodi answers, "Right before I left...(long pause)...I really don't recall about that night". She looks apologetic, but she needn't be. Nurmi's been over-sexed today.

Judge Stephens grants Nurmi's request for a break, and the afternoon recess begins. There are only twenty minutes left to Jodi's third day under direct. Jodi stands for the jury, and she immediately turns toward them, looks at them, and crosses her arms across her chest. This is significant in terms of body language. It signifies that she is feeling negative, defensive, and nervous.

After a brief recess, court is back in session.

Nurmi says, "Miss Arias, before we move completely past the convention in Oklahoma City, you had mentioned some incident that had made you upset during this convention". Jodi answers, "Yes". Nurmi continues, "It made you more upset than being treated as his buddy at this convention, right?". Jodi answers, "Yes, I can't say that just the way he treated me made me really upset, but it kind of bothered me".

Nurmi continues, "Okay. What was this incident that you're talking about that hurt your feelings so significantly?". Jodi responds, "Well, umm, we were...this was the night of the executive director banquet, and I went, again, with Travis that night. Umm, after that banquet, most people like to change out of their tuxedos and gowns and whatever, fancy dresses, whatever they're wearing, into clothing that is more comfortable. And, umm, so Travis and I did that, and I was in whatever, jeans, and he changed out to the same, and, umm, some people will stay in their dresses. There was one woman that came down the stairs from another level of the lobby, I guess. We were in the lobby area of the Sheraton Hotel, and she was very, very drunk, and she almost couldn't stand up, so she began to hang all over various men (Jodi Arias! This is Your Life!), and, umm, slurring things, making jokes that nobody really understood. Umm, everyone was laughing at her though (Jodi Arias! This is Your Life!), because it was kind of funny, umm, I thought it was kind of funny at the time too, so I flipped open my phone and started video recording her (bitch...hateful, mean spirited bitch), so I could show her the next day (no, so you could blackmail her by threatening to post it online). Umm, so everything was kind – we were just laughing, and she...am I allowed to say what she said?". Oh no, we were actually covering territory, and now we have the tortoise named Nurmi back in the game. He says, "Well, let me get specifically to, what was it about this, this drunk woman, as you describe her, did she have an interaction with Travis or something that made you upset?".

Jodi responds (and she's nervous...breathing deeply and visibly), "Yes. She was hanging all over two guys, and then, umm, after that, she kind of lurched over to Travis, and fell on him a little, and he held her up, and they were facing each other, very close, and he was holding her around the waist, and she had her arms around his shoulders, and she had this very sexy black gown on, and umm, very generous cleavage, umm, kind of pressed up against his chest (we get it...she's better looking than you...let's go), and he looked like he was loving every minute of it, and I was sitting down on a couch nearby, and he was probably about five feet in that direction (she points to her left), and I had already shut my phone at this point 'cause (she didn't want Travis to see her filming a vulnerable drunk woman, or she didn't want to see images of Travis embracing someone who was far more attractive than her) the video didn't last that long. I just got this feeling inside, like my stomach flip-flopped, I couldn't believe he was doing that (holding up a drunk woman? Oh, that it an awful offense, especially when we consider the fact that he is stone cold sober), umm, not just doing it, but doing it right in front of me (I don't get it. What did he do? Did he comment on her breasts? Did he lick his lips and stare into her eyes? What did he do?), in front of all of our friends (in front of all of HIS friends). I was under the impression that most of our friends, Dan was there, Aaron Dewey was there, that other people understood we were together, and I didn't feel that that behavior was appropriate (too easy...I'm not going to take shots at her chronically inappropriate behavior), umm, but I didn't want to make a scene, so I stood up. I was hurt. I felt like I wanted to cry, but I didn't really want anyone to see that, so I decided that I was going to go to the bathroom...umm, but in order to get to the bathroom, I had to walk right past them (yes, because you know how microscopic those convention capacity hotel lobbies can be), so I passed them, and they stopped me briefly, and I kind of...I don't remember what she was slurring (is the drunk woman going to vomit on Travis? How bad is Jodi going to make this woman sound? She did make it down a flight of stairs without breaking her neck, so I'm pretty sure she isn't really falling down drunk), but he was kind of laughing, and they were swaying, and like that, and I just said, smiled, I don't know if I said much (I call BS), and I kept walking after that. And, I went into the bathroom, and into a stall, and sat down on one of the toilets, and just started crying".

Why in the name of all that is holy would Nurmi have her recount this story? I have never gotten a clearer indication of how socially inept and completely possessive this woman is. That story put a new light on Jodi Arias (and SHE is the one who gave it to us!). It's more than the content, it's the way she told the story. The big buildup that led to nothing. I'm beginning to recognize that pattern in her – the crescendos that build, promising something big and memorable, but at their apex, you're left wondering if you actually missed the climax. Was she, at this point, just completely frustrated sexually. Forgive my crude language, but was this a case of blue balls? I'm serious. I know her hormone levels are probably not that of the average woman, and in her mind, he is withholding sex while at this convention. As a woman, I cannot believe that this type of nonsense is something that seriously offended her. So, he's holding up a drunk woman. She was also held up by several other men, according to Jodi. However, I didn't hear Jodi say that she heard sobs coming from the other bathroom stalls, so I assume the women attached to those men ascribed the value to this incident that it actually warranted. Nothing.

All of I can think of, at this point, is that the sex must have been amazing. Why else would a normal man entertain this level of crazy? I also find it very interesting that Jodi was quite ready to laugh at a woman who had a little too much to drink – so much so, that she was ready to record the woman. Suddenly, it all stopped being funny when Jodi's feelings came into play. Did she ever stop, even for a moment, to think of how the woman would feel knowing that some neophyte recorded her? Rhetorical. I know the answer to that. She's a sociopath.

Nurmi quizzes Jodi, again, on her level of hurt feelings. I'm beginning to wonder if he shouldn't hand Jodi a pain scale sheet. When you go to the hospital or a pain management doctor, there are those silly charts that ascribe numbers to levels of physical pain. For those with low reading comprehension, there are accompanying little faces wearing expressions that correlate to the level of pain being felt by the patient. They go from number one, which is a smiling face, to number ten, which is a boiled in oil face. Instead of physical pain, perhaps we can make it emotional pain. We could save a lot of time if Jodi and jury just had a copy of the emotional pain scale. Jodi could just say she was feeling like a four, or a two, or a nine. It's something to consider when feelings are being hurt all the time.

Jodi says her feelings were really hurt – I'm guessing a seven on the pain scale. She says, "I stayed in the bathroom for quite some time. Leslie Udy came in, I believe it was her, it sounded like her voice, a few times, but every time I heard the door open, I put my feet up so that no one could see me in the stall, because I didn't want anyone to understand, to know, that I was upset. So, she left, and after the second time she came in, and then left, I finally exited the stall, and...". Nurmi's going to interrupt, but not before I do. She was screaming for attention. She put her feet up? Well, maybe the locked stall door – very obvious in a woman's bathroom – was a clear indication that somebody was sitting on a toilet. Jodi runs to bathrooms when she's out of control in public. She had enough control not to kick holes in the wall, like she did at Ventana Inn when she couldn't convince another waitress to switch sections with her, but she couldn't do that at convention. You know what's particularly telling? She was in this bathroom long enough for one woman to come in twice, but Travis never sent an emissary to look for her. That's what would have bothered me.

Nurmi wants to know why she didn't want the other women to know that she was hiding in the bathroom. Get ready...here's her response: "I guess, I was, I felt ashamed for some reason that he was acting that way. I felt ashamed. I don't...I really can't explain why (we noticed), I just felt like maybe I would be perceived as maybe someone who didn't deserve anything better (self-pity much?), or someone who was, maybe, overly dramatic (getting warmer, Jodi), or over-reacting (bingo), or emotional, too emotional. Umm, I didn't want...I wanted to be perceived as someone who was just cool and calm (you have to be cool and calm to be perceived that way, chameleon). And like, shrug it off, like whatever, 'cause maybe there isn't any meaning behind it, but even though they were very physically suggestive, or, at least close, and pressing their bodies up against each other, and it lasted quite some time, I still was...thinking maybe there wasn't anything to that. I didn't want others to think I was overreacting".

Wow. Very damaged goods. What strikes me is that she seems to have issues with Travis and the fact that he doesn't want to be perceived as someone breaking the Law of Chastity. She seems to have difficulty with the fact that other people are concerned about the way they are perceived. In her world, it is all about her. Go back and read her response again. This woman is just putting her psychopathy on the table. She has no identity. She doesn't fit it. She just puts on one mask after the other. If a man wasn't dead, I could almost feel some measure of pity for her.

I think that Jodi was in that bathroom for more than a half an hour. She says, "she didn't want to give herself away", and with her puffy eyes and dissolved make-up, that took some work. She says she finally left the bathroom and headed for the elevator. Most of the group had dispersed, but some people were left. As she tried to get to the elevator, someone called her name. She said hello to the person. I'm not sure why this matters. She says that as she got near to the elevator, Travis texted her and asked her where she was. Jodi said, "I forgot one thing I did before he texted me". This is important to her, and she intends to get it in, but Nurmi wants to focus on the conversation with Travis.

Jodi said, "It (the conversation) actually took place...he was trying to get on the same elevator I was, but from his floor, so, we figured that out, and I rode the elevator up and he met me at the elevator...umm, as I came off the elevator...we are outside the elevator, umm, there's a long hallway, but then, before you, right before the hallway there is a small table and a chair, maybe two chairs. We were there...I had calmed down a lot, I didn't want to leave the bathroom until I was cool and collected, so I had calmed down a lot, but as he got me to talk about it, it got me upset even more, and I started crying some, and he reassured me...just said some nice things". I pieced together her testimony in the interest of brevity. This was probably four separate questions, but Jodi's pathology is much more interesting than Nurmi's and his questioning.

Everybody made nice. The convention ended. The next time Jodi saw Travis was when he came to a "recap event" in southern California. These events were held the weekend after the convention. Jodi also went to this recap convention, and by this point in her testimony, I don't think the defense is even trying to make anyone believe that her attendance at these events had anything to do with her business objectives. Travis and Jodi did not stay in a hotel room. She said he stayed with friends or family – but guess what? Jodi wrangled a bed in the same house Travis was staying in. What are the odds? Nurmi wants to go to sexual activity. Was there any? Jodi thinks, and says, "That night...(very long pause)...I think...we did...in that house...during those times...but I don't recall, specifically". Jodi tells us that this was the home of Chris and Sky Hughes' parents. Now, we all know that Chris and Sky don't share the same parents, so I'm reasonably sure that this issue will be cleared up – not that it matters.

Nurmi gets Jodi to say that she was "his buddy" at this event, that she doesn't recall if he flirted with women at this event, but it's possible, because he was always friendly with women. This home was a ranch, and the owners threw a large party after the "recap", and Jodi says that they socialized and eventually went to sleep. She claims they slept in the same room. Nurmi wants to know if Travis told everyone at this party that Jodi was his girlfriend, or whether he just said that she was his buddy.

Jodi is angry. She says, "He didn't introduce me at all". Nurmi pretends that he didn't hear her, but he just wants her to repeat what she said. She obliges, and says, "He didn't introduce me at all". Now Nurmi wants to know if she went home at the end of the party. Jodi says she left on Monday, but Travis wanted to meet up with her in Riverside, California, that night. Jodi says, "He told me to go to...I don't remember what it's called, a mission, or something, it's kind of a tourist destination in Riverside. He said it's a beautiful place for photographs, and I could get some nice pictures, umm, while he finishes up whatever he was doing at their house. So I had to...I had to go to Verizon, and then I went there, and took some pictures".

Jodi took her pictures, but Travis never met her at the mission. Instead, he gave her directions to his grandmother's house. It wasn't a nice visit. In fact, Jodi makes it sound quite awkward. They spent a few moments with his grandmother, Jodi was not introduced as Travis' girlfriend, and then the couple went to Barnes and Noble (Jodi is quick to add the this was the first of three meetings she had with Norma Sarvey). No sex.

Now, we're at Valentine's Day. They did not spend Valentine's Day together, and since they were only 12 days into their relationship, added to the fact that Jodi had to work, she was not expecting much. However, she claims that she received a package on her doorstep. The package was from Travis. Contained in that package were Valentine gifts. She said there were chocolates, Reese's peanut butter cups, fun size Hershey bars – all melted. She also mentions apparel. There was a shirt that she claims he was joking about for months, but then she changes it to "weeks" – it was the notorious "Travis Alexander's" shirt. There were also pink shorts, and Nurmi introduced a photo of the clothes.

Jodi says that under the shorts were boy's underwear – Spiderman underwear. "I was confused at first. They were still in the pkg. I don't know the size...". The rest of her verbatim testimony doesn't matter. She adds that there was also a nice letter.

We are then interrupted by a "may we approach" request. After a three minute bench conference, court is adjourned for the day.

CHAPTER FOUR

- Day 4 -

"Confusion hath now made his masterpiece."

William Shakespeare, Macbeth.

Jodi Arias takes the stand for the fourth day of direct examination.

Regarding her Valentine's Day gift box, I assume it's possible that Travis sent her something, but because of the messenger's messy history with the truth, most of us will chose to disbelieve her. We'll spend a lot of time hearing about a gift box that may be imaginary, but this is the Jodi Arias Show, and there's only one imagination that counts on this stage. What we do know is that Jodi wrote a lengthy email to Travis on Valentine's Day in 2007, and that email was sent around "4:45PM" (according to Juan Martinez and Jodi Arias). Interestingly, she makes no mention of the gift box in that email. Make of that what you will – I know what I've concluded.

In the box, Jodi claims, was a sweet letter, assorted (melted) chocolates, shorts, a T-shirt bearing the name Travis Alexander, and the now infamous, boy-sized, Spiderman underpants (still in their original package). I think we're going to hear a lot about those underpants.

Jodi's father, Bill Arias, is in court today. The Arias family tends to dress rather casually for court, and Bill is no exception. Again, the contrast between the two sides of the court room is obvious. Those supporting Travis are not fans of court casual wear. The women could be going to an office or a house of worship, and the men wear suits and ties. Tanisha Alexander Sorenson's husband, Harold, wears French cuffed shirts with cuff links. As we look at Bill Arias, we see that he is wearing the uniform of the defense supporter -- casual, but still a step above jeans and T-shirts. He's wearing a dark blue dress shirt with vertical white stripes. He's not wearing a tie; in fact, several of the top buttons of his shirt are unbuttoned. He is not wearing a sport jacket; instead, he's wearing outerwear – a dark blue windbreaker or jacket. The collar is pulled up around his neck, and it leaves the impression that he is trying to hide in plain sight. He looks shell shocked and distant, this dark figure with blue tinted eyeglass lenses.

Judge Stephens says, "Miss Arias, please take the stand". This affects Bill. Maybe the reality of what is happening to his daughter is threatening to overwhelm him. He looks directly at her. It is difficult to see his eyes because of the dark tinted lenses he wears, but I believe he may been fighting tears. He is in pain, that much is clear. He winces, very visibly, but not dramatically. He looks up toward the ceiling, and the expression on his face is one of utter defeat. This is the first time I have felt any sympathy for someone connected to Jodi Arias. He is far easier to read than his wife, Sandy. Her face could be on Mount Rushmore. It doesn't move, and only occasionally do we see a distinct frown.

The camera is focused on Jodi. As she takes her place on the witness stand, you might think you were watching a young woman settling in for a day of office work. She moves some things around on the tiny desktop, and she gets ready to testify. She actually looks quite professional today; a huge improvement over Thursday's silly junior wear top. Today, she is wearing an ivory colored sweater with a tiny ivory bow at the V-neckline. Underneath the sweater is a black camisole, apparently worn for modesty – either that, or because it has padded bra cups sewn into it. I'm not sure why, but she looks far more endowed today than she has in the past. She has a solid black jacket on. Her hair is parted on the side, and the jury has a great shot of the black scrunchie gathering her small side pony tail. Her ever present eyeglasses are in place, and from the neck up, she looks like she's ready for her eighth grade portrait to be snapped.

Jodi's brother is also in the court room. If you tweezed his eyebrows and grew out his hair, you'd be looking at Jodi (although I don't think his face is as long as her face). He's wearing a white dress shirt with tiny boxes all over it. It's buttoned up to his neck. If he had just added a tie, he'd be the best dressed male in the defense gallery. He actually looks like he is fighting emotion, as well. I assume it is not easy to see your sister being watched by armed guards while she is a defendant in a capital murder trial. It would have been preferable for this younger brother to have attended court on an earlier day – perhaps a day when Jodi was recalling her younger years. This testimony is getting more and more graphic, and it makes me uncomfortable to think of her younger brother hearing this kind of detail about his sister. But then again, the Alexander siblings are being forced to hear the same thing about their brother, so I guess all is fair.

As soon as the jury is seated, Jodi's jacket comes off. Yes, she is definitely wearing some kind of shape wear under that sweater. I guess she's putting the goods on display for the male members of the jury. After the usual preliminaries, Nurmi is instructed to continue with his direct examination.

He is on his feet, and he is holding a photograph in his hand. He begins, "Good morning, Jodi. Last week, when we ended, we were speaking about the gift you received for Valentine's Day, uh, from Mr. Alexander in 2007. And one of the things we talked about you receiving was, we talked about you receiving a few things, but I'm showing you exhibit number 417. The package you received contained this T-shirt and this pair of shorts or underwear, right?" I assume that the shorts are being displayed on Jodi's computer screen because she's doing her PTSD trigger face.

Oh, and just so you know, back at the defense table, Maria de la Rosa, the mitigation specialist, as is her custom, snapped up the opportunity to fill Jodi's empty chair next to Jennifer Willmott. After a small flurry of activity that includes moving some folders, she's secured a great camera angle.

I don't know how Jodi could appear to be traumatized by what we are now seeing displayed on the screen, but she is. The photograph is actually quite ridiculous. The shorts are laid out on a flat surface, back side facing up. They are neither sexy nor erotic, and they are certainly not the type of lingerie one would associate with young love on Valentine's Day. In fact, I feel like I am looking at a big, pink, adult diaper. On the thin, white waistband of the diaper-like shorts are the top portions of capital letters. Those letters would spell out, "LOVE LOVE LOVE". It gets better. On the area that would cover the left cheek, three, black capital letters have been attached – TRA. On the right cheek, there are three more letters – VIS. Oh, I can't forget the most important thing – the apostrophe added at the end – the one that indicates that this is the possessive form of the name. It looks like someone (probably Jodi) stuck some vinyl letters on a pair of women's briefs. I know where this is going, but I'm already having a very hard time believing that a man who wanted to keep his sexual relationship with this woman a secret would give her such a strong piece of tangible evidence to the contrary. I always thought it was Juan Martinez' exacting cross examination that was the slam dunk in this case, but I do have to admit that her own direct examination is pretty damning.

Oh, there's the top of the photo! It's a shirt – presumably something to go with the big sexy diaper shorts. I see a badly spaced group of letters applied to a typical gray, cotton T-shirt. One line says "Travis", and the other line says "Alexander's". Again, the possessive form is on display. This is worse than the shorts, in terms of evidence. Travis, the man who won't introduce Jodi to anybody, the man who steadfastly refused to hold her hand in public, the man who thinks of her as a "bud" (according to Nurmi) and will not call her a girlfriend, thought it would be good idea to give his "dirty little secret" a T-shirt like this? You know, maybe if Travis was a drinker, I could buy this. This would be the kind of sophomoric, ill-conceived idea that would only look good through the blur of alcohol soaked reasoning. He wasn't a drinker. He was sober. All the time.

Nurmi continues, "Is there a story behind this – why you received these particular items?". Yes, Nurmi, there's a story behind this, and that's exactly what you're going to get – a story. Jodi answers, "Umm, there's a story behind the T-shirt. The shorts were unexpected". Jodi continues, "Well, sometimes Travis would come out to California, and we would go to Super Saturdays in Anaheim together (did the man ever come for an exclusively social visit, or was every trip planned with a dual purpose in mind? We already know his trips to California to see Jodi are extremely limited – in the single digits from September, 2006 to June, 2007 – so putting the word 'sometimes' in this answer is kind of silly), and I was new, so there were people that would introduce me to other people in the company, and if it was a man, he always wanted to know what we were talking about. He would be very inquisitive. He started this joke, and he said I'm going to get you a T-shirt that says 'Travis Alexander's' so you can wear it to all the PrePaid Legal Events (wait...I thought he wouldn't introduce her as his girlfriend to anyone at the PPL events)".

Nurmi continues, "And this was the shirt that he joked about, right?". Jodi answers, "Yeah, well we just joked about it...he joked it about it, occasionally he would bring it up. Umm, he didn't attend all the Super Saturdays in California, so sometimes I would go and he would inquire what happened, who did I meet, that kind of thing, and so it was a joke that came up occasionally from December through January".

Jodi is in a great mood this morning. She must have spent the weekend doing something that made her happy. Maybe she likes her new sweater and shape wear. She is talking very rapidly, moving her hands all over the place, and she's looking directly at the jury. Still, one cannot not avoid noticing that this is a strange affect – she is almost laughing every time she says the word "joke". She is literally in the past. In Jodi's mind, we are back in 2007. Once in a while, she should fast forward to the end of this happy tale she's recounting. Maybe it would wipe the annoying smile off of her face.

Nurmi continues, "Now you were telling us last week that another item you received from Mr. Alexander was some Spiderman underwear. Umm, to be clear, could you describe it for us? Was this one pair? Was this several pairs?". Jodi answers, "It was a package. I don't remember how many were in the package, but there were three designs, I mean three styles, I mean they were all the same cut, but they had three different patterns. They were all Spiderman".

Nurmi asks, "And to your recollection, this package of underwear that we're talking about, what did it say? Was it women's, or men's, or girl's, or boy's? What did it say on it?" Jodi answers, "I don't remember the size, but they were definitely for little boys. I thought maybe he was, umm...". The voice of Prosecutor Juan Martinez breaks in: "Objection. Speculation". She's going to speculate here...please sustain the objection. I couldn't hear the ruling, but I believe Nurmi was told to rephrase.

Why is Maria de la Rosa smiling at the camera? We are now moving into the sickening, twisted, repulsive world of pedophilia. This is not the time for Cougarloucious (the professional mitigation specialist's twitter handle) to start posing for the camera. Why the hell is she smiling? My guess? She's been practicing faces in the mirror all weekend (between several trips to Sephora to get a make-over and purchase a pound of new cosmetics). She's found a few expressions she particularly likes, and she intends to keep displaying them so that she has a nice recording of how beautiful she looked at the Arias trial in 2013. One day, she'll have her own mitigation specialist website, and I guarantee these screen shots will show up on that site. What a cast of characters. They all, defendant included, deserve each other.

Nurmi asks, "Were you surprised?". Arias answers, "I was a little confused?". A little confused? If I were dating a man who sent me a package of young boy's underpants, I'd be more than a little confused, but then again, I'm relatively normal. I would know the brand, the size, and I'd be looking for a price tag. Then, I'd be on the phone with the sender, and if there wasn't a good explanation – what's a good explanation for this? – we'd have a problem. We'd have such a big problem that I'd change my phone number. If he sent this package, he sent something that required an immediate response from the recipient. Frankly, I don't believe he ever sent her this package. Did anyone look at Travis' bank statement to see where he was shopping in early February, 2007? Just like the Walmart gas can were traced, couldn't the purchase of boy's underwear be traced? Oh, he probably paid in cash, right?

Nurmi wants to know when she received the package. She says it was on Valentine's Day. Then, she says maybe it was a few days before, or maybe a few days after. No worries, it was right on "the holiday, or right near it". Well, sending a package usually requires a trip to the Post Office or Fed Ex. Were there any records of packages being sent from his zip code to her zip code in the five days she has just encapsulated?

Jodi takes a very deep, open mouthed breath as she continues this facade. Nurmi asks, "And did you speak with Mr. Alexander on the day that you received this gift?". Yes, she did. She's not going to talk about it now, but Juan Martinez will bring it up under cross. We will learn, courtesy of the prosecutor, that Jodi wrote Travis a long email complaining that her ex-live in lover, co-foreclosure victim, Darryl Brewer, had called her asking for money (money she owed him...money he wasn't going to get...money she planned to spend on a plane ticket to attend a MLM convention put on by a company that Travis was paid to work for, and she paid to be a part of). In that email to Travis, Jodi lamented that she didn't even want to get out of bed on Valentine's Day. She was so depressed and so miserable. How dare Darryl ask her if she had any of the money he owed her? That really depressed her. However, magical thinker that she is, she shifted gears and lightened considerably when she thought about Travis' voice and the things he said to her on the phone just a day earlier. She wrote that Travis was so strong, that he knew "The Secret" (a reference to the book about magical thinking), and how she wanted to comfort him. She talked about her dangerous anger, and how it had caused her to damage property. It's no wonder Nurmi decided to avoid the subject of the email of February 14, 2007, and instead decided to focus on a Valentine's package that nobody can prove ever existed.

Nurmi wants to know if Jodi felt anything beyond confusion when she received the boy's underwear. Jodi answers, "No. At the time, I received Victoria's Secret catalogs at my house (beyond wondering if the male jurors are now thinking about busty Jodi in Victoria's Secret lingerie, I'm also wondering how nice it must be to live rent/mortgage free for almost a year --Victoria's Secret, sushi, airplane tickets, long road trips, hotel rooms), and there was a trend in women's lingerie at the time that kind of had boy's briefs, boy styles, or men's briefs, but they were designed for women's bodies (she's pouring it on thick today), so I figured, I mean he also received Victoria's Secret catalogs (because you anonymously signed him up for them to make him appear to be the hypocritical Mormon who was interested in looking at women in lingerie – as though there's something unnatural about that), so I figured it was something to that effect (what effect? She's actually trying to sell the theory that she believed that Travis thought little boy's underpants were a reasonable substitute for pricey, silky boy shorts sold at Victoria's Secret? Really, this is the best she can do?), and he didn't understand the difference in body shapes, and I thought that he was kind of going with that trend...I thought, I was giving him the benefit of the doubt". What doubt? Where has she expressed a hint of doubt about what was in the alleged package?

I can't let this go. They really made a mistake with this. Nobody is believing that Travis Alexander had requested that Victoria's Secret add him to their mailing list (Jodi may have made the request, but nobody is believing that the Mormon priesthood holder with multiple male roommates solicited catalogs of women's lingerie). Secondly, if we are being asked to believe that he did request these catalogs, it stands to reason that he would have actually opened them and looked through the pages. Go ahead, put a Victoria's Secret catalog in the vicinity of a heterosexual male and tell me he's not going to open it. As a man, if you would like to see the distinct differences between your own body shape and that of a woman, a Victoria's Secret catalog would be your best textbook. Did she really just say that he got confused on the body shape issue? Well, his confusion would have dissolved by the time he got to page 3 of the Winter, 2006 catalog.

Nurmi asks if Jodi had any doubt that Travis intended to send these underpants to her. Jodi says, "After speaking to him, there was no doubt...Well, I called him, and we discussed what I received, and kind of laughed about it, and I said, what's with the Spideys...?". She is almost laughing, and she's flushed – this is not the reaction of a woman who has discovered, in retrospect, that this was the first piece of evidence to indicate her sexual partner's hidden pedophilia. I cannot express to you how absolutely counter to reality her affect is in the face of this subject matter. My God, she has a nickname, "Spideys", for what she is now claiming is evidence of her boyfriend's desire to molest children. I'm blown away...literally blown away. Juan Martinez, the lawyer in the room who prosecutes pedophiles, (as opposed to the public defender in the room who attempts to humanize them), breaks in with an objection. It's a hearsay objection, and I don't even care if it applies. As an attorney, I would have thrown any objection in at this point, just to stop the momentum. I would want the jury to sit there and look at that frozen smile on her face. Her last word, "Spideys", needs to hang in the air for a second or two. I'd want the jury to realize that she's smiling because she finds this perversion to be quite amusing.

Nurmi is ordered to ask another question. Thank you, Juan Martinez.

Nurmi's been thrown off script. He slowly thuds around the podium, head down, and he's trying to think of how to make Travis look like a pedophile, while making Jodi look like a woman who never saw it coming. Finally, he speaks: "Did he ever wish you to wear this underwear?". "Yes", says Jodi.

Okay. Travis was not an idiot. Travis had obviously mastered the concept of big and small. Consider big and small when you think about the explicit nude photos we've seen of a posing Jodi Arias. Beyond the fact that she is a full grown adult, a few of those photos are quite unflattering, and they do reflect some substantial heft around her thighs. Now, I want you to imagine the size of little boy's underwear. We are not talking about underwear for adolescent boys. It has been defined as "little boy's underwear". Those underpants are tiny. All little boy's underpants are tiny. There is no way on this earth that Travis Alexander thought one of Jodi's legs would fit into the leg hole of little boy's underwear.

We see the Alexander family. This is the first time that Steven has caught my eye before Samantha and Tanisha. He is livid --absolutely sickened and angry. The expression on his face is frightening. As I'm looking at him, I hear Nurmi ask, "Is this something that would fit on your body?".

Jodi answers, "He asked me to try them on, while he was on the phone...". Juan Martinez objects with "non-responsive". Nurmi says that Juan's objections are improper. Juan's objection is overruled, but this time we see Judge Stephen's face as the ruling is made. She is not happy. There is no lilt in her voice as she tells Nurmi to ask another question. I think she is sickened by this. If her voice and facial expression are any indication, I think on a human level, she hates this. She knows about the falsified, excluded letters, and she knows, just as we know, that what we are hearing isn't true. This is hollow. This is desperate. This is evil. She is looking at the faces of three tortured siblings while the criminal to her right has a field day on the public dime.

Nurmi trudges on: "He wanted you to try on these boy's underwear?". She says, "Yes". What happened to "little boy's underwear"? Is he convinced he's already planted that seed, the seed of kindergarten children, and now he can stop using that descriptor because Big Jodi is going to somehow fit into these little underpants?

Nurmi asks, "Did they fit?". Jodi responds, "The seat fit, but the leg holes, the openings, were too small". If you haven't looked at Jodi's thighs, look at them again. Look at her naked thighs. She never got those underpants over her thighs, and the seat did not fit. If we were talking about adolescent briefs, perhaps, but not children's underwear. These two friends have realized that somebody will pick up on the improbability of what she's alleging, so they'll think of something, however ridiculous. Oh, and just for your information, she's still smiling. I'd be hiding behind my hair curtain. Oh wait, her hair is pulled back today. There will be no need for a hair curtain.

Nurmi asks, "Did you advise him that they didn't fit?". Jodi answers, "I just told him that the leg openings were very tight". Nurmi asks, "Even though they did not fit, was there a continued insistence on Mr. Alexander's part that you try on, or that you make accommodation for that underwear so you could wear it".

There is another shot of the Alexander family. This time, it is Samantha Alexander who catches my eye. Her long, dark hair is covering one of her eyes, but the other is laser like, and it's staring directly at Jodi. I remember Jodi making a comment in one of her media interviews about looking at the Alexanders in court. She said she avoids making eye contact with them because they look like Travis, and she doesn't want to look at her abuser. After looking at that eye of Samantha's, I realize that Jodi's comment was partially true (although her reluctance to look at them had nothing to do with seeing, "her abuser". It was more like seeing her victim). I don't know how to express this without sounding overly dramatic, but for a second or two, Samantha's eye looked ghostly and frightening. I had the feeling that if Travis were in that courtroom (and I'm not suggesting for a moment that he was), this is the way he would be looking at Jodi.

Instead of replacing the underwear with a size that fit, Jodi claims that Travis "had some ideas...". She gets that far and Juan Martinez objects: "Hearsay". The judge tells Nurmi to ask another question. Nurmi argues that this is not for the truth of the matter asserted, and therefore it is not hearsay. Judge Stephens replies, "I understand. Ask another question". I realize that the judge is taking this very seriously.

Nurmi continues, "Did Travis encourage you to make these alterations?". "Yes", says Jodi. Nurmi continues, "Did he, as far as you could tell, express gratification when you had those underwear on?". Jodi continues to malign her dead victim: "Yes". Just a question? Was Travis allegedly playing this pedophile game alone, or was Jodi involved in modeling the object that aroused his alleged pedophilic lust? Seriously, this is a woman who dissects and over thinks everything about this fake relationship. We just heard about Travis swaying around with a busty, inebriated woman. That sent her into a panic attack. However, altering little boy's underwear so she could model them for him didn't set off any alarms? Right. Einstein, indeed.

Nurmi and Jodi were at the point in the script when he asked her if Travis was gratified by the fact that she wore the underwear. Jodi confirms that Travis was all kinds of gratified with the altered underwear, and Nurmi follows up with, "How so?".

Juan Martinez, knowing the entire back story that is being withheld from the jurors, is objecting pretty regularly now. He says, "Objection, lack of foundation! When?". The objection is sustained. Nurmi moves into smart ass territory now. His voice is dripping with contempt as he says, "WHEN you were talking on the phone with him, and he insisted that you try on these boy's underwear that didn't fit you because you're not a little boy (have you seen the photos, Nurmi? You really might want to rethink that gender comment), did he express gratification when you had them on your body?".

Well, that's that. Forget all of the BS about providing the best defense possible. That is not what's going on here. Nurmi has no interest in the truth. Nurmi has no interest in justice. Nurmi has no interest in the constitution. Nurmi has an interest in being the next Jose Baez – a garden variety, low level attorney, who wishes to rise to prominence by winning an unwinnable case. He should have been sanctioned for his disrespectful tone of voice as it was obviously used in reaction to a bench ruling he didn't like. And just to show his level of arrogance, after Jodi says that he did express gratification when she wore the underwear, he repeats the exact question that started the objection: "How so?".

Jodi says, "He said, 'That's hot'". Juan Martinez over talks her with, "Objection, hearsay". The objection is overruled. Nurmi asks, "He said, 'That's hot'?". Jodi, suddenly wearing her trauma face (it changes from second to second) says, "Yes". How about if we ask Jodi what Jodi said? I don't believe any of this happened, but since they're pretending it did, can we hear what Jodi had to say about parading around in little boy's underwear? Please? Just a thought or two?

There is more lying about Jodi being asked to wear the underwear during sexual activity. There are some fabrications about Jodi wearing the underwear during phone sex. There is no inquiry made as to whether the woman who felt "silly" and "not hot" actually climaxed during those phone conversations while her circulation was choked off by the altered, little boy's underwear, but remember, she's not on trial here -- Travis Alexander is.

Jodi claims that she was a little confused by the underwear, but the woman who engaged in anal sex with regularity, said she was trying to be "open minded". Open minded to what? Pedophilia? Did this legal team actually sit down and think this through? Even if anyone is buying this (and I assume there is a small fragment of society who are deranged or stoned enough to believe this), did it ever occur to the legal team that their client might be considered somewhat culpable here? We're not talking about driving the getaway car, we are talking about an alleged desire to victimize children. They are playing with a very dangerous topic, and they are doing so without a safety net of evidence.

Nurmi wants to know when they used the underpants in a sexual encounter. Jodi lies, "It was after several months. Somehow, I kept conveniently forgetting to bring them to his house. It was after I moved to Mesa (hey! Can we get to that and put the underpants in the laundry, Nurmi? Let's hear about how your poor client decided to move to the same town as the pedophile – after he dumped her. Can we get to that part? Somehow I think they'll be two questions about that multi-state move, as opposed to 200 about the non-existent, don't know where they are, can't produce them, underpants).

Nurmi's doing his penile/vaginal status report thing. As usual, negative. Oh, I suddenly made the connection. Male pedophiles who like little boys don't like vaginas. Oh my God, they actually put this together. That's the implication. At this point, it is hard to believe that Nurmi had the courage to go forward with this defense, but he did. He doesn't look uncomfortable. In fact, he looks like an angry gorilla.

Now we're going to get into Travis' violent tendencies. Nurmi wants to know if Travis had been violent with Jodi prior to February, 2007. She says no, but the obvious implication is that he was violent with her after February, 2007. Nurmi asks, "Had you seen instances of his temper prior to February, 2007". Jodi says, "Yes". I believe that. I would have beaten her to a bloody pulp after three months.

Essay question: Jodi will now describe a powerful temper incident. She says, "Well, it was over the phone, and I guess I heard it rather than saw it, but...". Juan Martinez wants a foundation established. The objection is sustained. Nurmi says, "Over the phone. Do you remember when this conversation was – other than prior to February, 2007?". Jodi answers, "It would have been around the same time, just around Valentine's Day".

Nurmi wants to know if Travis was yelling at Jodi. The short answer is no. Of course, she'll be allowed to embellish whenever necessary. She says, "He was yelling on the phone, but not at me (Oh, how dangerous! Run for your life, or call 911, or just hang up the phone). Well, he was very apologetic about it afterward. He seemed a little ashamed...". Another objection. She was asked if he yelled on the phone, not how he seemed. Nurmi will recalibrate. He asks her something like "how did it make you feel". He's mumbling, and it's inaudible.

Jodi replies, "It made me realize that he had a temper (says the woman who still owes Ventana Inn repair costs for the bathroom she destroyed in a fit of rage). We had discussed that he used to have one, before, more in his teens. He had mastered it, gotten control over it". When asked if she physically saw any instances of violence, the answer was no. Isn't it interesting that there are quite a few people who could get up and talk about witnessing Jodi's rage? But again, right now, Jodi isn't on trial.

We're back to when Jodi and Travis had penile/vaginal intercourse. If Nurmi was listening to his own client, he'd know what we know – that they had this "penile/vaginal intercourse" that Nurmi's so fond of bringing up, in the spring of 2007. Remember, it's May...no, it's April...no, I'm sure it's May...well, it could have been April...I am getting tired of Nurmi and Jodi thinking her stupid vagina is this important.

Nurmi wants to know where Jodi was when they did the deed. Jodi answers, "I was in his bed". Will Nurmi ask if there were standard pillow shams on the bed, or European? How can all of this dandruff be deemed so critically important when we're talking about a man left to decompose in his own shower? Let's talk a little bit more about how the murderer with the bow on her virginal white sweater feels about....well, everything and anything. Global warming? Politics? Fashion?

Nurmi seriously asked, "In his bed, where?". Well, let's see...what are the options? In his bed on the roof of the house? In his bed on the front lawn? In his bed in the trunk of the car? In his bed in the LDS baptismal font? In his bed in the little boy's underwear section of Walmart? In his bed at a Super Saturday event? Where they hell does he think the bed was?

Jodi actually answers, "In his bedroom, in his house in Mesa". Good. I'm glad they cleared that one up. I'm sure Travis Alexander had beds all over the western United States. Nurmi wants to know what happened. Before Jodi gets a chance to tell us how Travis rounded third and slid into home, we see Bill and Sandy Arias sitting in the front row.

They look they are being kept alive by machines; maybe a power cord plugged into the backs of their heads. There is no life in either of them. I believe an extra chair has been brought in for Bill, but there is a visible distance between the spouses. He could sit in the empty seat next to his wife, but he doesn't. They are broken and ashamed people. What they do later, publicly, while being buttressed by family and supporters, is radically different to what they are doing now. What they are doing now is looking at the abomination that is their creation. Are they silently blaming each other? Is he thinking it's her DNA? Is she thinking it's his DNA? Not only are they sitting there like two lifeless and expired people knowing that, despite their daughter's delusional thinking, the entire world hates their offspring, but now they have to process her obvious delight in recounting sexual exploits she enjoyed five years ago. She'll never have those types of exploits again (prison sex is in a different category). I don't know how parents deal with this type of monstrosity, but the solutions I'm thinking of are unprintable.

As though her parents are 1000 miles away, Jodi begins to explain how Travis penetrated her – just what every parent wants to hear. She begins, "Umm, we fell asleep, umm, and I woke up, and he was on top of me, and he had already penetrated, and started having sex with me". So now Travis is not just a pedophile, and a violent phone yeller, but he is also a sleep rapist! Wow. Let's hear how horrific this was. Do you think she received any rape counseling, or will this be another story of "well, I wanted to be open minded...well, I really liked him...well, I wasn't going to break up with him...well, he was very apologetic...well, he was bettering himself...well, well, well."?

Nurmi wants to back up a step (as usual). I think he wants to hear more about what happened at third base. Go, Nurmi. Ask your question: "That night, you said you were asleep, that night, before you feel asleep, you said you were asleep, did you engage in sexual activity with Mr. Alexander?". Good one, Nurmi! You used the word "asleep" three times in one sentence! That satisfies the three time rule (say it three times, and it will get into someone's head – in the case, a juror's). Jodi replies, "No". Nurmi continues, "Was he seeking sexual activity that night before he fell asleep?". Was he seeking sexual activity? What was he, a feral cat on the make? Jodi says, "No, we had prayed about our actions and tried to be more, tried to be like in line with the Law of Chastity. Just try to be less physical".

Okay, I'll be honest. At this point, I seriously do not believe she's told the truth about anything – from the mundane to the interesting. I believe some of these scenarios may have happened, but not as she's portraying them, and probably at different times than she is stating. If Travis had decided that he was going to try and honor the Mormon Law of Chastity (and I don't for a minute believe that Jodi Arias cared about any of the Mormon doctrines), then he wouldn't have wanted her sleeping in his bed. So, I don't believe they were at a point of trying to obey the Law of Chastity. That being said, at the very least, he'd ask her to wear something to bed – unless, of course, we are also being asked to believe that he removed her clothing prior to penetrating her. It isn't easy to remove someone's clothing without waking them up. He was able to easily penetrate her because she was either naked or it took no more than a pull to remove the clothing that kept him from his objective. If this fool thinks that anyone believes that she prayed about abstaining from sex (while climbing into his bed), then she can also add mental retardation to her psych profile.

Can we give her the low IQ number she just earned, please? Jodi has just clarified that their special "prayer" didn't actually occur on the night she was sleep raped...no, it occurred "recently", but not that day. That's the best she can do – recently. This is getting embarrassing. Whenever this prayer occurred, Nurmi would like to know what motivated it. Of course, it was the spiritual giant of the pair, Jodi Arias, who began to think they should be in prayer over their sexual behavior. She said, "I would hear things occasionally in church (like, you're not allowed to sleep with a guy you aren't married to – those deeper truths that are so hard to find in a conservative religion?) that didn't sound like they were in line with how Travis explained it to me (because the missionary statement of "abstain from all sex outside of a legal marriage" was one of those gray areas that needed serious magnification in order to be comprehended), so I asked him one time (right...ask the guy who's already given you the answer that you believe is wrong...don't ask Sky, the revered female Mormon in the group, because she's only useful when you've got some hot gossip you want to share), and I understood it, after we talked, that those standards are put in place to prevent people from going all the way (although going down your throat and up your rectum is just fine by Joseph Smith, because that's really believable and stuff), so as long as we aren't going all the way, we're sort of treading in a gray area, as long as we don't go all the

Jodi and Nurmi can keep repeating this foolishness until Jodi runs out of oxygen. It made no sense the first time, it made no sense the fifth time, and it isn't making sense now. Nobody believes this. I think they seriously miscalculated the value of much of this testimony. They are actually insulting the jury.

Nurmi is clarifying. He wants to be sure that no sexual activity took place before Jodi was sleep raped (you know he didn't use that phrase...I'm using it). She says, "Not prior to that". Oh, so she went with it? Of course. Nurmi wants to know if Jodi was clothed when she went to sleep. She says she was in pajamas. Hey, I'll bet they were pink, with hearts and kittens on them. Yes. Soft cotton. She was covered head to toe in cuteness and innocence. Nurmi again repeats, "So, you woke up with him inside you?". I really don't know why he has to ask this for the fifth time. It has become abundantly clear that this is what they want the jury to believe, but there comes a point where you either have confidence in your skill or you don't. Right now, he doesn't appear to be a very skilled litigator.

I have heard sexual assault cases that do not get this detailed. I keep thinking of Juan Martinez during his closing arguments. He said (paraphrased), "They have made this case about sex. Sex has nothing to do with it".

If you feel like the walls are closing in, it's because they are. We have crossed the threshold to Jodi Arias' vagina, and it sounds like our tour guide, Kirk Nurmi, plans to give us the extended tour. Before you gross out completely, zip up your HazMat suit and count your blessings. We could be taking a tour of her preferred and neighboring orifice, but that's a neighborhood I'm hoping to avoid.

We have heard about Jodi's encroaching epiphany that oral and anal sex might be at odds with the clearly stated "no premarital sex" rule, as expressed by the LDS church. Feeling conflicted, she did what any reasonable person would do -- she asked the person she claims gave her the original information that is now so troubling to her, if he gave her the right information the first time around. Get it? Neither does anyone else, but we'll have to play along for now. That's right – traveling in social and business circles filled with people who could recite the Law of Chastity in their sleep, Jodi decides to do the same thing she did before, but she's expecting a different outcome. Jodi said a prayer, put on her comfy pajamas, and hopped into Travis' bed. She hoped this would help her obey the "not going all the way" version of the Law of Chastity.

Now, Jodi was doing really well by abstaining from what Nurmi continues to label "penile/vaginal intercourse"; in fact, she was a beacon of obedience, until the fateful night she was sleep raped by Travis Alexander.

Nurmi asks if Travis had talked to Jodi about having – what else? – penile/vaginal intercourse (this man has single-handedly removed all of the mystique and wonder of sex). Jodi is quick to tell us that Travis did not speak to her about Penile/Vaginal (Penile/Vaginal) intercourse before she woke up and found him "inside her". Nurmi asks, "Is it something that you desired?". With a shrug of her shoulders and a facial expression that makes sexual intercourse look about as erotic as getting a pap smear, Jodi replies, "Maybe not, on a conscious level, it wasn't anything I was actively seeking. We were trying to abstain from it". Nurmi is satisfied, and he asks, "Because at this point in time, your mindset was that you both wanted to comport with the Law of Chastity, at least as to what your understanding of it was, is that right?". Jodi replies, "Somewhat. I wanted to comport (copied a word from Nurmi – probably didn't know what it meant, and figured it out by context) with the Law of Chastity, because I believed our relationship would be blessed if we did that". Well, first you have to actually have a relationship before it can be blessed. I'm wondering if Crazy Jodi has resorted to the magical practice of making deals with whatever deity might be listening (i.e., if I don't go all the way with him, you have to make him give me an engagement ring).

Nurmi continues, "When you say you woke up with him inside you, do you recall, were you dressed?". Jodi Arias will now repeat, for the third time, that she was dressed. Unless Nurmi wants to know if her pajama bottoms were halfway down her thighs, around her knees, or circling her ankles, what's the point of asking this question? He really needs some direction from the judge here. He is wasting time, and he does this a lot. He asks a question, gets an answer, asks the same question, and gets the same answer. It must make the jury feel the way it makes me feel: we're never going to progress, and this will never end.

Jodi answers, "I wore cotton shorts to sleep, and they were gone, and my shirt was pulled up...pretty high". How shocking. This was probably the first time Sister Jodi had ever been that physically exposed around a member of the opposite sex. We can only breathe a sigh of relief that her later mental affliction, "The Fog", hadn't yet come to full fruition during her sleep rape. If it had, we wouldn't know how high her shirt was pulled up, and without that information, how could the jury be expected to deliberate correctly? I wonder how she handled the shame. Nurmi, with the skill of a surgeon, presses on. He asks, "When you came to (did you say, "Uh-oh, I killed him?" Oh, sorry, my bad, that would have been something she would have said when she "came to" on June 4, 2008 – carry on, Nurmi), what was happening? When you woke up, what was happening?" Does Nurmi expect a thrust/withdrawal count? Does Mr. Nurmi have children? Does he know how human intercourse works?

Jodi responds, "Umm, he was in the act". The act? We laugh at that description, Jodi Arias. We want details. Nurmi asks, "In the act of what?". Oh, Nurmi...perhaps it was the act of painting the baseboards, or plunging the toilet, or opening the window. Oh...now, I see the strategy! Do you realize how many "acts" Travis might have been involved with while simultaneously perpetrating sleep rape? Thank goodness he's going to have her narrow down the options. Jodi responds, "Of...vaginal sex".

Nurmi continues, "When you woke up, how did you react?". Did she fly out of bed and kneel on the floor, begging Spirit for forgiveness? Yes, that's what she's going to say, right? She responds, "Well it took me a second to orient myself, and I realized it was Travis (yes, I guess in her sleepy haze, it could have been Bobby, Victor, Matt, or Darryl), so I didn't feel unsafe or anything. My first thought was uh-oh, not the act itself, but how it would affect our relationship, the consequences, the spiritual consequences of it". No blessing on the non-relationship. Darn. Time to find a new religion and a new adherent.

Nurmi is going to amp this up. He asks, "Did you consider the fact that he was having sex with you when you didn't want him to?". Jodi swivels around, purses her lips, and looks up. Before she gets a chance to answer, Juan Martinez breaks in with an objection. I really can't hear the objection or the response. However, Nurmi is ordered to rephrase the question. I assume the objection was based on the fact that Nurmi is trying, very obviously, to make this sound like Jodi had no choice in the matter.

Nurmi asks, "Did you want him to penetrate your vagina with his penis while you were sleeping?". I'm in fifth grade. I'm watching the "Your Menstruating Body" film. We're getting to the end of the movie, and the school nurse is handing out little booklets with light blue covers and the words,

"From the Makers of Kotex, Inc." on the front. We're learning how babies are made. Oh, sorry. Flashback to 1971. I thought this was the audio to a sex education film from yesteryear. It's not. It's Jodi Arias' trial. Forgive me.

Jodi responds, "Nothing I had thought about". Nurmi asks, "So when you woke up and found him penetrating your vagina with his penis, your concern was primarily about chastity, the Law of Chastity, excuse me". She answers, "The consequences". Nurmi continues, "Did you give thought to the idea that this man was having sex with you while you were not conscious?".

Oh, this is rich. These words are being uttered by the mouth of an attorney who uses the following words as bragging rights on his website: **"Sex Assault –NOT GUILTY, Sex Assault / Unlawful Imprisonment –NOT GUILTY ON ALL COUNTS, Sexual Exploitation of a Minor (10 counts) –NOT GUILTY ON ALL COUNTS, Sex Conduct with a Minor, Sexual Assault – ALL COUNTS DISMISSED".**

If Travis Alexander had been accused of sleep rape by Jodi Arias back in the spring of 2007, he wouldn't have to worry if Kirk Nurmi was his lawyer.

Nurmi would like to know how Jodi felt. She answers, "I felt, umm, I was partially responsible because I was wearing cute shorts, a little T-shirt. I don't know. We might have been cuddling when we fell asleep. I just felt partially responsible because I was in his bed, you know, I was sleeping there, and it wasn't entirely his fault, like maybe it was invited". A moment of clarity. A freaking moment of clarity. It is destined to live a short life, and it will ultimately die alone, but it did make an appearance in this direct examination.

Nurmi continues, "Invited, just by you being there, right?". Jodi answers, "Yes". Nurmi asks, "When you woke up, did you tell him to stop?". Jodi answers, "I don't think I said stop". Yes, saying "stop" isn't really what women do who are trying to achieve an orgasm. I'm concerned about that moment of clarity. I think it may already be weakening.

Nurmi asks, "What do you recall happening after you woke up?". Jodi answers, "I said his name, and I remember, he was on top of me and in me...I was on my stomach...and, he was kind of heavy, so I started to squirm a little bit to get out from underneath him, and I think, well, he began to quicken his pace, finally, I don't know if I pushed him off or if I scooted out from under him, and he rolled over and pulled me on top of him, and he started pushing my head and my shoulders under the covers (couldn't bear to look at the woman he was having intercourse with???)". Nurmi's blood pressure is rising as he asks, "He was pushing your head and shoulders under the covers – for what purpose?". This might be a good place of a speculation objection, but it won't matter. Jodi's story will prevail.

Jodi responds, "Well, I presumed, oral sex". Nurmi asks, "Did he ask for oral sex? Did he verbally say anything to that effect?". Jodi says, "No words were spoken". Nurmi asks, "Did you perform oral sex upon him, afterwards". Jodi replies, "Yes". Let me guess. Ejaculation, timing and method of, will now be explored.

Nurmi asks, "Why?". Jodi responds, "We had already been intimate before, so it wasn't anything new on that level, at least, and, you know, he's turned on, and I guess he just wants to finish it". Nurmi asks, "What was that?". Jodi replies, "I guess I just wanted to follow through, with, you know...". Nurmi, defender of all perverts in Arizona, asks, "Follow through with what he started when you were asleep?". Jodi answers, "Yes, what his aim was, I guess". Nurmi is pretending he is deaf again. He says, "What's that?". Realizing that this is her cue to be more explicit, Jodi replies, "Let him finish".

Nurmi asks, "Why was that important to you?". Jodi replies, "He had complained in the past about (big pause accompanied by a "you're not really asking me this" face)...he complained about blue balls (she's smiling and almost giggling, but I don't think it's particularly amusing)...and how painful it was if he has a sustained erection and doesn't ejaculate. That's my understanding of it".

Nurmi – will he say blue balls? – continues, "But, I have to ask, Jodi. Travis has sex with you while you're asleep, or, you certainly weren't in a position to say yes or no, why would you care about Travis' physical condition?". Umm, maybe because he had the right to throw her squatting ass into the street instead of letting her sleep in a comfortable, king sized bed with matching sheets? Maybe that's why she cared? Maybe because she had her eye set on the prize – the engagement ring, the wedding invitations, the white gown, the temple ceremony, the back yard reception, and the first class honeymoon? Maybe that's why dozing Jodi cared about Travis' blue balls.

Jodi responds, "At that point, I knew I loved him (she's moved on from the Crush Realm! Ultra Extreme! Super-Sized!), and I cared about him, so it felt, kind of natural, even if it was frustrating". Nurmi asks, "After this sexual intercourse, this activity, took place, did you ever confront him about what he had done (what THEY had done, Nurmi)?". Jodi responds, "No, we actually never talked about it". Nurmi asks, "Why not?". Nurmi, if they didn't talk about it, they certainly didn't have any conversation that focused on why they didn't talk about it.

Jodi answers, "Well, he never brought it up and...I guess I just didn't have the moral courage to bring it up and say, hey, what happened, kind of thing". Nurmi asks, "Why not simply pack your bags up in your car and go back to Palm Desert?". Nurmi, did you miss something? She never said she didn't like it. She never said she didn't go with it. She never even said she didn't welcome it.

Jodi answers, "Because I enjoyed spending time with him. I wouldn't have done that". Nurmi continues, "Because that would mark the end of the relationship?". Jodi says, "Not necessarily, maybe not the end of the relationship, but I just stayed the rest of the weekend that was planned for me to be there".

Nurmi hit on the truth there. It was quite by accident, but even a broken clock is right twice a day. It would have marked the end of the relationship, and General Arias was not about to give up this fight.

Jodi is in love with Travis. Despite everything she's told us about him, he's her guy. Jodi tells us that she fell in love with Travis in April, 2007, and now she is quite clear that "the incident" occurred in May, 2007. Jodi did not tell Travis that she loved him. I guess she lacked the "moral courage".

Nurmi asks, "You said after this incident, you spent the rest of the weekend with him, is that accurate?" Incident? Isn't that something police officers respond to – you know, when they fill out those incident reports? Attorney and client are playing quite a game here, incrementally increasing the inflammatory language. Instead of consensual intercourse followed by consensual oral sex offered by the "victim", we have "an incident". I have to remind myself that none of these techniques saved her from an Murder One conviction. Jodi answers, "Yes".

Because he has already completed his penile/vaginal status report, Nurmi will now complete his boyfriend/girlfriend status report. Were they boyfriend/girlfriend during the incident? I can answer that for you, Nurmi. YES! We'll know when they break up; that's when the crazy train really goes off the tracks. Nurmi continues, "When you...well, let me ask you this: what did you do the rest of the weekend?" Knowing that Travis won't take her out or even go to the grocery store when Jodi is at his house, I wonder, did Jodi starve and drink from the bathroom faucet during the remainder of this weekend, or did the sleep rapist feed his victim after defiling her? Let's see. Jodi answers, "I don't recall the specifics of that weekend (other than she was sleeping on her stomach, had her T-shirt pulled up, was sleep raped, and performed oral sex), but we would have gone to church...I believe that was the first time I went over to his friend's house. He went to his friend's house every Sunday for dinner, so I went with him that time....".

Now, wait just a minute. She already told us about Travis' standing Sunday dinner engagement. He went every week, according to the liar on the stand. After "convention" in March, she said they flew back to Mesa, and instead of going back to Palm Desert, she stayed at Travis' home that Sunday afternoon, and together, they attended a standing dinner engagement at his friend's house. Does she think we forgot about the fact that she claimed he introduced her to this family as a "kinda friend" back in March? Here we are in May, and she's now claiming that this is the first time she went to the home of this friend for Sunday dinner. I don't care if Nurmi tries to fix this or if she makes up some lie to cover it. She completely contradicted something she said on Thursday, and she just lied – or maybe she lied on Thursday. It's impossible to tell.

She continues talking about the weekend and what they did: "Just general things...hanging out". What kind of dull relationship is that? Please, can she define hanging out, because I'm beginning to believe it means "we did nothing". I knew Nurmi was going to pick up on Jodi's lie. He is now attempting to back-pedal, to send his client a sure sign that it's time to think on her feet. He's fooling nobody. He asks if this standing dinner engagement was at the home of the friend she recently told the jury about – the place where Travis wouldn't introduce her as his girlfriend. Let's see if Jodi can handle a fastball. She says, "Yes, at his friend's house he didn't introduce me. I was in their home, but he didn't introduce me". No, she is not an accomplished liar. She's just a persistent liar. She completely blew over the issue he was asking about. The question was not "and this was at the friend's home that you told us about earlier, where he didn't introduce you as his girlfriend?". She ignored the question, Nurmi knows she ignored the question, and he's pretending she answered it. They played the same game when he questioned her about the historically significant sites she couldn't remember seeing on the Magical Mormon Mystery Tour. He asked which sites she saw, and she answered those questions by telling him what major airports were closest to the cities they visited. They're both pretending these exchanges make sense.

Nurmi asks Jodi if Travis ever showed her affection in public. This is probably the fifteenth time he has asked this question. She responds, "No, not in Mesa". Nurmi makes it bigger: "...Anything you did, while you were in public, was there physical displays of affection that might lead someone to believe you were boyfriend-girlfriend?". Jodi looks at him. She is a very homely woman. The slightly crossed eye, the bulbous nose, the big mouth, and the long, horse face. I cannot find an attractive feature on her face. Not one. Beyond that, she has such a vacant, strange look in her eye. It is easy to see her as the reject who just wouldn't accept a message of rejection. Beyond that, when did it become illegal for a man to refuse to engage in public displays of affection with a woman he's sleeping with? It's not illegal, and he can waste another day implying that it is, but it won't make it so. Why can't he just move along? If the jury hasn't bought this yet, they're not going to.

Tell me that this wasn't a rehearsed answer – it was given in response to Nurmi's question about Travis' public displays of affection: "There were – when we were in other geographic locations". The use of the word geographic is useless here. It has been inserted to trick the jury into believing that they are listening to a woman who thinks the way she speaks. She does not think the way she speaks. She thinks in fragments – black, white, yes, no, stop, go, take, give, smile, cry, run, stay. Her verbal skills are copied. They are absorbed while she is in the presence of educated or gifted people, and she tries to speak these languages, but her attempts are stunted and at odds with her education level and station in life. Geographic locations? People don't talk that way – not even the highly educated. They might write that way, but they don't speak that way.

Jodi is suddenly talking about Disneyland. I don't know how Jodi started talking about Disneyland, but she did. Nurmi reigns her back in and says he only wants to hear about this one particular, "going all the way" weekend. Was there a single public display of affection? The woman who began this exchange by saying that she cannot specifically recall what they did that weekend, is suddenly certain that there was not a single public display of affection. Right. She can't recall what they did, but she can say with absolutely certainty that it did not involve a single instance of public affection.

I really cannot believe this. Around and around and around, we go. Nurmi asks if Travis has roommates. Yes, Nurmi. You know he had roommates. Did Travis display affection toward Jodi around those roommates? Of course not, Nurmi. You've already established that fact multiple times with the surviving half of this "boyfriend-girlfriend" couple. Did Travis show affection to Jodi after the bedroom door was locked? Well, of course, he did. Did Jodi sleep in Travis' bed? Not only did she sleep there, but we can tell you what she wore and what position she slept in. Seriously, how many times have we heard this same exchange? It's in the double digits, right? Guess what's next? You know what's coming. We haven't heard it about it in four minutes. It's our old friend "Penile/vaginal intercourse". Was there any more PVI that weekend? No, says Jodi.

They play this stupid game a little longer. Jodi claims she can't remember specifics, but "the event" is something she will never forget. Yes, I'm sure the event has given her many warm memories in her dank cell. Now, we're finally going to get to Jodi being forced out of her foreclosed home, although I'm sure Nurmi will never mention a marshal padlocking the door, but instead, it will be treated like a move to follow some non-existent career. How is this girl even going to get an apartment? She will be forced to impose on someone, I assume.

So, where does a homeless woman, who enjoys an estranged relationship with her parents, go when her "boyfriend" doesn't go for the bait and give her an invitation to move into his sprawling home? Well, she retraces her steps. She goes backward. In this case, that would mean Big Sur. In this case, that would mean Ventana Inn and Spa. Good thinking. Staff housing or a tent – either is relatively free. They'll be a big difference this time; Darryl Brewer will not be able to shield her from her work responsibilities. Unless she begins to sleep with another manager, she's going to have to work under the same conditions as everyone else. I wonder if a majority of the employees had left. It has been five years since she was last employed at Ventana. For the ones who may have retained their employment post 2002, this news must have been disturbing.

Listen to the way Jodi explains this move: "I had a job back at Ventana again. The position was open for me (was this a standing invitation to the woman who destroyed their bathroom, or did it require a little begging on her part?), and umm, staff housing, so the rent was free (did this woman ever, in her adult life, actually pay to have a roof over her head?), and it was just a way for me to get back on my feet". There's getting "back on your feet", and then there just getting into the race. She mismanaged what little money she had, and that's why she was in this position. Bad things happen to good, hardworking people, and for those people, it means something when they say they're "getting back on their feet". For a parasite like Arias, "getting back on her feet" simply means that she's hungry again, and she needs a new host.

Nurmi asks, "Now, from what we heard earlier, Ventana is the place where you met Mr. Brewer. Is that correct? Was Mr. Brewer working there that summer?". Jodi answers, "No, he was working on the peninsula – the Monterey peninsula". Nurmi continues, "You also told us about, last time, that you, uh, worked there, that you were dating Matt McCartney – oh, you were friends, excuse me (friends who had intercourse in a tent, but go ahead Nurmi, rewrite history), sharing a tent, right?". Jodi answers, "Yes, we were freshly broken up". Freshly broken up? She uses odd words...

Nurmi asks if Matt was working at Ventana during the summer of 2007? Jodi answers, "Yes, he was working there". Well, after five years, I hope he's been promoted. Nurmi doesn't ask what Matt's position at Ventana was. I would have been interested in hearing if he had any decision making power when it came to hiring servers. I do not have the impression that Jodi left Ventana with a stellar reference in her pocket. In fact, I remember wondering why someone with three years of experience at a luxury resort was suddenly serving microwaved, prepackaged food at whatever chain bar/restaurant subsequently employed her (in addition to her second job at a strip mall California Pizza Kitchen).

Nurmi asks if the pair shared staff housing. Jodi answers, "Yes, we did". Oh, if the jury is not seeing a very clear picture emerging here, they are either still sleeping or completely hypnotized. I wonder if she actually squatted in the staff housing while waiting for a position to open up. I'd even go as far as suspecting her of sabotaging another employee to get their job. I now believe her depth of depravity and animalistic sense of self-preservation knows no depth. I know Nurmi is going to ask if Jodi engaged in penile/vaginal intercourse with Matt while they shared their dorm room, and I know Jodi will deny it. However, we know better.

Nurmi, who, for some reason, likes to remind the jury that Jodi is not above living under canvas, asks if the two lived in a tent, or if they had other accommodations. Jodi answers, "No, we had better accommodations. We were in the red house, right on Highway One. It was actually a historic house that they let employers...employees stay there. We were in that house, with other roommates". Hey, just for fun, can Nurmi ask what Jodi's position was? Is she serving, or is she a chamber maid waiting for a server's job? Just curious, because the exquisite timing of this whole thing seems a little too convenient.

Even Nurmi is bored and lost by this rambling, irrelevant testimony. He asks if he is correct in stating that Jodi and Matt had been broken up for "about a year at this point". What is he thinking? Matt came before Darryl, and Darryl has occupied Jodi's mind for five years. We can't forget the fact that Travis followed Darryl, and that relationship, in whatever form, has now been going on for eight months. Wake up, Nurmi. If we have to listen, you have to listen.

Jodi may not know the names of historical Mormon sites, and she may not realize that you only get a single opportunity to show up at someone's house for dinner for the first time, but she does know her boyfriends. She says, "No, we broke up in 2001...". Nurmi jumps to the question concerning her "romantic involvement" with Matt. Jodi adjusts her eyeglasses (not because they needed adjusting), and says that they were "more like brother and sister at this point". Okay. I'm not sure that you can ever forge a sibling relationship with someone you lived with and slept with for over a year, but Jodi Arias has a very different view of the world and the people that populate it.

Nurmi asks, "Did Travis know that you were roommates with Matt?". Jodi answers, "Yes". Nurmi continues, "To your understanding, was he jealous or upset about this situation?". I highly doubt it. They are two and a half weeks from breaking up – and that's according to Jodi. He certainly didn't care enough to invite her to stay with him, now did he? I'd suggest Nurmi leave this subject alone. It only makes his client look less important to Travis than we already assume she was.

Jodi answers, "Surprisingly, no – he didn't mind that one". That one? How many co-habitations with former lovers have there been in the last eight months? Secondly, I see absolutely nothing in her prior testimony that would warrant her inclusion of the word "surprisingly" in that answer. Nurmi says, "You say, that one. Were there other instances of jealousy around this time period?". Nurmi, were you listening? Just eight weeks ago, Jealous Jodi ran away and hid in a hotel bathroom because Travis had his arm around his "drunk and slurring" female friend. Jodi hid for a half an hour in a public bathroom stall, sobbing, and raging, and, despite her assertion that Travis apologized for his "screw-up", and reassured her, Jealous Jodi had an encore performance in mind.

Referencing the March PPL convention, remember, the next morning, Jealous Jodi went to the executive director floor of the hotel, and followed Clancy Talbot, the "drunk and slurring woman" into the bathroom. There, she proceeded to spray her scent all over her perceived rival, who, by the way, was finally rescued by a friend who had to get Jodi out of the way of the bathroom door so that she could get in. Yes, Nurmi, there were instances of jealousy, and the only reason that the Clancy Talbot episode was admitted to by your client is because the "drunk and slurring woman" was on the prosecutor's witness list, and you wanted to strike first. However, you're looking for uncorroborated stories of the angry phone yeller/sleep rapist exhibiting jealous behavior toward a woman he didn't care about. Carry on.

Jodi answers, "Yes, there were". Here it comes, the frowny, serious face. The woman who smiled when thinking of Travis while posing for her mug shot, is so very adept at transforming her face into the mask of the forlorn on a second's notice. Essay question alert: "Describe those for us". I really don't mind her essay answers, because the more she speaks, the more she exposes herself. What I really hate is when Nurmi constantly interrupts the essay answers. Let's see how long he lets her go before he has to redirect her.

Jodi says (eyes down, not looking at the jury, and she's squirming in her chair): "There was one incident when I was going to drive to southern California and meet Travis...(long pause)...I think we were going to meet at the airport...for Disneyland...I don't remember which trip it was because it was while I was living in Big Sur (how many trips to Disneyland – or anywhere – could they have taken while they were officially boyfriend-girlfriend and she was living in Big Sur – there were literally 2 – 3 weeks of their official relationship left at this point) and all the water on the property at Ventana had been shut off, and I wanted to take a shower before I hit the road, so I called a friend who lived nearby (a male, obviously), and he said...well, he said he was in Monterey, but his house was open, so he gave me directions and his gate code (why do people give Jodi Arias codes to anything?), so I could drive up through the mountains to get to his house, shower, and hit the road, and when I told Travis, he flipped out on me for that".

Now, before we get to what we all know is coming, Nurmi's inquiry as to the definition of "flipped out", is it at all possible, if this even happened, that Travis was upset about something else? From all outward appearances, Travis is ultra-organized. He may have had this trip planned down to the minute. Along comes Jodi, who has to take a shower, and she is driving "through the mountains" to find a free place to take that shower. I don't think this was a three minute drive – it required directions and some mountain trekking. This may have thrown the schedule off, and that would be a plausible reason for Travis "flipping out".

Nurmi, predictable as ever, asks, "Well, you say flipped out. Was he yelling at you?". Yes, Nurmi. It's already been established by your client that Travis is an angry phone yeller. Jodi answers, "Yes". There's a long pause – Nurmi wants more, but he kind of likes the way Jodi looks when she's pretending to be too traumatized to give him the ugly details. So, Nurmi waits, and then he continues, "And you said jealousy. Was he, to your understanding, angry because he thought that this was something sexual in nature?". It always goes back to sex. Travis knew Jodi was easy, and now we know that Jodi is easy, but Nurmi should really stop reminding the jury of how easy she is. In any event, who cares if Travis yelled at Jodi for traveling mountain ranges to take a shower when she's supposed to be meeting him for a departure? Does that mean he deserved the death penalty?

Jodi says, "He was worried that it would lead to something sexual, or that I could be at risk (oh no...don't go there, please) because I had gone to somebody's house to shower". Ironic, isn't it? For Travis Alexander, there was a risk, a lethal risk, associated with taking a shower. For Jodi, it was just squatting and consuming as usual.

Who are these people on the defense side of the room? Do they all travel together to court in a van? They really are quite unappealing, for the most part. We are treated to the lovely visual of a woman sitting directly behind Bill and Sandy Arias. She is an Hispanic woman, and she's wearing a white camisole top with a red hoodie over it. Her stomach protrudes beyond her breasts by what looks to be five or six inches. She is large, her hair is a mess, and she is completely lost in the joy of sucking on her left index finger.

Nurmi wants to know what Jodi might be at risk of while showering in an empty house. Jodi says, "He didn't believe that the guy was in Monterey, he thought he could drive back, something could happen. He kinda made me feel vain for wanting to shower before we got on the road..he thought I could have showered later". Did he mean when they got to the hotel? Well, he's right. If she showers every day, and hadn't had sex with anyone the night before or morning of the trip, would it kill her to wait a few hours for a shower? It's not like she was jogging in the hot sun, or had just finished blacktopping a driveway.

Her inclusion of the word “vain” also clarifies the situation. Jodi is vain – top level, professionally vain (if appearance is important, she has to go to a lot of effort. In her natural state, she is a 3.5 out of 10. Made up, bleached, and from a distance, she's a 6.5 out of ten – although I'm sure she'd grade herself far more liberally). For Jodi, it wasn't about being clean – it was about being camera ready. After all, she's going to make sure that this trip ends with plenty of photos of her hanging all over Travis. Jodi goes nowhere without a full mask of make-up and fluffed hair. How long do you think it takes Jodi, the woman who wanted her make-up before she was arrested (and again, while she was being booked) to go from showering to walking out the door? This may have happened, but he wasn't afraid of what was going to happen to her. She was going to seriously delay the start of this trip. Actually, I think I believe this event occurred. This is why I like her essay answers. They are annoying, but they are chock full of clues.

Nurmi continues, “Now, now this jealousy you're talking about...was this expressed when you arrived...you were supposed to meet Mr. Alexander in southern California, right?”. Jodi answers, “Yes”. Nurmi continues, “Was this something that was discussed, displayed before you arrived there or when you got there, or perhaps both?”. Jodi answers, “Over the phone, on the way there”. The way where? To the free shower in the empty house or to the meeting place in southern California? It doesn't really matter; this argument obviously arose after she placed her “I'm going to be late” phone call, and he didn't appreciate waiting. So, I guess that means he was jealous.

Nurmi continues, “And do you recall, I know you don't remember which trip it was (because there were just too many to remember in this tiny period of time), do you recall how much, how long it took you to get to the place where you were going to meet Mr. Alexander?”. Nurmi is being misleading here. The correct question is how long it took her to get to the house with a shower, finish beautifying herself, and then get back onto the highway. Telling us how long it took her to get to the meeting place after the shower tells us nothing.

Jodi answers, “I left in the late morning (not very specific – probably more like 12:30), and arrived at sunset. I don't know...six, maybe seven hours”. She looks up, makes a “who knows?” face, and tilts her outstretched hand from left to right to show that's she's mentally measuring something. This is another indication that this trip was not to Disneyland. It is 5 - 6 hours from Big Sur to LAX - about the amount of time Jodi claims she drove. She said they were “meeting at the airport” to fly to Disneyland. Disneyland is under an hour from LAX.

Nurmi continues: “So, several hours later, when you get there (seven hours is not several hours), this jealousy about the shower, is this still an issue?” Jodi meekly says, “No”. Nurmi, he's an angry phone yeller. If there's no phone, he's not yelling. Get it?

She adds, “Not at the point. He was with Josh Ward, so he wasn't really displaying that”. Oh, a few more puzzle pieces just fell into place. Now we learn that Josh Ward, the roommate we know called Jodi a skank, is also a part of this "romantic get-away". Wow. He just couldn't wait to be alone with her, could he (why am I just assuming she injected herself into this trip)? It's safe to assume that Travis wasn't the only one being inconvenienced by Jodi's vanity, but Josh was as well. As for Jodi's assumption that Travis was no longer "displaying" his anger because Josh was there, well, does she expect us to believe that he told Josh to give him some privacy while he had his yelling phone conversation with Jodi? The two men shared a house – they obviously traveled to the meeting place together.

Nurmi asks, "Is this something that was brought up later during this trip?". Jodi, who has already admitted that she doesn't even know which trip this was, and who has also admitted that the sun is about to set on this official boyfriend-girlfriend relationship, says, "Well, it's something he didn't let me live down for a while, but it didn't lead to any major fights". That may be true. Every time she was around and a trip was mentioned, I assume she tried to secure an invitation, and he probably made public statements like, "Yeah, if we want to be four hours late, we'll make sure to invite you". I don't believe it was beyond him to make comments like this. There comes a point in a dying relationship when one party wants to move on, and the other is pretending that they aren't hearing what the other person is saying. Some people, and Travis may have been one of them, hate hurting other people, and they wrongly assume that delaying the inevitable is a kindness. It isn't. It's just delaying the inevitable. Add to that her threats of suicide or self-harm every time he tried to distance himself from her, and you've got a man with a lot of resentment building up. He's getting cagey, and when people get cagey, they tend to strike out. His mistake was in not cutting her off, and realizing that if she bled, she bled. At her age, she should have already built her own support system of family and friends. The problem was she had no world. She had no support system. She had a string of ex-lovers and some unidentified male friends. Beyond that, she was absorbing Travis' world and support system, and she was intent on pushing her way into that world in exactly the same way as she pushed her way into that bathroom on the executive director's floor.

Nurmi continues, "Now, this trip to Southern California, you say you don't recall where you were going (no, she doesn't, but she does know that this trip did not include any major fights), is that right?". Suddenly, she remembers. She says, "I think we were flying to New York at that point". You think? Did the lights just come on? Did Jodi suddenly realize that some juror might go home and do a google search of the distances she's quoting and realize that her trip to Disneyland makes no sense?

How is Jodi Arias financing this trip? She's talking about a trip across the country. Secondly, how is she getting time off of her newly secured job at Ventana to take this trip? Was she actually working there yet, or just staying there?

Nurmi continues, "And this was summer of 2007, correct?". Jodi answers, "Yes". Summer? Summer begins in on June 21. They broke up during on June 29. Now, it's entirely possible that these plans were made months before, and the trip did occur in the summer of 2007, but if Nurmi is going to level the "public displays of affection" complaint again, someone should clarify that they are a week from breaking up (according to Jodi). So, in the summer of 2007, they were barely an official couple, and that fact might be exactly why Travis took Josh Ward on the trip with them. Nurmi and Jodi are playing fast and loose with these dates and locations – "I can't remember, I do remember, Disneyland, New York" – and they are just melding things together to confuse the picture.

Nurmi repeats that Jodi did not tell Travis that she loved him in May, 2007. Now he asks her if she told him that she loved him by the time they were taking this trip. She says, "No". Nurmi asks, "Did Mr. Alexander tell you that he loved you?". Jodi says, "No, well, we did way back, before our relationship, but while we were dating, it wasn't, I love you, I love you, too – or anything". She just can't admit that he didn't love her, can she? Not even after she hated him enough to kill him. Not even when she's sitting on the stand trying to avoid a lethal injection. She cannot admit that he may have been attracted to her for a short period of time, but he never, ever loved her. Notice, however, she had no problem stating that she didn't tell him she loved him. That was easy. That puts her in a position of power – at least in her own mind.

Nurmi continues, "Now, you mentioned you were flying to New York. Why were the two of you flying to New York?". Jodi answers, "Well, there was more church history, places that were significant to the history of the church there (stalling), and I had won a trip to Huntington Beach for some of my production in PPL, so I put him on the ticket as the extra person, and we decided to use one of the flights to fly from Rochester to LAX instead of just driving there, so we could actually get out to New York for half the price, and then have PPL pay for our flight back".

Nurmi wants to be clear. Good, because I can't make heads or tails of this trip. He says, "So, to be clear, you said you flew into Rochester, NY (there are flights between Rochester and LAX, so that much could be true)...right?". Jodi answers, "Right...no,wait..I don't...we flew into Cleveland on the way there, flew back from Rochester to LAX". What? Seriously, what? What kind of prize was this? Were there no restrictions? Her arms are flying wildly, simulating airplanes flying. Nurmi seems to understand. I don't.

Nurmi asks, "Just for further clarification, was it just you and Travis on this trip to New York?". She answers, "Yes". Then why was Josh Ward even mentioned? The jury should be instructed to disregard all prior testimony regarding Josh Ward. After all, he was used as the reason for Travis' not displaying his temper on this trip. As it turns out, he wasn't even there.

I guess Nurmi wants to back away from the disaster. He says, "So, you said this was to be another church history trip, right?". Jodi answers, "Well, church history, and there were also other travel goals that we had, at that time". What time? Does it even matter?

Nurmi continues, "What do you mean by travel goals?". You know, Nurmi, the 1000 places to see before they died? It's beginning to sound like they had three down, 997 to go, but Jodi will make this book seem like importance is only overshadowed by the New Testament and The Book of Mormon. Jodi says, "In that same spring, Travis had discovered a book called, "1000 Places to See Before You Die", and he thought it would be a cool goal to have, maybe a lifetime goal, to try to check off as many places as he could, and I began to join him in that pursuit (invited or uninvited? Is there nothing she doesn't invade – she stole his goal?), and Niagara Falls is on the list, so while we were out east, we saw Niagara Falls, and the finger lakes in New York, and the Rock and Roll Hall of Fame in Cleveland, Ohio". There is something so perverse about this woman sitting there talking about Travis' life time goals. There is something equally perverse about her talking about "1000 Places to See Before You Die", and realizing that Jodi Arias murdered him before he could see any of those places without her.

I wonder if Jodi will mention visiting Palmyra, NY (about 25 miles from Rochester). This would be a very significant location as far as the history of the Mormon church is concerned. The Mormons believe that the angel Moroni directed their prophet, Joseph Smith, to farm land in Palmyra, and it was there that he uncovered the golden tablets that contained the words to the Book of Mormon. It would be the birthplace of their particular faith. Rather important, I'd say, and it should top Niagara Falls and the Rock and Roll Hall of Fame. Incidentally, anyone want to venture a bet as to whether or not Jodi mentioned eloping while in Niagara Falls?

Nurmi reiterates that this was a dual purpose trip. He asks Jodi if they were also in New York to see sites of religious, historical significance. Jodi responds, "Yes". Then, there is a very long pause. I assume that Nurmi is trying to decide if he should ask Jodi what these particular sites were. Based on the fact that she only offered an affirmation instead of elaborating, I think he does not trust his client to remember the religious places she visited.

Nurmi asks if he can approach the bench. After some time, he approaches Jodi with another exhibit. He tells Jodi that he just wants to know if she recognizes either of the photographs he's handing her. I assume these photos are not pornographic in nature. She doesn't handle them as if they are hot. She looks at them quickly, and then, with a voice that sounds like she's crying (she's nowhere near crying, it just sounds that way), she answers, "Yes". Nurmi continues, "I move to admit exhibits 432 and 435". I can see the photographs; they are close-up headshots of a platinum blond and a man. They are handed to Juan Martinez. He responds, "May I voir dire the witness, please". Judge Stephens responds, "You may".

Juan is on his feet. I feel invigorated. I hope this is more than one question. Jodi's stomach must be turning. Juan asks, "Ma'am, with regard to these photographs, exhibit number 435, was Mr. Alexander the person who took this photograph?". Jodi answers, "I believe he took both of those".

Martinez continues, "So, exhibit 432, he also took that? Umm, exhibit 435, is this the one from Niagara Falls?". Jodi responds, "If it's got the water in the background, it is". Martinez continues, "Right. And exhibit 432 has some trees in the back. Where was that?". She answers, "The Sacred Grove in Palmyra, NY". No objection.

Jodi is afraid of Juan Martinez. That is obvious. I cannot wait until he gets a real chance to question her. I understand why he questioned her. Maria de la Rosa is suddenly sitting up. She looks incredibly suspicious. She looks at Jennifer Willmott, and her expression belies her discomfort with Martinez' intrusion into the Jodi Show. She actually maintains that expression while Nurmi begins talking. She and Jennifer Willmott begin writing. They are all a little off balance now. They know that Jodi was asked this question for a particular reason, and it boxed her in. They don't why she was asked what she was asked.

Now we see the picture at Niagara Falls. There's a super close-up of bleach blond, Jodi Arias, thick lips painted with a brownish lipstick, huge, full toothy smile, and her face is pressed up against Travis Alexander's face. It is an excellent photo of Jodi Arias. She almost looks beautiful. Her eyes, typically askew in photographs, are completely focused and symmetrical. Her teeth are very white, and there isn't a hint of the poor orthodontia we know she is afflicted with. This may be the best photograph of her that I've seen. It actually makes me sad. I realize that with a different brain, she could have had a happy life. This picture should be entitled "Waste". By comparison, Travis is not wearing the full smile that Jodi's wearing. In fact, he is not even grinning. His eyes are narrowed, and his mouth is slightly open. He appears to have a cold sore on his bottom lip. If you were to judge who was the happier individual by the expressions on the two faces, there would be no contest; one is delighted, the other looks like the boat ride might be upsetting his stomach. I'm seriously not trying to biased. It's just the way the shot was captured. It may mean nothing. It may mean everything. By the way, Jodi is staring at the screen, and she will now attempt to cry. It's coming. I don't know if she will be successful or not, but she's trying to work up some emotion.

Nurmi points out that they look very much like a couple in this photograph. He wants to know if this photograph is a good representation of the trip. Jodi says, "This trip, we acted like that, but it was a pretense". I see no pretense on Travis Alexander's face. It is clear to me that he does not want the head of Jodi Arias up against his cheek. Nurmi asks, "What do you mean, a pretense". Jodi responds, "I found out on that trip that he was cheating on me".

She continues, "I just didn't want to bring all the drama because our tickets were bought and paid for. I couldn't refund them. I couldn't change his name on the ticket. I didn't want to be, he didn't want to be, I didn't want it to be totally miserable, even though I was miserable". Funny, she doesn't look miserable. The face of a thousand masks strikes again.

Back to Niagara Falls, NY. Jodi is unhappy. Nurmi asks, "In this photograph, it appears that you and Mr. Alexander are acting like a couple, physically affectionate, is that accurate?". Jodi answers,

"Yes". Well, look at that! Jodi finally got Travis to act like half of a physically affectionate couple", and he was doing this around other people. Granted, it was thousands of miles from Mesa, but it was still outside, and it was something she made sure was photographed (and, I'm sure, this photo ultimately found its way online for all to see).

Jodi looks defeated as she tells Nurmi that their happiness was a mere pretense. Really? It's even more shocking! Jodi says that she knew before they took the trip to Niagara Falls that he was cheating on her. Oh, so sad. His name was already on the tickets (she won), and she couldn't get a refund on the tickets (she won), and she was just flat out stuck with a sleep rapist/angry phone yeller/alterer of little boys underwear/cheater for this whole awful trip. She's a good faker, but being drama-free is very important to Jodi, she claims. Wow. She's just beaming in her pretense pics. What could the details be? I wonder, did she find out about his cheating ways by snooping through his property, or did she just interrogate his friends?

Jodi is so thoughtful. She just told us that even though she was miserable on this trip, she didn't want Travis to be miserable. She's almost super-human. I'll bet she even had sex with him – just to keep the drama and misery at bay. Jodi, sitting at her tiny desk, rubbing her right hand against the table top. She refuses to lift her head. She's being devastated right now. The sniffling is just starting, and her voice is breaking. There are no signs of tears.

In reference to Travis' cheating, Nurmi asks, "How did you discover that?". I don't know, Nurmi. Do you really want to give her that much latitude in answering a question? Apparently so. Jodi responds, "We were in, I think, Sandy, Utah, at his friend Dave's house, and we had just returned from Daniel Summit, which is a place up in the mountains, near Park City, and I had been getting my suspicions about things. He was treating me a little differently, a little more distant, a lot more flirty with other women, and it just made me uncomfortable. When I tried to talk to him about it, he blew up and got very defensive, even though I didn't accuse him of anything (calling him flirty and distant isn't accusatory?), so it was kind of a red flag (it wouldn't have mattered if the flag was red, black, white, or on fire – Jodi Arias was not going to pay attention to flags of any kind). He assured me that he was only dating me, and I left it at that. There were a couple of things that stuck out on the trip, too. Umm...at Daniel Summit, but I ignored it, and then we got back to Dave's house, and he was taking a nap one day, and he left his phone wedged between two cushions in the couch, in the living room (which is exactly where he wanted it while he was napping on the couch, and exactly where it should have stayed. Somehow, this phone is going to end up flying out from between these cushions, and it's going to land right into her hands, right?), and he was in another bedroom sleeping (no, he wasn't...that makes no sense for someone who was as socially and professionally connected as Travis), and, I just, I figured (here it comes...more theft of information), I didn't know if he was being honest with me – I had a feeling he wasn't, and I wanted (because that's the moral litmus test for her – does she want something) to know if I should continue in this relationship, or I should give him the benefit of the doubt (no, she had already decided there was no benefit of the doubt – now it was just a matter of collecting evidence), I'd been cheated on before (is she going to throw the kitchen sink in as well?), and I figured it was just past emotional baggage that I'm looking into and reading things that weren't there, so I saw his phone, and I debated on whether I should look at it, and I was kind of sitting there and tapping my fingers (wow, this is incredible), and finally I snatched it, and I ran into the bathroom, and I shut the door, and I was clicking around on his phone – he had a touchscreen, it was a smartphone, I didn't really know how to use it – but I found the text messages and began to read them".

Here's the Reader's Digest condensed version of that story: So as not to wake Travis, she slowly and carefully removed the phone, ran to the bathroom, and invaded his privacy...again. Her story of how the stars aligned perfectly to set the stage for this intrusion is just evidence of the fact that she knows normal people will fault her for doing this. By the way, what is it about Jodi Arias and bathrooms? She beats them up when she's angry, she hides in them when she's jealous, she uses them as her office when she's playing private detective, she follows women into them and holds them hostage when she feels she's been disrespected, and she kills people in them when she wants to murder someone.

Nurmi asks, "And without telling us what they said, based on those text messages on Mr. Alexander's phone, you believed he was not being faithful with you?". Jodi answers, "Yes". Nurmi continues, "Was there a particular person you believed he was dating after you saw these text messages?". Why do I feel like I'm in divorce court? So what? Who cares if he was dating every girl in Mesa? That's completely up to him. In fact, I'm beginning to wonder if Travis was trying to drive her away – perhaps ignoring her and being flirtatious was his way of trying to tell her that the bloom was off the rose. Sometimes, that's the way people break up with other people – they make it so uncomfortable and so humiliating that the other party gathers up their self-respect and calls it quits.

Jodi answers, "No, there weren't too many names, there were just a lot of phone numbers, and it wouldn't have been a person, it was several different people, many different phone numbers". Good for Travis. I hope these relationships brought him some joy.

Nurmi now tries to rehabilitate the snoop by repeating what he already said; she knew all about this, but she didn't want to cause any chaos or drama on their trip, so she kept all of her pain hidden, for his benefit, of course. Bad move on Nurmi's part, again. She caused plenty of chaos and drama – she was just biding her time and waiting for the right moment to exact her revenge. He really should strive to remember that these people he's underestimating already know how this story ends, even if Arias claims she doesn't remember any of it. Everybody knows exactly what happened. In short: normal, healthy, sexually repressed male, sees young, well made-up, bleach blond at a conference. The attraction is instant, but once he finds out that this woman has a decade long sexual past, and is currently five years into a live-in relationship, he crosses her off the potential wife list. She wants what he has, and she uses every charm – the ones that have worked with her assorted odd boyfriends in the past – and thinks she's going to be successful again. He sleeps with her. She's fine with that. Then, she becomes demanding, suffocating, and possessive. She invades every area of his life and privacy. He tries to disengage. They go back and forth. When it finally becomes obvious that he never intended to marry her, from day one forward, she kills him. It isn't much more complicated than that.

Nurmi continues, "This trip with him, this trip to New York, how long was it". Jodi answers, "I think we flew out on June 18, or something (eleven days to the official demise), and got back, I wanna say a week. I don't recall exactly". Nurmi asks, "Was there sexual interaction between you on this trip?". Jodi is still looking like she's ready to off herself, but she pulls herself together long enough to answer, "I think there was, but I don't recall specifics". Nurmi was hoping for some penile/vaginal intercourse, and I suspect he'd even settle for the Provo Push at this point. To that end, he asks, "Why do you say you think there was?". Jodi answers, "Because there usually was when we traveled". Yes, it was part of the deal – he'd go on trips with her, but she had to put out. If she didn't want that pattern established, she would have gone for a ride on the swings in the park instead of performing oral sex in the park, way back in September, 2006.
Nurmi continues, "Well, let me ask you, on these travels, did you share the same hotel room?". No, Nurmi, the sex they usually had when they traveled took place in alleys and elevators. Aren't some of these questions just a little stupid? Jodi answers, "Yes". Nurmi asks, "Same bed?". Jodi answers, "Yes". Nurmi asks, "Were you in love with Travis in this photograph?". Jodi answers, "Yes".

Now Nurmi shows Jodi exhibit 452, which I assume, is the Sacred Grove picture. Yes, that's the picture. We see Travis grinning while wearing a blue baseball hat. We see Jodi smiling – no teeth this time – and she appears to be standing slightly behind him. As usual, she is touching him. Her chin rests on his right shoulder, and her right hand is on his upper chest. She's not as happy in this picture as she was in the Niagara Falls photo, and he's not as blasé.

This is Jodi's moment to prove that she is a Mormon. Nurmi asks her what the significance is of the Sacred Grove. Jodi answers, "The Sacred Grove is an important place in the history of the church because it was where Joseph Smith received what is called the first vision, where he was in this grove praying, umm, I think it was in 1820, or somewhere around there, and, he, umm (she's losing it here, struggling to remember the script), he looked up, and two heavenly beings appeared before him, and it was the father and Jesus Christ". I feel like we should applaud – or at least give her an "A+" for her oral examination on Mormonism. She even got the year right, although I would have given her extra credit if she knew the season that this visitation allegedly took place.

Nurmi establishes that devout Jodi, anal gymnast, really wanted to see this grove of spiritual significance, and she did, so that's great. Now, what does any of this have to do with murder? Nurmi asks a ridiculous question: "Would it be considered a romantic spot for you and the members of your church?". Well, of course it would be considered a romantic spot, Nurmi! Don't most Catholics have candlelit dinners at the Vatican? Aren't Jews always exchanging love poems at the Wailing Wall? Isn't Mecca just another way to say, "I love you"? Why should the Mormons be left out of the romance of religion?

Holy cow, what is it with these Mormons? She didn't just say no. She thought about it, and then said, "I think, my understanding of it is that church members get engaged when they get there, and Travis had complained that that was a cliché (well, that's damnable!) before going, so I wasn't expecting any kind of romantic interaction". Nurmi rubs it in, "You mean, you weren't expecting a proposal?". Jodi answers, "Definitely not a proposal, not after reading his phone". It sounds like justice to me. Any woman who snoops through a man's personal space certainly isn't worthy of a proposal.

Guess who's not going to the chapel to get married? Jodi's energy level is so low that she appears to be in the depressed phase of a bi-polar episode. That could change at any moment – depending on the topic – but for now, picture the ivory sweater clad murderess as a rag doll tied to a chair. She's been depleted by recalling these sad memories.

Nurmi asks if Travis knew, while on the trip to New York, that he had "been caught". It would have been more accurate to ask if Travis figured out that Jodi had stolen his phone, but he has to take the onus off of his client and put it on her victim, because that's how defense attorneys roll. In a barely audible voice, Jodi responds, "I didn't tell him". We are treated to a side shot of Arias at her little desk. What's that on her computer screen? Oh, it's the Sacred Grove picture. Nurmi's making her look at a picture of her nuzzling the neck of her victim. There's a nice dramatic pause between attorney and client. Jodi uses that opportunity to turn her face from looking at the photograph. For good measure, she turns toward the jury before she drops her eyes.

Nurmi continues, "So, for seven days then, on this trip, you grin and bear it, so to speak, because you don't want to cause any kind of fight or any kind of confrontation during that week, right?". She's so sad, she can't even manage a proper "yes"; instead she responds, "Yeah. More or less". Nurmi continues, "And I say, specifically related to his being unfaithful, you didn't bring that up the whole week?". Jodi answers, "No". Nurmi asks, "The trip itself, was it then harmonious, or were there fights anyway?". Tell the truth, Jodi. There were fights anyway.

Jodi thinks before answering, "We did have a fight in Ohio. It was just a little...I don't remember...it was an argument, and he kept asking me throughout the trip, what's wrong, what's wrong, and I kept saying nothing. I was just trying to act like nothing, everything was okay". Yes. We all know how to play that passive-aggressive game of "What's wrong/Nothing". Now, why don't you tell the jury what you fought about, because you definitely remember.
Nurmi asks, "What was your plan? Were you just going to break up with him when you got back to California? Did you have a plan?". Jodi may not have much, but she always has a plan. She answers, "My initial plan, when I found the text messages on the phone, was to break up with him, but I didn't want to cause a lot of drama at Dave's house, so I decided I would wait 'til we got back

to Mesa (because she couldn't do it in the car), and we got back to Mesa, and Travis was kind of domineering, and I was worried about confronting him. He got very upset the last time I even hinted about it (mood changed duly noted. She's smiling), accusing him of anything, so...". Nurmi interrupts, with a "Hang on, hang on...".

Yes, hang on, Jodi. If she was so worried about confronting the domineering Travis, then why confront him at all? According to Jodi, she knew the truth. There wouldn't have been any confrontation if she simply got out of his car in Mesa, transported her luggage into her own car, and then, in a public place, like his driveway, she could tell the angry man, "I've given this a lot of thought. You're very special to me, but I think we both realize that there are too many differences between us for this to work on a permanent level. I want to get married and have a family, and that's what you want, too. I think we both know that this isn't going to work for us. Let's end this on good terms.". Then, before he has a chance to get in his car, throw it into reverse, and run her over in a jealous rage, she could run to her car, and leave for California. It may not have been easy, but it would have worked.

So, let's see if that's what Nurmi came up with.

With Jodi hanging on, Nurmi continues, "Wait a second, Jodi. Before you get too far down the road (I think I heard a few words I'd like to exploit a little further...yes, let's talk about , 'domineering', 'worried', and 'upset'), you said when you returned to Mesa, weren't you still living in Big Sur at the end of this trip?". Wow, sounds like Jodi is already too far down the road. Jodi responds, "Yeah, I'm sorry. We flew back to, umm, we flew to LAX that time (wow, Jodi's a jet setter – all these plane trips!), we did the Huntington Beach thing, we did Disneyland one more time, and then I was gonna do it".

Nurmi says, "Okay. So, obviously you didn't have to be back at your job in Big Sur for an extended period of time, right?". Jodi answers, "Yeah, about a week I think I took off". Wow. How does a newly hired waitress (mid-May, according to Jodi), secure a vacation after being employed for a month? Something isn't adding up; either she's squatting at Ventana Inn's Red House, waiting to start a job, or she's living with shower man in the mountains, and Nurmi didn't think it would be a good idea to tell the jury that Jodi was living with yet, another man. We'll never know, but Nurmi should at least understand that people, if they're listening, can figure out that something is off with this story.

Nurmi continues, "But you said you landed, and you went to Disneyland and that sort of thing – you didn't have a job to go back to?". What's going on here? Who is off script? Nurmi or Arias? Jodi replies, "I did". Nurmi asks, "But you still had some days off in LA?". Jodi said, "Yes". Busted. She either didn't answer the way he wanted, or while listening to her talk about this extended trip, he realized nobody was believing her. It's clear she's lying about having the job. It's all over her face.

Jodi continues, "We had four days, five nights in Huntington Beach". Actually, only in the Twilight Zone would you have a four day/five night vacation. They had five days/four nights in Huntington Beach. Added to the "about a week" trip to New York they just returned from, this gives Jodi almost two weeks off from her brand, spanking new job. Does anyone require more proof that she had no job to go back to? Why do I think she and Nurmi had a little tiff right before he left for a three courser at some restaurant, while she waited for her peanut butter to be served in her cage (a/k/a lunch)?

Nurmi asks, "The Huntington Beach trip, that was work related, right?". Oh, stop. We have a bird's eye view on the work situation. There isn't one at the moment. Perhaps Nurmi will now try and put the focus on the "reward" aspect of the Huntington Beach trip. Jodi answers, "It was a reward, being work related". They had better give some details here, because they have already made it clear that Jodi was very actively involved in PPL meetings, but made no money. No money.

Nurmi asks, "Was it strictly a vacation, or was it also a meeting?". Jodi looks upset with Nurmi. There is an odd vibe, for lack of a better word, between them. Jodi answers, "It was mostly vacation, mostly leisure. There was like maybe a few speeches given, but it wasn't centered on training or anything like that". So, it's a vacation with speeches, and it's a vacation with other PPL people there. I don't believe her. I don't believe anything they are saying about the way this trip evolved.

Nurmi asks, "Did you and Mr. Alexander share a hotel room in Huntington Beach?". Jodi looks right at the jury and says, "Yes". Nurmi asks, "Was there sexual activity during that meeting at Huntington Beach?". Jodi closes her eyes, and then answers, "I believe there was". I guess sex is not as thrilling anymore. Nurmi sounds just like Dr. Phil as he says, "I think the part that's hard to understand, Jodi, is this idea that you just didn't end it". Juan Martinez knows Dr. Phil when he hears him, and he objects. It's difficult to understand what he said, but it has something to do with Nurmi's use of the phrase "hard to understand". Nurmi gets his sentence in, just as he wanted to (because that was his way of telling the jury that he knows they're having a hard time with this story), and he's told to rephrase. He does. He continues, "Explain to us, why after a trip to New York, you're grinning and bearing it, you get back to California, why are you still willing to put up with this?" You know what Nurmi – it isn't difficult to understand, it's damn near impossible to understand.

Jodi answers, "I think I was in denial at the time. I knew what was going on, and I think it was a convenient reason to deny it, this vacation that was paid for, there was no refunding it, umm, if we had changed flights and things like that, it would have cost even more fees...". Nurmi interrupts with, "But I'm talking about when you got back...".

The trip to Huntington Beach may fall into the category of paid ticket. However, the trip across the country, which happened after she searched his phone, was not paid for by PPL. I know they are trying to weave two separate events into one, and they've almost succeeded – if you're not paying attention.

Nurmi continues, "I'm talking about Huntington Beach. You're back from New York, there's no flights, there's nuthin' (he actually said it that way)...". Jodi tries to interrupt Nurmi, but all that comes out of her mouth is, "Wha, wha...". Then Nurmi stops talking. Jodi raises her hands in the air, as if to say, "who knows?", but she finally responds, "I mean, I couldn't imagine kicking him off the trip and saying, get out of my room. He was there and...". Nurmi's getting aggressive: "Why not?". Jodi looks flustered, and she says, "Well, we had friends that were, well, there were a lot of things to do in Huntington Beach. There are shops on the sidewalks and restaurants. There's the beach itself, and there are pools, hot tubs...". Wait. If this is an event with friends and PPL associates, why would kicking him out of her room be a problem? I thought that all PPL events required them to have separate rooms due to the heavy Mormon crowd. Are these friends, listed as one of the reasons for not breaking up with a cheating boyfriend, non-Mormons? Beyond that, is she serious? She didn't break up with him because of shops on the sidewalks? Pools? Hot tubs? Why would you want to get into a hot tub with a man who was cheating on you? Who does that? Is this the best she can do? I do believe she has gone AWOL here. I think she's answering in ways that Nurmi was not prepared for.

Nurmi interrupts her again, and it is an interruption: "It sounds like a great place, and I'm sure you both wanted to be there, and Travis probably wanted to be there, but that really doesn't get to my question. My question is, why aren't you done with him at that point in time. Why don't you kick him out of your room?". I might believe this was all planned, if not for her responses. They are random. Jodi is not happy. She closes her eyes, swivels toward the jury, looks up and to the right (deceptive), and says, "I didn't have a lot of self-esteem at that time, and I just...I...I was kind of a door mat (the phone stealing doormat), and I didn't assert myself, and I was in denial, and I just...I knew it had to happen...I wanted to hurry up and get it over with because that was going to be the hard part...I knew the relationship couldn't continue like that...I was kind of waiting for the right moment to tell him...". So, which is it? Low self-esteem? Denial? Waiting for the right moment? Those are three distinctly differently reasons, but we'll pick "denial" because she's justified her behavior twice by using that excuse.

Jodi Arias was not in denial. Hardly. Jodi Arias has seen the evidence, and that's according to Jodi Arias. She did not claim to be in denial on the day she found the evidence of "his cheating" – evidence she retrieved from his phone. On the contrary, she was angry. Her reason for not dealing with it at the moment had nothing to do with "being in denial". In fact, she articulated very clearly why she didn't break up with Travis when she found her evidence, and her stated reason was that she didn't want to start drama at someone else's home. That is not the same as being in denial. When asked why she didn't deal with it before the trip to Huntington Beach, she said that she was "worried" what "domineering" Travis would do if she "confronted" him; in the past, he had become "upset" when she hinted at his cheating. This has nothing to do with denial. Denial would mean she saw the evidence and convinced herself that there was nothing to worry about. She has spent too much time in the company of sympathetic, gullible mental health professionals who were more interested in money than integrity, and she's learned a smattering of verbiage that she is now using without the benefit of definition.

Nurmi continues, "And while you're waiting for the right moment, you're still, to your recollection, not specific on dates and times, but you're still engaging in sexual activity with him while you're waiting for this right moment, right?". He sounds like he's mocking her. He sounds like a...a...a prosecutor. It's the tone of voice he's using. This will pass. It has to. Jodi answers, "Yes, on occasion". On occasion? What does that mean? She's waiting for the right moment on occasion, or she's engaging in sexual activity with him on occasion?

Nurmi asks, "Why was that okay with you?". Jodi answers, "Well, sometimes when we did those things, it made me feel loved, depending on how he acted during the incident". Nurmi clarified, "During the sexual interaction, right?". Jodi says, "Yeah". I don't know if he's trying to make her look like the doormat she claims to have been, but this is making her look incredibly stupid.

Nurmi says, "You felt, what you seem to be telling us, is that when you were engaging in sexual behavior with Mr. Alexander, you felt completely loved?". Jodi answers, "At times". Well, why not just pick one of the times she didn't feel loved and make that the "right moment"? What is she, a masochist?

Nurmi asks, "When you were not having sexual interactions with him, did you also feel, to use your words, completely loved?". Actually, she didn't say "completely loved"; Nurmi did. She said "feel loved". Let's not make this bigger than it is. Juan Martinez is on the ball. He objects with, "Those were counsel's words, not the witness' words. Completely loved". That has to be sustained. He'll be told to rephrase. Nurmi argues, "That's exactly what she said". No, it's not. Before Judge Stephens overrules the objection, which she does, could she at least ask Mike Babicky to read it back, because Juan is correct.

Jodi answers, "Will you repeat it, I'm sorry". Oh, there's Arias, giving the middle finger to Juan Martinez. She does this whenever Juan objects and Nurmi wins. Nurmi repeats what Juan objected to: "I'm gonna try (why is he not admonished for this smart ass behavior? He is dead wrong and acting like he's being thwarted at every juncture). You told us earlier that when you had these sexual encounters with Mr. Alexander, you felt completely loved, right?". Will Jodi lie too? Rhetorical.

With her best bitch face, and with eyes like a laser on Juan Martinez (something she rarely, if ever, does), she gives a strong and firm, "Yes". Wow. I cannot believe I just saw her do that. Nurmi continues, "And, what I was asking is, how about the times when the sexual interactions weren't going on? Did you feel that same sense of being completely loved?". I hope the judge realizes that she cannot give an unethical attorney and his lying client an inch. He is making this the centerpiece of the questioning now – this "completely loved" nonsense.

Jodi answers, "There were some moments, during that trip, where we connected. It was actually more painful when we connected than when we didn't (Oh, I bet Travis would completely agree...it was far more painful when you connected than when you didn't. But, the prosecutor will get to that part in due time)". Now, we're going back to analyzing Jodi's feelings. Nurmi asks, "What do you mean by that?". Jodi answers, "Because it was a reminder of how much I loved him, and when you weren't connected, it was easier to start distancing myself from him, even though that became kind of impossible. Umm, when we were getting along, it was almost like I could pretend that I never saw any of those things in his phone". Well, that's a classic case of denial, isn't it? Once in a while, but not often, she was able to pretend (deny) that she hadn't really seen the evidence. The rest of the time, the majority of the time, she couldn't pretend. Denial. Right.

Nurmi asks, "At this point in time, had he told you he loved you". Jodi looks up (and to the right) before answering, "Not since we had begun officially dating". Nurmi continues, "Now, apart from Huntington Beach, did you spend, did you and Mr. Alexander go anywhere else before you returned to Big Sur?". Jodi answers, "Yes, our (his) friend Jeff drove us to Disneyland, to Anaheim". Is this another day on top of Huntington Beach? Wow, some vacation policy at her new job.

Nurmi asks, "And you say that your friend drove you, did the three of you go to Disneyland, or was it just you and Travis?". Jodi answers, "Just Travis and I, he dropped us off". Nurmi asks if this is part of the Huntington Beach trip. Jodi says it was all part of the same trip, but I'd be interested to know if this is a separate leg of the trip.

When we last left Jodi, she was about to tell us about her trip to the Magic Kingdom. Jodi claims that while on this trip, she was waiting for "the right moment" to break up with Travis, her travel companion and boyfriend, because, as everyone knows, Disneyland has always been the perfect backdrop for break-ups. Park hopping will surely provide many wonderful opportunities for Jodi to seize the right moment. Maybe while enjoying all the brotherly love of "It's a Small World", she could bring it up ("Travis, speaking of small worlds, yours is about to get a little smaller"), or perhaps she needs the adrenaline surge guaranteed by the ride called Splash Mountain ("Travis, I just want you to know that from now on, that cave up ahead will be the largest opening you'll be entering"). We'll just have to see how things develop.

As we begin, it becomes clear that Nurmi will apply the same litmus test to Disneyland as he has to every other date, private or public. Were they holding hands? Were they acting like a couple? Did they appear to be boyfriend-girlfriend? Jodi answers, "Somewhat. It was kind of dull. The park just didn't have the same kind of magic as it did before, because of everything that was going on". On cue, Nurmi asks, "What do you mean, everything that was going on?". Has he been listening?

His client, the doormat in denial, felt betrayed, and all the hugs from Mickey and Goofy weren't putting a smile on her miserable face. Haven't we been listening to her version of "everything that was going on" for a half an hour now? Does Nurmi believe there was some dramatic event Jodi forgot to mention, and his brilliantly phrased question will elicit a shocking response? Does he think that Travis threw Jodi overboard on the steamboat ride? There was nothing dramatic going on. It was merely Jodi moping and trying to infect Travis with her misery because he was popular, well-liked, had options, and she didn't. That's what was going on.

While spinning her hands, she says, "Inside, like my inner turmoil, with the knowledge that I was, I guess, cursed with, sort of...you could say". No, you really couldn't say she was "cursed with knowledge". I assume she's referring to her knowledge of "the cheating". Actually, she didn't have that knowledge because of a curse – she had that knowledge because she decided to take it by force.

For the 9,463rd time, Nurmi prods, "Did you get along okay at Disneyland, or were there any arguments?". You know, Travis seems like a very outgoing, make the best of it, kind of guy – at least in every video I've seen of him. I'm hoping that he ignored her moping. I'm hoping that he had a great time in spite of the company he was forced to keep. Jodi responds, "I remember us getting along pretty well". So, despite the fact that Jodi was "cursed" with information and looking for the right moment to end this relationship, she remembers getting along with Travis pretty well. Right.

Nurmi asks, "So now this trip to Huntington Beach comes to an end – a few days later, I would assume, right? After you go to Disneyland?" Jodi purses her lips, swivels in her chair, and pretends to think. Then, she answers, "Yyyess...after Disneyland (her mouth is slowly twitching from left to right, and she makes some sort of clicking sound with her lips)...I don't remember where I stayed, but we hung out in Riverside for a while". This was all said in a very slow and deliberate fashion. I wonder, will Nurmi want to know what "a while" is? Will he ask how another few days off will affect her new job – especially in light of the fact that we know this trip has reached the two week point.

Nurmi says, "Eventually, there was gonna come a point in time, eventually, there came a point in time where you and Travis were gonna part company, right?". Nurmi has been trying to get to the end of this trip for a while. He knows it has gone on for far too long, and it makes her look like she lying about her job. Jodi doesn't want the trip to end – that's obvious. She has such a strange and unnerving look in her eye. As I pause the video, the look becomes even more evident. I find her eyes to be frightening. Jodi pauses, and finally answers, "Yes".

Nurmi moves on, "Now, you told us before that this was seemingly gonna be the moment in time when you told him, you're done, right?". Again, freezing the video shows a look of utter contempt in her eye. She is swiveling in her chair, looking down, looking at Nurmi, looking down, and then she simultaneously nods her head once, and says, "Yes". Nurmi asks, "Where, do you recall where the two of you were when you were to part ways?". Does it matter? Can Nurmi just ask her if she actually broke up with Travis, or is he going to help her look less ridiculous and desperate by allowing Jodi to make up some fake scenario that forced her to put her plan on hold?

Where were they when they parted company? Jodi answers, "Well, I planned to drop the bomb at, in Riverside, when I was dropping him off at his grandmother's house (oh, I see where this is going), and I couldn't get up the courage to tell him". She has a ridiculous, goofy (that's the only way I can describe it) smile on her face. For me, as a juror, this would be the end of her defense. I would know that whatever was coming was nothing more than her unwillingness to be bested by Travis Alexander.

If we are to believe any or all of what she is now claiming, we must also believe that Jodi, a 27 year old woman (I had a husband, two children under the age of five, and a home at 27), made a conscious decision to accept the situation. She, by her own admission, without being coerced or forced in any way, chose to stay with a man she claims raped her in her sleep, forced her to perform unwanted, painful sexual acts, seemed embarrassed to be around her in public, and as far as we know, has never taken her to an elegant lunch, let alone a beautiful dinner. He's given her no gifts of any value – except the pair of cheap, Victoria's Secret knock-off shorts and a gray cotton T-shirt (and we aren't even sure those came from him). Beyond that, he gave her the Book of Mormon. He doesn't, according to Jodi, pay for her to accompany him on any of these road trips and hotel get-aways. It is never on his dime, and she is never his guest. She is always responsible for paying her own way. He's called her a skank, wants her to wear little boy's underpants, has a flirtatious manner with other women, is making "plans" with a married Mormon woman, and is also dating "several" other single women.

He is, according to Jodi, confrontational, a yeller, domineering, suspicious about every man she talked to, and he was awkward and uncomfortable while introducing Jodi to his grandmother (and I can imagine, for a conservative, old-time Mormon, this obviously vain, bleach blond with figure enhancing clothes and mask of a make-up, was not the type of woman Norma Sarvey envisioned for her grandson. I've often wondered if that first encounter was not quickly aborted because Jodi was letting Norma Sarvey know, by the way she was touching Travis, that they had been intimate). In fact, according to Jodi, that first meeting was so uncomfortable, that Travis stood there not knowing what to say. If this is what she knew, and she couldn't break up with him, then this was her choice. Oh, and for the juror who thought that Jodi Arias was "normal" before meeting Travis Alexander, perhaps he should have been paying more attention to some of the other words in her testimony – words that didn't have anything to do with oral sex, anal sex, penile/vaginal sex, ejaculation, and erections.

This is not a woman who was confident, and then suddenly lost all of her self-worth by merely being the girlfriend of Travis Alexander (for four whole months). She was a user, and as a user, she was willing to accept certain drawbacks, certain negatives, if in so doing she was guaranteed access to something she really wanted. It is the pattern of her life. She was willing to live in filth and poverty with Bobby Juarez, if in so doing she was freed from high school and her parents' attempts to control her. She was willing to dump Bobby in favor of aimless Matt McCartney, until she realized how aimless Matt really was. She was willing to pick up and move hundreds of miles away to Big Sur and sleep in a tent, because she waiting on free housing to open at Ventana Inn and Spa. Once she got that housing, she set her eye on Darryl Brewer. She was willing to overlook his smoking, alcoholism, and ex-wife because with Darryl, she could become a homeowner. Jodi Arias, the woman who couldn't find the right moment to break up with a man she portrays as a hypocritical bully, had no problem sitting Darryl down at his own kitchen table to tell him that, in addition to assisting him in the ruination of his career and credit, she also needed to be free – by next Saturday, because her new object of desire wouldn't consider dating her if she wasn't unencumbered. This IS Jodi Arias. It has always been Jodi Arias. It is Jodi Arias today. Her treatment of Kirk Nurmi is a contemporary reminder of the use and move-on pattern of her life.

Remember, she has said, many times, "I'm not beneath sleeping in my car", but she'll only sleep in her car if she's doing so while on a road trip to see or obtain someone or something she wants. This is who Jodi Arias has always been. Her behavior and personality traits were set in stone years before she met Travis. He had nothing to do with the fact that she could act like a submissive when she needed to.

To believe her story, we'd have to believe that her entire adult personality has disintegrated in nine short months. That's not what happened. What happened was Jodi Arias was not going lose to the likes of Travis Alexander. Jodi did the leaving, and that's what happened.

We left Jodi with a question hanging. Why, after dropping Travis' at his grandmother's house in Riverside, did she not "drop the bomb". She cites a lack of courage. Nurmi asks, "So, you say you're at his grandma's house in Riverside, you're dropping him off, and you don't have the courage to tell him". Jodi responds, "Yes", and she punctuates that answer with another single nod of her head. Nurmi continues, "Are you leaving Riverside at that point, or are you staying with Mr. Alexander?". Oh, you better believe she's leaving town. There will be no cohabitation under Travis' grandmother's roof.

Jodi answers, "I'm leaving town and I'm driving back to...Big Sur (why did she have to obviously think about where she was driving back to? She says she lives in Big Sur, right?)". Nurmi asks, "Now, I believe you had told us earlier that you had met his grandmother three times, is that right?". Yes, that's right. I distinctly remember her saying that. Suddenly, Jodi needs to search her memory bank for information that literally rolled off of her tongue on Thursday. She answers, "Umm...I think...(very slowly)...I did meet her three times (hands spinning, talking rapidly), but I don't know if that was the second or third time". Translation: Three times sounded better than two, so she said three times when she was initially asked. It's clear to me that she did not meet the woman three times; in fact, I'm not even sure that this second encounter qualifies as a "meeting". I also have a suspicion that this encounter was nothing more than Jodi watching Travis as he walked away from her car while Norma Sarvey opened her door to greet him. I don't believe Jodi even went inside the house that day. Actually, I seem to recall that Samantha Alexander saying that Travis never introduced Jodi to his siblings, although she did meet their grandmother once (and the letter that a post-arrest Jodi wrote and sent to their grandmother upset her badly. If my recollection of Samantha's account is accurate, it was an incredibly long letter – I want to say eight pages – and it was thrown away).

Nurmi continues, "So, you're driving back to Riverside from Big Sur, and you never have this confrontation you've been planning to have for about a week? Right?". Jodi answers, "Yeah, more like two, two weeks".

The Alexanders are listening closely – well Stephen and Tanisha are. Steven is looking quizzically at Jodi through narrowed eyes, and Tanisha stares directly at her with angry eyes and pursed lips. Nurmi must still have the photograph of Travis and Jodi on the large screen. Imagine the pain of seeing a photograph of your murdered loved being hugged by their murderer. There it is, on the huge Jumbotron. It's been staring at you for a long time. It's hideous, and it's cruel. It's a tactic, and it is done with the hope that the survivors will crack under the emotional stress. Samantha's eyes are fixated on something on the right side of the room, and because her eyes are also lifted, I believe it is that photo she is looking at. Her shoulders are slumped, and her hands appear to be clasped in her lap. She looks tired, and she looks sad.

Now that the cat is out of the bag (the one week vacation was a two week vacation), Nurmi continues, "Well, what's the plan?". Doing her best mea culpa act, Jodi says, "I was really mad at myself. I wanted to...I wanted to do it in person (her hands and face are pleading with the jury to believe her), and now...now I didn't know when I was coming back to Arizona, to southern California...I didn't know when I would see him again, physically. So, I realized at that point, it would have to be on the phone".

This is asking too much. She just spent two weeks with a man, and she couldn't find the right moment to break up with him? She never intended to break up with him. In fact, there are many of Travis' friends who say that she did not break up with him – He broke up with her. That's what happened, and we all know it. Let me speculate as to what actually happened on this trip.

After disengaging with Jodi following two weeks of intense togetherness, probably the longest period of time that the pair had actually spent together, Travis realized that there was no way he was going to share a future with Jodi Arias. It's possible to hide your neuroses and disorders from another person for a weekend – even a three day weekend -- but two weeks? Two weeks is a long time, and it's enough to tell you if you can at least imagine yourself with the other person on a day in, day out basis. I believe Travis realized that this was something he couldn't do, so he gathered up his courage, and he made a phone call to Jodi. The purpose of the phone call was to let her down easy. I think he did it on the phone because he didn't want her to spend any more time or money driving the 1,370 mile round trip (11 hours, each way) from Big Sur, California, to Mesa, Arizona.

I don't think he intended to waste that type of time or money either. However, Jodi is the one who does the leaving. She'll change the conversation around, and she'll make it seem like she was the one initiating the break-up, but this pathetic storyteller will never convince me that her version of this story is the truth.

Nurmi asks, "Did you ever then, have the talk that you were dreading for so long?". Jodi says, "Yes, yes". Now I know why she looked so defeated, sad, and angry during this portion of the testimony. This was the last trip before he dumped her, and it's very likely that she felt, while on that trip, that he was going to try to break off the intimate relationship and reduce it to a friendship. She realized that friends rarely travel 11 hours to see each other – certainly not once or twice a month -- and even a friendship would ultimately be minimized to little more than Travis yelling, "Hey, Jodi! How you doin?'" while simultaneously giving her a friendly slap on the back if they crossed paths at future PPL conventions. Beyond that, their relationship would be no more than social media banter, available for all to see. There would be no more pursuits of his that she could join, and there would be no reason for them to ever close a door behind them.

Nurmi confirms that this conversation happened over the phone. Then, he says, "And tell us what you told him". Hang on, it's going to be a whopper. Jodi is going to "drop the bomb". She replies, "Umm...well, I said, there's some things I want to talk to you about (her fingers are interlocked, and that indicates her anxiety), and I told him that his phone has been...(she pauses while she tries to stifle a grin)...the source of the problem...and...everything came out...I told him what happened in Utah, and I apologized 'cause I felt really bad for violating his privacy, even though I felt justified (you either feel bad, or you feel justified – and I've never seen her fingers interlocked for this long during an answer), and I found out, and he was apologetic". This is about as pointed and memorable as their "boyfriend-girlfriend" conversation. This is Jodi Arias. There's always these lead ups, this crescendo, and then, you think you missed the apex.

The camera goes to Steven Alexander. We get a close up. I have never seen him make such a readable facial gesture. He makes very tiny back and forth movements with his head (as if to say "no"), and then, he just closes his eyes. He's right on the money.

Nobody believes this. What happened to the guy who gets aggressive when the subject of cheating comes up? Does that same guy remain calm when he's faced with the fact that some woman he's sleeping with has gone through his private messages so that she can confront him with the subject that makes him so aggressive ? Is he so calm, in fact, that HE apologizes to HER? What world does this woman think we live in?

This is good enough for Nurmi. The man who wants to know when Jodi Arias felt "completely loved" as opposed to merely "loved", is just fine with this level of detail. He says, "You said he was apologetic. Did you end up breaking up with him after this conversation?". Jodi replies, "The conversation evolved, his apology was weak, I thought...and...umm....I said...in an indirect way, I don't think either of us is ready to be in the kind of relationship that we thought we were having". Oh, please. Jodi said in "an indirect way"?

That's a short and direct sentence. I can't think of any way to make it indirect. She's using the word "indirect" because she is lying. She's the one with the pattern of spying and invading people's privacy (and not just in this relationship). Suddenly, she's the one who "doesn't think they're ready...."? She's suddenly the mature one?

My Theory: Travis said, "You expect me to apologize to you because you stole my phone and violated my privacy? Are you serious? You know what? If you're going through my personal things, then it's pretty clear that we shouldn't be having the kind of relationship you seem to think we're having".

Nurmi is tongue tied, "Was that, then, when you said, was that really, or was that conversation, was that really the end of yourself and Travis as a couple?". Jodi's demeanor has changed. She says, with her shoulders squared, her head up, and while swiveling in her chair, "As an official couple, yes". Where's the sadness? It's all gone. No, it's not – it's on Samantha's face. There's a close-up of her. She's sinking lower in her seat. She's completely hunched over now. Now I know why Jodi suddenly seems empowered. She feeds off the pain and misery of others. She is such a hateful, hateful being. She should have been put in an institution of some kind years and years ago.

I don't know what is going on with Jodi's mouth. I thought she might be chewing gum, and then I realized that if the sheriff didn't give it to her, she's not allowed to have it. Besides, unless you're sitting with the Yreka fan club in the front row, there is no snacking in court. In any event, her jaw keeps moving.

Nurmi continues, "You essentially broke up that day over the phone". Jodi answers, "Yes, that was our ending, you could say". She looks like she's talking about someone she despises when she says, "ending". She tosses her hands in the air and makes a distasteful expression. This was not Nurmi's finest hour. He either failed to prep his client, or she is just incorrigible. Everyone has had a break-up, and if the relationship was as serious as Jodi has tried to make this one sound, her account of the break-up indicates that she is either lying about the exclusivity of the relationship, or she isn't willing to tell the jury the details. This was a bad move...among many bad moves. Jodi, a woman on trial for her life, has made it very clear to anybody watching – her attorneys included – that these are HER memories, and she has chosen to keep them to herself. Her arrogance is the only thing about her that makes her special.

Jodi Arias, who gave us a mere 37 word answer to describe the romantic break-up she claims to have initiated, now wishes to announce that she remembers the exact date of the break-up – June 29, 2007. That was a Friday. By that point, would anyone believe that the hopeless borderline/sociopath cut the cord? It is beyond her ability to cut Travis off. I believe he dumped her. In fact, I believe he dumped her and left her to face a long, lonely weekend. Oh, and for your edification, Jodi claimed (in the twisted and sick letter she authored and sent to the Alexander family on what would have been Travis' 31st birthday) that Travis "begged her" to marry him the day she broke up with him. Sure, he did. In her fantasy world, I'm certain that's what happened.

There is a cute moment between Tanisha and her husband Harold, and since there isn't much that's cute about this trial, it's worth mentioning. Harold's having a hard time staying awake. Seriously, he's not blinking, he's actually dozing.
The man is probably exhausted. This is draining on so many levels, and he has been at Tanisha's side throughout this trauma. However, she must have heard his breathing rate change, and she probably realizes he's falling asleep. She turns her head to left and looks at him (as only a wife can). He immediately opens his eyes, and she turns her gaze back to Jodi. Harold makes a valiant effort, but he just keeps blinking excessively. You can just tell he would really love to have five minutes of sleep. Mormons really should rethink that coffee thing. It could really help.

Now that the relationship has been taken underground, Nurmi wants to know how long it was before Jodi spoke with Travis again. Jodi says, "He called me the next morning. He was still in southern California". Oh, here we go. Nurmi asks, "And just so we're clear, you were in Big Sur". Hey, does anyone think she's going to say that Travis was willing to drive the 6.5 hour, 350 mile trip to see Jodi before he leaves California for Arizona? Jodi confirms that she was in Big Sur.

Nurmi continues, "And, what was the subject matter of that conversation?". Jodi answers, "Well, I don't remember how it started, ummm...I think he was at his friend's house...". Just to let Arias know that he is listening to every word, Juan Martinez objects. He says, "Objection. Non-responsive. She was asked what the subject matter of the conversation was". I hope Judge Stephens admonishes the witness to answer the question, but I'm not holding out much hope. She seems to be giving Arias enough rope to hang herself. Nurmi says, "It's not his objection, your honor". The objection is overruled, and Nurmi is instructed to restate his question.

Nurmi restates his question: "You say he called you the next day. Do you know where he was calling you from?". Jodi answers, "I understood he was at his friend's house...Chris and Sky's house...in southern California". That's a trip he would make. It's a mere 45 minutes from Riverside to Murietta. Nurmi continues, "And (he always drags this word out, every time he says it, and he begins 80% of his questions with 'eeeyaaaahhnndd'), was he wanting to get together with you, was he wanting to continue the conversation? Tell us the subject matter of this conversation".

Jodi answers, "At first it was about what he was doing there, so that's why I figured he was there.

And then, we didn't continue the conversation from before. Umm, it was a lot less dramatic (dramatic? I heard no drama in her 37 word break-up conversation), and, well, I don't know what room he holed himself up in, but the conversation began to turn sexual, and umm...". She's doing her "what's a hot girl supposed to do when Captain Horny calls?" face. She's interrupted by Nurmi, who, as we all know, never lets the word "sexual" go by without asking for details. He asks, "What do you mean, sexual?".

Jodi answers, "Well, he began to say things like, he's been horny lately...". Lately? She just spent two weeks with him, and that trip ended about 40 hours ago, and she couldn't remember when they had sex, or how they had sex, but suddenly, he's ready for action. Another fatal mistake. Jodi Arias, if she gives into this, could really be classified as changing by the minute, or mentally retarded. You do not break up with a man after this passionate relationship, and the next morning agree to engage him in phone sex. This is beyond ridiculous. Once again, she is playing with the jury. I think she's probably picked her male prey in that jury box. She's tailoring this testimony to arouse someone. So, this is what justice looks like for a man who was left to melt down the drain of his own shower after he died an awful, painful, terrifying death...three times.

Juan Martinez objects. I cannot make out his objection, but I believe it is a hearsay objection. Nurmi, riding high on objections being overruled, sounds confident as he says, "It's not being offered as truth to the matter asserted, judge". I've heard this response to an objection many times, and I did start to research it. However, it would take a lot of space to try and explain it (and that explanation would be framed by my very limited understanding), so I'm going to leave it to the judge.

Judge Stephens says, "Approach". It is not a weak, "approach"; it's a hard, "approach". She is irritated. I don't know who she's irritated with, but she's not happy or lax. Jodi Arias, meanwhile, is most likely delighted that all of this legal drama is playing out because of her. I hope she enjoyed her moment in the spotlight – her many moments in the spotlight. She sitting in closed custody now, unless someone is visiting her to talk about how to keep her off death row and in prison forever. Works for me.

During this lengthy bench conference, we are shown the two sides of the courtroom. On one side, the Yreka fan club is taking the opportunity to catch up on conversation. Sandy whispers to Bill. Aunt Sue is pointing something out to Jodi's younger brother. This boy always wears a "deer in the headlights" look. She puts her hand up to her lips to block her mouth. Unfortunately, she puts her hand on the wrong side of her face, so they only people she's blocking from reading her lips are the people in the second row. Jodi's brother looks directly at the computer screen at the defense desk, so Aunt Sue is explaining something about that. Behind them, it's a small flurry of activity. There's just so much to say that cannot wait for lunch, and that's right around the corner.

On the other side of the courtroom, the Alexander family waits quietly with their supporters. They move a little, probably to revive their blood circulation, but there is no whispering. Again, it's quite a contrast. The Alexanders are still staring at Jodi. Jodi refuses to look up and face her accusers. She's a coward. When it becomes obvious that the microphones are back on and Nurmi is about to take his place at the podium, Jodi looks up. She looks at the Alexanders. I believe she was told not to look at them or taunt them in any way, but apparently Jodi cannot help herself.

Nurmi says, "You said that this conversation was sexual in nature, this day after you broke up, right?". Now, Jodi appears demure. The woman who just boldly used the word "horny" in open court, is playing with her fingernails and refusing to look up. Nurmi continues, "When you say sexual in nature, that could mean a lot of things, so why don't you clarify that a little bit". Jodi has been thwarted. She was having a good time talking about Captain Horny, and now she's not so sure she's ready to say what she wanted to say. She throws Nurmi a defiant look that says, "maybe I will, and maybe I won't". No kidding.

Jodi doesn't answer. Instead she puts her right hand on her face. Nurmi continues, "Was he talking about the two of you engaging in sexual behavior?". Jodi can hear these bench conferences. The fact that she waited when she would have normally answered is proof that she knew what to wait for. She answers, "Yes". At this point, if Jodi Arias agrees to have phone sex with the man she claims to have dumped yesterday, she is one of three things: a liar, a slut, or insane.

While Jodi continues to touch multiple areas of her face, Nurmi continues, "Did he talk about specific acts that he wanted to do, engage in with you?". Jodi answers, "I don't remember specifically (other than to say he was "feeling horny lately – that part she remembers quite specifically), I just remember, he was sexual, the things he was saying". Nurmi asks, "And you remember it related to the two of you interacting, right?". Jodi answers, "Somewhat, but I was on the phone, and I was out in the gravel driveway at the Red House at Ventana (homeless Jodi squats again)". Nurmi continues, "Alright. You had just broken up with him the night before, right". Jodi corrects him – it was the afternoon before. Nurmi continues, "Did you find it strange that the morning after your breakup, or the morning after, yes, the morning after your breakup, this man's on the phone with you trying to have dirty talk?". Dirty talk? Did he really just say that? Ick.

Jodi Arias, alien from another world, answers, "I felt it was strange, but also, he had....(long pause, stupid grin)...I really had low self-esteem at this point, and it made me feel better, actually". Somebody call the men in the white coats. Jodi Arias is walking around a gravel driveway at a luxury resort (notice, she's still not working), and she's willing to engage the boyfriend she just dumped (for cheating on her) in phone sex. Forget the fact that his apology was weak. Forget everything. Jodi has low self- esteem, and low self-esteem causes you to kick the gravel under your feet while you're talking to your ex-boyfriend on the phone (and the discussion involves his penis). It doesn't really sound like low-esteem to me. In fact, it sounds more like, "I operate a 1-900 phone sex line. May I have your credit card number, please".

Nurmi knows that if she doesn't explain this, the jury, including the men, will brand her a whore. So, Jodi explains, "Well, he had made promises to change. He said those women didn't mean anything (oh, and she did? Are they the ones he's calling to help him get through this alleged masturbatory session, or is easy Jodi the one he called? What does that tell you?), and that kind of thing". No, not "that kind of thing". This is a heavy and unproven accusation. The time for "that kind of thing" has come and gone. She should be forced to repeat the exact words, and she should take that stupid smile off of her face while she continues to use these open ended phrases that are intended to let the jurors' imaginations take over.

Juan Martinez is angry. He objects with "hearsay". Overruled.

Jodi thinks she's the attorney now. Having heard the ruling, she starts, at almost a whisper, "So, umm...". Nurmi interrupts. He says, "So, he told you these women didn't matter and you did? Is that what you're saying?". Jodi, who is appearing to be more abominable by the moment, says, "Yes". If this is true, and it may be true, at least at some point, the only reason she matters and the other women don't is based on what is in his hand. It is not a diamond ring – that would be for one of the "other women", but if he's holding his penis, he either has to urinate, or he's looking for the woman that does matter in this situation: Jodi Arias. And you know what? That's on her.

Jodi continues, "He said, I'll change, I'll change. Just give me a chance (probably all of the things she said to him)...so this way my...I still loved him, so this was...I don't know...I thought that he was serious about changing. So I continued to be intimate with him". Newsflash. Talking dirty on the phone, as Nurmi so eloquently puts it, is not intimacy. I think it $9.99 a minute.

Nurmi realizes that phone sex is not intimacy – especially when it's between two people who are not dating. He says, "Let's not get too past the phone call right now". She isn't, Nurmi, and you know it. He tries to rehabilitate this idiot on the stand. Go ahead, Nurmi, try to rehabilitate a woman with the morals of a dog in heat.

Nurmi asks, "Did you reciprocate the general tone of the conversation the day after you broke up". She responds, "At first I didn't know what to say (right, because she's a phone sex virgin), because he (she's just outright smiling and having a good time with this)...". Juan Martinez objects: "Non-responsive. It's yes or no". Please Judge...it really is yes or no. Stop making everyone listen to these drawn out answers.

Nurmi responds with another, "It's not his objection, your honor". Judge Stephens rules, "I'm going to sustain the objection. Ask another question". Thank you.

Nurmi asks, "The day after you broke up with him, was it your hope, did you say, I hope Travis calls and talks dirty to me?". Nurmi, mistake. She could have hung up. She didn't. Jodi answers, "No, I wasn't thinking that". Nurmi continues, "When he did start talking dirty to you, why not hang up the phone?". Any chance her answer will contain some random combination of, "Well, he said he was sorry, he said he was going to change, I really loved him, I had really low self-esteem, I was in denial..."?. Jodi responds, "I wouldn't have hung up on him. He wasn't being mean or anything".

Nurmi tries to fix this, "You just found out he was cheating, and you broke up with him, why, why, would you talk to the guy, Jodi?" Jodi answers, "He promised to change, and I still loved him". Right – just as we thought, she offers two of her prepared, pat answers for staying with a man she now claims was a brutal hypocrite. She gives Nurmi a defiant look. Apparently, he doesn't notice, because Nurmi just continues, "Let me back up a minute, and you may have already answered my question with what you just said, but why even pick up the phone to begin with?". Jodi answers, "I don't know, I guess it was habit. His ring tone came through. His picture was on the screen. I wasn't going to ignore the call".

She just won't admit it, will she? She won't admit that she never broke up with him – it was the other way around. Nobody ever feels good about breaking up with someone – even if they're the person ending the relationship. After the "it's over" conversation ends, the person who hurt the other person with the break-up is usually a little reluctant to pick up the phone when they realize that their ex is calling. It's an emotionally draining experience, and usually, it requires a little time before communication restarts. If she broke up with Travis, she would have heard his ring tone and thought, "Oh...I can't do this right now". She wouldn't say, "Oh, it's Travis. Let's see what he wants". She would look better if she'd just admit that he dumped her, and she was desperately hoping to get him back.

"Yeah it made me feel good that he still desired me and claimed that he didn't really care about anybody else...so I believed him", says Jodi. Why would she believe that? After two weeks of turmoil and a ruined vacation in The Magic-less Kingdom – all based on her knowledge of his cheating – she suddenly believed that everything was going to change? Did he say anything of the sort during her break-up phone conversation with him just 24 hours earlier? According to Jodi, his apology was weak. It didn't seem at all odd to her that he was calling her the very next day to engage in phone sex with her (while adding that everything was going to change, etc.)?

Nurmi wants to know what specific things Travis told her that made her feel so good. She claims she doesn't remember specifics. She says, "He was just saying very nice things to me, and they were erotic, and they were...they made me feel sexy, they made me feel attractive...so I stayed on the phone with him". Poor, poor Travis. He didn't realize that the pig he had just called – if he actually called – wanted more than his money. She wanted his house, his car, his reputation, and his last name. I say this with all sincerity – poor, poor Travis.

Nurmi wants to know what the next contact was. Jodi answers, "We began the routine again, and when he called me at night, and his calls began to get very late, almost to four in the morning, so I just went to sleep and waited for him to call". Nurmi feigns confusion. He wants to know if they

are back together again. Are they boyfriend-girlfriend? She answers, "We are talking about trying it again, but we are not back together again". This directly contradicts what she just said. She claimed that Travis made some pretty big statements – everything was going to change, and no other woman meant anything to him besides her. So, what was the point of saying those things if it wasn't to win her back? For phone sex? Please...
Travis Alexander was not a stupid man, but he didn't realize what he was dealing with. We've since learned from his friends and journal entries that he believed that she way too clingy and she cried too often. Other women he dated testified that Jodi followed Travis and his dates – either in her own car, or by running down the street after his car. Of course, Nurmi will not address any of the evidence – actual, firsthand information that will completely change the dynamic Jodi is now trying to paint. Nurmi won't talk about the journal entry Travis wrote the day Jodi finally left Mesa and went back to California in late March/early April 2008. Why would he? In that entry, Travis expresses relief that she is gone, and he is happy to have experienced an entire day without her.

To Jodi Arias, faux Mormon, this was life or death. Never before had she had a man of this caliber on her line. He was young, popular, successful, and he owned a home that impressed her. Her family home could have probably fit into any quadrant of his home. She wasn't willing to let this one get away. I don't believe he ever understood what the cost of playing with Jodi Arias would be. He trusted his God to protect him. I don't believe he viewed her as anything more than a troubled woman who would move on to another host. What I do believe is that Travis, a Mormon who was desperately conflicted and saddled with guilt, realized that there was no way he could marry this needly, fraudulent woman. If she had shown evidence of a true conversion, he may have overlooked a past that was sordid, according to his faith.

Nurmi throws in a curveball, "When he's wooing you back, is he telling you that he loves you? (who said he was "wooing her back)"? If any of this is true, he's using her, and she's willing to be used. Where's the problem? It's America – two consenting adults. No money is exchanged. This is legal, folks – if we believe any of it.

Jodi claims that Travis said he loved her. Odd, In the phone sex tape, I didn't hear the word, "love". In the multiple texts and emails from Travis, I didn't read the word "love" coming from him. I saw an entry in her journal that said she loved him so completely that she "didn't know any other way to be". Frankly, it all seems rather one-sided. Having gotten the "wooing you back" comment in under the radar, Nurmi begins piling it on. Suddenly, Jodi claims that Travis talked about love, marriage, family, and children frequently. She adds a troubling suffix – it was always in a joking manner. So, we've gone from raunchy phone sex to love, to marriage, to children.

Jodi claims that the two had a future. She believes Travis has the potential to change, and she was hoping he would. Suddenly, the late night phone calls, which come anywhere from midnight to near dawn, are not sexual in nature. No. These are honorable phone calls. According to the surviving half of this couple, the calls are loving, sweet, and he asks about her day. He continued to mention their future, and he always used the words "us" and "we" when speaking of the many years ahead of them. Phone sex was a thing of the past.

Guess how much time this metamorphosis from raunch to love took? It was early July. This miraculous change began to occur just three to seven days after their break-up. Now that's almost as miraculous as what supposedly happened to Joseph Smith at The Sacred Grove in Palmyra, New York.

Oh, hey, what about that job at Ventana Inn and Spa?

Nurmi asks if it was done for the season. Oh, so it was seasonal. Jodi tells us that, if she so desired, the job would have lasted for a year. But, Jodi says, the entire summer was slow for Big Sur. She says she picked up another job at The Big Sur Bakery to supplement her (non-existent) Ventana income. While she had a financial incentive to stay in Big Sur, she claims there was a more compelling reason to move.

Before we get to her move to Mesa, the judge calls the lunch recess. Get thee to thy cage, lying succubus...

I have a mental picture of Jodi Arias. She is on Highway One in California. She's standing right outside the Red House at Ventana Inn and Spa. She's taken a few professional photos of the gravel driveway, just so she can remember that special spot in which she enjoyed post break-up phone sex encounters. She's dragging her hefty bag of belongings behind her, and she's carrying a sign that says, "Mesa or Bust". No, not really. Jodi, employee of the Big Sur Bakery, and self professed, seasonal employee of the Inn, thanked Matt for the squatting rights, and, as she is so fond of saying, hit the road. Jodi, who doesn't have a home, a job, or much of anything else, always has two things: a car and a cellphone.

We're all waiting for the dungeon dweller to emerge from her cage so that she can share with us the "compelling" reason she had to embark on the 11 hour, 685 mile trip that will mark her next move to Mesa, Arizona. Imagine...Mesa, Arizona. Does Jodi even have a friend in Mesa (Travis' friends do not count)? So what's in Mesa...what's in Mesa...what's in Mesa? Hmm... could it be the elusive Mr. Alexander?

We begin with a shot of Judge Stephens. She says, "The record will reflect the presence of the defendant and all counsel. The jury is not present. Miss Arias, both here today, and last week, a number of times, there has been an objection that your answers are non-responsive. I'm going to ask that you listen very carefully to the questions and answer the question you are being asked".

Right. Is this supposed to mean anything to the killer on the stand and her overpaid public defender? Take a guess. The foul flower answers with a weak, “Yes”. Judge Stephens responds, “Let's bring in the jury”.

I assume this is why the pre-lunch bench conference was so long. My only issue with this admonition is that it was done outside of the presence of the jury. If the judge assigned credibility to the objections, perhaps she should have sustained them. The jury should know that according to the law, Jodi has a habit of being non-responsive. I assume my opinion obstructs her constitutional right to a three million dollar tax payer funded defense – oops – I probably shouldn't have mentioned the gold plated defense this common murderer managed to wrangle for herself. Too prejudicial, and all of that BS.

Nurmi begins, “Miss Arias, before we broke for lunch (rub it in Nurmi...you had lunch, she had kitchen scraps, a browning apple, and a stale cookie), we were talking about whether or not you were considering whether or not to move, or stay, in Big Sur, or move on, and when you started talking about moving on, you said that there was a compelling reason to move on. What was that compelling reason?”. Let me guess...Travis told her to? This should be good. I wonder how many hours it took this team of liars and fabricators to come up with something to legitimize stalking.

Jodi answers, “Do you mean move on, or move geographically?”. The arrogance of this woman is stunning. She was just admonished by the judge to stop being non-responsive, and the first answer out of the gate is non-responsive. She knows what Nurmi is referring to – in fact, he overstated it. She introduced the word “compelling”, and she introduced it to justify her move to Mesa. It was the last question before the recess. She isn't being asked about emotionally moving on, and she knows that.

Nurmi will now pretend to clarify the question that is already crystal clear to Jodi (and everyone else). He says, “Move on...move on and leave Big Sur”. Jodi answers, “So, move on, geographically (she does a hand and facial expression that says, “now that we've cleared that up...”). Umm, there were already plans, Travis and I were making plans for me to move to Mesa. He was very upset when I moved to Big Sur. He wanted me to either go to Mesa or stay in southern California, but not go so far. So, I had already made my commitments in Big Sur, and I decided to fulfill those, and, umm, they were expecting me, and the season wasn't panning out to what it was, so I gave my notice there, and my last day was going to be sometime in June or July...I don't remember when...and I was already making plans to move to Mesa, and then I discovered that he was cheating on me, so plans kind of halted, and I was going to move in with my friend, Rachel, and I kinda told her what was up. I didn't want to throw Travis under the bus, so I didn't go into a lot of detail, but I said things weren't really working out with him, and...you know...things weren't working out up here either, and she was encouraging me to come to Mesa anyway, and, umm...kind of make it 'My Mesa'...don't worry about Travis...and Travis was also...”. Interrupted by Nurmi. He says, “Well let's just, let's just stop right there for a minute, and clarify". Clarify? That's the code word for muddy the waters.

There are too many questions here. Jodi said she left her foreclosed home in mid-May, 2007. This was after the "exclusive" conversation she claims to have had with Travis. This was after breaking into his email and learning of his "plan" with racy Mrs. Mormon, as well as the fact that he was talking about a "wild experience" with another woman who sent him hearts and sparkles graphics.

This was after the convention that left Jodi crying for a half an hour in the bathroom. We have heard that he didn't treat her like his girlfriend, but we never heard that he was making plans for her to move to Mesa. She did not mention that – she didn't even hint at it. Now, we learn that she left her seasonal job in June or July. She only got there in May. What we know about June is that they went on their two week trip. What we know about the first week of July is that Travis completely changed and stopped having phone sex with her (after the phone sex incident she reported that would have been June 30, 2007). So, I have to ask, why wasn't this mentioned before?

When Nurmi was asking about their relationship, wouldn't it have been a good time to say, "Oh, by the way, I had to go to Big Sur to work, but Travis was really mad about that. He wanted me in Mesa (his back yard) or southern California (five hours away)" – which, by the way, is a hell of a difference in terms of location. This whole story is a complete fabrication. It also does not line up with what many of Travis' friends have publicly stated about this period of time. They claim that they did see his temper, and his temper was fueled after he found out that Jodi Arias had moved to Mesa. Several of his friends said they heard multiple arguments about that – both on the phone with Jodi, as well as face to face with her. He allegedly asked her why she moved there. According to witnesses, he told her there was absolutely no reason for her to be there. How does she do this? How does she sit in this type of courtroom, swear to tell the truth, and then proceed to absolutely fabricate a story that can be debunked by so many people?

Secondly, who is Rachel, and why would Rachel care if Jodi made Mesa her home? Is Rachel the woman who ultimately told Jodi she had to leave, the woman Jodi said was "a great girl, but a little flighty" during her interrogation? Rachel's flighty? I seem to remember Rachel was not too flighty to have secured her own lease on an apartment. Rachel wasn't the person looking for a life – Jodi was.

This must have been when Travis began to realize that he was in trouble. I don't think he realized it was the type of trouble that would lead to his death, but he must have started to think of ways to "handle" Jodi.

So, now Nurmi is going to "clarify". He'll clarify a work of fiction, but he'll clarify. He asks, "You had planned to move to Mesa before you moved to Big Sur in the summer, right?". Jodi answers, "Yes. We began to talk about that in the spring". Nurmi continues, "And, once you found out he was cheating on you, you then made a decision to go to Big Sur, is that right?". Jodi inhales deeply and says, "No. I moved to Big Sur prior to all of that".

She appears to be going off script. I'm beginning to wonder how often she does this. I'm also beginning to wonder if this is why nine days out of ten, Nurmi doesn't like her. She has so confused the story with dates and cities, that even going back and looking at her testimony is nearly useless in trying to piece things together.

Nurmi is painting the more accurate picture here. It is far more believable, after looking back over her testimony, that she moved to Big Sur because she discovered Travis was cheating on her. She attempts to put a final overall smudge on the dates by saying that she moved to Big Sur prior to "all of that". All of what?

We can go back to February, on the weekend that they became boyfriend-girlfriend, to find her first suspicion of cheating. She went to his home in February believing that he cheated on her with someone named Chelsea over the holidays. Then, after the "exclusive" conversation of February 2, 2007, she snooped through his emails, and she found a sexually suggestive email from Mrs. Mormon that indicated that Travis was "making plans" with a married woman. Jodi was so disturbed by this, that she reported it to Sky Hughes. This was the reason she was only happy for one day when they became a couple.

Then, we have Jodi saying she left her home in Palm Desert in mid-May. If plans were already in place to move to Mesa, having been made in the spring, then why not just go from Palm Desert to Mesa? Why go to Big Sur for seasonal work that never materialized? That is a very reasonable question if you look at the dates she reported. She gets to Big Sur in mid-May, she leaves on her two week trip in mid-June (she believes they boarded the plane on June 18), but then she reports that the seasonal work was over by June or July (probably June). So when did she have time to work at Ventana? Was it a three week job? Doubtful. In any event, according to Jodi, she knew about his cheating prior to that two week trip in June, and that's why the trip was so miserable. So, where in all of this is there room for a spring time conversation that resulted in plans for her to move to Mesa? According to Jodi, she always believed Travis was cheating on her – at least through all of the "official" months. Suddenly, the previously undisclosed plans to move to Mesa occurred "prior to all of that" (meaning his cheating)? Thank God these jurors were listening to the details.

Nurmi continues, "So, you were planning on staying in Big Sur until he had this conversation where he was loving with you, correct?". Jodi responds, "The plan was to stay in Big Sur, fulfill the commitments I made, and then move to Mesa". But, she didn't fulfill the commitments she made. If she was, as she claims, working at Ventana Inn and Spa, she gave them her notice and left before the end of the season. She claims that the season was slow, and while every rating and review site I've looked at has plenty of reviews up for the period she claims was so slow, if that was the case, they would let her go. She wouldn't have to submit her resignation. Secondly, what about her job at the Big Sur Bakery? Was that not an obligation? She obviously walked out on that obligation as well. She cannot make all of these scenarios fit.

We all know what happened. Jodi is not a planner. By her own admission, she crosses bridges when she comes to them. She knew her house was going to be padlocked, and she knew she could not stay there indefinitely without paying the mortgage. Instead of making firm plans, responsible plans, adult plans, she started whining to Travis about her impending eviction. She probably did hint around about moving to Mesa. That much, I do believe. However, I think he made it very clear that she wasn't staying with him, and that he could not give her money for a security deposit, and without a job, she couldn't pay rent. He was probably very practical about it, and that infuriated her (and led her to add the lie, the one she wishes were actually true, that Travis was very mad about her moving all the way to Big Sur. It never happened). That's when she called Matt, in an absolute panic, and asked if there was any work at Ventana. I don't believe Ventana wanted Jodi Arias back. I think Matt said she could stay with him for a little while, and it wasn't that difficult to pull off because half of the time she wouldn't even be there. But, I believe there came a time when Matt told her, early July to be precise, that she had to go. That's when I believe she got into her car and drove to Mesa. I have no idea where she stayed when she got there, and I'm actually quite curious to see what she comes up with.

Nurmi asks, "What were the commitments, in terms of time?". Good question, Nurmi. These jurors are adding up the months, and it's not making sense. Jodi answers, "In terms of time? About two months, two and half months". Again, impossible. Two months would mean that she was leaving Big Sur in mid-July. Two and half months would mean she was leaving in the beginning of August. Liar.

She just said she was out of there in June or July (which indicates, for most people, late June/early July). She could have recited exact dates, if the defense had just requested the employment records. I wonder why they didn't?

Nurmi continues, "So, you fulfilled your commitments. Why would you decide then, getting to my point, why would you decide that moving to Mesa would be a good idea, considering what had happened prior?". Oh, does he mean the cheating? Jodi answers, "Well, I was on the fence about it (oh, come on). I was going to move to Montclair (which would be 330 miles to the south). There was another woman, umm, that I was working with at the Big Sur Bakery that was moving there, and that's closer to, it's in southern California, it's closer to where I used to live (she's flying through this part of her testimony)...it's within an hour's drive from Palm Desert. Umm, so there were two choices, and I decided to go to Mesa because Travis painted a nice picture of all the benefits of moving to Mesa...he said it's a strong Mormon community, there are a lot of church members, umm...there are always other LDS single women looking for roommates...he said I could store all of my things at his house...he said that I could sock away more money...umm...just benefits, benefits".

Did Travis ever say, "Oh, wow. This might be fate. Move here, honey. I'll help you. Let's give this our best shot. Let's be together. Let's back up. Let's do this right. Let me show you what you mean to me. Let me take you to wonderful places...just the two of us. They don't even have to be wonderful places – they can be random camping sites, where we're alone and really getting to know each other. Let me introduce you to my family. We'll go to them, or better yet, I'll invite them here, and together, we'll make an amazing meal that will blow them out of the water. Let's go to exotic restaurants and just enjoy being served dishes we can't pronounce, or let's just pop in the car and go to McDonald's and gorge on milkshakes and French fries when the mood hits. Let's talk. Let's laugh. Let's listen to music together – the stuff I like, the stuff you like. Let's turn it up so loud that the floor is vibrating! I can't imagine having you so close that we could actually rent a movie, order Chinese food, turn off the cell phones, make some popcorn, and enjoy a Friday night together on the couch. Let me take you to church. Let's be a couple. I just have this feeling that we may have a beautiful destiny together. What do you say"?

No, according to Jodi, he was a storage unit, a bed to occupy once in a while, and a prospective roommate who could help subsidize the rent for young Mormon women waiting to be married in the temple.

Nurmi asks, "Benefits to you, or benefits to him?". Jodi answers, "Benefits to us both. Well, he was painting the benefits that I would reap, if I moved there". Nurmi continues, "Did you believe he was also seeking benefits?". Jodi answers, "Of course. He said we could hang out more and figure things out".

By now, we all know what "hang out" means when it comes from the mouth of Jodi Arias. It is her way of saying "foreplay". There is not one instance of "hanging out" that hasn't ended with Jodi engaging in some sexual act. Another mistake. You don't sit on the stand and, after being asked why you decided to make a drastic and long distance move, cite as your primary motive inclusion in a strong religious community which absolutely forbids all forms of premarital sex, and then claim that you'd also get to have more pre-marital sex once the move was completed. Every time I think of her excuse as to why she was engaging in premarital sex, I wonder why nobody on the jury simply asked, "Did it ever occur to you to google 'The Law of Chastity'? You said you were conflicted about it, and you certainly knew your way around the internet".

Nurmi read my mind. He asked, "Hanging out and figuring things out. Did hanging out involve sexual activity?". Jodi, lured in by the strong Mormon community with virginal women looking for roommates, said, "Yes". Nurmi continues, "When you moved to Mesa, how far from Travis were you?". Jodi adjusts her glasses, and replies, "I don't know if you know mileage, but Travis lived over by Signal Butte and Elliot, and I lived over by Greenfield and Broadway". Nurmi continues, "Do you have any idea how long it took you to drive over to Travis' house?". Jodi responds, "Well, depending on traffic, fifteen minutes, maybe twenty". In the large scale of things, that qualified as his backyard, no?

Nurmi asks, "So you live about 15 minutes away. We heard other witnesses testify, but tell us about where the ward was. Where you lived, was that in the same ward as Mr. Alexander?". Now, just wait a minute. Forget what ward she was living in, can we get some information as to where she's living, if she signed a lease, is she paying rent? Come on, there are more important details in this significant move than what ward she was in. Even a Mormon would agree with that.

Jodi answers, "No", to the ward question. That's supposed to comfort us. That's supposed to be proof that she wasn't stalking him. Nurmi continues, "Was that an issue to him, from your understanding?". Jodi responds, "Umm, it became an issue". Okay...moving right along. Nurmi asks, "Why to your understanding was that a concern?". Jodi answers, "Well, umm, as soon as I moved in with Rachel, about...I'd say a week and a half, she approached me and informed me that she and...". Juan Martinez objects. He says, "Hearsay". His objection is inaudible, and Nurmi is instructed to rephrase his question.

Nurmi asks, "Well, let's do it this way then. You moved, you mentioned a person named Rachel. Is that who you moved in with originally?". Jodi answers, "Yes...and her boyfriend". Oh, a living in sin situation. Here's the big difference, Jodi: this man is going to marry Rachel. She has a diamond ring on her finger. You, by contrast, will have your butt thrown into the street once their religion takes over – and it will.

Nurmi replies, "Okay. And how long did you live with Rachel and her boyfriend?". Jodi responds, "About a week and a half". Why did I just laugh? Did Jodi just say a week and a half? Isn't that technically ten days? Isn't Rachel the architect of the "My Mesa" campaign? Oh, I must hear the details of this ten day occupancy.

I guess Jodi didn't like the expressions on the jury members' faces. Nurmi is already saying "And...", while Jodi interrupts with, "Well, maybe two and a half weeks". Does Jodi think this type of huge move is more palatable is she has secured a roof over her head for twenty days as opposed to ten? Yes, I think that's what's she saying.

Nurmi continues, "Okay. And after this two and a half week period, it is time for you to move on, for personal reasons, is that what you're telling us?". Jodi responds, "Yes, they eloped". Yes, I remember something about this. It doesn't really matter, but it had something to do with an official ceremony, a temple ceremony, blah, blah, blah. Bottom line? This couple found some way to put Jodi Arias out on the street, and if the tenets of their faith helped them do that, more power to them.

Jodi is now expecting a jury to believe that Rachel Whoever coerced her to move to Mesa and make it her own Mesa, and Rachel, the person on the lease of the property, screwed Jodi Arias out of a roof over her head after 20 days? Please. A normal person might encounter two or three of these odd situations in a lifetime, but as it stands, the life of Jodi Arias is defined by these odd encounters. So, what's a California resident fraudulently lured to Arizona to do? Well, let's turn the page of this comic book to find out.

Nurmi ties the bow neatly on top of the package, and he says, “So they got married, and it was time for you to find a new place to live, right?”. Jodi says, “Yes, they were newlyweds”. How convenient. Nurmi continues, “And, you said the issue of ward boundaries, or, ward, errr, became an issue. Can you explain that to us?”. Well, of course she can, Mr. Nurmi. You've rehearsed this 16 times. Jodi responds, “Ahh, yes. It became imperative that I move out as quickly as possible...umm...they were going to have another civil wedding ceremony after eloping in Vegas. So, what I did, what I went to was an institute center, which was a place in the church where any young adults can go for scripture study, or things like that. There was a bulletin up there with different places for rent, so I wrote down a few price numbers that were in my price range. I called a girl, umm, I think she lived in Gilbert, she said that that listing was old, but she directed me to LDS Housing dot net, and so I went there, and I found a few within my price range – I called them all – umm...two returned my call. One was a girl named Brenda. She lived in Gilbert. She had a brand new house – she said she was looking for a roommate. She had not moved into the house yet because she was in the process of buying it, and the mortgage lender hadn't funded yet, and so, she didn't have her keys yet, but we went by the house together, we peeked in the windows, she showed me the property – it was brand new, it had never been lived in, it was a really great ward, she said everyone in the ward is really awesome...so, I was excited about that. But then, the days just go on and she wasn't getting her keys, and Rachel and her new husband were kind of like...uhhh...they kind of wanted their own space, so I went to LDS housing dot net again, and I called back the same number as before, not Brenda's, but the other one, and she told me that there was a room available for rent. So, I went and checked it out. The house was nice. It was in a great neighborhood, it was available immediately, it was in my price range, and I asked her which ward it was in, she told me it was in the University Six ward, which was not the ward that Travis was in at the time...”. ZZZzzzzzzzzz. Oh, excuse me. I dozed off. Nurmi's voice startled me. He asks, “Why did you ask which ward it was it was in?”. She over talks him at the end of his question, and she says, “I didn't want to land in the same ward as Travis”. Nurmi, in his smartass tone of voice, asks, “Why not?”.

How long will this game go on?

Jodi answers, “Well, one, I figured, he didn't treat me very well while I was at church (snore...sorry), and as his girlfriend, he ignored me, he didn't introduce me, he flirted with other women, so I figured if he was capable of treating me that way as his girlfriend, who knew what other humiliating behaviors we were capable of now that we were exes. I didn't want to show up at his ward like that”. Okay, right, whatever. So, Travis displayed this behavior for two church services. Wow, she's packed a lot of disrespect into two weeks.

Nurmi continues, "And to your understanding, did he not want you in his ward as well?". Jodi responds, "Umm...we had talked about it, yes. He had said that now that we are not together...". There's an objection from Juan Martinez. He says, "The question was whether or not she knows that he wants her there or not". I didn't hear the ruling. I heard Nurmi toss his pen on the podium.

Nurmi continues, "To your understanding, did Mr. Alexander want to make sure that you were in a different ward?". Jodi answers, "I don't know if he went that far. We just discussed being in different wards".

We begin with the judge summoning the attorneys to the bench. Nurmi has implied that Travis wanted Arias to wear a French maid's uniform to clean his house. We all know the implication: For $12.50 an hour, Travis wanted Jodi to clean his house in some Frederick's of Hollywood maid costume. Every man and every woman has their own personal image of what this may have actually looked like. The defense is counting on that. Juan Martinez has no problem with the photo that is attached to the email, but he has a problem with the text because it contains hearsay.

As the attorneys approach, the camera catches Mitigation Specialist, Maria de la Rosa. Once again, she's in the prime camera spot. She looks directly at Juan Martinez and gives him a look of disgust. This woman is completely unprofessional. It appears that she and Jodi have some sort of personal relationship developing.

As the white noise blares, we're treated to yet another shot of the Yreka Fan Club. Stunning. Bill and Sandy Arias are whispering and smiling about something. Even their Jodi-look-alike son cranes his neck toward his parents so he can get in on the first row fun. To his credit, he doesn't crack a smile. I don't know what these two middle-aged parents find so amusing. Their aimless, chronically unemployed, promiscuous daughter, indicted for first degree murder, is about to talk about some guy asking her to scrub his toilets and pair his sweat socks while she's parading around in stripper-wear for a whopping $12.50 an hour.
There's a shot of Jodi. She's waiting patiently for the bench conference to conclude. Her eyes had been fixed on the Yreka Fan Club, but now they are lowered. A shot of the Alexander family tells us why she will not look up. Samantha is staring right at her. Samantha has an intimidating stare, and, in my opinion, she is one of the siblings who bears the strongest resemblance to the victim. I love knowing that this is making Jodi squirm. I don't think she likes these white noise bench conferences. There's no Nurmi voice to focus on – nothing to shield her from the contemptuous stares of her "haters". If she thinks this is bad, just wait until she is finally marched down the corridors of Perryville Prison holding her folded blanket and mini-pillow in her hands. I'll bet those ladies will have a lot to say to her.

Nurmi begins, "Jodi, let's back up a step". French maid costume? Of course he wants to back up a little. We'll probably end up hearing about every inch of this non-existent costume. He continues,

"Mr. Alexander proposed this arrangement to you in August, 2007. Is that accurate?". Jodi responds, "Yes". Nurmi continues, "Did you accept this arrangement?". Jodi answers, "I hesitated, but when he said it's a few hundred extra a month, I said yes because I needed extra money". Sure, she hesitated. Can she make it sound plausible at least once? Can there be a single instance in which she says anything was her idea?

Juan Martinez is correct – she is non-responsive. The answer would be "yes". She certainly didn't need to add another nineteen words to that answer.

Somehow, she thinks that saying she hesitated prior to accepting, or that she accepted because needed the money, is going to alter the fact that she chose to be Travis' naughty cleaning lady.

Nurmi continues, "And at the time you accepted this offer that Mr. Alexander made to you, were you still sexually active with him?". If she says yes, then she really looks really bad. Sorry, if he's taking her to bed and only helping her out financially if she performs domestic chores, he's not trying to impress her. This is not a romantic relationship – it's quid pro quo. I cannot imagine my husband degrading me this way when we were dating. He would have said, "How much do you need every month?". Then again, I wasn't using him as an ATM. Now that I think about it, I remember cleaning his apartment a few times as a sign of affection (coupled with my distaste for messy bachelor apartments), not because it was my job.

Well, alright then; Jodi says that she was sexually active with her employer. She looks worse, if that's possible, than three minutes ago.

Jodi is doing something she doesn't normally do – she's touching various areas of her face. It started earlier in the testimony. Now the face touching has evolved into neck touching. Her hand continually moves to the side of her neck. She's doing this so consistently that I decided to look up the significance of this gesture. It's indicates deception. Big surprise.

Nurmi asks, "Did he ever express the desire to have sex with you while you were working for him?". Juan Martinez objects: "Mischaracterization (inaudible)". It certainly is a mischaracterization. She just said that they were sexually involved while she worked as his cleaning lady, so we already know the answer. What Nurmi is now implying is that he had sex with her while she working. May I ask, who the hell cares? Can we get to the day she brutally slaughtered him in his bathroom? Isn't that slightly more important than this nonsense?

The objection is overruled, and Jodi is free to add some more embellishments: "Umm, occasionally". Nurmi asks, "And how did you feel about that? You were there to clean his house, and he's having sex with you?". No Nurmi, I think you have that backwards. She was there to have sex with him, she complained that's she's overdrawn at the bank, and he lets her clean is house for a hundred bucks.

Let's get back to the fantasy (since it's going to be part of the court transcript): Travis is chasing Jodi and her bucket of soapy water all around the house with his cattle prod extended. Napoleon is nipping at his heels, but Travis is determined to get his house wench down the basement stairs because that's where his make-shift sex dungeon is all plugged in and ready to go. Did I go too far? What's next, allegations of white slavery?

As to the implied workplace sexual harassment, the slutty servant replies, "It didn't bother me. We were still intimate, he was paying attention to me, he was being nice, he focused on me, making me feel attractive, so it wasn't unpleasant". Forget scented candles to set the mood. If Arias is to be believed, an uncapped bottle of bleach or a spritz of ammonia are an economical alternative to aromatic enhancements. I wonder if Bill and Sandy are still smiling.

Nurmi, now that he's been forced to make his client admit that she willingly and happily blurred the lines between work and pleasure, will now bring up the French maid's outfit – again. However, this time around, it won't be nearly as kinky. This time around, it will sound like what it was: guy hires poverty stricken girl (who happens to be a suicidal friend and occasional carnal playmate) to clean his house because he is trying to teach her that you have to earn your money (unless he intends to marry her, in which case he would, most likely, give her the money without strings attached), and between loads of laundry, the two begin having sex, which, according to the girl, was their custom. One of them suggests lingerie to enhance their mutual arousal. Both agree that's it's a pretty cool idea. How scandalous! How X-Rated! How pornographic! If I'm not mistaken, lingerie companies bring in billions every year because couples of all stripes think this way (sans the housekeeping foreplay).

Nurmi asks, "Did he ever ask you to wear a particular uniform? Jodi answers, "Yes". Nurmi asks, "How would you describe that uniform for us?". Seriously? Nurmi is putting the word "uniform" on this? Frankly, if Travis Alexander wanted to pay someone from a topless maid service to clean his refrigerator, what business is it of Nurmi's (or Jodi's)?
Jodi was not compelled to do anything (beside move to Mesa). The only way this attempt to paint Jodi as a victim might work is if she had been certified as mentally impaired. That isn't the case. Her reading comprehension test proved that. She was completely free, able bodied, and of allegedly normal intelligence. Maybe the bigger issue, the one worth investigating, is why she chose to screw around while pretending to clean a house when she should have gotten herself a real job. If she had enough maturity and motivation to do that, we wouldn't be having this juvenile and pointless "uniform" discussion. Dissecting pillow talk, especially pillow talk that might have come from the mouth of a young man who has been forever silenced, is a grotesque intrusion. It doesn't sit well with me, and I believe it isn't sitting well with those charged with judging the gossipy murdereress disclosing the contents of very private conversations.

Jodi is ready to describe the proposed uniform. She begins, "The picture he sent me was a picture of a woman, a voluptuous woman with long blond hair in a low cut French maid outfit. She had, umm, stockings that went up to her thighs, stilettos, umm, it was a black and white outfit with a little apron, she had her foot up on something...". I wonder how many men in that jury box felt the need to adjust themselves by the time she got to "stockings that went up to her thighs, stilettos...". Even the old guys probably felt a jolt.

Welcome to the dark nether regions between every adolescent boy's mattress and box spring. So what?

Ironic, isn't it? Jodi doesn't remember shooting, stabbing, and slitting a man's throat, but she remembers the lingerie model had her foot "up on something". Well, to be fair, maybe she was pissed off about that and remembered feeling that it was unfair. After all, finding size 12 stilettos is no easy feat.

Nurmi continues, "Jodi, I'm going to show you a picture from exhibit 395...". Juan Martinez speaks up, "Objection. This is not in evidence. It cannot be published to the jury". Nurmi counters, "It just...well, he didn't object to it a few minutes ago". Judge Stephens is going to give the boys a time out. She says, "Counsel approach, please".

It's another lengthy bench conference. Jodi's quite interested. She wants that catalog picture published for the jury. She wants the men to be lulled into a state of sexual frustration. She wants their minds wandering. She's hoping they're remembering or conjuring sexual images, and suddenly they have to pull themselves back to court, flushed and embarrassed, hoping that the images they were just enjoying isn't showing on their faces. When that happens, they lose minutes of testimony. When that happens, they begin to connect Jodi Arias, on a subconscious level, to something very pleasant and desired.

The camera lands on the Yreka Fan Club again. Bill is confused about something. He wants Sandy to explain something to him. Her hands are moving...her daughter apparently shares that habit with her. Finally, Sandy gives up, and she mouths a very clear, "never mind". Bill obeys. He sits up and looks at his darling daughter.

I'm not certain what happened at the bench. We hear some stomping around, which, I assume, is Nurmi. The camera catches him back at home base – the defense table. He is looking at documents that are stapled together. He reads the first page, and then he flips to the second page. Jennifer Willmott takes her hot pink pen and begins to write large block letters on her note pad. Then, we see Juan Martinez, already seated and quietly staring at Jodi, and then toward the jury. Judge Stephens says, "Ladies and gentleman, you are free to stand in place. We have two minutes. Feel free to do so". That works for me, Judge Stephens. I'm game for anything that runs the clock out.

Lots of silence. I like the silence. Two minutes has morphed into thirteen minutes. Miscalculation? Stalling? Who knows, but the moment is gone. Nobody, male or female, is thinking about the voluptuous blond model in the thigh high stockings. Everybody is wondering why this feels more like a wake than a trial. Judge Stephens interrupts the silence: "Alright, ladies and gentleman. I'm going to ask that you go back to the jury room, and use your card to let yourselves in. We will be back with you shortly. I don't know what's happened. I'm going to go and find out". We can assume she'll be asking Nurmi. He's the only individual in the room doing anything besides staring in various directions. He's reading paperwork.

We all know that Judge Stephens is not about to go knocking on desks to find out what's happened. Everyone stands for the jury. Everyone sits when they have left the room. We hear some banging around, and then Nurmi's voice begins. He says, "Judge, we...". Judge Stephens says, "Why don't you come forward, please". Nurmi says, "Okay".

More silence. At the 17 minute mark, Jodi decides that her left breast needs adjusting. Apparently her push up bra or sewn in cups are irritating her. She scratches, she lifts, she adjusts. Her breast rises, and then it falls. Thank goodness the jury is not here to see her play with her left breast. After adjusting herself, Jodi is thirsty. Funny, when the jury is not here, she uses her right hand to grab her water cup. Her drinking looks normal. Actually, I figured out how she makes that weird contortion when she drinks with her left hand – and it is a contortion. Try this at home. It isn't dangerous, just slightly uncomfortable. Take your left hand and grab your glass. However, the trick is to extend your fingers around the glass so that they are completely visible to anyone on your right hand side – your fingertips should be at the 5 or 6 position on the clock. Now lift the cup and drink. You just did the Jodi Arias. She does this so that they jury – seated to her right – will hopefully notice her left ring finger (the one that will be forever without a wedding ring). She sliced tendons in that finger the day she killed Travis. The knife, wet with blood, slipped and cut her finger deeply. She has never admitted to that. She has given at least four different excuses for her very deformed finger (the latest being that Travis kicked it and broke it).

Almost twenty minutes have passed. The jury is back. Nurmi has been instructed to continue, and the judge says that an exhibit has been admitted.

Nurmi says, "Jodi, before we went on break, we talked about a picture you received. If I may approach your honor.". Your honor grants Nurmi's request. Nurmi continues while approaching the killer, "...of a woman in a French maid's uniform. Do you recognize that as being that picture?". Oh, will we get to see the scandalous image? Jodi looks at the exhibit and says, "Yes". Juan Martinez has some kind of interchange with the judge. It's inaudible. Nurmi places something on the overhead projector.

Oh, there's the tiny image. Nurmi's victory is a black and white photograph, and it's really small. Jodi forgot about the little cloth tiara type hat the French maid is wearing. I guess Jodi's a leg gal.

From what I can see, I'd tend to label that woman more of a Scandinavian maid – Swedish comes to mind. I'm smiling. I can't believe it took 20 minutes to get something more tame than what you'd see on a contemporary music video up on that screen. This is such a waste of time and money.

Just so you know, the flesh that is exposed on this woman is minimal – as far as lingerie goes. This "uniform" is reasonably easy to find if your google "modest French maid lingerie". In Nurmi's tiny black and white photo, the model's arms look like they're covered. They aren't, but unless you had the color copy, that would be difficult to determine. Oh, the gloves, stockings and shoes don't come with the package, which is currently selling on Ebay for $9.19, Australian currency.

Nurmi asks, "Did you receive this before or after you began working for him". Please don't tell me that Jodi is going to try and look offended by this image. This is not what I thought it was going to be, and I'm actually glad Nurmi was allowed to publish it. Anyway, Jodi answers, "It was after we made the agreement, but before I started".

Nurmi asks, "How did you feel in receiving this?". What did she receive? Was it the costume or the picture of the costume? Nurmi is implying that she received the costume, but she didn't – just the picture of the costume.

Nurmi asks, "You felt like he meant it as a joke?". What the hell is going on here? Is she defending him? Nurmi doesn't like Jodi's answers. He replies, "Did your feelings on the subject change when he was having sex with you, you know, when you were supposedly working for him". Umm, probably not, Nurmi. That outfit is not Jodi's speed. Jodi's not going for it. She makes a "meh, who knows?" expression and says, "Umm, on the uniform, no, but as far as the implication, I mean, I kinda knew that was implied, sometimes".

Nurmi is on a roll, after all, he fought a 20 minute battle – sitting down, of course – to get this picture published. He continues, "That that was kind of implied sometimes? Meaning, if you were available to have sex while cleaning his house, that was part of the deal?". Juan Martinez objects: leading. Nurmi is told to rephrase (although I wish the judge would tell just the defender of Arizona child molesters to stop with his phony moral indignation about a stupid, relatively modest, photo of lingerie that some guy allegedly suggested his chamber maid would wear the next time she was ready to perform oral sex on him).

Nurmi blathers on: "Did you believe, when you were working for him, that he was entitled to have sexual access to you?". Oh, come on. I'm not a lawyer, and I'm ready to object. If this isn't leading, what is? She was a willing participant in any sex they had – probably an aggressor most of the time. Can some adult in the room please stand up and put this nonsense into perspective? Yes, Nurmi, you may not like it, but he was absolutely entitled to have sexual access to her when she was offering it – and we all know she was offering it. It's called consensual sex between adults.

Jodi responds, "I wouldn't say that. I needed money. We were already...". Juan Martinez objects. He says, "She says she wouldn't say that". True enough, but who knows how the judge will rule. I would have let her finish. She's about to explain her morality to the world. She needed money. What currency does a morally bankrupt, barely employed, homeless, high school drop-out deal in? Does it really need to be spelled out? Seriously, she's not having an issue with sex for money. It's very clear.

Nurmi is told to ask another question. Nurmi asks, "Why did you not feel that way?". Jodi responds, "I was already intimate with him, and I had feelings for him, so it wasn't, it didn't, I didn't correlate the two. Usually, I stuck with my duties there. It was generally during the day. He worked also, and I didn't want to distract him from that (but ultimately she did distract him "from that", and he'll remain distracted until the earth disintegrates). Sometimes he would come to me, bump into me, suggestively, and he'd say, oh excuse me, and then it would happen again, and it would lead to something...sometimes he would just come up and kiss me".

Nurmi is hoping that the jurors are picturing all of this excusing and bumping while Jodi is wearing the maid's uniform. There isn't a hint of testimony or evidence that would lead any juror to believe this outfit was actually purchased, let alone worn.

Attorney and client seemed to be locked in a dispute. Attorney is telling his murdering client that she needs to act like Travis psychologically degraded her to the point of being his private prostitute. Murdering client will not wear that mask. Nope. Travis wanted her. She gave it up. He took nothing. Jodi Arias, the biggest "skin for stuff" woman we've seen on the witness stand in long time, does not want to be painted with the promiscuity brush. Fine. A rose by any other name...

Can we PLEASE get a little closer to the day she committed murder? Isn't that what this is about?

Nurmi continues, "How long did you clean his house? Work as his maid?". Jodi answers, "Almost the entire time I lived in Mesa". What a brute. He continued to support this low income, faux Mormon until he was finally able to drive her back to her northern California tribe in April, 2008. I repeat, what a brute.

Nurmi asks, "Did he always pay you?". Jodi answers, "He always paid me, in one form or another". Nurmi asks, "What do you mean by that?". Forget it, Nurmi. Jodi Arias has already made it clear that she will not make herself a prostitute. She will not ascribe a monetary value to any sexual acts he may have performed on her or vice versa. Suffice it to say that she wrote plenty of emails and journal entries that indicate that he allowed her to use his home and eat his food...whenever. That cost him money.

Oh, I just wanted to interject. I haven't seen Nurmi refer to the written portion of this French maid email. That's the portion Juan Martinez originally objected to. Hopefully, it's been precluded.

Jodi answers, "Sometimes (definition: occasionally, rather than all of the time), it was usually (definition: under normal conditions; generally – she can't have it both ways), but sometimes it was when we went on trips together, so sometimes...we always split the trips 50/50. He kept meticulous track of the cost. He could always figure it down to the dollar – who owed who what, and how he reached the figure, so sometimes if he owed me money for the house, he would just eat the cost on traveling". Nurmi has no issue with this, as long as Jodi was always compensated, which she claims she was.

In the nightmare that won't end, Nurmi says, "Now earlier today, you mentioned, when you moved back to Mesa, there was a clandestine relationship that went on behind closed doors. Was there a sexual relationship that took place in other places besides his bedroom?". Jodi answers, "Yes". Nurmi asks, "Where did those occur". Juan Martinez is right. This testimony is nothing but sex, sex, and more sex.

Jodi answers, "Usually when we...". Juan Martinez objects with lack of foundation. He wants specific date if she's going to talk about this. The objection is sustained. Juan's writing now. If Jodi gives a date, she had better be able to back it up under cross examination.

Nurmi asks, "Where else did you have sexual interaction with Mr. Alexander?". Jodi responds, " Umm, sometimes it was...". Nope, Jodi, that "sometimes" is not going to fly. Dates, dear. Please, be specific. Juan Martinez interrupts. He says, "Same objection. We just need to know when".

Nurmi responds, "Well,...". The objection is overruled. Why was the first objection as to dates sustained and the second overruled? This isn't making sense to me. Is it making sense to the jury? Jodi is advised by the judge that she may answer the question, and she may answer it as vaguely as she likes. Jodi responds, "Sometimes it was in my car, and sometimes it was in a parking lot, because it was when we traveled".

Alright, I'm going to say it. I do not want the judge replaced. That would be a disaster. However, I cannot understand how she was faced with two identical objections in the space of one minute and sustained one objection and overruled the other. I fear that she might have sent a message to the jury, and that message was that she wasn't sure how to handle the intricacies of this case. This has happened over and over again. I want to give her the benefit of the doubt, but I seriously wish this case had been overseen by a more experienced jurist (this was her first DP case).

Nurmi continues, "Now, when you mentioned your car, earlier in your testimony you told us about the interaction that took place after he gave you the Book of Mormon and you went to Starbucks, is that what we're talking about, or are we talking about other occasions in your car?". Jodi responds,

"Umm, other occasions, but the same kind of thing". Nurmi continues, "And did those occur before you moved to Mesa, or did they occur after you moved back to, moved to Mesa?". Jodi answers, "I know they occurred after I moved to Mesa".

More sex: "You also mentioned that sexual behavior was happening on these trips you took with him as well, right?". Jodi answers, "That's right". Again, so what? Nurmi continues, "And you also mentioned your house in Mesa. Is that the one you shared with Rachel, or are you speaking of the other home you moved into a couple of weeks later?". Jodi answers, "The other home. He wouldn't go to Rachel's house".

I'm starting to get seriously irritated by Jodi's ability to add prejudicial declarations to a majority of her answers. The correct answer to the last question was, "the other home". However, she had to throw another hint of hypocrisy in by adding the suffix, "he wouldn't go to Rachel's house". I completely understand Juan Martinez' repetitive statements of "yes or no". I completely understand his anger. It is justified. All the jury needs are facts.

A man is dead, and it seems like what really matters is that his killer is allowed to disguise herself as a meek, eyeglass wearing, intellectual human being, while throwing out anything that might help her save her own pathetic life. At this point, it feels great to know that she actually thought she'd serve a small sentence and walk out a free woman. She actually believed she'd make millions with her book, her art, and her photography.

Nurmi is just prurient. This line of questioning will do nothing to impact her guilt or innocence. This is nothing more than trying to incite the jurors to paint mind pictures of naked Jodi. He asks, "Is there a specific location in the home where this sexual activity took place?". Jodi answers, "In the bedroom". Wow, shocking, and so offbeat. Nurmi wants the jury to picture Jodi bending over in other areas of the house. Where else, he asks, did they have sexual activity? Jodi answers, "A couple of times...the front porch". Jodi had to be reined in here (probably because Travis' home did not have a front porch). She was about to describe the encounter, but Nurmi had to remind her that he only wanted the location.

Nurmi clarifies that the front porch sex happened at Jodi's house. We don't even know the name of the person Jodi was allegedly living with when she was renting a bedroom in a house that had a front porch. We haven't gotten that information – just some "great girl" from LDShousing.net who happened to live less than ten minutes from Travis Alexander.

This is so obviously rehearsed. Nurmi never asked her whose front porch they had sex on, but they both knew what she was referring to. Suddenly, Nurmi must have realized that the jurors were still back in Travis' bedroom, and he clarifies that the front porch was at Jodi's house. Anyway, in response to the question about the front porch sex, Jodi says, "It was something he wanted to try, since I had known him, since 2006, it was something he expressed that he wanted to do...umm, he had a list of fantasies that he wanted to fulfill...ummm, and he wanted to show up, get out of his car...". Thank God Juan Martinez objects with "Beyond the scope".

I guess Juan won that little battle. Nurmi is instructed to ask another question. Jodi apologizes. Nurmi, the arrogant loser, says, "No need to apologize, Jodi". Nurmi, if anyone in that courtroom needs to apologize, it's Jodi Arias.

Nurmi says, "Describe for us, if you will, this fantasy he had involving you being on the porch of your home". Jodi answers, "Okay...it was...it was...he wanted to drive up to the house...we couldn't do it in Palm Desert, so now that I was in Mesa, it was a different kind of porch, it was more private, there was a huge column, a huge square, a stucco column that offered more privacy, there was a big bush that created a shadow from the street lights, and this would occur at night, late at night, and so, he wanted to drive up to the home, he wanted to get out of the car, have me come out of the house, give him oral sex, and he wanted to ejaculate on my face, and then he wanted to get back in his car, and drive away without saying a single word".

She vacillates between looking embarrassed, looking aroused, and stifling a grin. I can think of two other bodily functions he may have suggested initiating on her person, neither involving reproductive organs, that might have sent her the same message – perhaps slightly more indelible, however. The message: "You are a whore". Ejaculate on her face? I just can't...

The camera just showed the Alexander family. I think Steven may cry.

We've seen how low Jodi was willing to go to please her man; a man she doesn't want to share a ward with because, based on his prior behavior, she had no idea what other humiliating experiences (rich choice of words, don't you think?) she might be subjected to if they actually shared the same public space. Let's see if she'll actually crawl around in the dirt for him.

Nurmi, who is beyond being comfortable with the gutter talk, wants to know if the fantasy she just described required her to be naked. Jodi says, "I was dressed". I found it interesting that she said Travis wanted to approach "the home". Most people would say, "the house". But, let's not forget, a house is not a home. A house is merely a structure, while a home is a place of family, warmth, comfort, and security. It's also pretty big on the Mormon Top Ten list.

Nurmi walks around his podium. He never ventures far from it. This may be a cheap shot, but he's got it coming: he reminds me of a baby elephant chained to a stake in the ground. He thuds around, we know he's moving, but we know he's not leaving that tiny area. His head is down. He's thinking. Finally, he says, "And how many times did he do this?". I wonder if Juan Martinez is going to try for the dates again. He won once, lost a second time. Maybe he'll go for two out of three.

Jodi answers, "Um, two or three...". Yes. Juan Martinez objects. He wants dates. Judge Stephens overrules his objection. I doubt this will discourage him. He'll probably continue making this objection every time he thinks it's applicable. Jodi finishes her answer: "Uh, two or three times. I can only remember two, specifically". If she only "remembers" two, why is she allowed to add another incident on top of the first two lies?

Nurmi continues, "Tell us about those two occasions?". Excuse me. Didn't she just finish doing that? Does he want more detail? How much more detail could he possibly extract from this? Seriously, what does he want to know?

While Jodi pretends to be thinking, Nurmi interrupts. He says, "Tell us about the first occasion". Jodi answers, "Well, the first occasion occurred just like I described, and we talked later the next day. The second occasion (she pauses and lets out an audible breath to let us all know she'd rather not be discussing this), after he was done, he dropped something down near me, and then he got in his car and left. And so I picked up whatever he dropped, and I took it inside to find out what it was (her expression is crazy as she ends that sentence. I think she shrugged her shoulders, but she definitely widened her eyes and retracted her lips while looking at Nurmi)." Nurmi asks, "What was it?". Jodi answers, "It was Toblerone".

Toblerone? As in that Swiss chocolate candy? Wouldn't the triangular packaging tell her it was Toblerone, even before she got inside the house? I'll cut her a break, she looks more like a domestic "half off the holiday candy" chocolate consumer. In any event, Travis should have thrown her an old Hershey kiss – he should have bounced it right off of her forehead. Scratch that. It would have been noted as an act of domestic violence.

Nurmi responds, "So, he ejaculated on your face and threw you some candy?". Jodi answers, "Pretty much". I'm being completely honest here – I just laughed out loud. What the hell am I listening to? Are these rap lyrics destined to become the issue of massive controversy? In order for this type of testimony to cause the kind of moral outrage this contemporary Abbott and Costello act are hoping to elicit, we would have to be hearing this from the mouth of a young girl who had been kidnapped and held prisoner by a sexual deviant. Because Jodi Arias was a willing participant in this alleged fantasy, it means nothing beyond the fact that Jodi Arias needed therapy and medication, not Toblerone.

As the pair wait for the impact to hit the jury, there's a short pause. Nurmi picks it up with, "Is this hard for you to describe?". Nurmi, get a new eyeglass prescription. She stifles grins while recounting this incident. Jodi says, "Yeah, in front of my mom and dad, it is". Oh well, darling, get used to it, because your real porn performance is just around the corner. Mom and Dad will be bursting with pride tomorrow listening to your phone sex encounter, memorialized on tape, secure in the knowledge that aged grandma and grandpa were on the other side of the bedroom wall while it was actually happening.

Nurmi is either losing his place consistently, or he's really overplaying the whole "do you people on the jury realize how difficult it is for this young woman to talk about this in front of mommy and daddy?" approach, because these gaps are getting longer. We all know her parents are there. We saw them laughing ten minutes ago. I don't know why Jodi didn't mention the presence of her brother. He's young, and he shouldn't be listening to this. No wonder he needed a medical marijuana card (an achievement he bragged about on social media). He probably went into a doctor's office and under "Chief Complaint", wrote "I am the brother of Jodi Arias". Prescription written – five refills.

Nurmi asks, "Did Mr. Alexander have other fantasies that he described for you? Can you tell us another one of those fantasies?". Jodi replies, "Um, he wanted to do the mile high, which we never did (hey, I called that earlier! You know, when Jodi was jet-setting all over the country? The only difference was I thought Jodi extended the invitation. Oh, and not that it means anything, but she must be pretty familiar with this. I've heard it called "The Mile High Club", but she's on a first name basis with it). Um, he wanted to pull off the side of a remote highway somewhere and have sex on the hood of the car (because everyone wants to lay their naked flesh on a hot car hood and have sex), which we didn't do (she smiles and shakes her head from side to side), and he also wanted to...ummm...(she appears to be chewing her cud before finishing the sentence, so I assume this one is going to be super aberrant) have sex on the freeway, while driving, which we did. Um, it was the 10 or the 40; we were driving east across Texas". Nurmi asks, "Oral sex?". Jodi answers, "No".

Now wait just a minute! What? How? Jodi continues, "I think it was vaginal". Okay, if there was ever a time for Nurmi to invite penile/vaginal to the party, this would be that time. Well, go figure. No inquiry. Please tell me that the jury does not believe she was bouncing on his lap while he was driving a car. That would be impossible.

Oh, Jodi isn't finished: "He wanted to me to wear the boy's underwear (question, fragile flower, why the hell did you pack the boy's underwear when you made this eleven hour move, especially if it was so completely confusing and ultimately embarrassing for you?)...umm, he had a lot of anal sex fantasies (he just didn't know that all of his deeply embedded anal sex fantasies required lubrication – Jodi's the one who educated him on that). He wanted me to wear the boy's underwear and have anal sex and he wanted to wear um – he had a lot of nice suits because he was in PrePaid Legal, and he had tailored shirts with his initials stitched into the cuffs (that would be a monogram, Einstein), and he wanted me to perform oral sex on him in his office while he was wearing those suits...umm...".

Well that last part is a variation on a theme. The editor at the National Enquirer, the individual who was approached by a begging Sandy Arias with the forged pedophile letters, mentioned this during a public interview. However, he said the letters claimed that the initials were on cuff links, not shirt cuff monograms, and Travis wanted Jodi to wear the shirt with the cuff links while she performed oral sex on him. The editor of the National Enquirer, who readily admitted that they have a very low journalistic standard, said that the letter referred to the fact that Travis wanted to see his initials as he was serviced. He found this scenario to be completely unbelievable. He said that it was obvious to him that a woman wrote the letters – not a man. That was merely one example he cited. Seems clear to me.

Jodi continues, "That one we did many times – probably his whole wardrobe". Nurmi starts again: "Now, we were talking about the boy's underwear and anal sex. Is this the boy's underwear that you received back on Valentine's Day?". Jodi answers, "Yes". Nurmi continues, "Did he ever explain to you why he wanted you to wear this underwear and why he wanted to have anal sex with you while you were wearing this underwear?". Jodi replies, "He just said it was hot".

No, he didn't. This is all going to lead to the big pedophile disclosure, right? As long as fantasies are the theme of the day, here's mine: Arias and her "counsel" should be locked in a small cement room with a bowl of water and a small box of cat food sitting between them. They should be left alone for three weeks while Law of Chastity teaching tapes loop over and over on a loudspeaker. Let's see who survives.

Nurmi asks, "He didn't offer any other explanation at the time?". Jodi replies, "Not at that time". Well, did she ask for further clarification? Most normal women would. Nurmi continues, "You mentioned...well, let me ask you this – how did you feel about having anal sex with Travis while you were wearing this boy's Spiderman underwear?". I'm wondering, if these altered Spiderman underwear got the amount of use she claims they did, how often were they laundered? I mean, seriously, wouldn't they fall apart after this six month period? Seriously, they've already been "altered" (whatever that means).

Jodi replies, "Well, after we began to do that more regularly, he used lubrication that time (what time? See, Juan Martinez is completely correct – dates matter, and this is why), it wasn't painful, and I don't know, I guess there were times when I enjoyed being with him, so I guess I was willing to do...I enjoyed making him happy, so I was willing to do things he liked to do, so while he was doing things that he liked to do, he was paying attention to me, so I got something out of it too, in that regard".

Who fed her that line of crap? Was it Samuels, the defense psychologist? Was it LaViolette, the defense domestic abuse expert? Was it something she read in her December, 2012, issue of "Psychology Today" magazine (a publication that one of her friends or family pays for her receive at the jail)? Is she hoping that the male members of the jury are thinking, "Wow. I wish my wife was like Jodi. She's willing to do things she doesn't like to do just to please her man".

Nurmi drones on, "Based on what you're telling us, are you saying that he treated you differently before, during, and after these encounters, or before, or – you say he was paying different amounts of attention to you. Can you explain what you mean by that?". Well, of course, she can, Mr. Nurmi. It won't be the standard answer – it will have nothing to do with the fact that sexually involved couples tend to act differently while having sex than they do while hosting a dinner party, but this is Jodi Arias, professional victim, we're talking about. So, let's ascribe far more meaning to this than it's worth. After all, you still have to get around that voice box severing she did, so you might as well talk about sexual lubricants and how Travis didn't give Jodi all of the public adoration she craved. Go right ahead. We're fascinated.

Jodi spins, "Well, when he was in the mood or turned on, then he was very nice and paid attention to me. Um, sometimes when we got together, he was very loving and romantic, and sometimes it was just animalistic. Afterward, when he was done, he was done. For a while".

Does she know why he was done...for a while? Perhaps because, as a Mormon, he was overcome with guilt and looking for the exfoliating soap to take to his scalding shower? While he was showering, he was telling himself this was the last time. Then, he probably wanted her lazy butt out of his bed so he could throw the sheets in the washing machine with two cups of bleach. She can try as hard as she wants to, and while I believe he had sex with her, I don't believe it was the type of sex she's describing, and I think it always ended the same way. No cuddling, no soft talk, just a look at the clock and an utterance of , "I have to be up early in the morning".

Nurmi asks, "You mean done sexually, or done being nice?". Both, Nurmi. He shouldn't prolong this. She looks mentally ill now. Despite the impression she's making, she answers, "Um...done...he didn't turn mean, but done being nice, I would say". So, which is it? Was he nice, or was he mean? I think the word she's looking for may be "indifferent".

Nurmi says, "Would it be fair to say that when he wanted sex again, he became nice?". Jodi nods her head as she answers, "Always".

Nurmi blows more hot air: "Once you moved back to Mesa (will he stop saying this – she never moved "back" to Mesa), you were having this clandestine sexual relationship, and you weren't his girlfriend, so why was this okay with you?".

This has been asked and answered more times than I can count. She was in denial. When he was nice to her, it made her feel good. She loved him. She had low self-esteem. What the hell is the point of asking this again and again? If there is something new here, something like "Well, I discovered I had a brain tumor that completely altered my personality and ability to make good decisions", then, by all means, ask again. But, honestly, what else is there to say about a slutty woman who offered herself up to someone she was trying to coerce into a commitment. She knew the rules, and she played the game to win. She lost. That doesn't mean she gets to kill her opponent...or boyfriend...or ex-boyfriend...or man who introduced her to the gospel...or whatever.

She answers, "I wasn't, well I was still in love with him. I would go on dates with other people occasionally, but there was no spark there. I think because Travis had my heart, and I didn't really, I – I'm a monogamist person (oh, no she didn't), and I'm sleeping with Travis, and so there's not really any room in my heart or my life, and I wasn't making room for anybody else. So, that's kind of just how it continued".

Nurmi asks, "Was there ever any thought in your head, this isn't right, I need to stop this relationship". She answers, "There were times when it seemed very unhealthy, and I had those thoughts". It was unhealthy, certainly. Interestingly, the person who suffered the greatest injury to their health is now buried.

Nurmi asks if Jodi ever vocalized those thoughts to Travis. She lies, "Eventually, I did, yes". Right, she did. Doesn't anyone remember the big break up she initiated back on June 29, 2007? You remember, a few weeks before she moved into his back yard? That's when she vocalized her thoughts and gave him his walking papers.

Nurmi wants to talk about something else.

Jodi just said that there were times that the relationship seemed unhealthy. Nurmi asks, "Did you ever vocalize those thoughts to Travis?". She answers, "Eventually, I did, yes". He continues, "Let's talk about this time period as well, because you mentioned that you were traveling with Mr. Alexander even after you moved back to Mesa, is that accurate?". No, Nurmi, it's not accurate. She did not move BACK to Mesa. She never lived in Mesa before the break-up. She moved there AFTER the break-up, but nice try...again.

Jodi answers, "Yes". Nurmi asks, "And, after you moved back to Mesa in later summer of 2007 (early summer, but who cares about the facts?), where did you and Travis travel to? Where were some of the destinations you went to?". Jodi adjusts her glasses and answers, "Well, first we went to Las Vegas for the convention, which was in early September, again (did he ever take her to Vegas when there wasn't a convention? You know, just the two of them? No.). Um, we...I went to the executive director banquet with him again (right...we know...convention...September, 2007. She was asked for locations, not itineraries). And after that, (we went to the restroom) the weekend following Las Vegas, there was going to be a recap, but we ditched that and went with Dan and Desiree to Havasupai (oh...she's referring to the trip Travis asked Dan Freeman to chaperone so he wouldn't be alone with Jodi Arias. Fine, that's technically a location, but it hardly seems romantic in nature)". Great. So we have one location, and a second location that followed on the heels on the first location. Wow, all of this traveling is really something – and in the space of a week, no less. I count two places (one mandatory for him) in all.

But wait, there's more! In October, they went to Albuquerque for the Balloon Fiesta. They went to Santa Fe to 10,000 Lakes Spa. They went to see Route 66. This is all one trip, obviously. If not, Nurmi would be putting new dates in front of every location. Jodi refers to "The List" – a nickname she says she and Travis had ascribed to the book, "1,000 Places to See Before you Die". These were all places she claims they were checking off "the list".

Nurmi says that before they get too far in discussing all of the places the pair traveled to, he wants to show her some photographs. Why am I assuming that we won't get back to the other places to which they traveled? Probably because there are no more. I can see the photos he's about to hand her. They are pictures of Jodi at the convention, dressed to attend the executive director banquet. Get comfortable – he's about to dissect that convention.

Nurmi asks her what she recognizes a certain photograph to be. She answers, "That's Travis and I at the executive director banquet in March, 2007". Well, great, finally some real evidence. However, the subject he's questioning her about has nothing to do with the period of time before she moved to Mesa. That was when they were in "official boyfriend/girlfriend" mode. This photograph has nothing to do with the premise of his question. If he wants to put up photographs of a convention she attended with Travis, let's see something from September, 2007 – the banquet she just said she attended with Travis while they were no longer official, but still traveling together. Nurmi is playing a legal game of bait and switch, and he's hoping the jury is too confused to catch the switch.

The other photo is of Travis and Jodi at the Balloon Fiesta in Albuquerque. Nurmi asks her to date that photo. She says it was October, 2007. Fair enough. At least that event relates to their postdating travels.

Nurmi says, "Now, you just mentioned the executive director's ball in 2007 (yes, she mentioned the one in September, 2007 – not the one from March 2007. The photo he is putting on the overhead projector is March). Um, is that what we're seeing here?". Jodi is all fake-sad. She mumbles, "Yes". Nurmi asks, "Is it hard for you to look at that picture?". No, it's not. The people dying while looking at this picture are the siblings, relatives, and friends of Travis Alexander. Before she can answer, Juan Martinez says, "Objection, relevance", and it's another "approach" and a bench conference. Believe me, a pattern has developed that allows me to confidently predict that she'll have all the time she wants to tell everyone how hard it is for her to look at this photograph.

The objection is overruled. She answers, "It's just very sentimental. It's about happier times (before she covered him in his own blood and heard his death rattle?). When you just look back, you just don't think that it would end up the way it did (because for most of us, it doesn't. For her, it did)". The last few words of her answer rise to that high pitched, just about to cry octave. She doesn't, of course.

Nurmi does an instant replay with the Balloon Fiesta picture. He puts it on the overhead, she barely looks at it, he wants to know if it's hard to look at, she says it is, he wants to know why...you get it. This time she adds, "We had a really bad fight that morning. It turned out better. We had a good day, afterward". No tears. Not one. It sounds like she's crying, but she's as dry as a bone.

This festival, or "Fiesta", the one held in 2007, was a 10 day event. Nurmi wants to know how long this trip was. She says she's not sure, but she thinks it was just the weekend. So, they stopped in to cover one leg of a three legged trip. Thrilling. Moving along.

Nurmi points out that the photograph shows them acting as a couple. She affirms his statement. He wants to know if this coupling ended when they got back to Mesa. She answers, "Yeah, it did". She takes her hand and pretends to wipe away a non-existent pool of tears that has supposedly collected on her chin and threatens to rain onto her little desk. Then, just in case the jury missed the imaginary waterworks, she reaches over and grabs not one, but two Kleenex tissues. She just holds them. Then she adds, "Well, it depends on the timing". Nurmi asks, "Well, what do you mean by that?". Oh, no...

She answers, "Um, I was (she pinches her nose with her tissues) still coming over to his house...um, his roommate tried to warn me that he was seeing other people (when?)...so I mean, it was...". She sniffs and looks at Nurmi. She has no intention of finishing that sentence. Nurmi helps her. He says, "Well, what I was asking you was if this public affection ended when you got back to Mesa". Okay, the photograph doesn't show public affection, per se. It could just as easily have been Travis' sister standing next to him in the photograph, but we see where Nurmi is headed. She's going to say yes. She has to say yes. She does say yes, however she adds this gem, "unless we were in his room". No Arias, you were in his house. He's the one with the house. You're the one with the room (in some still undisclosed location).

Nurmi says, "So affection was okay, as long as you were in your room or on your porch, where he was ejaculating on your face, right?". Hey, Nurmi – don't forget the Toblerone! He gave her Toblerone after he ejaculated on her face! That's not just a lowly, domestic Kit-Kat. Can we just not do this again, please?

We're going to do it again. She answers, "Well, yeah, uh, but the latter wasn't really affection, that much". Nurmi says, "Okay. That brings up a good point. You come out on the porch, you fulfill his fantasies, he ejaculates on your face (overkill, Nurmi, overkill), he throws chocolate at you – how do you feel after that?". We already know. We've already been on the front porch. We've already heard about her face and the candy. Why won't the judge tell him that there is a jury that has a life, and they'd like to get back to it? This needless, incessant rehashing of prior testimony is unfair. It can be stopped, but it isn't being stopped.

Jodi swipes her man-chin again with her man-hand and says, "I couldn't help thinking that it was kinda like a prostitute". Now, we're talking. In my heart of hearts, I believe Jodi Arias got through all of those jobless segments in her life by plying the oldest profession in the book. If we were able to see her bank records (which were deemed too prejudicial, with the exception of several transactions related to the premeditation aspect of her crime), she would not be able to explain how she supported herself. She was getting cash, and she was getting it somewhere (and it wasn't from her "art" or photography). She adds, "I just put that out of my mind. I just chalked it up to one of his little antics that he did".

One of his little antics? What woman allows herself to be used as a prostitute by her significant other and chalks it up to "little antics that he did"?

Nurmi says, "One of his little antics. Was there ever a point in time where you said, I'm done with these little antics?". Wait, wait, I know, I know! Pick me! Yes, Nurmi, there was. It was June 4, 2008. Why don't we just get to that point in time and stop acting like this woman, a willing participant, was a victim of anyone but herself.

Jodi pretends to sniff and says, "If anything, we increased...with antics, and things like that". Here we go again. Nurmi asks, "Well, had he been physically abusive with you up until this point in time – late summer, 2007". She says, "No", but then adds, "Well, he grabbed my wrist one time, but I didn't consider it abusive, so I don't know".

Nurmi is all over this new development. He says, "Well, when did that occur?". She says, "Well, at um, um, at the convention in Oklahoma City in March, 2007". Great, per Nurmi's request, she's about to describe those circumstances for us. Remember, this is the convention in March – so that means they were still an official couple – or as Nurmi likes to say, "official boyfriend/girlfriend". This is not the convention she included in her post break-up travels. I assume the jury is either so bored or so confused that they haven't made that distinction. They weren't supposed to.

She says, "I was...he and I were hanging out at the Sheraton ...this is two nights after the drunk lady fell all over him (she's still angry about that, and you can see it on her face. That's because the drunk lady – and I've seen her – was far more feminine and attractive when she was drunk than Jodi Arias was when she was bleached, covered in her make-up mask, and completely sober), so we were just hanging out with other colleagues and friends (HIS colleagues and friends – her colleagues and friends were bus boys, dishwashers, and men without last names who always had a bed for her to crash in at a second's notice), and I had to use the restroom. So, I ran to the same restroom that I ran to a few nights before (that would be on the executive director floor. Jodi Arias, lowest level PPL associate, was playing executive director that night). It's sort of by a bar. It's in the lobby, and this is Saturday night now. A lot of people are partying. Convention's over. Everyone's going to leave Sunday (can she just get to it? Are we going to hear about the color of the tiles in the bathroom and the amount of time it took her to empty her bladder – why does every answer require such a detailed set-up?). So, there were a lot of people, a big crowd (yes, a lot of people is called a crowd), a lot of people were drinking and having fun and just being social. And, I was making my way back through the crowd, I heard somebody call my name, and I stopped to look around and see who it was, and it was Abe – the guy I'd gone on a date with some months earlier. Um, and we talked briefly, and I don't remember if he had heard about what happened or if I told him about what happened (he heard about what happened. It isn't often that a lowly associate barricades a public bathroom door so that she can trap a higher level employee and read them the riot act about hanging on her boyfriend. That story made the rounds at that convention, but she's going to pretend she told Abe about it. Right.), but he was just listening, and he said you deserve better, and I said thanks. I said, it's okay – that kind of thing. So, then I went – we parted – and I made my way back through the crowd, and I was leaving the crowd, and I saw Travis standing at the edge of the crowd, um, waiting for me. I just smiled and walked up to him and went to grab his hand, and his hand shot out and grabbed my wrist instead".

Is she kidding? She cannot be serious. All of the ridiculous build-up for that? Abuse? She has since come to define that as abuse? There's more dialogue about this non-event. She said he didn't seem upset at first, but once she started talking to him, he was pretty mad. Now why would that be? Could it have anything to with her never ending talking, her unquenchable neediness, her never truthful assertions, and the fact the she was as good at trying to incite jealousy as she was at oral sex? Antics? Who's proficient in antics? I'm not dignifying anymore of this. You get the picture.

When we last left Jodi, she was recounting the incident that led to her becoming a victim of severe wrist abuse syndrome (SWAS, a new disorder underwritten by The Law Office of L. Kirk Nurmi, can be embarrassing to talk about, but Jodi Arias has courageously come forward to explain, in excruciating detail, how to recognize the signs of this abuse. She's a vanguard in the fight to enlighten and educate the masses who, like the professional victim herself, have innocently extended their hand and received abuse in return. Typically occurring in dark, crowded rooms filled with people, victims of SWAS do not realize, usually until it is too late, that what has befallen them will cause their lives to go off the proverbial rails. Thanks to L. Kirk Nurmi and Jodi Arias, victims of SWAS will now understand what has happened to them – and more, importantly, they will face a new dawn knowing that none of this was their fault. Get help now, or face the consequences of being a fugitive on the run or a resident of a dank cell in prison. Note: this syndrome may also affect victims who suffered a single wrist grab as opposed to a double wrist grab).

We're back in the past – the place Jodi will live forever. It's 2007! It's convention! It's Las Vegas! It's the Executive Director Banquet! Someone Nurmi keeps calling "Mr. Abaldahla" just approached Jodi and told her that she deserves better. I assume Abadahla/Abdelhadi is talking about Travis Alexander. The normal response to such a statement, coming from the mouth of a woman who claimed she loved the man being slandered, would not be "thanks". No, it would be something far more defensive than that. I know what I would say, and it wouldn't be "thanks". Picture your husband or significant other escorting you to a swanky event – a retirement dinner, a wedding...whatever. Some idiot comes up and tells you that you deserve better than the man you woke up with this morning. What are you going to say? Thanks?

Now, Jodi is about to tell us what Travis, who talked to her sternly under his breath, was mad about. Jodi looks like she's folding laundry while looking down at her little desk. Perhaps it is a Kleenex. Nurmi wants to get into the fact that "Jodi deserved better". He asks her if that was the discussion that she had with Abadahla/Abdelhadi. She says, "Yes".

Nurmi wants to go back to Mesa. He says, "Now, going back to Mesa, the sexual encounters, you said they were happening more frequently. Was this a daily basis, a near daily basis?". Jodi says, "I'd say, three to four times a week". Well, if Jodi says it, you have to do a little math to get to the truth. I'll be exceptionally gracious and say it might actually be three or four times a month.

Nurmi continues, "And apart from those instances on the porch, you mentioned incidents of his home. Um, how did that work?". Jodi plays with her Kleenex, adjusts her prescription-less lenses, and says, "If it was the middle of the day and nobody was home, then there wasn't as much of a need to, uhh, keep it a secret, or keep it within the confines of the bedroom, but if people were home, and his roommates were home, uhh, we had to be very quiet. He used to (past tense, because she killed him) complain that his house was a KB home, and the walls were thin, and his roommates could hear every sound, so we had to be quiet". Yes, we know. They had to be quiet. We've been hearing this refrain since she first claimed to have crossed the threshold to his bedroom. You know what Arias and Nurmi are? They are a campaign for abstinence. They have made sex, the very idea of it, absolutely mundane, routine, and pretty soon, I'll be putting my hands over my ears so I don't have to hear about it anymore.

Is not having a raging, surround-sound orgy in a home in which other people reside something to be ashamed of, because I'm certainly getting that impression. Just because a masturbating Jodi, safely under the roof of her grandparents' bungalow, chooses to snort and scream her way through phone sex while sounding like a chimpanzee whose banana has been stolen, it doesn't mean normal, discreet people carry on that way.

Nurmi incorrectly surmises that Jodi's presence "in the home" was supposed to be secret, and Jodi corrects him: "Well, mainly our activities. I parked right in the driveway". Nurmi doesn't miss an opportunity to inject sex into any sentence. He elaborates on the obvious, "So, it wasn't your presence in the home, it was the fact that he was having sex with you that was the secret". Jodi says, "Yeah", and nods her big head.

Nurmi continues, "Were precautions made? You mentioned daytime. Sometimes this happened at night as well, is that correct?". Jodi answers, "Yes". Nurmi's on a roll: "Okay, umm, were there precautions made for getting out the next morning, did you stay the night? How did that work?". Nurmi, he wanted her out before the sun came up. Everyone already knows that, but go ahead, have her repeat it. They're still going to find her guilty, even if he tied his 800 thread count sheets together and told her climb out the bedroom window.

Jodi answers, “I usually stayed the night, but I left pretty early”. No way. He doesn't want his roommates to hear a car pulling out in the morning, and he doesn't want his neighbors to see Jodi leaving his house in the light of day. If she's going to be the dirty little secret they're trying to portray, she should have stuck with the “by cover of night” exit.

Nurmi is smiling as he says, “Was this intentional to avoid letting the roommates know that you spent the night?”. Go ahead, Arias, speculate. If you say that Nurmi is correct, then you were a willing participant in this clandestine affair. If you say no, then Travis obviously didn't think he had anything to hide. Pick your poison.

Jodi answers, “Yes, because, well, yes, usually”. Usually. I wish this man had survived her attack. I wish he were here to tell his side of the story. Nurmi is still smiling his creepy, leering smile: “Did that state of affairs continue throughout the fall of 2007?”. Jodi answers, “Yes”. Jodi looks like someone who has just admitted to baking a kitten casserole. She's so humiliated, so completely convinced of her wrongdoing, so overwhelmed that she has been led astray, and frankly, it's sickening.

Nurmi would like to know if Jodi knew that Travis was dating other women during “this state of affairs” (he likes this phrase). Jodi says, “No, in fact he specifically told me the opposite”. I have to interject here. We have been listening to the “he used me/he was cheating on me” story for hours now. If Nurmi and his demon don't get to the point, in about fifteen minutes, it's going to become very clear that they are putting a dead man on trial for seeing several women at the same time (and that can mean taking one to dinner, one to church, and one to bed, if all parties are in agreement). It will become even more apparent that he was not judged by a jury of his peers, but by a jealous she-wolf who decided she didn't the like the contract she had willingly entered into. Ultimately, it will become clear that this man, who does what men on the jury have probably done at one point in their lives, has been convicted and executed. Let's take this down to its foundation: He won't commit = He dies. She murders = She deserves to resume her life. I cannot believe I'm even hearing this. Seriously, they should move on. I know that Nurmi is trying to create an image of a slowly degrading relationship that ultimately ended in justifiable homicide, but he lacks the skill and client to paint such a picture. The product of this argument will be that she is a combination of a jealous eighth grade girl and a disturbed, male thrill killer.

Nurmi asks, “So you assumed, while you were engaging in this sexual activity, that he wasn't dating anyone else?”. Jodi changes her “he specifically told me the opposite” answer. This time, she says, “Not exclusively. I assumed he went on dates with other people from his church...sometimes I'd go on group dates, but I definitely didn't have the impression that he was in a committed relationship with anybody”.

So, is it fair to say that Jodi did not answer Nurmi's question truthfully when he asked her whether she knew that Travis was dating other women during "this state of affairs"? She just said she thought he was dating people from his church, after saying that he told her "the opposite"? Which is it? If he wasn't dating women from his church, who was he dating? Men? In her lies, she has actually spoken the truth: Travis was not dating ANYONE exclusively, and Jodi Arias topped that list. So, by what right does she sit on this stand and act as though Travis Alexander owed her fidelity and commitment? She's spent quite a bit of time telling us how he used her, hid her in the bedroom, wouldn't be seen with her in public...so why would we now put her under in category of exclusive and committed? Why would SHE put herself in the category of exclusive and committed? They cannot have it both ways, but they continue to try.

Nurmi proves my point, "And you told us just a few moments ago, that you didn't believe, or you didn't characterize it as a committed relationship, right?". Jodi swivels toward the jury and answers, "No, I didn't". Instead of asking what should be asked (i.e., "So why would you assume he couldn't date other people if you were dating other people, and why would you even ask him if he was dating other people?), he asks, "Were YOU dating other people?". We already know the answer to this. Nurmi's asked her this question several times, but for old time's sake, let's hear it again: "I went on a few dates on occasion, but nothing that became that heated...nothing that blossomed into any kind of relationship". Is that this issue? Nobody else in their social/church circle was really interested in parading Jodi around as their girlfriend? Is that was this is all about?

What is the theory here? Because she couldn't strike up passion with another man, Travis wasn't allowed to try and ignite something with another woman? Apparently, he was quite successful in establishing a committed relationship with another woman – and Jodi will have plenty to say about that later. Right now, it has to be evident to every person listening to this testimony that Jodi Arias knew exactly what type of relationship she was having with Travis Alexander. No strings attached. Wow. Watch out guys...this can get you killed (and then dissected during your killer's trial).

Nurmi makes it dark and ugly. He asks, "Did Travis know about your dates with any of these other individuals?". Jodi answers, "He found out about one...umm...two actually, early on, if we're talking the same time period". Found out? Oh, let me guess: he got jealous. Let's say he got jealous, for the sake of argument. Here's the solution: walk away. That's why none of this rings true. That's why we are always forced to err on the side of Travis. She is pretending to be reasonable, but at the end of this relationship, she slaughters him. Slaughter makes us think of frenzy. Frenzy makes us think of disturbed and uncontrolled. Oversized eyeglasses, ponytails, and a junior high school wardrobe don't negate slaughter. If they put a strand of pearls on her, it still wouldn't cover the stench of blood.

Nurmi wants to know if Travis acted "positively or negatively" about the dates Jodi allegedly went on. She responds, "One, he just teased me, and the other one, very negatively". Nurmi will want to hone in on the very negative response, but he'll probably want the jury to sympathize with the mocked femme fatale, as well. He continues, "You weren't in a relationship with him, so what was the problem?". Good question, Nurmi. It's just a pity that he asks this when the problem has been ascribed to Travis. This would be a question that should have been asked when the problem was ascribed to Jodi. We would have liked to have heard this question asked when she was complaining about Travis dating other women. How predictable that he would ask it only when it came to Jodi dating other men.

Jodi answers, "The one that he reacted negatively to was the one that...he hated". Pardon me. That was not the question. Nurmi did not say, "Tell us about the date he reacted negatively to"; Nurmi asked, "You weren't in a relationship with him, so what was the problem?". Now Nurmi asks, "Who was that?". Jodi answers, "His name was John Dixon".

We are now back in John Dixon territory. We've been here before. Nurmi has gotten Jodi to say that Travis didn't like John Dixon. As a matter of fact, I think it was before they allegedly became exclusive. I have no idea if there was a second date with John Dixon, or if Nurmi is rehashing the first date with John Dixon. It doesn't matter. I'm glad that John Dixon got away from Jodi Arias with his life. Nurmi, on the other hand, is getting intense. He's making bold statements that indicate that Jodi was not to date John Dixon because Travis Alexander didn't like him. There are several objections from the prosecution, overruled on one, restate the question on the other. These objections make Nurmi mad. He becomes childish when he's challenged. He works up some passion here, and I suspect he'll be exhausted in a minute or two. Jodi says, "Not date him, and not even be his friend".

Nurmi continues, "Because Travis says so, right?". Jodi plays a role here. She's attempting to look like the abused woman, who, out of habit, still has to defend her abuser, but she's so close to becoming liberated that she actually speaks out against him, "He...well, yeah". Nurmi reinforces her, "Yeah! So, you could date who you wanted unless Travis told you no, right?". Jodi answers, "Yeah, it seemed that way". Yeah, and that's why she killed him.

The Alexanders come into focus. Samantha appears to be grinning, staring right at Arias.

Nurmi is as on fire. He says, "So all this time he's having sex with you behind closed doors or on your porch, right?". Juan Martinez objects. He doesn't get passionate with these objections. He is asking for dates, for foundation, and this might be what's really getting under Nurmi's skin. Nurmi is arguing emotion. Juan Martinez will stick with fact. I'm glad he's done his homework, because Nurmi has been given a lot of room to lead his client into discussions in which SHE isn't even sure of the time period (just recently, she said, "if that's the time period"). That is why the dates are important, and she's been allowed to talk without significant limit or boundary.

Juan Martinez wants to know when this sex was happening, and he wants to know what time period she was dating John Dixon. Nurmi actually says, "During this time period, judge". Juan Martinez is angry and replies, "No, he can't testify...she can". Thank God. Sustained.

Well, now you've got a pissed off pachyderm. Nurmi waves his arms around and says, "Fall of 2007, he comes over, he ejaculates on your face, he throws candy on you, has you having sex behind closed doors, and you're not in a committed relationship (Nurmi is now standing right in front of Juan Martinez. Both arms are fully extended), and this is in the fall of 2007. That's what we're talking about right?".

By contrast, Juan Martinez sits at his desk, his head supported by his right hand, as he watches Nurmi huff and puff. What Juan Martinez asked for was the time period that Jodi claimed to be on a date with John Dixon. According to what we've heard, Nurmi has reached back into the past and applied that date to fall of 2007, but all we've heard about is a date in the early spring 2007 (when Jodi first mentioned going on a date with John Dixon), and I believe that is exactly what Juan Martinez is trying to expose – or at least clarify.

Nurmi is bellowing, "That's the same time period you dared to defy Mr. Alexander and go out on a date with John Dixon, right?". Wow, hold your horses, Nurmi! Dared to defy? What are we back to wrist abuse again? He has not proven or even mentioned a single act of physical abuse, so why are we into the "dared to defy" category? Jodi mumbles, "Yes".

Juan Martinez says, "Objection, misstates the testimony. She didn't say she defied him. He was just upset about it. The characterization is what is objectionable". The objection is sustained, and Nurmi is told to rephrase.

Nurmi asks, "When did you go out with John Dixon?" Jodi answers, "It was right before the fall, actually the very last weekend in August". What year? Didn't we hear about this date in early 2007? It was while she was in Pasadena seeing a doctor, seeing Abe Abdelhadi, and seeing John Dixon and his clips from a movie? Perhaps she was playing fast and loose with those dates when she spoke of the date with John Dixon earlier. Either way, she should be forced to explain how many dates she went on with John Dixon, and she should be forced to say when those dates occurred. Was it in November, 2006? Was it February, 2007? Was it August, 2007? The prosecution deserves to know these dates (even approximate) if he is to effectively cross examine her. That's the rule of law.

Nurmi continues, "So, Mr. Alexander expressed his anger in the fall of 2007 about you going on a date with Mr. Dixon, right?". Jodi answers, "Yes, he found out the morning we were leaving for Havasupai". Havasupai? Wasn't that trip taken instead of attending the recap event that happened in September, 2007? Was she referring to a date with John Dixon that had happened months before, or a week before Havasupai?

Nurmi continues, "But it didn't stop him from having sex with you or ejaculating on your face, right?". Jodi answers, "No". Hey, why is Nurmi allowed to deflect? Forget "ejaculating on your face". We've heard it, and heard it, and heard it again. We want to know when Arias went on a date with John Dixon. From what I recall, it was long before the Freeman chaperoned Havasupai trip. Martinez says, "Objection, asked and answered". He is overruled again.

Jodi, the wilted weed, says, "No, it didn't stop him from that". As I understand it, the face ejaculation episode happened months earlier. Why don't dates matter here? I'm seriously confused, and I believe the judge is as well.

Nurmi says, "And it didn't stop him from going to Havasupai with you, right?". It could also be said that it didn't stop her from going to Havasupai with him, but what difference does that make? I'm surprised that Travis Alexander was able to drive anywhere – Havasupai or otherwise. Nurmi makes it sound like the man had an ejaculatory condition that prevented him from being in public.

Nurmi asks, "Did it stop you from dating John Dixon again?". Jodi answers, "Yes". Well, of course it did. There was only one date. He may have "found out" because she told him, but I believe they have successfully avoided exposing the fact that there was never a second date with John Dixon. If there had been, where was the detailed agenda of the date? We always find out what Jodi did on her dates. Sushi, movie clips, sex, visits to the restroom, etc.

Happily off of the subject of John Dixon, Nurmi asks, "Did it stop you from dating anyone else?". Did what stop her from dating anyone else? A bad mood? A stern voice under his breath. A wrist grab as she went to grab his hand in a crowded, dark room? Perhaps we are about to enter the world of choke outs and broken bones. He had better get there because he's looking like an obese puppet master who needs to sit down, and his client looks like a badly chiseled marionette.

Jodi answers, "Um, I went on a couple more dates at the time". Now wait a minute. Ten minutes ago she was able to recall one, and upon further reflection, two dates, she had gone on. Suddenly, there's several more dates she went on "during that time period". Let's hear about the other dates.

Before Nurmi can speak, she adds that there were several more through the next year: one to two, to a few more, to several more. This is a carefully crafted, carefully unfolding lie. It's taking place under oath in a court of law. There's the seal of the State of Arizona, and there's the American flag. I guess this means nothing to her, and from all appearances, it means nothing to Nurmi.

Nurmi asks, "Did you tell Travis, or did you try to keep those a secret?". Jodi answers, "No, I learned to stop telling him anything about my social life regarding that. I didn't tell him about John. He found out". I wish John Dixon had been called as a witness. I will never believe there was a late fall date with John Dixon, unless he actually says there was.

Nurmi wants to know why Jodi didn't cut the cord with the current "state of affairs". Jodi answers,

"Well, we're focusing on the negatives, but there were things he did that made me feel like a million dollars, um...". Nurmi interrupts, "Describe those things for us".

Jodi says, "It was more the things he did for me at times. He would say little things that were sentimental, things that had meaning between us. He got me little gifts – things that weren't expensive (details – we deserve details, after having to hear about his semen), it was the thought, and just the gestures that he did, and he still would allude to the fact that he wanted to marry me (despite the fact that she said it never came up unless he was joking), even though I don't know if he was very serious (bingo)".

Nurmi does a "come hither" gesture with his fingers and asks, "Kept telling you things you wanted to hear? (because every woman dismisses her beloved's mocking laughter after the subject of marriage comes up)". Jodi answers, "Yep. Yeah, he did". Nurmi fans the flames, "He kept promising you...come on, come on, Jodi, maybe I'll marry you some day?". Jodi answers, "No, it wasn't quite like that". Nurmi asks, "How was it (she's already told us how it was, but ask again, if you must)?". Jodi answers, "If I did something that he liked, or pleased him in some sort of way, he would...like...something I said, or something I did, he would just look at me with this enigmatic smile and say, marry me, and it wasn't like an actual proposal (she looks like a mother watching her 6 year old son hit a home run in little league – it's a "that's my boy" smile), you know, it was kind of a joke, but I took it as a compliment". This would be Nurmi's cue to say, "Was he ejaculating on your face while flashing the enigmatic smile and saying, 'marry me'?".

Nurmi asks, "Why, why would you take that as a compliment?". Jodi replies, "Because he only said those things when I did something that would merit me being a good wife, potentially". Well, it's safe to say she failed that test with flying colors. He's dead now.

Nurmi wants that last part repeated. Jodi complies, "Being a good wife, potentially. Like if I did something that might be in line with that, because that was my goal at the time, and that's what I wanted to become".

There's another foundational truth that escapes amidst the flood of lies: being his wife was her goal, and that's what she wanted to become.

Nurmi likes the wife talk. He asks, "Did you want to become his wife...Travis' wife?". Well, I hope so. He was ejaculating on her face, after all. Jodi answers, "That was my desire for a while until after Havasupai". Nurmi continues, "What changed after Havasupai that made you change your mind and say, I don't wanna marry this guy?". Um, maybe the fact that he brought chaperones? Just a guess.

Jodi answers, "My feelings for him didn't necessarily change, but in my mind, we had a very bad fight that morning, and he said some very ugly things to me, and it was a boundary we had never crossed before, and I couldn't imagine marrying somebody who had ever said those things to me, or raising children with a man who, had, who...their father had said those things to their mother, kind of thing...that's how I saw it".

Well, she got further in the mental process than Travis ever did. I don't believe he ever considered Jodi Arias, anal queen, to be the potential mother of his children. Secondly, for all of her family values and concern about the character of her fictitious offspring's' father, she still had no problem squealing about how she liked to be debased by him months after she had allegedly reached the conclusion that she couldn't breed with him. During that phone sex conversation in May, 2008, she also had no problem talking about the boring, vanilla Mormon husband she would actually end up with – while he ignored that particular subject on the other end of the phone.

Nurmi wants to know what "ugly things" Travis said. Juan Martinez immediately objects with "Hearsay". Nurmi goes through his "truth of the matter asserted, it goes to the effect on the listener". Judge Stephens says that it is time for the afternoon recess.

As Jodi gets ready for her final performance of Day Four, we see her whispering with Jennifer Willmott, her second chair attorney. I wish I could slow down this video. A lip reader could make out what Jodi is saying, but I'm not going to even try. Jodi is clad in her black jacket, and as she approaches the stage with her water glass in her right hand, we see Willmott following her. Nurmi says, "Jodi", and the actress turns around, and Willmott is there to whisper last minute directions into the diva's ear. Counsel is told to approach.

As Jodi stands for the jury, I look at her black blazer. It looks different than the one she was wearing this morning. Then I realize, the lapels and collar are not folded back. She looks like a priest without the white matchbook-like cover at the throat. Is she attempting to make a fashion statement, or is she just sloppy?

After standing for the jury, Jodi sits. Immediately, the jacket comes off, the boobs stick out, and the record will show the presence of the defendant, all counsel, and the jury. Nurmi may continue. He does: "Jodi, before the break, we were talking about an argument you had with Mr. Alexander before the Havasupai trip, and he had learned that you had gone out on a date with John Dixon, right?". Jodi answers, "Yes". Nurmi continues, "The argument you had with him, where did that take place?". While I'd rather know when and where the date with John Dixon took place, that ship has sailed, despite Juan Martinez' repeated and legitimate attempts to put the second date on the record.

In the minds of the jury, there were several dates involving Jodi Arias and John Dixon. I believe there was only one. If there were more than one, we would be drowning in details about it. The fact that the defense has avoided giving even a hint of detail is all the proof I need. Jodi has used that date with John Dixon as her foundation for the beginning of her "committed" relationship with Travis, and now she will use that date with John Dixon as her foundation to build a house called anger, control, and abuse.

Jodi answers, "I believe it started downstairs, over the backpack...that's kind of what started it...and I took the backpack back upstairs, into his bathroom, to look for my toothbrush. Everything had been repacked, so I didn't know what was what, and I just woke up, wanting to brush my teeth before we hit the road, and he came into the bathroom, and the argument escalated in the bathroom". I wonder how Jodi felt – if this happened – about being the victim of invasion and intrusion.

Nurmi continues, "Okay. This was the argument that Mr. Freeman testified to that was all about make-up and personal care products, right?". Right. Who takes cosmetics on a hike? Who applies make-up over the dust and dirt that will inevitably soil a hiker's hands and face? Jodi Arias, that's who. Have you ever seen a photo of an adult Jodi Arias – indoors or outdoors – prior to her booking photo – that doesn't feature fully painted lips?

Jodi responds, "Yes, but it wasn't make-up (yeah, it was make-up, and lots of it)". That's it? If it wasn't make-up, what was it? Nurmi and Jodi exchange a knowing smile, and suddenly, Jodi, who often looked like a drag queen in her blond bombshell days, suddenly wishes to adopt the fresh air persona of a natural, outdoors type who laughs at the vain women who worry about their hair and make-up while on hikes and camping trips. The jury may believe it. She looks like a Plain Jane right now.

Nurmi says, "What sort of things, you said that he said that Travis said (huh?) bad things to you up in the bathroom that made you realize that that wasn't the type of person you wanted to marry, right? Did I understand that correctly?". Jodi answers, "Yes".

Marriage? That was never on the table, Mr. Nurmi. By Jodi's own admission, Travis never used the words "Jodi" and "marry" in the same sentence without letting her know it was a joke. She has been consistent with that. I'm still trying to figure out if she's playing the marriage/joke card because it plays into their "dirty little secret" angle, or if it's because there are far too many people who would be willing to testify to that Travis did not want to marry Jodi. In any event, Nurmi just articulated a position that Travis Alexander held from very early on in this relationship: no marriage. The fact that Jodi is now pretending it was a decision she made in his bathroom in the fall of 2007, is ludicrous. Even if we believed what she is saying, we still have to wonder why she would come to that realization and still go on this trip. Had I been in the position she is trying to describe, I would have needed to go home and process my feelings. I don't think I could have gotten into the car with him.

Nurmi asks, "What things did he say to you that made you feel that way?". After taking a ridiculously fake deep breath, Jodi starts spinning her hands and replies, "It was only one thing specifically as our argument escalated more and more. At this point, I was brushing my teeth...and I had found my toothpaste, my toothbrush, and I was crying, he had found out about my date, because I wrote about it in my journal, regrettably, and he repacked it and read it, and it wasn't incredibly detailed, but it talked about the time I spent...".

Juan Martinez says, "Objection. Beyond the scope". Jodi is over talking Juan. She's saying "I'm sorry, I got distracted", while Juan is ignoring her and addressing the judge. Juan Martinez says, "She was asked about an argument, but now she's trying to tell us about a journal and that sort of thing". Nurmi puts his left hand up to make the universal "stop" sign. He looks like the court crossing guard as he pretends to be the voice of logic and reason. Unfortunately he just makes sounds, not words: "Judge, ahh...". Juan Martinez is angry. He continues to over talk Nurmi. Martinez plans on crossing this street. He says, "She's just not being responsive. So, objection, it's beyond the scope of the question. She's just being non-responsive". Judge Stephens nods her head in agreement, doesn't rule, and says to Nurmi, "Restate your question".

Nurmi is always angry when he's stifled in what is quickly becoming a free for all. He says, "Sure, Jodi. What did Travis say to you to make you realize that you didn't want to marry him? What specifically?" Jodi answers, "He said, fuck you". Well, let me join that chorus. Is there a single person who can blame him? I don't. I can't believe how long it took to pull out the king of all curse words.

Are we supposed to be shocked? Jodi is pretending to be traumatized. She's moving around in her chair, pushing items around on her little desk, looking up, looking down, and she wants everyone to believe that she doesn't use this type of language. Nurmi asks, "What else? Did he say anything else?". To give you a little context, you should picture two tough guys doing the pre-fight dance. Think of two adversaries ready to have a street fight, and one of them is using that "I dare you" tone of voice to egg their opponent on. It's a very distinct tone, and Nurmi uses it when he's ready to do battle with a dead man. This isn't the first time he's done it. Jodi answers, "Umm, well he said a lot of things about John. He was calling him John Dickhead instead of John Dixon – that was his nickname for him – for the last year. And, after he said F you, he turned on his heels and left the bathroom".

For the last year? Really? Where are we in this testimony? We're in September/October 2007. Where were Jodi and Travis a year earlier? They were, according to Jodi, engaging in drive by blow jobs and phone sex. Where were John Dixon and Travis in September, 2006? Well, according to Jodi, Travis, if had been calling Dixon a dickhead for a year, and that would have been something he was doing while Jodi was still living in Palm Desert, prior to the "official" start of their relationship on February 2, 3, or 4, of 2007. If we believe Jodi, Travis had issues with John Dixon long before Jodi had her date with him – the one that included an interrupting phone call from Travis – something that happened in Pasadena at the end of 2006. Interesting.

These few months don't make a year. In fact, I believe that Jodi went on her one date with Mr. Dickhead precisely because Travis called him Mr. Dickhead. She did it to arouse anger in Travis. The bad blood between Dixon and Travis Alexander had nothing to do with dating Jodi Arias. There was something else going on. Travis is dead, so we'll never hear his side of the story. John Dixon works pretty extensively in Hollywood as a stunt man, and my guess is that he will stay as far away from this pile of radioactive waste as possible.

This is another example of why these dates are so important, and why Juan Martinez must be allowed to reconcile the dates with the events. In allowing the defense to be this sloppy, the story is being altered.

Now that I realize how truly sick, disturbed, and manipulative this woman is, I believe it is well within the realm of reason to assume that she over packed on purpose, put her journal into the back pack, but before doing so, made sure to write a detailed entry about a date with John Dixon (imaginary date or business transaction). Knowing Jodi, if this happened, she drew comparisons between the two men, and she probably used Travis' name in this entry – if this was even the cause of the fight...if there even was a journal entry...if, if, if.

Nurmi asks, "Why did you still decide to go to Havasupai with him". Jodi answers, "Well, there was a lot of crying...that kind of thing...Dan came in the bathroom, I didn't realize he was there...".

Hold the phone, again. I have to interrupt. Dan was in Travis' master bathroom? Jodi didn't realize he was in there? How is that possible? Seriously, how is that possible? I've seen that bathroom. What's she saying is impossible. She not only knew Dan was there, Desiree was probably there first, and Jodi probably asked Desiree to get Dan, because, you know, Dan understands Travis. So, just picture it, Dan has walked through Travis' master bedroom, and he's in the master bath with a crying Jodi, who has just figured out that he's there: "...I was blowing my nose and crying. I was embarrassed, and, umm, to be arguing in front of him (so, is everyone in the bathroom now?), umm, so, Dan was kind of like, Dan and Desiree were sorta like the glue, that sorta said (glue talks?), hey, let's just calm down, let's just try to get along, let's just try to go on the trip. I wanted to go on the trip, but I, I, con..contemplated just going home (she's smiling and waving her arms) because it was really bad, and, umm...".

Nurmi interrupts, "Because he was really...what was that?". No, Nurmi, put your knife and fork away...she didn't say "he was really mad", she said, "it was really bad". Jodi continues, "It was really bad between us. I was mortified. We had never argued before to this extent, and much less in front of somebody else, and so, I was very embarrassed, and I felt very ashamed, and I stayed in the bathroom for a little while and trying to calm myself down, and I don't know how it all ended, but eventually we were all in the garage and in the car and we were beginning to drive off".

Wait a minute! This was the worst argument they had ever had? Really? I thought he choked her to near unconsciousness. I thought he kicked her in the ribs. I thought he broke her finger in a fit a rage (and then apologized by using a popsicle stick and tape to reset her broken bone). But this is the worst? Oh, maybe I have my abuse dates mixed up. At this point, it seems pointless to try to date any event. Whatever the defense says does not need a date attached. They've won that legal argument more times than they've lost it.

So, here we are. We're listening to yet another bathroom performance by Jodi Arias. Isn't it a shame that the Freeman siblings weren't available to forge peace on June 4, 2008? Frankly, those two give me the creeps. Sorry. They should have escorted Jodi out of that house and gone home.

Nurmi surmises, “So, the plan was to suck it up (yes, that was on Jodi's agenda), and go to Havasupai anyway, right?”. Jodi answers, “Right”. Juan Martinez objects with “leading”. Guess how that ruling came down? Right, overruled. Jodi answers again, “Yes”.

Nurmi continues, “And it sounds like during this trip, you two were acting like boyfriend-girlfriend again, right?”. Does Nurmi speak English? It sounds like, during this trip, they were acting like two people that hated each other. Maybe he knows something we don't. Maybe the magic love fairy descended on Havasupai and sprinkled happy sparkle heart dust on Travis and Jodi. Maybe a sparkling unicorn touched each of them with his magic horn while they were in their sleeping bags. Maybe Travis realized he thrived on manipulative fight scenes played out in public. Maybe the two had another fight of epic proportion. Maybe they had several.

Jodi answers, “During some parts, we were kind of, well, I felt, like my feelings were hurt, so I wasn't very responsive to him during that time (when was it established that he made single gesture of affection toward Jodi? What was there to respond to?). I wasn't ignoring him. I wasn't being rude to him, but I just felt like an emotion chasm between us”. Here is another prime example of the eleventh grade dropout reading words and using them before she's ever actually heard them spoken. Jodi says she felt an emotional “chasm” between them. She didn't pronounce the word as it should be pronounced (ka-zem). She pronounced it the way it looks (Cha-zem). This is hard to listen to.

Nurmi says, “Okay, and this trip was when again?”. Jodi answers, “Umm, this would be...probably the second weekend in September”. Nurmi says, “Okay, let's move back to the late part of 2007. We were talking about how the usual course of conduct was late night rendezvous, be they on your porch, be they in his bedroom, right? And you said that happened three to four times a week, right?”. Juan Martinez interjects: “Objection, asked and answered”. It WAS asked and answered. It's a 50/50 on the ruling. Juan is overdue for a sustained. Let's see....overruled, Jodi may answer.

Jodi answers, “Yes, that's correct”. Yes, we all knew that because it has already been asked and answered. Can the Powers that Be now remember that this particular question has been asked and answered...twice? Can the Powers that Be also make a note of the fact that is completely unnecessary for counsel to ask, for the eleventh time, if he ejaculated on her face? That's been asked and answered as well.

Nurmi continues, "And at this point in time, and now we're talking late 2007, has he been physically abusive with you...other than the one incident you told us about (you remember – SWAS)?". Jodi looks in the air, swivels in her chair, and pauses before she says, "Late 2007? There was a point in October, where he pushed me down on the ground, in his bedroom – but I landed on my knees, I didn't, like, fall over or anything".

Jodi is remembering a time in October, 2007, when she was in Travis' bedroom, and he pushed her on the ground. She says she landed on her knees. Nurmi asks, "Not that there would be any excuse for it, but what would be his reason for pushing you to the ground?". Juan Martinez objects: "Speculation. Not that there would be any excuse for it?". The objection is sustained. Nurmi, wearing a contemptuous sneer, rephrases his question, but essentially, he wants to know why Jodi was pushed to the ground. Jodi begins to answer, "We were arguing...", but Juan Martinez objects again. He says, "Judge, this is hearsay if she's going to tell us what he said". Overruled.

Jodi continues, "We were arguing, umm, and I got up to leave, and he wasn't done making his point, and he wanted to stay, or he wanted me to stay, I guess, so he could finish yelling at me". What a miserable, pointless, destructive relationship. Why wouldn't she just go away? He told her to go away. He sent her every hint in the book. Does anyone not believe that Jodi Arias drove to Travis' house on those Friday evening "fight nights" where he invited everyone but Jodi? I can see her sitting outside, or worse, peering into windows to see who was there. In this instance, I'd even venture a guess that he found her in his house – again – uninvited, and his point was "stay the hell out of my house". I can see her trying to walk away from that, and him telling her that he wasn't done making his point. Pushing her? I don't know, but I do know one thing: any woman who continues to degrade herself this way is destroying the very hope she holds so dear. He despises her at this point. He may continue to tolerate her for sex, but in his heart, he despises this woman. He despises her for who she is.

Jodi continues, "I got up to leave the bedroom, and he blocked the door. He grabbed my arms and shoved me down (very dramatic hand motions accompany this tale), and I landed on my knees. He said...". Juan Martinez is writing furiously. He doesn't bother to look up as he says, "Objection, hearsay". Jodi says, "Okay". Nurmi blathers on about "not being offered for the truth of the matter asserted, blah, blah, blah". There's a pause, and then, the attorneys are told to approach.

Good Lord, Nurmi is a worse actor than Jodi! Fresh from the bench with an "overruled" in his pocket, he literally yells, "What did Mr. Alexander say WHEN HE PUSHED YOU DOWN?!". Jodi's ready with, "He said, no, like five times fast, like, no, no, no, no, no. You're not going anywhere". Shocking! I'm speechless! Call Alyce Freaking LaViolette, and do it NOW! Jodi should be experiencing a PTSD trigger at any moment! She should be melting down, experiencing this nightmare all over again, feeling his hands on her arms, smelling his cologne, and she should be rubbing her knees because they hurt, all over again...poor, Jodi. She's gonna fall apart, right? Wrong. She smacks her lips and looks rather pleased with herself. I've never seen a PTSD trigger affect a victim this way.

Nurmi's pouring it on big time, now. He yells, **"YOU – WERE – NOT – ALLOWED – TO – LEAVE, RIGHT!?"**. Juan will try again, probably in vain, to get this melodrama under control. He says, "Objection, leading". Sustained? Did she just say sustained? She did. Well, that's good. I'm wondering if Jodi will use the time Nurmi needs to reformulate this accusation against a dead man by grabbing a Kleenex. She's supposed by upset and emotional when recalling this type of incident.

No time for a Kleenex grab -- Nurmi's too quick: "Were you allowed to leave?". Jodi looks around and does one of those "half a dozen of one/six of the other" facial expressions, lifts her hand, and says, "I didn't push the issue at that point. I tried to leave one more time, and he stopped me again, and then on the third time, he didn't try to stop me". I'm sure. He probably desperately wanted her to leave – forever. She wouldn't promise to do that, so he gave up and decided to be satisfied with what little he could get. By the way, where are the slaps, the kicks, the punches? Where is the abuse? Is it hiding under the bed? Is it in the bathroom? Where is the abuse?

Nurmi wants to know if he grabbed her and threw her down again when she tried to leave the second time. Jodi, sounding like she's describing the technique a paper hanger used while hanging wallpaper, says, "No, the second time he just put his hands on my shoulders". There is no emotion here. Nurmi's the one having the meltdown. He's the one who's seriously overplaying this. The alleged victim is just enjoying all of these important legal people arguing over her.

Nurmi wants to extract abuse, and dammit, he's going to do it. He asks, "Forcefully?". Jodi thinks, clicks her tongue, and says, "Umm...yes". Nurmi asks, "Did he call you names?". This might have happened. Her blasé attitude is gone, and now she looks sad. She says, "Yes". Nurmi asks, "Like what?".

Jodi closes her eyes, grabs the edge of her little desk, and says, "That was such an awful fight. I don't remember all the names he called me. I just remember...one thing that sticks out is that he was insulting my family". Well, if he was insulting her family, people he had never met, where does Nurmi think he got the ammunition from? Perhaps the only person in the relationship that knew her family? This is a stupid avenue to go down.

She's going to try and tell the jury what the names were, and Juan will probably object because this wasn't the question. Jodi says, "He, umm..". Juan objects and says, "Beyond the scope. She was asked if he called her names, not what he said about her family". Nurmi doesn't even wait for a ruling. He throws his arms up in the air and says sarcastically, "Okay. Let's ask this, was he insulting your family? Was he calling them names?". Jodi pretends to be sad as she responds, "Yes". Nurmi asks, "What was he saying about your family?". Hey, there's an objection on the floor.

Forgive me. I know these people didn't murder someone, but this was not the time to focus the camera on the three very strange looking people from Yreka sitting in the front row. You have two middle aged people who look like they're sleeping with their eyes open, and a boy with a grown out crew-cut, wearing big glasses, with his shirt buttoned up to his neck. He always looks like he doesn't know where he is, and he's always looking around the room. I'm ashamed to say that it seemed like a comedic set-up.

Jodi says, "He was saying that my brother was a faggot, because his name is Carl...(big exhale here, she's on the verge of tears, and she's playing with the edge of her little desk again)...". Apparently, Jodi cannot go on. It is too overwhelming. Travis said that hideous word...the worst of the worst...the F word. Faggot. It was fine when Jodi could barely hold it together talking about an effeminate, emotional man named Steve who was running around Crater Lake trying to warn Bianca that Jodi was in town, but suddenly, she's offended by anything that stereotypes gay men. Right. They need her support like they need a hole in the head.

Nurmi prods her along, "What else?". Jodi responds, "I told him that he was named after my grandfather (this might be it, folks. There might be tears here), and he said, your grandfather must be a faggot too, then".

I still don't see tears, but if couldn't see her, I would probably believe she was actually crying. She goes on, "That's just something that bothered me specifically (a big gasp here). It's not that...I wouldn't care if they were gay (does everyone always have to say that?), but Travis' way of issuing a deep insult...to him, that's insulting". Well, we're not here to talk about Travis' way of issuing deep insults, but we are here to talk about Jodi's way of issuing deep knife wounds, so, can we move this trash along?

Nurmi asks if Travis said anything about her other family members. Jodi says, "Not in that specific argument". Then he goes on, "Now this specific argument where he grabs ya, throws ya down, restrains you a second time when you get up to leave, what was the, what was the thing that was so important that Travis wanted to do? Insult your family, or is there something else?"

Oh, do I hear the "Jeopardy" theme music? I'm going for it! I'll take BS for $100, Nurmi! A Daily Double? I know this one! What is, ejaculating on her face!".

No, I was wrong. Jodi says, "He was just ranting and raving and yelling". No, I'm giving myself half of that daily double. Jodi's off script. Nurmi did not work up that sweat for "yelling and ranting". Nurmi prods her, "You don't remember about what?". He's right in her face, and that's unusual. He wants ejaculate, and he wants it now!

She shrugs her shoulders and says, "Honestly, my brain sorta went on freeze (she cups her hands on either side of her head and shakes them), and I don't remember a lot of what he was saying, he was just yelling".

Ladies and gentleman of the jury, meet "The Fog". This is just a teaser mind you, but you know where we're going. Jodi was traumatized during this argument, and so "SHE DOESN'T REMEMBER". Why does this moron think she knows better than her attorneys? They did finish high school, so they are slightly more qualified than her to write the script. She was supposed to say something else, but she decided to invoke "the fog".

Nurmi sounds like he's reading a domestic violence police report as he questions Jodi. He wants to know why she didn't leave Travis the day he grabbed her, pushed her down, wouldn't allow her to leave twice, yelled at her, and insulted her family. Why, he asks again, was this not the last day she ever saw Travis? She'll probably begin her answer with, "Well, it was going to be the last time, but...".

Jodi answers, "Well it was going to be, and I went downstairs and left, and well, he followed me out to my car to say one mean thing to me after another, and his tone changed to something very friendly, but it was artificial friendly, and he said, I have a great idea, and he said, how about you move to Antarctica and never call me again?". Understandable, from my vantage point. Good advice, actually. However, Jodi is showing real emotion here. She looks like a child pleading her case to the school principal after she hit somebody over the head for saying mean things to her on the playground. She's really feeling this. She's playing with her hands while she's speaking, and she reminds me of a nervous child. Travis seriously hurt her feelings, and she truly believes that his insults were uncalled for. He's doing everything he can to drive her away, but she refuses to hear him. This is rather disturbing. It isn't disturbing because Jodi is in pain; it's disturbing because this emotion – the one we're seeing – is very likely one of the ingredients in her recipe for committing, what was, in her mind, justifiable homicide.

She continues, "And I said, minus Antarctica, sure, and (there's a tiny pause, but something shifts here...I'm not seeing pain anymore) I was getting into the car and while I was getting my leg into the car, he slammed the door hard, and I started to drive away, so I thought we were not going to talk at that point. Umm, it was a very low point for me (she's back to being hurt, wow fast shifts happening)...throughout the fall I had been feeling suicidal (she almost just broke, her mouth showed a true indication of fighting back her need to cry – of course, it's her death she's speaking about), and I got to a point where I decided I wanted to go through with that, so, umm, I called my friend Matt because he had guns, and I was gonna ask him if I could borrow (will she be able to return it?) one because I wanted to kill myself, and he could tell...I don't know...he called a suicide hot line and had me call them, and he called my dad or my parents, and I was on the phone with Matt, and Travis began calling again as I was driving back home, and umm, I wanted to answer because Travis always apologized after he had been very mean, and I thought, maybe this is his apology. Umm, but sometimes it took a while for him to calm down, so it could have just been more of the same, of his anger, so I hung up anyway with Matt, and Travis was very sweet, and very calm, and he was telling me to come back and that he was too harsh on me, and I needed to help him make his bed. I had been there doing his laundry (a shot of Samantha shows her about to break out in laughter. Her grin is from ear to ear), and cleaning the house when the fight started, so I hadn't finished making his bed and all the sheets were out of the dryer...".

Oh, why would Matt call a suicide hotline? Let's see if we can figure it out. Ring, ring. "Hello". A voice answers, "Matt, it's Jodi (sniff, sniff, sob, cry). Can I borrow one of you guns?" It's called a cry for help. The problem is she never wanted the help she needed. She wanted Travis.

This woman is pure evil. For the first time, I felt just a few seconds of something besides pure revulsion for her, and by the time she's done elaborating, I loathe her more than I did before I felt a hint of anything that wasn't black and negative.

Let's paint the picture here: Jodi's having a tough couple of months. She's been thinking about killing herself. She's just gotten into her car, and she livid, panicked, and spinning out of control. Telling her to go back to Yreka is one thing – telling her to go to Antarctica is another. Nobody lives in Antarctica, and they both know that. He's telling her that she deserves isolation. She knows she's losing him. What does she do? Before she even gets home, while she's still driving the 5 – 10 minutes back to her house, she's calling Matt and asking for a gun. She holds people hostage by threatening suicide. These are the most awful, cruel, and manipulative people in the world: do it my way, or suffer the guilt of knowing you killed me. So, she thinks nothing of calling Matt – who is five/six hours away – and turning his world upside down with threats of suicide, and then she hangs up on him to talk to Travis.

If Travis called her, and again, that's a big if, it was because someone in her family was alerted to her suicidal threat, and they got his phone number and said that Jodi was going to kill herself because of the fight the two of them had. More likely, however, Jodi called Travis before she got down the street and starting screaming into the phone that she was going to go home and shoot herself, and he panicked and called her back. That's how the uninitiated would respond. Remember, this worked. Sky Hughes has said that every time Travis got some distance between them, Jodi threatened to kill herself. Sky tried to explain that Jodi wouldn't really do it, but Travis said he couldn't take that chance. Look who ended up dead.

If they think that phrases like "it took him a while to calm down" and "his anger" are what will stick with the jury, they're wrong. They are hearing a woman who was mentally ill talk about how she tried to control the people in her world with suicidal threats. Again, if I had been a juror, she'd be dead in the water with this tactic. I'm feeling sorry for the person living with these threats, not the person who's constantly threatening and never actually making even a faux attempt.

Jodi is composed now. Nurmi asks if Travis was actually telling her to come back and finish her duties as "his maid". He should remind the jury that paying Jodi to be a maid was an act of kindness on Travis' part. She was not cleaning his house for free. She was an uneducated, barely employed loser who ended up on his doorstep with her hand out.

There was nothing coercive in their employee/employer relationship – at least nothing I've heard. Jodi should have a job. In fact, Jodi should have five or six houses she cleans regularly. Jodi is a young, able bodied woman who should be working full time somewhere, or working part time while she finishes her education.

As to whether or not Jodi was supposed to go back and finish her work, she says, "Umm, the implication was more come help me make my bed so we can make up". Nurmi asks, "Make up so you can have sex?". Jodi says, "Yes".

Nurmi asks, "Did he request this French maid's outfit again?". A shot of the overhead projector shows the same tiny, grainy photo of the woman in the maid lingerie that Nurmi put up earlier. How long has that been up there? I assume it's been displayed since the subject turned to housekeeping. This is so wrong. Travis never "requested" that outfit. From the onset, Jodi made it clear that the entire subject was a joke. She never wore it. She never owned it, and neither did he. This is misleading the jury. I cannot believe this is legal in a court of law, this obvious manipulation of jurors with half-truths.

Jodi says "No". Nurmi continues, "So he makes this call, you begin to feel better (because suicide goes away when your boyfriend calls), did you go back over there?". Really, Nurmi? What the hell do you think?

Jodi answers, "Yes...I'm telling him no, but at the same time I'm turning around (she's almost smiling now) in the turnabout that's in my neighborhood". Nurmi asks, "What's that?". He heard her; he just wants the jury to hear it again. She repeats, "I'm saying no, I'm saying no while I'm actually doing it, I'm going through the turnabout on the way to my house, but instead of going all the way through it, I'm turning around and heading back". Nurmi spins his finger in tiny circles in the air, and then he asks, "Why'd you turn around, Jodi?". Jodi responds, "Umm, he was being the nice person that I was craving, I guess...I felt like a writhing ant under a magnifying glass for the last three hours. It was a long fight, and now he had relented, and he was being nice, and he was implying that his feelings would be hurt if I didn't come over...very sweet...almost baby talk, but not quite, so I came back, to his house".

A writhing ant under a microscope? She really shouldn't try to use colorful metaphors. That was lame, and also quite inaccurate. If anyone was the malicious kid holding a magnifying glass over a helpless ant, it was Jodi playing the role of the kid, and Travis playing the role of the ant. Anyway, we're all so glad that Travis adopted his baby voice and soothed the suicide right out of Jodi's sick and twisted head.

Nurmi asked the usual: did they have sex when she got back to his house? Jodi says they had sex. Nurmi wants to know about the sex. Jodi says, "We, umm, he, uh, we had anal sex that night, but he wasn't, it wasn't like, it wasn't, it wasn't loving, I mean, he said I love you, and he whispered those things in my ear and stuff like that, and, emm...". There's a long pause here. Maybe Nurmi wants to hear more, but she's not giving any more information.

Nurmi is now going to move onto Lisa Andrews. He asks if she remembers walking into Travis' house and seeing Lisa Andrews there. Oh, I'll bet she did. I bet it was on one of those nights that Lisa was typically at Travis' house.

Jodi answers, "I was...well, this might have been before New Mexico...it was all around the same time. I had been hired at PF Chang's in the summer, and his friend John was always talking about how he liked the honey chicken on their menu, it was his favorite dish, and one night, it was Monday night, which would have been Family Home Evening in the church, I worked though, for short, it's called FHE, and I got off work early because it was Monday night because it was slow (she always just happens to get off work early when she starts tracking her wayward boyfriends...amazing), and there was an extra honey chicken that was getting thrown away (wow, so here it is, early, and they already know that no one wants this honey chicken. So, before the shift even ends, the chef is willing to throw it away. No, what happened is, Jodi ordered it to take to Travis' house), so the chef said I could have it, so, it was still fresh, and I put it in a to-go container, and I'd taken food home before, and I always offered to split it with my roommates, but they never really wanted it, it was still early, so I knew, or I assumed that Travis was at church, so I didn't call him, but I called John, and asked, do you want half of this honey chicken, and he said yes, because he liked it, and so I was going to go over there, split it with him, and then go back home, because if you put it in the fridge it gets soggy because it's breaded and glazed, and so, I headed over there, oh...and he said Travis wasn't home, I asked him if Travis was home yet, and he said no. So, I started driving over to his house and I pulled into the driveway, in the same place I would always go, I came and went in his house without knocking, I'll show up...it's something I did, something a lot of friends did, so I walked into his house with the container, honey chicken in my hands, and I'm walking down, it's kind of a walkway with tile, there's a living room here, and as I was coming toward the kitchen just beyond that, there's a wall, just beyond that, I was going into the kitchen to get a plate for John, and John was on the couch over here watching TV, and I came around the kitchen and Travis was standing there with another girl, I didn't see who the girl was because I just saw hair, and he was standing in front of her, so I was mortified (huge grin on her face). I was like, oh my gosh, so I immediately turned and walked right straight out the front door, and I got in my car, and I left, and I was really embarrassed because I thought he wasn't home, and, umm, I started driving, and I drove west down Elliot, and I turned north on Signalview (people say left and right, not north and west, especially a woman who says she gets lost all the time), and right as I turned north on Signalview, there was a car that came right up behind me with their high beams on, and they were right up on the tail end of my car. I didn't know at first, but I thought it was somebody who had to go somewhere fast, so I was coming up on an LDS chapel that was on, on the left side of the street, and that was a turn out, so I assumed I was just gonna drive a few more yards, and the pull over on this turn out, but this car pulled over the double yellow line and sped up, and I thought, wow, they're really in a hurry, and then they pulled in front of me and braked really hard, and I saw the car, and that's when my headlights hit the paint, and I could see it was purple, it was a BMW, it was Travis' car. So, he pulled into the turnabout, and I assumed he wanted me to pull over because of that, and so I pulled over behind him".

That first part of her answer might qualify as the longest sentence in the world. Did you all learn enough about honey chicken? Do you know that it is breaded and glazed and will become soggy if you store it in the refrigerator? Did you know how important "to go" containers are when you plan to transport Chinese food to your boyfriend's house? Do you care that John's favorite PF Chang's dish is honey chicken? Do you have a good sense of the general street view of Travis' old neighborhood? Good, because that was all very critical information, and it has to be in the court transcript if justice is to be served.

Here's a translation: Despite her futile attempt to paint herself as the kindly Meals on Wheels lady, Jodi got word that Lisa was spending Friday nights at Travis' house with a bunch of other people. Jodi realized she had been excluded from the group. Jodi realized that there was a reason she had been excluded from that group, and that reason was a young woman named Lisa Andrews. Jodi knew that Travis had been getting closer to Lisa, and somehow, she knew that Travis would be leaving the hour long FHE meeting with Lisa. It's entirely possible that Lisa's car was in Travis' driveway when Jodi arrived at his house, and the two of them went to FHE together. Whatever the scenario was, you can be sure that Jodi knew Travis was attracted to Lisa, and he intended to date her. Jodi feigned illness at work so that she could get over to Travis' house, but not before she put in her order for honey chicken. Where was Travis' car, by the way? Was it in his driveway? Jodi hoped to be in his kitchen when Travis returned from FHE, and I'm not sure whether or not she expected Lisa to be there. So, she either wanted to sabotage their evening and she realized, after looking at Travis' face, that he was furious, or she knew that Travis was going to embarrass her in front of Lisa by telling her that she wasn't allowed to walk into his house anymore. Jodi ran out for a reason. Perhaps she wasn't willing to give Lisa, her adversary, the satisfaction of watching Travis telling Jodi that she was not allowed to walk into his house.

According to his friends, this was an argument the two had many times. He had experienced enough of Jodi, and that's why he got into the car to chase her. Whatever he said to her, he could have said on the phone, but he was emotional, and I think the emotion he was feeling was anger.

Nurmi asks, "Did he offer an explanation for what you just walked in on?". Why should he offer her an explanation? Unlike Jodi, Travis continued to make his mortgage payments, and so he actually owned his house. As the owner of a private residence, Travis could have been sliding down his Vaseline covered banister in a bikini while throwing Toblerone at the walls while reciting "The Night Before Christmas", and he STILL wouldn't have had to offer an explanation to anyone – not law enforcement, not the health inspector, and least of all, a manipulative, intrusive ex-girlfriend who, despite being told that she was no longer on his welcome list, refused to stop walking into his house as if she were named on the deed. Offer her an explanation? He could have had her arrested for trespassing, or, at the very least, he could have had a police officer explain to her that she was no longer allowed to walk into his house at will.

We all know that Jodi called ahead, found out that John was home, ordered the chicken, said she had an emergency and had to leave work, drove herself and the bait in a to-go container over to Travis' house, and she timed the whole thing so that'd she be serving food to his friend as Travis walked in the door. Yes. Because she really is all about her plan.

The longer her explanations are, the bigger the lie she's telling. Does it not insult this jury to hear this woman always painting herself in the best of all possible lights? She is on trial for a massive overkill, so it's safe to assume that she's got a temper and crosses boundaries. Yet once again, here we are, asked to believe that the planets just happened to align perfectly so that she could put herself exactly where she wanted to be. Jodi makes sure to throw in a sentence or two praising herself for her thoughtful behavior in bringing home food home for her roommates (plural and still nameless), and she wants everyone to admire her selflessness as she, after working a shift, thinks of John and his love affair with an order of honey chicken that's destined for the dumpster. Jodi even calls to make sure she won't run into Travis before walking into his house to deliver food to someone named John. There's even the implication that Travis really should have been at some church meeting, not at home. She would even like us to believe that she would also be at a church meeting, but she had to work on Mondays. She never misses an opportunity to make herself look like a missionary of charity and goodness. Is anybody wondering why she thought it was acceptable to walk into this man's house – especially in light of the ridiculous tale she had to weave to make it all seem acceptable?

If this resulting car chase scene ends up in sex, I'm going to throw my hands into the air.

So, did Travis "offer an explanation" for being alive and at home on that Monday evening? Jodi says, "Yeah", and then she takes a deep breath. Prepare yourself for another string of lies. Nurmi asks, "During that discussion, did he admit to you that he was dating Lisa Andrews?". Again, this falls under the category of "why should he?". He's not dating Jodi – she is a willing bed buddy, that's it.

Jodi answers, "No, he didn't say who it was. He just said it was a girl from his ward who was there and he wanted, she wanted to see his house, and he was just giving her a tour". Of course Travis didn't say who the girl was. He liked Lisa, and the last thing he needed was jealous Jodi honing in on someone she perceived as her competition. Jodi had no problem confronting women. The name Bianca comes to mind.

Nurmi continues, "Did he invite you back to the home?". Jodi answers, "Not at that point, but he gave me a hug, and he squeezed my butt, and said, you're coming over later tonight, right?". I now fully understand why Juan Martinez used that refrain "what's a girl to do?" as he literally mocked her during his closing argument. That is exactly the look she just gave Nurmi, and she added that shrug of the shoulder and lift of the hands to seal the deal. It's really as though she expects everyone to believe that she is some kind of sex slave, and all her master needs to do is whistle and she's panting and wagging her tail after bringing him his slippers. She's an embarrassment to women. Have some self-respect, or call it is what is it – prostitution or gold digging.

Nurmi asks, "What did that mean to you? What were you coming over later that evening for?". Jodi almost cuts Nurmi off because she's so ready to answer this question. She really thinks they're gaining steam with this whole strategy. She responds, "To hang out – sex, pretty much". Nurmi asks, "After he was done with this date with Lisa Andrews, after that you were supposed to come over and have sex with him? Is that what we're saying here?". Yes, Nurmi, that's what we're saying here. It's kind of like the situations most of your clients find themselves in, except this time, everyone involved is an adult.

Jodi looks down, and ponders Nurmi's questions. Finally, she lifts her hands and says, "Umm...yeah".

Nurmi says, "Now, late in 2007, and this relationship is going on and on and on, and uh, are you still living in Mesa in early 2008?". Jodi answers, "Yes". Which year are we talking about – 2007 or 2008? Nurmi asks, "Are you having sexual intercourse with Mr. Alexander in early 2008?". Jodi answers, "Yes, well, no, yes, not vaginal, so much". Um...what? Nurmi replies, "Not vaginal intercourse?". Jodi answers, "No".

Nurmi the gynecologist asks, "Was that, you'd had it before, was there a reason you weren't having it at that time?". Jodi answers, "Yes, after the...well, the first time I was asleep, the second time was in August, 2007, and that was consensual (they were both consensual, unless I missed the part of the sleep rape story where she jumped out of bed, grabbed her clothes, and fled into the night), and I knew we had gone all the way (all the way?), so that was pretty black and white, and I thought, okay, and I confided in Rachel, and I didn't want to tell her that we went all the way, but I said I think Travis and I might have gone too far, even though I knew we had gone too far, I wanted to get her advice, and she asked me how far we'd gone, so I thought oral sex was okay, so I threw that out there, and I said, well, we've had oral sex, and her jaw dropped almost to the floor, and she just freaked out and said you have to go to your bishop right now, and I didn't know that, and she said Travis has to go too, he needs to right away, he needs to get back on the right track, and go tell him right now, and wear your seatbelt, because you know, the implication being you don't want to be in a car accident and die until you repent (calling him on the phone would have alleviated the death threat, but I assume it's more fun to watch his face melt when she tells him that he's been outed). It was that serious to her (once again, the "what's a girl to do" expression makes an appearance), so I, I didn't know that (yes, we know, you've said that a few too many times now), and so I got in the car, called Travis, and went over there...".

I guess Juan Martinez realizes that it is completely pointless to even try to make Jodi tell us when this big event happened. Considering the fact that this testimony has been so mired in sex that I feel like I need a shot of penicillin, I don't think it's asking too much for her to give us a little clarification about the timing of this revelation. Once again, it begins with Nurmi talking about years, not months. It's 2007, it's 2008, it's the sleep rape date, no...actually, it's August 2007.

Jodi Arias has been engaging in all kinds of sex. Anal sex is a form of intercourse, and she's very well aware of that. I think the LDS church might have a bigger issue with that form of intercourse than vaginal intercourse. I did notice that Jodi, who thought anal sex was perfectly acceptable under the Law of Chastity, left that out of her confession to Rachel. That's not really fair, is it? It's not honest either. When Rachel asked her how far they had gone, she should have said that she wasn't going to answer that, but she would like to know what forms of intimacy were acceptable. Of course she wouldn't do that. This was about outing Travis. This was about telling on him. I hate the fact that we have to do so much parsing to get even a general hint of what the truth might be.

One thing is for sure – Jodi Arias is a hateful woman. She continues to show it the jury, and she continues to show it to the world. Don't do things her way, and she'll kill herself. Don't do things her way, and she'll disgrace you in front of your friends and church family. If after that, you still won't do things her way, she'll kill you.

Nurmi asks, "And you weren't having vaginal intercourse because of the Law of Chastity, right?". Jodi says, "Yes". This is just beyond the pale. It's too much. I am constantly amazed, literally amazed, that they thought she could sell this utter rot to the jury.

Nurmi asks if anything happened in January, 2008. Now, wait a minute. We just left Jodi, securely buckled in her car while in her pre-repentant state, and she was heading over to Travis' to tell him that they both needed to get to the Temple emergency room to have the sin extracted from their lives. What happened? How did he react? Are we just going to fly by that information? Didn't the domestic abuser beat her senseless when he found out she blew his cover? Wasn't there at least another round of gay slurs directed at Carl, Sr. and Carl, Jr.? Did she even tell Travis?

Since we're going to fast forward to January, 2008, I guess we can assume this is where the pedophilia accusation comes in. Now that Jodi is withholding sex – or at least she's implying that she's been made aware of the Law of Chastity in its entirety – will we stop hearing the salacious stories of sex? Will Travis now be forced to indulge in his base fantasies involving children? Is that where this is going?

Nurmi says, "Did something happen in January, 2008, that changed your relationship with Mr. Alexander". And here we go...oh, what an act this is. Jodi strikes a serious pose, and she's trying to look like one of the world's bad people has scarred her for life (she likes pretending she's one of the normal people). With her head down, and her voice lowered, she answers, "Yes". Nurmi asks, "What happened?". Jodi closes her eyes and slowly moves her head as if to say, "Please, please, don't make me think about this...".

Juan Martinez objects, and it upsets Jodi. She was ready to recite her lines on camera, and now the spell is broken. She'll have to get into character all over again. Juan says that he needs some foundation for this. He needs a specific time, not a month. Actually, that's all this man has been asking for. As the months and years roll by, all Martinez wants is a date. Just a date or an approximate date. He doesn't get many.

Nurmi, with his voice at a reasonable level because it is inappropriate to venture into such a sensitive and horrific subject while stamping and yelling, says, "I'm asking what happened in January, 2008. She can explain (thank you for that decision, Judge Nurmi, but that's what the lady in the black robe – the only person who remains seated when everyone else is standing for the jury -- is here for)". Judge Stephens says, "Counsel approach". The last time I checked, there were 31 days in January, and unless Jodi plans to start with New Year's Day and finish up the month, I think narrowing down the week is a reasonable request. I think it would be something you would remember – considering the subject matter.

I'm not sure who won that round, but Nurmi starts with, "Before we get into the particulars of it, can you remember where it occurred?". Jodi responds, "Yes, in his bedroom". Nurmi continues, "Do you remember the date it occurred?". Jodi answers, "It was on a Monday, and it was late January, 2008. I think it was around the 21st". Why didn't she just say that? If she knew the exact date all along, why not just say so?

Nurmi continues, "What did you see on the 21st, or late January, 2008, or I should say this, what HAPPENED on the 21st of January, 2008, that changed the course of your relationship with Travis". Nurmi stretched the question out long enough to allow Jodi to get back into her "pedophiles are bad" character.

Oops, another objection. Jodi will be forced to do her prep work for a third time while this is argued. Juan Martinez says, "There's still a lack of foundation. Can we have a time? Was it morning, noon, afternoon?". Once again, Nurmi puts on his judicial robe and says, "She can explain this story, judge". Judge Stephens says, "Alright. Overruled".

Jodi says, "I got off of work (her right hand is placed on the side of her face), I was working at (here we go, the telltale sign of lying. It doesn't matter where she worked. She waited tables. It doesn't matter if those tables were in Denny's or a Chinese restaurant. Her below minimum wage – plus tips – job is no more relevant than her testimony about honey chicken from PF Changs. She pauses, and lets out a big sigh, and with her hand still plastered to her face, she stares into the void)...Mimi's cafe, at that point, in Mesa. I got off work, and came over to his house, and helped him. He was loading big boxes into the attic, umm, he was just rearranging them, so I was just handing them up to him.. we were hanging out for a while. He disappeared into the attic, so I was waiting for him, and, umm, and then he kind of popped out and said boo and scared me, and we laughed about that (she's happy now...no more stress), and he came down the ladder, and he gave me a little white, porcelain angel that he had (attic junk he didn't want), and he handed it to me and called me an angel (she wishes), and he gave that to me, and I thought that was sweet, and so, umm, I went and put it next to my purse, which was in his bedroom, on the dresser, and we hung out a little bit longer downstairs in his office, and then I was leaving. So, I ran upstairs, got my purse, shut the bedroom door, after I had already said goodbye to him, and I left, and as I was driving back home, I realized I had left the porcelain angel there, and Travis, just knowing him, I knew he would call me (more smiles) and make me feel guilty about it, in a joking way but, I wouldn't live it down, for a while...".

Absolute fantasy, on many levels. Travis Alexander has not given Jodi anything significant in terms of a gift. He's given her religious items, but nothing feminine and nothing personal. Remember, he won't even pay for her to accompany him on trips. That bed she shares with him when they're in a hotel room? Yeah, she pays for her half of it. According to Jodi, she's been given melted chocolates, some cheap, tacky shorts, a cast off T-shirt, and while she's still allegedly hanging onto the threadbare remains of Spiderman underpants, there is nothing else to mention in terms of gifts – not even a tiny, inexpensive, silver cross on a chain that would have been an appropriate gift on "this spiritual day". Nothing.

Suddenly, he gives her a trinket, the equivalent of room dandruff – but still, something from his hand to her hand – a small, white angel that has just been liberated from the attic. She puts it next to her pocketbook, this angel that will probably end up swinging from her rear view mirror, and she forgets it? Why didn't she put it IN the pocketbook? Because she needed to have some reason to put herself back in that bedroom. I would love to hear her attempt to tell this story backwards. She couldn't do it. She's only memorized it one way.

Nurmi interrupts, "So, what, what, so what did you do?". The clock is ticking and he wants these jurors going home with pedophilia on their minds. He's got to get this verbal diarrhetic to the point. She answers, "Well, I thought of getting it later, but because of that pattern, I turned around to get it. And, I called him real quick on his cell phone (how do you call someone "real quick" as opposed to "real slow" – she always reveals herself with these stupid and invalid details), I called him real quick on his home phone, he didn't answer. I hadn't been gone ten minutes. I didn't think it was a big deal. I walked back in there, and I ran upstairs, and I went into his bedroom to grab it, and...".

She stops mid-sentence, looks up, licks her lips, and stares at Nurmi with excitement in her eyes. Nurmi is too slow. It wasn't seamless. He asks, "And what did you see when you got there?".

Jodi answers, "I walked in, and Travis was on the bed masturbating...ugh...ahh...and I got really embarrassed, even though we'd been intimate more times than I could count, it was just kind of awkward walking in on him like that, and umm, I was headed toward the dresser and I stopped, and I was thinking of something funny or witty that I could say like, do you still need my help, or something. Umm, he started grabbing at something on the bed, and I realized they were papers, and as he was grabbing the papers, one kind of went sailing off the bed, and it fell in that chaotic pattern that papers fall, it landed face up near my feet, and it was a photograph...umm". Nurmi missed his cue again, and left the lead actress looking at him to cue her for her next line.

Before we get to that next line, can we take a moment to examine what Jodi claims she saw? If you walk in on someone who, in the privacy of their own bedroom, is engaged in this type of incredibly private activity, what do you naturally do? I would say you utter an expletive and shut the door. Then you leave. You do not think, "What funny or witty thing can I say?" as you make your way to the dresser. In fact, you don't make your way to the dresser. And what was that ridiculous statement about a piece of paper that falls to the floor in a "chaotic pattern"? This paper certainly isn't a magic carpet, and after seeing the distance between his bed and his bedroom door, that is what it would need to be to sail through the air and land at her feet. If I have ever despised this woman, it is now. There are no words for what she is doing.

Nurmi picks up his line, as rehearsed: "What was the photograph of?". The monster answers, "It was a picture of a little boy". Please, can we leave it here? Please do not traumatize the people in the room who have been through this nightmare, and believe me, according to statistics, there are plenty. Will Nurmi be a human being, or is this a scorched earth attack?

Nurmi asks, "Can you guess how old for us the little boy was?". Scorched earth attack it is. Jodi answers, "Oh, five-ish, five, six. I'm not a good judge of age." Really? Then why all the stories about her little brother, the one born shortly after Jodi? Does she not know the difference between a four year old and an eight year old, because most people do. She knows the difference between roller skates and roller blades, but she doesn't know the difference between a five year old and an eight year old? This is the best this pair of clowns could come up with?

Nurmi asks, "Did you recognize the little boy?". Jodi answers, "No". How about this: Did she care about the little boy? Did she report this to anyone? If not, she's an accomplice to the "crime".

Nurmi asks, "Was the little boy dressed?". She answers, "He was dressed in underwear, like briefs". As a human being, I am sickened. This woman slaughtered a man; she slit his throat like he was an animal who was going to butchered and sold to a supermarket. She left him to rot. She lied about it. She lied about it a second time. She's lying about it now. Why is she allowed to talk about this if her phony pedophile letters have been precluded? This is an atrocity.

Nurmi wants to know what the monster did when she saw the photograph sitting next to those planks she calls feet. She says, "I was frozen there for a minute...well, maybe not a WHOLE minute, but I, I didn't know how to react. It kind of seemed like one of those dreams where's something's really off, but you can't, you can't figure it out, and so, I left the angel there on the dresser, and I turned to walk, and he called my name, and I just ran, and I didn't stay, and I got in my car and I started driving (this part is probably lifted from her leaving the kill site on June 4, 2008), and I went home, again, and I got...".

Nurmi asks, "Did you call his name, or did he call your name?". She answers, "He called my name".

Nurmi says, "So, I'm sorry...you were driving away from his home. How did you feel about what you saw?" The beast from hell answers, "Umm, I felt nauseated?". Did she drive to the police station? Did she do that? If not, who the hell cares how she felt?

There's no question, but the swine offers, "I drove all the way home. I was trying to drive fast enough to get to...well, trying not to pull over to throw up. I got home, and I was hitting the garage door opener about half a block away so that I could pull right into the garage, and ran inside and threw up inside the bathroom". How convenient. Most people don't have such control over visceral reactions to trauma. It's nice to know she didn't vomit in her car, on the street, or in the garage. She made it all the way to the safety of her own bathroom.

No, she did not. If you are shocked with something this horrific, if you see what she says she saw, you are in such a state that you cannot drive. When the full impact hits you, and it may take a minute or two, you will react, but everything is involuntary. Your brain is operating in a way that is unfamiliar to you. The sickening panic gives way to an awful, perverse reality. All you can do is say no, no, no. You fall to your knees or you vomit – maybe both. You cannot believe you've ever spoken to this person – let alone been intimate with them. You may even faint. Some people can operate on auto-pilot, but not most. You may be able to get into your car and drive, but if that is the case, you don't really remember it. You do not contact the pedophile. They are the enemy, and you feel no sympathy for them. You contact somebody who knows the ins and outs of this dark, sick, and twisted world. It may be a hotline. It may be the police. It may be a friend. What it isn't is the pedophile. You've already erected that wall. In a real trauma, you have to collect yourself, because dialing 911 can suddenly become something that is too difficult to figure out because your mind is racing and spinning. You cannot hold your stomach contents in for ten minutes if the bile is in your throat. You just can't...not if it's real. Normal people would react involuntarily. Enough people in this courtroom know what a disclosure like this did to them.

Nurmi asks, "Did you speak, did Travis ever make other attempts to call you after you saw what you saw?". The demon says – no, she whispers, "Yes". Nurmi asks, "How soon?". This abomination says, "After I cleaned myself up, I went, umm, I went back out to my car to get my purse and my phone, and I saw that there were some missed calls from him (she wipes away a tear – one that doesn't require the removal of her goggle sized glasses)...like four, like maybe three or four". She's looking at her missed calls?

Nurmi asks the creature lower than a maggot why this wasn't the moment in time she ended her relationship with Travis. It responds, "Well, I wasn't even thinking anything along those lines at the time. I was confused and I was crying, and I didn't really know what to make of all that. So, I went for a drive. Before, when I didn't answer the phone, and he would call repeatedly, he would come over to the house, 'cause I didn't live far, and I didn't want to be at the house when he came over, so I wasn't sure how to talk to him, or what to say, so I left, and I drove around Mesa for a while, and I ended up at the temple visitor center, and I hung out in there for a little while, and umm, I was just collecting my thoughts, and not really meditating, but just trying to figure out what to do next, and how to handle that".

For a woman who was acquainted with suicide hotlines, did it ever occur to her to google a child abuse hotline? Did she ever think, even for a moment, that this was bigger than her imagined romance? Of course not. This NEVER happened. I would bet my life on it. I know she is odd, unbalanced, and not normal, and because of that, we may assume that her reactions to things may not be status quo, but this is way outside the norm. She is sexually involved with this man. Her head should be about to literally explode. Drive a car? She should be sitting in the corner of a room sobbing.

Nurmi asks, "Did you come to a decision as to what to do next?". Jodi answers, "Umm, well, I couldn't imagine never talking to him again (BS...absolute BS. Not only wouldn't she want to talk to him again, she would be ashamed to admit she ever talked to him at all). That would just be, if we never spoke again after that point, I would feel unsettled, and, uhh, I don't know, I wanted to let him explain, at least".

She is being so abnormal in her response to this, I'm seriously wondering if she isn't a pedophile herself. I'm completely serious. She wanted to let him explain it? No, no, no.

It continues, "I went out, from the visitor's center, and I checked my phone again. There were like frantic voice mails from him...and they were, come over and talk to me, that kind of thing, and so...". Nurmi interrupts, "Again, Jodi, let me address the question, and perhaps it's difficult, but why would it be, from what you've told us, you saw him masturbating to the image of a child? Why would it have been a problem for you, in other words, why couldn't you imagine not having any more contact with him at that point in time?".

She's off script again, and Samantha knows it. A shot of her face shows a grin. Jodi doesn't realize that pedophilia is a deal breaker – regardless of the connection between the pedophile and the person who discovers what they are. None of this rings true. Again, if anything is being reinforced, it is that this whole story is a lie, or we are listening to a pedophile excuse their own behavior.

She lies, "As I was thinking in the temple, I mean, I've heard in the past that usually people who have problems like that were hurt when they were children, and I kept thinking, what if he was hurt when he was a kid, and it made me angry to think of somebody hurting him when he was a kid, so I tried to mitigate it that way (nope, not real...mitigate is a legal term she's throwing around), and I wanted to talk to him, and find out what was wrong with him, what was going on with him, so...I called him back, finally, after a while and we decided, we agreed to meet up, we were going to swap cars for family home evening (pedophilia...swap cars...family home evening...no way), and umm...".

I have never seen someone go from a near break-down to then talking about the logistics of switching cars this quickly. I'm talking seconds.

Even Nurmi sounds incredulous as he says, "You were swapping cars for family...home...evening?". She answers, "Yes". Nurmi asks, "Is that what you just told us?". She repeats, "Yes". He continues, "So he could have your car or you could have his?". She answers, "Both. He didn't want to drive my car to church with other people...he wanted to take his own car".

So, what was the rush to get back to the house to pick up the angel? She just said that she was going to be back at his house a few hours later to swap cars with him. Couldn't she have just picked up the angel then? Now, if this hole in the story is addressed, she will say that Travis would have never let her live down the fact that she left the angel there in the first place. However, she did return to retrieve the angel, and he was going to realize that. So, there was no way to get around the fact that she forgot the angel. Whether she picked it up ten minutes after leaving the first time, or whether she picked it up several hours later when she returned to swap cars, the fact remains – she forgot the angel, and he was going to know that.

Nurmi wants to reiterate: Travis was the one who wanted to go to FHE on the same day he was caught masturbating to images of young boys. Nurmi wants to know how that happened, in the wake of the day's events. Did she just take his car and leave, or did they see each other. She responds, "We never hooked up before family home evening. I had a migraine, and I needed to just sleep, and, uhh, and I don't know...I woke up later in the evening, and I just went over to his house later that night".

Nurmi continues, "You go to his house later that night. Do you talk with him?". She says she did. Nurmi asks, "Do you ask him about what you saw?". She says, "I didn't really have to ask him. I let him do the talking, mostly...". There is a hearsay objection from Juan Martinez, and another bench conference follows.

After a lengthy bench conference, Nurmi says, "This conversation...after you viewed him masturbating to the image of a young boy, a child, what was the subject matter of the conversation?". Jodi responds, "Umm, mostly about, he was explaining to me...". Nurmi wants details, but Juan Martinez objects. He says, "Objection. Hearsay. She said he was explaining, and she's telling us what he said. She can talk about what the subject matter was...which is what we discussed". Sustained.

Nurmi continues, "After that conversation, did you come away with the understanding that Mr. Alexander had a sexual interest in children?". Jodi answers, "Yes". Nurmi continues, "Did you come away with the understanding that it was boys and girls, or was it just one or the other?". There is another objection. Juan Martinez says that the objection has something to do with "her understanding". Nurmi is told to rephrase.

He asks, "Did you believe him to have an interest in young boys?". Objection, hearsay, overruled. Jodi answers, "Yes". Nurmi asks, "Did you believe him to have an interest in young girls?". She thinks for a moment, and then replies, "I already knew he was interested in young girls, but they were sexually mature girls, but minors". Doubtful. That's not the way this works.

Nurmi goes through the nonsensical questioning of "did Jodi think she could help him". Jodi says, "That's the impression he gave me". Nurmi asks, "What was your impression of how you were to help him with this problem?". The liar answers, "He preferred sex with women. He preferred sex with women. It made him feel normal, more normal". Again, that's not the way it works.

Nurmi asks if, during this conversation, there was any discussion about the boy's Spiderman underwear. She answers, "That was the reason for it, apparently...that's what he said". Nurmi says, "The reason being, if I understand it correctly, he liked pretending that you were a young boy". The snake answers, "I didn't ask what he was visualizing".

Jodi's really pouring it on. She's barely audible, her head is in her hands, and she's been wiping away tears for the last five minutes. Nurmi asks, "Is this the last time you ever spoke with Travis Alexander?". She answers, No". If any of this were true, the answer would be, "Of course".

Nurmi asks, "Did you leave right away after this discussion?". She answers, "No". Nurmi continues, "Did you have, did you submit to a sexual interaction with Mr. Alexander after this discussion?". She answers, "Yes". Well, that's it for me folks. Jodi Arias is a pedophile. If that conversation got her in the mood, she's a pedophile.

Nurmi will now go into the realm of the grotesque by asking, "What sort of interaction was that?". The pile of human feces responds, "It was sex. It was anal sex".

Nurmi asks, "Why Jodi, were you willing to submit yourself to sexual interaction with Mr. Alexander having seen and having heard everything you saw and heard that day?". Because she's either a liar or pervert. One thing she is not? A victim.

It answers, "It's hard to describe because it's really embarrassing, but he seemed very, very ashamed with himself, and like, he didn't want to be that way. It was something he struggled with, and it's not who he wanted to be, it's not who he wanted to be in the future, and he was trying to deal with it, and when he had sex with women, he felt like a normal, heterosexual man, and that's what he wanted to be, and that's what he said he was, and that's what I believed him to be, so when he had sex with women, it was normal, and it was preferable to his other deviant urges". A woman married to a man for 20 years who had several children with him would not this be this forgiving. No, it makes no sense. In my estimation, it was a travesty that any of this was allowed to be introduce to a jury.

Secondly, it is interesting that Jodi uses the plural term "women" when explaining why she continued to have sex with Travis after she allegedly discovered his penchant for children. She is implying that by having sex with him, she is engaging in a therapeutic exercise meant to help him feel like "a normal, heterosexual man". If she's so convinced that this is the cure (which is ridiculous), then why should she have such huge issues with Travis having sex (or making out) without women? Wouldn't that go along with the therapy Dr. Arias has prescribed?

Did she ever ask him if he had victimized anyone? That would be the first question. Why am I even asking? Jodi finds out her boyfriend is a pedophile, and her response is to let him sodomize her. Rrrrrright. There is ridiculous banter between attorney and client about helping him, loving him, whatever....yes, she loved him. Nope. Impossible.

Nurmi would like to know if she helped him in any other way beside sticking her ass in the air and handing him the KY (I'm paraphrasing, obviously). She says, "Yes, before I moved back to California, I gave him a pamphlet that I found. There was a stack of them in a mall, umm, and I picked up a few of them because it was about mental illnesses. I don't remember what the name of it was. It had an 800 number, and it also had a 602 number (now do you believe her?), and, umm, it might have had other phone numbers and a website, but it looked like it was for services that were complimentary, or maybe not free, but cheap or affordable, or something to that affect. I thought that maybe he would just talk to some people. I thought it was confidential, and that there would be somebody who could counsel him, or there would be somebody that had a degree in psychology, or some kind of certification in mental health counseling...".

Jodi says that she didn't find this pamphlet until March, 2008. I guess we're all supposed to guess at how many sexual encounters Jodi had with her "pedophile" boyfriend between this exposure and the pamphlet. At least five weeks have gone by.

Let's just skip right on by those weeks between Travis being discovered and the pamphlet. Now Nurmi wants to know how Travis reacted to being handed the pamphlet from the mall. Jodi says, "He was upset. It led to an argument. We argued about several subjects that day...it started off verbal, and then it became physical".

Oh, so the best friend of a "pedophile" is going to be physically abused? The keeper of the secret that could destroy his life is about the be beaten? Just get to it, Jodi Arias. I can't take much more. She says, "This incident was in April, and yes, he was physically abusive before that...".

Nurmi is moving backwards now. He wants to know when Travis was physically abusive after the wrist grab at convention.

She answers, "It would have been the time I got up to leave three times...when he pushed me down...the pamphlet came later, the third incident was when I walked in on him". Nurmi says, "Okay, the day after you walked in on him, you mentioned you had sex that night. Did you leave that night?". She says, "Yes". Nurmi asks, "Where did you see Mr. Alexander the next day". Jodi answers, "Umm, I was getting ready to leave for California, and before I left, I wanted to see if he was okay. I figured, if that were me, I would want to go jump off a bridge (or shoot yourself, but it wasn't her). I wanted to make sure that he was okay." How long does it take Jodi Arias to get ready to leave for California? She didn't leave until April, 2008, but here she is saying that she showed up at his house on January 22, 2008, to check on him because she was getting ready to leave for California (in another eight or nine weeks).
Nurmi responds, "And you said that before you leave for California, where were you going?". She answers, "Umm...I think I was going, San Diego might have been a few weeks later. I was either going there, or I was going back to Palm Desert. My neighbor still had some things of mine, umm, in her garage...that I hadn't picked up yet (does she pay for anything, even storage?)."

Suddenly, Nurmi is back to January 22, 2008. He asks what happened when Jodi went over to check on him the next day. She says, "Umm, I went over there just to see how he was doing. We were talking in his bedroom, and he told me he needed to borrow, I think it was $200, and umm, I didn't have it. I had just lent him 699 and I...like a few days prior, and I had just enough money to pay for the gas on my trip, and maybe some food and get back. All my credit cards were, at that point, were shot, from my house. So I told him, I didn't really snap at him because he had reacted very badly in the past when I snapped at him, but I did say, I just lent you $700. OH, he called ME selfish, because I didn't have it because I was going to California, and if I didn't have it then maybe I shouldn't go to California, maybe I should stay in Mesa, and pick up more shifts, because that's not a lot of money, and if I don't have it, that's a problem, a problem, a reflection on my own personal finances. So, I thought, umm, how can you call me selfish? I just lent you $700, and when I said that, he got angry, and he crossed the room, and he started shaking me, and said, fucking sick of you (oh, me too), and he was screaming it real loud, and some of his spit got in my face, and I mean, he wasn't spitting on me (that's to make it sound believable – Jodi Arias would never embellish), but as I was talking, he body slammed me on the floor at the foot of his bed (there's a dramatic pause here for Nurmi to ask the next question, but I'm going to skip that and keep going with what she said)...well, it startled me, but it didn't hurt, but it startled me, and I kind of let out an unexpected sound. It could be best described as a yelp. I can't explain it, but it startled me, and the impact, and the sound came out, and I think he misinterpreted and he said, don't act like that hurts, and he called me a bitch, and he kicked me in the ribs, and that hurt, for real, and he went to kick me again, but I put my hands out, to block his foot, and it clipped my hand, and hit my finger...(Nurmi asks if hit her finger)...yes, my left hand".

Nurmi pontificates: "So, he kicked you once in the ribs, and he goes to kick you in the ribs again, and you go to stop him with your hand, and he kicks your finger, right?". She's got her mouth open now, and she's breathing in and out. She answers, "Yes, on the second kick". Nurmi asks, "What happened after that second kick?". Jodi answers, "I screamed. Really loud. I think I yelled out, my finger, or my hand, something to that affect". Something to that affect? Sure.

Jodi claims Travis stormed out of the room and went downstairs after that, despite the fact that her finger was swelling up. She kind of peeked around the bedroom door, and down onto the landing. Then, the doorbell rang. He sent whoever it was away. Then Travis came back upstairs, and, being visibly more calm, he wanted to see Jodi's hand.

There's some more ridiculous banter, but ultimately, Jodi says, "He was calmer, and he asked to see my hand, but I kind of pulled back a little, just as a reaction, and then he said, let me see it, but he said it in kind of snappy, stern way, so I didn't want to provoke him anymore, so I just let him look at my hand". Did anyone ever teach Jodi Arias how to dial 911? She still has nine more fingers.

Nurmi asks if there was a particular part of her hand that was injured. She responds, "Umm, yes. The ring finger on my left hand. The ring finger". Nurmi asks if she received medical attention for this injury. No, of course not. Her excuse is, "I didn't have medical insurance, for one thing, and two, I was worried that the police would get involved if I went down there, and I mean, I guess I could have made up a story (obviously), but Travis made a splint for my finger. I was at his house, and we just stayed with that. It was swelling, but we put ice on it, and he had like two little, or three little, popsicle sticks that he broke that were like the length of my finger, and he tied it onto my finger".

Nurmi asks why she didn't call the police. The liar with "the secret" in her heart says, "I would have never called the police on Travis...I was, I couldn't imagine doing something like that...it would have felt like treachery. I wouldn't have betrayed him. I was loyal to him".

Nurmi wants to know about this "loyalty". He asks, "Given all that you went through, what did you have to be loyal to?". She answers, "Well, I looked at him as someone who had his own issues that he was struggling with, and I didn't see him as a bad person. I just saw him as a person who had issues, like everyone has issues. He just had different issues, and I wanted him to get help. That was one of the conditions we had made the day before (that she conveniently forgot to mention when talking about the day before). Of course he didn't want me to say anything, and I promised him I wouldn't (was that before or after she vomited?), and I said I wouldn't say anything, of course (of course? This is pedophilia we're talking about), and he said he would. And so, umm, I just couldn't imagine doing anything to betray him".

There is no medical evidence, but Jodi says she believes her finger was broken. Here's the joke of the day: Nurmi asks if the injury is still visible today. Satan's personal assistant says, "I think so. It's still crooked today". That finger should have been entered into evidence. She has been displaying it since the day she took the stand, and probably before.

Nurmi has Jodi do a show and tell with her finger. Higher, Jodi...hold it higher. Yes, that's what you get when you go stab a man over and over with a blood drenched knife. Tough. I hope it hurts...every day.

Nurmi asks, "What do you think about when you see that injury on your hand?". He can't be serious. She thinks about trapping him, stabbing him, the way the blood felt spraying on her body, the fact that blood has a metallic smell, and that she had better get some bandages somewhere before she goes to Ryan Burns house to see if there is any chemistry between them. She was amped up after the murder. She needed a sexual release, and no gimped finger was going to stop her from climaxing. That's what she was thinking.

There's an objection, but Nurmi argues it. Juan Martinez doesn't give up. It's an objection as to the relevance of the question. They are told to approach.

Jodi is told to hold her finger up again, and she does. When she's asked what it reminds her of, she says she tries not to think about "the incident" because it was "unpleasant". Nurmi asks her if she is scared when she thinks of that incident. She says she doesn't go too far into that memory because it was a very negative experience. She says, "I wish I handled it differently". Yeah, I'll bet. She's got a gimped finger. His fingers? Don't even think about the condition they're in now.

What does Jodi mean by that – handled it differently? She says, "Umm, sometimes I regret not making a record of these things (sometimes? Is that what the domestic violence champion just said? Sometimes?), and sometimes I regret not getting medical help because at least it would have healed correctly (it doesn't matter, inmate...nobody will slipping a diamond or a gold band on that finger, so what the hell is difference?)..maybe not...it feels arthritic (good), as opposed to any of my other joints...". She makes some weak, wimpy noise. Excuse me, but are we at the funeral of Jodi Arias' left ring finger, because it certainly feels that way. One finger. Are we supposed to grieve for her finger after what she did to the man who ended up in a coffin? Seriously?

Nurmi tries twice to get this question in, and ultimately he is successful: Did Jodi want to make sure Travis didn't get into trouble for everything he did? Jodi answers, "I definitely didn't want him to get in trouble, and I didn't want anyone to know that that happened between us". Nurmi finishes up with, "Because you were embarrassed that he beat you up, right?". Nurmi is in her face, and he's pointing his finger at her. He looks like an idiot.

There's an objection as to leading the witness. It's sustained, but that just causes Nurmi to rephrase. The killer says, "I was more ashamed (because that's what the domestic violence literature tells her she supposed to be feeling)". Nurmi says, "Ashamed. You felt shame. Right?". Another objection. Another rephrase. Nurmi rephrases, but Juan Martinez objects again. It's sustained again.

Finally, in a voice *dripping* with sarcasm, Nurmi asks, "Were you thrilled and happy that Travis beat you up?". It answers, "No". He goes on, with his arms spread wide, "Did you want to shout it from the rooftops?". She's a sad sack of gloom, and she answers, "No". Nurmi asks, "Why not?". She answers, "I just felt, I guess embarrassment isn't an accurate word, but I just felt, it was stronger than embarrassment. I felt very ashamed, and I didn't want people to know that we had this kind of drama in our relationship, this level of problems, and I also felt like, I used to judge women who would get into situations like that...". **HOW ABOUT A "PEDOPHILE" ON THE LOOSE** – Did that mean anything to Jodi Arias?

This is sickening.

Juan Martinez has had enough. He objects again. He doesn't believe this is relevant. He is overruled. The rodent continues, "I used to think that women who got into situations like that, that it was partially, if not equally their fault, because they stayed. They kept staying there, and I went home (that's not something true victims of domestic violence have as an option, but Jodi Arias is a special case), and I just felt disgusted with myself, and I was just thinking, here I am in this situation, and I am just staying, and I've become that thing that I used to judge". Nurmi says, "You realized, at this point in time, that you were one of these people. Is that what you're telling us?". The cockroach hisses, "Yes".

The evening recess is called. The jury is told to have a nice evening. For Arias, the best part of the day has come and gone. She will be taken back to her basement cell, her street clothes will be removed, she will be put back in her jail stripes, she will be put into a van, and with a SWAT team for her own protection surrounding her, and she will be driven back to her cage at the Estrella Jail. She'll be strip searched, the guard will attempt to ignore – again – the size of her anus, and she'll be marched back to her cell in restraints. She'll be given whatever nutrients the FDA mandates, and then, she will recline on her metal slab and tell herself that today was a huge success, and it's just a matter of time.

Surely one of those women on the jury has been a victim of pedophilia or domestic violence. Right? At least one man wants to make it all better for her.

She truly believed that...

The intention of the author was to compile the entirety of this direct examination in one volume. Unfortunately, that goal proved impossible unless the reader was ready to invest in a tome, not a book. The full testimony and accompanying comments would have consumed over 1.200 pages. If you are interested in following the balance of the direct testimony of Jodi Arias (conducted by L. Kirk Nurmi, her public defender), Volume II will be available following the release of this volume. It is the hope of the author that Jodi Arias will be exposed for what she is, and the author further hopes that this type of non-linear, hopscotch-like, repetitive testimony – all of which assault a jury – will be addressed by the courts all across our country in the future.

Volume II covers days 5-8 of Jodi Arias' direct examination. Volume II is available on amazon.com.

You can contact the author and get updates through her website at:

www.KimAWhittemore.com
Or join in the continuing discussion at:
www.facebook.com/BehindTheWordsBook

ABOUT THE AUTHOR

Kim Anne Whittemore has a love of the written word, satire, and an interest in human nature. She spent years in the business world, and her primary responsibility was putting words to the thoughts of others.

She has been married to her husband for 33 years, and is the mother of two adult children, and the proud grandmother of a little boy.

This is her first venture into the world of publishing, and it is the first time she has credited herself for own work.

You can contact the author and get updates through her website at:
www.KimAWhittemore.com or KimAWhittemore@gmail.com

Or join in the continuing discussion at: *www.facebook.com/BehindTheWordsBook*

Made in the USA
Lexington, KY
19 June 2015